D0049227

The Reporter
Who Would Be King

The Reporter
Who Would Be King

A Biography of

Richard Harding Davis

Arthur Lubow

Charles Scribner's Sons
New York

Maxwell Macmillan Canada
Toronto

Maxwell Macmillan International
New York   Oxford   Singapore   Sydney

Charles Scribner's Sons
Macmillan Publishing Company
866 Third Avenue
New York, NY 10022

Maxwell Macmillan Canada, Inc.
1200 Eglinton Avenue East
Suite 200
Don Mills, Ontario M3C 3N1

Macmillan Publishing Company is part of the Maxwell Communication Group of Companies.

Library of Congress Cataloging-in-Publication Data

Lubow, Arthur.
    The reporter who would be king: a biography of Richard Harding
Davis/Arthur Lubow.
        p.   cm.
    Includes bibliographical references and index.
    ISBN 0-684-19404-X
    1. Davis, Richard Harding, 1864–1916—Biography.   2. Authors,
American—19th century—Biography.   3. Journalists—United
States—Biography.   I. Title.
PS1523.L8   1992   92-15971   CIP
070'.92—dc20
[B]

Macmillan Books are available at special discounts for bulk purchases for sales promotions, premiums, fund-raising, or educational use. For details, contact:

Special Sales Director
Macmillan Publishing Company
866 Third Avenue
New York, NY 10022

10 9 8 7 6 5 4 3 2 1

Printed in the United States of America

DESIGN BY DIANE STEVENSON / SNAP·HAUS GRAPHICS

*For my mother
and in memory of my father*

Contents

The Reporter
Who Would Be King

Introduction

The Celebrity

A MONTH BEFORE HIS UNEXPECTED DEATH, *Town and Country* wrote: "Richard Harding Davis is unique in that he has lived to see, while still in the prime of life, his own cycle of romance form about him. . . . To conceive a map of New York without his direct and indirect influence, his personality, his friends and his enemies, would be like an automobile map of Long Island without the Jericho Turnpike."[1] It wasn't simply that, at the turn of the century, Richard Harding Davis knew virtually everyone who was prominent in popular literature, the theater, and New York society. Davis was a landmark, a point of reference—a hero to many, a joke to some, but recognized everywhere.

To be famous virtually all one's adult life and forgotten promptly at death: this is celebrity in its purest form. Time, washing away the merely fashionable, has erased all impressions of Richard Harding Davis. We remember those of his contemporaries who seem precociously "modern"; and so, we read Henry James and Stephen Crane, Ambrose Bierce and Jack London. But if we seek the flavor of a lost time, we must recapture the fripperies and tinsel, the snippets of slang and popular songs, the fads and crazes, the popular heroes. The ephemeral becomes essential.

To a college boy in the 1890s, Richard Harding Davis glowed with an unrivaled glamour. "His stalwart good looks were as familiar to us as were those of our own football captain; we knew his face as we knew the face of the President of the United States, but we infinitely preferred Davis's," Booth Tarkington recalled. "When the Waldorf was wondrously completed, and we cut an exam. in Cuneiform Inscriptions for an excursion to see the world at lunch in its new magnificence, and Richard Harding Davis came into the Palm Room—then, oh, then, our day was radiant! That was the top of our fortune; we could never have hoped for so much. Of all the great people of every continent, this was the one we most desired to see."[2]

Richard Harding Davis reported on wars and other great events; he wrote best-selling fiction and hit plays. But all of that is beside the central point. Davis sparked the fantasies of a generation of Americans. Boys and young men dreamed of becoming him, girls and young women imagined marrying him. They were enraptured by the image of a well-bred, handsome, clean-living man who was equally at home at a dinner party or on a battlefield. In both his life and his fiction, Davis consciously created that image. He knew that a star reporter must not only observe but be observed.

He had been attracting attention since earliest childhood, in ever widening circles. Raised in a genteel literary household in gray, tradition-bound Philadelphia, he developed a personality so flamboyant that he had to escape. "I expect to leave the Quaker City if I succeed," he wrote at the age of twenty-one, "if I don't I will stay there and vegetate."[3] New York was his natural destination; and there, in November 1889, he emerged dramatically from his cocoon. In his first day of work as a reporter for the *Evening Sun*, he wrote an article that tickled the town. It was the story of a greenhorn, new to New York, who outwits a predatory crook. Typically, Davis himself (the greenhorn) had the starring role in his narrative. "In one day he became famous," observed Edward W. Bok, the editor of the *Ladies' Home Journal*.[4]

He was still only a twenty-six-year-old newspaperman the next year when, with his short story, "Gallegher," he founded a genre (the newsroom adventure tale) and catapulted abruptly into the ranks of "leading young authors." Adding to his popularity, he wrote a series of wry fictional sketches about a debonair clubman called Van Bibber, who spends his time getting into and out of minor scrapes. Languid, overdressed, and witty, Van Bibber was the popular notion of a society swell. Van Bibber, too, bore more than a casual resemblance to his creator.

As Davis grew more prolific and popular, it was often remarked that he modeled his fictional heroes on his own chivalrous personality. That wasn't quite right. What he did was construct his own life and the lives of his fictional characters according to the same formulas. Davis and Davis heroes alike chased adventure, charmed society, and glorified women. Above all, they were scrupulously clean in body and mind. "In a certain sense he was living a life of make-believe, wherein he was the hero of the story, and in which he was bound by his ideas always to act as he would have the hero of his story act," observed his friend, the cartoonist John D. McCutcheon.[5]

The confusion between the author and his protagonists was complete when Charles Dana Gibson sketched an idealized Davis as the square-jawed, clean-cut young man who, arm in arm with the Gibson Girl, defined masculine beauty at the turn of the century. College boys and their sisters posted sketches of Davis on their walls. Or were they portraits of Davis heroes? It was impossible to distinguish.

Successfully courting the public, Davis modeled his gestures and projected his emotions for the rear balcony. He sacrificed tonal gradations and subtleties in favor of bold colors that would "carry." His costume was an ulster and yellow gloves in his youth, English tweeds and khakis in his maturity. He found his speaking voice—an aristocratic drawl—and a square-shouldered, rolling gait. Once he had mastered these mannerisms, he proceeded to write his own part. Maybe he couldn't be quite as dashing as his fictional heroes. But he tried. He became the greatest war correspondent of his time.

While there were other prominent war correspondents who preceded him, it was Davis who invented a particular type: the reporter who brings a folding bathtub and dinner jacket to the front so that he can dress properly in the evening. It was Davis who inspired a series of greater American writers, from Frank Norris to Jack London to Ernest Hemingway, to take up journalism as a way of learning about life. He was a brilliant reporter. "His powers of observation were the most remarkable I have ever known . . . ," one colleague observed. "In addition he possessed a remarkable nose for news. He seemed to have a natural instinct for picking out the right point to make for when in search of a really good story."[6] He was equally adept, once he reached the correct vantage point, at selecting the most evocative details to report.

He covered all manner of warfare. He cut his teeth on the Greco-Turkish War of 1896–97, a "comic opera" sort of conflict in which picturesquely garbed peasants chased each other to little effect in the scenic Macedonian hills. He made his greatest success in the Spanish-American War of 1898, writing the classic account of his friend Theodore Roosevelt's charge up Kettle Hill. He went to South Africa two years later to report the Boer War, and antagonized many of his upper-class English friends by championing the Bible-thumping, courtly Afrikaners over their imperial (and imperious) foes.

With the Boer War at the century's hinge, the door clanged shut on the free-roving war correspondent. Traveling to the Far East in 1905 to cover the Russo-Japanese War, Davis saw nothing: the Japanese, precocious as ever, had extended government censorship to new levels. A reporter on the modern battlefield was required to fit smoothly in a designated compartment of the juggernaut. By the First World War, which was Davis's last assignment, a career counselor listing the talents of a successful war correspondent would have placed the ability to finesse War Department bureaucrats and rearguard newspaper editors far ahead of a vivid prose style or keen eye.

Davis reported on wars as the ultimate spectacle. When no war was playing, he checked the newspapers for the best available show. He enjoyed athletic contests—the similarities between football and martial skirmishes were not lost on him—and in the tranquil days of his youth, he was highly regarded as a chronicler of college sports. He was already famous in 1895 when William Randolph Hearst, waging the all-out circulation battle of yellow journalism, paid him the unheard-of sum of five hundred dollars to cover the Harvard-Princeton game; as the edition sold out, it was money well spent.

Even better than football was royalty. A connoisseur of pageants and costumes, Davis was attracted to kings and queens much as we are today drawn to snow leopards, quetzals, and other gorgeous endangered species. He witnessed the coronation of Nicholas and Alexandra of Russia, the Diamond Jubilee of Queen Victoria, the millennial celebration of the Hungarian monarchy, and the crowning of King Alfonso XIII of Spain. He described all these occasions with a boyish enthusiasm that never flagged. Even when he wrote about routine subjects—such as Paris, a city that to rich New Yorkers was more familiar than the Bronx—he displayed the same wide-eyed wonderment he had for the Congo. According to a gibe of the time, Mr. Davis's ignorance must have been acquired, since no one could possibly have been born with so large a stock of it.[7]

Perhaps it was a pose, just as the world-weary cynicism of the following generation was a pose. If so, he adopted the pose so early that his temperament adhered to it like a vine on a trellis. Where others saw dirt, he picked out the picturesque. We remember the decade that we call the gay nineties as a whirl of boys riding bicycles and girls wearing pompadours. We forget that it was also a period of bloody strikes, anarchist bombings, and financial panic. By focusing on what was jolly, we are following the example of Richard Harding Davis.

Today we prefer our writers to suffer publicly, to storm and rant, to break down in boozy delirium or crushing melancholy. These stigmata are prized as hallmarks of artistic authenticity. A century ago, what was valued was a stiff upper lip. Victorian writers struggled to sustain a sunny demeanor. Davis was typical in succumbing to fits of depression, at times taking to his bed. But this was a private face that he did not share with his readers. In public, he was a hero, and a hero betrayed no personal weakness. It may have required a genuinely heroic effort to keep smiling, but the struggle took place backstage. No one must see.

As a reward for his steadfast self-control, he enjoyed enormous popularity. Davis reassured the privileged classes, who, bruised and jostled by the accelerating modern world, worried endlessly about their own effeteness and degeneracy. In his life and his art (who could tell them apart?) Davis exemplified the survival of upper-class virility.[8] He combined his adherence to traditional values and his fondness for modern luxuries with a manly, athletic vigor. He was not a literary critic or a professor; he was a correspondent. As a reporter, he traveled to dangerous and uncomfortable places, having adventures that he could later recount wittily. In a set of stockbrokers and lawyers, this made him a lively addition. Lest anyone miss the point, he created a series of fictional protagonists who were as handy with a fish fork as they were with a Colt revolver. The heroes in vogue in the Victorian era were typically salvaged from a glorious, mythical past: Greeks and Romans, Norsemen and Celts, valiant King Arthur and chivalrous medieval knights.[9] What was captivating about Davis's chevaliers is that they wore modern dress and talked like New Yorkers. They worked as journalists or engineers, and they conquered villains and rescued maidens in Central America, not Camelot.

Davis's virile heroes not only reassured; they instructed. New York society in the late nineteenth century was dominated by a new elite of self-made men who had amassed huge fortunes after the Civil War. Over the centuries it has been demonstrated that people who suddenly come into a great deal of money need to be taught how to enjoy themselves. Davis was the ideal teacher because he was himself a student—a very gifted student—of the art of consumption. Like the new rich, he was looking to be something he was not. He shared their fascination with English manners and style. He was very impressed by the exclusive Ivy League colleges (which he did not attend) and by distinguished family lineages (which he could not claim). He loved to drink champagne and fine clarets, to smoke expensive cigars, to order elaborate French meals at the best restaurants. He adored bespoke English suits and debonair military uniforms. Following his instincts, he established himself, in the memorable words of one critic, as "the prose laureate of the snobocracy."[10]

The creation of his own personality was Davis's greatest achievement. His romantic image brought him fame and wealth in his lifetime; but without the whirligig of his charm, his posthumous name plummeted to oblivion. In 1898, when his renown was at its zenith, a popular American writer named Winston Churchill wrote a novel, *The Celebrity*, with a protagonist obviously based on Davis. The Celebrity is a young man whose short stories have made him a household name. He smokes cigarettes out of a gold case, he wears rough-spun knickerbockers and diamond-patterned stockings, he travels incognito but plants newspaper items about his whereabouts, and at any opportunity, he readily confesses to being an "eccentric." However, as the narrator observes: "There was nothing Bohemian in that character; it yearned after the eminently respectable. Its very eccentricities were within the limits of good form."[11] So with Davis. His excesses were never excessive; his unconventionality tweaked, but never defied, convention. He went as far as his time would permit, and no further. Which is why the story of his life illustrates so well the contours of his era, and why, once his time had passed, he was so soon forgotten.

1

His Mother's Son

*H*IS MOTHER WAS THE MOST IMPORTANT PERSON in Richard's life. Like him, she dreamed in her youth that, by writing professionally, she could escape to another world. And, like him, she succeeded. There the similarities end. By the time Richard began to publish, the literary figures of his mother's era seemed as historical as Greek statues, layered with an inch of dust.

Rebecca Blaine Harding was born on June 24, 1831, in an old stone house that was the finest dwelling in the small western Pennsylvania town of Washington. Her mother, Rachel Wilson, had left Washington a year before to elope with Richard Harding, an Irish immigrant apparently of English stock. The young couple tried their luck in the cotton plantation country of Alabama, but the experiment was going badly. They were visiting this stone house in Washington, which belonged to Rachel's eldest sister, for the birth of their first baby.

When Rebecca was still a toddler, the Hardings abandoned the South and moved to Wheeling in what was then western Virginia. Next to the pastoral hills and farms of Washington, Wheeling represented the brusque, rude face of the modern commercial world. That, in fact, was why the Hardings had moved there, for the fast-growing town offered Richard Harding a chance to prosper; and prosper he did, in the hotel and insurance businesses. By 1850 he was city treasurer.

Since Wheeling was a place for money, not culture, Rebecca spent three years with her aunt and namesake, Rebecca Blaine, in the old stone house in Washington, studying at the Washington Female Seminary. After graduating first in her class, she returned to Wheeling, where she wondered what her preparation had prepared her for. The Hardings were affluent and employed servants, so that even after tutoring her four younger brothers and sisters, Rebecca had the time to read and write. What she wanted was a husband and a publisher, but in Wheeling, she was unlikely to find either.[1]

It was a town, she once wrote, in which even the residences "smelt of trade," having shops on the ground floor; a town in which the only trees were Lombardy poplars that grew straight and narrow, "knowing their best policy was to keep out of the way." Walking to the city outskirts, she found mills, not cottages. Even the churches announced their yearly alms in the newspapers.[2] Rebecca was already thirty when she wrote "Life in the Iron Mills," the story with which our own story really begins. She was attractive, with a broad high forehead, wide-set brown eyes, a determined-looking chin, and plump, sturdy shoulders and arms. But at that advanced age, she was probably fated for spinsterhood in Wheeling.

Recently rediscovered by feminist critics, "Life in the Iron Mills" was one of the earliest pieces of American fiction to look realistically at the urban poor.[3] Its protagonist, Hugh Wolfe, is a tubercular iron-puddler who in his few free moments sculpts anguished human figures out of korl, the porous, flesh-colored residue of processed iron ore. Awakened by a careless reformer who admires his talent, and enticed by a crippled girl who adores him, he participates in a muddled theft. Sentenced to nineteen years in prison, he cuts his wrists with the tool he once used to carve korl. What's remarkable about the story isn't the plot: the predicament of a stifled artist has always been popular with writers like Rebecca who feel alienated themselves. The startling feature of "Life in the Iron Mills" is Rebecca's unsentimental depiction of the potato-eating, ale-drinking, vice-ridden mill workers, and their hellish world.

In an act that was slightly presumptuous for an unknown woman in a provincial town, she sent the manuscript to the editor of the *Atlantic Monthly* in Boston. Boston in 1861 was the self-proclaimed Athens of America, the home of Emerson and Hawthorne, the city in which mind was exalted above matter. And when the sages of Boston deigned to commit their airy thoughts to paper, the *Atlantic* was their chosen medium. Rebecca carried the letter of reply in her pocket, seal unbroken, for a full day, convinced that it contained a polite refusal. When she finally tore it open, she saw to her astonishment an enthusiastic acceptance from editor James T. Fields, a check for fifty dollars, and a request for other stories.[4]

"Life in the Iron Mills" was so grim that Oliver Wendell Holmes, the *Atlantic*'s popular "autocrat of the breakfast table," thought the author must be European.[5] When the *Atlantic* literati learned that R. B. Harding was a young woman from the West, they clamored to meet her. Fields, the editor, was a large, bearded, tweedy man who had risen through the bookselling business to become the junior partner in the publishing house of Ticknor and Fields and then the part-owner and editor of the nation's most prestigious magazine. In 1854, when he was thirty-eight, he had married Annie Adams, a beautiful young woman half his age. Annie was an amateur poet with a great gift for friendship. She began a correspondence with Rebecca that rapidly intensified and deepened.[6]

The Fieldses pressed for a face-to-face meeting, but the timing was bad. In April 1861, the month that the *Atlantic* published "Life in the Iron Mills," shots sounded at Fort Sumter and the Civil War began. When a convention of Western Virginians in Wheeling voted to secede from their state rather than from the Union, the federal government immediately rushed troops to the city and established headquarters in a stately old house across the street from the Hardings. In that volatile atmosphere, Rebecca hesitated to leave home.[7] Added to that were the usual complications: the uncertain health of her father, whom she doted on, and the troublesome need of an escort. "How good it must be to be a man when you want to travel!" she told James Fields.[8]

For a year she vacillated, submitting more fiction and exchanging photographs. Then on May 1, 1862, two weeks after telling her would-be hosts that a visit that spring would be impossible, Rebecca reversed course. She was "very much in the mind of going to Philadelphia in June," she wrote mysteriously, and she could stop first in Boston. As promised, that month a self-described "very determined looking female," accompanied by her favorite younger brother, Hugh Wilson "Wilse" Harding, boarded a train north.[9] "I *must* say it—I do hope you will all like me," Rebecca blurted out nervously in a letter to Annie. When she arrived at 37 Charles Street and stood at the portal through which Emerson, Hawthorne, and even Thackeray had passed, how relieved she was to see long-haired, outgoing Annie come to the door and, with a warm greeting, dispel her "downrightly scared and lonesome" mood.[10]

For Rebecca, crossing this cultured threshold was an epiphany. It stirred her with the thrill of arrival and acceptance that her son would later feel in the millionaires' mansions of New York. The Fieldses' walls and shelves were covered and cluttered with authors' letters and other framed relics, as well as portraits and busts (all done from life, of course) of Pope, Dickens, Thackeray, and Wordsworth.[11] And the master and mistress of the house could not have been more gracious. Over the next two weeks, they introduced Rebecca to saltwater fish—she especially loved salmon—and chowder; to the beach at Nahant, thrilling to one who before this trip had never seen the sea; and to the literary sages of Boston and Concord, who largely disappointed her.[12]

A talented young writer from the West bringing first-hand news of the war was welcome everywhere. Ralph Waldo Emerson, Nathaniel Hawthorne, and Bronson Alcott all invited Rebecca to their homes. She was awed, but not for long. Their talk, distorted and insubstantial, floated over her head like soap bubbles. Their rhetoric glorifying the war—about which, she soon realized, they knew nothing—particularly infuriated her.[13] As an old woman, she would recall that only one of these eminences appealed to her: Nathaniel Hawthorne, a short, powerfully built, low-voiced, melancholy man.

Hawthorne and his wife took Rebecca on a walk through the fields of rural Concord, and ended up at the Sleepy Hollow Valley, where the people of Concord had begun to bury their dead. It was a cool, misty morning, with sheaves of sunlight sifting through the clouds. Pink blossoms peeked up from the mossy ground. A woodsy smell floated in the soft air. On a grassy bank, Hawthorne sat down with his hands clasped about his knees and said with a smile: "Yes—it *is* pleasant. The most beautiful pleasure grounds you will find in New England are our graveyards. *We* only begin to enjoy ourselves when we're dead." That night, bidding her farewell, Hawthorne hesitated, and then, holding out his hand, said shyly: "I am sorry you are going away. It seems as if we had known you always." That goodbye remained one of her dearest memories. All her life she kept a piece of moss that Hawthorne stripped off and gave her that morning. She never saw him again. Two years later he lay beneath the moss of Sleepy Hollow.[14]

Rebecca left Boston impressed—who would not be?—by a society in which America's leading writers addressed each other in their work and on the street. Looking back, she would find it even more remarkable. The American literary scene was about to swell unrecognizably, engorged by the large sums of money that accompanied the birth of a national audience. The contrast between high-minded Boston and money-grubbing Wheeling would blur. As it happened, neither city would be Rebecca's ultimate destination.

The sages of Boston were not the only appreciative readers of "Life in the Iron Mills." In Philadelphia, a young lawyer with literary predilections admired the story enough to write a fan letter to the author; and when, receiving a reply, he discovered that this personage was a woman (the story was unsigned), he began a correspondence. That went well—so well that this gentleman, who was named L. (for Lemuel) Clarke Davis, visited the Hardings in Wheeling. Probably he went in late April 1862, the month that Rebecca reversed herself and decided to journey north without further delay.

Clarke Davis was almost four years Rebecca's junior, a thin young man with the sunken eyes and prematurely pained face of a Romantic poet. He wore his long brown hair swept back above a high forehead. A fine nose jutted out over hollow cheeks. His lower lip was pinched with a touch of hauteur, or fanaticism, or sickness, or neurosis. It was the face of Hamlet. In what Rebecca described as "a happy week" in Philadelphia, he rowed her down the Wissahickon Creek in the gray light of dawn, and told her, with tears in his eyes, "You—every woman has a right to summer days in her life."[15] Their engagement may have been sealed on that visit. If not, it was decided within the next few months. Discussing the days of their courtship, Clarke later joked: "Of those there were *three*—though you are not to tell. We married in haste, but mean to give the lie to the old adage by repenting, *never*."[16]

By stepping out into the world of letters, beyond the confines of dollar-hungry Wheeling, Rebecca had found a kindred spirit. Clarke loved books, not money. He was a man of principle, perhaps to excess: he would rather be right than be anything else. His manners were courtly in a way that would soon be old-fashioned. He had a sentimental nature that grew fervent at the thought of the helpless and oppressed, that puffed with admiration at a noble gesture or chivalrous deed. And to the discerning eye, he displayed a quiet determination, a self-effacing ambition. He would rise to the top rank of Philadelphia journalism, ending his career as the editor of the city's most respected newspaper. His death would be mourned by such friends as President Grover Cleveland and Secretary of State John Hay.

His beginnings, though, were modest. He was born on September 23, 1835, on a farm in what is today the city of Sandusky, Ohio, but was then Indian territory on the banks of Lake Erie. The Davises had ventured west in a Conestoga wagon, until, like the Hardings in Alabama, they reassessed and retreated to more civilized parts. It may have been Mrs. Davis's health that brought them back, for in Maryland, she died. After that calamity, the widower lifted stakes once again, resettling with three sons and a daughter in Philadelphia. Clarke was sent to a suburban boarding school run by Samuel Aaron, a prominent abolitionist whose viewpoint was contagious, and then to the fashionable Episcopal Academy in town. At nineteen he graduated (his father had died three years earlier), and began work in a law office, winning admission to the Pennsylvania bar. He spent much of his day on real-estate transactions, which he found fatiguing and ungratifying. At the same time, drawn to journalism, he worked for little pay helping to edit *Law Reports* and the *Legal Intelligencer* and soon became the editor of both. After his engagement to Rebecca, recognizing that he hadn't the income to support a family, he took on yet another job, as a post-office clerk. His drawn look at the time of his wedding could probably be blamed in part on overwork.[17]

Originally scheduled for Christmas, the wedding was postponed due to the illness of Rebecca's uncle and performed quietly on March 5, 1863. Only Rebecca's closest family attended.[18] The Davises started off humbly, boarding with Clarke's widowed sister, Carrie Cooper, and her children, who lived in a comfortable but unstylish northern district of Philadelphia that was just being urbanized into tiers of row houses. Mrs. Cooper's house was large, so they would have their own rooms. Because she was eager to get to know her new sister-in-law, Rebecca declined to take a honeymoon. On the day of their wedding, the Davises departed for Mrs. Cooper's.[19]

Having attracted her new husband with her literary talent, Rebecca never dreamed that being a wife would prevent her from being a writer. "It is a necessity for me to write—well or ill—you know every animal has speech and that is mine," she told Annie Fields, shortly before her marriage.[20] But the practical demands of married life would radically change the quality of her work. She was no longer writing exclusively for the *Atlantic*. When still just a pen pal, Clarke had referred Rebecca to his friend Charles J. Peterson, the proprietor of a popular magazine based in Philadelphia; and she started writing mysteries and melodramas for *Peterson's* in November 1861. It was less prestigious but better paying work, and it steadily soaked up more of Rebecca's time. While she disliked writing potboilers, even anonymously—"It does me no good and for others is neither harmful nor helpful"—she admitted that "as times are, I am not justified in refusing the higher price."[21]

If it was difficult to resist hack-work assignments before her marriage—and the seven stories that Miss Harding wrote anonymously for *Peterson's* suggest that it was—it became that much harder once she had wed a man who was overworked in a profession he loathed.[22] Harder still when, because of their penury, they were living in a situation that was quickly growing intolerable. A newlywed moving into the home of her widowed sister-in-law must anticipate a few rough patches, but life at Mrs. Cooper's was positively scabrous. Infectious disease, always a frequent visitor in the era before antibiotics, seems to have set up permanent residence at Mrs. Cooper's. Like her brother Clarke, Carrie had a propensity for real and imagined illness (a tendency which would persist in future Davis generations). The sickroom smell of bay rum filled the house. Worn out by nursing, with no time to read let alone write, prevented from traveling by Carrie's precarious health, Rebecca sickened, too. Not used to city life, she pined for the woods like a caged animal.[23]

Boxed in, she was trying to cope with a larger problem: how, at an age when habits have hardened, to mesh her life with another. She had married a man she barely knew. He was in fact as retiring and bookish as she had hoped, with a firm faith in a merciful God. But life consists of more than books and beliefs. For example, he smoked, a habit she hoped to break by substituting ice cream for tobacco. More troubling, and less amenable to cure (not that she ever broke his tobacco addiction), was his habit of mind. Clarke was a zealot. On the Civil War, he was as vociferous as the fiercest Boston fire-eater. "These are grand days to live in—sublime ones to die in—if death comes under the old Flag . . . ," he trumpeted toward the end of the war.[24] Rebecca had a novelist's temperament: "If you could only see the other side enough to see the wrong the tyranny on both!" she wrote in August 1862. The war filled her with "inexpressible loathing."[25]

Early in the marriage, she joked that all would be well if she could persuade Clarke that the war was in God's hands, not his. By July 1863, her sense of humor had vanished. That month, the Confederate army invaded Pennsylvania, raising war anxiety in Philadelphia to new heights. Adding to her worries was the draft, which Lincoln had instituted to replenish his army. In July, Clarke's name was called. For three hundred dollars, a draftee could buy his way out, but Clarke agonized over the correct moral course of action. With a sour edge, Rebecca observed that while Clarke spoke very heroically, he was assiduously nursing rheumatism into one foot.* Meanwhile, to assure herself a central role in this grim drama, Carrie predictably collapsed in her room, requiring Rebecca to attend to her. Each morning, after Clarke left for the office, Rebecca would listen for the postman's ring, anxiously wondering who still thought of her in the world from which she felt so cut off.[26]

The breakdown came later that summer. Its occasion was one more emotional shock, one that, to a calmer mind, would have been simply a cause for rejoicing. Rebecca was pregnant. The reason this blessed event plunged her into depression is suggested by a short story that she published a year later. In "The Wife's Story," as she aptly titled it, an aspiring opera singer and composer sacrifices her career to become a wife and mother— until, offered a production of her opera in New York, she abandons her family. The opera proves to be a fiasco. The wife wanders toward the waterfront to end her life—and then she wakes. It has all been a dream, a fever of the brain brought on by the producer's temptation. Given another chance, she tearfully rejoins her husband and infant, and shoulders her womanly obligations. Despite the unconvincing resolution, the conflict between career and family in the woman's soul rings true.[27]

Like her protagonist, Rebecca in the late summer of 1863 collapsed from a fever that almost killed her. Her doctor, the leading Philadelphia physician (and writer) S. Weir Mitchell, forbade "the least reading or writing for fear of bringing back the trouble in my head," and she languished in a state "so like the valley of the shadow of death" that she feared her life was ending. To bolster her spirits, Clarke promised that, if she recovered, they would move into a place of their own.[28] And, slowly, she did recover. To convalesce, she went to her parents' home in Wheeling. Although still "enough weak to feel my heart beat," she was gaining strength.[29]

If only the mood in Wheeling were a little brighter. Rebecca's revival contrasted sharply with the failing health of her father. After she returned from her Wheeling sojourn in the fall, Richard Harding with morbid determination urged her to come back for Christmas. Extricating himself from professional commitments, Clarke went with her, but they found the old man nervous and depressed. It was not a merry holiday.[30] Because of her advancing pregnancy, Rebecca could not make another trip west. She wasn't told when, on March 20, at the age of seventy-two, Richard Harding died of "congestion of the brain." Four weeks after her husband's death, Rachel Harding traveled to Philadelphia to inform her daughter. It is said that the instant she saw her mother's face, Rebecca knew. All night she was ill. The next day, April 18, 1864, she gave birth to a son, and named him after her father: Richard Harding Davis.[31] She would pour into this child not only

---

*How Clarke avoided the army is unclear; but avoid it he did.

the excessive love that is the firstborn's birthright, but the devotion she had felt for his namesake. Much of her artistic energy, too, would be drained off into the creation of this grand work, her son.

For two weeks after the birth, Rebecca's life was in danger, and for a month she didn't leave her room. Her mother, worn out when she arrived, was stricken seriously soon after the baby's birth. Not to be outdone, Mrs. Cooper fell ill also, leaving poor Clarke—with the help of nurses—to administer this women's hospital. The baby, Rebecca reported, was "the smallest tiredest little thing. And homely too only with big dark eyes. . . ." But a month later he was fattening up nicely, "with an uncompromising snub nose and great serious eyes that grow terribly frightened if a stranger looks at him."[32]

To buck up the strength of the whole family (by now, Clarke was ill himself), the Davises left Philadelphia for the summer and moved into rooms in an old farmhouse on the Manasquan River, near the village of Point Pleasant, New Jersey. Bordered by a thick woods and a broad blue river, with the Atlantic moaning in the background, it was a village of fishermen. As fishing was Clarke's favorite recreation, he quickly grew red and happy. For Rebecca, the rituals of washing the baby in the morning and putting him to sleep in the evening soothed her spirit with a deep maternal satisfaction. Best of all, she loved the moments "when half asleep he looks up terrified in my arms and finding who has him nestles down with a bright little smile." Drifting from day to day, the new parents could forget the press of business and the painful news of the war.[33]

Shattering this idyll would have been unbearable but for the long-awaited promise of fall. The Davises were finally leaving Mrs. Cooper's. After a year and a half of boarding, they were renting a place of their own: a North Philadelphia brick row house that was, in Rebecca's words, "flanked by one or two hundred twin brothers of itself—like it to a nail."[34] Over the next six years, they would move twice more. In the fall of 1866, they exchanged their row house for one of its many twins—one with cleaner paint and wallpaper—just around the block.[35] Four years later, having saved and sacrificed, they bought a home of their own, a three-story brick Greek Revival row house at 230 South Twenty-first Street, in central Philadelphia, only two blocks west of fashionable Rittenhouse Square. After that, there were no more moves. In this house, which they dubbed "the Center of the Universe," they raised their family and lived until their deaths.[36]

With equal tenacity, for more than twenty-five years they returned every summer to the Manasquan River. They rented and eventually bought a small cottage connected to the old farmhouse. It consisted of just two low-beamed rooms with a vine-covered porch; Clarke later added two small bedrooms. He acquired a sailboat, the *Vagabond*, and christened the cottage

Vagabond's Rest. Although Manasquan was remote—the trip from Philadelphia required a steam ferry, two separate railroads, and a three-hour stagecoach ride—it became increasingly popular, especially with Philadelphia's theatrical community. For Clarke, that made 'Squan truly paradise, since his other great passion, along with fishing, was for the theater. It was at 'Squan that Richard would meet his lifelong friend, Ethel Barrymore, as well as her mother, Georgie Drew Barrymore, and grandparents John and Louisa Drew—the first family of the American theater.[37]

Whether in Philadelphia or at the seashore, Rebecca continued to write. With a costly house and a growing family, she had to. Clarke's salary was increasing, but not as fast as their expenses. In 1870, he obtained his first full-time newspaper job as managing editor of the Philadelphia *Inquirer*. Rebecca had joined the staff of the New York *Tribune* the previous year as an editorial feature writer, a post she retained for almost two decades.* She was also steadily manufacturing stories for *Peterson's* and its many dreary counterparts. As a novice author, she had rejected a hundred-dollar advance from the *Atlantic* for fear that she would write something "broad and deep just $100—and no more;—dollarish all over."[38] These scruples were long gone. To salve her literary conscience, she continued to write for the *Atlantic*, at half the price per page she commanded elsewhere; but in November 1866, to her great mortification, she scanned the list of next year's contributors and saw that her own name (that is, "The Author of *Margret Howth*," one of her novels) had been unceremoniously dropped. She was no longer one of the elect.[39]

Sadly, she never equaled her first story. In "Life in the Iron Mills," she had molded raw reportage to a moral framework. In her later work, she was less fresh, less honest. Hugh's love interest in "Iron Mills" had been merely suggested, buried in the story as it was submerged in his numbed life. To satisfy the editors (and, presumably, the readers) of the better-paying magazines, Rebecca now constructed her tales around conventional romances, in which the heroine always got her man. How depressing too that, less than two years after describing the torn horse-blanket and straw-heap on the slimy, mossy floor of Hugh's room, Rebecca should depict the tenement apartment of an opium-addicted harlot (who is tending an angelic little brother) as a "clean, pure room" with "walls she had whitewashed herself." Whitewashed, indeed. Of this story, which Fields understandably found overdrawn, Rebecca said, "I am sure my heart never wrote one as much before."[40]

Her heart had usurped the place of her eye. Rebecca's writing suffered from the move to Philadelphia. In provincial Wheeling, she had been free to move among all classes, and the scrape of reality sandpapered off some

---

*She resigned when asked not to harp on a subject that offended advertisers: the need of sick people in the South for drugs that were being retained for industrial use in the North.

of her sentimentality; but in Philadelphia, she was boxed alongside people she learned to dislike but never got to know.[41] As her primary reader, Clarke must also bear some responsibility for the mawkishness which increasingly suffused his wife's work. What Clarke had liked most in "Iron Mills" was its theme that even the lowest human creature contains a divine spark. It wasn't what made the story distinguished, but it was the one feature which persisted through all of Rebecca's later work. Characteristically, Clarke had suggested the hoary plot of the tale of the young harlot: a God-fearing man on Christmas rejects the plea of a fallen woman—a woman who, as fate and cliché would have it, is actually his niece. Abstract and rigid, Clarke's principles didn't foster good fiction. Probably realizing it (for he always deferred to his wife's superior literary talent), he refused to read her stories before they appeared in print.[42] But a woman far duller than Rebecca could predict easily what he would favor.

Unlike the great men of Boston, Rebecca had to balance family and work. Exhausted by a long day of writing and mothering, she would wait for Clarke to return from the newspaper, ready with dinner or, on his late nights, a pot of tea and oysters.[43] At daybreak she would be awakened by one of her growing brood. Little Harding was not an only child for long. On January 24, 1866, a brother arrived. Conceived the month the war ended, the new baby was named Charles Belmont Davis, after Clarke's brother Charles, who was killed at the battle of Belmont, Missouri—a living memorial to both the fallen warrior and the triumphant cause.[44] (Clarke's other brother also died in the war.) Rebecca wrote to Annie Fields: "Nobody was enthusiastic about Charley[;] his brother had carried off all the plaudits as first child and first grandchild, and this boy was a sequel to the story—an afterpiece—an every-day matter."[45] The family circle was closed on October 16, 1872, with the arrival of a daughter, Nora. Harding had enough of a head start over Nora always to regard her as a pet or plaything, a role she took too much to heart. Charlie was close enough in years to become a sidekick, a position that he too assumed as his life's work.

There was something about little Harding—a delight in being alive, a sunniness—that encouraged others to fall into orbit as his satellites. "He is never still an instant: nervous living—hot tempered and fond of his own way," his mother observed. "I don't know if he is brighter than other children but he has a frank boy-way about him that wins everybody at once."[46] Rebecca let no one else put the infant to sleep. "Some little things I always want to reserve the right of doing," she explained. "I fancy it will bring us nearer hereafter."[47] Perhaps it did. Certainly, his values, his vocation, his choice of a bride—all the crucial decisions that he made—bear the imprint of his formidable mother. She, in turn, doted on him always. "In the evening I put the boys to bed & going in to kiss them once more, frightened Hardy," she recorded in her diary. " 'I'm so sorry,' I said. 'Don't you be sorry you dear Mamma. You come frighten me every night if you want to kiss me.' With his arms around my neck and his eyes shut."[48] Even as a baby he was charming.

On the grand day that the Union army veterans returned to Philadelphia, baby Harding was taken to see the parade. Rebecca rejoiced that her son would grow up in peacetime. "I am glad the smell of gunpowder will have gone before he is older," she wrote. "Fresh air will be better for his lungs, I think. I used to look with real sorrow on the boys who saw war as part of the daily business of life and not a savage necessity—far off and never to be reached perhaps."[49] What she didn't foresee was that in the crass commercial world that the war engendered, the acrid odor of gunsmoke would seem bracing and pure to those like her infant son who had never smelled it.

If war was the ultimate spectacle, little Harding—who had a love of spectacle that he never lost—would have to wait for it. Meanwhile, he could enjoy a tamer show. He was not yet three when Clarke took him to a pantomime. At the last minute, Rebecca, who had never seen one, decided to accompany them. It was the first time the three had gone out together. The little boy sat awestruck through the performance, eyes fixed on the stage. Only when they returned to the safety of home did he release his feelings, dancing like a very awkward Columbine and charging at the wall like Harlequin. He talked of it for months.[50]

Stagestruck, he never recovered. It was a passion he inherited from his father, who often stopped at the theater on the way home from work. At a time when New York had not yet bullied the rest of the country's theaters into obscurity, Philadelphia was a dramatic center, and Clarke was one of the most prominent men on the aisle. His office was decorated with engravings of leading actors—men who were his friends, as well as his idols.[51] Similarly, Richard and his brother, Charles, adorned their bedroom with cabinet photographs of actors and actresses, which they collected as avidly as later generations of boys bought baseball cards. When rainy weather kept them indoors, they would perform melodramas written and produced by Richard. Invariably, he would play the hero and throttle Charles, the villain.[52]

Beyond his improvised sets, Richard saw the world as a stage. "Every little incident is a 'venture,'" Rebecca noted when he was seven, "every twopennysworth of candy becomes a tea-party, every pleasure the most trifling is converted into a 'surprise.'" Almost as soon as he could talk, he became "the most entertaining of storytellers"—perhaps *too* inventive, Rebecca worried. "Harding gave us great distress to-day by telling an untruth," she wrote in her diary. "I'd rather see him dead I think than a liar. But he is too young to know the difference between a lie and 'a story' & I never saw a child with the imagination he shows."[53]

If she feared that her son would not develop a moral sense, she was worrying needlessly. Richard took to religion with enthusiasm. Rebecca told him to think of his prayers as "talking to the Lord Jesus": once she over-heard his request to make his baby brother talk.[54] Her own faith, like her husband's, was nonsectarian. Contemptuous of religious cant (many of the villains in her stories are narrow-minded Methodists), she valued a hard-headed, practical sort of Christianity. Richard was his mother's son when, as a teenager, he dropped into a church collection plate the money she had given him to buy glycerine for his chapped skin. "The minister said it was a sin if anyone went away with out giving something and as I have never sinned yet I don't want to commence now so I just put it in," he explained. "It would do more good being spent for red flannel shirts for the little heathen than for my hands, anyway."[55] Rebecca, who was no slouch when it came to worrying, fretted that his sense of sin might be too vivid. His melancholy side emerged precociously. Early one morning when he was almost seven, Rebecca entered his room to find him awake in bed. "Mamma, I have so much more to think about now," he told her. Rebecca thought that he spent too much time alone. "The child lies awake thinking of all that has been read or told him until his imagination is morbid," she wrote in her diary.[56]

One thing for him to think about was his academic performance. It was abysmal. As Charles later recalled, "his weekly report never failed to fill the whole house with an impenetrable gloom and ever-increasing fears as to the possibilities of his future."[57] Two years shy of graduation, he withdrew from his father's alma mater, the Episcopal Academy in Philadel-phia. Hoping that personal attention might save him, the Davises entrusted him in the fall of 1878 to his uncle Wilse Harding, Rebecca's younger brother, who was now an affable, goateed, bachelor professor of physics at Lehigh University in South Bethlehem, Pennsylvania. After a year of tu-toring, Wilse thought his nephew was doing well enough to merit another year. "So that is settled thank God!" Rebecca wrote in her diary. "I feel as if that boy was on the way to a useful happy manhood at last."[58]

After another year of Wilse's tutoring, Richard tried a year on his own at the Swarthmore College Preparatory School near Philadelphia. That experiment failed so dismally that he returned to Bethlehem the following fall to enroll in Ulrich's Preparatory School, a feeder school for Lehigh University. Boosted by Ulrich's instruction and his uncle's connections, Richard, having passed all the entrance exams but mathematics, entered Lehigh in September 1882, as a special student in the Latin-Scientific course.[59] It was a markedly undersubscribed course of study: about 90 percent of the Lehigh boys were engineering majors. The university had been founded in 1865 by Judge Asa Packer, who made his fortune building the Lehigh Valley Railroad through the coal and iron country of eastern Pennsylvania. As a practical man, Packer envisioned a practical university—primarily, though not exclusively, an engineering school. The Bethlehem Iron Company opened its first blast furnace in 1862. Many of the men who would run the mills in Bethlehem learned their business first in South Bethlehem. Indeed, Lehigh had trouble holding them until graduation.[60]

Through South Bethlehem's sober streets, Richard strutted like a peacock in a chicken coop. You could tell from a distance that this was no engineering student. Assembling a theatrical character, he began with an ultra-English costume: gloves, Norfolk jacket, knickerbockers, tam-o'-shanter, and ulster, with a briarwood pipe in his mouth and a crooked cane over his arm. His accent was a strange drawl, somewhere between the tones of upper-class Philadelphia and the diction of the English actor. Even his walk was guaranteed to draw attention. He described it (in an early story about a football hero) as a "straight military walk, with shoulders squared and head erect." He was a well-built, handsome young man, so the whole effect was quite striking; but understandably it struck some people, especially those who didn't know him, the wrong way.[61]

His personality was as overblown as his appearance. A lily-white rectitude—which in later years became synonymous with the name of Richard Harding Davis—was the showy hybrid flower of his religious and theatrical impulses. From boyhood on, he had a flair for seeing and exploiting every opportunity for moral melodrama. At Swarthmore, the seven boys at his dining table were once called before the president on suspicion of stealing a sugar bowl. All the boys protested their innocence, except for Richard, who smiled his gravest smile and said nothing. "The only boy that doesn't deny it is Davis," said the president. "Davis, you are excused. I wish to talk to the rest of thee." In recounting this victory Richard generously gave credit to the president for living up to a gentleman's code. Richard had refused to respond because to deny stealing, one must first be accused; and such an insult would force him to withdraw from the school.[62] The same logic that guided him at fifteen would also govern him at fifty.

It didn't take him long to find a moral dilemma at Lehigh. The university had a venerable tradition—as venerable as any tradition could be in a school not two decades old—known as the Cane Rush, in which the sophomore class would attempt to wrest possession of a cane from the freshmen. The Cane Rush may have had its athletic aspects when the student body numbered a few dozen, but by the time Richard got there, it had degenerated into a bloody brawl. In letters to local newspapers and in speeches before college audiences, Richard denounced this barbaric behavior. He was asking for trouble, and it came in the form of another dubious college tradition—hazing, the ritual humiliation of freshmen by sophomores. Hazing struck Richard as not only "brutal" but (even worse) "silly and undignified." He would not submit.

Thanks to a tip, he was prepared for what happened as he left the opera house alone on a rainy Friday night. A group of observers, also in the know, watched as a sophomore grabbed his arm. "If this means hazing, I'm not with you," Richard proclaimed loudly. "There's not enough men here to haze me, but there's enough to thrash me, and I'd rather be thrashed than hazed." Protesting that he misjudged them, a dozen sophomores dogged Richard's heels. When he turned defiantly, four jumped him. He had time for only one blow before they had him in the gutter, pounding his head. Wet and muddy, his face stinging, Richard rose. He saw that except for his four assailants, the sophomores seemed embarrassed that things had gone so far. "Now, you're not able to haze me, and I can't thrash twelve of you, but I'll fight any one man you bring out," he declared. He was elaborating on his principled opposition to hazing when two policemen came out of the night to break it up.

Suddenly, he was a hero. He showed up for a student election the next day, intending to vote, not run. To his surprise, he heard his own name placed in nomination—and by a sophomore, no less. As each candidate rose for identification, the audience roundly booed; until Richard stood, with his reddened eye, and the sophomores cheered and stamped. He withdrew his name, but the moral was evident. As he told his father, "one gets taken care of in this world if you do what's the right thing, even if it is only a street fight." Along with his reputation, he made his point. The university president forbade hazing for the year. And the following fall, Richard's classmates (now sophomores) abjured the Cane Rush, which was then abolished by faculty decree.[63]

Richard was also triumphant on that usual testing ground for the adolescent boy, the athletic field, where he compensated for his dearth of talent with a nonstop gush of enthusiasm. He quickly endorsed the merits of football, a game still in its crude infancy. (The first match of American football was waged in 1871 between Harvard and McGill.)[64] Played without helmets or padding, football was as bloody as any Cane Rush.[65] In the fall of 1883, Richard was part of the sophomore team which lost to the freshmen, 10–0, in the first football match played at Lehigh. No one had much idea of what was going on. Two weeks later, despite unspecified but well-publicized injuries, Richard played in Lehigh's first intercollegiate game. Anticipating an experienced squad of sophomores from the University of Pennsylvania, the Lehigh boys fastidiously rubbed their new white uniforms with dirt before the game. They needn't have bothered. The contest was fought in the rain on a field which had not yet had time to nurture grass. Three hundred spectators watched the sophs of Pennsylvania trounce Lehigh, 16–0, in eight inches of mud, mud so thick that the players' feet sank into it. After the game, Richard insisted that his teammates stop at a tintype photographer to pose in their dripping uniforms.[66]

Despite these murky beginnings, football advanced at Lehigh. The next year a varsity squad was formed. It began by losing to neighboring Lafayette College, 52–0. That lopsided score forecast the season, in which the valiant but feckless men of Lehigh totaled 16 points to their opponents' 181. For Richard, this ignominy was softened by the glorious fact that when Lehigh finally did score her first touchdown, he was the man carrying the ball. Seven years later, by which time he had some more celebrated accomplishments to his credit, he wrote that he took "a keener satisfaction in the fact that he scored the first touchdown for Lehigh than in all the verses or short stories he [had] ever written."[67] Although that was just the sort of upper-class, self-deprecating remark that Richard could be counted upon to make, in this case it might have been true.

At Lehigh, Richard also discovered tennis. British in origin, tennis was played in dashing costumes with socially prominent partners—in short, it was made for him. The business elite of Bethlehem had taken up the sport, and by the end of his year at Ulrich's, Richard was a regular on their courts on fashionable Fountain Hill. He played often with William W. Thurston, the president of the Bethlehem Iron Company, whose court he considered "a perfect dream of what a court should be, like a billiard table." J. Davis Brodhead, a leading attorney and Democratic congressman, became another good friend. The grandees of Bethlehem dated their fortunes back no further than the anthracite industry's beginnings in the War of 1812; and, in most cases, back only as far as the founding of the Bethlehem Iron Company just before the Civil War. They welcomed bright newcomers, unlike the patrician Philadelphians whose ossified circles Richard never could crack.[68]

Had he attended a university which more closely approached his ideal (say, Princeton), Richard might have beamed more of his charm on his fellow students. But the engineering majors of Lehigh refused to conform to his fantasies. When he first arrived in Bethlehem, as a fourteen-year-old pupil of his Uncle Wilse, he had been disheartened to discover that only four Lehigh men had dress suits—and one of those was hired.[69] If things were improving, he could take some of the credit. Objecting on principle to the fraternity system (with considerable regret, he declined an offer from a prestigious one), he instead started organizations that met his standards. He helped to found both an eating club, the Pipe and Bowl, and a dramatic society, the Mustard and Cheese.[70] Admiring the Anglophile ritual of the undergraduate regatta, he organized something called the Hefty Club to sponsor a mile race of four boats, each with a two-man crew sporting colored jerseys. "The boat race gave the club immense prestige as it was given with such 'form,' " Richard related happily to his parents. "All the crews looked well and dressed well. The club will be pretty close next year and outsiders won't get in easily."[71]

A prig, a snob, an affected little ass—one can see how his enemies arrived at their epithets. Yet there was also something touching in Richard's attempt to rewrite his prosaic reality into a romantic lyric. Having matriculated at a provincial engineering school that was a year younger than he was himself, when all his fantasies of undergraduate life came from the stage and English literature, Richard did his best to transform his stay at Lehigh into a facsimile of Oxbridge life—or what he knew of that life from such sources as a favorite novel, William Thackeray's *Pendennis*. He didn't always succeed, but he was working on obstinate material. It took him a while to realize how much easier it would be just to pick up a pen and—not metaphorically, but literally—rewrite his life. So began a literary career. A literary vocation, really, for as Charles later wrote of him, "no other career was ever considered."[72]

The earliest surviving narrative of Richard Harding Davis is a small volume which he titled, with characteristic misspelling, "The Boys in the Adariondacks," and presented to his parents on his return from a hunting trip that he took with Charles in July 1881. At seventeen, he had already found his subject matter and tone of voice. Told in the third person, "The Boys in the Adariondacks" chronicles the waggish exploits of Richard and his Sancho Panza, Charlie, whose voracious appetite is a recurrent source of humor. Richard's own deeds—outwitting a coach driver, shooting a buck, splitting his knickerbockers, finessing a track meet—are related with a self-belittling drollery. With the enthusiasm Rebecca had noted in him from the first, Richard turned every incident into a "'venture," and strung them together into a mock-epic, with himself in the leading role.[73]

A year later, he lighted on the clever notion of christening his hero with a name other than his own. So "Conway Maur" was invented; he first appeared in October 1882, in the pages of the Lehigh *Burr*, a student monthly which filled the roles of newspaper and literary magazine. In Conway Maur, Richard created a protagonist who, under different names and varying circumstances, would persist throughout the Davis literary canon. Conway Maur, a brash freshman, was obviously a caricature of Davis himself. To blur the distinction further, Richard even wrote pieces for the *Burr* under Conway's byline. Having fashioned an image for himself on campus as extravagant as a fictional character, Richard created an imaginary youth in that image, and made him a little more bumptious, a little more extreme; and so inoculated himself against painful personal criticism by gently laughing at the same traits himself.

He established the pattern with his first story. Looking for sketch subjects for his art-class assignments, Conway worms his way into neighboring households by pretending to be an illustrator for *Century* magazine. Eventually, he stumbles on a house in which the university president is dining. Fearing exposure, he runs out so quickly he forgets his cane. Until the appearance of the university president, this was basically a true story: Richard himself had entered strange homes on a similar pretext.[74] In subsequent stories, Conway lands on his nose in various embarrassing scrapes. He invites several friends to the Hop, sure that none will accept—but they all do. He pursues a couple of attractive girls, calling at their house, he says, by error—but his ruse is discovered. He takes a minor role in an *Uncle*

Tom's Cabin road company—only to lose his watch when the bankrupt thespians can't pay their hotel bill. As he recounts his misadventures to a patient upperclassman, Conway is alternately rueful and cheerful: the discomfort he has suffered is probably exaggerated and, in any event, his delight in telling the story more than makes up for it.[75]

Richard wrote seven Conway Maur stories in his freshman year and one the following fall. He published six of these stories, illustrated by a classmate, under the title *The Adventures of My Freshman*. His parents defrayed the cost, with the help of advertisements that Richard sold to local merchants. The small volume, its cover an antique green, was sold in Bethlehem for twenty-five cents a copy. With some alarm, the author noted that "everybody has read it but they have an unfortunate way of borrowing it from each other." He was thrilled when the edition sold out, then puzzled and hurt that his parents refused to finance a second printing. Some years later, when he found the entire first edition neatly stacked in their attic, he understood their reluctance. Or such was the story he told—and a perfect Conway Maur story it was.[76]

In January of his junior year, Richard was assigned by the Philadelphia *Inquirer* (whose managing editor just happened to be his father) to accompany Col. Alexander K. McClure, the proprietor of the Philadelphia *Times*, on a trip through the New South. The destination was the World's Industrial and Cotton Exposition in New Orleans, designed to showcase the business potential of the South after Reconstruction. Along with McClure, Philadelphia was sending an even more venerable relic—the Liberty Bell.[77] Although the fair did not impress Richard as a spectacle, New Orleans did. He was especially intrigued by the privately owned Louisiana lottery, the nation's only legal gambling operation. Plugged into municipal life, the lottery donated generously to charity—and, less publicly, to the bank accounts of Louisiana's leaders. "I have been fighting that lottery since I was a young man," a prominent judge told Richard, "but they can buy our legislature and we are helpless." He then confessed that of course he bought the tickets himself. Who could resist them?[78] The lottery was a good story— too big a topic for a novice journalist to tackle, but one he would store away for the future.

Richard returned to South Bethlehem to confront what would be his grandest—and final—moral challenge at Lehigh. The battlefield was the *Burr*, which, by May 1885, numbered only four editors. That month three of the four, including Richard, wrote a review savaging the college yearbook for its "bad taste." The sole holdout, William Cooke, was understandably peeved: he was an editor of the yearbook. He was also managing editor of the *Burr*, which gave him, he maintained, authority to suppress the review. So he did. With the tyranny of King John I reverberating in his freshly educated mind, Richard led the outraged three in demanding that Cooke resign. Instead, Cooke made off with the engraved plates for the *Burr*'s cover and threatened to renege on a printer's bill if the rebels' *Burr* were published. In turn, Richard retained his friend, the lawyer Davis Brodhead, to promise the printer a lawsuit if Cooke's *Burr* appeared.

It was getting very grown-up. In a power play familiar to the iron companies that usually occupied his time, Brodhead bought up all the printer's available cover stock. He then requisitioned all the *Burr*-style type for a hymn book, leaving over just enough type to print one issue of the *Burr*—Richard's. As a backup, Richard knew that the university administration, which held final authority, would side with him if asked. Before this barrage Cooke crumbled. His name was expunged from the masthead, replaced by Richard's in the top spot. On behalf of the victorious editors, Richard presented a cane to Brodhead. The Bethlehem *Times* reported the gift on page 1.[79]

It was a shame that this unbroken string of undergraduate moral achievement couldn't counterbalance Richard's failing grades. He was quick-witted but restless, and he lacked the patience to read. He had begun college with a flourish of optimism, confident that he had faltered in prep school because the work was beneath him.[80] Having failed the entrance exams in arithmetic, algebra, and geometry, he entered Lehigh as a special student. He never did attempt a course in mathematics; he had a hard enough time with French, German, Latin, and chemistry, all of which he flunked repeatedly. Even in English, a subject required of the entire freshman class, he was fifty-fourth in a class of sixty-nine. That was in English, competing against engineers! In Latin, taken only by those in the Classical or Latin-Scientific courses, he usually finished last. The only subject in which he excelled was Greek history.[81]

Many years later, near the end of his life, Richard Harding Davis wrote an undistinguished story for the *Saturday Evening Post* called "The Grand Cross of the Crescent." Undistinguished, that is, except for one thing—it was his only fiction set in an American college other than Harvard, Yale, or Princeton. The protagonist is a young man who flunks out of Stillwater College, a new university much like Lehigh. When he is given a chance to take the exam again, after a summer that he should have devoted to study, he flunks once more, and says with a laugh, "I got working for something worth while—and I forgot about the degree."[82]

By the time he wrote that story, Davis had gained some of the equanimity that accompanies success. Still, though he muffled the memory with humor, he could not truly forget about the degree. He never earned a college diploma. At the end of his junior year, his grades were as shameful as always (near the bottom of his class for almost every subject), and the faculty requested that he withdraw. He responded with bitter incredulity. "You do not think me worthy to remain in this school," he proclaimed to a meeting of the Lehigh faculty. "But in a few years you will find that I have gone further than you will ever go."[83]

2

The Muddy Road
to Johnstown

*F*OR VOCATIONAL GUIDANCE, CLARKE TOOK HIS SON to Talcott Williams, who was managing editor of the Philadelphia *Press*. Richard might have expected this veteran journalist to welcome him immediately into the ranks. Williams did not. Probably prompted by Clarke, who didn't want his son to become a newspaperman,[1] Williams urged a year, preferably two, of study in the social sciences at Johns Hopkins University, to be followed by an apprenticeship of four or five years of newspaper reporting.[2] Ignoring the lessons of his personal history, Richard accepted this advice and packed his book satchel for Baltimore.

At Johns Hopkins, Richard took courses in diplomatic history with Herbert Baxter Adams and in political economy with Richard T. Ely. Both were star professors, and neither could teach him much. With Adams, he studied Spanish-American relations. A prescient choice, in view of his later exploits in Cuba; or so you might think, until you discovered that the high point of his term was his hour-long oral report on Spanish-American treaties, in which he waved a piece of chalk and thought to himself, "As no one knows anything about it, Adams least of all, I can say pretty much what I wish and none will call me to account."[3] From Ely, he acquired a vague Tory socialism. This meant that while Richard supported strict enforcement of the eight-hour day, he disdained the urban poor, especially the immigrants. Concluding that "democracy is a failure," he complained, "For myself I'm sick of a country that is content to go on making money while Aldermen steal, Senators use the language of barrooms and Catholic Irish rule their cities."[4]

One thing that Richard learned for certain at Johns Hopkins was cricket, a game that Clarke had enjoyed at Point Pleasant in the 1860s.[5] Popular in America since colonial times, cricket was at first favored mainly by English-born workingmen. In the 1850s, the athletic boys of the proper Wister family of Philadelphia took up the game, and they and their friends cleansed it of its lower-class swearing, betting, and drinking. After the Civil War, when baseball replaced cricket in the heart of the American laborer, cricket was free to flourish in genteel districts.[6] Somehow the sport had escaped Richard until he reached Baltimore. Promptly ordering a suit of flannels, he joined a cricket club and reported that "the hours of practice and the men who play are just what suit me best."[7]

Baltimore society resisted Richard's charms until, close to Christmastime, he won an invitation to his first German, a dance for the town belles and their beaux.[8] One invitation was all the opening he needed. By spring he was racing so fast around the social circuit that he had to ask his parents to send him an extra supply of visiting cards.[9] "Girls are rising in my opinion as bright individuals," he wrote home. "I think very few men could tell as many funny or witty stories as they did and ones which showed so clear an insight into what was ludicrous and absurd."[10] At Hopkins, as at Lehigh, he was popular with many girls but the special favorite of none. He was absurdly chivalrous. Like most of his lifelong traits, he had picked up chivalry as a child. At six, riding with his mother on a streetcar, he insisted on giving his seat to every lady, stating loudly, "Men ought to stand." By the time he was fifteen and living with his uncle in Bethlehem, he was (his mother observed) "in love with all the pretty girls & good well bred women from eighteen to forty that he knows."[11] He was at Johns Hopkins still a very young man, and there was nothing unusual in his playing at love. Only later was it apparent that he would do so for most of his life.

Richard tried during his year at Hopkins to sell articles to national publications. He systematically mailed manuscripts to editors, addressing three or four envelopes at a time in a realistic anticipation of rejection.[12] Occasionally, he was happily surprised. *Life*, the humor magazine, printed a poem.[13] An obscure Chicago fortnightly, *The Current*, published his ponderous tirade against—oh, irony—the lightweight fiction that was ruining the "literary palate."[14] Reading the *Current* essay, Richard's most faithful critic offered a shrewd assessment. "I think you are going to take a high place among American authors, but I do *not* think you are going to do it by articles like that you sent to *The Current*," Rebecca wrote to her son. "The qualities which I think will bring it to you, you don't seem to value at all. They are your dramatic eye. I mean your quick perceptions of character and of the way character shows itself in looks, tones, dress, etc., and in your keen sympathy, with all kinds of people. Now, *there* are the requisites for a novelist. Added to that your humour. You ought to make a novelist of the first class."[15]

Although she encouraged her son to write, Rebecca wished that he were less quick to publish under his own name. While he was at Hopkins, Richard scored his first big success—selling a short story to *St. Nicholas*, a respected juvenile magazine to which Rebecca sometimes contributed.

"Richard Carr's Baby" tells of a Princeton football captain who accidentally injures a sickly young fan and then, by showering him with attention and paying for doctors, restores him to perfect health.[16] Thinking her son capable of better, Rebecca urged him to publish the story anonymously. She cited the advice of Josiah Gilbert Holland, who helped found *Scribner's Monthly* in 1870. By rushing into print, Holland cautioned, young people would produce inferior work, or would achieve a public success they could never again equal; either way, Rebecca said, meant "sure ruin to their lasting fame."[17] Rebecca had insisted that her own first novel, *Margret Howth, A Story of Today*, be published anonymously, and had forbade James Fields to include her name on a list of *Atlantic* contributors. Only in late 1866, at Clarke's urging, did she finally request an *Atlantic* byline, as "Mrs. R. H. Davis."[18]

Some of Rebecca's early reticence might be attributed to an unmarried woman's modesty. Clarke, however, was at least as shy of celebrity. In an age of great newspaper editors, Clarke, said a eulogist after his death, probably "was personally less known to this generation than almost any editor of a large newspaper." He labored in an "obscure and hidden station," said another, "screened from the view of all save a very small part of the public."[19] Rebecca and Clarke both came from a world in which a genteel writer sought lasting fame, not celebrity. It was the ideal of Concord, of Emerson and Hawthorne. What mattered was the judgment of one's peers, and one's peers all knew who had composed the unsigned pieces that ran in the *Atlantic*.

Richard wasn't interested in publishing anonymously. He was of a different generation. By the time he began sending out his first manuscripts, the scruples of gentility seemed as old-fashioned as bustles. There was a large national audience that could be reached only with the megaphone of the media. From the start Richard aimed to be a famous writer. "I am going to write a story that will raise my name to fame above that of Mark Twain, Max Adler, Danbury news man and Joakin Miller," he bragged to his father when he was fourteen.[20] Five years later, sending a fan letter to an author, he advised, with joking confidence: "Preserve this as a literary curiosity until the autograph is sufficiently valuable to make it marketable."[21]

It didn't take Richard long to realize that Johns Hopkins wasn't the place to realize his ambitions. "I was never made for a student," he wrote home. "Nature put too much vitality into my limbs and too much imaginative ideas in my head to allow me to sit still for eight hours a day and think of serious things in books." He might manage four and a half hours of study every morning, but in the afternoon, he could remain in a chair for no more than an hour at a time. "I feel creeping up my back and aches in my legs and fidgets all over," he admitted, "and I have to get up and fence with an imaginary villian [*sic*], or twang the guitar or write a long winded letter to a suffering family."[22] It was an honest self-assessment; and by now, he was old enough to act on it. In the spring of 1886, he decided not to return to Johns Hopkins in the fall. What part his grades played in this resolution cannot be determined, as the university records were later destroyed in a fire, but it seems unlikely that his grades would have argued against the move. He returned to his parents' home in Philadelphia, intending to look for newspaper work.[23]

Before he could begin, however, he received an irresistible invitation: to accompany his old friend William W. Thurston, president of the Bethlehem Iron Company, on a trip to Santiago on Cuba's southeastern coast. Thurston's company had recently begun mining iron in the village of Siboney near Santiago, and the boss wanted to inspect the operation. It was a long way from the drab grid of Philadelphia. For Richard, this trip left an enchanted impression of pastel houses, royal palms, and a glinting blue harbor—a tropical vision that forever represented an escape from the worries and routines of everyday life. He stayed with Thurston in La Cruz, a mansion overlooking Santiago harbor. They traveled together to the Siboney mines on a narrow-gauge railroad cut into the limestone cliffs, so near the sea that the salt spray dashed over the open cars. Richard met the chief engineer, Dave Kirkpatrick, who had come from Pittsburgh to oversee first the clearing of the jungle and then the construction, not only of the railroad, but of the pier at the little village of Daiquirí, where the ore was loaded onto ships. A few years later, Richard would write from memory about the house, the mines, and the engineers, in what would be his most popular novel. And a few years after that, he would see a different view of Santiago harbor, from the flagship of the American squadron that was blockading it; and he would revisit the beach of Daiquirí, as thousands of American troops landed there by night to invade Cuba in the Spanish-American War.[24]

Returning to Philadelphia, Richard, with Clarke's help, found a newspaper job at the *Record*. Like many young reporters breaking into the business, he wrote for space: he waited in the newsroom to receive an assignment from the city editor, and earned a specified amount for each column inch that appeared in the paper.[25] Cub reporters did not usually receive the choicest assignments. As an illustration, here is one of Richard's efforts, "A Tobacconist Disappears," in its entirety: "On August 30 Charles P Goodwin, a tobacconist at the corner of Master and Camac streets, left his home and has not been heard from since. His family can assign no reason for his disappearance, as his business affairs were in a flourishing condition. Goodwin had been in ill health for some time, and it is supposed that his mind has become affected."[26]

Although it was tedious spinning out such tripe, Richard didn't let it inhibit his personal style. He woke up each day at half past seven and played tennis all morning before he was due at the office at 1:00 P.M. "They could send me anywhere they pleased," he later explained. "It made no difference. They could not take my fun from me, because I'd already had it."[27] Nor did he give up his heavy cane, quickly dubbed "the Davis railroad tie," or his long yellow ulster with the light green stripes. However hot the weather, he wore kid gloves in the newsroom. He was on call to cover fires and labor meetings, but he was dressed for an afternoon tea. What interested him most was sports, and he could usually be found away from his desk, musing over the latest scores with the sports editor. For three months, James S. Chambers, Jr., the city editor, seethed quietly. Then one night, he snapped at the sight of the young man leaning over the sports desk, his notes for his overdue story still in his pocket. Ordered to remove his gloves and coat and get down to work, Richard sat down but the gloves stayed on. After reading the story, the furious city editor told the youth he was wasting his time in a newspaper office and he was being granted a long vacation, beginning immediately.

"Well, I guess I am fired," Richard said. "Is that it?"

"Well, that's the English of it," Chambers replied.

"Well, old chap," he said, "I suppose I'll have to take my medicine." He extended his hand—still gloved—and walked out of the building.

It was an inauspicious beginning for a newspaper career, but happily enough it was the low point. Walking out of the *Record* office in a daze, Richard reached the corner before he realized the enormity of what had happened to him. He stood in the middle of the car tracks on Chestnut Street and looked up at the lit windows of the *Record* building. The word "fired" reverberated in his head. "You are a failure," he said to himself. "The idea of your being fired!" That moment he resolved to reform. From now on he would work as hard as he could on any assignment he was handed. He peeled off the provocative gloves and gave the cane a long rest.[28]

When he applied bare-handed for a job on the Philadelphia *Press* in December 1886, he was hired on the spot, even though his old mentor, Talcott Williams, had stepped down as managing editor. True to his silent vow, he now approached each story, no matter how banal, as a chance to prove himself. A cub reporter, he was often drafted to produce the obligatory newspaper pieces that commemorate every holiday. He spent Christmas at a home for retired actors, Easter in the park and zoo, Thanksgiving at the hospitals and asylums. Even Arbor Day found him plying his trade at a tree-planting ceremony outside a grammar school. On each of these tired occasions, he sniffed out a human element to animate his story: for Arbor Day, it was the sweating educator waiting by an arboreal hole for his tardy superintendent to arrive. Assuming that what fascinated him would interest others, Richard devoted much of a story on a proposed toboggan slide in Fairmount Park to a minute description of fashionable Canadian tobogganing costumes. When a story was hopelessly dull, he tried to invent some sparkle, as when, faced with a routine assignment on a visiting French warship, he concocted a lighthearted tale of officers threatening mutiny if one more Philadelphian greeted them with the "Boulanger March."[29]

Recognizing his talent, the *Press* editors quickly entrusted Richard with more important feature stories. His fellow reporters viewed him with less enthusiasm. It wasn't simply his dress style (although that didn't help). His whole manner set him apart from the hard-drinking fraternity of newsmen. Arriving late one time to cover a meeting of the Irish Land League, he walked slowly to the reporters' table at the front of the room, laying down his cane and taking his seat with a melodramatic flourish. As the delegates reported how much money they had raised to free Ireland from the British yoke, Richard ostentatiously thumbed through his copies of the *Spectator* and the London *Athenaeum*, two upper-class English periodicals. The speakers seemed not to notice, but the press corps did.[30] Because he was formal and mannered, he was thought to be "uppish," and no doubt he did consider himself superior to most of his colleagues. Lining up for assignments in the morning and waiting late at night to be released from duty, he would chat with the other *Press* reporters. But even when he doffed the ulster, he remained cloaked in reserve. "I say, Davis, what's your first name anyhow?" a new recruit once asked him. "Mister," he replied.[31]

He made few friends; but in the almost three years that he worked for the *Press*, Richard learned the reporter's trade. It was immeasurably more to his liking than the classroom had been. Reporting was like a game. With no advance preparation, the newsman would be dispatched to the scene of a story. In a few hours, he would have to find the right people and ask them the right questions; then rush back to the office to scribble a coherent account.[32] (Typewriters didn't supersede pencils in the newsroom until the twentieth century.) A press card was a passport into every social realm and a letter of introduction to every social lion. As a *Press* reporter, Richard spent a night with shad fishermen on the Delaware River. He visited a condemned murderer in prison and skeptically observed the man's apparent insanity.[33] He wrote about leading actors, such as Henry Dixey and Creston Clarke. He profiled the most prominent Third Street stockbrokers.[34]

Later in life, discussing those interviews in which a cub reporter attempts to place his own words in the mouth of some prominent person, Davis remarked, "You can't expect a fifteen-dollar-a-week brain to describe a thousand-dollar-a-week brain."[35] He might have been thinking of his own first encounter with Walt Whitman, when the *Press* sent him to Camden to press for a reaction to Swinburne's recent "Whitmania" attack. "I haven't read the article," the placid old poet demurred. Neither had Richard, but he had read the *Critic*'s extract from the *Pall Mall Gazette*'s review of the article. He pulled that out of his pocket. The amiable Whitman lit the gas, donned his spectacles, read the vituperative paragraphs without expression, and then said, "I don't think I want to say anything about it."

"But did you read this?" asked the importunate young man, excitedly reciting some of Swinburne's fiercest aspersions. "I would rather not say anything about it," Whitman repeated mildly. "There may be things of value in the article. It is often that we obtain more good from those fellows who criticise us than those who eulogize."

At this point, recognizing that the old bard wasn't going to help, Richard tried providing him with a ready-made response that he need only endorse. "He says that you are absolutely deficient in rhythm, meter, and cadence," the young man explained. "In your article which recently appeared in the *Press* you forestall this by saying you must not be judged by the rules of art or aestheticism. That argument will apply in answer, will it not?"

"I won't say so," the poet retorted good-humoredly, deflating Richard's last hope. "Mr. Rice cabled me from London, asking me to answer this article in the *North American Review* and his editor has telegraphed me four times since urging me to write; but I do not care to write, and even after I have read the whole article, I know that I will not feel any more inclined to do so."

"It wouldn't be hard to retaliate in kind on the man who wrote 'Laus Veneris' and 'In the Orchard'?" Richard threw out as a desperate parting suggestion. Whitman was silent. As the young man rose to leave, Whitman said serenely, "I'm sorry you've had your trip for nothing. Remember me to the boys, those that know me and those that don't, and tell them the latch string is always out and that I will always be very glad to see them."[36]

Whitman found Davis's report of this interview "very cute."[37] A year later Richard returned to Mickle Street to describe Whitman's recuperation from a stroke.[38] "So you say that was the son of Rebecca Harding Davis?" the white-bearded seer remarked to Horace Traubel after Richard had gone, apparently not remembering the previous visit. "I thought him an Irish boy: I liked him—he was so candid, so interesting. Such tall, wholesome looking fellows are rare among American youngsters."[39] As for Richard's view of Whitman: he couldn't recognize that he was marching beneath Whitman's banner, that the grizzled prophet was the model for the theatrical, self-aggrandizing American writer. A decade later, Richard congratulated his mother on writing an essay which, while conceding Whitman's poetic talent, derided the man as "coarse by nature and vulgar by breeding." Richard thought that was the "coup de grace."[40]

Like many young men of the *Press*, Richard ranked the romantic Robert Louis Stevenson highest among living writers. (All his life, he considered Stevenson's "A Lodging for the Night" to be one of the finest stories in the English language.)[41] He sent Stevenson his favorite piece of *Press* work: a maudlin account of a friendless boy who, heartsick at the sudden death of his collie, shoots himself in the head at the dog's graveside. The famous writer sent Richard a letter. "The tale of the suicide is excellently droll," Stevenson wrote, "and your letter, you may be sure, will be preserved. If you are to escape unhurt out of your present business, you must be very careful, and you must find in your heart much constancy. The swiftly done work of the journalist, and the cheap finish and ready made methods to which it leads, you must try to counteract in private by writing with the most considerate slowness and on the most ambitious models. And when I say 'writing'—O, believe me, it is rewriting that I have chiefly in my mind. If you will do this I hope to hear of you some day."[42] It was good advice. Richard had it framed.

Press credentials gave Richard entrée to poor, crime-ridden neighborhoods, but his leeway was restricted. Unlike the Wheeling of Rebecca's youth, where the classes bumped together in daily contact, and a sensitive observer from the upper classes could write with empathy of the less fortunate, Philadelphia was a large modern city, in which the poor lived apart, in districts which outsiders need never enter. Often the poor were immigrants whose foreign ways isolated them further. To these exotic districts Richard went expectantly, in search of the colorful haunts and picaresque characters of literature.

He found that people didn't always live up to their parts. Richard was distressed when a murderer, on hearing the fatal word *guilty*, failed to perform as he would in a stage melodrama. "He had gazed in a rather vacant way at the foreman of the jury," Richard wrote, "and when the announcement that meant he must hang was made he dropped his hands by his side and sat down as if he had not heard the verdict."[43] Similarly, a hangout for thieves was no subterranean den out of Dickens, but "a cozy, cheerful place, as light as day, comfortably warm—not even picturesquely criminal."[44] From the start, Richard as a reporter was sharp enough, and honest enough, to note when reality didn't match his theatrical preconceptions; but to the end it was this congruence, or lack of it, that impressed him.

A few months after Richard arrived, the *Press* beefed up its crime coverage. A newly elected mayor had campaigned on a vow to close down the "policy shops," where bookmakers placed bets, and the "dives," where prostitutes found clients. The mayor's inauguration was scheduled for April 1, 1887. In late March, the *Press* investigated the policy shops; the series was so successful that a sequel on the racier dives followed. These dives, in an innocent earlier life, had been respectable German music halls, until the honky-tonk crush of the 1876 Centennial Exposition abased them. To find out how low they had sunk, Richard was dispatched one midnight into the inferno. His companion was his best friend on the *Press*, F. Jennings Crute, a brilliant young man with the soft voice, shy demeanor, and slight figure of a girl. Like Richard, Crute was a writer as well as a reporter. When he was only a boy, he began publishing vivid descriptive stories in a rural Delaware weekly, stories good enough to win him a job on the *Press*. From his Southern family, he had inherited a colonial pedigree and a wasting tuberculosis, two romantic attributes that must have appealed to Richard's imagination.[45]

The red-light district was ordinarily off limits to such immaculate youths, and rarely has vice seemed so unattractive as it does in their *Press* accounts. In ill-lit, ill-smelling rooms hung with suggestive pictures, drunken women threw themselves on drunken men. Blacks drank "reds" (whiskeys) alongside whites. Scantily clad women sang. In one bar, the singer was a man in a blond wig, makeup, and a stage-girl's dress—"the lowest creature in all the world." Interviewing one of the girls, the reporters learned that a clog dancer was paid about three dollars a week. A room in the neighborhood rented for about three dollars a week. How the dancers supplemented their rent money was not a subject the youths chose to broach directly; but otherwise, their questions were quite pointed. "Do you ever take opium?" they asked their voluble clog dancer. (On the way to the dives, they had passed a crazed Chinese addict pounding on a door.) "Opium! No, indeed," she replied. "I haven't got that far yet. A man was telling me the other night how he took one of the girls out and gave her opium. The things she did when she'd smoked was too much for me. No; I've not got that far yet." At 2:00 A.M., with the sound of "vacant laughter" in their ears and the hot, foul stench in their nostrils, the reporters called an end to their research.

They were delighted, on their next incognito visit to the dives, to hear the response to their first story. Mr. Hennessy, the jovial proprietor of one saloon, apologized to Richard and Jennings that his girls were in street clothes. "I'm sorry the ladies ain't looking their best tonight," he said, "but you see, gentlemen, I told 'em not to put on their stage clothes because times is rather ticklish now with this new chief of police comin' in and the newspapers. We don't know what minute we may have to get out of this by the little back door." At which point, he pulled on a bolt and revealed that one of the wall panels was actually a hinged door that opened onto a back alley. "These newspapers, as you say, ought to mind their own business," murmured one reporter, in a voice that sounded very much like Richard's. "That's just what I do say," Mr. Hennessy agreed warmly. "What good did the *Press* do with its policy showing-up? Only got a little advertising, that's all. That's all they do it for, I think." In their story, the journalists answered that with a smug rejoinder; but here, a century later, let Mr. Hennessy have the final word. The dives closed, at least temporarily; and the circulation of the *Press* no doubt rose, temporarily, as well.[46]

Richard so enjoyed his day-trips into the demimonde that nine months later he risked a longer sojourn. Copying a stage costume worn by Henry Dixey, he appeared one evening at a thieves' den called Sweeney's saloon in a flannel shirt and a turned-up coat collar, with a cap pulled down over one eye and a cigar butt jutting above an unshaven chin. Even he thought his appearance was "a trifle too villainous."[47] But he pulled it off. He told two men loitering outside the bar that he was "Buck" Meiley of New York and he was looking for his chum Gus Clemens. (He knew from police files that Clemens, a burglar, was in Baltimore.) He bought the men drinks and soon "Buck" was confiding his disreputable projects. Although his new friends didn't know Clemens, they pointed out someone who might: Charley Toohey, a man whom Davis was most eager to meet.

Even younger than Richard himself, Toohey had established himself as a nonpareil con man on the strength of a glib tongue and a frank smile. As these were among Richard's chief assets, the two young men might have been expected to hit it off. They did. Toohey remembered Clemens well. "He lifted some stuff from a young gent on Walnut Street late in the evening," he said, "and before he had time to pawn it they had the 'rap' out and he had to go back to Baltimore to fence it." Richard inched out a little further on his limb. This was bad news, he said. He would have to abandon the schemes he had plotted with Clemens when they were both serving time in "Moya" (or Moyamensing Prison, as it was usually known in Rittenhouse Square).

Moving to a more discreet side table, Richard asked if Toohey could steer him to any opportunities. Under questioning, he admitted ignorance of film-flamming (fast-talking a storekeeper into giving the wrong change) and working the shells (palming an India rubber ball as your mark tried to track it beneath three moving walnut shells). But recognizing a talented novice, Toohey over the next eleven days taught "Buck" these and other arcane specialties. By the end of his charade, Richard felt "a most sincere and pernicious admiration" for Toohey. Paying his last visit to Sweeney's on a Saturday night, he bought Toohey one more beer. "I'll see you Monday morning, then," said the con man in parting. His own con job completed, Richard nodded, even though he knew that "Buck" Meiley would not be seen by anyone ever again. The Sunday *Press* devoted almost a full page—bursting with details and real names—to Richard's report of his yeggman days. The sensational story established young Davis's reputation in Philadelphia. Later, his stunt was said to be the first instance of a reporter's infiltrating a band of thieves. It became part of his legend, the first of his many journalistic exploits.[48] Less fortunate, Toohey apparently went to jail.[49]

Over the years, as the story took on rococo embellishments, Richard was said to have plotted a burglary with his larcenous colleagues and, at the final moment, turned them in to the police. Another story, one which Davis told himself, may be equally apocryphal but it is a characteristic Davis yarn. Leaving his parents' house in a dinner jacket, sometime after "Buck" had been laid to rest, Richard ran into a man he had known at Sweeney's. His old acquaintance winked knowingly. "What are you doing here?" he whispered. "Are you butler in this house?" Richard nodded. "When you rob it, don't forget me," the hoodlum continued. "I'll be in it with you." Delighted to have been exposed, not as a duplicitous reporter but as a crooked butler, Richard shook hands on it.[50]

He was less successful at combining acting with journalism the next fall when, with young publishing scions Morton MacMichael III and Barclay

Warburton, he founded a breezy, gossipy theatrical weekly. Lacking capital of his own, he received one-tenth ownership in return for supplying articles. With MacMichael as editor and Davis and Warburton as associate editors, the first issue of the *Stage* appeared on September 29, 1888.[51] Richard's chief contribution was a weekly column, "The Lime Light Man." For the first two months, he assumed the fictional persona of the man in the second gallery who operates the limelight. (In those literal days, that meant heating calcium in a flame to generate a brilliant white light, and modulating it with colored glass shades.) He then shucked that silly constraint and continued to write, unfettered, about the subjects that interested him: theater etiquette, public relations, and celebrity, for starters. He was also remarkably knowledgeable about props, costumes, and bits of stage business. In its heyday, the commercial theater indulged a taste for verisimilitude regardless of cost. Richard adored these splashes of authenticity: real cows, horses, and lions; real wagons loaded with real hay; and real champagne uncorked by real waiters. In one production, real dirty dishes were rinsed in a real washtub; and in another, a real horse was shod at a real forge. The most exhaustive display of realism occurred nightly in *The Stowaway*, when for eight silent minutes two Sing Sing alumni applied their safecracking skills to a recalcitrant vault.[52] The injection of the "real" added greatly to the impact of the drama. As a renowned connoisseur of spectacles, Richard would one day praise "real" pageants in which noblemen wore their age-old costumes and peasant soldiers marched in storybook uniforms. Memorably, he would record the scene as a young czar donned a gem-studded crown in an ancient chapel. And he would discover that, by the standards of "real" play-acting, there was something even more impressive than royalty: war.

Richard left the *Stage* in May 1889, as the paper became more and more MacMichael's one-man show.[53] For much of that May, he was bedridden with a nervous complaint.[54] In the late nineteenth century, nervous exhaustion was common among the upper classes; indeed, neurasthenia (literally, weak nerves) was thought by some experts to be a sign of refinement, an ailment that all the best people endured. Throughout his life Richard would suffer from these periodic "nerve storms." He would take shelter in his bed, and eventually they would pass. This time, though, a storm of a different sort roused him from his refuge. It was a real-life epic too big to fit beneath a proscenium arch, a historical event that was the first major story of his reporting career.

The first word of the disaster that had struck Johnstown, Pennsylvania, came at about 6:00 P.M. on Friday, May 31, 1889, some three hours after the dam broke at South Fork. Heavy rains had been flooding western Pennsylvania for days. On the afternoon of May 31, an official of the Pennsylvania Railroad attached a private car to a passenger train and left

Pittsburgh to inspect damage to the tracks. He reached Sang Hollow, about
four miles from Johnstown, at about 4:00 P.M.; on orders from the tower
operator, he stopped there. The telegraph lines to the east were dead. Not
long afterward, debris began rushing down the swollen Conemaugh River—
horrible debris, with people clinging to it. After waiting two hours, the
railroad official ordered his train back to Pittsburgh. Before departing, he
wired the Pittsburgh newspapers that the South Fork dam had failed and
Johnstown was catastrophically flooded.[55]

To a professional ear, that telegram was a call to battle. In newsrooms
around the country, reporters began leaving for Johnstown. The first private
train, chartered by newspapers, pulled out of Pittsburgh a little after 7:00
P.M. Another soon departed. Responding to the news on the Associated
Press wire, reporters set out that night from New York, Boston, Chicago,
St. Louis, Cleveland, and Philadelphia. As they approached Johnstown,
they found that the disaster scene would not be easy to reach. The two
trains from Pittsburgh were halted at Bolivar, some twenty miles from
Johnstown, at about 10:30 P.M.

As the son of a newspaper editor, Richard probably heard the news
early. Certainly he knew by the time he read the *Press* of Saturday, June 1.
"Hundreds Dead," the headline proclaimed. Although no reporters had
yet reached Johnstown, the *Press* correctly judged that the city was "the
scene of one of the most appalling disasters in American history."[56] By the
time this newspaper appeared, two *Press* reporters were speeding—or trying
to speed—to the scene. Henry S. Brown, upon reading the first telegraphed
report Friday evening, hurried to the Broad Street station of the Pennsylvania Railroad and, at 11:25 P.M., boarded the first train headed west. He got
as far as Harrisburg. Everything was blocked to the west. All day Saturday
and into Sunday he waited, until, in desperation, he tried another railroad,
the Cumberland Valley. That got him fifty miles southwest, to Cham-
bersburg, where he thought of driving. Exhausting six relay teams of horses,
he drove 105 miles of rain-gouged mountain roads in twenty-eight hours,
to arrive in Johnstown from the south on Monday night.[57] Ten minutes
after his arrival, he met Richard's friend and fellow *Press* reporter, Jennings
Crute, who had left Philadelphia the same night as Brown. Taking a much
more circuitous course, all of it by rail, Crute reached Johnstown at sunset
Monday, about an hour before Brown arrived. Crute's first sight of the
devastated city was the Cambria Iron Works, "crushed and mashed into a
fearful mass."[58]

All weekend Richard fretted in Philadelphia, reading the second-hand
news accounts originating from cities near Johnstown. This was the biggest
story since Lincoln's assassination, and he was missing it! He pleaded with
the managing editor to send him, and at last he won an assignment. Like
smelling salts, the scent of a good story usually shocked him out of depression. On Tuesday, bubbling with excitement, he was traveling on the Balti-

more and Ohio Railroad through a desolate West Virginia landscape. Two days before, part of the road on which he passed had been submerged beneath eight feet of water. Now the receding flood waters unveiled, in place of corn fields, a terrain of mud, water, and giant stones. Stained with muck, the leaves of even the tallest trees along the Potomac were as brown as in November. The train crawled; and although Richard had thought he would get to Johnstown at midnight, he didn't arrive until sometime Thursday.[59]

He saw a city that had been blotted out. Much of it was washed away, and most of what remained had been smashed and dirtied until it was barely recognizable, let alone useful. The death toll could never be fixed with certainty, but 2,209 is the generally accepted estimate. By the time Richard arrived, the city stank from the decomposing bodies of people and animals. Along with the stench rose fears of typhus. The weather had turned unseasonably cool, which was fortunate for disease control but uncomfortable otherwise. The first wave of reporters set up shop in a drafty old brick kiln with an earth floor, improvising tables out of boards laid on barrels. The advantage of this dump was its location, close by the telegraph office that had been jerry-rigged at the west end of the stone bridge over the Conemaugh. Nine telegraph wires to the west had survived the deluge. In a hovel once used to store oil barrels, its floor slimy with old grease and its air still reeking, in darkness punctured only by flickering tallow candles, the telegraph operators took the reporters' copy and transmitted the awful news to the world beyond.[60]

There were no hotels, restaurants, or stores standing in Johnstown. When Richard left the train, he greatly amused the crowd of reporters by asking the way to the nearest restaurant. Told he had to live off the land, he triggered new hysterics by inquiring how he could hire a horse and wagon. Funniest of all was his final question: Where might he buy a white shirt? "A boiled shirt is as rare here as a mince pie in Africa," noted a man from the New York *Times*.[61] The first carloads of emergency provisions had arrived, but they were earmarked for the survivors—not for the newspaper reporters. Slipping between the slats of the organized relief effort, many of the journalists wheedled food from poor workmen. About the time Richard arrived, a generous correspondent of the New York *Herald* imported $150 of food from Pittsburgh to supply a local cook whose house had withstood the flood, and Johnstown once again had a restaurant. For fifty cents a meal, the grateful reporters could dine there. In a reporter's day of slogging through town for news, competing for a place on the telegraph wire, and bedding down in barns, the rituals of breakfast and dinner at the Café Hungaria marked the bright spots.[62]

As a junior reporter coming late on the scene, Richard drew a peripheral assignment—the charitable efforts of Philadelphians. The news of the calamity had inspired an extraordinary national relief campaign: Americans donated $3.6 million for the relief of Johnstown, with the largest share, $600,000, coming from Philadelphia. "The act of feeding 12,000 a day lacks the easy grace of an afternoon tea," Richard remarked, "and the way canned meats, sardine boxes, loaves of bread and bundles of tea fly through the air and are shoved into the baskets of the refugees would make a delicately organized nature lose its appetite for a week."[63] He was most impressed by Miss Helen Hinckley, a socially prominent Philadelphian who, while administering the efforts of the Children's Aid Society from an office facing the morgue, managed to look "as neat and fresh as if she had stepped that moment from the Quaker City's Rittenhouse Square." He also admired a Philadelphia Club member who, in his role as a National Guard first lieutenant, cheerfully hoisted barrels of flour. In this sweating, public-spirited aristocrat, one may discern the prototype of a Roosevelt Rough Rider.[64]

Richard was most distressed when a gentleman failed to live up to the code. On the day he arrived in Johnstown, he saw a local deputy sheriff attempt to quiet a drunken National Guard first lieutenant. Although the deputy sheriff had lost everything—wife, baby, and home—in the flood, he calmly withstood the drunk's insults. A burly passerby, however, overheard the dispute and took a swing at the guardsman. At this point, Richard, who with the delicate Crute had been observing the quarrel, intervened to break it up. When the lieutenant fumbled for his pistol, the sheriff wrestled him to the ground. Instead of arresting the lout, the sheriff told him to return immediately to barracks. And there it might have ended, had the *Press* not run the story the next day. Instead, the lieutenant was stripped of his sword and court-martialed. Both Crute and Davis testified at the hearing.[65]

As an epilogue, some months later, the lieutenant sued for libel.[66] By then Davis was the only remaining *Press* witness. His health undermined by the hardships he endured at Johnstown, Jennings Crute died six months afterward. Despite his chronic tuberculosis, and his exhaustion from a hard winter, Crute hadn't hesitated to rush to Johnstown, arriving on the scene before any other Philadelphian. He continued to work in the chill and wet, among the rotting corpses, subsisting on such rations as soda crackers filled with jam, after many of his colleagues had been furloughed. "I knew I had my death-blow," he reportedly said later, "but there was so much to do there!" A short time after his return to Philadelphia, while covering troop maneuvers, he collapsed, and never left the hospital.[67] His death moved Richard deeply. Jennings was his closest friend. Beyond that, in his dedication to the newsman's craft, Crute displayed an inspiring chivalry. When Rebecca eulogized young Crute in the *Independent*, saying his courageous life exemplified the "often heroic service" of the reporter, her grateful son wrote her, "I cannot tell you how it pleased me except to say that loving him as I did I would not have changed a word in it."[68]

According to Rebecca, two other reporters died from their Johnstown ordeals, and few escaped serious illness. It was in the flooded city that Richard apparently contracted sciatica, an inflammation of a lumbar nerve root that periodically crippled his right leg. It would crop up throughout his life; but then, so would the comparisons to Johnstown, which, as the first major story he reported, remained the standard of reference for all to come. When an event was truly of the first water, Richard would write that it was as wonderful or as terrible as the Johnstown flood.[69]

The cause of the disaster, which emerged as the mopping-up proceeded, must also have made an impression upon the recent student of political economy. A break in a dam caused the flood, but it wasn't engineers who were at fault. The dam at South Fork wasn't the work of engineers. To understand why the disaster occurred, one must quickly survey the history of that dam. It had been built to create a reservoir to fill a canal, which would link Johnstown to Pittsburgh, even in the dry summers; but by the time it was completed in 1852, the western spur of the Pennsylvania Railroad made it already obsolete. Unused, the earthwork dam deteriorated for almost thirty years until a Pittsburgh real-estate broker bought it and decided to reconstruct it, making the fish-stocked lake the centerpiece of a summer colony for wealthy Pittsburgh businessmen. He formed a club, which included Andrew Carnegie and Henry Clay Frick, and from the members raised about seventeen thousand dollars to rebuild the dam. He didn't bother to replace the discharge pipes (which had long ago been sold for scrap), so there was no way to lower the water level if it rose dangerously. He didn't call in engineers to reconstruct the dam itself, which was badly battered from fire and neglect. Instead, he had it patched with mud, rocks, hay, even horse manure. To permit a road to cross the breast of the dam, he lowered its height, thereby effectively reducing the capacity of the only emergency outlet, the spillway. Finally, in an act that took on resonance after the catastrophe, he erected a screen of rods at the mouth of the spillway, to keep the stock of fish from escaping. Under normal conditions, the screen would not have impeded the flow of water. Once it was clogged with debris, however, the screen became a plug. Arrogantly eschewing the scientific advice of engineers, a group of selfish, pleasure-loving businessmen had imperiled an entire community so they could enjoy a bit of sport. That was the national lesson of Johnstown.[70]

There was a more personal lesson, too, for a young man who insisted religiously on his daily bath and boiled white shirt. Richard's code of chivalry, good manners, and clean living shielded him from the temptations and terrors that lurked beyond the limits of civilized society. As a symbol of what happens if reserve and restraint collapse, what could be more powerful than the torrent of filth unloosed when the dam broke above Johnstown?

3

Famous Overnight

*I*N THE SUMMER OF 1889, not long after the Johnstown flood, Richard
accompanied the Philadelphia championship cricket team on a tour of
England. Another *Press* reporter had snatched this plum assignment, but
Richard (probably with Clarke's help) obtained credentials from the *Evening Telegraph*.[1] Sometimes one must get away from a place to realize
how oppressive it is. Philadelphia's Quaker plainness cramped Richard's
flamboyant style, and its fusty deference to old families choked his social
ambition. On his first trip to Europe, the rudeness of the class-conscious
British dismayed him. More painfully, he was oppressed by the blue-
blooded Philadelphian cricketeers, who snubbed him because of his Western parents, his undistinguished college, and his grand affectations. Their
teasing drove him to tears. In England he realized that back in Philadelphia,
the houses he wanted to enter would never welcome him.[2] When he returned home in August, he itched to leave. The destination was never in
doubt.

Then as now, New York was the place for a socially ambitious young
American. While Philadelphia society resembled an arboretum, with every
family tree precisely labeled and all permissible paths explicitly laid out,
New York was a promiscuous jungle. Luxuriant new species sprang up
alongside manicured older specimens, and the accidents of cross-pollination
produced a state of excitement and surprise. In other Eastern cities, the old
families had maintained their grip on local society. But in New York, the
weight of the enormous Gilded Age fortunes was too much for ancient
bedrock to bear. Shut out of Knickerbocker circles, the new New York
millionaires created a society of their own. Their houses and parties were
so lavish that, throughout the booming cities of the West, New York became
a mecca for the wives (husbands in tow) of other new millionaires. Their
society became Society.

For convenience, one might point to 1883 as the year the balance tipped. That year Mrs. William Kissam Vanderbilt, of recent but enormous wealth, staged a lavish costume party at her new $3 million Renaissance mansion on Fifth Avenue. Mrs. William Astor, the doyenne of New York society, had studiously snubbed the upstart Vanderbilts at every opportunity; but now, her daughter was so crestfallen at not receiving an invitation to the party that Mrs. Astor swallowed her principles and paid a call on Mrs. Vanderbilt. The Astors promptly received their invitation to the Vanderbilt bash—and the following January, the Vanderbilts attended Mrs. Astor's annual ball.

Along with Mrs. Astor's visit to Mrs. Vanderbilt, which resounded in New York society as an updated pilgrimage to Canossa, 1883 saw the opening of the Metropolitan Opera House. Tired of being shut out of the small, exclusive Academy of Music, where the eighteen boxes were handed down like family heirlooms, the new rich simply built a bigger auditorium of their own, and it fast eclipsed the old.[3] The grandiose Metropolitan Opera House stood as a cenotaph for the society of old New York. Those Knickerbocker families unable or unwilling to indulge in the increasingly extravagant entertainments just dropped out of sight.[4] They were like aborigines, wrote their leading literary chronicler, Edith Wharton; and they were "doomed to rapid extinction with the advance of the invading race."[5]

New York's fashionable elite were dubbed the Four Hundred by Ward McAllister, a professional courtier who helped reorganize the city's social life after the Civil War. When, in 1892, he finally divulged the Four Hundred roster (it contained only 273 names), one-third of the elect were revealed to be from undistinguished families, admitted on the basis of money or celebrity.[6] In Philadelphia, one's social position was fixed for life, unaffected by changes in fortune or achievement.[7] Volatile New York society revolved around entertainments. If a newcomer was entertaining enough (and one could entertain with witty conversation as well as with extravagant banquets), he might expect to rise in the great metropolis.[8]

New York was also the place for a newspaperman. Its newspapers were the largest, the most exciting, and (not incidentally) the most profitable in the country. Here once again the year 1883 marked a turning point. That was when Hungarian immigrant Joseph Pulitzer took control of the New York *World*, and revolutionized the business with eye-grabbing headlines and snappy graphics. The *World*'s ever-increasing circulation and profits won the grudging respect of its rivals. Realizing that they had to spend money to make money, publishers shelled out startling amounts on everything from telegraph fees to wages. The salaries of first-rate editors and reporters in New York almost doubled in fifteen years. At least twenty reporters were earning $3,000 to $5,000 a year; one managing editor was paid $12,000, and five or more others were topping $6,000. No wonder that young men and women from all over the country applied to New York newspapers for jobs.[9]

This golden age of newspapers would have been impossible without a series of technological breakthroughs that permitted the cheap and rapid production of great numbers of papers. In the early nineteenth century, printing was a preindustrial craft. A printer composed a page of type by drawing each letter out of a box, and then printed the page by hand-feeding sheets of paper into a flatbed press. After the Civil War, this antiquated system changed radically. The flatbed press gave way to an ever-improving sequence of rotating-cylinder presses; by the early 1870s, the web-perfecting press was able to print both sides of a continuous roll ("web") of paper and then cut it into sheets. On these presses the printer placed curved stereotyped plates, an innovation of the news-hungry days of the Civil War. A printer could make many plates of the same page and run it off on multiple presses simultaneously. Fast-flowing inks quickened the printing, and the triangular form folder (introduced in 1881) facilitated the assembly of the newspaper. In 1886, Ottmar Morgenthaler eliminated the worst bottleneck in the process by inventing the Linotype machine. Instead of composing and justifying each line from precast letters in a printer's box, a keyboard operator could now type out a story on reusable type.

The development of the half-tone process of photoreproduction in 1880 enabled publishers to liven up their papers; by the mid-1880s, Pulitzer's *World* regularly featured illustrations, political cartoons, and comic strips. Modern science even altered the paper the news was printed on. Newspapers before the Civil War were made of expensive rag-fiber paper. After the war, the manufacture of cheap paper from wood pulp was perfected, and the price of paper fell from nine to three cents a pound.[10]

These technological advances made possible the rise of a mass press. They did not create it. Indeed, it was the demand for cheap popular newspapers that stoked the engines of invention. Before the Civil War, the great newspaper proprietors, men like Horace Greeley and Charles Dana, hungered for influence over the minds of educated people. Dana even dreamed of someday publishing a newspaper which excluded all advertising.[11] Their ambitions, while large, did not require a large readership. In this distinguished pack of newspaper proprietors, there was one joker: the unorthodox James Gordon Bennett, who introduced the new strain in American journalism with his New York *Herald*, a lurid sheet that made him rich. Compared to what followed, however, Bennett's operation was small potatoes. The *Herald* at the start of the Civil War proclaimed a circulation of 77,000, the highest in the world.[12] A generation later, at the time of Richard's arrival in New York, Pulitzer's *World* boasted a circulation of 250,000.[13]

No longer directed at opinion makers, the New York newspaper now catered to shoppers.[14] The same sort of industrial innovations that permitted the creation of cheap newspapers had given birth to mountains of cheap consumer goods. The department store grew up to sell them. The newspaper grew up to advertise them. The staid and "objective" newspaper, typified by the New York *Times*, and the screeching, sensation-mongering sheet, represented by Pulitzer's *World*, appeared totally different, but they were alternative responses to the same new conditions. The nonpartisan *Times* appealed to all political persuasions of the well educated and well off. The populist *World* penetrated the homes of the working poor. Each provided a valid advertising environment; it all depended on what you were selling.

In years to come, as radio and television came to alienate the affections of working people, the newspapers that catered to them would wither and die. But when Richard moved to New York, those papers were booming. Three weeks before he arrived, ground was broken for the construction of Pulitzer's new World Building. When completed a year later, it towered at least six stories above any other New York building. The New York *Sun* sneered that it resembled a brass-head tack.[15] However, as Pulitzer pointed out, from the top of his tower he could spit on the *Sun*.[16] To reporters in lesser cities, the golden dome of the *World* beckoned like the Statue of Liberty with the promise of a better life.

On his return from London, Richard traveled to New York, armed with a letter of recommendation from George W. Childs, the proprietor of the Philadelphia *Public Ledger*. This was another family connection: in October 1889, Clarke went to work for Childs as associate editor of the *Public Ledger*, the most prestigious paper in the city. (He became managing editor four years later.)[17] Despite Richard's illustrious references, he was turned down by several papers. Walking in frustration down Park Row, where New York's newspapers had their headquarters, he resigned himself to taking the train back to Philadelphia in failure. Until, with the luck that characterized his career, he ran into Arthur Brisbane, and his plans changed.[18]

Davis had met Brisbane, then the English correspondent of the New York *Sun*, that summer in London. Six months younger than Davis, Brisbane was a brilliant young man cut from the same cloth: handsome and foppish, with exquisite, artificial manners and a love of ostentation. Unlike Richard, though, Arthur hadn't acquired all of his pretentions from literature and the theater. He had spent his adolescence in Europe, attending school in Paris and Stuttgart. His father, Albert Brisbane, was a Fourierist socialist of independent means, an earnest man who was a close associate of Horace Greeley, the proprietor of the New York *Tribune*. Arthur inherited his father's love of journalism, if not his socialism or his earnestness. It was as a last effort to rescue Arthur from a life of frivolity that Albert Brisbane asked Charles A. Dana, whom he knew from their *Tribune* days together, to take on the boy. In 1883, Dana hired the nineteen-year-old Arthur as a fifteen-dollar-a-week cub reporter for his New York *Sun*.[19]

Dana's *Sun* was widely regarded as the best-written newspaper in America, "the newspaperman's newspaper." From the time he bought the paper in 1868, Dana attracted talented young writers to his staff. He instructed his exchange editor, who scanned other papers for reprintable items, to be on the lookout for any inspired writing, even a paragraph, so he could lure the author to the *Sun*.[20] Harvard-educated himself, Dana did not share the typical editor's prejudice against college boys. He recommended that all reporters read Shakespeare, Milton, and, for its admirable terseness, the Bible. "I had rather take a young fellow who knows the 'Ajax' of Sophocles, and has read Tacitus, and can scan every ode of Horace—I would rather take him to report a prize-fight or a spelling match, for instance, than to take one who has never had those advantages," Dana said.[21] He also thought that for a true command of English, a grasp of the old Teutonic provided a helpful supplement to Greek and Latin.[22]

Although he held his native tongue in high regard, Dana was not a donnish, diffident fellow. He honored the language as a rifleman respects his weapon. Choosing his targets fearlessly, he outraged virtually everyone. Within a decade of his purchase of the *Sun*, it was banned from the reading rooms of respectable clubs, such as the Century. "It is read by horse-car drivers," said the priggish.[23] In fact, it was read by everyone worth talking to. "Make the paper interesting," was Dana's credo.[24] He succeeded magnificently.

Young Brisbane worked for Dana for eighteen months and then quit to join his father in Europe. But he missed the *Sun*. Dana suggested that as long as he was over there, Arthur might like to become the *Sun*'s London correspondent, which was then a low-paying, low-profile position. Brisbane took the job and transformed it. He rented an expensive suite at the Victoria Hotel, sent out fancy announcements, and, in every way, dressed and acted the part of a grand young gentleman. Londoners who ordinarily ignored the representatives of American papers began to take notice. Back home, *Sun* readers responded favorably to Brisbane's reports on the gruesome murders of Jack the Ripper and the miseries of the Whitechapel slums. Enlarging his bailiwick, Brisbane traveled to Paris and Rome; it was in Chantilly, France, on March 10, 1888, that he made his reputation with his coverage of the prizefight between John L. Sullivan and Charlie Mitchell. Not long after meeting Davis in the summer of 1889, Brisbane heard of an attractive opening back in the home office. For such a young man, it was a very long shot, but he applied—and succeeded. Remarkably, at the age of twenty-four, he became the managing editor of the *Evening Sun*. Which is how, at their fortuitous meeting, he was in a position to offer Richard a job.[25]

The *Evening Sun* was an afternoon paper that Dana started in March 1887, at the urging of his associate, William M. Laffan.[26] Spritely and well written like its parent, the *Evening Sun* was a bit more raffish in its tastes. For an *Evening Sun* reporter, whatever his knowledge of Tacitus, the best place to scrounge up news was in the city's police courts. The murder of a respectable person merited a series. The revenge or suicide of an outraged young woman would be lovingly detailed. Brawls among immigrants, fires in tenements, freaks of nature, fits of madness—the *Evening Sun* played up the weird, the piteous, the startling. It was the sort of newspaper that promoted itself with stories of its newsboys catching babies dropped from tenement windows.[27] The tone was set by the first editor, Amos J. Cummings, a former printer who had risen at the *Tribune* to city editor until he was fired for his profanity and hired by Dana.[28] The tone was nicely maintained by the second editor, the fun-loving, sensation-seeking Brisbane. Many years later, when William Randolph Hearst had made him the most highly paid editor in the country, Brisbane was asked by a young journalist for advice. "In a man's early years enthusiasm and general interest help him, and if he has moderate ability he is likely to do well enough," Brisbane said. "Around thirty he is in danger of becoming too seriously interested in something and thereby becoming heavy and monotonous." Brisbane pointed to a heavily laden bookshelf that was built into his automobile. "Do you see those books?" he said. "It is an encyclopedia; there are thirty volumes; I began at the left, have read straight through fifteen volumes, and shall read straight through the rest. There is a little on every subject under the sun. Young man, if you would succeed in journalism, never lose your ... *superficiality.*"[29]

The *Sun* and *Evening Sun* were housed in a ramshackle five-story building that had once been home for Tammany Hall. Legend claimed that it was built on shifting sand. One mechanic boasted that he could bring it down using only a shovel. Repeatedly condemned by the health board, often set afire, infested with rats and enormous cockroaches, it somehow survived. Dana had bought it in 1868, the year he took over the *Sun*, and he presided in a bare office behind a black walnut table. The most striking decoration in his office was a stuffed owl, a fitting alter ego for the cranky, bearded editor. In the newsroom, which occupied almost all of the third floor, the reporters sat at two rows of small desks, with the managing editor, city editor, and copy readers occupying the choice seats near the five windows facing City Hall Park. They wrote by hand, dipping pens into violet ink. Electric lights had recently been introduced, a big improvement over the gas jets suspended many feet above the desks. The room was poorly ventilated, and on hot summer nights, the thermometer often exceeded a hundred degrees.[30]

Brisbane ran the afternoon edition from a cubbyhole, in which, hoping (in vain) that he might occasionally catch some sleep, he had installed a cot.[31] A *Sun* reporter was typically on duty for ten to twelve hours a day, his editor even longer.[32] Better paid than other newsmen, widely regarded as the elite, the *Sun* men lengthened their days further by socializing when work was done. The French bistro Mouquin's on Fulton Street was a favorite hangout, where a dinner with wine and a ten-cent cigar could be had for under a dollar. After hours, Perry's drugstore, on the ground floor of the *Sun* building, was a popular gathering spot: if you knew the management, you could obtain drink stronger than soda behind the Prescriptions screen.[33] To be asked to join the *Sun*, even the *Evening Sun*, was to be invited into the most exclusive fraternity in journalism. As Brisbane scornfully remarked, "to put a good newspaper man on a Philadelphia newspaper is like inviting a good musician to prove his skill on the jew's-harp."[34] Richard gleefully accepted Brisbane's offer.

With mixed emotions, the Davises received a jubilant telegram and prepared for the departure of the eldest son. Richard returned home for two days to pack up his things. Like all such inevitabilities, Richard's quitting Philadelphia, when it finally happened, seemed very sudden. Rebecca could not hide her dismay. To reassure her, Richard promised that his move to New York was temporary. "I am not surprised that you were sad if you thought I was going away for good," he wrote her, in a note dashed off at the railroad station. "I could not think of it myself. I am only going to make a little reputation and to learn enough of the business to enable me to live at home in the centre of the universe with you."[35] This blatantly insincere vow did little to reassure her.

Six feet tall and weighing 180 pounds, with a square face, a straight nose and mouth, and a round, dimpled chin, the youthful Davis glowed with a sense of athletic well-being[36] (although a sensitive observer might detect "extreme nervous tension, almost exhaustion, in the lines around the mouth and expression of the eyes"[37]). He seemed too wholesome to be a New Yorker.

Crossing City Hall Park on the way to his first day of work, Richard, carrying a hat box and a bundle of canes, was stopped by a stranger in a beaver coat who addressed him warmly as "Mr. Williams." Having recently taken a course in con artistry, Richard replied smoothly that the man was mistaken. His name was Norris and he was the son of a Philadelphia woolen-goods manufacturer. He was not at all surprised a few moments later when another stranger came up and greeted him as "Mr. Norris." The man identified himself as the nephew of George Wanamaker, a Philadelphia department store mogul who was postmaster general. Since Mr. Wanamaker's first name was actually John, here was another tip that not all was aboveboard. Young Wanamaker said that he was his uncle's New York agent and asked "Norris" to come inspect some woolen samples.

Richard excused himself and ran to the *Sun* office. He told the city editor that a bunco steerer was waiting outside. Would he please assign him to be buncoed? He obtained the assignment. Young Wanamaker, attending patiently, then took him in a streetcar to Mulberry Street, where they entered a building prominently marked 17, even though it was on the even-numbered side of the street. The interior of the building was made up as a ticket office, with timetables, photographs of express trains, and railroad scenery. Wanamaker bought a "scalp ticket" from an ersatz agent and presented "Norris" with a box of fabric. Richard was fingering the cloth when a loud, dirty man with a sombrero and a spurious Southern accent charged in and requested a ticket to Mobile, Alabama. Before long, this self-described Southern cattle king was losing heavily in cards to Wanamaker and inviting "Norris" to join in. "Norris" easily won a thousand dollars before the cattle king challenged him: "How do I know that you've got a thousand dollars about you?" Admitting that he hadn't, Richard offered to go to the posh Astor House, where he said he had left his trunk. Wanamaker accompanied him to the hotel and waited outside.

In the lobby, Richard frantically but unsuccessfully looked for a policeman. He would have to act on his own. Rejoining Wanamaker, he suddenly tackled the man, grabbing him around the neck in an illegal football hold. He held him until a policeman came up and escorted them to the police station, where "Wanamaker" was recognized as Sheeny Mike, a notorious con artist who preyed on ingenuous out-of-towners. Young Davis with his hatbox had seemed a likely mark. When the judge at the police court asked Davis his profession, and the youth replied, "A reporter on the *Evening Sun*," the spectators in the courthouse shouted their approval, and even the judge laughed. Because the newcomer to New York was unable to locate the phony ticket-office, Sheeny Mike could be convicted only of disorderly conduct. Still, he was sentenced to six months in jail.

Returning to the office, Richard wrote up the story and gave it to Brisbane, who was so enthusiastic that he took it personally to Dana's partner, William Laffan. Laffan was delighted with it. Under the title "Our Green Reporter," it ran in a long column down the front page. The other *Evening Sun* reporters gathered to congratulate Richard, and rival newspapers published their own versions of the amusing incident. It was the talk of the town.[38] In his first day at work, Richard had triumphed. Lucky, certainly, but it was no fluke. "Our Green Reporter" fit squarely in the Davis tradition, a genre he had established in the Adirondack narrative and the Conway Maur tales. It was a yarn of adventure with Richard himself as the protagonist. "I thought I would get on here after a while," Richard wrote his parents, "but I really did not think I would have my name on the newspaper bulletins on the second day of my arrival."[39]

Richard's starting salary on the *Evening Sun* was thirty dollars a week.[40] For four dollars a week, he rented a temporary room at 116 West Twenty-second Street while he hunted for an apartment.[41] Then as now, New York was a city best appreciated by the young, who could overlook the bumps on the ride, and by the rich, who could cushion themselves. Things moved fast in New York. A man ran for the tram he wanted, dodging the ones he didn't; and then, to the conductor's refrain of "Step lively," he jumped off at his stop.[42] Prices soared. Newspapers bulged. There was an excess of money and a surfeit of news. Houses rose and fell and rose again: the wreckers and the builders worked in harmony. As far back as 1856, an editor wrote that New York was "notoriously the largest and the least loved of any of our great cities" because it was "never the same city for a dozen years altogether."[43] Ten years before Richard's arrival, there had been only scattered shanties and a few market gardens north of Fifty-ninth Street. Now large tracts were developed for housing. Buffeted by fashion, propelled by greed, the city lurched northward, consuming whatever got in its way.

The air of New York seemed to stimulate rapid growth and change. Even the trees in Central Park, thought one European, had too much leafage for the size of their trunks.[44] Along with the rush came the noise. Writing at the turn of the century of a disease he labeled "Newyorkitis," a physician compared the assault of sound endured by the New Yorker to the position of a boilermaker hammering rivets on the inside of a boiler. "The New Yorker has become so accustomed to noise," wrote the doctor, "that he requires it at all times, even at his meals."[45]

In soil that is likely to be bulldozed at any moment, a well-adapted plant will devote more energy to blooming than to rooting. New York effloresced riotously. It was a city of short-lived sensations, in which a song, a play, or a performer would for a while dominate all discussion, and then vanish. Three months before Richard, an obscure Spanish dancer had arrived in New York in a creaky extravaganza that featured a chorus line of Greeks and Amazons. When Julian Ralph wrote a rave in the *Sun*, Carmencita—as the young dancer called herself—became a phenomenon. Ladies who did not ordinarily attend vaudeville would wait outside Koster and Bial's in their carriages until 9:50 at night, when a man would escort them to their box to see the star take the stage. Or, for a hundred dollars, they would have the dancer, accompanied by two musicians, perform in their home. This being New York, not too many months elapsed before a rival, Otero, was imported to the Eden Musée across the street from Koster and Bial's; and with her more blatantly sensuous dancing, Otero became the hot new act in town. Carmencita gave her American farewell performance in 1893 and disappeared into the European wilds. One admirer later tracked her down to a sparsely furnished boarding-house room in London, where she lived penuriously with her guitarist husband.[46]

Among the fashionable young people of New York, each moment had its craze. Around the time Richard arrived in New York, it was the baseball team the Giants, and the faddists would greet each other with the stadium cheer, "Who are the people?" to which the correct reply was "We are!" or "Us!" Then it was Carmencita, followed by Otero, who in turn was eclipsed by the little boy jockey Willie Wilson who jumped big horses over big hurdles at the Horse Show in Madison Square Garden. The flickering needle next came to rest upon Maggie Cline and her rendition of "Throw Him Down, McCloskey," a boisterous ballad of an Irishman who begins his prizefight according to the Queensberry rules but quickly descends into mayhem; each time Maggie trumpeted the chorus line, the enraptured audience at Tony Pastor's would bellow, "T'row him down, McCloskey!" right along with her.[47] Less talented, and certainly less wholesome, but nonetheless extremely popular, was the "nude" model at the Standard Theatre, who usurped Maggie's place as *the* subject of conversation. The Fire Department halted ticket sales at the door because the demand was so overwhelming. She came on at the start of the third act—at 9:07, to be precise, and at that time, the house would be packed, with men outnumbering women by five to one. Her face and her arms were bare, but she wore bright pink tights and a striped silk chemisette—it was the *idea* that she was impersonating an artist's nude model that was naughty enough to create a furor. "She looked as much like a nude model as a boiled lobster looks like a live lobster," wrote one disgusted critic.[48] Her day soon passed. Far more authentic was the next attraction in town—Signor Giovanni Succi, an Italian hunger artist who conducted a forty-five-day public fast. This early pioneer of performance art arrived in New York fresh from a forty-day engagement in London. Admitted from 10:00 A.M. until midnight, the curious public paid fifty cents apiece to see him lying in bed, growing ever more yellow and waxy. To quell hunger pangs, he would light a cigar. If that failed, he would take a swig of his own discovery, Liquore Medicale Succi; he displayed certificates attesting that it lacked any nutritive value.[49]

In this universe of shooting stars, Richard felt right at home. His fancy clothes raised no eyebrows: New York was full of dandies and dudes.[50] Delighted by the instant success of his protégé, Arthur Brisbane happily inducted Richard into his regular tour of New York's high life, which included afternoons at the racetrack, theater first nights, late-night poker games, and country weekends. "It is no wonder he is popular," Richard observed. "He is a most remarkable young man I think."[51]

Richard spent many of his happiest evenings in New York at the theater. Through his father's connections and his own work on the *Stage*, he knew virtually all the leading actors of the day. He was especially friendly with the comedians Francis Wilson and De Wolfe Hopper, who were each performing regularly in comic operas at the Broadway Theatre. Charles, who was working in a tedious job at the Pennsylvania Railroad, often came up from Philadelphia to visit his older brother, and the two would end their Saturday night frolics at the Broadway.[52] "There is a smell about the painty and gassy and dusty place that I love as much as fresh earth and newly cut hay," Richard wrote his mother, "and the girls look so pretty and bold lying around in the sets and the men so out of focus and with such startling cheeks and lips."[53] Actors, like newspapermen, lived on the borderline of polite society. If they came from impeccable families, or if they were extremely successful at their craft—and preferably, both—they might pass muster. This social insecurity brought the two groups together, as did their odd hours. They tended to work when other people played, and play while others worked.*[54]

Unlike some reporters, Richard did not loiter in theaters hoping to meet chorus girls. His relations with women were scrupulously correct. He arrived knowing the three Shippen sisters, who summered across the Hudson in fashionable Sea Bright, New Jersey. He would visit them regularly with Brisbane, strumming his banjo and singing the tunes of the moment as they sat around a fire.[55] On a grander scale, he also took up with Helen Benedict, a wealthy and witty young woman who was considered the best female harness driver in the country. Thanks to her father's fortune, Helen had nine horses with which to practice. Elias C. Benedict preferred to be called Commodore, in deference to the yacht that in warm weather he sailed daily at 5:00 P.M. from the Twenty-sixth Street wharf, on a two-hour voyage to his country house in Greenwich, Connecticut. "It is a magnificent boat with everything about it you could think of and innumerable things I never would have thought of," Richard told his mother.[56] At the Benedicts', Richard would take riding lessons, eat dinner, go driving in the moonlight, and then catch a late train back to New York. Socially, he had come a long way from Lehigh.

He saw many young women, and his behavior was always impeccable. He hadn't changed much since his days as a romantic fifteen-year-old pupil at Ulrich's. Consorting with a sophisticated crowd, he maintained a peculiar innocence—and, when it came to sex, a deep reticence. Just how reticent he was can be guessed from "The Goddess in Mid-Air," a very suggestive story that he wrote for the *Evening Sun*. It is a romantic fantasy with a quirk that removes even the possibility of sex.

Hiram, the protagonist of the tale, is a country boy who comes to New York in an unsuccessful attempt to find work. His only solace is a beautiful red-headed girl who sits on display outside a Bowery dime museum. The first time he approaches the girl's booth, Hiram is horrified to see that "the

---

*A year after coming to New York, Richard applied successfully to the Players Club, a society of actors and acting enthusiasts. (His nomination was seconded by Grover Cleveland, a fishing companion of Clarke's, who, in between White House terms, worked in a New York law firm.) Edwin Booth, the great Shakespearean actor and the brother of Lincoln's assassin, founded the Players, and his Gramercy Park townhouse served as its clubhouse. Booth was among the small party to celebrate Richard's induction—a gathering which became a permanent part of Players lore. Seeing the collection of theatrical programs which adorned the club's walls, Richard thoughtlessly exclaimed, "Why, I have an interesting theatrical relic which I would like to give to the club. It is the playbill used at Ford's Theatre in Washington on the night that Lincoln was—" At which point Booth threw up his hands in horror and retreated to his rooms upstairs. Appalled at his gaffe, Richard followed the great man to beg his pardon. "Do not apologize," Booth said graciously. "I really took satisfaction in your forgetting. It shows that at last there are some people in the world who do not associate me with Lincoln's death."

lower part of her body was cut completely away." As he recoils with "sudden pity and disgust" that "a woman who was so good to look at should have been born in this way," he hears two men discussing how lights and mirrors create the trick, and he blushes "in anguish at his own inexperience." The rest of the story relates his courtship of this exceptional girl. Even though they had intended him for the Methodist minister's youngest daughter, his parents happily welcome Hiram with his new bride back to the farm.[57]

Did Richard think this was what his own parents wished—for him to marry a woman who seemed not to exist below the waist? His eventual choice of a wife suggests so. And it is interesting too that Rebecca, while liking the story, was also worried by it: worried not that her son feared the female sex, but rather, that he might, like Hiram, marry impulsively. To dispel her anxiety, Richard wrote a long letter that deserves quoting, because it illustrates the gift for mimicry and slang that enlivened his conversation. "He talked a great deal," one friend remarked, "and he talked even better than he wrote."[58]

I went to the Brooklyn Handicap race yesterday. It is one of the three biggest races of the year, and a man stood in front of me in the paddock in a white hat. Another man asked him what he was "playing."

"Well," he said, "I fancy Fides myself."

"Fides!" said his friend, "why, she ain't in it. She won't see home. Raceland's the horse for your money; she's favorite, and there isn't any second choice. But Fides! Why, she's simply impossible. Raceland beat *her* last Suburban."

"Yes, I remember," said the man in the white hat, "but I fancy Fides."

Then another chap said to him, "Fides is all good enough on a dust track on a sunny, pleasant day, but she can't run in the mud. She hasn't got the staying powers. She's a pretty one to look at, but she's just a 'grandstand' ladies' choice. She ain't in it with Raceland or Erica. The horse *you* want is not a pretty, dainty flyer, but a stayer, that is sure and that brings in good money, not big odds, but good money. Why, I can name you a dozen better'n Fides."

"Still, somehow, I like Fides best," said the obstinate man in the white hat.

"But Fides will take the bit in her mouth and run away, or throw the jock or break into the fence. She isn't steady. She's all right to have a little bet on, just enough for a flyer, but she's not the horse to plunge on. If you're a millionaire with money to throw away, why, you might put some of it up on her, but, as it is, you want to put your money where it will be sure of a 'place,' anyway. Now, let me mark your card for you?"

"No," said the man, "what you all say is reasonable, I see that; but, somehow, I rather fancy Fides best."

I've forgotten now whether Fides won or not, and whether she landed the man who just fancied her without knowing why a winner or sent him home broke. But, in any event, that is quite immaterial, the story simply shows how obstinate men are as regards horses and—other uncertain critters. I have no doubt but that the Methodist minister's daughter would have made Hiram happy if he had loved her, but he didn't. No doubt Anne Cummins, Nan Webb, Katy Shippen and Maude Hoyt would have made me happy if they would have consented to have me and I happened to love them, but I fancied Fides.

But now since I have scared you sufficiently, let me add for your peace of mind that I've not enough money to back any horses just at present, and before I put any money up on any one of them for the Matrimonial stakes, I will ask you first to look over the card and give me a few pointers. I mayn't follow them, you know, but I'll give you a fair warning, at any rate.

"You're my sweetheart, I'm your beau."[59]

Years later, when he finally did mark his card, Richard was true to his word.

A dutiful son, he continued to spend weekends with his family in Philadelphia. *Evening Sun* reporters were required to work six days a week, but if they wrote a feature in advance for Saturday's paper, they could take the day off. These were the economic conditions that spawned Davis's first famous literary creation. Later, to snatch a bit of the credit, Brisbane said that he had read a tale in a French magazine about an amusing boulevardier and suggested that Davis attempt an American version.[60] Whatever the conception, however, the product was pure Davis—the sort of yarn he had been spinning since his Lehigh days. Like Conway Maur of *Adventures of My Freshman*, Davis's new protagonist was always getting into the most hilarious kinds of trouble. Exquisitely dressed, devoutly fashionable, he was, like Maur, a caricature of Richard himself—or, to insert another set of mirrors, a caricature of the image that Richard cultivated. He was a clubman, a gregarious bachelor with independent means and unlimited leisure. His name was Cortlandt Van Bibber, and, making his debut on March 1, 1890, he caused an immediate sensation.

At first, he was just a figure of fun. Despite the Dutch name, he definitely did not belong to the old, retiring Knickerbocker aristocracy. He was a drawling dude who arose at 2:30 P.M. (leaving him barely enough time to dress for dinner) and anxiously ducked the various demands of the florist, two young ladies, and his father.[61] Still self-obsessed and fashion-crazed when he reappeared two months later, Van Bibber now was nevertheless more sympathetic—unmistakably ripe for redemption. Buying a box at the circus because it was the thing to do, and then discovering that all his friends were busy that night, he impulsively treated a few urchins and "felt a queer sensation of satisfaction in someone else's pleasure."[62] As if to emphasize Van Bibber's humanity (or because he was low on inspiration), Davis the next month reused the plot (a plot, by the way, borrowed from

Thackeray's *Pendennis*).[63] This time it was three lower East Side girls, whom Van Bibber took on a swan boat in the Central Park lake.[64]

Over the next months, Van Bibber matured until the family resemblance was unmistakable: he was a rich older cousin of Conway Maur. Summarizing the plots of the Van Bibber stories cannot convey their charm, which comes from their amused tone, their droll asides, their quick rhythm. They are lighter than air; when compressed, they come off flat. Van Bibber, accosted three times by the same beggar, who claims not to have eaten in a day, forces the man to consume an enormous breakfast in a restaurant and pay for it with his fraudulently obtained alms. Van Bibber, prevented by a series of accidents from placing his bets at the track, happily reckons that he has made $625—the wagers he would have lost (an accounting method, incidentally, that Richard Carstone thought of earlier in Dickens's *Bleak House*). Van Bibber decides to economize, taking public transportation and eating at a greasy spoon; but in the end, he spends more money than he would have had he followed his typical extravagant routine. Van Bibber stumbles upon an eloping young couple (he knows the boy's older brother) and arranges a proper, albeit last-minute, wedding. Van Bibber single-handedly captures a burglar and then, softened by the man's hard-luck story, releases him and even buys him a railroad ticket to the West.[65] No longer a bumbler, Van Bibber was now an affable, handsome, debonair bachelor. In short, he was an idealized portrait of Richard.[66]

The stories (which Davis sometimes dashed off in under an hour)[67] resembled one-act plays, buoyed by breezy dialogue. Typically, Van Bibber would deliver a curtain line at the end. Adding to the stagey appeal was a generous supply of sets and props, all "authentic" in a theatrical way. In a style that a century later has become familiar, the Van Bibber tales often included scenes in well-known places, particularly upper-class watering holes. They were as fresh as the news that was printed alongside them.

It is true that Van Bibber, as one wag put it, was "the office boy's idea of a gentleman."[68] To less sophisticated readers, the Van Bibber stories offered a privileged peek into the mansions of the glamorous. But Van Bibber was also, strangely enough, a paragon for the new rich themselves. "The sham aristocracy indulge in mushroom-manners," sniffed one etiquette authority.[69] The new rich had no eye for subtleties. Instead of the aristocratic, delicate eglantine, they adored the long-stemmed, bright-red American Beauty rose, the trendy flower of the 1890s. They favored the grand gesture. They could be generous, but not self-effacing: their names were tagged onto their public bequests. When they learned that modesty was an upper-class virtue, they called attention to their modesty. So they adored Van Bibber. "Van Bibber is the new American swell, not precisely as he is in life, but as he would like to be, and as his sisters and his friends' sisters would greatly like to have him," wrote one of Davis's most astute critics. By addressing himself to "the still nebulous and inchoate" fragments of a unifying upper class, Davis was "writing for a body of readers to whom no American author has ever before appealed."[70] Van Bibber was "a photograph most marvelously retouched to flatter the subject of it."[71]

Most of all, Van Bibber was young, and his insouciance, his swagger, his daring, and his wit appealed to the young. It was the young, for the most part, who had the energy and inclination to run after fashion. Their parents, or at least their fathers, were preoccupied with making the money to fund this pursuit. Businessmen and financiers were drab figures. They were like the stagehands in a Kabuki play; and throughout his career in fiction, Davis did his best to ignore them. He was young, and he wrote for the young. "Older people don't care for epigrams and quaint ideas I find so much," he told his mother, explaining why the "brightest talkers" were young. "Not that the younger ones pose but that the older ones find it pleasanter to listen."[72] Richard preferred to talk. And when he addressed his young readers, he did so in a clean, wholesome way that reassured their parents. "Mr. Davis's stories prove," wrote one appreciative critic, "that the public does not demand that a new writer should be horrifying or disgusting in order to attract its attention and receive its favors."[73]

Even when he was reporting on the seedier byways of the city, Davis retained his clean vision. The word "slumming" entered the language in the mid-1880s, as groups of fashionable people, emboldened by curiosity or charity, ventured into the disreputable parts of town. The Bowery's reputation was so great by 1890 that a saloonkeeper named Ahearn hired youths to accost the new arrivals at Grand Central Terminal with shouts of "Show you the Bowery for a dollar, mister?"—a tour that ended with supper at Ahearn's.[74] Like Philadelphia a few years earlier, New York when Richard arrived was in a spasm of reform. A coalition of civic-minded gentlemen and ministers, under the leadership of Anthony Comstock, had declared war on vice and the political machine, the two aspects of immigrant Irish culture that threatened and repelled them the most. Cultivating both Comstock and the police,[75] Davis was on hand when the authorities revoked the liquor license of a notorious Tenderloin dive, the Haymarket. Since the Haymarket made its profit on the overpriced drinks that prostitutes and their clients consumed on the way to contract, this was like cutting off its blood supply. Davis heartily approved.[76]

Charmed by this enthusiastic young reporter, police officials provided a detective escort whenever he wanted to show visitors the Bowery or the East Side. Even more flattering, the captain of the Bowery precinct cancelled the privilege less than six months after Davis's arrival in New York, declaring that the reporter was so well known in the downtown slums that his guests were perfectly safe.[77] Richard's standard nighttime tour of the slums began at police headquarters on Mulberry Street, where swells in evening dress were so old hat that the napping doorman barely stirred to admit them. After displaying some photographs of famous criminals, a detective would lead the party to the office of the legendary chief of detectives, Thomas Byrnes. At that hour, Byrnes would not be in evidence, but his office merited a look, especially the artwork: a larger-than-life photograph of a criminal being held by the hair and ears. Across the hall from Byrnes's lair was a museum, its large glass cases filled with crime memorabilia. Of grisly interest were pieces from the ropes used to hang famous murderers— still warm when they arrived at headquarters, the detective observed, to appreciative shudders. There was a life-sized photograph of the face of one killer, and a slightly smaller shot of the limbs of his victim, whom he had sawed into four pieces and shipped west in a trunk. The detective described how the inspector had invited the arrested murderer out of his cell and motioned him to have a seat on the bloodstained sofa. Confronted with the telltale couch on which he had carved up his victim, the man confessed.

Having seen the indoor exhibits, the party was now ready to observe the fauna in the field. By this time, it would be 9:00 P.M. They would check out a local saloon and a nearby Chinatown opium den before heading for the Bismarck, an enormous flophouse with three levels of accommodation. At the first landing, in a room heated to a suffocating temperature by a huge iron stove, twelve cents bought a night on a hammocklike bed of rubber cloth. The beds were filled with exhausted men, in rags or naked, the soles of their feet blackened with filth. On the floor above, other men had paid ten cents to sleep on boards. Those on the top floor, for seven cents, lay on the floor. The Bismarck was a memorable sight, but no place to end the tour. To dispel any gloom, the group would proceed to a series of wine cellars, public balls, and beer gardens, so that the parting impression was jolly. Slumming was supposed to be fun.[78]

So were Richard's slum stories. He began by writing an impressionistic piece on the summer frolics of poor, ethnic New Yorkers, especially the Irish families of Cherry Street. In a pulsating sidewalk scene of gossiping, drinking, brawling Irishmen, he focused on one family, the Regens, and their son, "Rags." He ended the story with Rags's dramatic return from a gang fight. Blood on his face, a knife in his hands, the youth barely eludes two policemen. Watching it all, Mrs. Regen weeps. "And then she went out," Richard concluded, "and in a fit of feeling washed Rag's [sic] blood off the front stoop, an act that was considered unnecessarily punctilious by the other tenants and as liable to render the steps damp."[79] Somewhere between a newspaper story and a short story, this was the first of several vignettes of working-class life that Richard published in the *Evening Sun*. Good-humored and sentimental, his stories disarmed poverty by rendering it picturesque. He developed the character of Rags Raegen (even the name grew) in subsequent tales; another hero, Hefty Burke, was slightly less tough and equally big-hearted. The stories were popular. It was even said that Davis "knows his East side and all the rest of the underside of his New York as Dickens knew his London or Victor Hugo his Paris."[80]

The young men of the *Sun* considered themselves to be writers. Their assignments they saw as Life. They held a widespread belief, which remains popular to this day, that newspaper reporting is the best apprenticeship for a young writer; that, in the words of *Saturday Evening Post* editor George Horace Lorimer, "The daily newspaper sustains the same relationship to the young writer as the hospital to the medical student. It is the first great school of practical experience."[81] Stephen Crane, Lincoln Steffens, and David Graham Phillips, among Davis's contemporaries, Theodore Dreiser, Frank Norris, and Jack London, among his juniors, all believed it. They thought, as Davis put it, that a reporter in just three years of work "has crowded the experiences of the lifetime of the ordinary young business man, doctor or lawyer, or man about town."[82] Certainly, the big-city reporter met a wide variety of people and heard of a great many queer events. But what did it add up to, the mornings in police court, the hour-long interviews with statesmen and financiers, the chase for the "beat" and the new? Like a magpie, the reporter swooped down on the scintillating and flew off for more. The job demanded and developed a quick eye and mind. It required cleverness, not wisdom. As Brisbane said, the good reporter never loses his superficiality.

Ideally, the reporter would relate purely what he has observed. More often he recounts what he has been told, attributing it to a source if he is punctilious. All too frequently, though, the reporter hasn't seen what he wants to know, and can't talk to anyone who has. What then? In Richard's day, the answer was clear: make it up. An 1894 correspondence course in journalism advised a tyro reporter to use his imagination if he can't get the facts. "Truth in essentials, imagination in non-essentials, is considered a legitimate rule of action in every office," the novice was told. "The paramount object is to make an interesting story."[83] Richard had been at the *Evening Sun* almost a year when he was sent to cover the suicide of a young and, of course, pretty woman. She had gassed herself in the luxurious Tenderloin flat provided by her lover, who called himself Mr. Bradley. Devoting most of his story to a description of the apartment, Richard revealed that it was not the hodgepodge of velveteen sofas, gilded bird-cages, and suggestive photographs that one might expect. Instead, it was tastefully furnished with leather armchairs, books, Turkish rugs, and signed etchings. Apparently, it had been decorated to the taste of the man who paid for it; but who or where he was, no one could say. After keeping his mistress for three years, "Bradley" abandoned her. Suicide was her response.

It was the pathetic sort of story that Richard relished, and he wrote it up with flair. Too much flair, perhaps. As a malicious compliment, Brisbane suggested (Richard anxiously told Charles) that the story "would lead any-one to suppose that my evenings were spent in the boudoirs of the horizon-tales of 34th Street." In fact, the police had barred him from the room—

"and I don't know whether it abounded in signed etchings or Bougoreau's [sic] nymphs." He simply invented the scene. "It is hardly the fair thing," he complained, "to suppose that a man must have an intimate acquaintance with whatever he writes of intimately."[84] Working on deadline, the accomplished journalist pretended to a deeper knowledge than he could possibly have gained through reporting.

A surface cynicism, which was as much a part of the reporter's outfit as his cigars and pocket flask, helped him appear very knowing.[85] "I have never seen anything that could not be explained or attributed directly to some known cause, such as crime or poverty or drink," says a reporter in a short story that Richard wrote for the *Evening Sun*. "You may think at first that you have stumbled on something strange and romantic, but it comes to nothing." As the hard-bitten newsman summarizes: "It is all commonplace and vulgar, and always ends in a police court or with a 'found drowned' in the North River."[86] Although Davis never adopted that cynical pose (he retained an enthusiasm that irritated many other newsmen the way a child's piping voice grates on a man with a hangover),[87] he came close. He was an ironist, not a cynic. He poked fun at hypocrisy but didn't impugn all higher motives. Without denying that a man might affect the course of events, he preferred to write about the peculiar twists of fate beyond any man's control.

One morning when news was slow, Davis was sent to investigate an unpromising item on the police blotter: a tenement fire in the Tenderloin District. By the time he got there, the fire was out and the crowd had dispersed. The fire had merely singed the top floor. "Nothing here," the policeman on duty told him. "Only $500 damage and a bum lodger asphyxiated. He's in that room." Peeping through the door, Richard saw the stiff body in the bed. The story was worth a paragraph. Then, as he walked about the smoky room, he observed an alarm clock, still ticking. It had been set to go off at 7:00 A.M. "What time did you break in here?" he asked the policeman. "Let me see," the man said with a yawn. "Seven o'clock it was. I remember because that alarm was going off just as I got inside." "That's my story," Davis said happily. Had the man set his alarm just half an hour earlier, he would be alive today. That was how Richard began his story, and it made the front page.[88]

For an *Evening Sun* reporter, sex and crime were the lodes to mine, and a story that mixed the two was a bonanza. The biggest *Evening Sun* story during Richard's tenure began as a sex crime—although as sex crimes went, it was a rather ordinary one, barely worth a feature. In a drunken quarrel, William Kemmler had killed his lover, a married woman for whom he had left his own wife two years before. True, he had done the bloody deed with a hatchet, in the presence of her young daughter, but these were details, a paragraph or two. Not the crime but its aftermath had whipped the New York papers into a competitive frenzy. Kemmler's importance was as victim, not criminal. It was his hapless distinction to be the first New York sentenced to die in the electric chair. For a newspaper—at least, for a New York afternoon paper at the turn of the century—there could not be a better story. The big-city reporters went after it with gusto.

Some three years before, a three-man panel under Elbridge T. Gerry had been empowered by the state legislature to find a more humane form of capital punishment than hanging. With admirable Victorian thoroughness, the commission examined forty modes of execution, including crucifixion and breaking on the wheel. The four finalists were injection of poison, such as Prussic acid; the garotte; the guillotine; and electricity. Opinions were solicited, and electricity got the nod. Experiments on dogs, cats, cows, and horses proceeded under the supervision of electrical expert Harold P. Brown, described by one reporter as "a tall young man, who looked as if his face had been cast in a waxen mould and some of the wax had adhered to it in spots."

The wheels of justice had turned with great speed for Kemmler. The murder occurred on March 29, 1889. He was tried and convicted a month later, sentenced to die in the electric chair on May 14, and sent to Auburn prison. The date of execution was set for the week of June 24. At that point, the system jammed. Electrician Brown, who was designing the chair, announced that the alternating current used in Westinghouse dynamos was more deadly than direct current. He was planning to buy three Westinghouse devices, one for each New York prison that imposed the death penalty. This was not the sort of publicity that Westinghouse sought. Even without it, the public viewed with a wary eye the rapid electrification of American cities, a process marked with alarming regularity by accidental deaths from fallen wires. In the New York metropolitan area alone, about thirty people had died this way. Taking the offensive, George F. Westinghouse, Jr., attacked Brown's work, which had been performed in the lab of Westinghouse rival Thomas Edison. At the height of the argument, Brown proposed what he called an electrical duel, in which he and Westinghouse, in the presence of experts, would submit, respectively, to charges of direct and alternating current. The jolts would begin at one hundred volts and increase by increments of fifty, until one man should cry enough. Instead of taking up this challenge, Westinghouse proclaimed that the company would not sell its dynamos for lethal purposes. The company said that its machines were all numbered and that it knew the whereabouts of each. In response, the state hired several intermediaries to buy the dynamos. It then obliterated the identifying numbers.

While this comedy was proceeding, Kemmler's lawyer brought in a prominent attorney, W. Bourke Cockran, to argue that execution by electricity constituted cruel and unusual punishment. Westinghouse supported Cockran's position, while companies using direct current took the opposing view. As this was to be the first use of an electric chair, the judge decided to solicit some opinions. He appointed a commission, which met daily throughout July and August. After considering their findings, he upheld Kemmler's sentence. Cockran kept appealing, but when the state's highest court, on March 21, 1890, declined to overturn the sentence, it seemed, as the *Evening Sun*'s headline writer put it, that "Kemmler Must Die."

What fun the papers had with the story! For starters, there was the chance to describe the macabre apparatus. The heavy wooden chair, if one disregarded the leather straps, was "shaped something like a deck chair used on an ocean steamship"; the footrest, except for its metal plates, was "something like that used with a barber's chair"; and the executioner, standing in an adjoining room, would complete the circuit by turning "a lever like a hideous exaggeration of a telegraph key." Mundane items, monstrously transformed—like the electrical power itself. To test the current's strength, a homely board of two dozen incandescent light bulbs had been constructed as a more expressive backup to the traditional voltmeter. The dynamo was connected by one set of wires to the chair, by another to the light board. Before the fatal shock was administered, the current would surge into the light board and, with a blaze of illumination, verify that there was enough juice to kill a man. The naïveté of the light board candidly reflected the approximate nature of the whole enterprise. Why measure the electricity precisely when no one could say for certain how much was needed? The only human experiments up until that time had been highly uncontrolled—namely, accidents. How could one be confident of administering a lethal dose and yet avoid, as the *Evening Sun* rather indelicately put it, "the horrible features of roasting and burning"? That was one of the questions adding excitement to the impending event.

At the center, the inconspicuous seed of this black pearl, was the hapless Kemmler, a man with the mental capacity of a child. Until his arrest, he had been illiterate, but the warden's wife had taught him to write his name, which he now signed happily on everything brought within arm's reach. Using Christian books, the warden's wife had also instructed him in reading. Until then, he had never been told of the life of Jesus; now, he said what he most regretted was not having heard those "stories" earlier. "If I had known about that Saviour story, I never would have killed her," he said. "I would have gone away from her." While the newsmen impatiently awaited the main act, this sideshow kept the ink flowing. As docile as the cattle that had preceded him to the electric chair, Kemmler seemed not to doubt the official assurances that his death would be instantaneous and painless. The members of the press were far more skeptical.

The news corps gathered in the upstate New York town of Auburn at the end of April. Disgusted with the press circus, Warden Charles F. Durston refused to announce the date of execution. However, everyone knew that his soft-hearted wife, wishing to distance herself from the scene of her husband pulling the switch on her prize pupil, had bid Kemmler farewell and left for New York City on Saturday, April 26. Somehow, everyone also knew that the Warden had told her she could return on Wednesday. The popular view was that the execution would be held on Monday night. Auburn's main hotel, the Osborne House, was crammed with out-of-towners over the weekend, so that it resembled a political convention. There were the various experts and the twenty-seven invited guests. There were telegraph operators, including those privately retained by the New York *World* and the New York *Sun*, archrivals for such a sensational story. And there were about forty reporters snuffling for news; and, when they couldn't find any news, drinking and carousing.

Richard was included in the *Sun* contingent. Without any particular assignment, he enjoyed himself at the carnival. Adding to the playground atmosphere was a tight legal restriction on press coverage of the execution. In consequence, all the reporters engaged in a hilarious charade, assuming false names and pretending to some other profession. "The World have a reporter disguised as an electrician's assistant or lineman or something of the sort and the two factions are fighting tooth and nail," Richard gleefully reported to his family. "Brisbane has exposed the World's scheme and the World have exposed Brisbane and the schemes and whisperings are equal to the plans of Napoleon." After a day of it, he was caught up in the farce. "The Plots Thicken!" he wrote home. "I may not sign this letter for I do not know who I am or if I do I must not tell anyone. Never in the whole history of journalism has there been so much mystery conspiracy and secrecy. You go up to your best friend and he stares coldly at you and says *'Excuse* me, sir, but you have the advantage of me. I am Charles P. Dusenberg of Rochester N.Y.' Another man with whom you spent an hour in the office on the day previous passes you by without recognition and then whistles to you from a distance and tells you behind a corner that he is a lawyer's clerk and that you musten't [*sic*] recognize so and so if you ran across him because he is an electrical expert nor such an one because he is a prisoner doing corridor work. Whenever a train arrives all the newspaper men rush to the register and proclaim the real names of the men who have signed false ones and every five minutes you are beckoned to a quiet corner or read a mysterious letter, which you are instructed to tear up, appointing an interview." The joke was that if a reporter wanted lamb chops and peas for dinner, he would ask for beef and onions. Rumors flew about, rumors of tunnels into Kemmler's cell, of reporters disguised as convicts, of carrier pigeons ready to fly to New York. A man with mumps got no sympathy; people assumed he had infected himself as a disguise. If a correspondent condescended to speak, he would pretend he was in Auburn for any other reason—perhaps to see relatives in a neighboring town. One man made himself famous by responding to the usual, "Well, have you come to do the execution, too?" with a mysterious and solemn, "No, I came up to do something else." Richard hadn't laughed so much for months.

For the reporters, the suspense centered on the race to get the news to New York. The first newspaper to unleash its "Extra!"-shouting newsboys on the streets would be the winner. To accomplish that, the men of the *Evening Sun*, under Brisbane's generalship, had devised an elaborate system. First they had enlisted a confederate within the prison and instructed him to wave a handkerchief at the moment of Kemmler's death. An *Evening Sun* man was perched atop a watch tower that had been specially built on two telegraph poles opposite the prison. From there he could see into the death chamber. As soon as he saw the waving handkerchief, he would shout to the telegraph operator—a virtuoso who had outclassed the competition at the national fast-sending tournament—who was waiting just below him in the tower. The operator would convey the news instantly to New York. An open telephone line was reserved to provide further details for later editions.

Everything was assured, except the cooperation of the courts. On Tuesday morning a U.S. circuit judge issued a stay of execution. Waiting until he actually received the papers, Warden Durston announced this at 2:00 P.M. to the crowd of reporters waiting at the prison. Like water through a sluicegate, they rushed down the iron steps to the front courtyard, where the one-armed gatekeeper leisurely turned the key in the lock to let them out. Kemmler was praying, and Durston waited for him to finish before conveying the news. He waited almost two hours as the reporters grew more and more impatient. At 3:48, an *Evening Sun* man—probably Brisbane—pointed out that "humanity and the interests of the afternoon press demanded that the good news be no longer held back." As the warden compliantly went off on his mission, the reporter urged him to remember, for history's sake, every word of the ensuing conversation, which would be "quite as notable, perhaps, as that between Voltaire and Frederick the Great." Durston promised; and when he returned, he related his brief interview. "Well, William, they've granted a writ of habeas corpus to you, and that carries you over into June," he told the reprieved man. "You're safe now for the present." "Is that so?" Kemmler replied. "Well, I'm easier in my mind now." He was "about as much elated," wrote the *Evening Sun* reporter, "as a man who hears that the express man has finally turned up with his trunk from Jersey City."

The Kemmler saga dragged on until the U.S. Supreme Court on May 23 refused to intercede. Cockran obtained another month's delay on a procedural question. Then the machinery of death began once more to crank up. The execution was scheduled for the week of August 4. Reporters flocked back to Auburn, which was now in the grip of a stifling heat wave. The dynamo was retested; it still worked. Shrunken, shriveled, expressionless, Kemmler was said to be oblivious to the noisy preparations in the next room. Not everything was in perfect working order. The dial voltmeter was broken; and if the light board could be trusted, the current was erratic. In the third test, the charge reached as high as one thousand volts, but it frequently dipped to little more than one hundred. "If applied it might kill like a thunderbolt," the *Evening Sun* opined. "Then again at the very moment of the application it might drop away and inflict a torture beyond words and make that death chamber a scene too awful to describe." Harassed and anxious, Warden Durston traveled to Albany for a consultation with electrical expert Harold Brown. The press waited eagerly for the invitations to be sent out—the visible sign of the coming execution.

Mailed out on August 1, the invitations asked the twenty-seven guests to report to the warden on the evening of Tuesday, August 5. Like locusts rubbing their legs, the reporters buzzed excitedly. The dynamo seemed to be working better. Although it had yet to reach the desired level of twelve hundred volts, it was no longer dropping as precipitously. Now the nervous warden had another worry. In the latest version of the electric chair, the current was applied through wet sponges at the two electrodes. The one on the victim's head was held in place with a copper spring. The one at the base of his spine was not. Should the prisoner shift in his seat, a space would prevent the completion of the circuit. In these final hours, Durston hastily arranged for a spring attachment for the spinal sponge.

Early on Wednesday morning, the witnesses were woken for a hasty breakfast and then led to the execution chamber. At 6:20 Kemmler appeared. "This is William Kemmler," the warden announced. "How do you do?" Kemmler addressed the crowd. "Sit down, William," said Durston, pointing to a conventional chair alongside the fatal one. He asked if Kemmler had anything to say. "Yes, I wish you all good luck in this world and in the next," the prisoner said. "I think I am going to a good place. The newspapers have not treated me right. That is the only thing I have to say. I wish you all very good luck." Without a blush, the newspapers reported his words.

Following instructions, Kemmler stood and removed his coat and vest, placing them on the chair he had just vacated. The witnesses could then see that his trousers had been slit from the waistband down, to permit the application of an electrode to his spine. As the warden and his assistant arranged the straps, Kemmler several times said, "Take your time. Don't be in a hurry. Be sure that everything is all right." The assistant buckled one strap about his body, two around his legs and one on his right arm. Then he fastened Kemmler's head to the head-rest with a handkerchief that covered his eyes. At that point, Kemmler spoke up: "Joe, you forgot to strap the other arm." Trembling, the guard corrected his oversight. "Goodbye and good luck to you all," Kemmler said loudly. Durston held Kemmler's head as the assistant pressed down on it the rubber cup containing the sponge. When it was in place, Kemmler said, "Oh, you'd better press that down further. Press that down." They unclamped it and redid it. "Well, I want to do the best I can," Kemmler said. "I can't do any better than that."

The warden adjusted a leather muzzle over his head. An electrical expert entered and, with a syringe, moistened the two sponges with saltwater. The preparation had taken about twenty minutes.

At 6:45 the warden gave the signal to the man at the switchboard. "Those who were looking at the strapped-down man," the *Evening Sun* reported, "saw a sudden twitch pass over the body, the limbs seemed to shrink up about an inch or so, and there was dreadful contortion of the body. The mouth worked convulsively, saliva spattered out, and it seemed as if the writhing form would tear itself away from the binding straps." Even the physicians averted their eyes. A heavy sigh escaped from Kemmler's body—"as if the soul was glad to be freed," thought the impressionable *Evening Sun* man—and then it was still. The supervising physician studied a stop watch. After ten seconds of electricity had flowed through the prisoner's body, he called out "Stop!" to the man at the lever. He then stepped forward, and after a brief examination, pronounced Kemmler dead. The electrodes were removed from Kemmler's head. The witnesses rose from their seats and hurried to the chair. Someone turned to the warden and said, "Warden Durston, I congratulate you upon the success of your—" He never completed the sentence.

A deep, groaning breath heaved out of the form strapped in the chair. The body once again twisted in convulsions, the mouth frothing and chewing. The United Press man turned a ghastly white and fainted to the floor. The other witnesses stood dumbstruck with horror. Quickly the guard put the rubber cap back on Kemmler's head. The warden hurried into the adjoining room to tell the man at the switch to pull the lever again. As the current flowed for seventeen seconds, a nauseating stench of burning flesh and hair filled the room. Once again, Kemmler was examined, and this time, without question, he was dead. The post-mortem consensus deemed it a mistake to apply the electrode to the thick hair on the head. Kemmler was pronounced dead at 6:48 A.M. The *Evening Sun* was on the street at 6:56 A.M. Its headline writer admirably summarized the story in one capitalized word: WRITHED.[89]

The Kemmler execution was the biggest story of Richard's *Evening Sun* tenure. Yet when the switch was pulled, he wasn't in Auburn to see it. The story, great though it was, wasn't *his* story. When he was younger, that wouldn't have stopped him. He had fought to go to Johnstown just to see the flood, knowing that his paper's senior newsmen would commandeer the headlines and reduce him to sidebars. Now he knew that this was no way to build a career. Rather than witness the Kemmler execution as part of a team, he was back in New York writing on his own about two other crimes: one real, one imagined. In truth, both were imagined, although one was presented as real. That was the way crime was reported at the turn of the century—a sketchy outline of fact overlaid with a thick impasto of the clichés of fiction. The coverage of the Kemmler execution was so exceptionally vivid because, in a state-sponsored murder, the reporters could be there. They didn't have to imagine it. They had only to describe it.

Far more usual was the death of Annie Goodwin, the true-life crime story that detained Richard in New York. The death of Annie Goodwin was distinguished only by Richard's energetic depiction of it. He put so much energy into describing this mundane tragedy that, at the end of the year, the *Evening Sun* declared it to be one of the two most-discussed crimes of 1890.⁹⁰ The other was the murder of a well-known businessman by a young woman who said he had drugged and raped her. Without Richard's embellishments, the sorry story of Annie Goodwin pales alongside that.

The death of the young woman—"of rare beauty," it goes almost (but never) without saying—came to the attention of the police by chance. A man on an elevated train overheard two people discussing a cigarette factory girl named Annie Goodwin, who had been "in trouble," underwent an operation in Harlem, and disappeared. The eavesdropper passed the word to a Harlem police detective, who learned that Goodwin had been turned out of her sister's house after taking up with a young playboy. From there the police tracked her steps to a boarding-house, where, they believed, an abortion was performed by Dr. Henry G. McGonegal, a Harlem practitioner with a specialty in dubious obstetrics. According to police witnesses, McGonegal had returned at night to remove the ailing woman to another apartment in Harlem, where, on July 12, the eve of her twenty-first birthday, she died. The next morning at 2:00 A.M., the old doctor returned to the Harlem apartment, and emerged carrying a large, awkward bundle, which he placed beside him on the seat of the gig. "The something that sat beside him, wrapped in the bed quilt," Davis wrote excitedly, "as he drove through the silent streets in the glimmering gray of that early dawn, past policemen on their beats, past a thousand sleepers secure in their beds, between rows of lamps that blinked knowingly at him and at his odd company, that something was a corpse, the body of the murdered Annie Goodwin, if the story told by the witnesses was true." Like a child's hand on a helium balloon, that little concluding attribution barely grounded Richard's free-flying reconstruction.

The day that his story appeared, Davis accompanied an official delegation to a Long Island cemetery. The police had located a death certificate signed by McGonegal for a woman of a different name; under interrogation, the doctor admitted that the woman was in fact Annie Goodwin. Her body would now be exhumed. In the graveyard party was Gus Harrison, the "coarse," chain-smoking young man who had been her lover. "Young Harrison is such an ill-favored youth," the handsome reporter noted waspishly, "with a nose of extraordinary size and weak, watery eyes, that it is hard to see how the girl became attracted to him." The grave was dug up, the pine coffin raised, its lid opened. In the first edition of the afternoon paper, Richard's story was restrained. "There was nothing left to show that the girl had once been beautiful," he wrote. By the second edition, the story had been rewritten, perhaps by the city editor. Now the reader learned that the open coffin disclosed "a loathsome, pulpy face as black in one part as a negro's, as yellow in another as a mulattoe's, with wide, staring eyes and a distended mouth that showed the lips and gums a hideous black and purple." The *Evening Sun* had declared war on Dr. McGonegal. The human voice of the reporter, recognizably Richard's, could no longer be heard in the distorted blare of the megaphone. This is how the later edition described the moment when a gravedigger located the coffin: "He had struck a nickel-plated screw of the coffin, and at that moment the bell over the superintendent's house began to toll. They were very near your secret then, Dr. McGonegal—very near. And the bell that tolled for the funeral passing through the gate of the cemetery was just a coincidence, but it sounded like a knell, Dr. McGonegal—very like a knell." On two consecutive days, the *Evening Sun* published editorials denouncing the court system for having released McGonegal in the past. At the conclusion of his luridly reported trial, the seventy-year-old McGonegal was convicted of first-degree manslaughter and sentenced to fourteen years of hard labor.[91]

During that overheated summer, as he was conjuring up the final days of Annie Goodwin and sealing the fate of Dr. McGonegal, Richard was also reviewing the proofs of another crime story, a work of fiction that would lift him above the ranks of the journeyman reporters who chronicle the misfortunes of the Goodwins and McGonegals of this world. He had begun the story in Philadelphia. Its hero was a *Press* office boy, a tough, sweet urchin named Gallagher, who would entertain the reporters by performing a tap dance on the table, or by rushing down from the telegraph room and shouting, "Gentlemen, I has de honor to announce dat de Phillies winned de game."[92] Years later, it was said that Gallagher once accompanied Davis to a prizefight between Jack Dempsey the Nonpareil of New York, and Mike Mallon of Pittsburgh. (Since telephones were still a rarity, copy boys would be sent out with reporters to bring back the first part of a story.) Prizefighting then was an illegal sport. The bare-knuckled boxers would slug it out in a clandestine ring that had been hastily constructed in a barn or roadhouse, before an audience of high rollers. At the Dempsey-Mallon fight, the police got wind of the action and staged a raid, arresting the reporters along with the other spectators. Before he was taken away, Davis quick-wittedly slipped his copy to Gallagher—who, being young and small, was able to sneak unnoticed through the police cordon and return to the *Press* in time to make the morning edition.[93] This event may have actually occurred to Richard in Philadelphia. Certainly it occurred to him when it came time to write his story.

The other adventure that the young writer bestowed on his youthful protagonist was an even more unlikely one: a crime story, faintly redolent of the work of Robert Louis Stevenson. A secretary had murdered his wealthy employer in New York and escaped with two hundred thousand dollars. The whole country wondered where he was. The murderer was a nondescript fellow, except for one feature: he was missing the trigger finger on his right hand, blown off in a childhood shooting accident. The inspiration for this telltale deformity was a Philadelphia stock actor who had lost the same finger in a stage fight gone awry. In the last "Lime Light Man" column that he wrote for the *Stage*, Richard said of this actor: "He used to complain that no matter how well made up he might be, the audience was always sure to recognize him through his absent finger."[94] In the same way, the fugitive murderer is spotted—by Gallagher, of course, who, as a devotee of crimes and criminals, has correctly surmised that his quarry will be dressed as a gentleman, complete with gloves to disguise his deficiency. Studying the hands of each passerby, Gallagher finally sees the one he seeks, its fingers curved about a cane handle, except for one incriminating digit that juts straight out.

As coincidence would have it, the culprit is hiding out in the very roadhouse in the north Philadelphia suburbs where the big fight is being staged. Gallagher leads a New York detective and the *Press* sports editor to the scene. The Philadelphia police raid the fight. The New York detective makes his collar, and without revealing the culprit's identity to his Philadelphia counterparts, takes the wretch away. The sports editor, arrested, watches in desperate impotence. He has scored two beats, neither of which will appear in the morning edition. Then he sees Gallagher at his side, deftly picking his pocket, and he realizes he has a chance. The story concludes with Gallagher stealing a waiting cab and galloping through the freezing snow a few paces ahead of the police. Davis had once commandeered a hansom from a drunken cabby and driven himself back to the office. When he began composing his newspaper story, he remembered that incident. "I saw that a man driving at night under those circumstances through the falling sleet was interesting," he explained, "but make it a little boy who did it, and it became dramatic."[95] Gallagher returns to the *Press* office with the big story just in time to make the paper.

"Gallegher"—for that is how the inveterate misspeller labeled his hero and his story—was a thoroughly implausible, romantic tale embellished with the gritty language and urban settings of realistic fiction.[96] In its style, as well as its subject, it inaugurated the genre of newspaper fiction, that bon-bon school of hard exteriors and soft, syrupy fillings, in which tough characters behave in the most sentimental fashion, all for the love of the paper. "Gallegher" and its successors—from Jesse Lynch Williams's "The Stolen Story" to Charles MacArthur and Ben Hecht's *The Front Page*—would be invaluable recruitment tools for many generations of city editors.[97] Richard worked on the story for more than a year. "Have you done anything at Gallegher?" his mother wrote him in the summer of 1888. "That is by far the best work you've done—oh, *by far*. Send that to Gilder. In old times The Century would not print the word 'brandy.' But those days are over."[98] Rebecca was too kind to the *Century*. As late as 1896, its editor, Richard Watson Gilder, balked at this sentence in a story: "The bullet had left a little blue mark over the brown nipple." In vain the writer argued that the nipple was male, and therefore not prurient. The story was not printed in the *Century*.[99] American fiction was typically read by young girls, and an editor would excise anything that might make them blush. Since young girls tended to blush easily, the prohibition list was long and comprehensive. After a quick reading, Gilder rejected "Gallegher," on the grounds that it was too slangy. For the rest of his life, he regretted his error.[100] He could draw some comfort from the fact that he was not alone. Two other editors also turned it down.[101]

There were four "quality" magazines in the United States in 1890. The unillustrated *Atlantic* continued in James T. Fields's tradition, catering to an elite but small readership. The handsomely illustrated *Harper's Magazine* appealed to a wider audience. The *Century*, noted for its beautiful pictures as well as its high literary standards, had been started by the Scribner publishing house, but was sold and renamed in 1881. As a condition of the sale, the house of Scribner agreed not to start another magazine for five years; but as soon as the stipulated time elapsed, the Scribners began planning a new *Scribner's Monthly*, which premiered in January 1887.[102]

In the post–Civil War publishing world, a monthly magazine was an essential part of a successful literary publishing house. By offering a contract for combined book and serial rights, a publisher could better compete for authors. At first, the magazine serials were chiefly a good way to promote the novels; but as advertising revenues increased, the magazines started wagging the dog. Writing for magazines became more remunerative than writing books. It was the fat fees from magazines, in fact, that allowed American writers to make a living from their art, without necessarily relying on private fortunes, public offices, teaching, or editorial work. And while the old-fashioned public continued to believe otherwise, the best in belles lettres first saw print in magazines. It was the inferior work, including many of the best-selling novels, that bypassed the periodicals and came out immediately in book form.[103]

"Gallegher" appeared in the new *Scribner's Magazine*. After requesting revisions, editor E. L. Burlingame accepted the story on March 17, 1890, and paid $175 for it.[104] "I am so glad I could cry," Rebecca wrote her son. "I knew Gallegher would go. It is a *great* story—and so the public will say."[105] A month after the acceptance of "Gallegher," Richard scored again, this time with *Harper's Magazine*, the chief rival of *Scribner's*. In the Van Bibber genre, but with more sentiment than humor, "A Walk up the Avenue" described the second thoughts of a young man who has just engineered the break-up of his engagement. Davis wrote it at one sitting, on the hotel piazza in Auburn, while waiting in vain for Kemmler to be executed.[106] When he accepted the story, *Harper's* editor Henry Mills Alden summoned Richard to his office and assured him that William Dean Howells had never written anything finer. "It is light," he said, "light in a grand and noble way. It shows the power to feel and to stand apart and touch these feelings delicately. We have had no such writer in this country. The French have them but America has wanted them for years and you are the man." Slightly dazed, Richard at one point asked if Alden was referring to him. Telling Richard that he could do for New York what Maupassant had done for Paris, Alden urged him to send all his fiction to the house of Harper. Richard floated out of the office, feeling himself "a most obnoxiously cocky individual."[107] When he later learned that "A Walk up the Avenue" would appear the same month as "Gallegher," he was delighted, "as it should show people that I can write about other things than newspaper beats and detectives."[108] In the spring of 1890, *St. Nicholas* accepted a boys' story on a tennis tournament, to be published in September; and Gilder bought a story, less vulgar than "Gallegher" and less original, "The Cynical Miss Catherwaight," to appear in the *Century* towards the end of the year.

"Perhaps it never rains but it pours," Richard remarked to his mother.[109] Certainly it was a soaking spring, with the promise of a bountiful summer. In May, Richard's likeness, slightly idealized but completely recognizable, appeared on the cover of the humor magazine *Life*, as drawn by his friend, Charles Dana Gibson.[110] Gibson, who was doing the illustrations for "Gallegher," had met Davis in the smoking room of the Victoria Hotel in London the previous July. It was after midnight, and Richard was dressed as a Thames boatman, in a rough brown suit, a soft hat, and a handkerchief about his neck.[111] For an artist seeking to illustrate the athletic vigor of American youth, he was the perfect model; and when the two men became reacquainted in New York, Richard was happy to pose for him. The young men that Gibson depicted, like the ones of whom Davis wrote, were rarely engaged in business, or in work of any sort. They were in dinner dress at the table, or around the piano, or at the opera, or by the bar.[112] Their chief function apparently was to escort the Gibson girl, that robust beauty who made her debut in 1890 and tantalized the American public for the rest of the decade.[113] The broad-shouldered, clean-cut Davis was her ideal companion. At the same time as his literary reputation was building, Richard Harding Davis was becoming known as the up-to-the-minute, thoroughly modern paradigm of male beauty.

The publication of "Gallegher" in August 1890 made him Byronically famous overnight. His Van Bibber pieces and the Gibson portraits had stirred some favorable talk. But with his first publication in a major magazine, he was, quite abruptly, a leading literary figure. "Gallegher" was "a success from the moment it appeared," observed Edward W. Bok, editor of the *Ladies' Home Journal*.[114] William Dean Howells deemed it "an excellent piece of work,"[115] and Gilder, belatedly making amends, declared that Davis had written "some of the strongest romances that have lately appeared."[116] The French writer Paul Bourget proclaimed "Gallegher" a "masterpiece" drawn with "a few strokes of matchless precision" from "an observation terribly keen and yet pathetic, darkly realistic and yet lighthearted."[117] It was easy to believe that Davis was at the start of a brilliant literary career.

His youth was definitely an advantage. The dazzling advent of Rudyard Kipling encouraged patriotic Americans to be on the lookout for a young laureate of their own. Kipling had arrived on a tour of the United States in 1889, twenty-three years old and virtually unknown. Despite his literary success in London, he was unable to interest reputable American publishers in his work. Pirated versions of his stories and poems, however, began appearing the following year. By the fall of 1890, he was all the rage; and a pirated version of *The Light That Failed*—brought out just before the international copyright agreement took effect on July 1, 1891—confirmed Kipling's popular reputation as a youthful genius. He was a year and a half Richard's junior. "I think it is disgusting that a boy like that should write such stories," Richard told his mother. "He hasn't left himself anything to do when he gets old."[118]

A fan of Kipling's fiction, Davis was also fascinated by the French, especially by the ironic tales of Maupassant and by the Symbolist prose poems that Stuart Merrill, an American expatriate in Paris, had translated and published that year under the title *Pastels in Prose*.[119] A few weeks after *Scribner's* accepted "Gallegher," Davis talked to a few editors there about trying his hand at the form. He worried, though, that American literary taste had not yet advanced so far. "People do not understand it over here," he told his mother. "They want a plot, they don't want a bit of descriptive work and an idea. They want characters with names and they want to see them married or killed off. They ask 'Is that all[,] why I was just getting interested.' "[120] He wrote a few prose-poems, which he feared "read like imitations." Feeling the same way, both *Scribner's* and *Harper's* declined them, although *Harper's Weekly* published one that described a summer night at Battery Park, with the boats floating by on the river, and the people, many of them immigrants, promenading side by side without speaking.[121]

Battery Park was not where Richard was whiling away his summer nights. He spent much of the golden August in which "Gallegher" appeared at Sea Bright, where he and Brisbane had rented a cottage. Leaving the office at three got them to Sea Bright in time for an early evening swim with the Shippen girls. They would all go for a ride through the countryside, followed by a seven o'clock dinner, after which they would retire to the porch, or around the fire if it was cool, to hear Richard sing for half an hour. Then the girls would go to read novels, and Richard would write until ten or ten-thirty. It was, he judged, "a perfect way of living and they are all such thoroughbreds."[122]

In these pleasant environs, he was composing a story of life on the scruffy East Side. Responding to the first rumbles of the "Gallegher" uproar, Burlingame had commissioned a story for the *Scribner's* Christmas issue, due in three weeks.[123] To comply, Richard revived an old character, Rags Raegan, in a vehicle that had been creaky since Bret Harte's "The Luck of Roaring Camp." In the new story, Rags is on the lam from a murder charge, hiding out in an abandoned apartment whose usual tenants have been sent to Blackwell's Island. Somehow, everybody has forgotten about the jailbirds' baby daughter, an adorable creature who is Rags's salvation. To get her a doctor, Rags surrenders to the police. Naturally, all ends well, and he is acquitted. When last seen, he has forsaken crime for a steady job and seems to have adopted the little girl.

With its theme of the moral redemption of an outcast, "My Disreputable Friend, Mr. Raegen" enraptured Richard's parents. "He has written a *great* story," Clarke told his wife. "How does a boy like that know the thoughts that are in that?" Rebecca found it superior to "Gallegher" because "it touches deeper feelings." Richard had to agree that it was "the best I have ever written by all and long odds." In fact, it was an early example of the sort of story that he would write on deadline throughout his career: easy to read, sentimental, hackneyed. Calling it "not startlingly novel," editor Burlingame accepted it. Already, he knew the Richard Harding Davis name would sell.[124]

Confident of Davis's talent, and eager to tie him to the house of Scribner, Burlingame immediately commissioned him to write a sort of prose poem, but one of a length and importance way beyond anything the young man had envisioned. *Scribner's* was planning a series of magazine articles on the great streets of the world, to be published eventually as a book. Henry James was doing the Grand Canal, Andrew Lang had Piccadilly. Burlingame wanted Richard to take on Broadway as the leadoff. "Of course it is an immense thing and as he points out the first must give the tone to all of the others and he wants it pitched very high," Richard informed his mother, his own pitch a bit heightened with excitement and anxiety. "He wants it treated from the human point of view. I consider it the most important piece of work I have had and I confess to being sadly rattled over it."[125] Reading a half-completed version in October, Burlingame thought it made too much of the obvious and needed more of "the moralizing and philosophy of the street."[126] In response, Richard pumped up the ending with a melodramatic account of a lovelorn young man who shoots himself behind a tree in Madison Square. Burlingame was pleased.[127] *Scribner's* ran it in May 1891.

"Broadway" is Davis's first piece of travel writing, a genre which became one of his specialties. Like the later examples, it is breezy and chatty. If a little less cocky, it was, after all, his first try—and it was hard to take a full swing when you knew you were leading off for Henry James. To give his essay some structure, Davis followed Broadway geographically, tracing how it changed as it moved north. Less obviously, he also advanced in time, beginning in the early morning and ending at night. He started in the fast-paced business district, where thousands of foot soldiers in "the battle of business" arrived each morning before eight, to be "chained before roller-top desks, or bound down in the arms of swivel-chairs," until at six they are released "and are allowed to run up town overnight, on their promise to return again, and are given three hours in which to become acquainted with their children." This was Davis's dour view of the business world, a jailyard that he not only shunned personally, but even avoided writing about. He much preferred the shopping district, populated by women, to this "very grim and very real" masculine business center. The stores were bargain joints between Tenth and Fourteenth streets, becoming more fashionable and more to his liking further north. At Twenty-third lay the cosmopolitan heart of the city, where lively Broadway crossed respectable Fifth Avenue to form Madison Square. Although Broadway continued north through the Tenderloin District and into the dusty suburbs, Richard ended his tour at Madison Square, near which he had recently moved.[128] On the edge of the square stood a building, decorated with broad white window shades and tropical plants in iron urns, that was a sort of living pantheon of the city's leading socialites, actors, businessmen, sportsmen, writers, and wastrels. This was Delmonico's, the most fashionable restaurant in town. It was run like a club, operating on the credit system: a customer was handed a check only at his request. (But, if he didn't ask for a bill around the first of the month, after he was seated and his order graciously taken, he would never—no matter how long he waited or how loudly he protested—be served.) Tracing its lineage back to an 1836 watering hole on Beaver Street, Delmonico's since 1876 had been based on the south side of Twenty-sixth between Fifth and Broadway in an establishment that— with its frescoed ceilings, silver chandeliers, flower-decked fountain, and French *haute cuisine*—realized all the fantasies of the new rich. The restaurant had been the scene of some of the grandest private entertainments of the 1870s and 1880s, those Lucullan banquets that later seemed to epitomize the Gilded Age.[129] When Richard first came to New York, Delmonico's was his idea of heaven.[130]

Yet during his first six months in New York, he went there only a couple of times.[131] Not because of the expense (all his life he spent his money as fast as he earned it), but because of his workload. When he wasn't writing stories, he was performing the duties of a full-time reporter for the *Evening Sun*. Typically, he was in the *Sun* offices one day in September

1890, reviewing the *Scribner's* galleys for "My Disreputable Friend, Mr. Raegen." He had worked on the story for three weeks; it would make up nine pages in the magazine; at ten dollars a page, that would bring him ninety dollars—or thirty dollars a week, just what the *Evening Sun* was paying him. Distracted by these delicious calculations, he looked up to see a thin, light-haired young man with a thick moustache and a bustling manner. The stranger slapped his business card on Davis's desk and announced, "I am S. S. McClure. I have sent my London representative to Berlin and my New York man to London. Will you take charge of my New York end?"

Unrattled, in the same perfunctory tone, Davis replied, "Bring your New York representative back and send me to London, and I'll consider it. As long as I am in New York, I will not leave the *Evening Sun.*"

"Edmund Gosse is my London representative," McClure replied. "You can have the same work here. Come out and take lunch!"

"Thanks, I can't, I'll see you on Tuesday."

"All right," McClure replied. "Think of what I say. I'll make your fortune. You won't have anything to do but ask people to write novels and edit them. I'll send you abroad later if you don't like New York. Can you write any children's stories for me?"

"No," Davis said. "See you Tuesday."[132]

McClure was a publishing phenomenon. Six years earlier he had started a newspaper syndicate, in which he bought works of fiction from prominent authors and sold the publication rights to newspapers. Since newspapers were far less prestigious than the top literary magazines, McClure had to pay, and he paid generously. For example, he gave Mark Twain a thousand dollars each for six letters from Europe, and William Dean Howells ten thousand dollars for the newspaper serial rights to *The Quality of Mercy.*[133] To keep his client newspapers happy, McClure scrambled to keep signing up new writers. Anyone with a name he could promote was useful. Earlier that year he had engaged Frances Hodgson Burnett, author of *Little Lord Fauntleroy*, as a figurehead for his new Youth's Department.[134]

He could not permit Davis—the young man whose story "Gallegher" was on everyone's lips, whose form (as drawn by Gibson) was in everyone's heart—to escape him. At their lunch, he dangled the tempting sum of seventy-five dollars a week. Davis considered it; but he decided to stay at the *Evening Sun*, using McClure's offer as a lever to jack up his salary. "I couldn't afford to put myself on a shelf at present," he reasoned privately. "There are several parts of the world I have not yet seen."[135] Brisbane guaranteed him a raise to fifty dollars a week by October 1. Even better, there was a chance that Davis might replace Brisbane as managing editor or become a London correspondent. "The more I thought of the McClure offer the less I thought of it," he concluded, "and the more I heard of McClure the less I thought of him."[136] Not a man who gave up easily,

McClure came back with a new proposal. He would pay Davis fifty dollars to write a weekly syndicated letter. The work would take two days, Richard estimated, leaving him "five days of absolute freedom." It was such a good offer that he might have been unable to refuse it, had another, even more impressive position not been offered him at the same time. To his amazement, he was asked to become the managing editor of *Harper's Weekly*.[137]

4

The Young Man's Epoch

*B*Y OFFERING A MAJOR PUBLICATION to someone whose only editorial credit was one issue of the Lehigh *Burr,* the house of Harper acknowledged that the *Weekly* needed a jolt. *Harper's Weekly* was an old man's newspaper in a young man's era. It had been founded in the heated political climate before the Civil War. In peacetime, it foundered. Like other genteel Republicans, editor George William Curtis progressed from abolitionism to civil-service reform—a passion that was not only dull but treacherous. It led him to desert his party in the 1884 presidential election for Grover Cleveland's Democrats, permanently alienating many loyal Republican *Weekly* readers. As the decade closed, Curtis was "only an occasional visitor" to the Harper offices in Franklin Square. The *Weekly* was run by managing editor John Foord, whose departure opened the way for Davis.[1]

At the end of 1890, having achieved an astonishing success in New York in little more than a year, Davis left his reporter's job at the *Evening Sun* to take command of *Harper's Weekly.*[2] As Richard Watson Gilder portentously put it, he began "at once to influence, editorially, American literature of the future."[3] Understandably, J. Henry Harper and his older, less active cousin, Joseph Wesley Harper, Jr., turned to a well-connected young man who was the literary darling of the moment. It enhanced his allure that the Scribners—led by Charles Scribner, with the help of his younger brother, Arthur—were wooing Davis so assiduously. Just a month before he began working at the *Weekly,* Richard informed the Harpers that he was declining their offer to publish his first book of short stories in favor of the Scribner firm, which "has shown the most interest in my work and has put the most work in my way."[4]

Polite but not friendly rivals, Harpers and Scribners in 1890 were the two most prestigious American publishers. They had coexisted uneasily since 1881, when the older Harper firm disputed Scribner's contract to publish Thomas Carlyle's *Reminiscences* in the United States. Harper published a competing edition of the memoir. Then, untrammeled by copyright restrictions, the Harpers spitefully violated "trade courtesy" and published cheap editions of several of Scribner's most profitable English titles. Scribner took the high road and did not retaliate. Although Harper soon stopped its raids, the acrimony lingered for a decade.[5] So it was a startling show of one-upmanship for the Harpers, having lost the competition to publish Davis's stories, to acquire Davis himself. In the future, he would be required to submit his short stories first to his new employer.[6]

As for Richard, who turned down McClure to accept the Harper offer—the *Weekly* position was just too prestigious to refuse.[7] Like McClure's original editorial proposal, the job would keep him "on the shelf." But it was a much higher and classier shelf. The position of managing editor of *Harper's Weekly* conveyed political importance and literary substance. The title on one's calling card would provide automatic admittance virtually anywhere a gentleman might wish to go. Although he was temperamentally and intellectually ill-suited for editing, Richard had a weakness for honors and for tradition.

He took up his new duties at the Harper offices in Franklin Square, a small bulge on Pearl Street on the lower East Side. It was an inconvenient and unfashionable part of town, choked and rattled by the elevated train and deafened further by the commotion of the Brooklyn Bridge. Back in 1853, when a great fire destroyed their plant (the fourth disastrous blaze in the firm's history), the four founding Harper brothers considered a move uptown, to a block on Broadway facing Madison Square. Clearly, New York City was heading in that direction. But after reflection, they made their usual mistake and bowed to tradition, remaining on the site they had occupied since 1825. To avoid any future conflagrations, they commissioned one of the earliest iron-and-glass buildings, probably inspired by the Crystal Palace of London. Eliminating the shafts and stairways that nourish a blaze, they dictated their office's quaintest feature. The only communication between the four stories was by an iron spiral staircase that was enclosed in a stucco-faced brick tower in the interior courtyard. The staircase connected to the landings of the front and rear buildings by iron bridges, which in winter were slick with ice and snow. The *Weekly* offices were located on the second floor facing on the courtyard.[8]

It was entirely appropriate that to these offices, built in a "modern" style that was old-fashioned the moment the last brick was laid, the Harpers now brought a "modern" editor whose amazing popularity derived from his embrace of old forms and values against the barrage of the new. Of course, neither Davis nor his admirers thought of it that way. Davis was so ostentatiously youthful and fashionably up-to-date that his conservative allegiances could be overlooked. His flair for the new made him exciting, his ties to the old made him safe. It was a recipe for popular success.

The end of the last century was very much "the young man's epoch." The phrase is novelist Gertrude Atherton's; one of her characters remarks, "A man feels a failure nowadays if he hasn't distinguished himself before thirty."[9] Those men who could no longer be young at least tried to look young by shaving off their beards. ("No one should wear a beard unless he have a preternaturally ugly mouth and chin," declared a fashion authority in the late 1880s.) Until Grover Cleveland defeated the bearded James Blaine in 1884, every President since the Civil War had worn a beard; after Cleveland, not one did.[10] As Booth Tarkington would later recall, a generation of young men and women "found [in Davis] their prophet and gladly perceived that a prophet is not always cowled and bearded, but may be a gallant young gentleman."[11]

In retrospect, we can see that at the same time that the nation was glorifying youth and energy, it was gripped with anxiety about depletion and loss. That is what is so poignant about the turn of the century. The national physiognomy resembled Davis's own: an exuberantly self-confident grin, masking weary, troubled eyes. Between 1898 and 1900, in a burst of aggressive expansion that climaxed in the Spanish-American War, the United States would acquire nearly all of her territory outside the North American continent: the Philippines, Hawaii, eastern Samoa, Guam, and Puerto Rico. It was also in the 1890s, however, that Americans mourned the closing of the frontier and the death of the mythical West. (In his famous paper of 1893, the historian Frederick Jackson Turner crystallized the public perception, if not the geographical reality, by declaring that the West was full up.)[12] The era of the Gibson Girl, the bicycle, and the American Beauty rose was also the time of the economic depression that began in 1893 and set off a series of convulsions: Populist agitation in the farmlands, violent labor disputes like the Pullman and Homestead strikes in the cities. Everywhere that a student of turn-of-the-century America looks, he finds an obsession with degeneration, exhaustion, and depletion. Morals were falling down, nerves were wearing thin, natural resources were running out. Very sensitive to these concerns, Davis expressed them by negating and denying them. A grateful literary establishment saluted him for "a certain unique vigor, healthy and hearty and masculine, in the work, rare in these days of sickly prurience and pessimism."[13]

As his new employers expected, Davis tried to transform *Harper's Weekly* into a young man's paper. "I want to wake up the sleepers of Franklin Square with a great big bang," he told his friend, the journalist Stephen Bonsal.[14] Because he had inherited a six-month backlog of manuscripts from Foord, he resigned himself to a long fuse before the explosion.[15] In the meantime, he enjoyed playing editor. He found that he could "trot around and bluff off whiskey and watery writers" and discourage beginners "as though I had been in the chair all my life."[16]

Seeking young men to write on topics that interested young men, he went first to his friends. Caspar Whitney began a regular column on amateur sports, and Mark Antony De Wolfe Howe (who was perhaps older than his years) wrote on Phillips Brooks. But he didn't stop at his friends. Prickled by a report that he had obtained his job through personal connections, and that the New York press boasted at least twenty young writers with more talent, Davis pursued these prodigies, getting many to write for the *Weekly*: David Graham Phillips, a brilliant young reporter for the *Sun* who later won fame as a novelist, contributed two pieces during Davis's first month on the job. Richard himself began a series on heroic young men, ranging from a British lieutenant who crushed a horde of "semi-barbarous natives" in India, to the more homespun example of a Harvard football captain who raised the depraved moral tone on campus. As part of his youthfest, Richard produced a supplement on "Young Men of New York" that featured friends and prospective friends: Bonsal, Brisbane, and a civil-service commissioner named Theodore Roosevelt.[17]

In the youth-oriented 1890s, no one was more youth-oriented than Davis. As early as his nineteenth birthday, he had confessed that he felt "abominably old."[18] Acutely sensitive to the erosions of time, he rebelled in a way that, had he been older, might have seemed pathetic or heroic. Since he was still in his twenties, his defiance was comic. He maintained the fanaticism for sports that had undermined his first job on the Philadelphia *Record*, but channeled it into writing savvy football stories for the *Evening Sun* and *Week's Sport*. He was regarded as the best writer on the game in New York.[19] Football had changed since his college days. The long passes of the 1880s had been superseded by a "scientific"—and brutal— game of rushing.[20] Although he preferred the passing game of his youth, Richard consistently opposed restrictions on the sport. As managing editor of the *Weekly*, he printed a large illustration of an injured football player being carried from the field, but he added a short piece of his own under the same title: "Out of the Game." The boy would be back on the turf tomorrow, Davis wrote. Pity instead the sad-eyed men in the stands, many not yet thirty, who were "out of the game in earnest." He was twenty-seven when he wrote those words, and already feeling like a "young old fogy."[21]

In the years since Davis played, football had become supremely popular as a spectator sport. The Thanksgiving Day game between Princeton and Yale was a major social event of the season. "You would go to see the English Derby whether you cared for horse racing or not, wouldn't you?" wrote an *Evening Sun* reporter, probably Richard, before the 1890 Thanksgiving Day game. "Well, then, you've got to go to the American Derby, to the greatest sporting event in the country, where there will be more people and more noise and more excitement and more to see and hear for your money than you can find anywhere else on Thanksgiving Day, or any other day in the year."[22] On the big weekend, all New York seemed decked out in blue or in orange and black. Coaches on their way uptown to Manhattan

Field in Harlem would pass tenements with a strip of colored cloth hanging from an eight-floor window and townhouses draped with large silk banners. Every shop window featured photographs of the players. When Davis was a student, only devotees of sport braved the cold to watch the game. Young men outnumbered young women by about fifty to one, and no more than twenty men were profligate enough to drive out in a cab and watch the proceedings perched on the driver's box. By 1893, it was necessary to reserve a cab a full year in advance, and to pay twenty dollars for a place to park it.[23]

Richard's favorite companion in the football bleachers was his brother, Charles. In the summer of 1891, Charles quit his job at the Reading line of the Pennsylvania Railroad—a job that left him too depressed even to lift a tennis racket—and moved to New York.[24] Richard found him a place with Brisbane as a reporter on the *Evening Sun*, beginning at the end of July. The two brothers took rooms together at 10 East Twenty-eighth Street, two blocks north of Delmonico's and Madison Square.[25] They lived together (when not abroad) until marriage eventually sundered them, and they remained the closest of friends throughout their lives. A stouter, duller, tamer version of his brother, Charles played Sancho Panza to the dashing don. He was Richard's trusted confidant and his reliable assistant. He seemed to run on Richard's motive force, showing up in all the same places, always a few steps behind. In addition to emulating Richard as a reporter, Charles tried his hand at writing short stories, boosted by his brother's enthusiastic suggestions and, to a lesser extent, by his editorial connections.[26]

Richard's comments to Charles are the closest he ever came to tabulating a literary creed. In the early 1890s, when both he and the world believed that his literary future was brilliant, he wrote his best short stories, and he gave much thought to his art. He would remain a conscientious and painstaking writer, but he would come to realize, as he grew older, that he was a craftsman, not an artist. A cabinetmaker, once he has acquired a style, makes chairs; he disdains to philosophize about the aesthetics of seating.

The theory of fiction that Richard adopted in his youth was, we might say, market driven. He believed that a character should not disappoint the reader. Reviewing a story by Charles, he complained that it was one thing to have the American girl flirt with a "monkey count," quite another for her to reject her American suitor. Charles "ought to show the danger American girls run without making a horrible example of anyone of them." We are a long way here from Henry James. Richard thought that Charles was too influenced by Maupassant's "cold blooded view of life." "You want to put in a little more of the humanity of which you are full and not make us pity people so much but laugh with them more," he advised.[27] This sounds so much like those "smiling aspects of life" that William Dean Howells thought most American that Howells's own advice to Davis, transmitted publicly in his *Harper's Magazine* column, is worth recording: "What we could desire this brilliant writer, if we had our wishing-cap on, would be a perfect unconsciousness of his reader's presence, and an entire willingness to trust others with his facts as simply as providence confided them to him." He should portray the thing as it is and not "as he thinks his reader would like it to be."[28]

With that shrewd wish, Howells identified the character trait that crippled Davis's talent: his deepest instinct was to please. He had learned early how to charm a doting mother. He did not intend now to disappoint his adoring public. Intuitively, he knew just how far he could go. He staked out the furthest boundary a few weeks after he began work in Franklin Square, when he published (in *Scribner's*) a story with a theme that one associates more with Edith Wharton than with Richard Harding Davis: the conflict between desire and convention in an upper-class New Yorker at the turn of the century. Even its name—"The Other Woman"—hardly sounds like Davis.[29]

Instead of the usual soldier, writer, or adventurer, the hero of "The Other Woman" is a wealthy young lawyer named Latimer, who has gone to ask for the hand of the bishop's daughter, Ellen. The bishop throws him off balance with this question: If Latimer had but a month to live and was promised impunity from all laws of God and man, would he choose Ellen or some other woman to share his last days? Latimer at first refuses to answer, arguing that beyond the borders of civilization, men can't be judged; then he concedes that another, unsuitable woman had a prior claim on his affections. Overhearing the conversation, Ellen orders Latimer to leave. Bitterly, he replies that "whatever good there is in me is due to that temptation and to the fact that I beat it and overcame it and kept myself honest and clean." Being another man, the bishop understands completely. Being a woman, Ellen rejects him. As he leaves, Latimer looks wistfully toward the neighborhood of the other woman, then controls himself and heads home.

In "The Other Woman," Davis made his strongest statement of his favorite theme. For the sake of civilization, men must repress themselves; the goodness that is a woman's gift comes to man only through struggle. As Latimer says to Ellen: "It's easy enough for you to draw your skirts around you, but what can a woman bred as you have been bred know of what I've had to fight against and keep under and cut away?" That Davis was not the only young person in late-nineteenth-century America preoccupied with the issue of sexual repression was made evident by the reaction to his story. Everywhere he went people asked him about it. "I shun society I hesitate to open letters and I fly from every new acquaintance," he joked.[30] "The Other Woman" was "the most discussed" of Davis's stories, a critic wrote six years later, because it "makes one think and wonder."[31] Burlingame at *Scribner's* declared with delight that it was the best work Davis had done.[32]

There was a war waged in American literature in the 1890s between the realists and the romancers—between those who sought to portray the startling facts of modern life without disguise, and those who hoped to remold new truths into comforting old forms.[33] It's obvious, knowing his tastes and disposition (and aided by hindsight), that Richard would opt for romance; but in his youth, at the time of "The Other Woman," it still seemed possible that he would follow his mother (that is, the Rebecca of "Life in the Iron Mills") and land in the realist camp. The more or less realistic stories—"The Other Woman," "Gallegher," and "A Walk up the Avenue"—were the standouts in the April 1891 Scribner collection, *Gallegher and Other Stories*, that Richard dedicated to his mother. However (as Rebecca had warned at the start of his literary career), Richard would strive to duplicate not his youthful achievement but his precocious success, and he would abandon realism in favor of more certain crowdpleasers. The response to *Gallegher* might have spoiled anyone: the first edition sold out within the month.[34] In the first year, Scribners reported sales of 15,346 copies.[35] One happy evening, as they left the Twenty-eighth Street apartment for a modest dinner, the Davis brothers saw the distinctive long Scribner envelope in the mail on the mantel: a royalty check. Richard guessed it would be for $190; Charles, despite doubts, loyally suggested $300. Fingers trembling, Richard tore it open, and announced, with whoops of glee and a dance around the hall table, that it was for $919.23! That night they dined at Delmonico's.[36]

Throughout her life, Rebecca would try to steer Richard away from the sentimental commercialism that had blighted her career. She argued vehemently against an offer of $1,000 from Edward Bok for a series of short sketches in the *Ladies' Home Journal*. "For one thing, you will lose prestige writing for Bok's paper," she explained. "For another, I dread beyond everything your beginning to do hack work for money. It is the beginning of decadence both in work & reputation for you. I know by my own and a thousand other people. Begin to work because it 'is a lot of money' & you stop doing your best work[.] You make your work common and your prices will soon go down."[37] That was a piercing summary of her own literary progression. Richard told Bok no.

He succumbed, however, to the persistent McClure. For $300 (almost twice what *Harper's Monthly* had paid for the longest Van Bibber tale) he sold to McClure "The Reporter Who Made Himself King."[38] It was a lighthearted mock-epic about a Yale dropout who provokes an international incident on an obscure Pacific island. To justify his high fees, McClure squeezed out every drop of promotional value for the circulation of his client newspaper. He had appalled his favorite author, Robert Louis Stevenson, with his shameless puffery of a children's story, "The Black Arrow."[39] Now he did the same to Davis. "This story which was never anything but a story for boys has been heralded in this country as 'the best thing I have done' and the English papers and my friends there have written about it to the most alarming extent," Richard complained. "The English papers have made it a sort of 'test case' and say that in the title I have virtually challenged comparison with Kipling and his 'The Man Who Made Himself King.'* This is all very absurd but exceedingly annoying."[40] It wouldn't be the last time that Davis, working for a less prestigious publisher at an advantageous price, would express outrage at the outcome.

He craved the love of the reviewers as well as the readers. While the Scribners wanted to issue another volume of stories immediately, Richard feared "criticisms of 'falling off' in interest and quality."[41] Persuaded to take advantage of the "Gallegher" phenomenon, he relented in time for the Christmas trade; with deliberate deprecation he called the book *Stories for Boys*. At the same time, he had not forgotten his new employers. For the Harpers he assembled a collection called *Van Bibber and Others* that appeared in April 1892. In the space of a year, he had published three volumes of short stories. He was making his work more common, but his popularity was soaring. The first edition of four thousand copies of *Van Bibber and Others* sold out by noon of the second day.[42]

Although he named the collection after his tongue-in-check alter ego Van Bibber, Davis, bolstered by his sudden success, would from now on create fictional self-portraits that were less humorous and more unabashedly heroic. In fact, the key story in *Van Bibber and Others* is not one of the old boulevardier tales, but a drawing-room adventure yarn that served as a prototype for much of Davis's later work. It is a tale of derring-do narrated in an upper-class English salon: a Kipling picture in a Stevenson frame. The gentleman who could fight his way through the jungle and then wittily describe his escapades at the dinner table was the classic Davis hero; and Gordon, the protagonist of "An Unfinished Story," was his first personification.[43] Like Gibson's flattering line drawings, Gordon was a fantasy figure whose resemblance to Davis couldn't be missed.

At a fashionable London dinner party, the Stevensonian question, Which is stranger, fact or fiction? provokes the young American explorer (and onetime foreign correspondent) Gordon to lean back in his chair and tell of a man he recently rescued in Africa. Hoping to prove himself worthy of his rich, patrician fiancée, this man embarked on a daredevil expedition. Gordon found him in the jungle near death and brought him back, but he was too weak to survive the voyage to London. Had he lived, Gordon concludes his story—and it is a much more colorful saga than we have room for here—the hapless lover would have returned to find his adored one engaged to an English aristocrat. As the narrative advances, the reader realizes that the faithless woman is the other American at the dinner,

---

*The name of Kipling's story is "The Man Who Would Be King." In selecting the title of this book, I have corrected Davis's error.

escorted by her new betrothed. But only at the conclusion of this cleverly wrought tale is it clear that there was no other man who died. Gordon is telling his own story. (Indeed, for some of Davis's more obtuse or juvenile readers, who wrote perplexed to the author, that was never clear.[44]) In later years, when, just as his mother had feared, he was producing fiction to pay off his creditors, Davis would drum out endless hackneyed variations on the theme of assumed or mistaken identity. But in "An Unfinished Story," as in the Conway Maur and Van Bibber tales, the idea still bounces on rust-free springs.

The theme was fresh because he was still young. With a change of costume, he might himself take on another life, another identity. Fidgeting in the overstuffed editor's chair, he looked about for alternative paths. The probable model for Gordon was an acquaintance of Richard's, William Astor Chanler, who (unlike Gordon) was as rich and upper-class as one might ask. Three years Richard's junior, Chanler in 1889 had led a party of 120 men on a successful safari to Masai country near Mount Kilimanjaro, where no American had ever hunted before. In the summer of 1891, when Davis was writing "An Unfinished Story," Chanler in London was planning another, even more ambitious African expedition. Richard vacationed in London that September, and later wrote an envious description of Chanler's gear.[45] Could a magazine editor, in comparison, be said to be living? On returning from his three-week holiday in London, Davis called on Grover Cleveland, who was living on Madison Avenue, to inquire about a political career. Cleveland thought that Richard could be elected to Congress, but that it would be "the greatest folly to go there." As Davis reported: "He seemed to think breaking stones as a means of getting fame and fortune was quicker and more genteel."[46]

It was predictable, perhaps inevitable, that like so many young Americans before him, Davis would address his need for excitement and adventure by looking west to the frontier. And it was preordained that he would be let down by what he saw. Out West, and later around the world, his travels would only reinforce Davis's personal sensation of ebbing youth. Wherever he went, he was always too late. At the end of the century, the westward urge was an exercise in nostalgia and irony. The true descendants of the California gold rushers are the miners who later in the 1890s journeyed to the treacherous Alaskan Klondike, hoping for quick wealth. Texas, the Great Plains, and the Rockies lured a different, tamer breed: those who had grown up on the stories of Bret Harte and sought romance more than fortune. Although the Indians had staged their last stand and the territories were fast becoming states, the afterimage of the Wild West flickered on. The West attracted Eastern scions longing for invigoration, English aristocrats lusting for exotic recreation, artists searching for new material, and bankrupts hoping for another chance. In January 1892, the West embraced the enervated young editor of *Harper's Weekly*, who was fleeing the humdrum routine and icy weather of New York.

After almost a year of editorial work, Davis had worked out a writing deal with the Harpers. He would go west for the winter, return briefly to New York, then sail off to London. For the Western articles (plus photographs), he would be paid $1,000 and $550 in expenses; for the London ones, $1,000 and $200 in expenses.[47] The articles would later be collected into two books, producing further income in the form of royalties.

It is of course an absurd idea to travel to a vast territory about which one knows next to nothing, spend less than three months there, and write a book about it. Still, writers did it then and do it now. When a reporter ventures into remote lands, the exotic subject matter compensates for the quick study. But the West was hardly mysterious in 1892. It was reliably, if tediously, accessible by the railroads that crisscrossed the continent. It had been mythologized and demythologized. In a spasm of self-confident elation, a young writer could imagine that he would find what others had overlooked, or that he would take what they had found and make it his own. In fits of depression, he would remember that this once virgin land had long ago been deflowered. As Richard bid his parents farewell in Philadelphia, his mood swayed sharply. "You dear old fraud, kissing your hand and laughing," his mother wrote him. "You did not fool me with your laugh."[48]

As an *Evening Sun* reporter, Davis, in a lampoon of Matthew Arnold's famously superficial railroad tour of America, had described the sights visible from a train window between Philadelphia and New York.[49] He would now be seeing the West in much the way he had ridiculed. The only way to deal with this conspicuous shortcoming was to joke about it: he called his Western book *The West from a Car-Window*.[50] The main destination of his three-month journey was Texas, where he hoped to accompany the U.S. troops commanded by Captain Hardie in pursuit of the Mexican revolutionary or brigand (it depended on whom you spoke to) Caterino Garza. Chased out of Mexico, where the government had tagged a three-hundred-thousand-dollar price on his head, Garza was spending most of his time in the wild Texas country near the Rio Grande.[51] In an eleven-day visit, Davis had about as much chance of spotting him as a Himalayan trekker does of glimpsing a snow leopard. "Tell mother that for one month 500 men have been hunting for Garza," Richard wrote home, "in that time one man has been wounded therefore my chance of being wounded is 15000th of one."[52] Reading railroad literature on the train to St. Louis, Davis learned belatedly just how large Texas was.[53] The enormous expanses of space, of interminable, undistinguished, maddening space, would be a revelation of his trip.

His first disappointment was the weather. The landscape was buried in snow all the way to St. Louis. When at last he reached San Antonio, Davis found the muddy city gripped by the coldest winter in a decade. "Tin cans in the gardens of the mansions and snow around the palms and palmettos," he reported gloomily. Even the Mexicans were "merely dirty and not picturesque." Those were his private complaints to his family. Preserving his smiling public face, he vowed not to write anything until he felt a bit more cheerful.[54] And, as if by magic, the next day the sun came out, the mud dried up, and he toured the Alamo in summer clothes.[55] In his first article for *Harper's Weekly*, he apologized for telling the "more than thrice-told story" of the Alamo's last stand, with the doddering excuse that it "cannot be told too often."[56] Had he been more candid, he could have supported his statement with a personal anecdote. Not long after the publication of *Gallegher*, he was invited to a dinner party at the Madison Avenue house of Theodore Roosevelt, who was then a civil-service commissioner and one of the bright young men of New York. Over dinner, Roosevelt spoke of the Alamo and Davis said he had never heard of it. Roosevelt, "most kindly indignant," then told him the story. Many years later, Davis recalled: "It was his rebuke that made me write about the Alamo when I shortly afterwards went to San Antonio."[57]

From San Antonio, Richard endured a wearisome two-day journey on a jerky, narrow-gauge freight train through the red soil and scrub of South Texas chaparral country. A young trooper escorted him on horseback from the tiny rail station to Captain Hardie's camp. Upon arrival, they found that Hardie had left that morning. For the next few days, Davis toughened his muscles to the saddle and deadened his stomach to the diet of fat bacon, undrinkable coffee, and alkaline water.[58] Things changed little after Hardie and his men returned. Davis rode with them for more than a week in dazing heat through country that was "more like the ocean than anything else and drives one crazy with its monotony." Garza was nowhere to be seen, and Davis worried that his articles would be as dreary as the landscape. "If we could have a fight or something that would excuse and make a climax for all this marching and reconnoitering and discomfort the story would have a suitable finale and a raison d'etre," he wrote wistfully to his mother.[59] The only cowboys he saw were roping wild horses for the amusement of Eastern visitors at the seven-hundred-thousand-acre King Ranch; the ranch manager called out the foot for them to snare like a pool player naming the ball and pocket. Elsewhere, Texas Rangers demonstrated their remarkable shooting prowess. But it was all display, all merely show.[60]

After resting up in San Antonio, Davis proceeded to Oklahoma City, where he was able to observe in one setting everything he loathed most about the West. Only three years had passed since the opening of the Oklahoma Territory to white settlers. Looking at the rows of remarkably solid buildings, Richard was reminded of the lightning crayon artists in New York who fashioned a portrait in ten minutes: one has seen better portraits, but not done while you wait. On closer examination, he saw that Oklahoma City was swarming with lawyers and real-estate agents, there to assist the frantic "Sooners" in their snatching of government land. Real-estate speculation was the civic passion. "It was all raw and mean, and greedy for money," he thought, "and a man is much better off in every way in a tenement on Second Avenue than the 'owner of his own home' in one of these mushroom cities."[61]

From Oklahoma City he traveled by stagecoach to Fort Reno in the Oklahoma Territory to visit an Indian reservation. Riding by red canyons and bluffs as sharp as a razor against the blue sky, he felt for the first time that he was in the West, the West as he knew it from the illustrated papers. Unfortunately, he arrived at Fort Reno, as at so many of his destinations, a few hours too late. To see the beef issue to the Indians, which promised to be one of the few "events" in his humdrum journey, he took another stagecoach to Anadarko.[62] What he saw there was not so much picturesque as it was poignant—a vivid tableau of what had happened to the Old West. Each steer that the government supplied was supposed to furnish twenty-five Indians with two weeks of beef. That calculation presumed that each steer weighed a thousand to twelve hundred pounds, but the steers that Davis saw delivered at Anadarko carried only about five hundred pounds, and they were so weak with hunger that they stumbled when they tried to run. "They were nothing but hide and ribs and two horns," he wrote angrily. He would have preferred to tell a simple story of the red man battling a mean-spirited administration, of a proud people squeezed into dependence and poverty. Unfortunately, more than land and wealth had been wrung out of the Indians. The ritual of the beef issue was a pathetic reminder of diminished glory. The cattle, driven into a pen, were greeted by mischievous Indian boys in beaded buckskin shirts and silver-buttoned leather leggings. Sitting two to a pony, each boy held a bow and arrow. When the enfeebled steers staggered into view, the boys would shoot at them, from a distance of ten feet. The arrows stuck quivering in the animals' flanks and necks, not big enough to kill, merely sufficient to hurt. Then the boys' fathers, who were taking possession of the cattle, would shoot at them with Winchesters, wounding them repeatedly; until, bleeding profusely, and nipped by packs of dogs, the exhausted steers keeled over and the squaws rushed in to carve them up. It was a degraded parody of buffalo hunting, painful to watch.[63]

So much of the West seemed to mock Richard's preconceptions. Soon after he arrived in Texas, he heard that a deputy sheriff had just been murdered. Since he knew from his reading that murders in Texas were as common as dust storms, he paid little attention—until he saw South Texas reporters who had traveled more than a hundred miles to cover the killing of this unimportant official. When four days later the people of the county passed a resolution denouncing lawlessness, he thought back to the twenty-five accused murderers languishing without fanfare in the Tombs in New York and wondered what had happened to the Wild West of his fantasies.[64] He felt the same disappointment on the stagecoach to Anadarko, finding discomfort unsweetened by romance. He felt it in southwestern Texas, when he learned that the cowboy was an anachronism—a casualty of barbed-wire fencing, which impeded cattle drives, and railroads, which made them unnecessary. He sought everywhere the colorful desperado, but the closest he came was to talk to those who had arrested, shot, or lynched one of the breed, and he was forced to conclude sadly that the desperado was another victim of the progress of civilization. Had the civilization been attractive, imposing, entertaining—in other words, had it resembled New York—he might have sympathized. Instead, it was "uncouthness and pretentious imitation and cheap things at big prices," and he recoiled in disgust.[65]

He ended his trip in Denver. It was a fine city, with a citizenry "just like Eastern people," a theater with red velvet seats, and—the surest gauge of its civilized standards—a great appreciation for Richard Harding Davis.[66] He lunched with the mayor and with other visiting dignities, such as President Charles W. Eliot of Harvard.[67] Seeking material, he traveled to the nearby town of Creede, where silver had recently been discovered. His head full of fictional visions of "the chivalric extravagant days" of the '49 California gold rush, he was predictably disappointed to find no "auburn-haired giants in red shirts." The silver miners of Creede "were dim and commonplace, and lacked the sharp, clear-cut personality of Bret Harte's men and scenes." As he photographed them with his Kodak, he thought, "They were like the negative of a photograph which has been under-exposed, and which no amount of touching up will make clear."[68] Creede was a village of new-cut pine, without one brick or awning. Nor was there a hotel bed available. For a less celebrated journalist, finding a spare bed in a boomtown would have been worrisome. Not for Richard. The youthful editor of a Creede newspaper met him at the station, and took him home— home being a ten-by-eight-foot Grub Stake cabin shared with two boys from Harvard. For them, it was an unexpected privilege: a large picture of Davis adorned their raw wall.[69] The Creede that Richard saw resembled a Hasty Pudding or Triangle Club production of a Harte story. Dining in a Creede "eating-house," he noticed four very rough-looking men of different ages, who had marked out a map with an iron fork on a soiled tablecloth. They were scowling so blackly and gesturing so vigorously that he wondered if they were about to start shooting over a disputed claim. Finishing his meal, he passed their table on the way out and eavesdropped on their conversation. Pointing to the map, the oldest man was exclaiming: "Then Thompson passed the ball back to me—no, not your Thompson; Thompson of '79 I mean—and I carried it down the field all the way to the twenty-five-yard line. Canfield, who was playing full, tackled me; but I shook him off, and—" Richard left before learning whether the man had made his touchdown.[70] He never got to see any silver nuggets in Creede, either, although he did observe a pie-eating contest, a prizefight, and a Mexican circus.[71]

Ending his Western trip, he worried that he had seen nothing but play-acting and parody. So he was wild-eyed when he heard of an expedition of "thoroughbred sports" who were departing Denver for Mexico on April 1 in search of a remote tribe that worshipped idols, wore gowns of bird-feathers, and owned immense gold mines. Although he remained skeptical about the gold, Davis yearned to join this party. He had failed to see anything out of Bret Harte; perhaps he could witness a few scenes from H. Rider Haggard. Sensibly, the Harpers didn't subscribe to this vision. Richard returned to New York on schedule at the end of March.[72]

Had the Harpers approved his wild goose chase, Richard would have missed the social season in London. That would have forced him to postpone his trip, because the whole point, three years after that dismal tour with the Philadelphia cricket team, was to enter English society. May was set aside for the boat races at Oxford. June was the London horse-racing season at Epsom Downs and Ascot. To meet these deadlines, Richard had only a week in New York to gather his letters of introduction before boarding the ship to England in early May. "I forsee that I am going to be a *great social success*," he wrote his family when he reached London. He was sending out his letters *"at once."*[73]

The England that greeted the precocious managing editor of an eminent American magazine was unknown territory for the former junior cricket reporter of the Philadelphia *Evening Telegraph*. Richard was about to see England at the height of her empire, in the late glow of the Victorian summer. After the Great War, the upper classes would look back on these years as a prolonged garden party before the deluge. Davis had journeyed to the American West a decade or two too late, and had seen only debased versions of the West's heroic period. He reached England in time. Much of his delight in England, which he retained all his life, came from the knowledge that he was seeing the storybook kingdom that he knew from Thackeray novels and Gilbert and Sullivan operettas. His pleasure was sharpened by the intuition that he had gotten there at the last moment, that soon this picturesque England would be as irretrievably lost as the fabled American West.

He began at Oxford and stayed until the end of spring term. Oxford obviously was everything that Lehigh was not. It was the difference between Gothic and Gothic Revival, between gentlemen of leisure with Shakespearean-sounding titles and aspiring engineers with rented dress suits. Richard's infatuation with Oxford was total, and totally predictable. Far more surprising was Oxford's embrace of him. At twenty-eight, he should have seemed ancient to a college student, but (as should now be apparent) he was an unusually youthful twenty-eight. He arrived on the scene with the family of

Arthur Peel, who was the Speaker of the House of Commons. Peel's son was a Balliol man. So was the son of the earl of Carlisle, Hubert Howard, who invited Richard to stay a week in his rooms.[74] After a few days, Richard decided that the prank-loving, game-playing, thoroughly unintellectual young Tories of Oxford were the most hospitable people in England.[75] That he recognized them from *Tom Brown at Oxford* only enhanced his enjoyment.[76]

At the end of the Oxford term, Richard moved to rented rooms in the Albany, the most desirable bachelors' digs in London. His ultra-English flat peered out at Piccadilly through a clutter of old silver, Hogarth prints, Zulu weapons, fur rugs, and silk-upholstered easy chairs. Richard even inherited a manservant who, besides running errands and cooking dinner, kept guard so vigilantly that one night he turned away Arthur Balfour, the leader of the House of Commons, who had stopped by unannounced to see if Richard was free for supper.[77] Balfour and his mostly younger circle called themselves the Souls. It was a tribute to Richard's charm and connections that he so quickly endeared himself to this brightest and most fashionable of sets. Among the philistine Tory nobility, the Souls distinguished themselves by befriending artists and writers, hoping to create an English counterpart to the Faubourg Saint Germain. Witty conversationalists and sexual intriguers, they were a late Victorian prototype for the Bloomsbury circle (although they were far more aristocratic and far less productive). Their privileged world was shattered by the Great War.[78]

The quintessential Soul was Harry Cust. At Eton, his tutors had thought him the boy most likely to become prime minister. Instead, he won more temporary fame as a philanderer. Fair-haired and blue-eyed, he was a brilliant talker: the same year that Davis met him, Cust so entranced the American expatriate William Waldorf Astor over dinner that Astor offered him the editorship of the *Pall Mall Gazette*. Without any experience, Cust made that paper a literary showplace. "Noblest and Best of Editors," H. G. Wells called him.[79] Margot Asquith, a fellow Soul, thought him (with the exception of her stepson Raymond Asquith) the most brilliant young man she had ever met.[80] Had women not pursued him so ardently, or had he resisted them a little more, he might have accomplished a great deal. Instead, he adorned innumerable dinner parties and country-house week-ends, and sired innumerable illegitimate children.

One wonders how much Davis knew of Cust's private life when they met and hit it off in the summer of 1892. Probably next to nothing. The talented, beautiful, and very pregnant Violet, Lady Granby, sketched Davis's portrait.[81] Did anyone tell him that she was Cust's mistress, and that the child she was carrying that summer was fathered not by the marquess of Granby (later the eighth duke of Rutland)—but by Cust? (The child subsequently won a celebrity of her own as Lady Diana Cooper, née Manners.) In June 1892, Cust was not only privately anticipating the birth of a baby, he was also publicly contemplating his election to the House of Commons. During the third course of a London luncheon, Cust asked Davis if he would like to attend a political rally that night in Lincolnshire and have his head broken.[82] Book material! Richard jumped at the offer.*[83]

Cust was the nephew of the earl of Brownlow, a Lincolnshire grandee. The ancestral family home, Belton House, is considered to be the masterpiece of Restoration country-house architecture, and Richard found it "the most noble place I have seen here." Within a seventy-mile radius, it was known simply as "The House."[84] Dinner was served on gold plate, within view of the golden oar that an early earl of Brownlow had given to Queen Elizabeth, and a portrait of William III that that monarch had left after spending the night. The present earl couldn't understand half of what Richard said and thought the other half hilariously funny, a combination which had the rare effect of reducing Richard to silence.[85] Lady Brownlow, however, was "sweet and good and tries very hard to be amusing." Richard liked her "immensely."[86]

For Davis, the appeal of this race was Cust's ancestral ties to his region. It was as close as one could still get to a Thackerayan squirearchy. The night of their arrival, Cust spoke first to a small audience in a little schoolhouse. To Richard's delight, the farm workers looked "exactly like the agricultural laborers in the *Chatterbox* of our childhood and in the *Graphic* Christmas numbers of today. They had red, sunburnt faces, and a fringe of whiskers under the chin, and hair that would not lie down." Davis thought Cust's speech was very clever, and he continued to think so after hearing it repeated at four villages a night over the next two weeks. There was no head-breaking. At the strongly Radical village that Cust feared might be boisterous, the crowd was larded with hecklers, but their abuse didn't veer beyond the verbal.

By day, Cust and his entourage traveled by special train; they took moonlit rides by night. Charlie Davis, who had joined his brother in England on holiday, came up to Lincolnshire to share the fun. The day before the election, Cust and company traveled thirty miles in a carriage that was drawn by four white horses and manned by whip-cracking postilions in red jackets and green velvet caps. An unabashedly Tory display, it thrilled

---

* Also at the luncheon was Oscar Wilde, who declined the same invitation. Most likely, this was the luncheon at which Davis bested Wilde at the other man's game—repartee. Hearing that Richard was from Philadelphia, Wilde remarked that Washington was buried there. "Nonsense," Davis replied, "he's buried at Mount Vernon." Even egos far smaller than Wilde's find it irksome to be corrected. A little later, when the conversation turned to a French painter, Wilde brayed loudly, "Do let's hear what Mr. Davis thinks of him. Americans always talk so amusingly of art." Laying down his fork, Richard replied, "I never talk about things when I don't know the facts." A silence fell over the table as Wilde pondered his rejoinder. "That must limit your conversation fearfully," he finally replied, but he said it a few beats too late.

Richard as only a living anachronism could. The Tory villages had laid out large luncheons for their candidate, which Cust himself couldn't be bothered to eat. Fortunately, his entourage covered for him, in village after village. When Richard recounted the story in print, the rotund Charlie once again took the comic role of the glutton, a part he had filled since the adolescent Richard chronicled their trip to the Adirondacks.[87]

On election day, the votes were gathered in the villages and brought to town in tin boxes for counting. Even though it was a Radical town, the crowd roared with excitement when Cust was declared the victor. The coach with four white horses transported him home, stopping at each village on the way. It was 6:00 P.M. by the time they reached the open iron gates of the House and rode down the mile-long avenue of elms. All the tenants, servants, and neighbors stood there, and alone in the center was Lady Brownlow in a cloak of red silk, the Tory color. Cust jumped out of the coach first, ran up the stairs, stooped, and kissed her hand. As Richard watched in admiration, he noticed that Lady Brownlow stared out at the park, lest she betray her emotion in public with a tear.[88]

When he returned to New York, Davis tried to keep in touch with Cust, but his letters went unanswered.[89] Cust may have been too socially distracted to write. As his five-year affair with Lady Granby flickered out, he fell in love with Pamela Wyndham, the young sister of two central figures in the Souls. He would have married Pamela, had he not been pressured into wedding another woman who claimed to be carrying his child.[90] (She either lied or miscarried, for no baby evolved.) The summer he met Davis proved to be the zenith of Cust's flashy trajectory. In 1896, he was dismissed as editor of the *Pall Mall Gazette*. By that time, he had resigned his seat in Lincolnshire; though he later returned to Parliament, it was as a dilettante. He began drinking heavily. His life took on the sour smell of curdled youthful promise—not a story for Richard Harding Davis.

Davis's account of the Cust election (omitting the names of the principals) is the high point of *Our English Cousins*, which first appeared in *Harper's Magazine* and then as a book in March 1894. Much of *Our English Cousins* is lightweight filler: a roundup of the London attractions that an American tourist should be sure to see, and a quick Saturday-night ramble through the East End slums. Even such familiar stuff, however, benefited from Richard's style. "I record my first impressions," he once explained to an interviewer. When the critics groaned that he seemed to think he had discovered London or Paris, "they totally miss the point." He was describing the place "exactly as it impressed me, not as I happen to think it ought to impress either myself or the public or any one else, nor as I expected it to impress me." During his newspaper days, he had too often listened to the colorful, amusing tale of a colleague just back from an assignment, only to read the same man's bloodless, boring story in the next day's paper. Writing it up, the reporter left out everything that was personal and interesting. Richard did not make such a mistake himself. He knew that those details that amuse the listener also entertain the reader.[91]

In writing travel pieces, he kept in mind the American reader who had never left home. "Instead of saying, for instance, that a certain object is as high as St. Peter's in Rome, which means nothing to a man who has never seen St. Peter's, I compare it to some building in America, such as Trinity Church, or the Washington monument," he remarked. He also assumed that people preferred to read about places they expected to visit. "If I say in one of my books that the savages of a certain tribe in Africa bend backward instead of forward when they bow, the average man does not care a rap," he observed, "whereas if I say, 'You don't want to go to Rotten Row in the mornings any more; no one rides there now; they're all at Chelsea Park, cycling,' the average man will say, 'By Jove! is that so?' and he'll read on, interested." During his trip to Texas, Richard had eagerly opened a new copy of *Harper's* to two articles that intrigued him: one on Chicago, and one on hunting in India. He read the one on Chicago first; and, as always, he generalized from his own example.[92]

When he returned to New York from London in August, he discovered that his friends were also reading and talking about Chicago. For fashionable New Yorkers, Chicago had been "Porkopolis," a rude settlement squatting by the abbatoirs. But in 1890, to New York's dismay, Chicago won the competition to host the World's Columbian Exposition, a fair commemorating the four hundredth anniversary of the discovery of America. Now the exposition buildings were rising on what had been six hundred acres of swamp and sand at the edge of Lake Michigan. And with admiration first grudging, then awestruck, New York applauded Chicago's achievement.

The fair was huge: one building alone had thirty-two acres of floor space, and the restaurants could feed seventeen thousand people at a time.[93] These stupendous numbers, however, merely reinforced the image of Chicago as a place where wealth and ambition knew no limits. Traveling to the dedication exercises in October 1892, Richard, like so many Eastern sophisticates, was caught off guard. With its Greek peristyles, Roman monuments, Renaissance cupolas, and Baroque fountains, the "White City" embodied his notions of refined taste. A visitor told him that it was the fair one might have expected to see in Paris in 1889, the world's last great exposition. Agreeing, Richard found it paradoxical that "the city of art and letters of the Madeleine and of the Beaux-Arts should have fallen down and worshipped an Eiffel Tower and Edison electric lightings, and that the city of grain-elevators and pork should have reared a second city as classic in its beauty as the Athens of today. . . ."[94]

Indeed, that was the paradox of the White City, but he misunderstood its significance. On the defensive over Chicago's materialistic image, Daniel Burnham and his corps of architects constructed a fake city that ignored Chicago—and, what's more, turned its back on the New World that Colum-

bus had discovered. In egregious taste, these temples to business and agri-
culture proved to be enormously influential. As Davis predicted, "the
architecture of every new State or Federal building" would bear the stamp
of the White City.[95] Louis Sullivan, whose red Transportation Building was
a lonely standout at the exposition, sneered that the "virus of the World's
Fair," bred in a culture "snobbish and alien to the land," later spread east
in "a violent outbreak of the Classic and the Renaissance."[96] He was speaking only of architecture, but the virus was not that specific. The Chicago
Columbian Exposition is an evocative symbol of American culture at the
turn of the century: a pastiche of old styles, a pile of polished forms
irrelevant to their surroundings, and, here and there, an isolated suggestion
of a new order. In its pretentious aping of an older tradition, there is
something touchingly adolescent about it. Dressing up in foreign costume,
American culture gained the self-confidence to strike out later on its own.

As a visiting dignitary, Davis spoke at the dedication exercises, winning
a longer ovation than Vice President Levi P. Morton or New York governor
Roswell P. Flower.[97] The fair didn't open to the public until May, so on his
first trip Richard was swooning over the façades. To see the full show, he
returned the following autumn in the exposition's last days. By then, the
country was racked by an economic depression, but the fair played on.[98]

What lingered most in his memory was not any particular exhibit, and
not even the spectacle of the White City, with its electric lights reflecting
at night in the black water of the lagoon. The most remarkable thing about
the fair, to Davis's mind, was its evanescence. The fair was as much of a
romance as any Richard Harding Davis story. The glorious decorations
and exotic pavilions placed it outside the commerce-driven, anxiety-ridden
American reality. As a price for this exemption, however, the makers of the
exposition had agreed—as in a fairy tale—that at the preordained hour,
the buildings would be razed and the dream would be over.[99]

C h a p t e r

5

Footloose and Nervous

THINGS WERE NOT PERFECT IN FRANKLIN SQUARE. For Richard, the chief drawback to being managing editor of *Harper's Weekly* was the recurring obligation to edit. The second problem was the Harpers themselves. Just four months after taking the position, Richard confided that he preferred publishing with the Scribners.[1] Even when traveling, which was the feature of the job he most enjoyed, he resented office frugality. On the trip to the Chicago Exposition dedication exercises, he was outraged to be booked into a deserted hotel way outside town, "on the seventh floor without a bathroom or electric button."[2] On their side, while they recognized the advantages of having a well-known editor, the Harpers also knew there was something to be said for experience. Shortly before the Chicago trip, Davis rejected Richard Henry Stoddard's verse eulogy of the *Weekly*'s sainted and recently deceased editor, George William Curtis. By the time the head of the firm, J. Henry Harper, learned of the error, the poem had been accepted elsewhere.[3] On another occasion, Richard published a short story that had appeared earlier in a small literary magazine. It was an obscure journal, and any editor might have made the mistake; but Davis was especially sensitive to suggestions of incompetence.[4]

Indeed, since he preferred detective to literary work, he became perhaps overly zealous that he not be duped again. He feared (as he wrote in a slightly fictionalized account) that his enemies would trap him into printing previously published pieces, for the purpose of "pointing out by this fact how little read he was, and how unfit to occupy the swivel-chair into which he had so lately dropped."[5] His vigilance paid off one day when he received a poem that he remembered under a different byline from the *Century*. Enlisting his friend Stephen Bonsal, he paid an unannounced visit to the Morningside Heights apartment of the plagiarist and surprised the man into a remorseful confession. Davis and Bonsal were on the way out when they unfortunately ran into the miscreant's sweet and beautiful wife. As they gazed at her, their fantasy of exposing the scoundrel evaporated in a cloud of chivalry. (Davis instead wrote a short story inspired by the episode.)[6]

In January 1893, having been back from London only five months (some of which he had spent in Chicago), Davis proposed that he go off again in February on a six-month journey to write two series of articles: on the Mediterranean for the *Weekly*, and on Paris for the *Monthly*. For each forty-thousand-word series, he requested one thousand dollars, the same price paid for his Western and English articles. However, he asked double the expense money, having learned that writing travel books was "much harder work than . . . anticipated" and that the research expenses for an article "frequently consumed a third of the price paid for it".[7] The Harpers immediately agreed to all of that. But in response to Davis's stated expectation of resuming his editorial duties in August, they preferred "that this question be left open until your return" and that "both parties . . . be entirely free in this respect."[8] They reminded him that *Harper's Magazine* travel writer Theodore Childs had recently died of typhoid fever in Persia. Perhaps Davis would like to replace him?

Alarmed, Richard replied at once that he could not undertake the travel pieces if his job were not safeguarded. The status of managing editor of *Harper's Weekly* provided "a distinct standing in and among journalists and in social and political affairs." He observed: "If I went to Egypt or India as the author of Hefty Burke stories, I would be trying to trade on something of which no one had heard, but if I go as the head of a big periodical they would show me courtesy and sights." The Harper position also furnished a reliable income; a travel writer, on the other hand, could be incapacitated by accident or illness. Nor were the benefits wholly one-sided. "I think that the fact that a young man is at the head of it attracts contributions and subscriptions for that reason," he argued. "I also think the paper gets more or less advertising out of the fact that I am connected with it."[9] Retreating before this ardent barrage, the Harpers allowed Davis to embark on his trip as managing editor of the *Weekly*. How to reconcile his ambitions to their needs was a problem that would have to await his return.

On February 4, 1893, Richard sailed for the Mediterranean, fleeing an unusually frigid winter: one week in January, the *average* temperature in New York was only seven degrees.[10] He was confident that he would avoid the dull stretches that plagued him out West. "Even if I know no one," he reasoned, "you can *see* the difference between Tunis and Oklahoma City."[11] He felt "miserably mean" about reneging on a promise to take his sister, Nora, but he wanted to be totally free to change direction at the first scent of a story. You couldn't do that if you were chaperoning your kid sister.[12]

Davis was trolling the Mediterranean in pursuit of the picturesque. He wanted people and landscapes that, while not posed, were worth painting. In practice, this notion of the picturesque as a scene that *should* be painted

was degraded by Richard into one that *has* been painted. He was forever
hungering to see a view that he had admired in the *Graphic* or meet a
character that he had applauded in the theater. Traveling off-season on a
small German steamer instead of one of the floating English palaces that
plied the seas during spring and summer, he was delighted to meet Americans of a sort that he thought existed only on the stage. His favorite was a
Tammany sachem whom he loved to mimic. "That's me," the man would
say. "That's what I do. When I have insomnia, I don't believe in your
sleeping draughts. I get up and go round to Jake Stewart's on Fourteenth
Street and eat a fry or a porterhouse steak and then I sleep good—that's
me." Also bound for Morocco and Egypt, and dining with Davis at the
captain's table, was Dr. Henry M. Field, the editor of the *Evangelist*. "I
have promised to show him life with a capital L, and he is afraid as death
of me," Richard teased. Most of the other passengers made a favorable first
impression by asking Richard to autograph their copies of *Gallegher* or *The
West from a Car-Window*.[13]

He enjoyed the stopover in Gibraltar, where he lodged at the British
garrison as the guest of a younger brother of Cust. He relished eating with
the young men of the Thirteenth Somerset Light Infantry in their gold-
braided red-and-black uniforms. "I had often seen pictures of it," Richard
wrote his mother, "and I enjoyed it all the more for that. They were so like
what they should have been. . . ."[14] He was similarly charmed by the little
of Spain he saw on a ride with young Cust: "It was like a colored number
of *Le Figaro*."[15]

Far less satisfying was Tangier, which he reached by ferry from Gibraltar. He was seeking an Africa "as dark and as silent as the Sphinx that
typifies it."[16] Instead, the first thing he saw in the harbor was an enormous
blue-and-white sign advertising the English provisions store.[17] Tangier was
"a very fine place spoiled by civilization," a disappointed Richard reported
to his mother. "Not nice civilization but the dregs of it. . . . [The foreigners]
hunt and play cricket and gamble and do nothing to maintain what is
best in the place or to help what is worst." In contrast, the Moors were
"wonderfully well made and fine looking and selfrespecting." In short:
"The color is very beautiful but the foreign element spoils it at every turn."[18]
Somehow he failed to see that he was part of that foreign element when he
visited the market and purchased two long guns, three three-foot pistols,
and "a Moorish costume for afternoon teas."[19]

Desperately seeking a sight that was not overrun by Westerners, he
zeroed in on the main prison, which was said to be crowded with half-
naked wretches in chains. The seventy-year-old Dr. Field, who was also in
Tangier, shared his interest. Warned by the bashaw, or Moorish governor,
that Muslim fanatics would probably tear a Westerner to pieces, Davis and
Field grew even more eager. They were taken by the bashaw's soldiers to
a barred doorway through which you could either crawl in on hands and

knees, or, clutching an upper crossbar, swing in feet first. "It impressed me as a particularly embarrassing way to make an entrance among a lot of people who meditated tearing you to pieces," Davis wrote in his Tangier article. "I pointed this out to the doctor, but he was determined, though pale." Richard went first. If the bashaw can be trusted, Richard's yellow riding boots were the first bit of Christian seen by the prisoners in a decade.

Richard viewed a straw-littered courtyard "about as big as the stage of a New York theatre," illuminated by a skylight. The fifty or sixty prisoners were shackled, but not chained to the walls, and while they were haggard, dirty, and half-naked, they were neither diseased nor starving. Once again, reality had failed to measure up to legend. But when they later learned of the exploit, some of the British residents mocked that the Americans had merely toured the anteroom—a show-prison. To dispel nagging fears that he had missed the story, Richard on the morning of his departure from Tangier crawled over a roof to photograph the top of the prison and prove there was no hidden chamber. Then a horrible doubt seized him. What if the building that he was standing on was in fact an annex to the prison— the secret ward spoken of by the English residents? An old woman in the garden below had been jumping up and down in distress as he tossed coins to quiet her. Richard sent his guide to ask why she was so upset and what was the building on which he was trespassing. The guide returned to say it was a harem, and the woman thought that Richard was flirting with the wives. He dropped back down and left Tangier with a good conscience.[20]

Richard spent ten days in Gibraltar, trapped by a cholera outbreak that played havoc with the ship schedules. "I want Zulus and lions," he said plaintively. Instead, he had "eating and drinking and loafing about in knickerbockers and riding clothes."[21] Much of the challenge of travel lies in minimizing the time squandered in getting from one point to the next. Richard sailed to Malta as a way station to Tunis, which he understood was "unspoiled and not like Tangier or Algiers."[22] Unfortunately, when he reached Malta he learned that the price of a visit to Tunis was ten days in quarantine for cholera before one could depart. So, sacrificing Tunis, he rejoined his steamer and continued directly to Cairo.

His first impressions of Cairo were mixed. The weather was unpleasantly cold for a city of palms: astrakhan coats clashed with white helmets. On the bright side, *Gallegher* was on sale across the street from Shepheard's Hotel. The real problem with Cairo was that Davis didn't discover it. "I am selfish in my sightseeing," he confessed, "and want to see things others do not."[23] So many people were taking photographs in Cairo that they had stripped away most of what was picturesque. Cairo was a popular destination for Americans who wanted to depart just a little bit from the well-worn path through Europe. They bore in on all the famous sights—including the famous writer, Richard Harding Davis. He couldn't sit down a minute before a stranger accosted him with the bright opening line, "I had no idea you were so young a man." Richard admitted to his mother that "I am becoming particular because I find if I don't people impose on me and hang on my neck."[24] He was hardening that stiff-necked posture which his enemies called snootiness, his friends shyness.

Preferring the less frequented places where "nothing you see is done for show" and "if [the people] make pictures of themselves, they do so unconsciously," Richard put off visiting the Pyramids until embarrassment drove him there. As he anticipated, climbing a Pyramid was a mockery of an adventure. He bought a ticket at the Pyramid of Cheops from "the sheik of the pyramids," who assigned him three guides—two to push, and one "to dilate on the view." When they finally stood wheezing and sweating at the summit, the guides feebly pretended that although the feat had often been attempted, no one before had ever managed to pull it off so triumphantly. "I would rather go into Central Africa then [*sic*] do it again," Richard told his mother. Luckily, he ran into the architect Stanford White and other Americans he knew. White pointed out that they were a hundred feet higher than the top of the statue of Diana on Madison Square Garden— just the sort of comparison Richard appreciated.[25]

What disappointed Davis the tourist worried Davis the writer. Ordering restaurant dishes that had been named for Stanley and Gordon, Richard had the queasy sensation that he was an impostor about to be exposed. He felt terribly ignorant, a sightseer in a hugely complicated place. "It makes you feel like such a faker and as if it were better to turn correspondent for the N.Y. *Herald*, Paris edition, and send back the names of those who are staying at the hotels," he admitted to his mother. "That is really all you can speak with authority about. . . . Everybody travels and everybody sees as much as you do and says nothing of it, certainly does not presume to write a book about it."[26]

Concluding that Egypt's politics were less widely known than her monuments, Davis arranged a private audience with the khedive, the young Egyptian who ruled the country within parameters set by the British. In the English press, the khedive was depicted as a sulky boy. In person, Richard found him a likable, fat little fellow, fluent in several languages, and—but for his red fez and his attendants—like any young man of New York or Paris. When Richard urged him to retain some American officers, especially those who had worked with Indians and Negroes, the khedive sadly replied that the English would never allow it. He seemed very dejected about his subservient status. In Egypt Davis saw colonialism for the first time, and disliked it. Seven years later, when he reported the Boer War, some would be surprised by his anti-British stance, not realizing that despite his Anglophilia, he was consistently anti-imperialist. He reviled England's appetite for other people's countries and her pretense to altruistic motives. He objected to the "bullying insolent way of treating Egypt" and thought it "would be just as mean if we took Hawii [*sic*]."[27]

After receiving permission, Richard sent the khedive copies of his books.[28] Perhaps that cheered up the stout little boy.

At his next stop, Athens, Richard was delighted by the dearth of tourists and guides. Even on the Acropolis, he could roam unharassed.[29] There, one moonlit evening, he saw a woman so lovely that he followed her back to her hotel to discover that she was Princess Alix of Hesse-Darmstadt, whose beauty dazzled the eyes of high society that season. Her image drove all other thoughts from his mind, he told a friend.[30] Princess Alix was destined to play a romantic role in his fiction (and an even more romantic part in world history). Athens, however, occupied only five days on his itinerary. He declined a brief interview with King Constantine because the date would have disrupted his schedule. "I didn't think five minutes with a salaried King was worth three days in Constantinople or Vienna," he told his mother.[31]

In Constantinople, he would have welcomed an audience with the potentate, but that was out of the question. The picturesque sultan (no constitutional monarch he) feared assassination too much to entertain strangers. Richard was reduced to routine tourism. One cold, rainy afternoon, he sat in a clubroom writing to his parents and consuming a three-parter in the *Graphic* on the Nile expedition in search of Gordon. He was facing a dreary evening and four bleak days in the company of the American minister, a "block of wood." Suddenly, he bolted. In an hour and a half, he collected his things and caught the twice-weekly train to Paris. He was free.[32] But as he congratulated himself on his escape and admired the car-window view of the picturesque Balkans, he fretted bitterly about his reporting. His book was to be titled *The Rulers of the Mediterranean*. Having failed to visit Algiers or Tunis, he could not speak at all about French colonialists; in Greece and Turkey, he hadn't made contact with the kings. He was right to worry. As early as Cairo, he had suggested to the Harpers "a less presumptuous title which people and reviewers would take less seriously, like 'From Sandy Hook to the Bosphorus' or 'From the North River to the Nile,' or 'From Gibraltar to Egypt and Beyond,' or 'The Shores of the Mediterranean.' "[33] As in so many other matters, the Harpers ignored his pleas. "I mean to call the Mediterranean book My First Failure and Where I Made It," Richard joked gloomily to Charles.[34]

In Paris he found an apartment (cheaper than a hotel: his expense money was running out), then hopped over to London for a fortnight with friends.[35] His London popularity was so great—two or three dinner invitations a night, with the likes of Cust, Herbert Asquith, and J. M. Barrie—that he had to return a gift of theater tickets from Oscar Wilde.[36] Everything was grand; except, once again, the Harpers. Waiting for Richard in London was a set of proofs of the first installment of his *Harper's Weekly* Mediterranean series. To his horror, the pages included two depictions of Davis himself—and second-rate ones that were "not only ridiculous but neither of them look like me or even like the other." To Davis, already disgruntled that neither the Harpers nor their editors had commented on his Mediterranean articles, the rotten illustrations were a final insult.[37]

Illustrations were always a sensitive point with him. "A bad illustration is like a bad cigar," he believed, "it is worse than nothing."[38] Visually *au courant*, he brought back from this trip a dozen French posters to inspire Edward Penfield, the head of the Harper art department, to advertise *Our English Cousins*; they were the first French posters that Penfield, the earliest and perhaps greatest of the American poster artists of the 1890s, had ever seen.[39] From a strictly financial viewpoint, Davis thought that Frederic Remington's drawings had sold half the copies of *The West from a Car-Window*.[40] But money aside, he felt that shoddy illustrations made his writing look cheap. He had thrown a similar tantrum when the Scribners used pictures he disliked (such as an inaccurately drawn Princeton football uniform) in *Stories for Boys*. But Charles Scribner was exquisitely tender to Davis's swollen ego. Having scrupulously kept his author informed of each stage of the publishing process, he responded with injured innocence.[41] J. Henry Harper regarded Davis more as an employee, which of course he was, than as the prima donna he also was. "[The Harpers] have made me very tired this trip," Richard wrote Charles.[42]

Richard was also peeved that Charles hadn't commented on the proofs of his articles.[43] But Charles was uncharacteristically preoccupied with his own business affairs. Floundering as a journalist and short-story writer, he began thinking, like many young men with connections and no vocation, of a diplomatic career. The previous fall, after Grover Cleveland's victory, Clarke transmitted his son's request for an appointment as second secretary in a European capital, preferably London or Paris. While sympathetic, Cleveland cautioned that he was constrained by the staffing desires of each minister.[44] He was also inundated with patronage requests. By May, two months after moving back to the White House, Cleveland had to request that Senators and Representatives stop bringing job applicants to the periods set aside for congressional visits, because he was spending almost all of his time "listening to applications for office, which have been bewildering in volume, perplexing and exhausting in their iteration, and impossible of remembrance."[45]

From his far-off vantage point, Richard couldn't understand what was taking so long. In Paris, the new American minister, James B. Eustis, precluded the nepotism of others by making his own son second secretary. That left London. Naming the distinguished statesman Thomas F. Bayard to be his ambassador there (the first time an American minister had carried such an august title), Cleveland gently but futilely prodded him to choose Charles. After much dithering, Bayard concluded in October that he needed a more experienced man and retained the current second secretary. Charles was left with nothing—but not for long. "I wonder if we might not have two strings to our bow," Cleveland had suggested as early as May. "Would Charley like that same position in another place—either in Europe or Asia?"[46] With England definitely unavailable, a new niche was found quickly. At the end of 1893, Charles took up residence in Florence as the American consul.

Ironically (or perhaps typically) the Eustises, who had blunted Charles's progress, smoothed the way for Richard in Paris. James Eustis had three children—Tina, Newton, and James—whom Richard saw often. By the end of his six-week sojourn, he was lunching with them almost daily, and dining virtually every night with prominent Americans. "I feel like one of those little India rubber balls in the jet of a fountain being turned and twisted and not allowed to rest," he told his mother.[47] His social schedule was also boosted by the arrival of Basil Blackwood, a young Englishman whose modesty had greatly impressed him when they met in Oxford. Having known Blackwood a couple of weeks, Davis, on a visit to his college rooms, had pointed to a portrait of a prominent diplomat and asked, "Why do you have such a large picture of Lord Dufferin here? Do you admire him as much as that?" "He's my father," Blackwood had explained apologetically. Lord Dufferin was now England's ambassador to France, and at his table, Richard met some specimens of the elusive French aristocracy.[48] Even so, he found Paris society much harder to crack than London's.[49] The language barrier was one problem: his four hours of French lessons a week didn't really suffice.[50] On top of that, French society was even more tightly woven than English, so that outsiders couldn't normally slip through.[51]

Richard spent most of his time with the expatriate community, particularly the American and English painters. In consequence, his most intimate view of Paris was tinted mauve. Soon after arriving, he visited Kenneth Frazier, an acquaintance from Lehigh, and to his embarrassment was asked what he thought of Frazier's studio. The room was so bare it seemed blighted by the direst poverty. The only furniture consisted of three chairs, a low bookcase, and a straight-legged table. A blue-and-white jar, a gold Buddha, and a jade bottle stood on the table. On one of the gray walls Frazier had hung a gray silk poke-bonnet, of the sort that was stylish in 1830. An empty gold frame adorned another wall. There was nothing else in the room. Delicately, Richard said that he admired the view from the window. When Frazier replied that he had spent a year and a half decorating this room and wanted Richard's opinion, Davis was incredulous. "But there is nothing in it," he protested.

Frazier smiled a gently superior smile. "I am afraid that you are one of those people who like studios filled with tapestries and armor and palms and huge, hideous chests of carved wood," he said. "You are probably the sort of person who would hang a tennis-racket on his wall and consider it decorative. *We* believe in lines and subdued colors and broad, bare surfaces. There is nothing in this room that has not a meaning of its own."

As Davis happily confessed when he wrote of his encounter, Frazier had correctly divined his taste in interior design. Frazier's rooms were recognizably modern: they anticipated the future. Davis's preferences were for the overstuffed jumbles that the twentieth century was about to sweep away. Soon after his return from Europe, he would refurnish his rooms on Twenty-eighth Street with precisely the high Victorian excess that Frazier abhorred. A Turkish rug and a bearskin would cover much of the dyed black walnut floor. A piano, two lounges, lots of cushions, and a mother-of-pearl table with a silver tea set would clutter the living room. His collection of medals would be displayed on the fireplace mantel. On the walls he would hang a hodgepodge of literary portraits, guns, autographs, photographs of Napoleon, and two large coaching prints. It was perhaps the thought of his own large collection that prompted his next question. Why didn't Frazier put a picture in the frame? he asked gingerly.

"Ah, exactly! that shows exactly what you are; you are an American philistine," Frazier crowed. "You cannot see that a picture is a beautiful thing in itself, and that a dead-gold frame with its four straight lines is beautiful also; but together they might not be beautiful. That gray wall needs a spot on it, and so I hung that gold frame there, not because it was a frame, but because it was beautiful; for the same reason I hung that eighteen-thirty bonnet on the other wall. The two grays harmonize. People do not generally hang bonnets on walls, but that is because they regard them as things of use, and not as things of beauty."

Richard pointed his walking-stick at the table, and asked, "Then if you were to put the blue and white jar on the right of the Buddha, instead of on the left, the whole room would feel the shock?"

"Of course," said Frazier. "Can't even you see that?" Recounting the incident, Richard wrote: "I tried to see it, but I could not. I had only just arrived in Paris."[52]

Richard carried a letter of introduction (perhaps from their mutual Philadelphia friend, Logan Pearsall Smith) to the young English artist, Will Rothenstein, who drew his portrait and introduced him to the community's god, James McNeill Whistler. Cynical at twenty-one, Rothenstein chuckled at Davis, this "robust flower of American muscular Christianity—healthy, wealthy, and, in America, wise." Dressing and talking like a famous writer (although Rothenstein had never heard of his books), Davis bought a couple of pastels and tried to convert Rothenstein into "a sort of artistic boy-scout" who would energetically turn out "good, wholesome work." Rothenstein thought that Davis was so puzzled by the young artists of Paris that "he even at times had doubts in regard to himself; but these doubts, when in the morning before his glass he brushed his rich, shining hair and shaved his firm, fresh chin and called to mind the sums his short stories brought him, proved fleeting as last night's dream."[53]

Although he was enjoying himself, Davis wasn't getting much of a story. "I see nothing of Paris but the outside," he confessed, "and it does seem like a waste of time." His Paris was a vast amusement park for foreign sightseers. Even the slums had been ruined by tourism. "They like the other things are all as obvious as a theatre," he reported, "you pay so much to see them." Americans bent on slumming were taken to the Château Rouge and Père Lunette, which survived solely on the patronage of tourists and adjoined houses of "hopeless respectability." He concluded ludicrously that the boulevards of Paris were too wide and well lit to permit the breeding of full-fledged slums. "Even the thieves pose, the detectives pose, and the artists pose and it is all uncharitableness and cynicism," he groused.[54]

As in Cairo, he eyed his fellow American tourists with distaste. Coach-loads of them blocked his view of the Arc de Triomphe. Their gleeful shouts to each other on the Champs-Élysées drowned out the sound of French. Instead of wandering along the Seine, they took tea to the sound of a Hungarian band, ordering up "Daisy Bell" and the other hits to simulate the ambience of the Hotel Waldorf. They carried their own environment with them like a protective bell jar: many spent all their time leaving their visiting-cards, watching polo, playing lawn tennis, or going to the track, just as if they were at Newport or Narragansett Pier.

Much as he scorned these risible travelers, however, they were fundamentally his own people, and he preferred them to the expatriates of the American colony. He thought the United States was well rid of effete creatures who scorned the "crudeness" of their native civilization and had wound up neither American nor French. What offended him most about the expatriates was their pretense to French morals. Despite the many hints of adulterous intrigues, Richard believed that the American women hadn't the courage to emulate the French example. In public, they told risqué stories and spoke scandalously of each other. In private, he was sure, they were all excellent wives and mothers. This inverted hypocrisy—the tribute virtue paid to vice—sickened him.[55] He understood "modern" morality no better than he did modern interior design.

His discussion of Americans abroad is by far the best part of Davis's book, *About Paris*. The French mystified him: "a useless, flippant people who never sleep and yet do nothing while awake."[56] Although his friend Bonsal reassured Davis that his articles would be interesting because "no one yet has ever genuinely disliked Paris," Davis knew that he hadn't gathered enough material for a book.[57] "I never was made for a flâneur," he wrote his mother.[58] He decided it had been a mistake to go to France after such a long stretch of traveling, and he asked the Harpers for permission to sail home on July 1 and then return to Paris for more material in September and October. "The city is dead now," he argued, "and nothing to see but sun and dust and empty streets."[59] Plus he was running out of money.[60]

Upon Richard's return, the firm's ruling cousins, J. Henry and Joseph

W. Harper, met with him for four hours to discuss his duties at the *Weekly*, and agreed to let him keep the title of managing editor and receive four months of vacation, during which he would write for Harper periodicals at the lucrative rate of two thousand dollars for forty thousand words. "I consider this the most conspicuously pleasant position in America," Richard told his mother.[61] He held it for less than two months. In late September, after he had returned from the closing days of the Chicago Exposition, the Harpers took him aside once more, and when that meeting ended, Richard had surrendered his glorious title. He would now be called an associate editor, essentially a part-time job which paid seventy-five dollars weekly. He agreed to solicit "articles from well known people on important topics" and to contribute two columns of copy a week. The Harpers emphasized that "the trial be purely experimental & subject to termination at will by either party."[62] Richard reassured his father that the new editorship was "about as agreeable a position as I can want."[63] He was more candid with Charles: "The *Weekly* is beneath consideration in my opinion. It is neither man, nor woman, nor priest."[64]

He may be forgiven for clinging to an unsatisfactory job, because the fall of 1893 was an unsettling time, personally and nationally. The whole country's nerves were stretched by a stock-market crash which had developed over the summer into a major depression. "Helen has gone to cheer her father who is standing ready to catch the sign of E. C. Benedict & Co. when it drops," Richard joked to his mother. "As Patty Fairchild is also expecting to have to teach kindergarten for a living in case her father fails it would seem that I had better transfer my affections to others less doubtful."[65] The depression—in which more than two million people (about 18 percent of the work force) lost their jobs, almost six hundred banks collapsed, and more than fifteen thousand companies failed—was no laughing matter.[66] Coming after a sequence of alarming eruptions of anarchist and labor violence, it seemed a culmination, not an aberration. The future was up in the air. How much this wind of anxiety cut through Davis is hard to calculate. Although he was temperamentally conservative and queasy at the notion of unrest, he was not one to make sweeping sociopolitical judgments. So he didn't take a public position on the social cataclysm—but his *Weekly* did. For instance, in July 1892, when Carnegie Steel workers battled Pinkerton guards and the Pennsylvania militia at Homestead, *Harper's Weekly* criticized the state and the press for not supporting management with enough vigor.[67]

In this unstable world, Richard was himself fighting a breakdown in the summer of 1893. After a bout of severe depression, he went up to Newport, where he ran into a wealthy acquaintance. She assured him that she had just gotten over a nervous attack exactly like his and was now as gay as a bird. Richard had feared that Newport would be "too exciting," but he was determined to "take it very carefully and rest all the time."[68]

Too much excitement was thought in the late nineteenth century to be the cause of nervous breakdowns. The very term "nervous exhaustion," which was the medical diagnosis, implied a depletion of limited resources that bed rest might restore. Unlike depression in our day, nervous exhaustion was not something to hide shamefully. Dr. George Miller Beard, the foremost American theorist of nervous exhaustion, associated the ailment (which he termed "neurasthenia") with an advanced stage of civilization. America suffered from it particularly, he believed, because America was so progressive. He cheerfully admitted that he himself was neurasthenic, and he reported that four-fifths of his patients came from "the higher orders." A nervous predisposition was associated with a fine temperament and a superior intelligence. It was a mark of sensitivity.[69] "The characteristic of our modern civilisation is sensitiveness, or, as the doctors say, nervousness," Charles Dudley Warner wrote in 1881, the same year that Dr. Beard published *American Nervousness*. Like many others, Warner saw all around him, in the ceaseless assault that constituted modern life, an explanation for the epidemic of nervousness. Even the telegraph, by monstrously expanding the amount of news available, exposed every reading person to "the excitements, the ills, the troubles, of all the world." The fact that so much of the news concerned violent strikes and anarchist bombings didn't help the situation at all.[70]

If present-day psychologists are to be believed, depression is the result not of overwork or overexcitement, but of internalized, unexpressed anger. In support of that view, one observes that many of the late nineteenth century's most relentless American optimists—Booth Tarkington, Lincoln Steffens, and William Lyon Phelps, for example—suffered from crippling spells of depression.[71] Private pain was the cost of Davis's constant public smile. Lacking an outlet for less happy emotions, he would work strenuously for long periods and then sputter out dramatically.[72] His was the unexamined life.

When he fell into a funk the previous Christmas, Richard assured his mother that his depression "always goes just as suddenly as it comes."[73] But this time, on his return from Newport, he waited in vain for "that tired feeling" to lift.[74] He consulted Dr. Louis Starr, who had treated Rebecca for nervous problems thirty years before. Starr concluded that the patient was fine except for "nervous imaginations and a touch of gout." On his advice, Richard swore off alcohol temporarily.[75] Feeling less nervous than he had for months, he went to Madison Square Garden for the annual horse show—that display of the pedigreed for the delectation of the parvenu, which opened the New York winter social season.[76] Then abruptly, just before Christmas, like an unsprung toy, he collapsed.

He arrived at his parents' house in Philadelphia on Christmas Eve and stayed there until January 2. He was "so blue" that he couldn't even eat.[77] Reckoning that his loathing of Philadelphia was only depressing him further, he took the train back to New York, wiring theater producer Charles Frohman for a ticket to an opening that night. When Richard's manservant John (the most expensive and best of a series of three) arrived that evening at Delmonico's bearing a sixth-row aisle seat from Frohman, Richard, who was dining alone, exulted, "I would rather have a 'pull' in New York than be a king in London."[78]

He threw himself into the social scene in defiance of his shaky nerves. He led the visiting French writer Paul Bourget on a "slumming" tour of the lower East Side, then hosted a dinner for Bourget and his wife at Delmonico's.[79] The next week he was in Washington, paying a call on Mrs. Cleveland at the White House during the day and attending a diplomatic reception at night.[80] Back in New York, doing only the things he wanted, he declared—in his best moments—that his nervousness was gone, "never to return I hope."[81] Other times he confessed that he was "half well and jumping from fits of blues to fits of joy."[82]

He forgot the admonitions against overexcitement. One night, he attended the Patriarchs' Ball, the highest ceremony of the Four Hundred, and then repaired to the rowdier French Ball at Madison Square Garden. In a large group that included actor Sam Sothern, publisher Richard Russell, and Stanford White, the only sober members were White's architect partner William McKim, a chorus girl named Saidie McDonald, and Davis. One very wealthy and married woman slipped a high-heeled slipper to Davis, and told her escort that she had put it in her purse because it pinched her toe. Another married woman so excited her admirers that one man punched another bloody just outside in the corridor, while Richard talked as quickly and wittily as he could to distract the other ladies.

It was the kind of scene that, if your mother found out you were there, you might excuse on the grounds that you were only gathering material. In Richard's case, that would be largely true. He loved the hubbub and spectacle of these gay nineties parties, but his chastity and (at least for the moment) his sobriety meant that he was largely an observer. As that night wore down, a young girl who had fallen asleep on her feet asked Davis what color ribbon was in her hair. "Pink," he said. "That's all right," she murmured. "*I* know who *I* am. Saidie McDonald was to wear blue and Florrie wear white and I was to wear pink. I know which I am. I belong to box 9." Richard led her back to box 9, and then, with the help of Miss McDonald, he sent her home in a cab. "She's a goose," Saidie told him. "If you want fun, you'se want to keep sober."[83]

Richard wrote it all down. A little more than a week afterward, he crumpled again.

This time it began with a flare-up of the sciatica that he had contracted in Johnstown. A week in bed, with his servant John pouring medicine down his throat and reading to him from *The Boy Travellers in the Far East*, failed to do the trick, so Richard returned to his parents in Philadelphia. Planning to spend two weeks on the horizontal with his leg in splints, he stayed more than a month. In a way, the sciatica seemed "providential," for he "had really forgotten *how* to keep still." Far more serious than the leg pain was a persistent fatigue—"like a man pulling on himself for a spurt and finding that he's left nothing there to pull on"—and an underlying "morbidness." The doctor recommended a summer out West, but there was no chance Richard would return to that accursed region. Instead, he relaxed by reading light literature and pasting articles about himself in a scrapbook.[84]

When he began working again, it was on a short novel in the genre of *The Prisoner of Zenda*, Anthony Hope Hawkins's wildly popular romance about a princess of an imaginary Balkan realm who falls in love with a young Englishman. The germ of Richard's story was his quasi-encounter with Princess Alix of Hesse-Darmstadt the summer before on the Acropolis.[85] That had led to nothing, not even an introduction; but now, in the rich seedbed of his fallow imagination, it sprang up as a full-grown love story. And, true to its real-life source, it was a love story without incident. Morton Carlton, a rich young American artist, becomes enamored of the photograph of a German princess and follows her to London, Paris, Constantinople, and Athens. While traveling, he meets an American girl who helps all she can. Aided by the princess's brother, who admires his art, he is tantalizingly close to receiving an introduction, when the American girl is called home suddenly by a cable. He discovers he loves her, and proposes in the hotel garden that night. As Richard, in a letter from his convalescent bed, described the ending to Charles: "The Princess Aliene who has not spoken throughout the story but is only described sees them from her balcony and goes in and takes out some pictures he has drawn for the Grand Duke and a likeness of him she has cut from a paper and tears them up and throws them into the garden and then goes into her room saying to her sister, 'I am tired of this travelling and sightseeing and living in hotels. . . .' "[86]

He had given poetic form (light verse, not lyric) to his mad crush on Princess Alix. He had invented a purpose for his London-to-Constantinople wandering, a motive more idealistic than the prosaic obligation to publish another travel book. He had, as he had done since boyhood, recast the events of his life into an adventure yarn or fairy tale with himself as the hero. (Although the protagonist, Morton Carlton, is a fashionable young portrait painter and not a writer, he has, like Davis, been an international celebrity from the age of twenty-six.) *The Princess Aline* is a charming piece of fluff. Not only charming, but crafty. It would be one of the ten best-selling American novels of 1895 because it ingeniously fulfilled all the fantasies of its reader, the American girl. With his imaginary duchy and royal entourage, Davis whisked up a confection frothier than plain American ingredients could produce; and then, in a tour de force, he handed the love of his hero not to the poor foreign princess, who secretly longed for it—but to the true heroine, the loyal, sturdy, sensible American girl who was standing in for the reader.[87]

Davis was almost thirty when he wrote *The Princess Aline*. He had by this time written many romances, yet he had lived through none personally. Morton Carlton is speaking for the author when he tells his American-girl confidante, "Do you know, Miss Morris, that I believe I'm not able to care for a woman as other men do—at least as some men do; it's just lacking in me, and always will be lacking. It's like an ear for music; if you haven't got it, if it isn't born in you, you'll never have it. It's not a thing you can cultivate, and I feel that it's not only a misfortune, but a fault."[88] This heartfelt confession rings with conviction, unlike the convenient transformation that produces a happy ending for the story.

Female affection rained down on Davis like water on a stone. Young women idolized him from afar—and, when they got the chance, from close up. At Ladies' Day at the Players' Club, they buzzed around him like bees; and when he attended an exhibition of portraits of women, he was so besieged by schoolgirls and their mothers that he had to flee the scene. He joked that he was going to run for president on the Women's Ticket.[89] Yet, despite many female friends—mainly rich young women, like Helen Benedict and Patty Fairchild, and actresses, like Maude Adams and Ethel Barrymore (who had grown up since her toddler days at Point Pleasant)—he had no girlfriends. He was an escort, not a lover. Since Richard never wrote of any love affairs or infatuations—not even (until very late in life) in the letters to his most intimate friend, his brother, Charles—the best insight into his amorous feelings comes from the portrayal of women in his fiction. It is not a fetching portrait. Falling in love sounds very much like landing in jail. Marriage precludes excitement. "The Romance in the Life of Hefty Burke," which was published in *Harper's Magazine* in January 1893, reveals its theme immediately in the double entendre of its title: the mutual antagonism between the romance of a woman's love and the romance of male adventure. Hefty (whom Richard revived from the *Evening Sun* days) has the chance to join a beautiful young woman in a gun-smuggling mission to her uncle, the overthrown president of Ecuador. Hefty's vows to his fiancée hold him back. In a final twist, he restrains another river rat from turning in the filibusters (although his personal share of the reward would be more than enough to satisfy his demanding fiancée) because he has been smitten by the beauty and nobility of the Ecuadoran. Once more, he has been hung up by a woman.[90]

The idea that women keep men from doing the boyish things they like (the Huck Finn complaint) runs through the Davis canon. In "Miss Delamar's Understudy," which he wrote in early December 1894, the protagonist wishes he could have a test run before proposing marriage to the beautiful, but dull, Miss Delamar. That, of course, is impossible in the 1890s. But when he returns from a pleasant bachelor outing to find that she has sent him a life-size photograph of herself, he sets the picture up in a chair and dines with it, imagining her side of the conversation. Over dinner, he realizes that he has "given up the chance of meeting fresh experiences" and that his "real life seemed to have stopped." That night, "radiant, happy, and excited, like a boy back from school for the holidays," he resolves to go the next morning to Abyssinia.[91]

What he is fleeing is not imagined in gory detail, but at about this time, Davis published a nonfiction report on the life of young marrieds in the Long Island suburbs. It was a bleak prospectus. On the ferry to Long Island City and the train, the homebound commuters greeted each other with such pleasantries as, "Your wife asked me if I met you in town to tell you not to forget the salted almonds." The breadwinner would be met at the train station by his wife, whose chiding, superior manner was intended "to show you how well he is trained." A stop at the bakery and the little grocery, enlivened by gossip about the stove that needs repair and the horse that limps, would be followed by a long drive down a rutted road to a house that was half a mile from its nearest neighbor. If you were a New York bachelor visiting suburban friends, Davis wrote, you inevitably thought, as you sat before an open fire reading magazines and listening to arrangements for the Hunt Club ball committee, that "at that hour in New York you would be lazily considering whether or not you had not better leave the club and go home to dress, and that you would have nothing before you for the evening but a succession of amusing things, each within a few blocks distance of the others." Ostensibly poking fun at suburban provincialism, Davis's little essay was really contrasting the joys of bachelor life with the servitude of the married man.[92]

Davis's chivalry was so overwrought and so artificial that—at least to modern eyes—it calls attention to the resentment beneath its lacquered finish. It's a resentment that he expressed obliquely but unmistakably, and indeed, inevitably. If women embody men's higher instincts, if they constantly remind their earthier consorts of the more spiritual life, they must expect a little bitterness along with the gratitude. The epidemic of neurasthenia among upper-class American men at the turn of the century was partly a case of swallowed bile.

In "His Bad Angel," a story published in *Harper's Magazine* in August 1893, Davis put a novel spin on the old theme of a good woman saving a man who has gone astray. This time his alter ego is a Harvard-educated young composer who has been demoralized and disillusioned by great popular success. An old friend whom he once loved (a woman who "never excused a weakness in herself or in others" and who "would 'never let up on him' when he offered excuses") sees him in London and urges him to return to the United States with her family. He refuses. But that night, out carousing with an English officer and a couple of loose women, he provokes a hysterical reaction with a song about his own degradation and despair. His date, furious, tells him that like so many women, she had idolized him from afar as the one good man in the world. Now she sees that he is just as low-minded as the rest. Her rebuke reaches him where his upper-class friends could not. He prepares to leave immediately for America—and, no doubt, the purer life he once knew.[93]

Probably all Davis intended was the surface moral: even a "bad" woman retains the finer spirit that can lift a man up. Interestingly, though, the way that the composer appalls his friends is by exposing his genuine sentiments. As in so many Davis tales, the subtext of "His Bad Angel" argues the social necessity of repression: self-censorship in one's art, self-control in one's private affairs. Like his fictional alter egos, Davis crafted his art to satisfy his female readers, and he curbed his behavior to conform to what he saw as female morality.

Throughout his life, Richard impressed those he knew with his rigorous code of cleanliness. His body, his thoughts, his writing—he scrubbed them all as hard as he could. His friend Gouverneur Morris thought that "cleanliness" was his salient characteristic.[94] "He never appears on the street that he does not look like an advertisement for a safety razor," another friend observed.[95] Cleanliness is an ideal that a little boy learns from the person who bathes him—his mother. Davis's friends recognized who had inspired his hostility to dirt. As the equally mothered John Fox, Jr., wrote after Davis's death: "I never heard a word pass his lips that his own mother could not hear."[96]

His mother was always on his mind. He relied on her to correct his manuscripts before publication.[97] He valued her opinion above all others. The desire to be worthy of her overwhelming love dominated him from his childhood until her death. His hunger for public approval seems closely linked to his need for maternal sanction. He was addicted to positive reinforcement, but no one could ever match the love of his mother, a love rooted in loss: first, the death of her father, Richard's namesake, and then, the withering of her literary career. She took great vicarious pleasure from Richard's professional success, as if seeing in it the extension of her own interrupted flight.

The extraordinary closeness of mother and son was often remarked upon by Richard's friends. Gouverneur Morris once witnessed a reunion in which Richard and Rebecca "threw their arms about each other and rocked to and fro for a long time"; the odd thing, Morris thought, was that Richard had only been for a walk in the woods, and was gone less than three hours.[98] When Richard embarked on an actual journey, his effusions became positively torrential. For instance, when he left for his Mediterranean trip in February 1893, he wrote his mother on the eve of his departure:

"But as *you* say, we understand and do not have to write love letters; you have given me all that is worth while in me, and I love you so that I look forward already over miles and days and months, and just see us sitting together . . . and telling each other how good it is to be together again and to hold each other's hands. I don't believe you really know how *happy* I am in loving you, dear, and in hearing you say nice things about me. God bless you, dearest, and may I never do anything to make you feel less proud of your wicked son."[99] In looking for a cause for Richard's depressions, which afflicted him from childhood, one thinks first of this enveloping maternal love, a love which left no room for rivals and no ground for rebellion.

Not that it is fair to blame everything on his mother. There was also his father. Clarke Davis was plagued by nervous ailments and hypochondria; and from the time he was a little boy, Richard was accustomed to reassuring his melancholy father. "I am so sorry you are so gloomy about your voyage," Richard, still a schoolboy, wrote when Clarke was about to sail for England. "Your [*sic*] going off to have a hard earned holiday and not to be un-happy."[100] Travel particularly agitated Clarke; so that, in the summer of 1891, when he was touring Europe with his wife and daughter, he worried himself sick through Italy and Switzerland, fearing that his inability to speak foreign languages was keeping them from having the best possible time.[101]

Clarke had an excitable temperament, flaring up at the slightest outrage or smallest worry, and then guttering into gloom. He was a loving and affectionate father, but a somber streak ran through it all. He was fifty-six, with twelve more years to live, when he wrote this morbid letter of thanks to Richard, who had dedicated his book of short stories, *Van Bibber and Others*, to his father. "I am glad to be associated with my dear boy and with his work even in that brief way," Clarke wrote. "You may not yet have thought about it after this fashion, but I have thought a good deal about it. Reports come to me of you from many sources, and they are all good, and they all reflect honor upon me—upon me as I'm getting ready to salute the world, as our French friends say. It is very pleasant to me as I think it over to feel and to know that my boy has honored my name, that he has done something good and useful in the world and for the world. I have something more than pride in you. I am grateful to you. . . . My greatest pride in you, that which has added some sweetness and joy to a life that has had little of either in it, has been the recognition that something of the divine element was given you, and that your voice rang out sweet and pure at a time when other voices were sounding the fascination of impurity; that like Christ you taught humanity. Don't be afraid of being thought 'fresh,' fear to be thought 'knowing.' Life isn't much worth at best; it is worth nothing at all unless some good be done in it, the more the better. Don't make it too serious either. Enjoy it as you go, but after a fashion that will bring no reproach to your man hood."[102] It's hard to imagine a weaker injunction to enjoyment, or a stronger prescription for depression.

Like his father, Richard, when dejected, developed a morbid aversion to travel. He wasted a great deal of his scarce energies in the early spring of 1894 worrying whether to embark for Europe. In fact, there was no way he was going to Europe. He was still so skittish that, at the last moment, he scrapped a plan to go on the road with a theater company to research a Van Bibber story. Leaving New York for only a week was more than he could contemplate.[103] To discipline himself, he locked himself two days later into an express train to Philadelphia and, to his delight, emerged with his nerves intact. "There were days when I would have no sooner gone into a car which did not stop for two hours than I would have gone diving for pralinés off the Paris in midocean," he wrote Charles.[104]

This revulsion from travel did not prevent him from enjoying himself in New York. His evenings there were brightened by a new friendship with a young married English couple, Seymour Hicks and Ellaline Terriss. At twenty-two, Hicks had already written and starred in a number of London hit comedies. "I think he is a Richard Sheridan," Richard exclaimed.[105] Hicks was enthusiastic about everything, constantly scribbling notes on his cuffs for future gags or stage business, chuckling over each one with great glee. When he went to see *The Country Sport*, a hit comedy, he declared it the funniest thing he had ever seen: his cuffs were black. As he bubbled and giggled, dancing to himself and practicing songs, his beautiful young wife would say very little. Drowsy from a full day of rehearsals for her starring role as Cinderella (the occasion that had brought them to New York), she would smile sleepily or laugh "a low shy laugh that is like bells."[106] Richard especially loved to watch her at a street corner as a cable car passed by. "Oooh," she would cry, jumping up and down, "exactly like a child when a man puts a rug over his head and plays he's a bear."[107] Davis and the Hickses would stay out past two every night.

They would stop in first at one or more of the season's hit plays. In the 1890s, theater tickets were cheap, and competing forms of public entertainment didn't exist. For the middle and upper classes, the theater permeated everyday life in the way that television does today. Most of the theater at the turn of the century was no more intelligent than television, but it was more convivial. Theater, unlike television, all happened in public. One ran into friends at the theater and, later, one discussed with other friends the shared theatrical experience. Everyone saw everything, and the key phrases from the hit shows or variety acts became part of the "smart" lingo of the moment. So that for a while, Richard and his friends called each other "Aleck," after the character played by Pete Dailey in *The Country Sport*.[108] As they went from one nightspot to the next, they would shout to each other, "You can't lose me, Charlie," echoing a number on the variety stage. And they borrowed another line from Lottie Gibson, who sang a well-received song in the music-hall genre that began, "She's a very nice girl, She's a very nice girl, Not a bit stuck up, But every inch a lady," and then continued: "It's true she took my Jack from me *but there are others. Oh there are others.*" In the spring of 1894, on the most remote of pretexts, a smart young New Yorker might be heard to cry, "Oh there are others," to the merriment of his companions.[109] Such were the joys of the bachelor life that Davis preferred to suburban wedlock.

Trying to understand the chilling depression that swept over Davis in the winter and spring of 1894, one mustn't overlook a milestone that goes totally unacknowledged in his letters to his parents and his brother. On April 18, he turned thirty years old. Of course, he was still young, but he was no longer *that* young. For a public personality whose image radiated vigorous American youth, turning thirty was no trivial matter. Davis had feared growing old since the tender age of nineteen, and he would hate it all his life. He exercised regularly, avoided domestic entanglements, and cultivated a boyish enthusiasm, all in an effort to stay young.

Pranks, wagers, and impersonations glued his bachelor circle. One frequent companion in the mid-1890s was the publisher Robert Russell, a wealthy young clubman known for his distinctive chortle—a "fearsome sea-lion roar."[110] Like Davis's fictional Travers, Russell would bet on anything: that within ten minutes he could worm out the name of a married woman from her male companion, or that Davis wouldn't dare insult ten men on Broadway between Eighteenth and Thirty-fourth streets from the hours of nine to ten. He was "one of the funniest and deadest game sports" that Richard had ever met.[111] On train trips with Russell or others of that clique, Richard would tell alarmingly suspenseful stories for the purpose of being overheard, or pretend that one of their party was a prisoner being transported to jail. "So you can see," Richard told Charles, "that we are still young."[112]

One morning Richard read in the newspaper that his friend John Drew was performing in Harlem, then a white middle-class community and virtually a suburban venue. He immediately sent off a telegram saying that he was organizing a relief expedition to rescue Drew from the wilderness. At noon, having solicited Russell's support, he dispatched another telegram: "Natives from interior of Harlem report having seen Davis Relief Expeditionary Force crossing Central Park, all well. Robert Howard Russell." By the time the "explorers" reached the theater that night—heralded by many telegrams, decked out in safari costumes, and accompanied by two of Russell's black servants dressed in gold robes and turbans—the actor was so rattled that he mumbled through his role until the curtain mercifully dropped. "Mr. Drew, I presume," Davis said. And Drew replied, "Mr. Davis, I believe. I am saved!"[113]

It was some solace that as he aged, Davis was still a hero among the truly young. When he was inducted into the Clio Society at Princeton University, the undergraduates, having merely applauded the other dignitaries, cheered, howled, and waved their hats for Davis.[114] It helped as well when friends said that "The Exiles," his short story in the May number of *Harper's Magazine*, was his finest yet. "I was getting tired of hearing that Gallegher was my best work," Richard remarked. "I ought to have improved on the first thing I ever did."[115]

Thematically, there was little new in "The Exiles." Like so much of Davis's fiction of the 1890s, it argued that social forces shape a man's character. What attracted attention was its exotic embroidery. Set in Tangier, "The Exiles" was inspired by a conversation Davis once had with the dupes of an embezzler who had fled beyond extradition to Brazil. Davis asked the victims if they would like him to go down there and bring back the money—the germ not of an action but of a fantasy.[116] When he actually wrote his story, however, he did not model the protagonist in his own image (that is, a precocious and celebrated artist). He made him instead a morally rigid lawyer, whose transformation would illustrate the story's theme: Tangier is a place where "we can learn . . . just how far a man of cultivation lapses into barbarism when he associates with savages."[117] By savages, Davis meant not the native Moors, but the European and American flotsam who were attracted by Tangier's lack of extradition treaties. In Tangier, these social outcasts found a place where "there's no law and no religion and no relations nor newspapers to poke into what you do nor how you live."[118] Indeed, it's the very place that the bishop had conjectured and Latimer had declared inconceivable in "The Other Woman."

The notions of self-control and social repression were much on Richard's mind throughout the winter and spring of 1894. Struggling with depression, he sought the willpower to return to Europe. "I am like a chap who has been thrown and who is content to walk instead of ride for a while," he wrote to Charles, who was hoping for a visit in Florence. "I *could* ride but I prefer to walk. When I *prefer* to ride I will take the first steamer going."[119] He felt he had no more control over his "nerve storms"— as his meteorological metaphor suggests—than he did over the weather. "You understand that when I get these nerve storms I am quite silly about it and am most unhappy until I get my face turned towards my home," he told Charles. Dr. Starr thought his "nerves [were] completely shattered."[120]

Somehow in late June, almost a year after his previous visit, he made it back to Paris. Charles came from Florence to meet him. Richard arrived in Paris just at the time that French president M. F. S. Carnot was assassinated by a madman—a convenient tragedy, for it provided the material that Richard needed to complete his book. With relief he left on July 2 for London, to relax among his English friends the Hickses and Sam Sothern, and the crowd of Americans, including Dana Gibson and Robert Russell, who were over for the season. He was "enjoying everything with the greatest keenness" and felt that he was "on the road to a recovery of [his] senses."[121] Dividing his time between the tailor and the theater, he spent almost a month in London. Returning to the United States in high spirits, he proceeded without delay to Marion, Massachusetts, a seaside resort which had been attracting him and his parents since 1890. There he spent the month of August.[122]

The Davises had abandoned Manasquan for Marion in search of a seashore not yet despoiled. As early as 1890, Rebecca was complaining about the commercialization of Manasquan. "That was a sad little letter you sent me," Richard replied to one lament. "I am afraid the old place is changed indeed and irretrievably. Still, as you say the ocean is always there."[123] The very modern sense that an influx of people was ruining all the best places, from the seaside of New Jersey to the pyramids of Egypt, from the prairies of the West to the cafés of Paris—this was a favorite complaint of Richard's, and a commonplace among the affluent a century ago. Indeed, the enormous interest in the outdoors that is so characteristic of the 1890s stems from a sense of depletion. Like so many of his class, Davis developed his passion for rural life, which would consume much of his time and money in later years, in revulsion from an urban degradation that seemed to have gotten as bad as it could get. (It hadn't.)

In the larger political sphere, the perception that the nation's resources were running out nurtured the conservation movement. (The nation's first national park, Yellowstone, was established in 1872; and Congress passed the National Park Service Act in 1916.) On a personal level, wealthy Eastern urbanites at the turn of the century hied to the countryside. They built grand summer cottages at such resorts as Southampton and Bar Harbor; even more remarkably, they frequently spent all the summer months in these places. Some actually moved to the country year-round and commuted by rail to work. "If there is anything new under the sun it is the contemporary practice of living from twenty to a hundred miles distant from the place of earning one's daily bread," wrote one social observer in 1893. "The possibility of doing such a thing was never offered to any generation before ours. That hundreds of thousands of people should travel from three to five hours every day to and from their work in New York is a thing that would be hardly credible if one read it in a book, and needs to be observed to be realized."[124] Of course, the more people congregated in the unspoiled countryside, the more that countryside was spoiled, and the further afield the anxious urban refugees had to travel.

Richer and remoter than Manasquan, Marion had resisted the tinsel of the modern world more successfully. A drowsy village perched on Buzzards Bay, it attracted the kind of artistic people Richard liked: professionals with good manners and few cultural pretensions. He did "not believe in knowing literary lights unless they have other qualities to introduce them," he once said, explaining: "There is no reason why you should if you are a shoemaker associate with other shoemakers except to talk shop, but one does not go out in the evening to talk shop."[125] (Throughout his life he refused to join any club or organization of authors.)[126] In the 1890s, Marion was the frequent summer destination of Charles Dana Gibson, Gouverneur Morris, Stephen Bonsal, and John Fox, Jr.—all of them gentlemen first, writers and artists second. (Grover Cleveland, like his friend, actor Joseph Jefferson, lived in the nearby village of Buzzards Bay.)

Of course, not all the summer residents of Marion were New York literati. One of the finest houses in town belonged to the Clark family of Chicago—a family that would play an important role in Richard's life. John Marshall Clark was a wealthy businessman, and his wife, Louise, was a gifted amateur pianist. They too had been coming to Marion since 1890, when they stayed, as was the style, at the Hotel Sippican. After fashion decreed that one must summer at home, not at a hotel, they built a sprawling Queen Anne summer "cottage" on Water Street.[127] Although John Clark could only come out when business permitted, his wife spent the summers there, with their son, Bruce, and daughter, Cecil. Louise took a great liking to Richard, and he spent many evenings singing popular songs to her piano accompaniment. He paid less attention to Cecil. She was attractive and athletic, and she already bristled with the talent and dedication it takes to become a successful painter. But, after all, she was only a teenager.

Richard saw much of the Clarks that August. As he played tennis in the summer sun, though, his thoughts wandered away from the sleepy village of Marion to the other side of the world. Since he was a little boy, he had wanted to see a real war. There was a war on that summer, but it could not have been more inconvenient: the belligerents were China and Japan. While this might have discouraged someone who four months earlier had viewed the train ride from New York to Philadelphia as a test of nerve, Richard was fascinated by Japan. Like so many Americans and Englishmen of his generation, he had been captivated by Gilbert and Sullivan's *The Mikado*, which toured the United States in 1885 and left, bobbing in its wake, souvenir *Mikado* glassware, china, buttons, and greeting cards.[128] Even without the intercession of an English operetta, the Japanese had delicately marked all aspects of American culture, from the poster art of Edward Penfield to the chrysanthemum displays at horticultural shows. Now on the battlefields of Korea, they were proving as adept at war as they were at flower arranging.

The newspaper accounts of the war made it almost impossible for Richard to work. "It is like trying to do a latin exercise with the other boys playing football outside on the campus," he wrote.[129] No longer bound to the Harpers, he offered the Scribners a series of articles on the war, to be collected later as a forty-thousand-word book, and they immediately agreed to pay three thousand dollars for the serial and book rights, plus a 15 percent book royalty and five hundred dollars for expenses. He bought a complete war correspondent's kit and prepared excitedly to go. The night before his train left New York for Canada on the first leg of the journey, Eddie Sothern staged a surprise farewell party. In a dining room decorated with Japanese lanterns and artificial flowers, five of Richard's friends and six of the prettiest actresses in New York had transformed themselves into characters from *The Mikado*. The men were dressed in gorgeous embroidered silk robes, and were made up with pigtails and bald foreheads. The women, in elaborate kimonos, had their faces painted, their eyebrows drawn in slashes, and their hair piled up high off their necks and stuck through with tiny fans. When Richard entered the room, the ersatz Japanese all began to bob and bow. The dinner went on for six hours, and the guest of honor was both delighted and touched.[130]

But in the morning, by the time his train reached Harlem, Davis was already quivering with doubts. The boring three-week journey stretched grimly before him. Stopping in Montreal on his way to Vancouver, he realized that his heart wasn't in this. He continued as far as Ottawa and then, "travel-surfeited," turned back.[131] "I waited too long to be a war correspondent and my enthusiasm palled before 21 more days of railroad tracks and water I did not want to go over but I thought I ought to," he wrote Charles, "and was more sorry to leave New York there and my friends than I can tell. When I am tired of that place and of being still I will start forth again but if it is to WAR the WAR will have to be nearer by twenty days than Tokio."[132] Oscillating like a hypermagnetized compass needle, he seriously reconsidered traveling to the Far East the next month, but abandoned the project once and for all when he heard that the correspondents already there were stranded in Tokyo, unable to reach the battlefront.[133] The whole affair left a sour taste in his mouth. In early December, he confessed that he had still not gotten over "the retreat from Ottawa and it has made me miserable and nervous."[134]

Burrowing into New York, he took pleasure in the redecoration of his apartment. He justified the expense, with Van Bibber logic, by citing all the restaurant dinner parties he would no longer have to give. He dedicated the space absented by Charles to entertainment, and installed furnishings that were "artfully calculated to interest the old friend, and to stun the stranger with what a Hell of a man I am." The entertaining space was quite small, limiting the size of his parties; but as his friends were a mixed lot, he thought that was all to the good. He inaugurated the new digs with a practice supper for John and Louisa Drew and their granddaughter Ethel Barrymore. The table held just the plates, red candles, and little bowls of pickled walnuts and dried ginger. On a mahogany tea table were two trays with cold chicken and cold tongue and celery. All of this "bully spread," including champagne purchased at wholesale rates and served in gold glasses, cost him a mere five dollars, which was a fraction of what Delmonico's would have exacted. It was a grand success.[135]

Money was on Richard's mind because he had undertaken the writing of a novel. This book would prove to be the most lucrative project of his life, but he had no way of knowing that when he began. And until it was finished, he was short on cash. His short stories earned him three hundred dollars (from *Harper's*) and four hundred dollars (from *Scribner's*).[136] He was sacrificing that income to work on a book for which he had received no advance.[137] Even parties catered at home cost money, and Davis was never good at economizing. For a man with profligate tastes and dwindling income, New York was (and is) a hazardous environment. The city "takes more out of one and gives less than any place on this earth," Davis observed.[138]

As the days shortened and the temperatures dropped, New York's allure faded. Even though it had been a warm winter so far, with no snow, Davis's leg was beginning to twitch with sciatica and his mood was darkening.[139] Somers Somerset, the twenty-year-old heir to the dukedom of Beaufort, had breezed through town in October on the way to Nassau, and tried futilely to cajole his Oxford friend into accompanying him.[140] In December, however, when Somerset suggested a South American journey, Richard was more receptive.[141] His novel-in-progress took place in a mythical Latin American country, a landscape he had conjured up from memories of the trip to Cuba he made in his Lehigh days. Those reminiscences could stand freshening up.

So he was already gravitating southward when, one night at Delmonico's, a man stopped by the table at which he was dining alone, and asked, "Do you remember me? I met you once in a smoking-car in Texas. Well, I've got a story now that's better than any you'll find lying around here in New York. You want to go to a little bay called Puerto Cortés, on the eastern coast of Honduras, in Central America, and look over the exiled Louisiana State Lottery there. It used to be the biggest gambling concern in the world, but now it's been banished to a single house on a mud-bank covered with palm-trees, and from there it reaches out all over the United States, and sucks in thousands and thousands of victims like a great octopus. You want to go there and write a story about it. Good-night."

Richard remembered the lottery well from his boyhood trip to New Orleans. At that time, it was the only legal gambling operation in the United States, and through a clever mixture of bribes (to legislators) and charity (to the church), it had the city of New Orleans in its thrall. But in 1890, it was finally forced to surrender its Louisiana base and retreat to Honduras. From that exotic outpost, it used the U.S. mail to run a lottery-in-exile. Although its advertisements were a familiar feature in New York theater programs, its actual operations were obscured, as if by a palm-frond curtain. Like the elusive Garza, the exiled lottery sounded like a great excuse for escaping the New York winter.[142]

Some days later, Richard was again at Delmonico's making last-minute travel arrangements with Somerset, when Lloyd Griscom came in and joined them. At twenty-two, Griscom, like Somerset, was much Richard's junior. The son of a Philadelphia shipping magnate, he had met Richard in London while working as an unsalaried secretary to Ambassador Bayard. Soon after their introduction, Griscom was at a ball when the Prince of Wales, who often sprinkled a few words on members of the diplomatic corps, stuck out his royal hand and said, "I'm very glad to see you." As the august personage moved on, Griscom felt a tap on his shoulder, and a cheery American voice said: "Lord, some people are lucky. Here you've been in London only a few weeks, the Prince of Wales has spoken to you, and you've the foremost reporter in America to spread the news." It was, of course, Davis, and so began their friendship.[143] At the Delmonico's dinner that December night, after much mysterious fidgeting, Richard revealed his plans and invited Griscom to come along. Ingeniously, Lloyd won his father's consent by recalling that the elder Griscom had been asked to head a company seeking to build a canal through Nicaragua. Lloyd volunteered to make a first-hand inspection.[144] The trio of gringos (as Davis dubbed them in his book about the trip)*[145]—joined by Somerset's cadaverous valet, Charlwood, who Griscom thought was the least likely candidate for roughing it that he had ever seen—sailed on January 9 from New Orleans to Puerto Cortés.[146]

There they soon learned that the lottery was run scrupulously. Except for the overwhelming odds against the participants, there was nothing to expose. Aggravating Richard's predicament, the gringos foolishly boarded at the cleanest and finest building in town—the lottery headquarters. Having accepted the gracious hospitality of the lottery manager and his wife, how could Richard vilify their business? "I can write the story so as not to hurt anyone," he assured his mother, "it has been written by local reporters before and as we pay our way here it is not as though we were their guests although I shall consider myself so in writing the story."[147] Polite to a fault, Davis had hesitated to describe the London social scene in *Our English Cousins* for fear of "criticizing those who have been civil to him."[148] He was really too much the gentleman to be an investigative reporter.†[149]

Also staying at the lottery headquarters was Charles Jeffs, a thickset, muscular young American mining engineer from Minneapolis who had been living in Honduras for eleven years. Jeffs offered to accompany the three gringos to the Honduran capital of Tegucigalpa; and lucky he did, for the route to Tegucigalpa was more a mule path than a highway. They would never have made it on their own. With deceptive ease, the expedition began on the only railroad in Honduras. The track extended thirty-seven miles

---

*The word *gringo*, according to Davis, comes from an old song, "Green Grow the Rushes, Oh!" that English-speaking frontiersmen once sang on the Mexican border. The Mexicans introduced the word *gringo* to refer to these men. One should add, however, that Davis was no philologist.

†The Honduras lottery was finally closed down in 1907. It was the last legal lottery to operate in the United States until the modern renaissance of state-sponsored gambling.

inland to San Pedro Sula before it stopped, the victim of a stock swindle; so instead of unifying the country, the train transported bananas to market. To Davis, the unfinished railroad exemplified the inability of Central Americans to get things done.

They stopped for four days in San Pedro Sula so Jeffs could procure mules and *mosos* (mule handlers). Disembarking from the train, Davis, to his astonishment, recognized a man who approached with a sheaf of handbills. It was Garland Howland, a young social lion he had met long ago, on a visit to Newport in his Lehigh days. Ten years back, Howland disappeared, "having as I thought drunk himself to death," Davis said. Howland was about as far from Broadway as he would have been in Hades, but he was very much alive. He invited Davis to dinner at his thatch-roofed and mud-floored house, and there he told his strange tale. After some unspecified disgrace (Davis thought it involved forgery as well as drink), he had bounced around the world, doing everything—acting in a *Pinafore* company in Valparaíso, ranching in Patagonia, waiting on tables in Seattle, and blacking boots in Australia. For the past two years, he had been the stationmaster of San Pedro Sula. His boss, a Pittsburgh engineer who managed the railroad, told Davis to tell Howland's father that Garland "had stopped drinking absolutely but had every other vice known to man." He was a real-life illustration of what happened to a man's character outside the bounds of civilization. "[Howland's] colored 'missus' sat with us at the table and played with a beetle during the three hours I stayed there," Richard reported. She spoke no English. Two little children of mixed race frolicked outside. In this incongruous setting, Howland pumped Davis for news of the actress Marie Jansen, who he said had ruined him.[150]

The trail out of San Pedro Sula was so steep and narrow that at times the gringos had to climb up steps that had been carved in the rock. Although there were no murderous rhinos or hostile Masai, as had threatened young Chanler in East Africa, there were still adventures, or at least discomforts. The steamy green landscape was dripping with insects. Most common were the *garrapatas*, little ticks that buried themselves into the skin and festered if they were not removed. Most feared was the *chigre*, a species of flea that worked its way under a toenail and deposited its eggs in a sac, causing the toe to swell. If the egg sac broke, the *mosos* grimly warned, the best one could hope for was the loss of a foot. One evening Somers examined his big toe, which had been itching, and saw that it was a little red. His friends called over the *mosos* to take a look. "*Chigre!*" they shouted in unison. The victim alone remained calm, telling Griscom, the custodian of the medical kit, that he would have to operate. The *mosos* set water to boil while Griscom prepared bandages. Somerset lay on his back on a blanket and the *mosos* held down his leg. Rolling up his sleeves, the amateur medic traced the path of his incision in a deep curve all around the swelling. He swabbed the toe in antispetic, dipped a razor in boiling water, took a deep breath, and, with one slice, cut off a good-sized portion of toe. Somerset cursed loudly, but even he raised himself to observe the biopsy. Griscom slit open the piece of tissue and found, intact, a sac of tiny white eggs. The operation had been a success.[151]

Davis was fond of his companions. Somerset had a puckish sense of humor. Griscom was "a terrible kid," but he was good-natured about being kidded. Both boys were suitably impressed that even in darkest Honduras, the name of Richard Harding Davis was known. When ravenous insects forced the gringos to seek nighttime shelter in private houses, Richard's calling card opened more doors than did their letters from secretaries and ambassadors.[152] "As a rule [new acquaintances] will not believe us as to our only coming here for fun and that we are who we say we are," Richard remarked. "They always think it is a joke." Once, Jeffs intruded on an American who had stopped overnight on business in a native village, to ask if the three travelers could swing their hammocks in his shack. Told the name of one of his prospective boarders, the man replied merrily, "Certainly, Richard Harding Davis can come in and so can the governors of North and South Carolina."[153]

Tegucigalpa was a letdown, filthy yet colorless. There was nothing here for tourists, and the new arrivals realized quickly what held the small American expatriate community. One man had been the state treasurer of Louisiana, until he absconded with a few hundred thousand dollars. Another was wanted in Chicago for the murder of his wife. For all of them, the irresistible appeal of Honduras was its lack of an extradition treaty with the United States.[154]

Davis was unimpressed as well by the natives of Central America. He found the leaders to be preoccupied with waging or repelling revolutions, and the populace to be apathetic, indolent, and, in dealing with Americans, surly. "The Central-American citizen is no more fit for a republican form of government than he is for an arctic expedition, and what he needs is to have a protectorate established over him, either by the United States or by another power . . . ," he wrote. The frequent political revolutions in these states caused little bloodshed, but the political instability so discouraged capital investment that progress was impossible. He thought a canal should be built across Nicaragua or Panama—and "it will have to be some other man than a native-born Central-American who is to do it."[155]

Bound for Nicaragua, the young men journeyed four days to the Pacific coast, where they left Jeffs and the mules, and took an open boat to the island of Amapala, the chief Pacific port of Honduras. To their horror, they found on arrival that Amapala had been quarantined with yellow fever, a disease that was highly contagious and usually fatal. In a near panic, they bribed the owner of a small fishing boat to take them on a stomach-churning, heat-blasted, twenty-four-hour ride to Corinto, Nicaragua.[156] As their boat floated into Corinto harbor, the townspeople first thought they were shipwrecks, then revolutionaries. Fortunately, two American boys were in Corinto at the time, working their way through Central America by demonstrating a strange new invention called a phonograph. One had once sung in the Princeton glee club. They happily vouched for the character of the celebrated Richard Harding Davis. The gates of Corinto swung open.[157]

At this point, the Central American expedition, which had been sailing along nicely, drifted into the doldrums. To see Panama and Venezuela, the visitors depended on steamers; and no steamers stopped. They traveled inland to the capital of Managua, so that Griscom could discharge his filial duty of investigating the prospects of a Nicaraguan canal. (The consensus was that the likelihood of earthquakes made construction there a bad bet.)[158] For fear of missing a steamer, they hurried back to Corinto, where they waited in frustration for ten days at their hotel until a decrepit cargo boat, the *Barracouta* (so unseaworthy that not long afterward it went down with all hands) transported them to Panama City. After the disappointment of the Honduran lottery, Davis was hoping in Panama to see something newsworthy: the ill-fated French canal, which had bogged down first in bankruptcy and then in scandal. After construction stopped, engines and machinery worth thousands of dollars were left to rust in the rain. Or so Davis had read before arriving in Panama. When he made an inspection tour, he found all the locomotives painted, oiled, and shedded. The machine works likewise seemed in perfect order. He wrote dryly that "it would have given me a better chance for descriptive writing had I found the ruins of gigantic dredging-machines buried in the morasses, and millions of dollars' worth of delicate machinery blistering and rusting under the palm-trees; but, as a rule, it is better to describe things just as you saw them, and not as it is the fashion to see them, even though your way be not so picturesque."[159]

For a romancer who delighted in legends and traditions, Davis had a surprising habit of poking his finger in the gap between the expected and the actual. As an *Evening Sun* reporter, he had rushed with a lawyer to the jailhouse to announce the last-minute commutation of a death sentence. With an embarrassed laugh and a smile, the reprieved man shook the lawyer's hand, and then Richard's. "That's good," he said finally. "That's good." Lest anyone miss the point, Davis made it explicit: "that it is only on the stage and in novels that people talk as the newspapers would like to make them at dramatic moments."[160] Years later, in France for *Harper's Weekly*, Davis remarked that correspondents were cabling all over the world of the grief and rage of the Parisians at the assassination of President Carnot when, in fact, the Parisians were drinking and dancing in the cafés as if nothing had happened. He chided that "in writing of facts it is more interesting to report things as they happened than as they should have happened."[161] Had he subscribed to this policy when composing fiction, his fiction might still be read today.

The news in Panama was not the stalled canal, but a simmering revolution. (Panama was a part of Colombia.) The young son of the American consul conducted Griscom furtively to the bayside law library of a young Cornell graduate named Rojas. Vehemently condemning the ruling government, Rojas was about to give details on the next coup attempt when a knock on the door interrupted him. Five soldiers burst into the room. "Señor Rojas, you are under arrest," said the officer in command. Because they lacked a warrant, Rojas refused to go with them. One soldier kept guard in the outer office, while the others went off to procure the papers. "Well, they've got me," Rojas told Griscom, with philosophical resignation.

But to Griscom, this was a new game. "Suppose there were a boat under this window," he said. "You could drop into it and row out to the *Barracouta*." Rojas pointed out that it was too great a drop without a rope. Promising to procure one, Griscom hurried back to Davis and Somerset, who wholeheartedly endorsed this adventure. "We knew nothing of the rights or the wrongs of the revolutionists," Davis later wrote, "but we considered that a man who was going down a rope into a small boat while three soldiers sat waiting for him in an outer room was performing a sporting act that called for our active sympathy."[162] That is a succinct statement of the political principles of Richard Harding Davis. His attraction to the underdog and to the grand gesture would guide his sympathies through the major conflicts of his lifetime: the Spanish-American War, the Boer War, and the First World War.

The gringo conspirators smuggled in a rope on a dinner tray, but when they returned at nightfall in a hired boat, Rojas was gone. All his new allies could do was send him an ample supply of cigarettes in prison. (They didn't learn of his fate until many years and many revolutions later, when Griscom saw his picture in a newspaper photograph of Panamanian officials. Perhaps Rojas knew what he was doing when he accepted the news of his arrest so calmly.)[163] Their friendship with an imprisoned revolutionary having been duly noted by the authorities, the visitors crossed the isthmus to Colón on the Atlantic side, and boarded a ship to Venezuela. Here, too, Davis found political instability, of an even more exciting variety. Venezuela was in a bitter dispute with Great Britain over the boundary of British Guiana. Concurrently, she had just expelled the British, French, and German foreign ministers for criticizing her debt repayment schedule and her failure to honor concessions. By virtue of a ten-day layover, Davis could supply a timely on-scene report.

He and his friends brought back from Caracas their most prized souvenirs of the trip: each received the Order of the Bust of Bolívar the Liberator of Venezuela, of the Fourth Class. Even more valuable, Davis sailed home to New York buoyed by a renewed self-confidence. "All the things I was nervous about have been done," he told his mother, "and should I get nerves again as I suppose I always will in one form or another

I can get rid of them by remembering how I got rid of them before during this most peculiar excursion."[164] But to the historian with an eye on the big picture, the most important thing that Davis carried back to New York was a basket of alligator pears—better known today as avocados. He thought they were so good that he took samples to Charles Delmonico, who secured a steady supply and placed the exotic fruit on the menu. The rest is culinary history.[165]

In New York, Richard worked first on finishing his *Harper's Magazine* articles, published in book form as *Three Gringos in Venezuela and Central America*. Tart and amusing, the book is his best travel collection, in part because of the unfamiliarity of the territory. As one reviewer remarked: "Mr. Davis always has a way of giving an air of novelty to what he has seen, and in this book, as the scenes which he describes are wholly novel to most of us, he is doubly interesting."[166]

The book also had the good fortune to appear just as the dispute over the British Guiana boundary flared up into a war scare. In December 1895, shortly after the appearance of Davis's reportage in the magazine and before its publication as a book, President Cleveland delivered a bellicose anti-British speech. "My article was a very lucky thing and is greatly quoted," Richard told Charles, "and in social gatherings I am appealed to as a final authority."[167] If so, his friends had a feeble grasp of foreign policy. After President Cleveland's message, Davis wrote: "It may be true, as the foreign powers have pointed out, that the aggressions of Great Britain are none of our business, but as we have made them our business, it concerns no one but Great Britain and ourselves, and now having failed to avoid the entrance to a quarrel, and being in, we must bear ourselves so that the enemy may beware of us, and see that we issue forth again with honor, and without having stooped to the sin of war."[168] It would be difficult to find a more comical illustration of the adage that muddled writing betrays muddled thinking.

He was much better at imagining derring-do than he was at prescribing policy. Throughout 1895, when he wasn't recounting his Central American expedition, Richard was working on the novel that he had begun beforehand. He finished it at the end of the year.[169] The setting of *Soldiers of Fortune* is a fictional Cuba, as Davis remembered it from his adolescent visit with William Thurston, the Bethlehem Iron executive who was inspecting the construction of a small railroad to bring out ore from a mine on Cuba's south coast.[170] The building of that railroad is at the heart of *Soldiers*. The novel's atmosphere of Latin American politics, however, is colored by Davis's observations on his recent trip.

Soldiers of Fortune was the most popular book of Davis's career.[171] Published in early 1897 (it had appeared first as a magazine serial), this novel about a revolution in a quasi-Cuba became the second-best-selling book of the year.[172] Like *Three Gringos*, it came out at an opportune time: the American people were becoming increasingly agitated over Cuba's rebellion against her Spanish colonial masters. Today, Davis's novel is remembered—when it is remembered—as an illustration of two genres that have fallen from fashion. It was an action novel full of fighting. ("I never *saw* such men," Davis's friend Eddie Sothern remarked. "They are *always* *fighting*.")[173] And it was an imperialistic rhapsody, celebrating the triumph of the North American hero over his lethargic and corrupt Latin neighbors. *Soldiers* was so widely read that, in some unquantifiable way, it doubtless helped prime the national psyche for the collective adventure in Cuba. But it wasn't the crude racist tract that some later commentators have made it out to be.[174] It's a typical Richard Harding Davis novel, with a dashing young handsome hero who outmaneuvers everyone and gets the right girl. The girl, in fact, is the character who at the time provoked the most comment, because she was an early version of the athletic American type that Charles Dana Gibson idealized in sketches, as Davis did in prose.

Although the Central American society in which *Soldiers* unfolds is indeed treacherous, venal, and backward, that's not slander—it's reportage. In the late nineteenth century, the dictators of the small Central American "republics" were typically puppets of powerful European or United States commercial interests. The native president, as Davis wrote in *Three Gringos*, could only "pretend to rule his country." The real dictators sat in New York or London or Berlin, running the steamship firm or coffee company that controlled the local economy. When the president required money or weapons, they supplied him. If the president balked at their demands, they found a revolution-minded rival to replace him.[175] In *Soldiers of Fortune*, the native politicians and the American capitalists are equally corrupt. Significantly, the hero, Robert Clay, is an engineer with no commercial interests and no political ties.

In all of Davis's fiction, not one hero is a businessman or a politician. For Davis, as for many idealistic Americans, those professions were tainted; and although he admired some individual politicians and businessmen, he preferred, when creating an alter ego, to conjure up an artist, an explorer, a soldier—or an engineer, like Robert Clay.[176] In its use of an engineer as a hero, *Soldiers of Fortune* was very up-to-date. Davis had been impressed by the vast ambition of the engineers when he visited the site of the Panama Canal and saw the unfinished work—work that had been betrayed by the chicanery of French capitalists and politicians. He was also moved by the rows of wooden markers in the many cemeteries of Panama, signifying the ultimate self-sacrifice of the "young soldiers of the transit and sailors of the dredging-scow" who had fallen, without banners or bugles, but for a cause as chivalrous as a crusade.[177] Unlike soldiering or exploring, engineering wasn't the least bit anachronistic. Yet, as Davis (along with such disparate thinkers as Thorstein Veblen and Hart Crane) realized, the accomplishments of the engineer at the turn of the century were grandly heroic.

Like so many Davis tales, *Soldiers of Fortune* begins at a dinner party. The engineer Clay is seated next to a society beauty, Alice Langham, whose life he has been following in the newspapers and whose picture he has been carrying in his pocket watch. (So far, he resembles Morton Carlton in *The Princess Aline*.) Clay is about to sail to Olancho in South America to open a huge iron-ore mine for the Valencia Mining Company. He doesn't know that Alice's father secretly owns the company. Eventually, all the Langhams turn up in Olancho: Alice, her siblings, Hope and Ted, and the old man himself, who has been sent south to rest his nerves.

Olancho proves to be no place for the nervous; it's on the edge of revolution. President Alvarez, who has granted the mining company its concession in return for a 10 percent government commission, is being challenged by General Mendoza, who demands 50 percent for the government. (Lest we think that Mendoza is an honest patriot, he offers to back down for a sixty-thousand-dollar bribe.) There is an uprising, in which Alvarez is killed; but Clay topples Mendoza and replaces him with Alvarez's vice president, a popular politician whose integrity has kept him from higher office. In the midst of all this gunplay, Clay has enough time to realize that Alice has been spoiled by society and is better matched to Reggie King (named Roosevelt in the first draft), the yachtsman who is wooing her.[178] He falls in love instead with her tomboy sister, Hope, who, in a feat of driving worthy of Helen Benedict, rescues Clay and another man by picking them up in her carriage beneath a rain of gunfire. At the novel's end, Clay returns to America with the Langhams to marry Hope.

To its many enthusiasts, *Soldiers of Fortune* was memorable for its gunfights and its lovemaking. Those seem awfully insipid to the reader of today. We are more interested in the depiction of the natives of Olancho, even though—indeed, because—they play a distinctly subsidiary role. "They were of a people who better appreciated the amenities of life than its sacrifices," Davis wrote. They had discovered the large deposit of iron ore, but they were "too lazy to ever work it themselves."[179] In the scene in which Clay proves Mendoza's venality, Davis baldly contrasted the energetic, straightforward North Americans with their indolent, shifty cousins to the south. Shaking his finger in the general's face, Clay warns, "Try to break that concession; try it. It was made by one Government to a body of honest, decent business men, with a Government of their own back of them, and if you interfere with our conceded rights to work those mines, I'll have a man-of-war down here with white paint on her hull, and she'll blow you and your little republic back up there into the mountains."[180] A man-of-war with white paint on her hull was a powerful symbol of an intimidating United States. More than any other Davis work, *Soldiers of Fortune* glorified ascendant American power.

Chapter

6

First Love, First War

*D*AVIS WROTE MUCH OF THE BELLICOSE *SOLDIERS* in 1895 during a halcyon summer in Marion, Massachusetts. When he wasn't at his desk, he could often be found, as in the previous summer, with Louise Clark and her daughter, Cecil. He developed a comfortable routine. After breakfasting at the Hotel Sippican, he would work for two hours, and then walk the elm-shaded streets to pick up the mail and join the Clarks for a swim. Following lunch, he would work until four, when Cecil would arrive to take him driving until suppertime. He would read after supper and then pay a final call on the Clarks before bedtime.[1]

It was during this summer in Marion that Richard's gaze shifted from the amiable Louise Clark to Cecil, who was now an attractive young woman of eighteen, doted upon by a wealthy father. Cecil was an unusual woman. As a child, she had once badly wanted a horse and cart for harness driving, but her parents told her she was still too young. So this teenaged girl marched down to the Chicago jail and received permission to draw the prisoners. By selling her sketches to a newspaper, she raised enough money to buy the horse and cart herself.[2] That was a popular anecdote in the Clark family, for it summed up Cecil's salient features: her love of animals and sports, her talent for art, and her will of iron. An excellent rider and a standout billiards player, she could have been the model for the tomboy Hope Langham in *Soldiers of Fortune*. When Richard read her the scene in which Hope chafes to go to a ball in Olancho but can't, because she has not yet "come out" in New York, Cecil "thought Hope's feelings in the matter correct."[3] Like Hope, she loved to do the unconventional thing. On a brief trip to New York with her mother in late September, Richard took her on his popular tour of police headquarters. He reported that she "was in the 7th heaven of happiness and would hardly leave the place."[4]

She was, in short, the very picture of the new American girl—that dazzling creature whose afterimage lingers in roadside antique shops on the calendars, candy boxes, and magazine covers of the 1890s. This new American girl was (or so said the New York *Herald*) "better dressed, better mannered, more lovable and lovelier than any maiden of Europe."[5] Her hair was swept up, her neck was long, her bust was small, her bearing was erect. She resembled, as much as she was able, the pen-and-ink illustrations of Charles Dana Gibson. Whether Gibson started out by drawing the girls he saw is hard to say. His drawings became so popular so quickly that the country soon was brimming with young women for him to draw—women who had modeled themselves after the Gibson Girl. Had Gibson's sketches been in color, one might have detected a blush of sun on the maidens' cheeks; no longer the mark of the field hand, a feminine tan in the 1890s became fashionably associated with bathing beaches and tennis courts.[6] The American girl insisted on being active. On his travels through America in 1894, Paul Bourget drafted a taxonomy of girls: the socially ambitious, the politically committed, the intellectually voracious—and, most distinctive, the tomboy. "The tomboy is a sort of young woman who in general excels in all sports, wears tailor-made gowns, walks erect, plays billiards, and finds much less pleasure in being courted than in devising some new excitement, such as a ride at full speed on the cow-catcher of a locomotive," he wrote.[7] This is such a striking portrait of Cecil Clark that she might have sat for it.

In Hope Langham, the heroine of *Soldiers of Fortune*, Davis created his most memorable rendition of the new American girl. (The illustrations by Gibson surely added to her appeal.) Speaking of her younger sister, Alice Langham says, "She is a most energetic child; I think sometimes she should have been a boy."[8] In the Clark family, the same thing was often said of Cecil, who was markedly brighter and tougher than her brother, Bruce.[9] Just as Irene Langhorne, the Virginia belle who became Mrs. Charles Dana Gibson, seemed to be a Gibson Girl come to life, so Cecil Clark resembled many of the young women invented by Richard Harding Davis. Throughout Davis's fiction, the heroine has "the tall, slim figure of a boy" or a "slight, boyish figure" or "brave, boyish eyes."[10] She is someone "who could understand what you were trying to say before you said it, who could take an interest in rates of exchange and preside at a dinner table."[11] The greatest compliment that you can pay her is to address her as you would a man.[12] She in turn will respond "frankly, proudly, without embarrassment, without fear of being misconstrued, as a man might speak to a man."[13] She nurtures a man's finer instincts but does not arouse his feverish ardor. She is, in short, his best and noblest friend.

He preached the gospel of a wife who would also be a comrade, but Richard was too much the reporter to ignore how the convention of marriage left its mark, even on unconventional people. Although wives could theoretically be comrades, they all too rarely were. In *Soldiers of Fortune*, when Clay leaves Olancho to marry his new American girl, a fellow engineer casts a dreary shadow on his horizon. He says: "You will grow fat, Clay, and live on Fifth Avenue and wear a high silk hat, and some day when you're sitting in your club you'll read a paragraph in a newspaper with a queer Spanish date-line to it, and this will all come back to you,—this heat, and the palms, and the fever, and the days when you lived on plantains and we watched our trestles grow out across the canyons, and you'll be willing to give your hand to sleep in a hammock again, and to feel the sweat running down your back, and you'll want to chuck your gun up against your chin and shoot into a line of men, and the policemen won't let you, and your wife won't let you. That's what you're giving up."[14] Side by side, like defensemen guarding the end zone, the policeman and the wife will bar him from excitement.

This depiction of the grind of middle-aged domesticity strikes home. Even without a wife, Davis in his early thirties was saddled with an intimidating list of expenses. At the end of 1895, just in time for Christmas, he sold *Soldiers of Fortune* for an advance of seventy-five hundred dollars. Although he complained to Charles that it was "not as much as I think I should have got for it," the first installment of two thousand dollars helped pay the bills.[15]

He was also pleased that the book went to the Scribners; his relationship with the Harpers had totally deteriorated. He was humiliated when *Harper's Weekly* rejected two of his unsolicited articles.[16] He also resented the way *Harper's Monthly* handled his Central American pieces. The slipshod proofreading infuriated him: he deliberately misspelled Rio de Janeiro to see if anyone would catch it (no one did).[17] Even worse, the series was so poorly advertised that he thought the Harpers seemed ashamed of it. "Personally I do not care to take that much trouble and go through that much discomfort unless the work I bring back is placed in such a way that it may be seen and that some one will know about it," he explained testily. "I do not take trips in order to write about them I write about them in order that I may get the money to take the trips but I naturally want to write for who ever will present what I do write the most conspicuously."[18]

Success might have made Davis more confident of his achievements and less sensitive to perceived slights. It did not. Only his family and closest friends recognized the depth of his insecurity and his addiction to praise. Because of his pretentions, which became notorious, his critics lambasted his arrogance. When the New York *Sun*'s Edward W. Townsend sneered at errors in Davis's Paris reportage, the *World* announced that the aggrieved Davis had challenged Townsend to a duel.[19] His large ego—and skin so thin it might have been stretched to cover it—made a very tempting target. One of the better shots was this piece of doggerel:

'Good morning, Mr. Davis.' 'Harding Davis, if you please.'
'Oh! pardon! Mr. Harding Hyphen Davis, if you please.
I only called to say how much I like your journalese.

> *A little more familiar and a little less at ease*
> *With the rules of English grammar than would suit a Bostonese,*
> *'T is yet a fitting instrument to render thoughts like these,—*
> *The thoughts of Mr. Davis.' 'Harding Davis, if you please.'*[20]

So many derogatory paragraphs appeared in the press that for a time Davis collected them in a scrapbook, thinking he would respond to them as a block.

However, his forbearance was shattered by an item announcing that he had become terribly ashamed of his newspaper years and wished that people would forget his authorship of "Gallegher." These words were placed in his mouth: "That story was all very well, but it has a reportorial curtness and crystallization about it that I have now soared far beyond. 'Gallegher' has the thumb-marks of the poor, pawn-ticketed, free-lunched hack reporter on its pages. I want to forget that part of my existence. I want to wipe off the newspaper-shop part of my life. I will sacrifice 'Gallegher' and the royalties thereon if people will forget that I was once that scorned thing—a reporter!" As a quote, this was preposterous; but as an indication of the resentment and scorn that Davis's affectations provoked on Park Row, it was not so easily dismissed. In a plaintive open letter, Davis protested that "people who do not know me in any way are creating a personality for me which is becoming generally accepted by those who have no other means of learning anything about me." That personality was "snobbish and contemptible," reeking of "the most fatuous conceit."[21] "If I thought I was like the man the newspapers make me out to be," he told an interviewer, "I would not only cut my own acquaintance; I'd cut my own throat."[22]

It was odd that Davis should be accused of trying to hush up his newspaper background at the very time that he was re-establishing his newspaper ties. He had graduated from newsprint to glossy stock in the normal course of advancement, since magazines reached a larger audience and paid higher fees.[23] But in the mid-1890s, the economics of publishing underwent a seismic change. The source of the earthquake was a tall, basset-faced, pipsqueak-voiced, loudly dressed young man who came to New York in 1895 with the gumptious notion that he could topple Joseph Pulitzer's *World*. William Randolph Hearst had studied Pulitzer's circulation-building techniques firsthand in New York, apprenticing as a reporter at the *World* after Harvard expelled him for a characteristic prank: he sent his professors chamber pots with their names inscribed on the porcelain bottoms. After his stint on the *World*, Willie returned to his native San Francisco. There he persuaded his father, a mining and real-estate millionaire, to give him control of a moribund newspaper acquired as an afterthought in fulfillment of a debt. The *Examiner* barely registered on the senior Hearst's balance books; but to Willie, it was a stage on which to play out his peculiar genius. He brought to the *Examiner* the gigantic headlines and oversized illustrations that Pulitzer had pioneered. More outrageous still were the stories he assigned. He had a reporter jump off a ferry and time how long it took to be rescued. He had a clergyman marry a young couple in an *Examiner* balloon high above San Francisco. He dispatched a reporter to southern California to trap a grizzly bear and bring it back to the city. One staffer had himself committed to an insane asylum and then wrote an account of his terrifying month. Hearst invested huge sums of money, but his madness worked. Circulation soared.[24]

Great as his accomplishments were, Hearst could not regard himself as a successful newspaper publisher until he proved his mettle in New York. In October 1895, for the modest price of $180,000, he bought the New York *Journal*, a paper as sickly as the pre-Hearst *Examiner*. There he quickly established himself as a rival to his erstwhile mentor Pulitzer. He cut the sales price of the *Journal* to a penny, which was half the cost of the *World*, and he expanded the paper to sixteen pages. Then he promoted the *Journal* at a pitch that even New York, the noisiest of cities, had never heard. Billboards over vacant lots and sandwich men in crowded streets broadcast the virtues of the new *Journal*. Posters on delivery wagons and giant ads in rival papers alerted nonsubscribers to what they were missing. Pennies were mailed to registered voters to underscore how little the *Journal* cost. As a promotion for a feature on cheating husbands, wives received a postcard suggesting that they do themselves a favor and buy the *Journal*—signed, "A Friend."[25] These attention-grabbing ploys succeeded. By the end of the year, circulation was up from seventy-seven thousand to over one hundred thousand.[26]

One sure way that a new publication can attract attention is by hiring famous writers. About a month after taking over the *Journal*, Hearst asked Davis to cover an annual event that the reporter had described many times in his youth—the Thanksgiving Day football game between Yale and Princeton. Davis had seen a lot of the world since he covered The Game for the *Evening Sun* and *Harper's Weekly*. Football no longer seemed quite so epic. And if he wanted to write about it, he could find half a dozen more prestigious outlets without even looking. Not wanting to respond with a flat no, he said he would do it if Hearst met his price—and he named the preposterous sum of five hundred dollars. To his astonishment, the young publisher accepted his terms at once. The figure was generally said to be the highest sum ever paid to a reporter for an account of a single event.[27] Hearst, however, got his money's worth. He splashed the story, along with an enormous byline and a half-page of line drawings, over the entire front page of the Sunday paper.[28] The edition sold out.[29]

The publisher was so delighted that he pursued Davis doggedly, asking him to name his foreign assignment and his terms. The *Journal* was "the only [newspaper] now to stick to," Richard told Charles at the end of 1895. "They are trying to get all the well known men at big prices."[30] Along with money, Hearst lured his stars with bylines, a frill of magazine journalism which newspapers normally disdained, but which jibed neatly with Hearst's promotion schemes. Over the next couple of years, he hired Stephen Crane to write on vice in New York and Mark Twain to describe Queen Victoria's Diamond Jubilee in London. He raided competing papers for their best men, eventually snaring James Creelman, Murat Halstead, Robert H. Davis, and many other top journalists of the time. He preyed with special voracity on the *World*—stealing, in one stroke, the editor and entire staff of the popular *Sunday World* magazine. The most famous *World* defector was R. F. Outcault, who drew the popular comic strip "Hogan's Alley." Since the *World* owned the rights, Pulitzer simply handed "Hogan's Alley" over to another artist; but Outcault continued his strip at the *Journal*, rechristening it for its leading character, a gap-toothed urchin in a yellow gown who was known as the Yellow Kid. The appearance of the Yellow Kid in the Sunday editions of New York's two most sensational newspapers inspired the editor of the New York *Press* to coin the phrase "yellow-kid journalism." In these hurried times, it was quickly shortened to "yellow journalism."[31]

Had the tension between the United States and Great Britain over the Venezuela boundary dispute snapped into war, Davis would have covered the fighting on a private yacht for Hearst's *Journal*.[32] When the crisis cooled, he had a free agenda. He had been promising for more than a year to visit Charles in Florence. The original idea had been to go during the summer, after he finished writing *Three Gringos*. But while he was traveling in Central America, his mother, on his instructions, had opened his mail. She was so aghast at the stack of bills that she implored him not to incur any more expenses until he completed *Soldiers of Fortune*. He tried to explain that his creditors were tranquil, but she was not reassured.[33] Six months later, however, although the money was still rushing out for dinners, gifts, room furnishings, and the other drains on the affluent, money was also flowing in. In addition to *Soldiers of Fortune*, the Scribners were publishing a volume of Davis stories. (Richard was going to name this collection *The Reporter Who Made Himself King*, after the longest story in it, until his mother pointed out that he was setting himself up as a fat target for his critics. He judiciously titled the book *Cinderella* instead.)[34] With all this book money in hand, he felt that he could now go in good conscience to Europe.

Besides the long-awaited visit with his brother, Europe held another attraction for Davis. In May, in a pageant of anachronistic splendor, the Czar of All the Russias was to be crowned in Moscow. By his side would be the new czarina—who was none other than Princess Alix of Hesse-Darmstadt, the inspiration for Princess Aline. Even without a crystal-ball glimpse of the couple's sorry future, Davis knew that at a time when royalty was an imperiled species, there was a fin-de-siècle pathos about the coronation of Nicholas and Alexandra. "A hundred years from now there will be no more kings and queens," says Davis's alter-ego protagonist,

Morton Carlton, in *The Princess Aline*, "and the writers of that day will envy us, just as the writers of this day envy the men who wrote of chivalry and tournaments, and they will have to choose their heroes from bank presidents, and their heroines from lady lawyers and girl politicians and type-writers. What a stupid world it will be then!"[35] This revulsion from the spread of all that was gray, humdrum, and businesslike made Davis willfully believe in "such beautiful things as buried treasures and hidden cities and shooting men against stone walls and filibusters."[36] A nostalgia for the fading present and the recent past—a very fin-de-siècle sentiment— was at the heart of his romantic idealism. To his dismay, President Cleveland turned down his request to attend the Russian ceremony as an accredited representative of the United States. Instead, he traveled to Europe in the spring of 1896 with commissions from the *Journal* and *Harper's Magazine*, but without any assurance that he would be able to witness the historical event.[37]

After visiting with Charles in Florence—a time he described immedi- ately afterward as "the happiest in my life"[38]—Richard proceeded on a five- day train trip to Moscow. When he got there, only a fifth of the other eminent visitors had arrived, but the city was already in pandemonium. Ninety correspondents had come to Moscow. Only twelve would be permit- ted to see the coronation. The American minister, Clifton Breckinridge, had graciously added Davis's name to the list of *étrangers de distinction* ("distinguished strangers," in Davis's translation), but the decision on ad- mission rested with Count Daschoff, the minister of the court. Richard went to see him, accompanied by Augustus Trowbridge, a linguist (and later dean of graduate studies at Princeton University) who enabled the philologically retarded reporter to communicate in Moscow with people who were not considerate enough to speak English. Count Daschoff was a splendid figure in an astrakhan hat, gray uniform, white cloak, high boots, and three rows of medals. As it turned out, he spoke English perfectly. What he said, however, was not to Richard's liking. Politely shrugging off his supplicant's claims to eminence, he sent him to the bureau of correspondents, to receive, like all the others, a badge and a photo identification card. "We were frantic, and I went back to Breckenridge and wrote him a long letter explaining what had happened, and that what I wrote would 'live,' that I was advertised and had been advertised to write this story for months," Richard recounted to Charles. "I dropped *The Journal* altogether, and begged him to represent me as a literary light of the finest color." Breckin- ridge wrote Daschoff a strong letter. The Count did not respond.

Moscow was seething with journalistic intrigue, much like Auburn in the days before Kemmler's execution. Davis had given the good-natured Trowbridge a crash course in reportorial wiles, emphasizing that "we did not want a fair chance—we wanted an unfair advantage over every one else." One tactic was to win over the director of the telegraph bureau, who determined the critical sequence in which newspaper stories would be dispatched. On the pretext of wishing to learn if his handwriting was legible, Davis had the man read his cable to the *Journal*, which ended, "Recommend ample recognition of special facilities afforded by telegraph official." Grinning all over, the man said the writing was legible indeed. Later, when sending off his first scene-setter, Davis would slip the man two hundred rubles—about six months' wages—on the pretense that the *Journal* had authorized the payment. That would assure him first place on the all-important day of the coronation.[39]

But unless Davis wormed his way in, he would have nothing worth cabling. "There is not a wire we have not pulled, or a leg, either," he wrote Charles, "and we go dashing about all day in a bath-chair, with a driver in a bell hat and a blue nightgown, leaving cards and writing notes and giving drinks and having secretaries to lunch and buying flowers for wives and segar boxes for husbands, and threatening the Minister with Cleveland's name. . . ."[40] The Americans in Moscow came to view their compatriot's quest as a sporting proposition, and even those that Davis disliked were rooting and scheming for him to get in. His campaign succeeded. "They made it a personal matter," he wrote, "and when I got my little blue badge, the women kissed me and each other, and cheered, and the men came to congratulate me, and acted exactly as though they had got it themselves."[41]

Only six official representatives of the United States and two American correspondents won that precious blue badge.[42] On the morning of May 26, they were among the eight hundred people crowded into the chapel-sized Church of the Assumption, a building that was meant to hold a hundred—"much smaller than the Little Church Around the Corner in New York City," in a typical Davis comparison. No one was ever more than fifteen feet from the czar, although four immense pillars obstructed much of the view. In the compacted blur of uniforms and jewels, what stood out to Davis's eye was the image of the young czarina entering the church. Her hair was dressed in two long plaits, her gown was white and silver, and her only jewelry was a single string of pearls. "Of all the women there she was the most simply robed," he wrote, "and of all the women there she was by far the most beautiful." He was thrilled to see once again—and for the last time—that lovely melancholy face, "more like Iphigenia going to the sacrifice than the queen of the most powerful empire in the world waiting to be crowned." She possessed "the personal beauty which the queens of our day seem to have lost." After the coronation, he watched with amusement while the royal personages in attendance bowed as awkwardly as did those humbly born.[43]

Davis's account of the five-hour ceremony adorned the first two pages of the *Journal*. The drawing of the author was as large as the illustration of a half-American girl who was a maid of honor to the czarina.[44] Hearst was not one to hide his lights under a bushel. In boldface type, he had introduced

Davis's previous dispatch with the announcement that the author was "easily the ablest of the army of correspondents now gathered in Moscow."[45] Hearst's hype had contributed to the strain of the assignment. And while the publisher was lavish with blandishments, he was stingy with money. He didn't advance a penny for the expensive telegraph fees until it was so late that the banks were closed. "Imagine having to write a story and to fight to be allowed a chance to write it, and at the same time to be pressed for money for expenses and tolls so that you were worn out by that alone," Davis complained to Charles. He was also annoyed by the "impertinent cables" from Julian Ralph, the Hearst London correspondent.[46]

Unfortunately, in delivering his scrupulous account of the elaborate rituals, Davis totally missed the great news story of the coronation. It happened the next day, after the *étrangers de distinction* had exhausted themselves dancing at the coronation ball. A vast celebration for the ordinary Russian was scheduled for the morning at the Khodynka Field, a meadow just outside Moscow. Half a million people showed up, attracted in part by the promise of free liquor. Somehow, a rumor ignited: there wasn't enough beer, and only those who got to the wagons first would be able to sample it. The crowd abruptly became a mob. In the stampede, hundreds were killed, thousands injured. By the time the shocking news reached the distinguished celebrants, Richard had already left town, bound for another glorious pageant: the Banderium in Budapest, in which the nobles swore fealty to the king of Hungary (better known as the Austrian emperor) on the thousandth anniversary of the kingdom. Impressed though he was by the array of costumes at the Banderium, Davis was sorry to have missed the disaster. "It must have been more terrible than Johnstown," he reflected wistfully.[47]

The Budapest Banderium completed his list of assignments. He took most of the summer off, spending July and August in London, then catching the tail end of the season bicycling in Marion.[48] The summer of 1896 was the peak of the cycle craze in the United States.[49] Design improvements in the late 1880s had led to the introduction of the "safety bicycle," which was much easier and safer to ride than its predecessor. The safety bicycle was not limited to athletes. It wasn't even restricted to men. In Europe, English royal princesses and Parisian belles had demonstrated that cycling was an acceptable sport for ladies.[50] The taste for cycling had wafted across the Atlantic on the highest social stratum, as Americans who enjoyed "riding the wheel" on the asphalt pavements and smooth drives of the Bois de Boulogne saw no reason to relinquish the pleasure once they returned home. Touting the health benefits of cycling, prominent New York doctors encouraged them. In the spring of 1894, the leading school of bicycle instruction in New York became crowded. That summer, in Bar Harbor, Southampton, and especially Newport, the fruits of this learning became apparent.[51]

Davis didn't take up the sport until June of 1895, a full season after society's vanguard.[52] Trying to get the knack at the Benedict estate in Greenwich, he broke two of the "silent steeds" and tore up the front lawn. There had to be a better way. He paid fifty cents to a young instructor at the Madison Square Garden, and in ten minutes, he was pedaling on his own. "I came back to the room wringing with perspiration and feeling great and now I need not punch bags or take long tiresome walks for exercise," he reported.[53] At Marion that summer, he joined Maude Adams, Ethel Barrymore, Charles Dana Gibson, and his other modish friends on the wheel.[54] By the next summer, in England after the coronation, he was exhibiting American bicycling tricks at the country house of Seymour Hicks and Ellaline Terriss, his actor friends. "I was introducing the game of follow your leader at Seymour's to some men and a lot of girls," he wrote Charles, "and after we had destroyed several flower beds and a tennis net and run over a dog of Ellaline's without anyone having failed to follow the leader which was me I made to go between two pillars with flower pots on top and I did get through all right but could not turn and went on into a geranium bed and a wooden trellis, the next man rode over my back and drove his head through the trellis and the next man being a girl clasped both the flower pots in order to stop herself and brought them and the pillars and herself down on us like Samson. Tableau Vivant, there's a picture for you! My leg looked as if someone had lammed it three times with a rake and we broke two of the bicycles!"[55]

Like the Gibson Girl and the American Beauty rose, the bicycle remains imprinted in our image of the gay nineties. From an estimated 150,000 riders in the United States in 1890, the number of cyclists increased to about four million by 1896.[56] When something new takes hold so swiftly, everyone notices; and the bicycle was rhapsodized in song, depicted in illustrations, and debated in the press. In the future, Americans would take up bicycling as children. The hilarity of the cycle craze in the 1890s arose from the fact that for the first and last time, a generation had discovered the joys of bicycling only upon reaching adulthood.

Even for the rich, of course, not all was fun and games in the fall of 1896. There was a presidential election being fought; and, like a ritual reenactment of the recent economic crisis, it was waged openly along the lines of class hatred. To the horror of the creditor class (particularly New York bankers), the Democrats nominated William Jennings Bryan, who wanted to take America off the gold standard and accept silver, which was more plentiful, as another backing for currency. The resulting inflation would permit debtors to pay back their loans in devalued dollars. Uniting behind Ohio governor William McKinley, the distinguished-looking but rather dim Republican candidate, the financiers predicted that unemployment, foreclosures, and general ruin would follow a Bryan victory. The official organs of opinion endorsed McKinley almost unanimously.

Always on the side of stability and order, Davis was a McKinley stalwart. Shortly before the election, he, Gibson, and a contingent of three hundred from Harper and Brothers put on yellow sashes and four-inch gold-bug hatpins and marched with one hundred thousand other "sound money men" in a Republican parade down Fifth Avenue. Fifth Avenue, Broadway, and the cross streets between them were all draped with flags, as far north as Forty-second Street. Davis hung out two from his apartment window. His landlord, as well as flying five flags, gilded all the silver decoration on the house. Even the churches hung out flags, something that had not been done since the Civil War.

On election night, Madison Square was thronged with people awaiting the election results. Because of the frenzied interest, the newspapers set up elaborate display stations to announce the incoming returns. The ones on Broadway north of Madison Square featured cinematographs with life-sized figures in motion—McKinley walking in his garden, for example. At Hearst's splashy *Journal*, a map of the United States stretched the crosstown block from Broadway to Fifth Avenue, with the states illuminated in electric lights—the number of lights indicating each state's electoral votes, and the color (yellow or white) representing the choice of gold or silver. "It was the most remarkable sight ever witnessed in New York," Richard gushed to Charles. From eight at night until two in the morning, Davis and Gibson escorted four women through the congested streets, with four other men forming a football-style wedge in front of them. After McKinley's election by a wide margin, Davis joined in the plutocratic sigh of relief. "I did not know how unhappy it had made me until it was passed," he wrote Charles, "it was almost personal satisfaction."[57]

Of all the important newspapers in the East, only Hearst's *Journal* endorsed Bryan. The usually Democratic *World* couldn't stomach him. Even though Hearst disagreed with Bryan on free silver, which was the nub of the campaign, he was a liberal. Beyond that, he was very shrewd. He recognized that the *Journal*, by standing up alone for Bryan, could stake a claim to the workingman's loyalty. Rising readership was at the heart of the Hearst strategy. During the election campaign, as it peppered McKinley with insulting cartoons and abusive stories, the *Journal* lost advertising but gained circulation. Just after the election, celebrating the first anniversary of his move to New York, the proprietor of the *Journal* could boast that he had overtaken the *Sun*, the *Times*, the *Herald*, and the *Tribune*. Only the *World* still outsold the *Journal*.[58] And the restless Hearst did not mean to be number two for long.

As he sought to catch the jaded eye of his fickle public, Hearst alighted on the notion of sending Davis to Cuba. It was a surefire combination: the country's most flamboyant reporter assigned to the tensest, hottest story.

The Cuban rebellion—or, rather, sequence of rebellions—had been disturbing the peace for about half a century; but in February 1895, the revolution entered a new, more serious phase. Aware that something significant was happening on this island ninety miles from Key West, the *Journal* by October was reporting atrocities by Spanish troops. The paper lacked firsthand observers in Cuba, but that was a minor handicap: it simply attached Havana datelines to the propaganda manufactured in New York by the exiled Cuban supporters of the revolution.[59]

In February 1896, Spain tried to tighten her slipping hold on Cuba by appointing a new governor-general, Valeriano Weyler y Nicolau, a soldier with a reputation for ruthlessness. Weyler arrived in Havana on exactly the day that Joseph Pulitzer bowed to the one-cent *Journal* and halved the *World*'s sales price to match it. (The *Journal* ran a five-column cartoon of the big-beaked Pulitzer as a bedraggled bird climbing down from a "Two Cent Perch" to a "One Cent Stand.") Waging a superheated circulation war, the New York newspapers realized that the fighting in Cuba demanded on-the-scene coverage. Hearst sent his first star reporter, the distinguished Murat Halstead, to Havana about the same time as Weyler arrived. Also that year, the *Herald*'s George Bronson Rea and the *World*'s Sylvester Scovel each spent about ten months with the insurgents, and the *Journal*'s Grover Flint spent about four.[60]

At the end of 1896, wanting a big name to promote, Hearst offered Davis three thousand dollars plus all expenses for a month of reporting on the Cuban rebels. Davis would be accompanied by the artist Frederic Remington, famous for his depictions of the West, and by *Journal* man Charles Michelson, a veteran (for a few hours) of Weyler's jails. A fast steam yacht, the *Vamoose*, would transport the team to rebel-controlled territory.[61] Even though Davis had in Moscow resented the *Journal* for interfering where it wasn't wanted and disappearing when it was, he could not resist this temptation. He had been daydreaming about war since he was a little boy.

Fearing his mother's agitated pleas, Richard departed unannounced on December 19 for Key West. From there, the trio of *Journal* men planned to hop the *Vamoose* to Santa Clara province in Cuba. Writing from the train to Florida, Richard asked his mother to telegraph him in Key West "that you forgive me for running away." He pointed out how profitable the trip would be (in addition to the *Journal*'s largesse, he had lined up a six-hundred-dollar commission from *Harper's Magazine* and a book contract from Robert Russell). He stressed that there was no fever this time of year and that he would not be anywhere near gunfire. "I have bought at *The Journal*'s expense a fifty dollar field glass which is a new invention and the best made," he wrote. "I have marked it so that you can see a man five miles off and as soon as I see him I mean to begin to ride or run the other way—no one loves himself more than I do so you leave me to take care of myself." The only potential danger was "the problem of getting there and getting away again, and that is now removed by *The Journal's* yacht."[62]

Or so he thought until he arrived in Key West and found no sign of the *Vamoose*. When the small, mackerel-shaped speedboat did show up a day or two later, the captain was mysteriously disinclined to start out. Richard thought the crew simply wanted to spend Christmas on shore; but the day after Christmas, when the *Vamoose* was scheduled to depart, the crew went on strike, saying they feared being arrested in Havana. "I don't know what they would have done had they known they were going further," Richard wrote home.[63] On the night of December 30, with a new crew, the *Vamoose* finally sailed from Key West. The sea was so rough that Remington and Davis lay in the scuppers, clinging to the rail to keep from being swept overboard. As they hung on, they watched the Chinese cook lashing together some boxes and a door to construct a rude raft. Davis suggested that perhaps they should do the same. "Lie still," Remington responded. "You and I don't know how to do that. Let him make his raft. If we capsize, I'll throttle him and take it from him." When questioned later about this episode, Remington brushed off any moral objections to his scheme. "Why, Davis alone was worth a dozen sea-cooks," he remarked. "I don't have to talk of myself."[64] Twenty miles out, the captain declared the *Vamoose* unseaworthy and turned back. Davis was so frustrated that he lay on the deck and cried. "Guess I am done with Journal forever," he wired his mother.[65]

To make amends, the *Journal* sent Davis one thousand dollars and authorized him to buy or lease any boat on the coast.[66] It was no easy task. While Michelson cabled boatyards in an effort to locate a vessel, Davis was bored to the edge of madness. "I shall be so glad to get to Cuba that I will dance with glee," he wrote. Remington wanted to go home, but Davis— still smarting from his "retreat from Ottawa" en route to the Sino-Japanese War—would not consider it.[67]

The endless delay, however, exacerbated Davis's hostility toward Hearst. In Key West at the same time, also waiting to go to Cuba, was Ralph D. Paine, a young man two years out of Yale whose assignment was more characteristic of Hearst's so-called new journalism. Hearst had acquired a presentation sword with a gold- and diamond-encrusted ivory handle as a gift for General Máximo Gómez, the commander-in-chief of the Cuban rebels. After exhibiting the sword in the Madison Square Garden and reproducing it, almost full size, in the *Journal*, the publisher was faced with the problem of delivering it. Desperately eager to go to Cuba, Paine volunteered; so he was now in Key West, lugging around a large and expensive weapon. Also in Key West was another *Journal* minion, this one a surgeon with two large cases of medicine for Gómez. "I don't see why we don't take him a Christmas tree," Davis grumbled. "This new journalism is beyond my finding out. It is not news they want. They send Gómez a two-thousand-dollar sword and two medicine chests and a keg of rum, every correspondent takes him something and then the Journal publishes pictures of the sword and the *Vamoose* and the other fake freaks, and lets the news be written in the office or Key West."*[68]

Davis had signed on with Hearst, a man he mistrusted, only because of the promised ship.[69] Once Hearst's yacht dematerialized, reaching Cuba illicitly became difficult and hazardous. As if to underline that point, on January 2, some fifteen miles off the coast of Florida, the *Commodore*, a filibuster ship, foundered and sank. On board, along with crates of rifles, cartridges, and dynamite, was the novelist Stephen Crane, on assignment for the Bacheller Syndicate. The sinking of the *Commodore* made headlines in the New York press and, unlike most daily news, it is still remembered today, thanks to Crane's brilliant short story "The Open Boat."[70] For Davis, who had promised his mother that he would take no serious risks, the *Commodore* disaster narrowed the options. Either he could return to New York ignominiously, or he could travel to Cuba in a more conventional fashion. On January 9, he and Remington abandoned their attempts to filibuster and took the *Olivette*, the regular passenger liner to Havana. "Had we not wanted to go so much neither of us would have put up with the way we have been treated," Davis wrote; but they were "anxious to pull a sort of success out of a failure."[71]

The day after their arrival in Havana, Gen. Fitzhugh Lee, the American consul-general, took them to meet General Weyler. This was the same Weyler who was well known to *Journal* readers as "Butcher" Weyler, the man whom one *Journal* reporter later described as "the most sinister figure of the nineteenth century," a brute with a "malignant countenance" and "the eyes of an angry wolf."[72] On first meeting, Davis found him to be "a dignified and impressive soldier" who received them "with courtesy and consideration." He granted them permission to travel all over the island or to accompany him on his next campaign.[73] Since Weyler was not planning to set off anytime soon, Davis accepted an invitation from the proprietor of a sugar plantation in Cienfuegos, southeast of Havana in Santa Clara province. He was eager to see the countryside. "They have segars to burn in this city and good food but it is not an interesting city," he decided after a day of reconnoitering Havana.[74]

The *Journal* team (which included an interpreter) got as far as Matanzas, the province between Havana and Santa Clara, when Remington decided that he had had enough. The month which they had promised to Hearst was now up. According to one of the most famous stories in Ameri-

---

*Paine never did get the sword to Gómez. He handed it on to Michelson, who also failed to complete the delivery. After the war, Gómez finally received it. According to Paine, he exclaimed, "Those imbeciles in New York, with two thousand dollars wasted! It would have bought shoes for my barefooted men, shirts for their naked backs, cartridges for their useless rifles. Take it away!"

can journalism, the disgruntled Remington cabled his boss: "Everything is quiet. There is no trouble here. There will be no war. I wish to return. Remington." He received this reply: "Please remain. You furnish the pictures, and I'll furnish the war. W. R. Hearst." The sole source for this splendid anecdote is *Journal* correspondent James Creelman.[75] The Hearst files have never been opened to researchers, and no one has demonstrated that this telegram was sent. Hearst himself, writing a decade later, denounced as "clotted nonsense" the notion that "there was [such] a letter in existence . . . [and] that Mr. Hearst was chiefly responsible for the Spanish war."[76] But the wording of his denial isn't airtight. His role in fomenting the war is indeed debatable; and by then, of course, the communication might have been destroyed, leaving it no longer "in existence." Because it so colorfully expresses Hearst's personality and his "journalism that acts," the telegram—spurious or genuine—lives on.

Remington left Cuba for New York on January 15. Davis was as relieved "as though I had won five thousand dollars."[77] A brilliant artist who had effectively illustrated Davis's book on the West, Remington was also a trying companion. Big, fat, and vehement, with a love of the military, he was conspicuously macho even in an age not known for male sensitivity: at Yale, he had dipped his football uniform into a pool of slaughterhouse blood.[78] He was also a crude and strident racist. Anticipating a war between the United States and Spain over Cuba, he wrote, "It does seem tough that so many Americans have had to be and have still got to be killed to free a lot of d—— niggers who are better off under the yoke."[79] But what annoyed Davis most about traveling with Remington was the man's childishness. "He always wanted to talk it over and that had to be done in the nearest or the most distant café, and it always took him fifteen minutes before he got his cocktails to suit him," Davis complained. "He always did as I wanted in the end but I am not used to giving reasons or to travelling in pairs."[80] Proceeding through Cuba was thorny enough without having to unsnag Remington. "He is very excitable and a firebrand and makes the worst of everything," Davis noted. "I would rather manage an Italian Opera Company than him."[81]

All foreign travelers in Cuba were required to use public transportation, either steamers or trains. With Weyler's pass, Davis toured the western provinces in an armored train, accompanied by a Swiss-born interpreter who referred to Davis as "my lord" and to himself as a valet. It was pleasant enough. "Only when you remember the way I was invited to see Cuba and expected to see it, and now the way I am seeing it from car windows with a *valet*," he mused. "What would the new school of yellow kid journalists say if they knew that."[82]

It was the most beautiful country he had ever seen; but everywhere he looked, smoke columns rose higher than palm trees above the burning cane fields.[83] Having accepted many kindnesses from his Spanish hosts, gentlemanly Davis hesitated to condemn them and wished to "be fair to both sides."[84] In his published account, he scrupulously pointed out that both the Spanish and the rebels routinely burned crops; however, he assigned ultimate responsibility for the "wholesale devastation" to the Spanish.[85] Battling a native insurgency, Weyler in Cuba initiated many of the techniques that the Americans would employ—with similar results—seventy-five years later in Vietnam. Able to control the cities but not the countryside, the Spanish were burning homes and fields to force the peasants into what were called reconcentration camps. Most of the able men promptly fled to join the rebel army, leaving behind the women and children, many of whom succumbed to fever in the squalid camps. Conditions there were worse than in the Johnstown Flood, Davis thought.[86] His first *Journal* dispatch was a description—rare for the time—of the suffering of the *reconcentrados*.[87] But the plight of a multitude is never as gripping as an individual's ordeal. In the town of Trinidad, on the south coast just east of Cienfuegos, Davis chanced on a far better story.

"The Death of Rodriguez," first published in the *Journal*,[88] is a sentimental account of a brave soldier's death, told in an understated, reportorial language: the dry pathos anticipates the work of Hemingway. Since Davis spoke no Spanish, his narrative unrolls without dialogue like a silent movie. Adolfo Rodríguez was a twenty-year-old farm boy in Santa Clara province who had been captured with a band of insurgents and sentenced to death by a military court. For maximum impact, the thirty condemned men were executed individually on successive mornings. On the day that Rodríguez was to die, Davis followed the procession of three hundred soldiers on a march half a mile out of town. He was relieved to see Rodríguez walking erect with a quick step. As the doomed man came closer, Davis noticed that a cigarette dangled between his lips, "not arrogantly nor with bravado, but with the nonchalance of a man who meets his punishment fearlessly, and who will let his enemies see that they can kill but cannot frighten him."

Placed in the center of the square, Rodríguez let the cigarette drop (his hands were bound) and kissed the crucifix that a priest held. The firing squad readied itself. And then, just before the shots, the captain realized that as his men were positioned, they could shoot each other. So instead of a bullet, Rodríguez felt the captain's hand on his shoulder, telling him that he had to move. Throughout, the youth retained his heroic self-control, reminding Davis of the statue of Nathan Hale in City Hall Park. Then the soldiers fired. "At the report," Davis wrote, "the Cuban's head snapped back almost between his shoulders, but his body fell slowly, as though some one had pushed him gently forward from behind and he had stumbled. He sank on his side in the wet grass without a struggle or sound, and did not move again." The soldiers marched away, leaving the body where it lay. As Davis walked by, he saw that "the cigarette still burned, a tiny ring of living fire, at the place where the figure had first stood."[89] Through innumerable reincarnations, in novels and in movies, that final cigarette of the condemned man has burned on.

Davis still hoped to join the insurgents, but twice his Cuban escorts backed out, fearing that they were being watched by Spanish spies.[90] As a last try, Davis arranged to meet two seasoned reporters with a reputation for recklessness—the *Herald*'s George Bronson Rea and the *World*'s Sylvester Scovel—in a small seaside town, from which a guide would escort them to the rebels. When Scovel arrived at the rendezvous, however, he was waving a copy of the January 17 *Journal*. "Your paper has queered you, Davis," he shouted. "I never knew a case of a paper's treating a correspondent worse."[91] In a full-page story, the *Journal* informed its readers that Davis and Remington had "reached the insurgent army on the island of Cuba."[92] It was an outrageous lie, and a deliberate one, since Hearst knew that Remington was on his way home. Rea and Scovel—disguised with dyed hair—apologetically told Davis he would have to drop out. They could not assume the risk of added scrutiny on what was already a hazardous mission.[93] "If I had been an escaping cashier of the *Journal*'s they could not have queered me better," Richard raged to Charles.[94]

Using Weyler's pass to take him places that Weyler never intended, Davis managed to view the Spanish fortification lines.[95] Nonetheless, he concluded that the whole Cuba trip was "a failure from the beginning," and if he was lucky, the authorities would expel him once they read the *Journal* of January 17. "I haven't heard a shot fired or seen an insurgent," he wrote his mother. "I am just 'not in it' and I am torn between coming home and making your dear heart stop worrying and getting one story to justify me being here and that damn silly page of the Journals." He had no fondness for his employer. "All Hearst wants is my name and I will give him that only it will be signed to a different sort of a story from those they have been printing," he remarked. "I am not writing for the *Journal*, the *Journal* is printing what I write."[96] He thought he was too big a man for Hearst to manipulate. He was self-deluded.

He sailed home from Havana on the *Olivette*, the American passenger ship that had brought him to Cuba. Living up to the Davis tradition, he was at the dinner table of the *Olivette* when he scored the most memorable scoop of his trip. One of his shipboard companions was Clemencia Arango, a young Cuban woman whose brother commanded the insurgent forces near Havana. She was a cultivated, upper-class woman—as Davis described her, she "spoke three languages and dressed as you see girls dress on Fifth avenue after church on Sunday." Over dinner, she told Davis the story of her recent ordeal, a tale of woe that would soon shock millions of Americans. In these harder times, when the shrine of womanly purity has grown weedy through neglect, and the roster of outrages against innocents unrolls to ever greater lengths, we may have to struggle a bit to feel the fervor that Señorita Arango's tale aroused.

Suspecting, quite rightly, that she was aiding the insurgents, the Spanish authorities expelled Clemencia Arango, along with her sister, young brother, and two other women. On the day of departure, when the women arrived at the dock, Spanish detectives directed them into an inspection-house, where they were stripped and searched. A few hours later they boarded the *Olivette*. As they strolled on the deck, the police arrived again and ordered them to be taken into a cabin, where they were strip-searched once more. The group was then permitted to depart for the United States.*[97] These were the basic facts that Davis reported, in an overwrought story that he filed in Tampa. Outraged that respectable young women could be treated in this way on an American vessel, he ended with an inflammatory appeal to President Cleveland to punish Spain for her insults to the United States flag.

This dispatch set all bells ringing when it arrived at the *Journal* office in New York. Of the many Spanish atrocity stories that he printed, none pleased Hearst so much as the reports of outrages against women. He had already enlightened his fellow Americans on the arrest of nuns, the trussing of women captives, and the suffering of the female *reconcentrados*.[98] But these horrors paled next to the indignities endured by Señorita Arango. He splashed the story over the first two pages of his newspaper. "Does Our Flag Shield Women?" the headline asked rhetorically. On the second page, under the caption "Spaniards Search Women on American Steamers," he ran a Remington illustration of three Spaniards in straw hats surrounding a naked young woman. He intended the article to cause a sensation, and it did.

The tone of the uproar changed, however, when the rival *World* took the initiative to interview Miss Arango in Tampa. She revealed that no lecherous Spaniards ogled her naked body; she was searched by a matron.[99] The *World* jumped gleefully on this chance to discomfit Hearst. "Association for a few short weeks with the Journal has led Mr. Davis to write over his signature an atrociously exaggerated story of an alleged Spanish outrage upon a woman . . . ," the *Evening World* editorialized. "Mr. Davis and Mr. Remington should be well quarantined before they are allowed to mingle again with reputable newspaper men."[100] Another New York paper, the *Commercial Advertiser*, which favored a hands-off policy on Cuba, condemned the *Olivette* story as the "most monstrous falsehood that has yet appeared even in the new journalism."[101]

It was hard to embarrass Hearst, but Davis was mortified—and furious. He disclaimed all responsibility, blaming Remington and Hearst for the misleading illustration. "I never wrote that she was searched by men," he

---

*The police were looking for messages to the leaders of the Cuban Junta in Key West and Tampa. They found none, although Miss Arango later confirmed that she had indeed smuggled papers out.

declared to the *World*. Indeed, he had not. He wrote, however, that the Spanish officers "had them undressed and searched," and later "searched them thoroughly, even to the length of taking off their shoes and stockings," and finally, "demanded that a cabin should be furnished them to which the girls might be taken, and [there] they were again undressed and searched." Amid all this detail, he never bothered to mention that the actual inspections were performed by a woman. Perhaps he was vague intentionally; if Miss Arango didn't volunteer the gender of her searchers, the chivalrous Davis probably would have thought it improper to inquire. At the very least, however, his report was misleading. Remington's eye-opening sketch plausibly illustrated Davis's text.[102]

After his ill-starred trip to Cuba, Davis made up his mind about two things. First, he would never again work for Hearst.[103] Second, he now believed that a war between the United States and Spain over Cuba was inevitable; and, since the suffering in Cuba would continue until it occurred, the war should start as soon as possible. While he was in Cuba, Davis had waffled back and forth on the question of American intervention.[104] It's curious how bellicose he became as soon as he returned to the United States. Writing in Florida, fresh off the *Olivette*, he concluded his article on the strip-search of Señorita Arango with a diatribe as scorching as the standard fare served up in Hearst's kitchen. The United States could justify intervention, he contended, by virtue of "the thousand insults, open or covered, that the Spanish in Cuba are putting upon our citizens and on our flag." By acting forcefully, the lame-duck President Cleveland would end the "state of anarchy" and save "thousands of innocent lives."[105]

Davis's provocative tone can't be attributed to Hearst's editors. After his break with Hearst, Davis revised his articles for a small volume, *Cuba in War Time*, that was even more bellicose. "We have tolerated what no European power would have tolerated," he wrote, "we have been patient with men who have put back the hand of time for centuries, who lie to our representatives daily, who butcher innocent people, who gamble with the lives of their own soldiers. . . ." As in every war he covered, he sided emotionally with the underdogs."[106]

On his return from Cuba, Davis resumed his reportage of bloodless spectacles: the inauguration of President William McKinley and the Diamond Jubilee celebration of Queen Victoria. Reckoning that these reports would form a book with his articles on the Russian coronation and Hungarian Banderium (and thereby achieve a financial second life), he approached the Scribners and the Harpers. He preferred the Scribners; but the Harpers replied sooner, and he accepted their bid.[107]

McKinley's inauguration was a low-watt spectacle for a man who had seen the coronation of the Czar of All the Russias. The ceremony lasted six minutes. "The yellow kid papers are comparing it to the coronation and calling it extravagant display because it cost $75,000," Richard wrote to Charles. "The coronation cost forty millions and the harness alone cost more than the entire inauguration."[108] In his published account, Davis downplayed these invidious comparisons and depicted the inauguration as "a sort of family gathering." With his highly developed filial sense, he focused with pleasure on McKinley's white-haired, gold-spectacled mother.[109] He turned his spotlight away from McKinley's invalid wife, of whom he wrote privately: "Mrs. McKinley has epileptic fits and can only walk with the help of someone. She is also weak minded like a little girl of ten but her sufferings have given her a really beautiful face. She dressed the part exquisitely in blue velvet but it was a pathetic spectacle."[110] All of that was suppressed in his published account, on the principle that he was "not saying anything to hurt anybody's feeling but praising wherever I can."[111]

This gentlemanly code, which seems so old-fashioned, ruled American journalism until quite recently. The press's willful blindness to Franklin Roosevelt's wheelchair, for instance, is more difficult to justify than the chivalry shown Mrs. McKinley. Even in this genteel context, however, Davis stood out. Not trusting his own prodigious sense of discretion, he sent his manuscript on the inauguration to his mother with instructions to "cut out things you think are in bad taste as it is always best to leave out than to make trouble and if there is any doubt about a thing the blue pencil should have the benefit of the doubt."[112]

Davis wrote his *Harper's* piece about the inauguration while sailing to England for the Jubilee. On arrival in London, he was hailed by an interviewer from the *Daily Mail* as "a fine type of the Anglo-Saxon as they make him in the States" and the "most brilliant of the younger American writers."[113] The compliment was particularly welcome, since in London at the time was another candidate for the laurels of "most brilliant of the younger American writers": Stephen Crane. The paths of Crane and Davis, which had almost intersected a few months before in Florida, would cross many times over the next few years. In some ways they were rivals; although, to Davis's credit, he never doubted Crane's literary superiority. On reading *The Red Badge of Courage*, which was published in late 1895 to ever-increasing acclaim, Richard wrote to Charles, "Stephen Crane seems to me to have written the last word as far as battles or fighting is concerned."[114] Meeting him now in London, Davis was favorably impressed. "He is very modest sturdy and shy," he reported. "Quiet [*sic*] unlike what I imagined."[115]

Considering how fundamentally different they were, Crane and Davis had a surprising amount in common. Crane had attended Lafayette College in Easton, Pennsylvania, which was (and still is) the archrival of nearby Lehigh. At Lafayette, he flamboyantly resisted hazing.[116] Like Davis, he never graduated from college. Also like Davis, he was an enthusiastic college athlete. "I am rather more proud of my baseball ability than of some other

things," he said, after *The Red Badge of Courage* had made him famous.[117]
Davis once said much the same thing about having scored Lehigh's first
touchdown. Both writers moved to New York, where, working as newspapermen, they discovered the raw material to use in their fiction. And at this
point, the disparities become too numerous to keep the images superim-
posed. Davis and Crane stand at the end of the century like figures on a
weather vane, pointing in opposite directions. With his ever-ready blue
pencil, repressing the unclean and the unpleasant, Davis looked back to the
popular literature of the Victorians. What Davis avoided, Crane mined. His
realistic fiction prepared the ground for Norris, Dreiser, Dos Passos. The
realism of Crane was the literature of the future. Davis's idealism was
doomed.[118]

But if in retrospect they seem to be literary opponents, only Crane was
astute enough to perceive the battle lines. Before they ever met, he declared
that Davis had "the intelligence of the average saw-log." He despised the
readers who idolized Davis: those who "hang upon the out-skirts of good
society and chant 143 masses per day to the social gods and think because
they have money they are well-bred."[119] On his side, Davis saw in Crane
simply a writer of genius. In London, with his personal charm and no
doubt a large dose of flattery, he overcame Crane's prejudices. He hosted a
luncheon in Crane's honor at the Savoy, attended by Anthony Hope
Hawkins (author of *The Prisoner of Zenda*), Harold Frederic (author of *The
Damnation of Theron Ware* and an early supporter of Crane), and James
Barrie (author of *The Little Minister* and *Peter Pan*).[120] The next day Davis
and Crane crossed the English Channel together, bound for Paris. With
Crane was a woman whom Davis described as "a bi-roxide blonde who
seemed to be attending to his luggage for him and whom I did not meet."[121]
He probably ducked an introduction. Everything about the woman was
questionable, even her name. She was born Cora Howorth; her second and
current marriage identified her as Cora Stewart; but in Jacksonville, Florida,
where she worked as a nightclub hostess, she was known as Cora Taylor.
It was in Jacksonville that Crane had met her that winter, as he tried
without success to get to Cuba. She followed him to Europe. Today she is
remembered by the name of Cora Crane.[122]

Crane was bound for Greece, to cover the Greco-Turkish War for
Hearst's *Journal*. This absurd little war, which at another time would have
occasioned yawns, began when Athens sent a regiment to Crete to support
a rebellion against Turkish rule. Foreign squadrons quickly moved to block-
ade Crete and force the matter into arbitration. Not conceding so quickly,
the Greeks then sent troops by land to the Macedonian border, and the
Turks mobilized on the other side. Except for the Russo-Turkish War of
1877–78, there hadn't been a European war since the great Franco-Prussian
conflict of 1870–71. Hungry for any war, no matter how trivial, the ranks
of would-be war correspondents stirred and started east.[123] During his stay

in London, Davis had been invited to report from the northeastern Greek frontier for the London *Times*. Although terribly flattered to be courted by what was then the world's greatest newspaper, he declined to go unless war actually broke out. He intended, after a stopover in Paris, to pay Charles a long visit in Florence, before returning to London for the Jubilee.[124]

He spent more than two weeks with Charles, whose political appointment was ending with the lame-duck Cleveland administration. They toured Tuscany and traveled as far as Monte Carlo, where in two days at the tables Richard won enough to pay all their expenses, with six hundred francs to spare.[125] But on April 17, their perfect holiday was truncated by Turkey's declaration of war on Greece. Armies were now on the move, and correspondents (including Stephen Crane) were moving after them. Lusting after his first battle, and knowing that a description of a war would give a little spine to his book, Richard decided to sacrifice his preparation time in London so he could shoehorn in a battle tour of Greece.[126] With little idea of where he was going, he rushed off in the general direction of the war. "I have no credentials from the Greeks or Turks," he told Charles, "but I guess my winning ways and the Times letters will do."[127]

Leaving before he had the chance to communicate with the *Times*, he received a cable from his editor at his first stop on the Greek island of Corfu. The *Times* wanted him to join the Turks at Ioannina (which was then part of Turkey) and wait for the Greek column to attack. Davis balked. His excuse was that he lacked Turkish credentials and a Turkish interpreter; however, he possessed no Greek credentials, either. What he really lacked was sympathy for the Turkish side. He chose instead to try to reach the Greeks at Arta and accompany them on the march north to Ioannina. "No correspondents are in this part of the land so it is the more sporting proposition of the two," he reasoned. "If there is no fight I get left but if there is I have it all my own way."[128]

For a week he rode along the northern frontier, sometimes on the Greek side, other times on the Turkish, looking for trouble which he could not find. He saw only one bombardment. Still, he was having a wonderful time. This, his first war, would prove to be his best. In Cuba, where he was regarded by the authorities as a dangerous nuisance, he had received a preview of the life of a twentieth-century war correspondent: restricted, mistrusted, manacled in red tape. The joy of the Greco-Turkish conflict was that it was a nineteenth-century war. "I am treated like an ambassador and sleep in the mayor's house in each village and seldom move without an escort of soldiers and am [given] my transport and food free and welcome," he reported. Although he had no credentials, no one asked to see any. He "marched with the men and picniced with the generals." In Greece, the correspondent was "the woman in the camp."[129]

As for the fighting, he thought "this opera bouffe warfare [was] like a duel between two gentlemen in the Bois," especially after the Cuban insurrection, which he compared to "a slave-holder beating a slave's head in with a whip."[130] The fighting in Greece was not only chivalrous, it was rare. Davis followed the Greeks into Turkey, heading for the battle of the Five Wells; but on the way, they met the Greek forces in retreat, and backtracked with them across the Gulf of Arta to Greek soil.[131] Although disappointed, Davis couldn't be unhappy. Riding and walking all day long, and living on brown bread and cheese and goat's milk, he was becoming "tanned and almost thin."[132] The landscape through which he traveled was a fairy-tale confection of old stone houses and fortresses, mountains covered with grazing sheep and goats, and fields of blue flax and buttercups. The people, who dressed like "grand opera brigands," were too kind. After one uneventful march, the commander "seriously apologized for not bombarding while I was there and I said not to mention it."[133]

Yet he was always conscious of the other correspondents crisscrossing Greece. Crane particularly worried him. They had left England together on April 1, Davis bound for Florence, Crane for Greece. Meeting up with him again in Athens at the end of April, Davis was delighted to learn that Crane had been in Crete. "So that he is not a day ahead of me as we start from here together," Richard wrote his mother from Athens. "He is writing to the *Journal* poor devil. He has not seen as much as I have either for several reasons but then when a man can describe battles as well as he does without seeing them why should he care."[134] Davis blamed Cora for distracting Crane from the news. Commissioned like Crane by the *Journal*, she accompanied Crane and Davis on the journey to the northeastern front in Thessaly, along with young John Bass, who was the head of the *Journal* war team.[135]

The Greeks, led by their hapless Prince Constantine, had just scurried in undignified retreat to the east. Heading in that direction, Davis hoped he would finally see some shooting.[136] He and his comrades of the press stopped over at the village of Velestino, which the Turks had unsuccessfully attacked three times, most recently a week before. The Greek troops were now entrenched to defend a village that the villagers had abandoned. No one knew if the Turks would return. Betting that they wouldn't, the other reporters on May 3 left Velestino, Crane in the company of Cora. "She is a commonplace dull woman old enough to have been his mother [in fact, she was only five or six years older than Crane] and with dyed yellow hair," Davis wrote home. "He seems a genius with no responsibilities of any sort to anyone and I and Bass got shut of them at Velestinos after having had to travel with them for four days."[137] Of all the correspondents, only Bass and Davis remained behind in Velestino. In what had been the mayor's residence, Bass prepared dinner and Davis made the beds. On the morning of May 4, they were awakened by the sound of cannon fire. They shook hands in jubilation. They were going to see a battle.[138]

Rushing outside, they found that the noise they heard was the entire Greek battery (six mountain guns) on an isolated hill between the town and the open plain stretching to the north and west. Across this plain advanced the Turks, who at this distance appeared as a green blotch topped by occasional puffs of smoke. In four creases of green hills to the south and east of the village, Greek soldiers were dug into trenches. Heading for the trenches, Davis and Bass met one of the few villagers who hadn't fled: a redheaded, freckled peasant boy in dirty white petticoats, aquiver with excitement at the impending battle. Talking and laughing, he guided the reporters along the footpaths up the hills with the solicitousness of a squire showing visitors his estate. He mimicked the rustling sound of the Turkish bullets flying overhead; and whenever a shell struck near him, he would run and retrieve the pieces and place them at the feet of an officer. Asked where his parents were, he said with amusement that they had run away, but he had stayed behind to see what a Turkish army looked like. In the gray pages of war journalism, full of troop movements and battlefield topography, the little redheaded boy stands out like an exclamation point. He provides the human interest that makes Davis's report from Velestino a minor classic of battle reportage.[139]

The men in the front trench, which was the only one with a view of the Turks, welcomed Bass and Davis, spreading blankets to protect the American visitors from the damp earth. The day was brilliantly sunny and hot, with occasional drenching showers. The Turkish army as it drew closer became identifiably blue (the color of the Turkish uniform), but not recognizably human. The Turkish shells and bullets landed among the trenches with increasing accuracy, killing and maiming. Instead of the "shrieking shrapnel" that was a cliché of war reporting, the shells made a sound that reminded Davis of the whistle of telegraph wires when someone throws a stone at the pole. Coming closer, the shells whooshed like two trains passing each other rapidly in opposite directions. As for the bullets, they sounded like hummingbirds on a summer's day, or rustling silk—or, most of all, like the two wheels of silk that were spun backstage to imitate the sound of the wind in a theater. The Greeks shot back at the Turks, but they lacked visible targets; until, at dusk, lines of Turkish soldiers in fezzes suddenly emerged from a long gully below. "On the moment, the smiling landscape changed like a scene in a theatre," Davis wrote, "and hundreds of men rose from what had apparently been deserted hilltops and stood outlined in silhouette against the sunset. . . ."[140] Davis and Bass lay face down in the trench as shells and bullets rained from above. One shell struck three feet from Davis, knocking him over and filling his nose and mouth with pebbles. A man standing up next to him to clean his rifle was fatally shot in the chest. "At times the firing was so fierce," Davis wrote his family, "that if you had raised your arm above your head, the hand would have been instantly torn off."[141] After only five minutes, the volleys slackened and the bullets rustled fitfully by. The Turks were withdrawing for the night.

The next day, the Turks returned in force. So, unfortunately, did the other war correspondents, who made the twelve-mile journey from the seaport of Volo. Among them was Stephen Crane.[142] "Crane came up for fifteen minutes and wrote a 1300 word story on that," Davis wrote home. "He was never near the front but don't say I said so. He would have come but he had a toothache which kept him in bed. It was hard luck but on the other hand if he had not had that woman with him he would have been with us and not at Volo and could have seen the show toothache or no toothache."[143] (In addition to toothache, the sickly Crane was suffering from dysentery.[144]) Later, after the fighting was over, Bass wanted to write a story for the *Journal* on Davis's conduct under fire, but Davis vetoed the idea. "In the first place they would probably have said I was there for the Journal and made silly pictures," Davis explained to his family, "and then as I pointed out to him why should he describe how the Times correspondent acted and say nothing about Crane who was there for the Journal. But there was nothing to be said about what Crane did except that he ought to be ashamed of himself."[145]

The fighting that Crane was too sick to see went on most of the day. The Greeks were holding their own; but over at Pharsala, their comrades had retreated before the Turks. Without Pharsala, Velestino lacked strategic significance. And so, the Greeks received word to abandon the position, leaving Velestino to be burned by the Turks. The foreign reporters accompanied the Greek army on its retreat to Volo, where they could catch a steamer to Athens. At Volo, suffering a severe attack of sciatica brought on in the trenches, Davis boarded a hospital ship for Athens with 116 wounded men. On his right was a soldier whose ankles had been shot off, and the one on the left had a bullet in his side. "They groaned all night and so did I," Davis wrote. "Then when the sun rose they sang, which was worse."

In Athens, he spent two days in bed (visited by the minister, the consul, and all the officers of the U.S. warship *San Francisco*, from the admiral on down) before he could go on to Florence. Despite this painful coda, he was exultant about his Greek adventure. "It was the most satisfactory trip all round I ever had," he said. "I have been twenty years trying to be in a battle and it will be 20 more before I will want to be in another."[146] Moberly Bell, the manager of the *Times*, told him that his dispatch from Velestino was the best writing done in the war.[147] Substantiating that flattery, he asked Davis, an American, to describe the ceremonies and parade for Queen Victoria's Jubilee Day—an offer that Davis had to decline because of his commitment to the Harpers.[148]

Richard spent three final days in Florence with Charles, who was about to return to New York, before traveling to Jubilee-fevered London (making an overnight stop in the relative calm of Paris to dine at Laurent with Louise and Cecil Clark).[149] London was overrun with a million and a half visitors, and every building on the parade route was laced with scaffolding for spectators' stands. Richard observed that instead of soft coal, London smelled of green pine. One advantage to his late arrival was that the inflated market for observation stations had collapsed. For $25, Davis bought a seat facing St. Paul's Cathedral that had been advertised for $125. From there, he had a full view of the uniforms, the processions, and the spectacle.[150]

After the celebrations subsided and the ugly pine boards came off the historic façades, Richard stayed in London for most of the summer. There he wrote his *Harper's* articles on the Greek war and the Jubilee.[151] That summer ended the year that he commemorated in *A Year from a Reporter's Note-book*, a collection of his journalism that began with the coronation of the czar and included the Budapest Banderium, the Washington inauguration, the insurrection in Cuba, the war in Greece, and finally, the Queen's Jubilee. It had been a very busy year. Unavoidably, the pieces on strife are more interesting than the ones on ceremonies and parades. Davis had a talent for descriptive writing, but most readers will not share his fascination with court costumes and military uniforms. He attempted to provide themes for the articles by relating the flavor of the celebration to a national trait: the Jubilee went smoothly thanks to the English conservatism and respect for order; at the homespun inauguration, the American people were the principal actors—that sort of thing. Although the reported details of these festivities are valuable to historians, it is the war pieces—especially, "The Death of Rodriguez" and "With the Greek Soldiers"—that deserve to be remembered. They belong in any collection of American war reportage.

When Davis returned to the United States in late summer, he visited Marion and again saw Cecil Clark. Because their letters have not survived, what she thought of her dashing and increasingly serious suitor is unknown. But on his side, Davis let his imagination run free, attaching to Cecil all the most desirable qualities of the modern American girl. Gradually he was making his intentions apparent. When *A Year from a Reporter's Note-book* was published on December 7, 1897, it was dedicated to Cecil Clark.[152]

That fall in New York, Davis directed his energies toward a long-held ambition—the writing of a full-length play. The American commercial theater was booming; like many other writers of his time, Davis dreamed of inventing a perpetual-money machine like William Gillette's *Secret Service*, a play that would generate rich author's royalties into the distant future. As a writer of popular fiction, he was courted by theater producers, many of whom were his friends. In the 1890s, the great producers, like Charles Frohman and David Belasco, had their own acting companies. Other companies, like those of Nat Goodwin and Eddie Sothern, were managed by their star. All were looking for fresh material.

As early as the fall of 1892, Eddie Sothern starred in a one-act play that he and Davis crafted out of "My Disreputable Friend, Mr. Raegen." Although Sothern soon dropped it as too gloomy and too strenuous, the play was promising enough to lead Frohman, Goodwin, and Sothern each to ask Davis to write a full-length play.[153] As a warm-up, Davis in 1893 dramatized "The Other Woman" as a one-acter, which was poorly received.[154] Early in 1894, he was approached by another friend, John Drew, who asked for a Van Bibber play—an offer which Davis seriously considered.[155] At the time, though, he was in bed in Philadelphia, grappling with nervous depression and *The Princess Aline*. Over the next two months, he worked on a play, but nothing came of it.[156]

Not until the end of 1894, when Robert Hilliard successfully adapted the Van Bibber story "Her First Appearance" into a three-character play, did Davis finally enjoy the real reward of a life in the theater—royalties. Hilliard paid him twenty-five dollars a week to produce the play in Cleveland, and opened in New York to modest acclaim the following fall. "It has convinced me that I must write a play," Richard wrote to Charles. "Sitting in New York and having others go round working is the way to live."[157] With Eddie Sothern's help, he wrote a one-act play based on his story "The Boy Orator of Zepata City," and Sothern produced it once for a benefit in mid-November 1895.[158] But if he wanted to be a rich playwright, Davis would have to quit converting short stories into one-act plays and start transforming novels into full-length dramas. Late in 1896, when Sothern again urged him to create a play, Davis suggested an adaptation of *Soldiers of Fortune*.[159] By early December, he had completed a first act.[160] Happening to see Charles Frohman, the most important producer in New York, at Delmonico's, he mentioned his work. Frohman asked to read it. Davis demurred, saying he would like to wait until he had completed two acts. When Frohman left, another man at the table exclaimed, "I've known Frohman ten years and I never heard him ask a man to send him a play yet. You're taking big chances in refusing."[161]

Before Davis had time to write a second act, fate—in the guise of William Randolph Hearst—intervened. The *Journal* trip to Cuba ate up half of December and most of January. Then in March Richard was on the road again. Not until late summer of 1897, with his hectic year of wars and ceremonies at an end, did he settle back into his domestic routine and resume work on the play. On October 2, he read it to Frohman. Although he bravely declared that "it does not matter at all to me whether Frohman likes it or not," because what was important was "that I have learned in writing it how to write a really good play when I will have no novel to hamper me," he was shaken when Frohman declared disapprovingly that the play "talked too much and did not do enough."[162] Hoping for a more detailed critique, Davis gave the producer the manuscript, which he had just dictated to a stenographer (or typewriter, as they were called). "Go to work on it, that is all I can say," Frohman told him after a second look.[163] Bewildered by this direction, "which might mean anything," Davis attempted to cut free of the novel and plot out the play independently. He worked on it all fall, without success, spending most of the time at his parents' in the uncongenial city of Philadelphia. Discouraged and disappointed, he decided that he had better chuck it. On December 1, he sailed for London.[164]

In the cold, smoky fog of London, far from the mocking lights of Broadway, his spirits lifted. He completed a novella, *The King's Jackal*, about the scheming and double-dealing of a toppled monarch out to recapture his Balkan domain.[165] The inspiration was not his recent trip to northern Greece, but most likely (as contemporary critics observed) Alphonse Daudet's *Kings in Exile*.[166] *The King's Jackal* has much in common with Davis's previous light entertainment *The Princess Aline*; but where in *Aline* Davis cleverly kept the imaginary European kingdom in the background, in the *Jackal* he planted both feet in a fantasy world, and the product is as waxen as an artificial rose. Davis's best stories are romances based on life, not on other romances. He once urged his brother to "keep your mind in the way of constantly seeing 'stories' in everything."[167] This had been his guiding philosophy since early childhood.

How successful he was at alchemizing life into romance was demonstrated once again that winter in London, when he and Ethel Barrymore departed from Christmas dinner at the home of vaudeville star Cissie Loftus in a hansom cab around eleven. A light fog was descending. "I said that all sorts of things ought to happen in a fog but that no one ever did have adventures nowadays," Richard recounted to his family afterward. "At that we rode straight into a bank of fog that makes those on the Fishing Banks look like Spring sunshine. You could not see the houses, nor the street, nor the horse, not even his tail. All you could see were gas jets, but not the iron that supported them. The cabman discovered the fact that he was lost and turned around in circles and the horse slipped on the asphalt which was thick with frost, and then we backed into lamp-posts and curbs until Ethel got so scared she bit her under lip until it bled. You could not tell if you were going into a house or over a precipice or into a sea."

When the horse backed up a flight of steps and fell down, bumping the cabman against a front door, Richard decided it was time that he and Ethel got out. Groping through a yellow mist, they saw a square block of light suddenly open in midair, and four terrified women standing in the doorway of a house. The women invited the intruders to enter. Because the room was hot, Davis removed his fur coat, forgetting that he was wearing all his medals and decorations for the holiday. He remarked to Ethel that it would be folly to try to drive her home and they should return to the "Duchess's" for the night. "Yes, Duke," Ethel replied calmly. At this moment, Davis "became conscious of the fact that the eyes of the four women were riveted on my fur coat and decorations." The women ran off and returned a moment later with all the children, servants, and men of the house, who stared wide-eyed at their distinguished visitors. They dispatched

Richard and Ethel with minutely detailed directions as to where "Your Grace" and "Your Ladyship" should turn. "For years no doubt on Christmas Day the story will be told in that house, wherever it may be in the millions of other houses of London, how a beautiful Countess and a wicked Duke were pitched into their front door out of a hansom cab, and having partaken of their Christmas supper, disappeared again into a sea of fog," Richard concluded.[168] Since the house's location remained a mystery, the accuracy of his prediction could not be tested. What is certain, however, is that the incident inspired Richard four years later to write one of his most popular stories, "In the Fog." Another tale of adventure narrated in a drawing room, "In the Fog" is indebted to Robert Louis Stevenson (whose "New Arabian Nights" theme of the impossibility of adventure in modern times had been on Richard's mind that misty evening).[169]

Davis would write "In the Fog" years later in sunny Marion. That winter in London, he was trying to undertake a novel; and after a couple of false starts, he began a book he called *Captain Macklin*. Although it might at first sound like his typical adventure yarn, *Captain Macklin* was actually an ambitious departure for him. The eponymous narrator was a young Irish-American filibuster "who is always in love and always in trouble." Instead of an idealized version of Davis, Macklin was full of "vanity and vulgarity and commonness and bravado." Richard wanted to "show the young man's character" rather than write "a book of adventure." And in the end, Macklin would not "become a fine person because of a woman—but because his finer qualities come out as he grows older in years and experience."[170]

"It is rather amusing writing in the first person and making yourself out no end of a cad," Richard remarked.[171] Ethel Barrymore, Anthony Hope Hawkins, and Sam Sothern all thought that the first pages were his best writing yet; and Richard was "scared lest I can't keep it up."[172] He almost interrupted his writing to go to the Sudan, where the British were waging a war, but at the last minute Lord Kitchener barred correspondents from following the British regiments.[173] So Richard stayed in London, doing work he enjoyed during the day, seeing his English friends in the evening. "I am really more genuinely happy and having a better time here than I have been for years," he wrote his mother, "all the morbidness and things have gone. . . ."[174]

And then—on February 15, 1898, the U.S.S. *Maine* exploded and sank in Havana harbor. It was the gunshot that finally goes off in a tense, hushed room. After all the blather about war, war now seemed inevitable. Davis was in Paris an hour away from taking a train to Belgrade, for a journey through Serbia and Bulgaria, when he saw the headlines in an afternoon paper. He canceled the trip, anxiously monitoring the news reports to decide how soon he should return home. He was afraid that Charles would shirk the responsibility of telling him to come at once. "If I do miss it," he warned, "I shall be wild."[175] He did not miss it.

7

Teddy's Brave an' Fluent

Bodyguard

E VENTS DID NOT MOVE AS QUICKLY as a young man expected. Resisting the pressure to rush into war, President McKinley cautiously appointed a commission of inquiry to investigate the loss of the ship and 268 American lives. The commission's report was not presented to Congress until March 28. When it appeared, the report was inconclusive. To this day, no one is sure whether the *Maine* blew up from a fuel explosion or the detonation of a mine. If it was a mine, there is no evidence to suggest that the Spanish authorities were responsible. But the writers of the report suspected a mine; and after six weeks of incendiary stories in the yellow press, only a clear finding that the disaster was accidental could conceivably have kept the peace. The key opponents of war were the leaders of Wall Street, who feared that the rickety economy couldn't support it. Reflecting popular sentiment, Davis wrote an impassioned short story in which a U.S. Senator, inspired by a young, committed engineer to visit Cuba and publicize the horrors, turns back at the last minute under pressure from financiers ("the money-changers in the temple of this great republic"). By the middle of March, the mood on Wall Street had changed. Even the money changers wanted war, preferring military intervention to permanent instability.[1]

The stately march to battle gave Davis ample time to arrange his journalistic commissions. He sailed home from England with credentials from the *Times* of London. When the *Times*, without consulting him, agreed to share his dispatches with the New York *Herald* and its syndicate of fourteen American newspapers, Davis renegotiated his salary to four hundred dollars a week, plus expenses. He was happy with the *Herald*: no yellow journal, it had showed great restraint in its coverage of Cuba. All he needed now was a magazine affiliation. In the midst of discussions with the Harpers, he learned that they were also talking with his friend Stephen Bonsal. He withdrew at once and accepted a Scribner offer of ten cents a word: three eight-thousand-word pieces would net him twenty-four hundred dollars. On top of that there would be royalties from the eventual book. "I expect to make myself rich on this campaign," he wrote his family.[2]

In anticipation of imminent hostilities, he outfitted himself in London and New York with an elaborate war kit, which included top boots, a canvas shooting jacket, a revolver and cartridge belt, a leather flask, and a jaunty cap. Predictably, he had himself photographed, and the publication of the picture in the *Critic* provoked nationwide comment, mainly of amused derision. "If he were cut up into small pieces," jeered the Springfield *Republican*, "he would furnish the insurgents with arms and equipments for a whole winter"; without doubt, "there will be a terrific inkshed when he reaches the front." The Memphis *Commercial Appeal* declared he was "as impressive as a golf hero and as haughty as Emperor Bill." The Boston *Herald*, which belonged to the syndicate receiving his dispatches, naturally offered a more generous assessment: "he is the picture of an intrepid war-correspondent who is in for a long siege."[3]

Davis headed for Key West in April. The last time he was there, he was waiting impatiently for the *Journal* to transport him to the Cuban rebels. Now he was waiting impatiently for McKinley to ask Congress to declare war. The little Florida town was jammed with officers and correspondents, many of them there since the *Maine* went down in February. On the afternoon of April 21, Davis was sweltering in 103 degree heat on the crowded porch of the Key West Hotel when a messenger boy bicycled up with a telegram for his *Herald* colleague. The *Herald* man read it with a shudder. Then, realizing that half the row of officers and journalists was watching him, he calmly took his codebook from his pocket and showed Davis the cable—"Rain and hail"—and its meaning: "War is declared, fleet ordered to sea."

A few minutes later, the porch of the Key West Hotel was empty and the lobby was piled up with suitcases. On the waterfront, launches and cutters streaked across the bay, and yellow-and-red signal flags fluttered in the air. Not the *Herald* cable, but one delivered half an hour earlier to Captain William Sampson, had electrified the sleepy scene. Along with a promotion to rear admiral, the telegram gave Sampson his orders: to block-ade the northwest coast of Cuba. When Sampson commenced the coaling of his ships, the Key West press contingent needed no codebook to decipher the meaning.

The United States had not fought a war since 1865, the year one-year-old Richard watched the returning veterans parade through Philadelphia. Armies, like weapons, rust from disuse. With a belligerent roar, Congress declared on April 19 that the United States would use military force to free Cuba from Spain. President McKinley signed the joint resolution the next day. And then came an embarrassing silence. Less than a week before the war resolution, McKinley had learned that the United States would require two months to assemble a force capable of invading Cuba.[4] Unhappily, that date in late June coincided with the onset of the rainy season and, with it, the annual epidemic of yellow fever. Short of postponing the invasion until the fall (a policy favored by the commanding general of the army, Nelson Miles), the president would have to swallow these unpleasant complications, just as he had choked down his reluctance to lead the nation into war.

Because the navy, unlike the army, was ready to move, McKinley opened hostilities with a blockade. Two lines of gray warships cruised out of Key West at dawn on April 22. Bobbing like corks in their wake were the press dispatch boats. From the *Herald*'s *Sommers N. Smith*, Davis witnessed the first shot of the war, fired across the bow of a Spanish tramp steamer. What a reporter could see from the faraway press boat, however, was hardly worth mentioning. "It was like reporting the burning of the Waldorf-Astoria from the Brooklyn Bridge," Davis wrote. "The observer in the distance might see much smoke and some flame, but whether the cause of the fire were accidental or incendiary, whether there were loss of life or deeds of heroism, he could only guess."[5] Davis wanted to be on the deck of the flagship, the *New York*. With the help of a letter from the assistant secretary of the navy, Theodore Roosevelt—"the longest and strongest letter on the subject a man could write instructing the Admiral to take me on as I was writing history"—he believed that he was close to success. However, in the stampede that followed the signal to sail, his application was forgotten.[6]

He was on the *Sommers N. Smith* when he learned that Bonsal, representing *McClure's* magazine, had made it aboard the *New York*. Accompanied by Rufus Zogbaum, a prominent *Harper's Weekly* illustrator, Davis proceeded to the *New York* on a mailboat and persuaded Admiral Sampson on April 25 to let them on, too. Now Davis was in his element. He messed with the officers (not with the middies, as did the Associated Press man and Ralph Paine, the *World* stringer). Whenever a suspicious ship came into view, the *New York* went after it. Two times a day, a band played. "It is like a luxurious yacht, with none of the ennui of a yacht," Davis wrote home. "The other night, when we were heading off a steamer and firing six-pounders across her bows, the band was playing the 'star' song from the Meistersinger. Wagner and War struck me as the most fin de siecle idea of war that I had ever heard of."[7]

When he left Key West on the mailboat, Davis told his colleagues that he was bound for Tampa to investigate the army camp—"lying just on the principle that it is no other newspaper-man's business where you are going." But the lie backfired. Hearing that rival newsmen had weaseled onto the flagship, and ignorant that Davis was among them, the *Herald* man in Key West protested to Secretary of the Navy John Long. Long then cabled Sampson to put the interlopers ashore at once: there must be no favoritism.

Davis sent word to Sampson on the morning of April 27 that he would be leaving the ship and wished to pay his respects. A thin, professorial man with a gray beard and erect bearing, the admiral quickly ascertained that Davis was departing because he had heard about Long's cable and didn't want to embarrass Sampson by staying. Visibly angry at Long, Sampson said he had received three conflicting orders about correspondents and Davis was free to stay until they were cleared up. Also in the cabin was the ship's commanding officer, Captain French E. Chadwick, who said, "Perhaps Mr. Davis had better remain another twenty-four hours." As if to settle the matter, Sampson added, "Ships are going to Key West daily." So Davis stayed, and about an hour later, he witnessed the bombardment of Matanzas—the first military engagement of the war.[8]

The Spanish batteries at Matanzas triggered the bombardment by aiming a few rounds at the *New York*, which had ventured close to the coast on a reconnaissance mission. Supported by a monitor and cruiser, the flagship fired back, and in eighteen minutes, silenced the Spanish batteries.[9] The Spanish rounds missed their target, except for one round of shrapnel that broke over the main mast and reminded Davis of the fighting in Greece. Having nervously awaited the first shelling, Davis was relieved to find it "much less of a strain than [he] expected, there was no standing on your toes nor keeping your mouth open or putting wadding in your ears." Instead, he was "thrown up off the deck just as you are when an elevator starts with a sharp jerk and there was an awful noise like the worst clap of thunder you ever heard close to your ears, then the smoke covered everything and you could hear the shot going through the air like a giant rocket."[10] Because of the noise and smoke, the fifteen minutes of shelling were more exhausting than the two days of it he had endured at Velestino. At Velestino, he had moved to duck shrapnel; on the *New York* he moved involuntarily.[11]

The first part of a newspaperman's task is getting the news. Then he must write it. Finally, and perhaps most importantly, he must transmit it to the home office. The *Sommers N. Smith* was the only press dispatch boat within twenty miles of the engagement. Paine watched sorrowfully as Davis placed his manuscript (written in fifteen minutes) in a weighted envelope and tossed it onto the deck of the dispatch boat. The boat, which also carried Sampson's official report, tore off at top speed for Key West. Although it was a trivial engagement, it was the first of the war, and it was a grand "beat" for Davis.[12]

Two days later, Paine himself was tossed off the *New York*, replaced by the *World*'s Stephen Crane.[13] Crane was less popular than Paine. "I don't like him myself," Davis admitted.[14] On the same day, Remington (another man Davis viewed ambivalently) came aboard the flagship, bitter that he had missed the bombardment.[15] Even on the *New York*, news was scarce. The big headlines of the war came from Manila, where on May 1 Commodore George Dewey destroyed Spain's Pacific fleet. Compared to that sideshow, the featured presentation in the Caribbean dragged on colorlessly. Still, Davis was content, dining in good company and lionized by the

New York officers. He sent home for a dozen photographs of himself in his Greek campaign uniform and another dozen in his Central American kit of two years before. He wanted to give them to the many officers who had, he said, requested one.[16]

Richard was outraged when Secretary Long on May 2 ordered all correspondents but W. A. Goode of the Associated Press off the *New York*. Long said he was acting on a complaint from the Harper Brothers. (Cabled by their disgruntled former employee, the Harpers denied it; however, Davis later concluded that the Harpers were indeed responsible, and he added this to his list of grievances against them.)[17] Bitterly, but futilely, Davis protested to Long. "Some men are trained to fight and some to write," he argued. "I have been ten years learning to write, and it is possible that I can describe events more correctly than others or that I have learned how to place them on paper. I claim that trained writers are just as important to this war as trained fighters." In this distinguished literary cadre, he placed Crane, Bonsal, Remington, and Zogbaum—all of them, like himself, ordered off the *New York*.[18] When Long refused to reconsider, Davis gave up on covering the naval operation, which, even from the *New York*, was barely worthwhile. He departed for Tampa, where the army was struggling to assemble an invasion force.

Secretary of War Russell A. Alger might have mobilized the army more quickly had victory over Spain been his only task. Too many of his countrymen, however, viewed the defeat of senescent Spain as a foregone conclusion.[19] With that settled, they felt free to press the War Office with their political and social demands. Alger was so busy seeing congressmen and other influential citizens that he had to relegate war business to nights and Sundays.[20] Patriotic fervor crossed class lines: workingmen lined up to enlist, and the rich formed oversubscribed volunteer regiments. (Davis's useful friend, Assistant Secretary of the Navy Roosevelt, was one of the first to leave his job and form a regiment.) The conflict was an opportunity to reconcile regions as well as classes. McKinley gave key commands to generals whose Confederate credentials were impeccable, but whose ability to prosecute a war in 1898 remained to be proven.

Guided by political concerns, the president placed atop his shaky pyramid the bulky figure of William Rufus Shafter. Grossly fat, with short legs and a massive head, Shafter was a man of few words. When he spoke, it was in a pipsqueak voice, and what he had to say was often crude. According to an aide, he "couldn't walk two miles in an hour, just beastly obese." He was an anti-hero cast as the leading man; by the time the drama ended, he would be, in Davis's version, the arch-villain. On May 2, 1898, when he assumed command of the forces at Tampa, Shafter had completed almost thirty-seven years of army service, but his chief qualification for commanding the invasion of Cuba was a negative one: he was not Nelson A. Miles.[21]

Miles, the commanding general of the army since 1895, had like Shafter begun his military career by volunteering for the Union. He won fame after the war as an Indian fighter. Unlike Shafter, Miles was the image of a soldier: tall, well built, and fit. He was also pompous, conceited, publicity-hungry, and quarrelsome. He feuded particularly—and this cost him the commander's slot—with Secretary of War Alger, an orphan farm boy who had made millions in the Michigan lumber business. It augured ill for their relationship that, as governor of Michigan, Alger blocked the presidential ambitions of Ohio senator John Sherman, who was the uncle of Miles's wife. Like Miles, Alger was vain, sensitive, and selfish. An impressive-looking man, he stood tall and straight, and wore an elegant white moustache and goatee. But he had no real training in large-scale military administration and scant experience in politics.[22]

This was the political background to the state of inertia that greeted Davis in Tampa. For the extravagant sum of six dollars a day, he obtained a room with adjoining bath at the Tampa Bay Hotel. A Moorish-style confection opened in 1891 by Henry B. Plant, a railroad tycoon eager to develop Tampa as a railroad terminal point, the Tampa Bay Hotel was a five-story red-brick structure nine miles inland from the port. The hotel covered six acres and contained nearly five hundred rooms. The tapestries, statuary, ebony-and-gold furniture, and other furnishings were imported from Europe at the cost of over a million dollars. Diversions included a golf course, a casino, and an indoor swimming pool. Peacocks strutted through the exotic gardens.[23] In a hot, sandy city of derelict wooden houses, the Tampa Bay Hotel—with its illuminated silver minarets, crescents in the woodwork and plaster, and arabesques over the doors and windows—hovered like a fever dream. On rocking chairs on the wide porches, the commanding generals and their staff mingled with hordes of reporters. They drank gallons of iced tea, haggled over ponies with the horse-dealers who paraded outside, and crowded around the bulletin board to read the latest telegrams. After many false rumors of departure, the men unpacked their evening clothes and summoned their wives and daughters to join them. In the evenings, they would dance in the ballroom, or gather in the large rotunda to hear a regimental band. "This was the rocking-chair period of the war," Davis quipped, giving it a label that stuck. "It was an army of occupation, but it occupied the piazza of a big hotel."[24]

While their superiors paced the porches of the Tampa Bay Hotel, the rank-and-file troops gathered at the port and in the pine woods behind the city. About 25,000 men congregated in Tampa during the month of May. After the smooth-running machinery of the navy, Davis was aghast at the disorder of the army. "The army will have to do a lot of fighting to make itself solid with me," he wrote to his sister, Nora.[25] He found the army regulars to be well trained, but they were now a minority in a force engorged with 125,000 volunteers. The standing U.S. army was limited by law to about 28,000 soldiers, of whom many were required to defend the coast and maintain Western garrisons. In the weeks leading up to the outbreak of war, the incorporation of citizen soldiers into the existing army had been a contentious process. The states jealously protected their control over the National Guard units, and Congress, responsive to lobbying, refused to break up the state militias and distribute the men to skeletonized units of the regular army. Instead, the states sent their units of amateur soldiers mostly intact, under the command of officers who were politically connected but militarily unseasoned. Not that the command of the regular army was so much better: during the long stretch of peace, an unmeritocratic system of advancement had drained off most of the talented officers, leaving behind the unambitious and the superannuated. In the test of battle, some of the newly commissioned officers would outshine the veterans.

As friends of his, like Roosevelt and William Astor Chanler, donned their uniforms, Davis fretted over whether he should do the same. Having waited thirty-four years for a war, he knew that he might never have another opportunity to bear arms for his country. Would he get more out of the war as a correspondent or as a captain? When he won an assignment on the *Segurança*, the flagship of the invading army, he congratulated himself that he would be in a privileged position to cover the action. "I have a chance to make myself for life . . . ," he told Charles. "I wouldn't if I was on a tug seeing nothing but being at the very heart of it I would be less than a fool to let go. I can do much more as a correspondent than as a staff officer. There will be a thousand staff officers but only one *Times* correspondent."[26] He busied himself finding a horse and a Spanish-speaking courier to take with him to Cuba.[27] (Because of the transport shortage, he would wind up leaving both behind.)

In mid-May, however, he was commissioned as a captain, and his resolution disintegrated. He had applied for a commission, but when advised to marshal his connections, he had snootily replied that he had none, "and that if the question had degenerated to that I withdrew my application." So he was surprised when the appointment was announced. Visions of military glory obliterated all his other aspirations. He turned his argument of a unique opportunity on its head; and reasoned that while he would have many chances to cover wars, this might be his only shot at fighting in one. "I can be a correspondent any time," he told his mother, "but having been in the army will be a great satisfaction to me always, and it would be foolish to let the chance go." He approached the generals of his acquaintance to ask for a staff position.[28]

After talking to a few military men, however, he flip-flopped once more. His task, he learned, would be "to keep books and count canteens and soda crackers." Remington and Captain Arthur Lee, the British military attaché, talked with him for two hours in Remington's bedroom. Both were dead set against it, and they convinced him that a military appointment for a man without military training would be "sort of borrowed plumage and play acting." Lee remarked that he himself might write a dozen short stories, but he would always be regarded as an officer; and while Davis might outrank him by grace of the president, he could not persuade Lee or anyone else that he was a soldier. Remington chimed in that it was unfair to twenty-year veterans that he be appointed to the same rank at the same time as they were. Even more persuasive than their logic was their tone. They regarded the whole affair as a joke.[29] Afterward, Davis went out to visit the men of Troop G, Third Cavalry, whom he had met six years before on his trip to the West. They hailed him "as though I was a German Emperor." Each man he had mentioned in his book was celebrated for that fact; and they had kept the horse he rode, and led it out for a reunion. "I was one of the events in the existence of the regiment, but I didn't dare tell them I was a captain," he remarked. "I felt silly at the idea of it. They wouldn't have respected me as a captain, but they did for what I was."[30] Back at the hotel, Lee helped him compose a telegram to the president declining the commission.[31]

Almost immediately, clouds of doubt rolled in. As he watched the excited young militiamen arrive in Tampa, he berated himself for being "weak not to chance it." He had been scared off not by the perils of war, but by the prospect of humdrum servitude. The invasion could well be postponed until the end of the unhealthy rainy season in Cuba; and glorious victory might be followed by a tedious military occupation of Havana. "The whole thing would bore me if I thought I had to keep at it for a year or more," Richard wrote Charles. "That is the fault of my having had too much excitement and freedom. It spoils me to make sacrifices that other men can make. Whichever way it comes out I shall be sorry and feel I did not do the right thing." His choice threw into sharp relief the distinction between the man who acts and the man who writes about the actor—a distinction that discomfited Davis (as it does many journalists), but one that he never faced up to until the very end of his life. "It's all very well to say you are doing more by writing, but are you?" he mused. "It's an easy game to look on and pat the other chaps on the back with a few paragraphs, that is cheap patriotism. They're taking chances and you're not and when the war's over they'll be happy and I won't. The man that enlists or volunteers even if he doesn't get further than Chickamauga or Gretna Green and the man who doesn't enlist at all but minds his own business is much better off than I will be writing about what other men do and not doing it myself, especially as I had a chance of a life time, and declined it. I'll always feel I lost in character by not sticking to it whether I had to go to Arizona or Governor's Island." He mournfully concluded: "It was a great opportunity missed but the sad thing is that if it came again I doubt if I'd take it. I just don't want to make the sacrifice and I am sorry to find I am not of the stuff that can make it."[32] Although Davis told his parents that the other reporters did not impugn his courage, Stephen Crane on June 2 wrote, "It is now the fashion of all hotel porches at Tampa and Key West to run Davis down because he had declined a captaincy in the army in order to keep his contract with his paper. The teaparty has to have a topic."[33]

The tea party in Tampa dragged on through May into June. "As Sherman said 'War is hell,' " Davis wrote home, "it is when you spend it in a rocking chair growing soft and lazy and losing step after step."[34] First the army had to wait for the navy to locate and immobilize the Spanish fleet. Fortunately, Admiral Pascual Cervera y Topete brought his squadron into Santiago harbor, where the American navy found it and bottled it up. Now it was the problems of the unprofessional republican army itself that prevented departure. Grown tenfold, the army had a month to clothe and supply a force that by mid-August numbered 275,000 men. The cloth for blue uniforms that the quartermaster department obtained was anything but uniform: it was colored with impermanent dyes, so that from a distance, a regiment appeared as variegated as a Caribbean bird. Even worse, the cloth was wool, a dubious choice for a summer campaign in the tropics. Although the regular army had modern weapons, the volunteers had to make do with obsolete black-powder Springfields, which created clouds of telltale smoke for the enemy to fix on. When the War Department got its hands on these substandard supplies, it then struggled to distribute them through makeshift channels.[35]

By late May, the volunteers bound for Cuba joined the regular army in Tampa. Visiting the camps of five volunteer regiments under the command of General Fitzhugh Lee, Davis was appalled to see the men sleeping on blankets on the ground. No one had bothered to build rain trenches around the tents or gutters along the company streets. In one regiment's camp, the open latrines had been placed fifty feet from the first row of tents, on the windward side. The wind had been blowing steadily from that direction for a week. Garbage also was burned windward, so smoke and latrine odors swept across the camp. When Davis and his British friend, Arthur Lee, pointed out these errors to a colonel, the man replied airily, "Oh, well, they'll learn. It will be a good lesson for them." He revealed that he wasn't bothering to drill his men, since the ground was so rough with roots and palmettos. It didn't occur to him that the ground in Cuba would be much the same.[36]

Davis published a blistering account of the incompetence of the officers of the volunteer regiments. In it, he urged the president to appoint officers of the regular army to leadership positions in the volunteer regiments. However, he did not expose the ineptness of the War Department, which was even more newsworthy. He had been horrified to see the volunteers looking as ragtag as the Cuban army. Half the men he saw had no uniforms or shoes. The regulation shoe cut the instep. The pasteboard helmets were so flimsy that one tropical storm would smash them, and so light that the sun beat through them. The felt hats were just as bad: the brims too narrow to protect from sun or rain, and the felt so cheap that instead of shedding water, it became hard and heavy when wet. None of the American officers had ever before seen such things as Lee's khaki uniform and cork helmet. Davis, whose own kit was state-of-the-art, felt vindicated. "I have been so right about so many things these last five years, and was laughed at for making much of them," he wrote Charles. But he was holding his tongue. "I have written nothing for the paper," he explained, "because, if I started to tell the truth at all, it would do no good, and it would open up a hell of an outcry from all the families of the boys who have volunteered."[37]

He was the first reporter to describe at length the inadequacies of the volunteers, but that is as far as he would go. He would not state in print what he thought privately: that the whole war was being run "badly cheaply and without head or judgement."[38] He was defensive about his reticence; just how defensive he revealed when another reporter violated the unspoken conspiracy of self-censorship. Writing like Davis for the London *Times* and New York *Herald*, and also for *Harper's Weekly*, Poultney Bigelow denounced the state of the army. He started at the top with the "acephalous War Department in Washington," which had appointed such incompetent officers as the Confederate veterans Fitzhugh Lee and Joseph Wheeler. He then exposed the needlessly arduous railroad journey that the men of the First U.S. Infantry suffered in reaching Tampa, the total lack of preparation they found upon arrival, and the winter uniforms they wore and greasy pork and beans they ate in the ninety-eight-degree heat. Many had contracted dysentery. He claimed that not one regiment was ready to take the field.[39]

Bigelow's reports provoked an uproar. Although his charges closely duplicated Davis's private indictment, it was Davis who led the indignant outcry against him. By his own testimony, Davis at this stage of the war was thought by Generals Miles and Shafter to be "a sort of champion of the army."[40] In an article in the *Herald*, Davis wrote of Bigelow's *Harper's Weekly* story that it was "doubtful if anything has appeared in print since the beginning of the war, in even the yellow journals, so un-American, so untrue, or so calculated to give courage to the enemy." Lest anyone miss the insinuation, he flat out labeled Bigelow's account "treason." He said that Bigelow's "statements as to the condition of our army are absolutely false" and had been "universally condemned." Specifically, he defended the rations and the medical supervision at Tampa, both of which Bigelow had scathingly described. Davis concluded by writing: "That some official action will be taken in regard to this article is generally believed. Every one knows that mistakes have been made and that the condition of the volunteers is bad, but this is no time to print news of such a nature, and it is certainly not the time now, or later, to print reckless and untrue statements concerning our regular army."[41]

With our recent, unhappy memories of newspaper self-censorship to protect the military, in such cases as the New York *Times* on the Bay of Pigs invasion and *Time* during the Vietnam War, Davis's denunciation of Bigelow's dispatch (much of which he knew was true) is hard to defend. One can, perhaps, extenuate the offense. His angry dismissal of the message arose in part from his distaste for the messenger. Poultney Bigelow was a womanizer, a racist, and a lout. He was the sort of man who vilified blacks and Jews and bragged of deflowering foreign virgins.[42] The son of diplomat John Bigelow, he had grown up abroad and attended school with Kaiser Wilhelm of Germany. On first meeting in Tampa, he and Davis immediately disliked each other. Bigelow then cleverly manipulated Davis into declining to cover the *Gussie* expedition, an attempt by two companies of the First Infantry to deliver arms to the Cuban insurgents. By getting Davis's refusal, Bigelow was able to replace him among the reporters on the *Gussie*— which, although the mission was unsuccessful, still made a better story than most of the "piazza pieces" Davis was writing.[43] Pugnacious and arrogant, Bigelow was precisely the man to publish the information that his colleagues only whispered. "The trouble about Bigelow is that the man is crazy," Davis wrote home, "and that is the only thing you can't say about him in print. He is also right in many things he says, only it's no use saying them now."[44]

Some accused Davis of committing, in his article on the volunteer regiments, the same sin he vilified in Bigelow. In his own mind, though, the distinction was clear: ". . . I only complained of things that could be remedied he kicked against things that could not, and he also said things that were simply not true. He is like a man who goes around among the passengers on a sinking ship and tells them the captain and officers are incompetent and drunk. It does no good. It's too late then to ship a new captain. And it's worse if it happens to be untrue. There's lots to be written after the war is over but we're such a happy go lucky people that it won't matter."[45] The most damning explanation for Davis's self-censorship lies in that canny final assessment. He was right: the American people were too easygoing to worry about such matters. He knew that the man impolitic enough to squawk would be vilified. So he kept silent.

To the amusement of their peers, Bigelow continued to snap at Davis in the press.[46] It was his last chance to comment on the war. Punishing him for his heresies, the War Department revoked Bigelow's credentials and kept him from covering the invasion.[47] In hindsight, however, he comes off better than his adversary. As he argued in his own defense, the United States could postpone the invasion of Cuba at will. "If we were in a life and death struggle with the enemy at our gates I should hold my tongue and wait until after the war," he wrote. "But there is yet time to undo the mischief done."[48] His criticisms of the army were accurate and courageous. They would later be echoed by Davis, among others.

As Bigelow's punishment suggests, the blanket on criticism wasn't solely a matter of self-censorship on the part of correspondents. In late April, the government had appointed censors to man the cable office in Key West and each of the six major cable offices in New York. Censors were later installed in Tampa. But the mesh of the sieve was wide—until the *Gussie* fiasco. General Shafter blamed the *Gussie*'s failure on the newspapers, which had so publicized the plan that the Spanish were on the alert to prevent the ship from landing.[49] On his orders, the censors cracked down, and reporters began to complain about the difficulty of getting their stories through. Even if the censors passed a story, the telegraph operators could excise any portion they found questionable. The ultimate threat— and, as Bigelow's case illustrated, it was not an empty threat—was the power to refuse a reporter permission to accompany the invading army. Correspondents anticipating the glory of combat were understandably cautious.[50]

Aside from his article on the generally wretched shape of the volunteers, Davis in Tampa looked, as he always looked, for stories that would inspire and touch his readers. At a patriotic time, he wanted to help Americans feel proud of their country. War promised to provide in abundance the youthful idealism he sought futilely in routine life. With his snobbish prejudices, he preferred to give the leading roles in fact, as in his fiction, to the well bred and well educated. Inevitably, his gaze came to rest upon Theodore Roosevelt. In retrospect, it is obvious that Roosevelt in Cuba was the story that Davis's entire career had been leading up to. Part of Davis's genius as a reporter was his ability to foresee what the rest of us can appreciate only afterward.

He had met Roosevelt in New York when they were both making youthful reputations, Davis as a reporter for the *Evening Sun* and Roosevelt as a civil-service commissioner in Washington. Both were sharp dressers with a flair for self-promotion. Their introduction came at a dinner at the Madison Avenue house of Roosevelt's elder sister, Anna, probably in late 1890, and Roosevelt expressed his admiration for "Gallegher."[51] A couple of years later, Davis spent another evening with Roosevelt, this time in Washington. Roosevelt now was the president of the Civil Service Commission. They went out to a boxing match with two aristocratic young men attached to the British embassy, and they protested so loudly at the referee's decisions that they were almost thrown out. The possibility struck Davis as "humorous."

He would have been less amused had he known what Roosevelt thought of him privately. That month's issue of *Cosmopolitan* featured an article by Roosevelt attacking "vulgar rich" and "refined, fastidious" Americans who, motivated by snobbery or weakness, aped foreign customs.[52] This mimetic crowd—at least, the crass rich ones, if not the effete aesthetes—were precisely Davis's audience. At dinner, he berated Roosevelt in their defense. "[Davis] was of course stirred up to much wrath by my *Cosmopolitan* article, and was so entirely unintelligent that it was a little difficult to argue with him, as he apparently considered it a triumphant answer to my position to inquire if I believed in the American custom of chewing tobacco and spitting all over the floor," Roosevelt reported to his friend, Brander Matthews. "To this I deemed it wisest to respond that I did; and that in consequence the British Minister, who otherwise liked me, felt very badly about having me at the house, especially because I sat with my legs on the table during dinner. The man has the gift of narration; but when it comes to breeding, upon my word it is hardly too much to say that even Kipling could give him points."[53] A year later, Roosevelt exclaimed to Matthews, "What an everlasting cad R. H. Davis is!"[54]

But Roosevelt was too shrewd to reveal his distaste. Davis was a reporter, and Roosevelt cultivated journalists as an arborist tends fruit trees. He warmed them with the blaze of his nonstop activity; he watered them with flattering attentions and invitations; and, when it came time to harvest, he gathered bountiful fruit. As president of the New York police board, a position he assumed in 1895, Roosevelt declared himself the board's press spokesman and invited reporters to spend the day in his office. Since a day at the office could be dull, even in Roosevelt's office, he dreamed up the institution of "night patrols" to check up on cops on the beat. On an early "night patrol," Davis and Jacob A. Riis went along. "We would sit in a doorstep and take out our watches and time how long police talked to each other, or to citizens," Davis later reminisced. "Then R. would hurry up to them always asking first 'What is your post?' Before they recognized him [they] would laugh or swear and say What the hell's that to you? and then it was humorous for us to see their faces change as they recognized the spectacles and double rows of teeth and the fighting chin which the papers had already made familiar to them. Some of them were so frightened that they could not answer his questions. One man couldn't remember his own name." All of this made marvelous copy, which was a great help to hardworking reporters; and when Roosevelt needed assistance of his own, the press was there to provide it. Barely six months into the job, Roosevelt alienated Thomas Platt, the omnipotent boss of the New York Republican Party. A legislative prestidigitator, Platt resolved to make Roosevelt vanish by abolishing his office. After the New York *Times* in two front-page stories denounced these schemes of "sneaking cowards and hypocrites," Platt backed down in embarrassment, and Roosevelt was saved.[55]

Never has an American political figure better understood the needs and the uses of the press. When he brought his First Volunteer Cavalry from its preliminary camp in San Antonio to the embarkation center of Tampa, Roosevelt propelled himself at once onto the center of the stage.

Technically, the men were not his volunteers. Although offered the command of the regiment which he had organized, he modestly declined on account of his inexperience, and asked to be placed second under Colonel Leonard Wood, a seasoned soldier who was also the president's medical doctor. But while Wood outclassed Roosevelt as a military expert, when it came to personalities there was no contest. Cool and reserved, Wood had a temperament that deflected public attention. Not Roosevelt. As a contemporary observed, he "was a figure around which myths grew easily. About him the most picturesque simply must be the true account."[56] His regiment, which had been dubbed the Rough Riders, quickly became known as Roosevelt's Rough Riders. This was not a mere accident of alliteration; their other nickname was Teddy's Terrors.[57]

Even without Roosevelt, the Rough Riders were a natural story for Davis. The core of the regiment was composed of Western cowboys, the type he had admired on his tour of Texas. Added to them, like lace trim on a buckskin jacket, were scions of the best New York families. Reginald Ronalds, a descendant of tobacco king Pierre Lorillard, had played football for Yale, Horace Devereaux had played for Princeton, and Dudley Dean had captained a famous team for Harvard. Woodbury Kane, a cousin of John Jacob Astor (who finagled himself a regular army post as inspector general) was an outstanding yachtsman and polo champion—as well as a former Harvard football player. Another star polo player was Joseph Sampson Stevens of Newport. Dade Goodrich had captained the Harvard crew. Kenneth Robinson and Sumner Gerard excelled at golf. Bob Wrenn and Bill Larned were two of the top tennis players in the country. William Tiffany, the nephew of Mrs. August Belmont, and Hamilton Fish, the grandson of President Grant's secretary of state, were well-known New York men-about-town. Craig Wadsworth, a leader of the Genesee Valley hunts and New York City cotillions, was a baron of upstate New York.[58] Most of these "dudes" joined K Troop, which was organized in New York; yet they were integrated smoothly into the regiment. In less than a month of training in San Antonio, Wood and Roosevelt had sharpened the recruits to a fighting edge. "The camp is by far the best I've seen yet either regular or volunteer," Richard reported to Charles. "It's as neat as a surgeon's tray. 'Reggie' Ronalds, [Woodbury] Kane, 'Joe' Stevens, the Norman's, [Roscoe] Channing, [Jack] Greenway and about forty more tennis sharps and football cranks are working as they never did before and very happily."[59] There was something uplifting about seeing millionaires tramping through freight cars in the oppressive heat. "It is a great thing to bring classes together," Davis believed.[60] Plus, it made excellent copy.

Some of the Rough Riders knew Davis from softer days at Delmonico's. Those who didn't quickly befriended him, if for no other reason than his first-rate facilities. "They use my bathroom continuously," Richard told

Charles, "and I never open the door without finding a heap of dirty canvas on the floor and a cheery voice splashing about in the tub and calling out 'It's all right don't mind me. I'm one of Teddy's "Brownies." ' Then an utterly strange and utterly nude giant will appear from the bath room." Thanks to Wood's foresight, the Rough Riders were clothed in relatively light, brown canvas uniforms, instead of the suffocating blue wool worn by the rest of the army; and in place of the antiquated .45-caliber Springfield rifles firing black powder that the other volunteers received, they were issued the smokeless Krag-Jorgensen carbines of the regulars.[61] In his initial survey of the Rough Riders, Davis thought that "the discipline is the only danger." He was distressed to see Lieutenant-Colonel Roosevelt dining with two noncommissioned officers. "That stopped me from giving him a clean bill of health in the *Herald*," Davis confided. "It was a bad break, his Colonel, Wood, was at one table with the Commander in Chief, and the Lieutenant Colonel was dining with his sergeants, and of course the regular army officers present didn't miss a trick. Roosevelt gave the regiment a bad name by that one act that it does not deserve."[62] In San Antonio one day, Roosevelt had treated a whole squadron to unlimited beer, an infraction for which he sheepishly apologized to Wood.[63] Before he overcame his democratic instincts and conformed to military etiquette, he committed a chain of such errors that endeared him to his men.

Edith Roosevelt joined her husband in Tampa. When the cavalry regiments, including the Rough Riders, assembled on June 6 for a demonstration drill, Richard accompanied Edith and a group of foreign attachés to witness the spectacle. As he watched the two thousand mounted cavalrymen advancing in a two-mile-long line through the palm forest, their steel swords flashing and their red-and-white guidons fluttering, he was swept by a nostalgia for the present: by the sense that what he was seeing might never be seen again.[64] Whether or not Wagner was playing, this was a very fin-de-siècle war.*

On May 31 General Shafter received orders from Washington to proceed under naval convoy directly to Santiago. Although his destination remained a secret, the newsmen soon learned of the instructions to embark.[65] But logistical snags slowed Shafter down. For instance: the Plant System, which controlled the single track to Port Tampa, for a while refused to permit a rival railroad to pass over it; only after military authorities threatened to seize the line did Plant back down.[66] As days passed without incident, the more enterprising papers invented the departure that they were anxiously awaiting.

---

*Because of limited transports, Shafter ordered all the horses, except for those of the highest officers, to be left behind in Tampa. The cavalry, including the Rough Riders, went unmounted to Cuba.

Characteristically, Hearst took the lead. The *Journal* of June 2 announced that five thousand troops had departed the previous day for Santiago. Over the next week, the *Journal* reported an exciting sequence of landings, bombardments, and fleet battles, all admirably detailed, all entirely fictitious. The *Journal* was selling so well thanks to its apocryphal scoops that its rivals in desperation began to play the same game, often merely rewriting the accounts of the creative *Journal* writers. The low-water mark of journalism in the Spanish-American War was reached when the *Journal* on June 8 published a stirring account of the death of Colonel Reflipe W. Thenuz, an Austrian artillery expert who was fatally wounded while fighting for Spain. The next morning, at the end of a dispatch bearing the byline of Ralph D. Paine, the *World* also disclosed the demise of Colonel R. W. Thenuz, reprinted virtually verbatim from the *Journal*'s account. With what glee did the *Journal* squeal the next day, in a large page-three headline: "The *World* Confess to Stealing the News!" Colonel Reflipe W. Thenuz, Hearst's minions crowed, was an anagram for "We pilfer the news." They had set a trap to expose their competitors' thievery. The *Journal* men were too busy chortling to notice the real offense—that all the purloined copy was just as factitious as the death of Thenuz. It was in truth the death of the news.[67]

For the correspondents stuck in Tampa, this background static of phony news exacerbated the discomfort. "Iced tea and the heat and chiefly the inaction and strain is telling on the nerves of the men and the correspondents resign about twice a day," Davis wrote home.[68] On June 8, they were roused from their irritable lethargy by word of imminent embarkation. Along with the others, Davis traveled the nine miles from the city to the port of Tampa, where pandemonium awaited him. "Everything is at odds," he wrote home, "men sleeping all over the platforms and new regiments marching over them. It is the darndest confusion that ever happened." He camped out in a railroad office.[69] With trains shunting, drums beating, and bugles blaring, there was no chance of sleeping, so he stayed up all night watching the troops roll in. At 4:00 A.M., hearing that Shafter was about to arrive, he hired a small, leaky boat to take him to the *Segurança*. He was one of seven reporters to win a berth on the flagship; most of the eighty-nine accredited correspondents traveled on the *Olivette*.[70] "I would have died on the regular press boat," he wrote home, "as it is the men are interesting on our boat."[71] But the *Segurança* wasn't moving. Spanish warships had been reported a few miles offshore; until they were destroyed or otherwise removed from the scene, the transports could not sail.[72] A few hours later, when the animals were unloaded from the *Segurança* (after fifteen had perished from the below-deck heat), Davis took his cue and returned to the mainland to wait.[73]

There was another abortive start on the morning of June 10.[74] The incompetence of the staff work was now manifest. Provisions arrived un-marked on railroad cars, requiring that each crate be opened before loading. Regiments proceeding to their assigned ships were likely to discover that another regiment had already been placed in their bunks. With his usual zeal, Roosevelt rushed his Rough Riders to the *Yucatán*, which had also been promised to the Seventy-first Regiment, New York. When the Seventy-first appeared a little later, the deed had been accomplished. Watching with satisfaction as the rival regiment retreated, Roosevelt noticed Jim Blackton and Albert Smith, two young men with a movie camera who had signed on to accompany the Seventy-first. They were standing on the gangplank befuddled. "What are you young men up to?" he asked. "We are the Vitagraph Company, Colonel Roosevelt, and we are going over to Cuba to take moving pictures of the war." The genius of self-promotion beckoned them aboard. "I can't take care of a regiment," he said, "but I might be able to handle two more."[75]

Perhaps because of the false alarms, when the flotilla of thirty-two troop ships carrying some sixteen thousand men finally moved out of Tampa Bay on June 14, there were no crowds of weeping women waving handker-chiefs and no band playing "The Girl I Left Behind Me." Instead, Davis noted with disappointment, the *Segurança* was seen off by three black women, three soldiers, and a pack of sweating stevedores.[76] Prepared for the worst, Davis left behind a will at the hotel.[77] He was less prepared for the tedious discomfort of the *Segurança*. The voyage lasted a week, twice as long as it should have.[78] "No words can tell the discomforts and beastli-ness and boredom of the troop ship," Davis wrote his family. "The food is impossible and it is so overcrowded that never for an instant are you alone."[79]

He was as jubilant as a prisoner on parole when, for three hours on June 20, he and three other correspondents accompanied General Shafter and Admiral Sampson on a brief visit to Aserraderos, eighteen miles west of Santiago. In the party of twenty, two men required steeds: Shafter because of his bulk and Davis because of a sciatica attack. The others hiked the steep trail leading to a mountainside rendezvous, where the American com-manders conferred with the rebels' General Calixto García on where to land the American army. Nearby, the American bluejackets and the barefooted Cuban soldiers mingled with friendly curiosity. This was the high point of Cuban and American cooperation during the war.[80]

Two days later the Americans landed. The site selected was familiar to Davis—as it was to the thousands of readers of *Soldiers of Fortune*. By a strange coincidence, the American army launched its invasion of Cuba at Daiquirí, on the same strip of coast that Davis had visited as a Lehigh student and then reconstructed as the backdrop of his most famous novel.* When his ship drew near, Davis saw once again the iron-ore pier that paralleled the coast, and, rising in rows behind it, the company's corrugated-zinc shacks and the natives' thatched-roof huts. But there was no man or woman to be seen.[81]

As American artillery shells tore up the mountainside, the doughboys jumped from the ships onto heaving boats that carried them to shore. Since the boats weren't high enough to reach the ore dock, most of the men simply tumbled out into the breaking waves. (Two men drowned.) The sound of their cheers was relayed from ship to ship for miles over the sea. It made a pretty picture, but Davis was writing a book. With incredulous indignation, he learned that the reporters were ordered to remain aboard until the operation was completed. After the soldiers had been landed, the animals would be docked, and then the provisions. It was more than he could tolerate. As the small boats were being prepared, he walked up to the commanding general, who was standing on the promenade deck with the adjutant general, E. J. McClernand. "General, I see the order for disembarkation directs that none but fighting men be allowed in the boats of the first landing party," Davis said. "This will keep back reporters." Supervising the landing of his entire force on sketchily scouted enemy territory, Shafter was understandably tense. Even in more relaxed moments, he disliked reporters; personally, he believed they should not be allowed to accompany an army in wartime.[82] He informed Davis that this was true— not out of unfriendliness to reporters, but only to insure maximum return fire if any Spaniards were lurking in the wooded hills. Davis persisted, finally reverting to his old argument that he, and his select colleagues on the *Segurança*, were describing this campaign not for ephemeral newspapers but for the long view. He was not a reporter but a historian. Shafter's patience gave way. "I do not care a damn what you are," he retorted brusquely. "I'll treat all of you alike."[83]

Both Shafter and McClernand believed that this acidulous exchange soured Davis on Shafter and flavored all of his subsequent war dispatches.[84] In fact, the snub merely exacerbated Davis's existing contempt for the incompetent and unpicturesque general. None of the reporters liked Shafter; why should Davis be any different? When he belatedly reached the shore, Davis attached himself to Roosevelt, a commander he could respect. "You get more news with the other regiments," he wrote to Charles, "but the officers, even the Generals, are such narrow minded slipshod men that

---

*The invasion point was called "Baiquiri" in early news reports. While this was the first landing by the army, the army had been beaten by the marines. A force from the First Marine Division landed at Guantánamo Bay, about forty miles east of Santiago, on June 10. After some fighting, the marines took possession of the bay and established a coaling station for the ships that were blockading Santiago harbor.

we only visit them to pick up information."[85] Roosevelt was far more than a source. He was a legend in the making.

Almost half of the American force landed at Daiquirí on June 22. The next morning, learning that the Spanish had abandoned not only Daiquirí but also the more sheltered port of Siboney, the army disembarked most of the remaining troops there. Seven miles to the west, Siboney was that much closer to the eventual target of Santiago. When, on the morning of June 22, the Rough Riders were ordered to march from Daiquirí to Siboney, Davis accompanied them. Although they arrived well after nightfall, the transports were still disgorging their human loads. Watching until 2:00 A.M., Davis was reminded of a day at the beach at Coney Island—except that it was raining, it was after midnight, and the only light came from flickering campfires, beaming searchlights, and the pale moon. "It was one of the most weird and remarkable scenes of the war, probably of any war," he later wrote. "An army was being landed on an enemy's coast at the dead of night, but with somewhat more of cheers and shrieks and laughter than rise from the bathers in the surf at Coney Island on a hot Sunday. It was a pandemonium of noises. The men still to be landed from the 'prison hulks,' as they called the transports, were singing in chorus, the men already on shore were dancing naked around camp-fires on the beach, or shouting with delight as they plunged into the first bath that had offered in seven days, and those in the launches as they were pitched headfirst at the soil of Cuba, signalized their arrival by howls of triumph."[86]

In the middle of the night, as torrential rains washed out the camp-fires and softened the earth into oatmeal, Major-General Joseph Wheeler, the feisty old Confederate who commanded the Cavalry Division, summoned Colonel Wood and Wood's immediate superior, Brigadier-General S. B. M. Young. Shafter, who wanted to stand pat until the supply lines were flowing, had stayed behind on the *Segurança*. Wheeler, the ranking officer on the scene, was impatient to move. Seizing his opportunity, Wheeler ordered the troops to set out at daybreak. At this crucial strategy meeting, Davis was present—evidently the only reporter so honored.[87]

He had no chance to sleep before sunrise, when the troops moved out. Squadrons of regulars from the First and Tenth Cavalries struck out on the main road to Santiago, which ran along the upper rim of a valley. The Rough Riders were ordered to take a mountain trail about a half-mile or mile to its left, or west. On a plateau about three miles inland, the Rough Riders' mountain trail joined the regular cavalry's main road at a place which had no name but featured a stand of low, wide, nut-bearing trees called *guásimas*. The valley and impenetrable jungle divided the two trails.

The trail that the Rough Riders took was so steep that correspondent Edward Marshall of the New York *Journal* often had to cling to rocks and shrubs to pull himself up. Davis looked down on him from a privileged vantage point. Half-paralyzed by another sciatica attack, he had obtained use of one of the government's precious mules.[88] In the blistering heat, he was one of the few who could appreciate the luxuriant scenery. Riding alongside Roosevelt, who had never been in the tropics, he pointed out unfamiliar birds and trees. They agreed that it was impossible to comprehend that they were at war in the enemy's country.

Twenty minutes after leaving camp, Wood dispatched an advance guard of fifty men under Captain Allyn Capron, Jr. The rest of the column continued behind Wood, compressed into single file by the dense undergrowth and tangled vines that bordered the beaten trail. They had been proceeding for an hour and a half when Wood stopped the column and rode ahead to meet Capron, who was returning. Wood came back at once, leading his horse, and told Roosevelt: "Pass the word back to keep silence in the ranks." At the spot where they halted, the trail narrowed further and descended sharply. To the left was a five-stranded barbed-wire fence, cut through at this point, with fields of high grass beyond it. On the right side of the trail were dense bushes. Grateful for the rest, the weary men stirred a breeze with their hats and fantasized about beer.

Wood, after a ten-minute reconnaissance mission, fanned his troops out on either side of the trail: through the cut fence, into the bushes (virtually impenetrable, it turned out), and down the valley toward Young's regulars. He sent Capron's advance guard straight ahead down the trail. Although Davis knew what Wood was thinking, he personally believed that the Spanish, having offered no resistance at Daiquirí, would wait until Santiago before attacking in force. Roosevelt, reminiscing with Marshall about a luncheon hosted by Hearst in the Astor House, looked casually at the barbed-wire fence, then gasped. "My God! this wire has been cut today," he exclaimed: despite the heavy dew, the ends were unrusted. At that moment the surgeon, riding a mule, blundered up to the front. Shouting for quiet, Roosevelt made more noise still.[89]

The firing started suddenly on the right.

It sounded so close that Davis thought Capron's men must be shooting at random in search of an enemy. He ran after G Troop, which had been deployed in the thick undergrowth to the right of the trail, and found the men beating through bushes in an attempt to locate the source of the gunfire. "It was like forcing the walls of a maze," he wrote. "If each trooper had not kept in touch with the man on either hand he would have been lost in the thicket. At one moment the underbrush seemed swarming with troopers, and the next, except that you heard the twigs breaking, and the heavy breathing of the men, or a crash as a vine pulled someone down, there was not a sign of a human being anywhere."[90] After a few minutes, they all broke through into a small clearing that was closed by a curtain of entwined vines. Falling to one knee, the men began to return the gunfire that came, heavy and low, from no more than eighty yards away on the other side of that curtain. They could see no Spaniards. Fearing that Capron's men had lost their bearings and were firing in mistake, they called out to Capron that he was shooting at friends. "From this comes the frequently made—and false—statement that the Rough Riders had fired at each other," Davis later wrote. After the battle, the Rough Riders found hundreds of spent Spanish cartridges in front of G Troop's position.[91]

The shouting did, however, permit the Spanish to target the Rough Riders more accurately. As Spanish bullets whizzed in, nine men were seriously wounded in three minutes. A man near Davis was shot through the head. The soldiers crawled on their knees and stomachs, dragging the injured with them. Because of the smokeless powder, the enemy could not be seen. Arriving while the troop was holding fire for fear of shooting Capron's men, Roosevelt studied the jungle-covered mountain in front of him, searching vainly for a target, when Davis, who was standing by his side doing the same thing, suddenly said, "There they are, Colonel; look over there; I can see their hats near that glade." As Roosevelt later wrote: "It was Richard Harding Davis who gave us our first opportunity to shoot back with effect. He was behaving precisely like my officers, being on the extreme front of the line, and taking every opportunity to study with his glasses the ground where we thought the Spaniards were." Calling a few of his best marksmen, Roosevelt directed their fire and flushed out the enemy.[92]

Unable to advance in the jungle, G Troop moved back to the left and returned to the place where the column first halted. Pausing at that spot on the trail, where a dressing station had been set up for the wounded of G Troop, Davis saw a familiar figure he could not quite place. "A tall, gaunt young man with a cross on his arm was just coming back up the trail," he wrote. "His head was bent, and by some surgeon's trick he was advancing rapidly with great strides, and at the same time carrying a wounded man much heavier than himself across his shoulders. As I stepped out of the trail he raised his head, and smiled and nodded, and left me wondering where I had seen him before, smiling in the same cheery, confident way and moving in that same position. I knew it could not have been under the same conditions, and yet he was certainly associated with another time of excitement and rush and heat, and then I remembered him. He had been covered with blood and dirt and perspiration as he was now, only then he wore a canvas jacket and the man he carried on his shoulders was trying to hold him back from a white-washed line. And I recognized the young doctor with the blood bathing his breeches as 'Bob' Church of Princeton."[93] A Princeton football star on the field of battle—he might have burst, fully formed, out of the pages of a Davis story.[94]

While other troops spread to the right trying to link up to General Young's column of regulars, G Troop moved to the left, hurrying through the cut opening in the barbed-wire fence. "The advances were made in quick, desperate rushes—sometimes the ground gained was no more than a man covers in sliding for a base," Davis wrote. "At other times half a troop would rise and race forward and then burrow deep in the hot grass and fire. . . . The enemy were hidden in the shade of the jungle, while [the Rough Riders] had to fight in the open for every thicket they gained, crawling through grass which was as hot as a steam bath, and with their flesh and clothing torn by thorns and the sword-like blade of the Spanish 'bayonet.' The glare of the sun was full in their eyes and as fierce as a limelight."[95] G Troop advanced out of sight while Davis, stricken with sciatica, rested his bum leg at the dressing station. By the time he was ready to go, he could see no American soldiers in the field. He ran down the trail, which narrowed as it descended. Interlacing vines and boughs blocked out the sun. On either side, the rocks and rank grass were spattered and matted with blood. Blanket-rolls, haversacks, and canteens were strewn along the path, jettisoned in the heat by the Americans headed for the front. The spot was as silent as a graveyard, except for the whistling of the Spanish Mauser bullets and the scuttling of the hideous orchid-colored land crabs. Silent, but not unpopulated: casualties lay along the trail, the wounded as quiet as the dead.

At the sound of the stones kicked by Davis's feet, a hospital steward emerged from the underbrush, and called out: "Lieutenant Thomas is badly wounded in here, and we can't move him. We want to carry him out of the sun some place, where there is shade and a breeze." Davis followed the man and found Thomas, the first lieutenant of Capron's troop, lying on a blanket, half-naked and covered in blood. He had been shot through the thigh, and his leg was bound in a crude tourniquet of twigs and gaudy handkerchiefs. Raving and tossing in pain, he tried to sit upright when they raised the corners of the blanket to move him. "You're taking me to the front, aren't you?" he cried. "You said you would. They killed my captain— do you understand? They've killed Captain Capron. The ⸻ ⸻ ⸻ Mexicans! They've killed my captain." (Even in his notebook, Davis recorded Thomas's curses with dashes.) As the troopers carried him, assuring him that they were following his orders, they stumbled on roots and vines, cringing as they left a black streak of blood on the grass. But Thomas seemed not to notice. Raising his bloody hands, he cursed and pleaded to be taken to the front until the heat and loss of blood silenced him into a faint.

Thomas was right about Capron. Davis found him about fifty feet further down the trail, propped up against Bob Church. The surgeon was cutting away Capron's tunic to expose a black open wound in the chest "as white as a girl's." Nothing could be done; he was dying. Fifty yards beyond, around a turn, Davis found a boy with a bullet wound between the eyes. His chest was heaving with short, hoarse rattles. Lifting him, Davis tried to give him a drink, but water wouldn't pass between the clenched teeth. As he copied down the name written in a New Testament in the dying youth's pocket, another boy came down the trail and said, "It's no use, the surgeon has seen him; he says he is just the same as dead. He is my bunkie; we only met two weeks ago at San Antonio; but he and me had got to be such good friends—But there's nothing I can do now." Davis left him sitting on a rock beside his bunkie, weeping. As he proceeded down the trail, the firing sounded close. There were no more bodies or blanket-rolls by the side, making Davis think he had gone farther than the point at which Capron's column had left the trail. Running ahead, hoping to rejoin the men, he saw the body of a sergeant sprawled across the path. It was a hundred yards ahead of any of the others—evidently the first man killed. From his pocket, Davis took a silver watch with the inscription "God gives" and the initials "H.F." It was Hamilton Fish, the New York playboy who was the grandson of President Grant's secretary of state. A bullet had passed through his heart.[96] Davis closed the dead man's eyes.[97]

Borrowing a carbine from a wounded soldier, Davis joined the remnant of Capron's L Troop, now commanded by Second Lieutenant Richard Day. As a correspondent, Davis should have been a noncombatant; but he wasn't the only reporter to break the rule. Edward Marshall of the *Journal* had obtained smokeless-powder revolver cartridges in Tampa. Gleefully, he fired in the direction of the Spaniards, who were more than six hundred yards away. By Marshall's account, Davis, over to the right, was "pumping wildly" with his carbine.[98] Although he had met the regiment just the day before, Marshall "felt that every man who was hit was my personal friend, and there was nothing professional in the interest which I took in each one of them."[99] Feeling much the same way, and having known many of the men in their New York and Newport incarnations, Davis advanced alongside the Rough Riders through tall grass, in which thousands of Mauser cartridges glittered in the dazzling sun. The Spanish were in retreat, but it was a slow and punishing retreat. The Rough Riders struck by Mauser bullets lay where they fell, waiting for the hospital stewards to find them. Among the wounded was Marshall, shot through the body near the spine. Right after he was hit, Davis and Stephen Crane came up to him. He was in agony, racked with convulsions. "What can I do for you?" Crane asked him. "Well, you might file my despatches," Marshall replied. "I don't mean file 'em ahead of your own, old man—but just file 'em if you find it handy." Crane wrote afterward: "I immediately decided that he was doomed. No man could be so sublime in detail concerning the trade of journalism and not die. There was the solemnity of a funeral song in these absurd and fine sentences about despatches." Expected to die, Marshall recovered, but he was paralyzed by the bullet.[100] After assisting Marshall, Crane took the wounded man's copy back to Siboney, and filed to the *World* his own brief, undistinguished dispatch of the Rough Riders' "gallant blunder."[101]

After an hour of fighting, the Rough Riders' skirmish line reached more open country, which rose gradually to a wood. At the wood's edge stood a ruined *aguardiente* distillery which the Spanish held. Roosevelt and

Wood were advancing separately. Although they couldn't communicate easily with the captains, those men were intelligent enough to realize that this dilapidated shack was their target.[102] Davis also knew it. He urged Lieutenant Day to make the charge, and he ran with him, firing about twenty rounds.[103] "If the men had been regulars I would have sat in the rear as Crane did," he wrote his family, "but I knew every other one of them[,] had played football and all that sort of thing, with them, so I thought as an American I ought to help."[104] The Rough Riders' charge was a bluff—but it worked. The Spaniards assumed that the skirmish line which broke out from the bushes and trees must be the advance of a full regiment. They fired a few volleys and fled. The regulars of the First and Tenth Cavalries, coming up on the right, cinched the victory. Confirming that all danger had passed, the Cuban soldiers, who had mysteriously absented themselves during the combat, now reappeared, to scavenge the bedrolls that the Rough Riders had thrown off in the heat of battle. Thenceforth, the Americans viewed them with the same disgust they felt for the scuttling land crabs, which disfigured the fresh corpses by eating the eyes and lips.[105]

The fighting had lasted an hour and a half. It was fierce combat in brutal heat, fought by men who had slept only three hours on the wet ground after a cramped, fatiguing week on a transport ship. They had fought with unfamiliar Krag-Jorgensen carbines. They were outnumbered at least two to one by an enemy that, thanks to smokeless-powder Mausers, was virtually invisible.[106] And yet, they had won. The victory at Las Guási-mas—as the unnamed place was promptly christened—was a joint triumph for the Rough Riders and the regulars of the First and Tenth Cavalries. In the press accounts, and later in the history books, the regulars have attracted little attention. In part, that's because the Rough Riders, with their final charge, secured the victory, and did it in a dramatic way. Most of the explanation, though, falls under the category of press relations. The regulars fought the enemy without an attending bard to sing their praises. Even had a star reporter been on the scene, the story was inherently less compelling; to the New York newspaper audience, for whom the leading correspondents wrote, the regulars were nobodies. (In fact, the Tenth, which was cited for exceptional bravery, was a black unit.) The Rough Riders, particularly the dudes of K Troop, were familiar names to the readers of society and sports pages.

For a battle to seize the public imagination, as the Las Guásimas fight did, there must be at least one soldier of heroic stature, and at least one chronicler of descriptive power. The partnership of Roosevelt and Davis, forged at this nameless Cuban crossroads, was the high point of Davis's journalistic career, and the start of Roosevelt's final ascent to the White House. Each man instinctively recognized the importance of the other to his success. During a lull in the battle, Roosevelt urged the Associated Press correspondent (in vain) to cite Davis's courage in the fight.[107] In the afterglow of victory, he publicly praised Davis's contribution in detecting the hidden Spanish forces, and offered him a captaincy in the regiment whenever he wanted it.[108] Davis was one of three men to be named honorary members of the regiment's association.[109] Later, in his self-aggrandizing history of the regiment, Roosevelt once again commended Davis for his contributions during the fight. The satirist Finley Peter Dunne tweaked a pair of noses when he had his Mr. Dooley mimic Roosevelt's chronicle: "We had no sooner landed in Cubia than it became nicessry f'r me to take command iv th' ar-rmy which I did at wanst. A number of days was spint be me in reconnoitring, attinded on'y be me brave an' fluent body guard, Richard Harding Davis."[110]

Except for Marshall, who was crippled, J. P. Dunning of the A.P., who was colorless, and Crane, who was largely absent, Davis was the only reporter who saw the Rough Riders attacked at Las Guásimas.[111] In recounting the bloody events of the day, he had one ticklish question to resolve. There could be no doubt that the men had conducted themselves bravely in battle. But had they been prepared for the contest that they won? Or had they blundered into an ambush? In assessing the mettle of their leaders, Wood and Roosevelt, the answer was of paramount importance. The initial reports of the Guásimas fight had described a shocking ambush and defeat, with Wood dead and his men in disarray. These sketchy, confused eyewitness accounts had spread through Siboney, as the wounded arrived on their way to the hospital ship. Supplementing their unreliable testimony were the hysterical words of Adjutant Tom Hall, who, seeing Marshall fall in a spot where Wood had been standing, fled the battlefield in a panic. When he reached Siboney, he told the reporters gathered there that he had seen Wood drop and had taken down his dying message to his wife. Since those in a position to know better were still in combat, this version was unchallenged, and the reporters in the rear filed it to their papers.[112]

In the considered account of the battle that he later published in *Scribner's*, Davis blamed the reporters in the rear for accepting the word of the wounded and Hall when they wrote that the Rough Riders had stumbled blindly into an ambush at Las Guásimas. While he admitted that the enemy had lain in ambush, he claimed (and here he brandished his authority as a witness to the post-midnight planning session of Wheeler, Young, and Wood) that the Rough Riders had been warned; and he emphasized the "vast difference between blundering into an ambuscade and setting out with a full knowledge that you will find the enemy in ambush, and finding him, there and then driving him out of his ambush and before you for a mile and a half into a full retreat."[113] On paper, this distinction seemed sharp indeed. That it looked fuzzier in real life is obvious from reading Davis's own on-the-scene account.

His first dispatch, which appeared in the *Herald* two days after the fight, described "an ambush with the advantages all on the side of the enemy."[114] His second news account reiterated that the Rough Riders had been "surprised" in an "ambush."[115] Writing to his parents immediately after the battle, he similarly said, "We were caught in a clear case of ambush. Every precaution had been taken but they knew the ground and our men did not. It was the hottest, nastiest fight I ever imagined. We never saw the enemy except glimpses."[116] The next day, sending a detailed description of the battle to Charles, he wrote, "No one knew we were near Spaniards until both columns were on the place where the two trails meet."[117] Yet when it came time to write (as he would put it) not for the short-lived newspapers but for the history books, Davis erased any hint of an ambush. He ridiculed the very idea: as when, in a fawning letter to Roosevelt, he derided the account of a Las Guásimas ambush in Stephen Bonsal's book on the war. ("You have the matter as clear as a bell," Roosevelt replied.)[118] Modern historians concur with Davis's verdict.[119] However, had Shafter, not Wheeler, ordered the operation, in which sixteen Americans died and fifty-two were wounded, one wonders how Davis—and history—would have defined an ambush.[120]

Having secured the position of Las Guásimas on June 24, the army proceeded on the single trail which led to Santiago. Streams crossed the path in two places. The American outpost was established at the first ford and extended three miles to the rear. This stretch of the trail was a sunken wagon road, with banks that were three or four feet high. When it rained— as it did every afternoon, torrentially, for an hour—the trail became a huge gutter. For six days the American army encamped here. Rations were short. Instead of being served rice and beans, which are standard fare in the tropics, the men ate fried bacon and hardtack. They hunted for mangoes or coconuts to supplement their fatty diet. And tobacco, which had been scarce from the start of the campaign, was now unavailable. Although carried in the tranports, tobacco had been classified—along with canned peaches and lime juice—as a luxury, to be issued only after the bacon, hardtack, and coffee had reached the front. Himself down to a small cache of rough Durham tobacco, Davis observed the enlisted men smoking dried horse droppings, grass, roots, and tea. If it could be found, a plug of tobacco normally worth eight cents went for two dollars. "Tobacco to many people is a luxury, to men who smoke it is a necessity," Davis wrote. He would pound this point angrily in every subsequent war he covered.[121]

In these depressing surroundings, as the army spun its wheels in the mud, Davis's distaste for General Shafter swelled into loathing. The corpulent commander was conspicuously absent from the front. He was, Richard wrote his father, "an inexperienced, under-bred man and so fat that he can hardly walk."[122] Instead of walking, he lay on his cot cursing, Davis wrote;

"he insulted all of the foreign attachés collectively, and some individually, and he related stories in the presence of boy officers which would have been found offensive in the smoking-room of a steamer."[123] Starting with the botched departure from Tampa, everything Shafter touched had gone awry. The landing points of Daiquirí and Siboney had been "unnecessarily distant" from the goal of Santiago. It was a miracle that more men hadn't drowned at Daiquirí: the engineers who might have repaired the damaged pier had been sent that day by Shafter to build pontoon bridges for the Cubans thirty-six miles up the coast. At Siboney, where there was no pier at all, one was finally constructed, but so close to shore that supplies had to be laboriously unloaded from the transport ships and ferried in by lighters and tugs. Making matters worse, the captains of the transport ships retained their first loyalty to the ship owners, and not to the government which had leased the ships at great cost. They would scurry out to sea at the faintest sound of gunfire on shore, taking their badly needed supplies with them. "Had there been a strong man in command of the expedition," Davis wrote, "he would have ordered them into place, [and] stern and bow anchors would have kept them there. . . ."[124]

While Shafter dawdled on the *Seguança*, trying to unknot the tangled supply lines, the troops encamped on the road to Santiago had little to do but gaze at the scenery. Even the scenery was restricted. Officers were ordered not to explore further than a mile and a half beyond the outpost, where the hill called El Pozo afforded a view of the great valley that led to Santiago. From El Pozo, on the left one could see hills that hid the sea. On the right was the village of El Caney. Directly below El Pozo, a green forest stretched for a mile and a half, up to a meadow of high grass that ended after half a mile in a mountainous ridge called the San Juan hills. The hills looked prosperous, sunny, and peaceful; even that symbol of Spanish militarism, the blockhouse, resembled a Chinese pagoda at this distance. On June 27, the pretty view was ominously disturbed by the appearance of a long yellow pit in the San Juan hillside. With his field glasses, Davis could plainly see straw sombreros bobbing in these trenches. By the blockhouse, he detected blue-coated Spaniards riding on white ponies. Each day, the rifle pits grew longer and more numerous. Turning to his right, toward the village of El Caney, he could see street parades of Spanish soldiers. For four days he watched as the Spanish, unhindered, strengthened their defenses.

On June 30, surveying the terrain for the first time, Shafter rode out to El Pozo.[125] "He looks like he could carry the mule he was riding better than the mule could carry him," quipped one Rough Rider.[126] The heat on the three-mile ride prostrated the obese commander. According to Davis, he spent most of the remainder of his Cuban sojourn on his cot. "This is the offense that I impute to Shafter: that while he was not even able to rise and look at the city he had been sent to capture, he still clung to his authority," Davis later wrote.[127] But Shafter—although plagued by the heat and a gouty foot—was not quite as incapacitated as Davis claimed. While he was, by his own testimony, "nauseated and very dizzy" on June 30, and "very ill" the next day, he nonetheless remained, much of the time, in the saddle.[128] The battle plan, whatever one may think of it, was his plan.

After Shafter returned to his headquarters, he assembled his division commanders to outline the next day's attack. Among his replacements for officers felled by malarial fever were Colonel Wood, who took over General Young's brigade, and Roosevelt, who replaced Wood as colonel of the Rough Riders. Splitting his force in two, Shafter sent eight thousand men (including Roosevelt and Wood) down the main trail, which continued from the El Pozo outpost through a mile and a half of jungle and a half-mile meadow, until it reached the San Juan hills. Shafter directed Major-General H. J. Lawton to lead nearly seven thousand men to the northeast, or right side, of the trail, in an assault on the village of El Caney. Once they took El Caney—which, both Lawton and Shafter thought, should require no more than a couple of hours—Lawton would move his men to the primary battlefield, the San Juan hills. For the last four days, the Americans had watched impotently as the Spaniards entrenched the hills with rifle pits. This would be the major barrier to the taking of Santiago. It would also be the scene—in no small part thanks to Davis—of one of the most famous battles of American history.[129]

At about 4:00 P.M. on June 30, orders were issued to break camp. The word came simultaneously to some fifteen regiments. Imagine fifteen regiments camped along Fifth Avenue and directed at the same moment to march downtown, Davis wrote—and then think of it with Fifth Avenue only ten feet wide. Treading on each other's heels in three inches of mud, the troops stumbled slowly forward. The file was so interminable that someone joked it was a small group of men, marching in a circle around a hill to impress the Spaniards. They were still marching at midnight. Adding to the air of unreality was a huge signal balloon, imported from France, that floated at tree-top level above the gawking men.

Incapacitated by sciatica, Davis was driven by wagon to the front.[130] From the headquarters tent of Brigadier-General S. S. Sumner, who had replaced the fever-stricken Wheeler as the head of the Cavalry Division, he looked out at the white mist rising from the basin before the San Juan hills. Through the mist, the lights of Santiago were shining three miles away. He could see General Sumner and his staff making maps in pencil by candlelight. After filing a brief dispatch to the *Herald*, Davis turned in. He shared a blanket with a second lieutenant, who, after much tossing and a long silence, said, "So if anything happens to me, to-morrow, you'll see she gets them, won't you?" He was talking about letters, but Davis never delivered them. Although every sixth man was killed or wounded the next day, the second lieutenant was unhurt. When he married his fiancée in October, Davis sent him a silver flask engraved with the insignia of his troop.[131]

When they married in 1863, Rebecca Harding was a thirty-one-year-old writer who seemed fated to spinsterhood, and L. Clarke Davis was a twenty-seven-year-old lawyer who dreamed of becoming a journalist.
(Kehrig Collection)

Richard as an infant was (his mother said) "the smallest tiredest little thing. And homely too only with big dark eyes. . . ." (Kehrig Collection)

Even as a five-year-old, Richard adored dressing up in costumes. (Kehrig Collection)

Richard by age nine was both publicly charming and privately morbid. (Kehrig Collection)

Both Richard and his younger brother, Charles (back row, second and fourth from the right), played football for Lehigh in 1884–85. Richard later said that he took "a keener satisfaction in the fact that he scored the first touchdown" in Lehigh history than he did in all of his short stories.
(Special Collections, Lehigh University Libraries)

In his junior (and final) year at Lehigh, Richard (right) became an editor of the student newspaper, the Burr.
(Fairfax Downey, Richard Harding Davis: His Day*)*

In his first journalistic coup, twenty-three-year-old Richard dressed up as a burglar and infiltrated a ring of criminals. Even he admitted that his makeup was "a trifle too villainous."
(Kehrig Collection)

Davis (center) convulsed the other reporters in flood-devastated Johnstown when he asked where he might buy a white shirt.
(Fairfax Downey, Richard Harding Davis: His Day)

At twenty-eight, Davis was managing editor of Harper's Weekly *and one of the leading young men of New York.*

Davis outfitted himself fully before the Spanish-American War. When this photograph was publicized, one newspaper jeered, "There will be a terrific inkshed when he reaches the front." (Kehrig Collection)

During the Spanish-American War, Davis and Theodore Roosevelt forged a partnership that boosted both men's careers. (Culver Pictures)

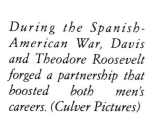

Idealized in drawings by his friend Charles Dana Gibson, Davis became the American masculine ideal at the turn of the century.

Among the members of the Davis wedding party in Marion on May 4, 1899, were maid of honor Ethel Barrymore (on Cecil's right) and best man Charles Davis (behind Barrymore). Louise Clark can be seen just behind her daughter, Cecil. Charles Dana Gibson stands behind Richard, to his left. Cecil's brother, Bruce, is at the extreme left in the back row. John Fox, Jr., is holding a cigarette at Richard's left. (Poett Collection)

After Richard married Cecil Clark, the twenty-three-room Clark "summer cottage" (since demolished), on fourteen waterfront acres in Marion, Massachusetts, was winterized for the newlyweds. It became their primary residence.
(Poett Collection)

Richard rented a small Marion house—a real cottage—
as his office.
(Kehrig Collection)

Cecil Clark made this sketch of Richard before their marriage. In general, she preferred to do portraits of women. (Poett Collection)

Cecil Clark Davis with her bull terrier, Jaggers, named for the messenger boy who carried Richard's engagement ring from London to Chicago.
(Poett Collection)

Morning broke on July 1 with the pounding of artillery. Allyn Capron, the captain whose namesake son had died at Las Guásimas, commanded the battery aimed at El Caney from a knoll about a mile and a half southeast of the village. The booming noise drifted across the miles of quiet jungle to El Pozo, where Captain George Grimes was setting up his battery, trained on the pagodalike Spanish blockhouse on the San Juan hills. Just behind his battery was a farmhouse, the only building for a mile around. There were Cubans inside, the Rough Riders (and Davis) in the yard, and a camp of cavalry regulars nearby. After each round, a telltale belch of black smoke lingered in the air for a full minute. To the first twenty shots, the Spaniards made no reply. When they did respond, their third shell landed among the Cubans, Rough Riders, and First and Tenth Cavalries, killing some and wounding many. The rest fled to safety.

"These casualties were utterly unnecessary," Davis fumed in print, "and were due to the stupidity of whoever placed the men within fifty yards of guns in action." Later, he asked who was responsible; Shafter, he was told. It was one more black mark against the fat man. Because only sixteen three-inch guns had been taken to Cuba (sixty were left behind in Tampa), this unfortunate incident was the only major participation of the artillery in the battle for Santiago. Here was another opportunity for criticism. Had the Americans pounded the San Juan hills with effective artillery, Davis claimed, the subsequent casualty rate among infantrymen would have been greatly reduced. "It was like going to a fire with a hook and ladder company," he wrote, "and leaving the hose and the steam-engines in the engine-house."[132]

About a quarter-hour after the El Pozo battery began to fire, one of Shafter's aides ordered the Cavalry Division to proceed down the Santiago trail to the edge of the woods, then halt at the beginning of the high grass and await further orders. The San Juan River, which despite its name was just a stream, crossed the trail at this point. Another brook ran across the trail about two hundred yards farther on. The troops were halted at the San Juan River; some crossed it and others went in single file to the right.

The grass, so high it blocked all wind, was suffocatingly hot. Some of the men were along the banks of the stream, others were in the grass, and many were in the bushes at the wood's edge, when the enemy opened fire, raining down bullets and shells for a mile to the rear. The men were ordered not to return the fire. For an hour they waited, as bullets cut through the high, waving grass. The place would henceforth be known as "bloody ford," "bloody bend," or "bloody angle." Bloody it was. Hospital stewards carried the wounded to the stream, laying them in long rows, feet at the water's edge and bodies on the muddy banks. Adding another dimension to the terror, sharpshooters and guerrillas hid in the trees above the streams and trail. Bullets came from every side. Because of the smokeless powder, and the din of shrieking shrapnel and spitting Mausers, the sharpshooters were invisible. A guerrilla wounded a Rough Rider who was helping Davis carry an injured captain. A second shot from the same tree almost hit the wounded man that they dropped on the ground. The wounded and the medics were preyed upon by snipers, and the surgeons dressed wounds with one eye on the trees. While the whining Mauser bullets passed too high for worry, the sharpshooter bullets splashed down among them. "The sounds of the two bullets," Davis wrote, "were as different as is the sharp pop of a soda-water bottle from the buzzing of an angry wasp."

In writing about the battle, Davis contrasted the gallantry of the fighting men with the stupidity of their commanders. The wounded lay uncomplaining. Losing his way, Davis came across Lieutenant Roberts of the Tenth Cavalry, a white officer of a black regiment. He was shot through the intestines, sitting upright, drenched in his own blood. Three of his soldiers, each shot in an arm or leg, sat with him. When the soldiers with Davis offered to carry Roberts back to the dressing station, the black troopers responded stiffly. "If the Lieutenant had been able to move, we would have carried him away long ago," said a sergeant, ignoring the fact that his arm was shattered. "Oh, don't bother the surgeons about me," Roberts added. "They must be very busy. I can wait."[133]

The men had been led into a trap. They could not retreat, because thousands of their comrades filled the trail behind them. They could not shoot, because their commanders forbade it—sensibly enough, since there were no targets. They waited, and they died. "This was endured for an hour, an hour of such hell of fire and heat, that the heat in itself, had there been no bullets, would have been remembered for its cruelty," Davis wrote vividly. "Men gasped on their backs, like fishes in the bottom of a boat, their heads burning inside and out, their limbs too heavy to move. They had been rushed here and rushed there wet with sweat and wet with fording the streams, under a sun that would have made moving a fan an effort, and they lay prostrate, gasping at the hot air, with faces aflame, and their tongues sticking out, and their eyes rolling. All through this the volleys from the rifle-pits sputtered and rattled, and the bullets sang continuously like the wind through the riggings in a gale, shrapnel whined and broke, and still no order came from General Shafter."[134] Lawton's division, which was supposed to have furnished reinforcement on the right, didn't arrive. Heavy firing from the direction of El Caney indicated that the battle hadn't been concluded as expeditiously as Lawton planned. "The situation," Davis wrote, "was desperate. . . . [A] series of military blunders had brought seven thousand American soldiers into a chute of death. . . ."[135]

Any reader of fiction will recognize that such a dire scene demands the appearance of a hero. Any student of American history will know the hero's name. Teddy Roosevelt had crossed the stream and halted his men in a sunken trail, with the First and Tenth Cavalries next to him. In front were the Ninth on the right, the Sixth in the center, and the Third on the left (although, the longer they waited in the jungle, the more the regiments overlapped). The trail continued between two hills. The further hill, on the left, was fortified with heavy blockhouses. As the main elevation in the San Juan hill range, it was called San Juan Hill. The closer knoll on the right contained some large ranch buildings and a conspicuous black iron kettle, causing the men to dub it Kettle Hill. From both hills, the Spaniards trained their Mausers on the Americans in the high grass.

Having waited in vain for a response to his repeated requests to advance, Roosevelt was about to act on his own when a lieutenant-colonel rode up with welcome instructions from General Sumner. Roosevelt should bring the Rough Riders forward to support the regulars in an assault on the two hills. At last! Like a dammed river, his pent-up energy thundered when released. Riding through the high grass, Roosevelt shouted and shoved his men into formation. Starting from the rear, where the colonel is supposed to remain, he pushed his way to the front, mobilizing as he rode. When he came to the head of his regiment, he ran into some of the troopers of the First and Ninth, who were lying on the ground, while their officers walked back and forth. He told the ranking captain that he had been ordered to take the hills, and that shooting would not do the job. They had to rush the Spaniards. When the officer hesitated to follow him in a charge, citing orders to keep his men where they were, Roosevelt brushed him aside, saying (as reported by Davis), "If you don't wish to go forward, let my men pass, please." Whatever the captain's doubts, the regulars, like iron filings to a moving magnet, rose from the grass to follow the charismatic colonel as the Rough Riders charged Kettle Hill.[136]

Watching, Davis was thrilled. So were the other observers, but the excitement comes across best in Davis's account of how "Roosevelt, mounted high on horseback, and charging the rifle-pits at a gallop and quite alone, made you feel that you would like to cheer. He wore on his sombrero a blue polka-dot handkerchief, *à la* Havelock, which, as he advanced, floated out straight behind his head, like a guidon." (After the battle, the Rough Riders adopted a polka-dot handkerchief as their badge.)[137] "No one who saw Roosevelt take that ride expected he would finish it alive," Davis wrote in the *Herald*. "As the only mounted man, he was the most conspicuous object in range of the rifle pits, then only two hundred yards ahead. It looked like foolhardiness, but, as a matter of fact, he set the pace with his horse and inspired the men to follow."[138] From a distance—which is how most correspondents saw it—the assault resembled a storybook picture; but from closer up, it was a scramble. Davis didn't make the charge. He stopped to help Morton Henry, a Philadelphia man who was lying wounded in the stream at "bloody bend," about three hundred yards to the rear. By the time he caught up with the Rough Riders, they were cheering in victory.[139]

But even while he was assisting Henry, Davis had one eye on the battle.

He recorded it with an eye trained to report things as they happened, not as they might have been expected to happen. He recalled afterward that there were so few men that his instinct was to call to them to come back, to shout that they were making a pathetic mistake. He was gripped not by a vision of heroism, but by the sight of colossal folly. Afterward, he remarked that he had seen many illustrations of the San Juan charge, depicting gallant men forming an invincible line. Although these pictures were magnificent, they were not of the war he witnessed. "[The Americans] had no glittering bayonets, they were not massed in regular array," he wrote. "There were a few men in advance, bunched together, and creeping up a steep, sunny hill, the tops of which roared and flashed with flame. The men held their guns pressed across their breasts and stepped heavily as they climbed. Behind these first few, spreading out like a fan, were single lines of men, slipping and scrambling in the smooth grass, moving forward with difficulty, as though they were wading waist-high through water, moving slowly, carefully, with strenuous effort. It was much more wonderful than any swinging charge could have been. They walked to greet death at every step, many of them, as they advanced, sinking suddenly or pitching forward and disappearing in the high grass, but the others waded on, stubbornly, forming a thin blue line that kept creeping higher and higher up the hill. It was as inevitable as the rising tide."*[140] As the bluecoats neared the top, the Spaniards suddenly appeared, silhouetted against the sky, and then they fled before the cresting wave that pursued them.

At the same time that the Rough Riders were charging Kettle Hill, the regular infantrymen—led by the gallant, white-haired General Hamilton S. Hawkins—stormed the key Spanish position of San Juan Hill. From the vantage point of Kettle Hill, which he had just secured, Roosevelt could see the hard fight proceeding. For a while, he had his men fire on the Spanish trenches. As the doughboys approached the crest, however, he had to hold fire. Wanting to be in at the finish, he called to his men to make a final rush down Kettle Hill and up the northern extension of San Juan Hill. Jumping over a wire fence, he charged. After a hundred yards, he turned around and saw to his dismay that only five men were following him. Running back, he taunted and berated his troopers, who looked at him with innocent consternation. "We didn't hear you, we didn't see you go, Colonel," they cried, "lead on now, we'll sure follow you." By the time Roosevelt and his men arrived at the enemy's stronghold, Hawkins had flushed out most of the Spaniards, except for a few diehards in the trenches (including one whom Roosevelt shot with a revolver).[141] Davis followed the Rough Riders up the crest of San Juan Hill. He went with the artillery and

---

*The phrase "thin blue line" is adapted from the great war correspondent William Howard Russell's phrase "thin red line," referring to the British troops in a battle of the Crimean War.

was still the first correspondent on the scene. The black powder of the American artillery drew the fire of every Spanish rifle within range. "The artillery ran away after occupying the crest three minutes," he wrote home. "I occupied it about three seconds."[142]

Although Roosevelt is popularly thought to have taken San Juan Hill, that distinction belongs to Hawkins. Kettle Hill, which Roosevelt rushed, was a smaller elevation in the San Juan ridge. Some of the general confusion can be attributed to Davis, who conflated the two assaults.[143] As Davis wrote, Hawkins and Roosevelt were the two "most conspicuous" figures in the battle for Santiago. Yet in Davis's report, Hawkins has a featured role, and Roosevelt is the star. Davis explained his emphasis on Roosevelt this way: "General Hawkins, with hair as white as snow, and yet far in advance of men thirty years his junior, was so noble a sight that you felt inclined to pray for his safety; on the other hand, Roosevelt, mounted high on horseback, and charging the rifle-pits at a gallop and quite alone, made you feel that you would like to cheer."[144] To put it another way: Hawkins, a Gettysburg veteran, was a gallant incarnation of the receding American past. Roosevelt was the coming man, the man of the future. "Roosevelt in the last fifteen years has played many parts—cowboy, big game hunter, Civil Service Commissioner, Police Commissioner, Assistant Secretary of the Navy and writer of American history," Davis wrote in the *Herald*. "He is now making American history, and making it very well."[145]

After abandoning San Juan Hill, the Spaniards retreated to a formidable position, some five hundred to a thousand yards closer to the city of Santiago. From that stronghold, they directed their fire on the trenches that they had just ceded to the Americans.[146] Once he fled the Spanish fire on the crest of San Juan Hill, Davis found himself on the Santiago road, which was under a crossfire. After about seventy-five yards, at a turn, he saw Colonel Wood and a group of Rough Riders digging a trench. At that moment, Stephen Crane came up with Jimmy Hare, a photographer. Walking to the crest, Crane—"as sharply outlined as a semaphore"—looked out over the enemy lines, immediately attracting a flurry of whistling Mauser bullets to himself and his companions. Wood, like everyone else, was crouched low, and he shouted to Crane to get down. Still standing, Crane moved away, as though to get out of earshot. Again, Wood ordered Crane down, crying, "You're drawing the fire on these men." Despite the heat, Crane was wearing a long India-rubber raincoat—which he didn't take off for fear of losing it—and he was smoking a pipe. "He appeared as cool as though he were looking down from a box at the opera," Davis later recalled. Knowing that Crane hated to seem a poseur, Davis called out, "You're not impressing any one by doing that, Crane." Instantly, Crane dropped to his knees. When he crawled over to where the other men lay, Davis said, "I knew that would fetch you." Crane grinned. "Oh, was that it?" he said.[147]

He took no offense. Later in the day, Davis was stricken with another attack of sciatica. Having nothing to eat and no place to sleep, he accepted Crane's offer of a blanket and coffee at his bivouac near El Pozo. Crane and Hare each put a shoulder under Davis's arms, and lumbered and reeled down the trail. Harassed by gunfire, Davis protested that the three men together made too large a target, and asked to be set down. He insisted he could make camp himself after dusk. They ignored him. When Davis lay down in the road and refused to budge unless they left him, Crane pointed out to Hare the effect of the setting sun against the palm trees. Reaching the camp, they left Davis to recoup his strength. Hare took advantage of his absence to ask Crane, "Who's this pal of yours we just brought down the hill?" "Beg pardon, Jimmy," Crane said. "I thought you knew him. That's Richard Harding Davis." Hare, of course, had heard many stories about Davis, most of them unfavorable. He particularly disapproved of Davis's ignoring his noncombatant status and firing a gun at Las Guásimas. But he was impressed by the man's white-faced persistence despite racking pain. The men who criticized Davis were still in the rear. The butt of their jokes was at the front.[148]

On the day after, despite the San Juan victory, the U.S. troops saw little cause to rejoice. Even in their captured trenches, they were vulnerable to punishing gunfire from thousands of Spanish soldiers in the valley below. On July 2 and 3, 134 Americans were killed or wounded.[149] The fire was sustained without respite; so, for a second consecutive night, the men went without much sleep.[150] The surgeons lacked cots, hammocks, rubber blankets, pillows, and clothing for the wounded men, who lay on the wet grass awaiting attention—a disgraceful and demoralizing tableau.[151]

Depressed by his losses and by an attack of malaria, which had laid him prostrate on his cot, Shafter wrote despondently for help to Admiral Sampson. Throughout the campaign, Sampson had positioned his ships outside Santiago harbor, bottling up the fleet of Admiral Cervera. To make sure that the Spanish ships could not escape, he had sent Assistant Naval Constructor Richmond P. Hobson to scuttle a coal ship in the narrow entrance to Santiago Bay. The mission had not come off perfectly—the *Merrimac* sank within the harbor, rather than in the channel, and Hobson and his seven-man crew were captured—but the hulk would slow down the Spanish fleet, should it be so foolhardy as to try to flee. However, the Americans were as stalled outside the bay as the Spanish were within. Because of mines, Sampson could not enter the harbor until Shafter took the city and disconnected the explosives.[152] The admiral reminded Shafter of that fact. Receiving this discouraging response (which, at this late stage, should hardly have come as news), Shafter on July 3 sent a bleak telegram to Washington, saying that he was contemplating a retreat to the high ground between the San Juan River and Siboney, about five miles back. In short, he was thinking of giving back the San Juan ridge that had, so far, cost 1,609 American casualties, more than 10 percent of the men engaged.[153]

In Washington, Secretary of War Alger, on receipt of the telegram, felt this was "the darkest day of the war."[154]

The mood was at least as bleak in the rifle pits. Rumors quickly spread of an imminent retreat. "One smelt disaster in the air," Davis wrote. The men hadn't had a night's sleep since June 30. They moved on their hands and knees to avoid enemy fire. They were cramped from bending over in the trenches, and weak from the sun. Their clothes were soaked with sweat, dew, rain, and stream water. ("My clothes smell so that I can't use them for a pillow . . . ," Richard wrote his mother.[155]) Every afternoon, the sky burst with torrential rains, followed by steamy heat. "They were hanging to the crest of the San Juan hills by their teeth and finger-nails," Davis wrote, "and it seemed as though at any moment their hold would relax and they would fall."[156] After touring the rifle pits and interviewing the commanding officers on July 3, Davis wrote a long dispatch to the *Herald* that was his most controversial article of the war. Probably because it was so inflammatory, the newspaper didn't print it until July 7, by which time the crisis was over. Even so, Davis was pilloried for it.

"Another such victory as that of July 1 and our troops must retreat," Davis stated bluntly. "The situation is exceedingly grave." The Spanish were defending Santiago with six-inch guns. The Americans had only sixteen three-inch guns, for the heavier artillery had still not been unloaded from the ships. "It is as impossible to take Santiago with the infantry now overlooking its walls," he wrote, "as to open a safe with a pocket pistol." Touring the trenches, he saw men who had not slept, bathed, or eaten properly in days. "Those who smoke—and they are in the majority—were suffering agonies from the lack of tobacco," he reported. Shrapnel and sharpshooter bullets plagued them without cease. "I do not see how men not made of iron can stand such a state of affairs much longer," he wrote. "It is not a question of weeks but hours. This may sound hysterical, yet it is written with the most serious and earnest intention." And should anyone question who was to blame for this disaster, Davis wasn't coy about spelling it out. "Truthfully the expedition was prepared in ignorance and conducted in a series of blunders," he wrote. "Its commanding general has not yet even been within two miles of the scene of operation. . . . The presence of some man with absolute authority is necessary at the front. . . . This is written with the sole purpose that the entire press of the country will force instant action at Washington to relieve the strained situation."[157]

When it appeared on July 7, the article caused a great sensation. Some accused Davis of treason. It was said that his dispatch had been sent from New York to the Paris *Herald*, and then forwarded to Madrid, where the authorities immediately transmitted it to General José Toral in Cuba to encourage the Spanish troops to hold out.[158] That was highly unlikely, since by July 7, the situation in Santiago had dramatically changed. On July 3, the same day that Davis wrote his gloomy article, Cervera's fleet attempted to escape from Santiago harbor and was totally destroyed. The naval victory boosted the morale of the Americans enormously. Before hearing the news, Secretary of War Alger had replied on July 3 to Shafter's telegram by deferring to the general's on-the-scene knowledge but requesting that the San Juan heights be held if possible. By the time Alger left his office late that night, the newsboys were shouting, "Full account of the destruction of Spanish fleet!"; and the Secretary of War was carrying home the latest message received from Shafter: "I shall hold my present position."[159]

But even though the outook was brighter, the Spanish still had not capitulated when Davis's story appeared. Shafter reacted angrily to a dispatch from Washington summarizing Davis's article. Had he actually seen the *Herald* article, he later wrote, he would have arrested Davis and ordered him out of Cuba.[160] In New York, the *Sun* published a biting editorial that ridiculed Davis as "the head of the marshmallow school of fiction" and the possessor of a "surprising private stock of misinformation."[161] At *Harper's Weekly*, where the staff was still smarting from Davis's slap at Poultney Bigelow's article in June, an editorialist asked which of the two men was more culpable of treason: "Mr. Bigelow, who warned the country against its unpreparedness for the undertaking, or Mr. Davis, who betrays it in the face of the enemy and while his shells are sowing death among our troops?"[162] By attacking another journalist's honest reporting as disloyal, Davis had left himself defenseless against that same charge.

Criticism would no doubt have stung sharper but for the truce that the Americans initiated unilaterally on July 4 after the destruction of Cervera's fleet. With their ships eliminated, how could the Spanish hold out? Or so the Americans thought at first. In the postbattle lull, provisions— including tobacco and two-week-old newspapers—were at last carried to the men at the front. Things that had been unavailable at any price were now to be had. (Most of the items for sale, such as the Spanish horse and saddle Davis bought, were stolen property.)[163] Despite these palliatives, it became increasingly apparent that the overall situation was discouraging. Repeatedly, Shafter asked General Toral to surrender; and consistently, the Spanish commander politely declined.

Although the Mauser bullets had ceased to rain, the American troopers faced a greater threat: fever. Already weakened by malaria, the men were now subject to the far deadlier yellow fever, which first appeared in the army on July 6. Three cases had been reported in Siboney by July 9. Four days later, the count was up to 150.[164] The stench from the dead men and horses, and the continued exposure to rain and heat, further darkened the soldiers' mood as they waited for something to happen. "We have got those Mexicans corraled now," said one Rough Rider. "Why in hell don't we brand them?" The soldiers had decorated their trenches with fluttering American flags, over the entire five-mile horseshoe curve of entrenchments. From that patriotic vantage point, they watched suspiciously as Shafter's peace emissaries, carrying white flags, went back and forth behind enemy lines. Comparing these missions to the war extras of a newspaper, the men would joke, "Is this the baseball edition coming out now, or is it an extry?"[165] Rumors spread that the "peace-at-any-price" men would permit Toral to evacuate Santiago with his troops, supplies, weapons, and ammunition. "We fight until we win the place," Davis grumbled to his family, "and then say, 'Why certainly go away and take your arms so as you can kill some more of us later on.' "[166] On July 9, President McKinley replied to Shafter's suggestion that Toral's terms be accepted: Absolutely not.[167] The refusal gave "a lift" to Davis and his friends. "It was to my mind a slap in the face for Shafter and Wheeler who were for getting in at any price and most keen to let them march out with all the honors of war," Richard wrote his mother. "When we heard it was referred to Washington we all thought of course they would accept. So we were greatly delighted when we learned there was to be unconditional surrender. We opened up for twenty minutes but they did not reply."[168]

In these days of uneasy truce, the most uplifting moment came on July 6, when a negotiated prisoner exchange brought the release of Hobson and the seven sailors who were captured after scuttling the *Merrimac* in Santiago harbor. Davis had met Hobson in the early days of the war, while living on the naval flagship, the *New York*. Because of Hobson's proud and haughty manner, no one but Davis would speak to him. "Now, they must feel queerly," the journalist reflected.[169] Freed five weeks after his capture, Hobson received a hero's welcome. As a waiting band struck up "The Star-Spangled Banner," the American soldiers silently rose and doffed their hats, looking up at Hobson. "It was," Davis wrote, "one of the most impressive things one could imagine." And then a red-headed, red-faced soldier shouted "Three cheers for Hobson!" and the mob erupted in jubilation.[170]

Along with Stephen Crane, Davis rode with Hobson from the front to General Shafter's headquarters at Siboney. His dispatch boat was waiting for him; but Crane's boat, the *Three Friends*, was not there. Laughing, Crane said he intended to keep Davis from finishing his story. He tried unsuccessfully to make Davis laugh, and then he began to tell a yarn about the Greek War. "Now, there was no one who could ever tell a story like Stephen Crane, and time after time I would find myself stopping to listen to the narrative," Davis reminisced after Crane's death. "Crane apparently was telling the story to others in the room, but in reality he was talking to me, and never was I so distracted in my work."[171] Perhaps Crane succeeded; at any rate, for some reason, Davis's story was delayed in transmission and didn't appear in print until three days after the event.[172] Now, almost a century later, when deadlines made or missed are a matter for footnotes, the quality of the two men's coverage is what counts. On pageantry, as on battles, Davis was unsurpassed. But for a glimpse of the true nature of the ordinary man, he was no match for Crane. Like Davis, Crane at first reacted emotionally to the Hobson parade. But before long, Crane observed with disgust that the hero was "bowing right and left like another Boulanger." For a more authentic human encounter, Crane watched the army wagon that conveyed the seven lesser seamen of the *Merrimac*. He later described "grinning heads stuck out from under the canvas cover of the wagon. And the army spoke to the navy. 'Well, Jackie, how does it feel?' And the navy up and answered: 'Great! Much obliged to you fellers for comin' here.' 'Say, Jackie, what did they arrest ye for anyhow? Stealin' a dawg?' The navy still grinned."[173] And the voices still ring true.

Once the president had rejected Toral's terms, Shafter, after giving the Spanish one more chance to surrender, resumed hostilities on the next day, July 10. But he had not abandoned hope of negotiating a peace. He suspended hostilities again the next afternoon; and this time, the truce held. There was much procrastination, as both generals, eager to end the suffering, sought to satisfy the demands of their more comfortable and implacable superiors back home. In the end, Toral surrendered his men and their weapons (although, at the Spaniard's insistence, the word *capitulate* was used instead of *surrender*). The United States undertook to transport the defeated men back to Spain. At a ceremony on July 17, Toral and Shafter rode out to a point midway between their lines for the formal capitulation. After Toral treated his conquerors to a lunch at the governor's palace, they repaired to the plaza to see the Spanish flag lowered and the American one raised in its place. The most startling occurrence wasn't part of the script, and so, none of the newspapermen reported it. When three officers scrambled onto the red-tiled roof of the palace to help change the flags, they were joined by an uninvited fourth man: the irrepressible Sylvester Scovel of the New York *World*. Shafter angrily ordered him down. Eyewitness accounts conflict. Scovel either hit or tried to hit Shafter, who either did or did not strike back. Arrested on the spot, Scovel could have been court-martialed and executed. But Shafter, showing there were limits to his provocation of the press, merely shipped the man home.[174]

Davis didn't see the scandalous confrontation. He was in Guantánamo Bay with Major-General Nelson A. Miles, the commanding general of the army, waiting to depart for Puerto Rico. "I left the army just in time," Richard wrote to Charles, "and for the very reason that I was afraid I'd do what Scovel did."[175] Viewed less histrionically, he embarked for Puerto Rico because the war in Santiago was all over except for the signatures, and he was hoping to collect more material for his articles and eventual book.[176]

The invasion of Puerto Rico was an anticlimax. To Davis, however, it was a controlled experiment—an opportunity to judge how an island assault might proceed under a different commander. His hatred for Shafter had become obsessive. "This expedition is a picnic on the Thames [compared] to the Santiago trip which still hangs over me like a nightmare," he wrote to Charles from Puerto Rico. "No one ever exposed a horse to the treatment Shafter gave us. The way he starved, and overworked, and ran us into danger like pigs down a chute to be converted into sausage. Hanging is too easy for that man."[177] Although Miles didn't cultivate the correspondents, Davis liked him anyway.[178] He admitted Puerto Rico's advantages over the Santiago campaign—dry weather, friendly civilians, unravaged countryside; but he still credited the smoothness of the operation to General Miles. "An eye-witness of both campaigns," he wrote, "must feel convinced that the great success of the one in Porto Rico was not due to climatic advantages and the co-operation of the natives, but to good management and good generalship."[179]

Miles's key decision, however, was an extremely dubious one. In a last-minute turnaround, he landed his force not on the north coast near San Juan, where he feared that press accounts had alerted the Spanish to resist him, but on the south coast near Ponce. To reach the Spanish stronghold at San Juan, his force had to march seventy miles on a mountain road, past natural fortifications that the enemy could have employed to great advantage. Fortunately, this grueling, pointless ordeal was obviated by Spain's timely surrender on August 12.[180] Needless to say, Davis did not criticize Miles's tactics. Instead, he wrote: "There was a beautiful contrast between the first landing on the soil of Porto Rico and the first landing of General Shafter's army at Baiquirí. . . . There was no confusion, no conflict of authority between the army and navy officers, as there was at Baiquirí."[181] It is hard to argue with success, and in this instance, Davis didn't want to.

For Davis, the high point of the Puerto Rico campaign was the taking of the town of Coamo. Along with three other correspondents, he overslept one morning and then raced toward Coamo, hoping to see the battle before it ended. Finding a short cut, the reporters galloped into the town, thinking that the infantry already occupied it. In fact, they were the first Yankees to enter. Luckily, the Puerto Ricans were even more terrified than the Americans. Waving white flags and carrying gifts of rum, wine, and cigars, they surrendered the town to Davis. The *alcalde* gave him the key to the *cartel*, a gold-and-ebony staff, and a fine Spanish flag. Reckoning that he was unlikely ever again to accept the surrender of a town of five thousand, Davis hid the flag in his poncho and strapped it to his saddle. When the Sixteenth Pennsylvania Volunteers occupied the town twenty minutes later, their commander asked Davis what he was doing there. Something in the tone of his voice made Davis reconsider keeping the flag. He pulled off his saddle and handed over the trophy, saying: "General, it's too long a story to tell you now, but here is the flag of the town. It's the first Spanish flag that has been captured."[182] Davis later included this tale in his collection, *Notes of a War Correspondent.* It would have fit in equally well in *Stories for Boys*, alongside "The Reporter Who Made Himself King."[183]

Davis returned from the war exhausted by fever and sciatica, but replenished in reputation. His news stories in the *Herald* had enhanced his credentials as a war correspondent, and his longer pieces for *Scribner's* were recognized, rightly, as some of the best writing of his career. When the *Scribner's* articles were collected into a book, the *Critic* hailed *The Cuban and Porto Rican Campaigns*: "Of all the literature of the war, this book is certainly one of the most entertaining and at the same time most instructive books that has fallen under our notice."[184] The prolix reviewer for the *Book Buyer* wrote: "It is hard not to believe, in rereading this excellently mingled narration and description of events in these two campaigns of the war, that Mr. Davis, his popular novels to the contrary notwithstanding, is at his best in this sort of thing."[185] E. L. Burlingame singled out Davis's Guásimas account as "a superlative piece of work" that he judged "unquestionably the best piece of war literature so far."[186]

Burlingame may have been limiting his purview to journalism; but in fact, the Spanish-American War inspired almost no distinguished fiction.[187] Only Stephen Crane rose to the occasion, with his book *Wounds in the Rain*—and, in particular, with his story of the death of a foot soldier, "The Price of the Harness." Davis was typically generous in acknowledging the superiority of his rival. "Of his power to make the public see what he sees it would be impertinent to speak," he wrote in *Harper's*. "His story of Nolan, the regular, bleeding to death on the San Juan hills, is so far as I have read, the most valuable contribution to literature that the war has produced. It is only necessary to imagine how other writers would have handled it, to appreciate that it could not have been better done."[188] Davis might have been thinking of his own hackneyed war story, "On the Fever Ship," about a wounded lieutenant who in his delirium imagines that the large German nurse on the hospital ship is "She"; and thinks, when the real "She" comes to meet the boat in New York, that he is still hallucinating.[189]

Afterward, Davis did publish one interesting story set during the Spanish-American War. "A Derelict" appeared in 1901, a year after the death of Stephen Crane; and in it, Davis attempted to reconcile his distaste for Crane's unstarched morality with his admiration for the man's talent. At the same time, he enjoyed himself by mocking the work of the Associated Press—which, for the sake of fiction, he called the Consolidated Press. At the center of "A Derelict" are two journalists who are very different men. Keating, the Consolidated Press reporter, "collected facts and his salary. He had no enthusiasms, he held no illusions." The other correspondents despise him. Contrasted with him is Channing, a popular but feckless fellow, who wrote passionately and poetically. What they have in common is that both men are drunkards. Unable to hold a job, Channing persuades Keating in Jamaica to take him on the Consolidated Press boat to see the blockade of Santiago harbor. Keating, smashed, grudgingly agrees. While they are there, Cervera's fleet attempts to escape and is destroyed, but the inebriated Keating sleeps through the battle. Out of pity for Keating's young wife, Channing writes a dazzling description of the engagement and signs Keating's name to it. He then collapses with fever. After six weeks' convalescence, he returns penniless to New York. He is about to be taken to a newsman's party when he discovers that it's to honor Keating for writing *the* story of the war. He begs off, and asks his companion to give Keating this message from him: "It's all right."[190]

When it was published, "A Derelict" angered the defenders of the Associated Press, one of whom called it "a dirty piece of work" that brought "honest journalism into unjust contempt." That particular critic also denounced Davis for romanticizing "an irresponsible drunkard"—Channing.[191] No one noticed or cared about the similarities between Channing and Crane. Later, as Crane's reputation posthumously grew, Davis was maligned for insulting the immortal Crane by depicting him as a souse. Indeed, after Davis's death, Crane's biographer Thomas Beer noted that "Mr. Davis suffered a deal of comment for which he was not responsible" and declared that Davis had firmly denied any intended resemblance between his fictional character and Crane.[192] The denial is hardly credible, but these fusillades in any case miss the central point—that Channing is the most sympathetic figure in the story.[193] He is irresponsible, but a gentleman; self-destructive, but a charmer; erratic, but a genius. His sins are venial, and his talents are prodigious. There is no bitterness, just a little envy mixed with admiration, in Davis's portrait of his rival.

For Davis had no reason at all to be bitter. Except for Roosevelt, no one had a better war. Roosevelt's subsequent career is well known. Capitalizing on a public perception (partly created by Davis) that he had single-handedly crushed the foe, he ran as McKinley's running mate in 1900. When, in September 1901, an assassin ended the president's life, the hard-driving colonel entered the White House, ahead of even his own ambitious schedule.

The war marked a critical turning-point not only in Roosevelt's life, but in the history of his country. It endowed America, like a blooded adolescent, with a new imperial authority. When it ended, the United States laid claim to the Spanish colonies of Puerto Rico and the Philippines, and simultaneously ratified the long-debated annexation of Hawaii. These faraway islands were irrelevant to the concept of continental integrity which had previously guided American expansion, but very relevant to the more modern notion of the U.S. as a commercial titan trading throughout the world. For business leaders, the glutted markets of the recent economic depression were far more horrifying than the yellow-kid newspaper reports of alleged Spanish atrocities.

The war had given Davis a grown-up sense of himself as well. Having proven his courage and his ability in two hot battles, he was working on a novel that he hoped would establish him as a "literary" writer. And he had other ambitions, too. Perhaps the experience of transcribing soldiers' messages for their wives and girlfriends had crystallized his thinking. When he went to Marion in August, he was contemplating marriage.

8

A Woman Well Bred, Wholesome, and Intelligent

RICHARD HAD KNOWN CECIL CLARK from her early adolescence. He watched her become a beautiful young woman in a transformation that resembled time-lapse photography—for the Davises normally saw the Clarks only during the summers at Marion. It was a friendship of families. Cecil gravitated to Nora, who was about her age. The Clark who first attracted Richard's attention was Cecil's mother, Louise, a lively woman who could always be counted on for a piano accompaniment when he felt like singing. How Cecil made the transition from quasi-sister to sweetheart is not clear. It's not even clear that she did.

Cecil's ambitions reached far beyond the hearth. In her early twenties, she was already a portrait painter of real talent. She loved animals, especially dogs, which she bred and showed, and horses, which she rode skillfully. Generally athletic, she was a champion billiards player. "The woman [Davis] really likes is the woman for whom he can have *camaraderie*," wrote Richard's friend Allen Sangree. "For her, in real life as well as in romance, he exerts every effort, every courtesy. . . . His is a woman well bred, wholesome and intelligent, one who delights in life, in the open air and exercise."[1] Such a woman was Cecil Clark.

Neither her breeding nor her intelligence could be faulted. Her father was John Marshall Clark, a Chicago businessman who had the good sense or good fortune to be an early backer of Alexander Graham Bell. An engineer by training, he served for a stint as president, and later as a director, of the Chicago Telephone Company. Politically active, he ran an unsuccessful race as the Republican candidate for mayor in 1881. By the end of the 1890s, he had served on the city council and the board of education, and he had been the president of the civil service commission and the collector of the port of Chicago. With his white hair and white moustache, his thin lips and prominent aquiline nose, he looked his part— a leading citizen of a major city.[2] He and Louise had two children: Bruce, who was the elder, and Cecil. Cecil was her father's darling, and she adored him in return. Her feelings toward her mother were more complicated and ambivalent. She preferred the company of articulate men and "advanced" women.[3]

When at the end of 1897 he dedicated his book *A Year from a Reporter's Note-book* to Cecil, Richard publicly announced his intentions. On his return from Cuba, he sought to make his wish come true. No record survives of the late summer and early fall of 1898 that Richard and Cecil spent in Marion. Richard was recuperating from both malarial fever and sciatica. At the end of the season, Cecil returned to Chicago, and Richard went to New York and then to Philadelphia, for treatment of his persistent sciatica. Their future relationship remained undecided. About the end of October, Richard wrote to John Clark, asking for Cecil's hand in marriage. He waited impatiently for a response; and when it came, it was not the answer he wanted. Although her mother strongly supported the match, Cecil felt unsure. She said no, but her no was tentative enough that Louise advised Richard not to despair. "At present it is hard," Richard wrote Louise, "but as long as she is alive, it is enough, and someday it will all come out right, I hope and pray."[4] To Cecil he sent an unsigned scrap of paper:

> Cecil Clark
> *There's A Name that's Never Spoken*
> *And a Young Man's Heart half Broken*
> *And a Photo that has Lost*
> *It's Silver Frame.*[5]

When he wasn't penning lovesick doggerel, he was lying in bed in Philadelphia, suffering from doctors who jabbed and froze his leg as "a counter irritant—a silly proposition—so it strikes me." All he had to do was lie still, which was the thing he found most difficult.[6]

Once the leg pain eased off, he traveled to Washington; but ominous twinges forced his retreat to an enervating routine of bathing, walking, and reading at the Homestead at Hot Springs, Virginia, a spa located near his mother's favorite, the less fashionable Warm Springs.[7] At the invitation of Louise, who was playing Cupid, he visited the Clarks in Chicago after Christmas. Despite sunny skies, his sciatica returned; still, he was happy to spend the week as a fussed-over invalid. "Being conspirators together has also helped to make me value all your goodness to me," he wrote Louise after returning home, "and it has made me take heart and be brave and wait." He asked her to keep him updated on "how you think things are going."[8]

Weakened by a flare-up of malaria and the nagging sciatica, Davis on February 1 sailed for London. In "the city of the world," as he called it, he never lacked for company.[9] Many of his friends, especially the actors and society women, were as bicoastal as their successors are today; only the coasts have changed. Beyond simple pleasure, Richard had an ulterior motive in going to London. He revealed his thinking in a transparently personal story completed shortly before his departure.[10]

The protagonist of "The Lion and the Unicorn" is a handsome young American playwright, Philip Carroll, who has come to London hoping to have a play produced. Also in London is Helen Cabot, a beautiful American portrait painter whom he has known since she was fourteen, when he was like her "elder brother." She has rebuffed his many declarations of love. "I care for nothing, and for no one but my art," she tells him, "and, poor as it is, it means everything to me, and you do not, and, of course, the man I am to marry must." When he persists, she reiterates. "It is very fine to think that any one can care for me like that, and very helpful," she says more gently. "But unless I cared in the same way it would be wicked of me to marry you, and besides . . . I don't want to marry you or anybody, and I never shall. I want to be free and to succeed in my work, just as you want to succeed in your work. So please never speak of this again."

There is a third character in this story, an English actress named Marion Cavendish (whose first name alludes to the place that brought Richard and Cecil together). Miss Cavendish sums up the situation in an analysis that seems the author's own. "You are too good a man to be treated the way that girl is treating you, and no one knows it better than she does," Marion tells Philip. "She'll change in time, but just now she thinks she wants to be independent. She's in love with this picture-painting idea, and with the people she meets. It's all new to her—the fuss they make over her and the titles, and the way she is asked about. We know she can't paint. We know they only give her commissions because she's so young and pretty, and American. She amuses them, that's all. Well, that cannot last; she'll find it out. She's too clever a girl, and she is too fine a girl to be content with that long. Then—she'll come back to you. She feels now that she has both you and the others, and she's making you wait; so wait and be cheerful. She's worth waiting for; she's young, that's all. She'll see the difference in time."

Those were the words that Carroll, and Davis, wanted to hear. "She could still keep her friends and marry me," Philip says to Marion, a bit petulantly. "I have told her that a hundred times. She could still paint miniatures and marry me. But she won't marry me." (The modern reader can't help noticing something that Davis seems to have missed: Helen may be unconvinced because she senses that Philip shares Marion's estimate of her artistic abilities.) In the end, Helen starts to come around when she hears that Philip plans to leave London. "Even if she had seen him but seldom," Davis wrote, "the fact that he was within call had been more of a comfort and a necessity to her than she understood." Once he threatens to go beyond her reach, she finally realizes how much she will miss him—and how much she loves him. With this background, Davis's own motives for traveling abroad take on a new coloring.[11]

As at home in London as he was in New York, Davis was made an honorary member of many of the best London clubs: the Beefsteak, the Bachelors', the Garrick, and the Reform.[12] His favorite dining room, however, remained the Savoy, and it was there, while lunching with Somers Somerset, that he came up with the outlandish wager that turned his romance with Cecil Clark into a transatlantic sensation. In London at that time, the District Messenger Service was a novelty that permitted those who were impatient and affluent to send a message to anyone in town without waiting for a regular mail delivery. One could simply call up a messenger, pay him, and dispatch him; or, as Davis had done, one could engage a boy by the week. Davis's messenger, fourteen-year-old William Thomas Jaggers, was as unflappable as Gallegher. He was so resourceful, Davis told Somerset, that if handed a letter with a Chicago address, he would deliver it without raising an eyebrow. In fact, Davis maintained, he would beat the regular mail. And that was the wager.[13] To be precise, there were two bets. First, that Jaggers would arrive in Chicago before the postman. Second, that after leaving London on March 11, he would return by April 5 with receipts from Charles in New York, Nora in Philadelphia, and Cecil in Chicago—the names on the three envelopes that Davis handed him.[14]

The bet began as a private affair, but as was so often the case with Davis, it quickly became a public phenomenon. According to the account Richard gave Charles, the messenger service leaked the story to the *Daily Mail*, describing Davis only as "an American gentleman." Nostrils flaring with the scent of human interest, the American correspondents in London pursued the lead without success until Jaggers's proud father wrote to the *Daily Mail*. Once they had Jaggers's name, it didn't take the reporters long to identify Davis. "At the Clubs I go to, the waiters *all* wait on me in order to have the latest developments," Richard wrote, "and when it was cabled over here that the Customs' people intended stopping him, indignation raged at the Foreign office."[15] Richard suggested that if the exploit hit the American press, Charles might milk it for more publicity by having his current employers, the vaudeville team of Weber and Fields, call Jaggers up on the stage. On second thought, though, he feared the press would mistake the caper for a showman's publicity gimmick. "It is regarded here now as a very serious, sporty bet, and if any theatrical company or person was mixed up in it, they would think I had fooled them into working up their interest in a bet, and then using it to advertise some American Star," he wrote Charles.[16] The only American Star he felt comfortable advertising was himself.

When Jaggers returned to London on March 29, he was greeted by a crowd of thousands. The duchess of Rutland pinned a gold medal to his chest; and later, at a garden party, he was presented to Queen Victoria.[17] "After he had received all his honors," Davis remarked, "just to show him he was still a messenger I sent him out to call a cab for me."[18]

But what was the message Jaggers had so faithfully delivered, the one to Cecil, the one that inflamed the imaginations of the sentimental paragraphers? It was not simply a letter, but a parcel. In it was an engagement ring. An exchange of telegrams—a proposal, and an acceptance—had preceded it.[19] Had Cecil, like the fictional Helen Cabot, "recognized that his absence meant to her a change in everything"? Had she "felt for the first time the peculiar place he held in her life"? It's possible; but more likely, Louise Clark, in Richard's absence, had been wearing down Cecil's resistance, until at some point during his London sojourn, she reconsidered the proposal of marriage, and said yes. Logic, rather than emotion, caused the change of heart. Richard Harding Davis was undeniably a good catch. He set the American standard for masculine glamour. His life was brimming over with interesting friends and unlikely adventures. He was a charming conversationalist who enlivened any dinner table. He earned a substantial income. His morals were universally conceded to be impeccable. How could she have refused him in the first place?

To the consternation of Louise Clark, Richard did not return to America immediately once Cecil agreed to be his bride. "I must ask you to trust me entirely and believe that I am doing what is best for both Cecil and myself," Richard wrote her reassuringly, if mysteriously. "Your long silence made me fear you disapproved of the delay. But I assure you I never gave to anything such earnest and sincere thought. It is the only thing I consider every hour and I am convinced we will both be happier by waiting. It has taught me, at least to love much more deeply and in a better way."[20] He arrived in New York on April 8, and he announced his engagement five days afterward.[21]

The wedding, which took place three weeks later on Thursday, May 4, 1899, was the grandest social event in the history of Marion. The day was generally declared a holiday. The townspeople gathered at the little rail station to meet the Boston express and watch the celebrated visitors board beach wagons that carried them to the Clark house on the waterfront. The wedding party included Ethel Barrymore, Cissie Loftus, Charles Dana Gibson, John Fox, Robert H. Russell, Lloyd Griscom, and Captain Arthur Lee. Charles Davis was his brother's best man. In a surrey drawn by two white horses, Cecil rode up to the tiny chapel of St. Gabriel's, which was decorated with palms, cherry blossoms, gilliflower, and white roses. After the ceremony, the guests returned to the twenty-three-room Clark "cottage," where they danced to the music of an orchestra that had been imported by train to Marion, and wandered across the great lawn and gardens of the fourteen-acre estate. At about five, all departed, leaving the newlyweds alone to begin their honeymoon.[22]

The discreet novelist, let alone the biographer, smiles politely at this point and pulls the shade. However, it would be wrong to suggest that even at the beginning, the marriage of Richard Harding Davis and Cecil Clark was a love match. A man who was thought to be a paragon of masculine beauty, who animated the fantasies of thousands of women, had chosen for his wife someone who did not find him sexually attractive. Not until Davis's death did the rumors make it into print, but the buzz began immediately. "It is unfortunate Cecil had such odd ideas," the couple's friends reportedly whispered. "Who ever heard of a platonic marriage?" Cecil had come around to accept her suitor's proposal, but she had laid down conditions. "A girl needs someone to take her about," she is supposed to have told Davis. "We will simply be as brother and sister."[23]

While this seems a preposterous concession for a young, healthy man to make, Richard was not the only man to do so. About the same time, a fashionable young woman in Cecil's hometown of Chicago asked an attorney to draft a contract in which her husband would vow not to consummate the union. When the lawyer reported this to a friend who practiced law in New York, that worthy replied, on March 9, 1898, that he had already been consulted in a dozen such cases.[24] This unenforceable contract was a way for an "advanced" woman to assert her feminist independence. It was also a shield for women who, because of a general sexual orientation or a specific physical revulsion, wanted to keep their distance from their husbands. Sex, especially for "nice girls," was shrouded in mystery in the 1890s. It is likely that Richard ascribed Cecil's reservations to a young virgin's timidity, and assumed that in time a more conventional marriage would unfold. If so, he was wrong. The passing years would not find Cecil any better disposed to a physical heterosexual relationship.

Viewed more positively, Cecil as a quasi-sibling could better be incorporated into the Davis clan than could a passionate bride. She would be like a daughter to Rebecca, not like a rival trying to possess the adored son. Neither Charles nor Nora married until after their mother's death in 1910; and Rebecca's relationship with her eldest child was the most intense of all. Richard had not changed much from the young writer who in 1890 imagined a youth in the sinful city falling in love with a "goddess in mid-air," a woman who appeared not to exist below the waist; and Rebecca was still the overly solicitous mother who swaddled her son with anxious love. He was forever trying to reassure her. On the occasion of his marriage, he redoubled his efforts. After she left Richard and Cecil behind at Marion, Rebecca wrote how much she missed him. He wrote back: "I would have it so that we all lived here, so that Dad could fish, and Nora and Cecil could discuss Life, and you and I could just take walks and chat. But because that cannot be, we are no further away than we ever were and when the pain to see you comes, I don't let it hurt and I don't kill it either for it is the sweetest pain I can feel."[25] Would a love so fierce make room willingly for another?

In the house that had been vacated, thoughtfully, by the senior Clarks, the newlyweds began their married life not in the bedroom but in the dining room. "We met downstairs, Cecil in her grandest dinner dress and 'diamonds!!' and I in the whitest and tightest of white waistcoats and the longest of dress coats, and we proceeded majestically into dinner," Richard wrote to his new mother-in-law. "There we found that the caterers had carried off all of the table linen and knives and forks and that the cook was helpless with champagne and that there was nothing to eat but ham and eggs.... At which we laughed and Cecil tucked up her train and cooked potatoes on the coals while I opened wine with an icepick and got so drenched that I had to disappear and get dressed again. It was most amusing." Around ten, a group of children gathered outside the house to serenade the couple, but they were chased away.[26] Richard and Cecil later that month invited the entire town to a seignorial party. They served the food themselves, dressed in their finery, and the appreciative townspeople cheered three times for Cecil and twice for Richard. "The thing that impressed them most was the 'free' segars . . . ," Richard wrote home. "Another thing that impressed them was Cecil who they had never seen in good clothes."[27]

In June, the Davises sailed for France, stopping first in Paris, and then in the fashionable spa of Aix-les-Bains, where Richard took an effective course of twenty-four baths for his still-aching leg. Pleading shyness, Cecil dreaded the final stretch of the honeymoon in London, and wanted at first to avoid Richard's celebrated English friends. "She really is nervous about meeting people until she meets them, and then she cannot help seeing how much superior she is to them and at once begins to put them at their ease," Richard wrote to Louise. "You would really not believe it was Cecil, if you saw her joking with Prime Ministers and guying the toilets of great ladies. I am so proud of her, and she outshines everyone so completely, that I am really afraid I married her under false pretenses and it would only be fair to her to let her get a divorce, and then ask her again, for I am quite too utterly unworthy of her." Ethel Barrymore, Anthony Hope Hawkins, and Finley Peter Dunne each gave dinners for the couple. They were pelted with invitations from Mrs. Joseph Chamberlain, Margot Asquith, and the duchess of Sutherland.[28] It was just as in *Soldiers of Fortune*, when Clay tells his fiancée, Hope, that on their honeymoon in London the grandees of Mayfair will be "giving dances in your honor, in honor of the beautiful American bride, whom every one wants to meet."[29]

They returned home in August. Marion was now their primary residence, for Richard, when he surrendered his bachelor state, also gave up his bachelor flat at 10 East Twenty-eighth Street. It was time to leave Madison Square, anyway; New York was marching northward. Two weeks before his wedding, Davis attended the closing of his favorite haunt, Delmonico's on Twenty-sixth Street. Although another Delmonico's restaurant had opened in November 1897, on Fifth Avenue and Forty-fourth Street, the Delmonico's era was over.* The Waldorf, which in 1893 made its appearance on Fifth Avenue between Thirty-third and Thirty-fourth streets, inaugurated a louder, showier, less exclusive style of entertainment. In the see-and-be-seen Waldorf, it didn't matter as much whom you were looking at or who was watching you. The Waldorf's main dining room, the Palm Garden, had glass walls and wall-to-ceiling mirrors. The corridor leading to it was called Peacock Alley: it was lined with seats from which one could watch the swells on their way to dinner. Although the plush rope blocking the doorway was a Waldorf invention, that exclusionary symbol was misleading, for Oscar, the famous maître d'hôtel, would smile with equal favor upon old-family New Yorkers, Midwestern parvenus, and beautiful actresses.

The decade from 1896 to 1906 was a golden age in the New York restaurant business, with Martin's, Sherry's, the Holland House, the Astoria (combining with its sister as the Waldorf-Astoria), the St. Regis, and the Savoy, all on Fifth Avenue; and, on even more promiscuous Broadway, the Astor Hotel, the Knickerbocker Grill, Shanley's, and Rector's.[30] Richard, so long a regular at Delmonico's, would be only an occasional visitor to these new pleasure palaces. Cecil lacked all taste for the New York nightlife. Responding to her influence, Richard detached himself from the glittering orbit of fashionable New York, and committed himself to a hardworking autumn in out-of-season Marion.

With marriage comes responsibility. With marriage to a rich young woman, more specifically, there comes a steady influx of bills. On the bright side, John Clark continued to pay for Cecil's clothes, many of which were purchased abroad. "I have nothing to [do] with that," wrote a relieved Richard, "it is a sacred matter between herself, her father and the dressmakers."[31] The Clarks also provided their house in Marion, which they winterized for the newlyweds. But the obligation of retaining a lady's maid, a cook, and, eventually, a kennelman and chauffeur, fell upon Richard. The administrative responsibility was also his, for Cecil had no interest in managing a household.[32] From the time of his marriage, right up until the time of his death, Richard never stopped worrying about how to earn enough money to maintain his new manner of life. He had gone from a bachelor existence, in which extravagant bursts could be followed by frugal retrenchment, to an inelastic regimen of steadily mounting expenses. His Van Bibber days were over.

He turned his mind immediately to ways of making money. Writing plays could be hugely lucrative, and after his wedding, Davis worked on dramatizations of the Van Bibber stories and "The Lion and the Unicorn."

---

*Delmonico's continued to cater to the stylish nightlife crowd until it buckled in 1923 under the weight of Prohibition.

One could reprocess old material with less effort by simply repackaging it in a new format. In the summer of 1899, the Harpers proposed reissuing *The Princess Aline* in a cheap edition, and Davis agreed with alacrity.[33] He suggested that his old publisher might want to give a lift to another moribund book, *The Rulers of the Mediterranean*, by distributing quantities to steamship lines for sale on board.[34] Anticipating a production of a Van Bibber play the next year, he urged the Harpers to publish a special edition of the stories (with photographs of the actors) for sale in the theaters.[35] He was going back to old olives for a second pressing of oil.

When he wasn't devising creative ways to pay the bills, he was trying to finish *Captain Macklin*, the fictional autobiography of a soldier of fortune that he had begun before the Spanish-American War. Once again, however, a real war intervened.

By the fall of 1899, the rumbling from South Africa was so ominous that fighting seemed unavoidable. Less than a month after his honeymoon, Richard was contemplating a trip there; but fearing that the English would mop up the Boers before he arrived, he stayed in Marion. The early reports of Boer victories convinced him that the war would last. He longed to cover it. Watching the British army in high gear would be "like taking a degree in war" and he felt "there will not be such a chance again, and there never has been one like it. I mean the use of modern weapons has been developed in this campaign for the first time."[36] Without telling his parents, he made preparations to go with Cecil at the end of December to cover the war for the New York *Herald*. Then, in the middle of the month, his sister, Nora, was stricken with pneumonia. While the Davises waited anxiously to see if she would recover, Richard kept his plans to himself, wishing to spare his mother additional nightmares. Happily, Nora pulled through, permitting Richard and Cecil to pull out. They sailed on January 10 back to London, the first stop on their trip halfway around the world.[37] More than the wedding trip to Aix, this South African journey would be their honeymoon. It defined the best time of their marriage as a bond of true comradeship.

Cecil insisted that Richard take the superior stateroom, which had the double bed, saying that she was tired of always getting the better room.[38] They read aloud to each other in Richard's cabin and played chess for a dollar a game when the weather got rough.[39] Everyone on board seemed fascinated by their South African plans—and particularly amazed that a woman was going to a war.[40] Being upstaged by a wife was an amusing novelty for Richard. In London, Cecil made a great social success. Margot Asquith gave her letters to two aristocratic ladies in Cape Town whose husbands were fighting in Mafeking. Cyril Maude sent her flowers, and Anthony Hope Hawkins gave a lunch for her to meet the duchess of Sutherland. At a dinner at Lady Jeune's, she was approached by a Lady

Arthur Butler, who said, "The Duke of Abercorn wants to meet you, shall I call him over?" "Is he amusing?" Cecil asked. Shocked, the woman said, "I really don't know." "Then I think I'd rather talk to you," Cecil said. At another dinner, she sat next to the fabulously wealthy South African Alfred Beit and charmed him. He sent her a book the next day and came to lunch the day after—"and has given us letters to all the millionaire Hebrews at the Cape[,] wives and all," Richard wrote his sister. Beit later had them over to lunch "at his palace in Park Lane," Richard reported, "and switched on fountains and electric lights and illuminated Romneys and Gainsboroughs."[41]

Richard's chief task was obtaining press credentials. The War Office turned him down, noting that too many reporters were already there. Using his connections, he directly petitioned Sir Evelyn Wood, the adjutant general in charge of mobilization, and Field Marshal Lord Wolseley, the commander in chief of the British army, to no avail. He thought of going down without credentials, of attaching himself to the Boers, or of giving up and going home.[42] He was sorting all this out when early one morning, Lord Alfred Harmsworth, the founder and proprietor of the London *Daily Mail*, woke him up with the news that George W. Steevens, the *Daily Mail*'s star correspondent in South Africa (and one of the greatest war reporters of all time) had died of typhoid in the besieged English garrison town of Ladysmith. Harmsworth asked if Davis was free to replace him. Wasting no time, he invited Davis to accompany him on his next appointment: a motorcar trip to the Surrey countryside to pay a condolence call on Steevens's widow. While Harmsworth talked to Mrs. Steevens, Davis stood outside in the garden. With news of the tragedy not yet cold, it was a little unseemly to present the dead man's replacement to the bereaved widow.[43]

Although he couldn't honorably relinquish his *Herald* assignment, Davis offered to represent both papers with different stories, if the *Herald*'s proprietor, James Gordon Bennett, Jr., approved. Davis dearly wanted the *Daily Mail* commission. With it, he could get credentials from the British army, plus a $150 weekly supplement to the *Herald*'s $300 salary. (On top of that, Davis was receiving ten cents a word for magazine stories and $1,000 in expenses, or over $3,000, from the Scribners.)[44] The challenge was gaining Bennett's assent in the few days before the next ship left for South Africa. An eccentric playboy, Bennett had fled New York two decades earlier, after allegedly urinating into a piano during a party at his fiancée's home. He lived hedonistically in Paris and the south of France. "We cannot get either a sane or sober reply from Bennett who cannot understand what we want, and who does not know what he wants or what his paper wants," Richard complained. As he saw it: "The proposition is Harmsworth—a sick old boy, peevish, fretful, sitting in the lap of Luxury with three hand telephones over his bed, and Bennett quite drunk at Monte Carlo sitting in Heaven knows who'se lap. It is enough to try the patience of any businesslike, energetic and sober young man who wants his job and who only asks to get started."[45] Bennett did at last agree; and with the help of Sir Evelyn Wood, Davis received Steevens's credentials.[46] "You have no idea how difficult it is to get a pass," Richard wrote Nora, "and had it not been for Steevens' death I should not have had one."[47]

While Davis did not sail to South Africa with an open mind on the conflict, he had what for a reporter might be the next best thing: a muddled mind. His education on the issues had commenced during his London sojourn in the summer of 1896. London then was preoccupied with the fate of Leander Starr Jameson, who had been captured leading a raid on the Boer city of Johannesburg and shipped back to London to stand trial. The revelations of the trial embarrassed both the arch-imperialist Cecil Rhodes, for whom Jameson worked, and the British government, whose interests were messily involved. Jameson was acting on behalf of the Uitlanders, the mostly English foreigners who flocked to the Boer republic of the Transvaal after gold was discovered in 1885 near what soon became Johannesburg. The longer they lived among the Dutch-descended Boers, who spoke a strange Afrikaans language and worshiped in a severe Dutch Reformed Church, the more disaffected the Uitlanders became. Since most were English, they naturally looked toward their British neighbors: the Cape Colony and the new British colony of Rhodesia, which (as its name suggests) was a virtual fiefdom of Rhodes's chartered company.

A group of Rhodes's associates established the Johannesburg Reform Committee and plotted an Uitlanders' revolt. At a signal that the rebellion had begun, Jameson was to lead a band of men across the border into Johannesburg. Waiting impatiently for an uprising that never occurred, Jameson on December 29, 1895, began his march on his own. He was trounced. Attending his trial in London, Davis saw Jameson as an underdog idealist who had been betrayed by the reform committee. He was especially contemptuous of John Hays Hammond, the one American member of the committee, whom Rhodes (for $125,000) had bailed out of a Transvaal prison. Hammond was now in London at the Savoy Hotel.

On the day that Jameson was sentenced to fifteen months' hard labor in Holloway Prison, Davis remarked that he "would rather be in Holloway with Jameson than in the Savoy with Hammond." He said it to a mutual friend who, rising to the bait, invited Davis to dine with Hammond at the Savoy. There, listening to Hammond's argument of how Jameson had irresponsibly jumped the gun, Davis performed the first of what would be many somersaults on the rights and wrongs of the South African conflict.[48] After corroborating the facts, he wrote a long article that gave the reformers' version of the Jameson raid.[49] Syndicated in some three hundred American newspapers, the story gave a great public-relations boost to the reformers, at a moment they badly needed it. In gratitude, Hammond presented Davis with a check for thirty thousand dollars—which Davis returned, saying that he was a journalist, not a public-relations bureau, and his five-hundred-dollar payment from the United Press Association was quite adequate.[50] Tailoring his gifts to suit Davis's scruples, Hammond was successful the next spring in making Davis accept some free stock options.[51]

Hammond and another South African, Barney Barnato (a gold and diamond mogul who rivaled Rhodes), urged Davis back in 1896 to go at once to Rhodesia, where the native Matabele had rebelled against the white settlers. "It can never be written later for it is changing every minute," Richard wrote his mother. "It would make a book like the 'West' which could not have been written by anyone at a later period for it has passed away."[52] Unfortunately, Rebecca trembled so loudly at the prospect of her son facing bullets that he backed down.[53] One advantage of Cecil over Rebecca was her enthusiasm for risky adventures.

Before leaving London, Davis gave an interview to Harmsworth's *Daily Mail*, in which he declared that the American public supported the British against the Boers. Along with the venerable tradition of British-American friendship, he noted the uprising of Filipinos against their new American masters. "Our experience in the Philippines is not so very unlike yours in the Transvaal, and when some people would talk of the power of a great Empire used to crush a little people they are silenced by the remembrance of our army of sixty thousand men in the Far East," he said diplomatically.[54] He did not mention that, personally, he had raised a Boer flag over the Clark cottage in Marion when war broke out in September.[55] His sporting sympathies lay with the underdog.

With a Belgian maid for Cecil hired in London, an English bull terrier they called Jaggers, and aspiring reporter Somers Somerset, the Davises sailed on January 27 for South Africa. Richard thought he would have three weeks to see Cecil settled comfortably in Cape Town. "I think her chance of getting to the front is extremely small—extremely so," he wrote from the ship.[56] His saying that only showed that he still didn't know her very well. During the very rough voyage, a great storm in the Bay of Biscay rocked the ship, and Cecil characteristically immersed herself in the action. "When Lord Dudley's horse was being knocked about the lower deck during the hurricane, all sorts of men went down to help the sailors, and Cecil stood on some riding bits and directed operations," Richard wrote to his mother-in-law. "It was very funny to see Lord Valentia and Lord Wolverton and Dudley, who is to be the next Viceroy of Ireland if he gets back from S.A. [South Africa], running up to Cecil for advice. One young man in rubber-boots and a seagoing reefer and cap was working very hard, and Cecil kept ordering him about and telling him where to put up a hoist and where to hang a tackle. After twenty minutes' work over the poor beast she asked the steward or 'bos'n' whose horse it was. 'It's mine,' he said. 'Yours?' exclaimed Cecil. 'I thought you belonged to the ship, that you were one of the ship's officers.' 'No, these are my yachting things,' he answered. 'I am

Dudley.' Cecil told me she had thought he was the chief steward and had treated him as such."[57] How long would such a woman be content rolling bandages with the officers' wives in Cape Town?

Hotel rooms were scarce in Cape Town, but with the help of Alfred Beit, the Davises found accommodations in the Mount Nelson Hotel—"a very, very smart hotel just like a West End club," Richard wrote approvingly. Cecil had a large bedroom and sitting room to herself, and Somerset, because of the crowding, shared Richard's room.[58] "Cape Town is a dusty wind ridden Western town with a mountain back of it which one man said was a badly painted backdrop," Davis wrote. The mountain and the Mount Nelson Hotel, he thought, were the only attractive sights in the city.[59] Also staying at the Mount Nelson was Rudyard Kipling, who—in an act of public intimacy that startled Richard—strolled through the hotel's elaborate gardens with his arm around the waist of his American wife. At first, Richard approved of Rudyard as "very friendly" but found the wife "a middle class cat."[60] On further acquaintance, however, he wrote off Kipling, too, saying "a more offensive little bounder it is difficult to imagine. He goes around in kharki 800 miles from the front and contradicts every general on every military question. He ought either to go to the front or go home."[61]

Planning his own trip to the front, Davis learned to his disappointment that Julian Ralph of the *Daily Mail* would be accompanying Field Marshal Lord Roberts, the commander in chief, and General Lord Kitchener, his chief of staff, on the march toward Bloemfontein. This advance of five divisions (about forty thousand men) on the capital of Orange Free State—one of the two Boer republics fighting the British—promised to be the big campaign of the war. But Ralph had been in South Africa for four months, and Davis could not in conscience even try to replace him. Instead, he settled for a chance at seeing the relief of Ladysmith, the beleaguered English garrison at the edge of Natal near Orange Free State. The Boers had cut off Ladysmith in early November. A relief force under General Sir Redvers Buller had been sent to lift the siege, but Buller had met unexpectedly fierce resistance on the way. As his men battled to advance, the outpost at Ladysmith struggled to survive.

Rushing to catch up with General Buller's column before Ladysmith either fell to the Boers or was relieved by the British, Richard departed Cape Town on February 17 on a ten-day journey by ship, rail, and two-wheeled, horse-drawn Cape cart.[62] Cecil was left behind in "quite the dullest and most uninteresting place I have ever been in." Almost all the foreign correspondents had left, except for the Kiplings—whom she, like Richard, despised. "The Kiplings are far from interesting," she wrote. "When he isn't telling people how he would have managed things he is asking questions of anyone and everybody, about things they could not know. She is rather pretty, very small, feels her great position as Kipling's wife and constantly tells him to put his feet down or stop biting his moustache or something;

but far the nicer of the two."[63] The only occupation open to Cecil was sketching the wounded soldiers in the hospital. That was a rare sign of war in a city in which, because of press censorship, the war seemed farther away than it had in London.[64] As in London, people in Cape Town talked of little else, but they spoke of it—if this was possible—even more stupidly.[65]

Meanwhile, Richard was racing toward Ladysmith. "It is just a question of minutes really and it seems hard to have come 1500 miles and then to miss it by an hour," he wrote.[66] His heart sank when the stationmaster at Frere Station woke the passengers with news from the wire: Ladysmith would be relieved at any moment. None of the passengers seemed pleased. The train was full of philanthropists, officers, and Tommies, all of them wanting to be in at the kill. When the captain of the Natal Carbineers opined, "I am afraid the good news is too premature," they agreed gratefully. Six hours later, shortly after sunrise, they reached Colenso. From a mile away they could hear the thud of naval guns, the hammering of Boer "pom-poms" (little one-pounder Maxims), and the spattering of Colt automatics. They traded guilty smiles. They had made it. Obviously, Ladysmith had not been relieved.[67]

What impressed Davis first was the bizarre topography of the battlefield, composed of large hills scattered without pattern. Below the hills curved the muddy yellow Tugela River. It was a landscape giving every advantage to the Boer guerrillas, who, knowing the country, could strike and then vanish.[68] On one of these hills, Bulwana Mountain, the Boers had installed a long-range gun ("Long Tom," the British called it) that shelled the garrison mercilessly. Enormously outnumbered, however, the Boers were flagging by the time Davis arrived on the scene. His introduction to the war was the battle of Pieters Hill on February 27. "It is terribly big and overwhelming like eighty of Barnum's circuses all going at once in eighty rings," Richard wrote home from the front, "and very hard to understand the geography."[69] Equally baffling was the British conduct of the war. Although they dislodged the foe from his stronghold of Pieters Hill, the British failed to drive home their victory. Davis watched for four hours as the Englishmen allowed the enemy to escape. Not wanting to see the Boers captured, but curious at this lack of initiative, he asked a staff officer, "Why don't you send out your cavalry and light artillery and take those wagons?" The officer giggled, and said, "They might kill us."[70]

Davis was repelled by the British officers, whom he privately denounced as mindless and class-bound. A few days before his arrival, the Inniskillings, Dublins, and Connaughts had made a disastrous frontal attack on Pieters Hill, only to be mowed down by the Boers' automatic weapons. "It is sheer straight waste of life through dogged stupidity," Richard wrote his mother.[71] While the rapid, tenacious Boers resembled terriers, the British seemed to have modeled their strategy after lemmings. Their leaders were contemptible. The sunburned officers stared as vacantly on the veldt as they gazed, in other months, on the dining room of the Savoy and out the windows of White's and the Bachelors' Club. "If they were bored then," Davis wrote, "they are unbearably bored now."[72]

The rigid inequities and anachronistic foolishness of the British class system, which had never troubled Davis much in London, infuriated him in South Africa. But, of course, the brilliant, talented Balfours and Custs were not the aristocrats who fought in South Africa. This was the class system at its worst: men given authority solely because of birth, and other men dying in consequence. "The whole thing is so 'class,' and full of 'form' and tradition and worrying over 'puttees' and etiquette and rank," Richard wrote his mother. "It is the most wonderful organization I ever imagined but it is like a beautiful locomotive without an engineer. The Boers out play them in intelligence every day. The whole army is officered by one class and that the dull one. It is like the House of Peers. You would not believe the mistakes they make, the awful way in which they sacrifice the lives of officers and men."[73] The Boer soldiers were invisible, but you could see every Englishman who was on a hill. "They walk along the skyline like ships on the horizon," Davis wrote.[74]

The Boers, having lost Pieters Hill, were forced to retreat to two further hills, and then to give up the field entirely. On the evening of February 28, British troops rode in and out of the beleaguered garrison at Ladysmith, ending the 181-day siege. But Davis didn't know that when, on the following morning, he set out for Ladysmith with two other correspondents. They rode up Pieters Hill; and as they scrambled down the other side, they saw British artillery and infantry regiments moving on the plain between Pieters and Bulwana. The siege had indeed fallen. As they advanced, they spied correspondents galloping back to the telegraph office to send their papers first word of Ladysmith's relief. Conceding the bulletins to their rivals, the three reporters continued on their way. They hoped to be the first newsmen inside Ladysmith.

When after a twelve-mile gallop they reached the the town (not quite the first correspondents to do so), they cried out in friendly jubilation.[75] Instead of the emotional response they craved, a Gordon Highlander standing guard called: "Halt, there! Where's your pass?" The lifting of a four-month siege had not taken the starch out of British protocol. Davis, despite his growing distaste for the British cause, couldn't help but be moved by the sight of Ladysmith. At first glance, the stone cottages and trimmed hedges of the main street gave the garrison town the air of a wealthy suburb. But while the appearance of Ladysmith had been maintained, the spirit of its people had dried up. Still hoping for a cheer, or even a nod, the three reporters rode past smart khaki-clad officers, small girls in white pinafores, and a man on a bicycle, all of whom averted their eyes.

On his way to file a brief dispatch with the military censor, Davis asked directions of two officers, who said they were heading that way. They rode together for a while in silence before one of the officers asked, "Are you from the outside?" When Davis admitted that he was, the other officer handed him a printed list of prices for food and tobacco during the siege. "He seemed to offer it as being in some way an official apology for his starved appearance," Davis wrote. The high price of cigars struck Davis as particularly cruel (stogies he had bought for two cents each in Cape Town were selling for $1.25 in Ladysmith), and he commented on it.[76] "I have not smoked a cigar in two months," the first officer said mournfully, staring straight ahead. Davis silently weighed the proud reserve of these Englishmen against their pitiful tobacco deprivation. Nervous lest he offend them, he nonetheless produced a fistful of cigars from his saddlebags and asked, "Will you have these?" The second officer started so violently that Davis thought his horse had stumbled. "Thank you, I will take one if I may—just one," said the first officer. "Are you sure I am not robbing you?" The second man also took only one. Davis gave them matches. "Then a beautiful thing happened," he wrote. "They lit the cigars and at the first taste of the smoke—and they were not good cigars—an almost human expression of peace and good-will and utter abandonment to joy spread over their yellow skins and cracked lips and fever-lit eyes. The first man dropped his reins and put his hands on his hips and threw back his head and shoulders and closed his eyelids. I felt that I had intruded at a moment which should have been left sacred." He soon gave out out all of his food and cigars. By his second day in Ladysmith, he was subsisting on a daily ration of four biscuits and an ounce each of coffee and tea.[77]

On March 3, Buller's entire column marched ceremonially through the recaptured town. "It was a most cruel assault upon one's feelings," Davis wrote to his mother. "The garrison lined the streets as a saluting guard of honor but only one regiment could stand it and the others all sat down on the curb only rising to cheer the head of each new regiment. They are yellow with fever their teeth protruding and the skin drawn tight over their skeletons—The incoming army had had fourteen days hard fighting at the end of three months campaigning but were robust and tanned ragged and caked with mud. As they came in they cheered and the garrison tried to cheer back but it was like a whisper." Standing alongside young Winston Churchill, who was beginning his long, varied career in the role of a war correspondent, Davis wept for an hour. "For the time you forgot Boers and the cause, or the lack of cause of it all, and saw only the side of it that was before you," he wrote. "The starving garrison relieved by men who had lost almost one out of every three in trying to help them."[78]

Davis spent five days in Ladysmith. By the end of it, the dirt and squalor had obscured the picturesque pathos of the scene. The garrison town, which at first seemed so charming, on closer inspection turned out to be "an unlovely, unhomelike place." The basic architectural unit was a one-story stone house with a corrugated zinc roof. When rain fell, the town oozed with mud. When the hot sun shone, the wind whipped yellow dust into a choking fog. "And when the dust is settled," Davis wrote, "all that you can see is so practical, hard, and ugly, that one almost wishes for the curtain of dust to rise again and hide it."[79] For four days, Davis went without a change of clothing—a violation of his code of cleanliness that always frayed his nerves and jaundiced his vision. "I can't complain now that I saw the raising of the siege," he wrote to his family. "But I hope we don't stay still. I want to see a lot quickly and get out. . . . I hate all the people about me and this dirty town and I wish I was back."[80] Ladysmith smelled—superlative of superlatives—as bad as Johnstown. "It was so foul and dirty and 'colonial' which means men who know that they would be scraping and saying 'Thank you sir' in England call you 'old man' and come sit on your bed and show their independence by being bad mannered," he grumbled once he left.[81]

The only Britishers he liked were the Tommies. The colonials in Cape Town bored him until his "scalp crawled." Those he met in Natal on the trip to Ladysmith whined constantly about property lost to the Boers. To show their gratitude to the Tommies who had traveled seven thousand miles to protect them, they charged the boys a shilling for a slice of bread and molasses. As for the officers commanding the Tommies, their stupidity and arrogance astounded him. "Sometimes they fight all day using seven or eight regiments and kill a terrible lot of fine soldiers and capture forty Boer farmers and two women," Richard wrote his mother. "It is not becoming that the British army should fight against women even if they are good shots. At least, it is not the kind of war I care to report."[82] When Buller announced that he would remain in Ladysmith for two or three weeks before advancing, Davis decided to return to Cape Town. Lord Roberts was planning to march from Bloemfontein all the way to Pretoria, the capital of Transvaal. If Roberts was ready to move, Davis would accompany him. If not, Richard and Cecil would say good riddance to South Africa and sail for London.[83]

To save three days, Richard came from Durban on the *Maine*, the American-sponsored hospital boat organized by Lady Randolph Churchill, Winston's American mother. On the way, Richard told the officers that he was confident Mrs. Davis would find a way to get him off the ship before any of the wounded men or even Lady Randolph herself. They laughed at him, saying it would be impossible to find a tug. When he sailed into Cape Town on March 22, Richard was vindicated: sitting in a rowboat about two miles out at sea, Cecil was there to greet him. She had gone all out for his homecoming. For days she had been arranging to have his room prepared and his clothes cleaned and pressed. She had bought his brand of cigars and ordered a dinner for the two of them, served in his sitting room, which she had filled with flowers. "Of course, it was a terrible experience," Richard wrote his mother, "but now that it is over I am so glad as without it I might never have known how much I needed her every minute and that she is what she is to me."[84]

Learning in Cape Town that Roberts wasn't leaving for three weeks, Davis decided to return to the United States. "There were other reasons [to come home]," he wrote his family, "the chief one being that the English irritated me and I had so little sympathy with them that I could not write with any pleasure of their work. My sporting blood refused to boil at the spectacle of such a monster Empire getting the worst of it from an untrained band of farmers. I found I admired the farmers."[85] He was representing an English paper, which made his affection for the "enemy" awkward, at the very least. Beyond that, he practiced a style of journalism—one that now seems as dated as the Gibson Girl's pompadour—which required him to take sides. As he increasingly favored the cause of the Boers, he realized that their story was the one he should report. If he could reach them, he would delay his return home.

Cecil agreed wholeheartedly. She too was disgusted with the British. "Their whole attitude about the war has been so contemptible I think," she wrote her father. "Now that the Boers are getting the worst of it they call them cowards & poor fighters & wont admit that there is anything to recommend them. When they themselves were being beaten their tone was quite different. In fact they are nothing but large bullies . . . the more I see of the English the more I admire the Boers—Dick agrees."[86] Davis supported imperialism only when it came clothed as chivalry. Back in 1891, when the American government mobilized vessels and the militia during a dispute with Chile, he had scornfully compared the preparations to "John L. Sullivan's going to Long Island to train to fight a man who had slapped his face on Broadway."[87] He had endorsed the war with Spain, but only on behalf of the brutalized Cuban patriots. He felt very differently about the conflict that continued to percolate in the Philippines. Of this war with the Filipino guerrillas, he wrote that Americans were "rightly ashamed."[88] The British assault on the Boers struck him as just as embarrassing—but the British knew no shame. The mighty British Empire was fighting for the Uitlanders, who had streamed into the Transvaal hoping for gold, not freedom. The most belligerent Englishmen were the owners of the huge mining concerns. The devout, homespun Boers appeared to be fighting to preserve their nation from the greedy, overbearing British.

Unsure that they would be admitted, the Davises embarked for Pretoria. (Failing, they would sail up the east coast of Africa and on to London.) Pulling many strings, they traversed the Portuguese colony of Mozambique, a strictly neutral buffer state. "Cecil is, of course, delighted," Richard wrote his family, "and as we will not leave Praetoria, that is, as I shall *not* go into the field I will be with her. . . ."[89] At Komatipoort, the first rail station within Boer territory, officials doffed their hats to Cecil and her maid, passed the Davises' luggage unopened, and presented a gift bottle of fine

French wine. Following manifold difficulties with the English and the Portuguese, the courtesies had the desired effect. "Go ahead and be as pro-Boer as you want," Richard wrote Rebecca soon after arriving. "They are God's own people, the few that are left who really worship him[—]a simple, sweet, pathetic people."[90]

In Pretoria, for a rent of two pounds a month, the government gave the Davises the comfortable four-bedroom house of a refugee Englishman. On top of that, for no charge at all they received the use of a carriage, driver, and two horses. What they couldn't find was domestic help—a problem Cecil solved by cooking the meals herself. "The people here are very much amused at our arriving six months after all the other women left in cattle trucks so eager were they to escape, and beginning to keep house," Richard reported. "It's the best fun we have had yet."[91]

The town oddly juxtaposed marble government buildings and thatched cottages. In the chief square of Pretoria, which was ringed with the most stately buildings, the Boers and blacks camped out with their large wagons and their oxen. This combination of city and country added to the charm. Despite the war, the Boers were conducting business as usual with no signs of hysterical patriotism. Their shop windows—unlike those in Cape Town, Durban, even London—did not bristle with battlefield relics or portraits of generals. Whenever the conversation turned to the war, they discussed the enemy with respect. "We love the Boers themselves dearly," Cecil wrote her mother soon after arriving, "they are entirely unlike any idea we had of them in America. . . . The way they take the war is so fine after the English method. They are so fair about it—and so just."[92]

The war, of course, was the reason the Davises were there, and they quickly disavowed their promise not to visit the front. Cecil was very eager to view a battle. "There is no red tape about those things on this side & many women have been up & seen engagements," she wrote to Nora.[93] On May 4, their first wedding anniversary, Richard gave Cecil a hat pin of the coat of arms of the Transvaal—but his real present was the chance to visit a war zone. That night they left Pretoria to join the Boer army.[94]

The Boers were fighting in Orange Free State, which was shrinking ominously before Lord Roberts's advance on Pretoria. Kroonstad, near the Transvaal border, had replaced Bloemfontein as the temporary capital of the Free State. The Davises traveled to Ventersburg, a town some twenty-five miles south of Kroonstad. Their guide was Captain Von Lossberg, a German baron and naturalized American citizen who had volunteered as an artillery captain for Orange Free State.[95] With him, they rode to the Boer laagers on the Sand River. Across the river, only six miles away, were the British. On the road the Davis party met the Free State's president, Marthinus Steyn, who gave Cecil a rose from his coat and spent most of his time talking to her. A woman on the front was a curiosity. The Boers would cluster around Cecil in swarms, first doffing their hats politely, and then staring, round-eyed and open-mouthed, for five minutes.

Rejoining his battery, Von Lossberg loaned the Davises a Cape cart, in which they explored the battlefront along the Sand River. One day, while Richard was riding to the rear of the cart, they were overtaken by three Boers. Richard threw up his hands immediately and shouted to Cecil to stop. Over the noise of the cart, she could not hear him. "I knew if I rode after her they would shoot at me, and that if she did not stop, as they were shouting at her to do, they would shoot her," he wrote home. "Under these trying circumstances I sat still. It caused quite a coolness on Cecil's part. However, the Boers could see I was trying to get her to halt, so they only rode around and headed her off." Overjoyed to see them, Richard annoyed the Boers by treating the arrest as a lark. They growled when he insisted on photographing them inspecting Cecil's passport. However, the Davises' enthusiasm, supported by their documents, convinced the Boers that they were friends. Richard and Cecil camped out on the veldt that night, near an encampment of Boer farmer-soldiers who were roasting ox meat and singing hymns. In an old-fashioned, flowery welcome speech, General Christiaan de Wet said that it was only to be expected that the greatest republic would help a little republic; but he hadn't hoped that the women would show their sympathy by coming over. "No English woman would dare do what you are doing," he told Cecil.

They were woken from "a cold storage sort of sleep" by the sound of pom-poms—the Boer Vickar-Maxim guns—going off overhead. Climbing a hill, they could see "the English coming in their usual solid formation stretching out for three miles." In their cart, they drove to a nearer *kopje*, or small hill; but they had no sooner reached it than the Boers abandoned it. Roberts's column was very close. They drove on further, toward the bridge. "I kept telling Cecil that the firing was all from the Boers as I did not want Christian [their driver] to bolt and run away with the cart and mules," Richard wrote his family. "But Cecil remembered the pictures in *Harper's Weekly* showing the shrapnel smoke making rings in the air and as she saw these floating over our head, she knew the English were firing on us, but said nothing for fear of scaring Christian. I had promised to get her under fire which was her one wish so I said that she was now well under fire for the first and the last time. To which she replied 'Pshaw!' I never saw anyone show such self-possession."

They halted the cart behind a deserted farmhouse and saddled Cecil's pony. "The shells were now falling all over the shop, and I was scared to distraction," Richard recounted. "But she took about five minutes to see that her saddle was properly tightened and then we rode up to the hill. It was a very hot place but Cecil was quite unmoved. We showed her the shells striking back of her and around her but she refused to be impressed with the danger. She went among the Boers begging them to make a stand very quietly and like one man to another and they took it in just that way and said, 'But we are very tired. We have been driven back for three days. We are only a thousand, they are twenty thousand.' " When the British came within five hundred yards of the Boer artillery, Richard announced to Cecil that they must flee. His edict gathered resonance when, at that moment, they saw the Boer troops a mile away suddenly stampede in retreat. Richard got Cecil on her pony and they raced back to Ventersburg, with Christian in the Cape cart well in the vanguard.

In Ventersburg, everyone was harnessing up frantically. Maintaining their sangfroid, the Davises lunched on scraps at the hotel. Then, surrounded by people who were jettisoning their possessions, Cecil went off to see if she could retrieve the hotel cook and bring her back to Pretoria. She succeeded. As British shells fell on the edge of town, Cecil gathered up her maid, along with a dog and a kitten. The party raced back to Kroonstad, a thirty-mile journey, in five hours without a halt. There Richard went to see President Steyn, who ordered a special car to take the Americans back to Pretoria at once. The English entered Kroonstad the next day.[96]

Pretoria remained calm, "completely indifferent to its fate."[97] Fully partisan by now, Davis bitterly resented the English shopkeepers, who had stayed open through the war: anticipating the arrival of their compatriots, they were replacing the Dutch photographs in their windows with chromos of the Queen of England and the Prince of Wales.[98] He wrote acidly of the captured British officers who, confined to a schoolhouse, destroyed books and insulted women strollers.[99] From these churlish, aristocratic prisoners, he selected for special obloquy the earl of Rosslyn—who happened to be the brother of one of his most popular and admired English friends, the duchess of Sutherland. Richard had met Rosslyn in early 1898, when the youth was squandering his inheritance at a fantastic rate (five hundred thousand dollars in six months, by Richard's estimate) and attempting a career on the stage.[100] Embracing journalism when war broke out, Rosslyn tried to gain a correspondent's credentials. Failing, he accepted a commission in Thorneycroft's Horse. He had met Davis in Ladysmith and told him this. He was in uniform at the time. Now the two men met again in Pretoria; and, to Davis's disgust, he heard Rosslyn protesting that he should be set free because he was a correspondent and a noncombatant. "It makes one wonder if Her Majesty is not in sore distress for officers," Davis wrote in the New York *Herald*, "if she gives commissions to peers of England who repudiate their oath of allegiance to her for the sake of their personal comfort."[101]

Having denounced the British, Davis eulogized as a crusader and virtually a saint the man who was ridiculed in all the British press as a belligerent buffoon—Paul Kruger, the president of the Transvaal republic. Kruger "will probably rank as a statesman with Lincoln, Bismarck, and

Gladstone," Davis wrote.[102] He praised the president's passion, his vigor, and, most of all, his simplicity. Much of the day, Kruger sat smoking a pipe and sipping coffee on the porch of his little whitewashed cottage, separated from the sidewalk only by a flowerbed. Kruger was a large, bulky man with a gray beard. In his ears he wore tiny gold rings, and he protected his eyes, which were reddened by disease, with gold-rimmed dark glasses. Interviewing him, Davis was struck by the contrast between Kruger's forceful gestures and speech, and the face "like a heavy waxen mask." He reminded Davis of Grover Cleveland, another man of great girth and stature.[103]

After returning from Ventersburg, Davis saw Kruger for the last time at a ceremony in the president's cottage on May 26. In three hours, Kruger would be fleeing Pretoria for Machadodorp in the mountains. He was giving last-minute instructions to his cabinet officers and generals. Still, he found time to accept a petition of sympathy signed by twenty-nine hundred Philadelphia schoolchildren and presented by a sixteen-year-old New York messenger, Jimmy Smith. "Kruger stooped and peered down at Jimmy Smith like a giant ogre," Davis reported. "One almost expected to see him pinch Jimmy Smith to find out if he were properly fattened for eating. But instead he took Jimmy's hand and shook it gravely." After Jimmy delivered his brief speech, another American gave Kruger a large leather box fastened by a lock. In it was a richly bound album of clippings and pictures of the Boer War. The box was quite secure, however, and for many embarrassing minutes, different men struggled to unlock it. When at last the case was opened, Kruger pushed forward and gazed at the great gold-and-vellum volume. He straightened himself with a sigh of pleasure and nodded approvingly. "It is a Bible," he said smiling. "The mistake was so in character," Davis wrote, "that as we grasped it and heard the simple note of real pleasure in his voice I believe every man in the room would have given half a month's wages to have changed that album into what Kruger believed it to be."[104]

During his seven weeks as their guest, Davis grew so fond of the anachronistic, fervent Boers that he had no desire to watch the British conquerors march into their capital. He and Cecil held tickets for June 4 on a ship traveling up the east coast of Africa. As that day approached, it became evident that Pretoria would fall a few days afterward. To see the triumphal entry, the Davises would be forced to miss their ship and wait a month under British martial law (and censorship) for the next passage out. Richard decided against it and left the city two days before Lord Roberts arrived.[105] In explanation, he wrote: "All I could have said of them was what the lady vindictively called after the burglar who had just swept her jewelry from her dressing-table, 'I think you might be in a better business.' "[106]

Writing about the war, Davis repeatedly likened the British to robbers and murderers, and the Boers to Crusaders, the children of Israel, and the minutemen of the American revolution. He acknowledged that some readers might find his tone "hysterical." He had come to South Africa freighted with conflicting sentiments: an affection for Great Britain, which was a land he loved to visit and the home of many of his friends; and a sympathy for the Boers as outmatched patriots, who were fighting the world's greatest empire to retain their independence.[107] Witnessing the war had burned away his ambivalence and left him ranting, the prophet of a hopeless cause. "One is really afraid to tell all the truth about the Boer because no one would believe you," he wrote his mother. "It's almost better to go mildly and then you may have some chance. But personally I know no class of men I admire so much or who today preserve the best and oldest ideas of charity, fairness, and good will to men."[108]

In part, his was the fervor of the convert, the penance of the onetime apologist for the Jameson Raiders. In 1896, after Jameson was captured and the leaders of the Johannesburg Reform Committee were indicted, Davis depicted the reformers as idealistic underdogs, who were defending the liberties of the British Uitlanders against the backward, boorish Boers. Now he ruefully concluded that he had been duped by British propagandists, and that the Boers' greatest failing was their inept public relations.[109] He no longer viewed the war as a political conflict. He saw it instead as a clash of cultures, and characteristically, he favored the old-fashioned and picturesque over the brutally modern.

Influenced by his stay in Pretoria, Davis forsook his usual analogies to New York City intersections and theatrical machinery, and plundered the Bible searching for suitable comparisons to the heroic Boer struggle. There was, of course, a perfunctory nod to the battle of David and Goliath. There were descriptions of old, white-bearded patriarchs. But his most extended trope was an uncharacteristic lapse into anti-Semitism. Though such bigotry was common in genteel circles, Davis virtually never indulged in it. (Even in this case, he expunged it when he republished the article in his book.) So it is startling to read that Lord Roberts has become "a janissary of the Jews," and that England "has kept the bargain she made with the money changers in her temples" (meaning Jewish gold barons like Alfred Beit, who was so helpful in furnishing Davis with Cape Town introductions). Hopping over to Shakespeare, Davis noted that England, like Shylock, "has awarded herself not only the gold, but the pound of flesh as well."[110] By raising the stereotype of the Jew, Davis intended to paint England as soulless and money-grubbing. Beyond that, he was implying that the English, like the financier Jews, spearheaded the assault of material "progress" on simple, traditional, rural cultures. The British clanged the bell of the modern era— crass, greedy, tawdry. There was a poignant inevitability to their suppression of the Bible-toting, long-bearded Boers. It was another case of chivalry squashed, of spirit trampled, of modernism triumphant.

Dejected and a bit bewildered, the Davises (with their dog, Jaggers, and their maid, Hubert) left Pretoria by train, not knowing if the Boers had destroyed the track which lay between them and the Portuguese border. The panic-stricken refugees, many of them bandaged soldiers, depressed Richard further.[111] The good news, however, was that the railroad was intact. The Davises took it to Portuguese territory and launched their journey up the east coast of Africa. Here at last was the Dark Continent of Richard's dreams, full of painted natives and roaring lions. In South Africa, he had half-seriously chided his black servants for refusing "to yield to [his] sense of the picturesque and go naked like their less effete brothers."[112] In South Africa, the natives were (for the most part) colorlessly civilized, and the landscape resembled Oklahoma or New Mexico.[113]

All of that began to change in the rough Portuguese port of Lourenço Marques, where the Davises boarded a German ship and steamed toward the Equator. "There are several English officers on board and the friction was rather tense for we talked painful truths and as they knew me in London it came with unusual soreness," Richard wrote his mother. "So, we know no one on board and play by ourselves."[114] Their first stop, Beira, reminded Richard of Asbury Park, New Jersey; but sailing on, they "struck the real thing" (as Cecil wrote) in the city of Mozambique.[115] In this town of faded blues and pinks, declining since the end of the slave trade, the few Portuguese residents emerged only after sundown, and the native women scarred and painted their faces and dyed their tongues yellow. "We took Jaggers into the market and the entire market fled in terror," Richard reported. "They think he is some sort of a lion. His impressions of Africa would be worth reading. He never moves without an escort of a dozen naked blacks who run up with great bravado and then if he looks at them run away shrieking and laughing."[116] (In fairness to the Africans, Jaggers was once described by an American correspondent as "the toughest looking English brindle bulldog that ever stepped upon American soil" with "a face that would give a stone image a nightmare.")[117]

Of his other ports of call, Davis most admired Zanzibar, a pulsating web of narrow streets and overhanging balconies that whites had made healthy, clean, and orderly "without destroying one flash of its local color, or one throb of its barbaric life . . . the native does not wear a derby hat with a kimona, as he does in Japan, nor offer you souvenirs of Zanzibar manufactured in Birmingham. . . ."[118] Less comfortable but even more exciting was the Davises' final stop on the mainland: Tanga, a German settlement just south of Mombasa. When they arrived, a blood-red sun was sinking behind a range of gloomy mountains. "It was a rank jungle dropping and dripping with hot moist water," Davis wrote. "Every leaf perspired and the silence was so great that you could hear the moisture slip and drip to the next leaf below." Here at last was the real Africa. Any doubts were dispelled when a man came to their hotel from three miles away, complaining bitterly about the "damned lions" that kept him awake all night at his camp.[119]

Because of an outbreak of bubonic plague, the Davises had to view the remaining ports from the deck of their ship.[120] The equatorial leg of the journey was fiendishly hot. Men, women, and children slept in a heap on the deck, hoping for a breeze. Cecil, who had the only single cabin on the ship, remained behind closed doors at night, even though she suffered greatly from the heat. Richard likewise shunned the "degrading" scene by sleeping in his cabin, on a sweaty mat that felt like a doormat after a thunderstorm. By the time they reached their destination of Aix-les-Bains, they had been traveling for six months. "It seems almost disloyal to the Boers to be glad to see newspapers only an hour old instead of six weeks old, and to welcome all the tyranny of collar buttons, scarf pins, watch chains, walking sticks and gloves even," Richard wrote.[121]

The Davises returned to the United States without stopping in London. That city did not take kindly to Richard's denunciation of the British war effort, and he was forced to resign from several of the elite clubs he so admired. "I am sorry my English friends have taken such an aversion to me—very sorry," Richard said. "Consequently I have made no attempt to try to solicit a return of their favor."[122] (Almost a decade would be required to heal the rift completely.) In the United States, however, Davis's articles generated favorable comment. He hurried publication of the book *With Both Armies in South Africa,* fearing that the Boer War was ephemeral news, already being eclipsed in the public consciousness by the Boxer Rebellion in China.[123] Because of the rush, *With Both Armies* is badly organized and marred by an unusual number of repetitions.[124] Still, most critics, like the reviewer for the Philadelphia *Times,* thought that Davis's volume gave "a clearer idea of the actual warfare and of the life and manners and methods of both the British and the Boers than any of the many war books that have been turned out."[125] It might well, judged the *Outlook,* be the best of the two dozen books to appear on the Boer War.[126]

Personally, as well as professionally, Richard's trip had been a success. During six months of traveling, he and Cecil had strengthened their bond of mutual affection and respect. And he had demonstrated—to himself, and to the world—that married life would not cramp his style. "We have shown that getting married has not made her keep me, nor made me keep myself from the place where things are happening," he wrote Rebecca.[127] With that settled, he could return to domestic tranquillity and finish the novel that he hoped would, after years of popular acclaim, at long last afford him literary prestige.

9

A Failure Drives Him
to Farces—and to Tokyo

O N RETURNING FROM SOUTH AFRICA, Richard and Cecil spent the fall
in Marion and, with some difficulty, moved in December to New
York. "You cannot imagine how awful were the flats and houses presented
to our view," Richard wrote his mother-in-law after three forlorn days of
New York househunting. But they did manage to find a small Manhattan
townhouse a block from Central Park at 172 West Fifty-eighth Street, and
a studio nearby for Cecil. They leased the house for three months. Bringing
with them a cook and Cecil's maid, they needed to hire only a messenger
boy (whom Richard dressed in blue livery with brass buttons and white
shoes) and a waitress.[1]

Richard was in New York to promote himself as a playwright, hoping
for the weekly royalty check that a successful play would provide. His
theatrical career advanced erratically on several fronts. During the previous
year, Edward Sothern, Richard Mansfield, and James K. Hackett had each
promised to open a Davis play. By the time Davis moved to New York, all
three productions were off. "From my brief experience as a would be
playwright, I know that this producing plays is the most uncertain game I
ever was up against," he complained.[2] His last live property, a "raging
melodrama" based on the Van Bibber stories, was set to go with Henry E.
Dixey as the star, until Robert Hilliard, who was still playing Van Bibber
in *The Littlest Girl,* threatened to sue.[3] So Davis's final theatrical hope
flickered out. "None of the plays will be produced and I am rather inclined
to give up thinking it is possible or worth while," he sighed. "The theatrical
manager and star on the question of a play try my nerves more than any
money could justify."[4]

But the money justified a great deal. As one historian of the time has
written, "1900 was the year of the dramatized novel. No successful fiction
was permitted to escape." Such popular novels as *David Harum, Richard
Carvel, The Pride of Jennico, Janice Meredith,* and *The Christian* went on

the boards. The practice persisted over the next several years. "[It] is antagonistic to good dramatic art," conceded producer Daniel Frohman, the older brother of Charles, "but it keeps the theatres filled."[5] Among all of Davis's works, *Soldiers of Fortune* was the obvious candidate for dramatization. Having failed on his own, Davis entrusted the job to an accomplished playwright, Augustus Thomas, who had been manufacturing hits steadily since his *Alabama* of 1891.[6] Thomas constructed a skillful four-act version. For his part, Davis insured that the actors wore uniforms tailored to his designs and that real coconuts hung from the fake palm trees.[7] After a brief tryout in New Haven, *Soldiers of Fortune* opened at the Savoy Theatre in New York on March 17, 1902. Starring the handsome, athletic Robert Edeson as Robert Clay, *Soldiers* was greeted with excellent reviews and resounding business. "How wonderful is the success of the Soldiers!!" Davis exulted. "It is one of those things you read about." Each week he received a royalty check for an amount between two hundred and three hundred dollars.[8]

Never able to save, Davis struck gold as a playwright at the very moment that he found a hole to drop it down. During New Haven rehearsals for *Soldiers*, he went to see a farm of over two hundred acres in the town of Mount Kisco, located a little more than an hour from New York City in northern Westchester County. Even in a blizzard, under three feet of snow, it captivated him. Cecil loved it, too. "It is great to think of owning that much of this little world, and a house over your head," Richard wrote his mother.[9] Why do writers so often mortgage their futures to country estates? Among turn-of-the-century Americans, Jack London's Wolf House, Stephen Crane's Brede Place, and of course Henry James's Lamb House immediately come to mind. None of these houses was merely a comfortable place to live and work. Each was a fantasy setting in which the writer could refashion his own image, treating himself like one of his fictional characters. "Crossroads Farm" was the name of Davis's property. On March 18, 1902, he purchased 204 acres. From that time on, his home absorbed a considerable fraction of his energies and a gigantic portion of his income—the price of becoming a Westchester squire.

In his mother's youth, publication in the *Atlantic* was reward enough; the fee, even when badly needed, was incidental. Such at least was the ideal of the Age of Emerson. Now, in the twentieth century, writers openly conformed to the gold standard. Their prestige depended upon their sales, and the popular writers lived like barons. A luxurious existence was the manifestation as well as the perquisite of success. The reward of writing that Richard most enjoyed in his youth was celebrity. In his maturity, it was money. His choice of journalistic assignments, his style of fiction writing, and his continued emphasis on playwriting all reflected his financial need.

The blockbuster mentality that dominates the publishing of our own day is not as new as we think. The great change in American bookselling came in 1891, when the United States Congress approved the international copyright law and ended the practice of literary piracy. By affording protection to the large respectable houses (which had mostly been the victims, not the perpetrators, of book bootlegging), the copyright law permitted the competitive bidding for top authors to rise unchecked.[10] The most popular writers demanded more (up to 20 percent royalties) because a commercial book by a brand-name author could earn huge sums for both writer and publisher. In the "book boom" of the late 1890s, a few new novels sold hundreds of thousands of copies. Publishers invested thousands to promote a single book, leaving the other titles on their lists to fend for themselves.[11]

The magazines were changing, too. Until the turn of the century, the literary magazines of the great publishing houses—*Harper's, Scribner's,* and the *Century*—dominated the field. They made a specialty of serialized novels, they published fine engravings of picturesque scenes, and they relied financially on subscriptions rather than advertising. In the early years of the twentieth century, cheap ten-cent weeklies like *McClure's* and *Collier's* achieved unprecedented circulations in the millions with muckraking journalism, topical fiction, and news photography.[12] By 1897, *McClure's* outsold *Harper's, Scribner's,* the *Century,* and the *Atlantic* combined.[13] The new cheap magazines were purchased primarily on the newsstands, not by subscription, and they made their money on advertising. Instead of restricting ads to a few pages in the back, the new periodicals featured advertising as prominently as the editorial copy. Manufacturers advertised in the high-circulation magazines to gain national attention for wares that were being mass-produced for the first time. Soaps, ready-made clothes, breakfast cereals, and particularly automobiles were celebrated in the paid columns of magazines (just as ads for the new department stores filled the newspapers). Because all this magazine advertising required the larding of editorial copy, the early twentieth century was a golden age, monetarily speaking, for short-story writers. The magazines could afford to pay great sums to the authors they wanted.[14]

Because of his celebrity, Davis had many suitors. *Collier's Weekly* captured him. Besides the money, the lure was the personality of Rob Collier, the attractive young man who ran the magazine with profligate charm. The Collier empire was of recent foundation, the work of Rob's father, Peter Fenelon Collier. Known as Pat by his friends, P. F. Collier had arrived in this country from Ireland with twenty-five cents. Selling Bibles door to door to poor Irish Catholics, he had his great inspiration one day when an old woman turned him down. "No, me boy," he later recalled her saying, "I would like yer Bible, but I have no dollar. If ye want to lave it here, I will give ye tin cints, and ye can come back some ither time and get the rist."[15] From this remark came the birth of the installment-plan book business—and (because his employer rejected the idea) of the Collier fortune. Pat went out on his own. He began by selling one book; eventually, he merchandised large library sets, which were offered on the installment plan by book agents and in series by mail order. In 1879 he started a printing plant, and in a few years, he was registering annual sales of three million volumes of reprints of standard sets.

As an offshoot of his successful business, P. F. Collier in 1888 started a magazine, called *Once a Week*, that was sold either on its own for seven cents or in conjunction with the biweekly *Collier's Library* of low-priced books. The magazine was a mix of readable fiction and increasing amounts of news. Rechristened *Collier's Weekly* in 1895, in imitation of *Harper's* and *Leslie's*, it improved steadily but unspectacularly until Rob Collier, fresh from Harvard, took command in 1898. A tall, handsome polo player with blue-black hair and soft blue eyes, Rob wrote poetry with a mystical tinge. He was (recalled the editor Mark Sullivan) "sentimental and high-spirited, quick to range from serious to gay, but usually gay." Both Sullivan and his wife thought Rob the most charming man they ever knew. A paragon of second-generation refinement, young Collier decided that the *Weekly* needed more literary flair. As one of his first editorial acts, he bought Henry James's "The Turn of the Screw" and retained Henry La Farge to illustrate it. For his first cover, he printed a picture of a Greek goddess mounting a hill, with a caption taken from the work of Sappho. "[I] was so afraid that someone would understand it," he later reminisced, "that I printed it in the original Greek."[16]

The Spanish-American War jolted Collier out of his aesthetic haze. He had the good sense to send to Cuba the photographer Jimmy Hare, who in this and later wars established himself as the greatest photojournalist of his day. With him as *Collier's* chief correspondent was Frederick Palmer, another young man at the start of a brilliant career. *Collier's* emerged from the war with a reputation that Rob Collier worked and spent to enhance. He had a taste for the best and a pocketbook to indulge it. Increasing the magazine's price to ten cents, he obtained articles by Rudyard Kipling, Sir Arthur Conan Doyle, Finley Peter Dunne, Robert W. Chambers, and Hall Caine. He enlisted Howard Chandler Christy, Frederic Remington, and Maxfield Parrish to illustrate his covers and stories. Perhaps his greatest coup came in 1903, when, for the unheard-of sum of a hundred thousand dollars, he commissioned Charles Dana Gibson to draw a hundred double-page cartoons for *Collier's* over the next four years. When Gibson wrote an acceptance letter stating the terms, Rob reprinted it everywhere and sent Gibson on a national promotion tour.[17]

Collier's was a natural environment for Richard to enter. The snare was sprung when Rob Collier began courting Charles Davis as well, eventually installing him as the *Weekly's* fiction editor. Since 1896, when the election of William McKinley abruptly terminated his diplomatic service, Charlie had been searching for a career, gleaning the fields of publishing and the theater that his older brother harvested so profitably. Charlie worked as an editor for Robert H. Russell, as a manager for the vaudeville company of Weber and Fields, and as a theatrical agent for some of Richard's plays. In between jobs he supported himself (barely) by writing short stories for magazines. Always portly, when he binged he grew quite fat. Psychologically, he veered alarmingly between highs and lows. His parents and brother dearly wished he would settle down. Richard had allied himself with Russell to advance Charlie's prospects, and he was happy now to do the same with *Collier's*.[18]

Back in 1901, Collier had wanted Davis to accompany Jimmy Hare to Venezuela after three American warships arrived ominously at La Guayra. The United States government was protesting President Cipriano Castro's plan to reassign an asphalt concession from one American company to another. Because Cecil didn't want to interrupt her painting, Richard at the last minute cancelled his plans to travel.[19] Instead, he provided *Collier's* with an analysis that supported the Venezuelan position. The Republican administration was bullying a friendly Latin American neighbor (he wrote) because the asphalt trust, which controlled the aggrieved company, was dominated by Republican party heavyweights. Would anyone even consider sending warships up the St. Lawrence River if two American firms were arguing over a Canadian concession? As he had when the American navy seized Hawaii to protect the interests of the sugar trust, Davis condemned a foreign policy that served the venal interests of a few well-connected American businessmen.[20] The Venezuelan minister of foreign affairs thanked him in the name of a "misjudged and ill treated people."[21] It's ironic that, because of his distaste for Latin American dictators and false revolutionaries, later generations regarded Davis as an apologist for imperialism, an American Kipling. In fact, in both his journalism and his fiction, he repeatedly criticized the high-handed foreign policy of the American government and the avaricious robber barons who manipulated it. He knew how often the white man's burden was a sack of gold.[22]

Later in 1901, Davis gave *Collier's* "In the Fog," a story inspired by his fogbound evening in London with Ethel Barrymore. The next year he provided an inferior Western tale, "Ranson's Folly," which he started to dramatize as soon as he was done writing it. The best short story of this period, however, he gave to his old friends, the Scribners. "The Bar Sinister" is one of the all-time great dog stories (admittedly a back vestibule in the house of literature). Davis finished it at the very end of 1901.[23] Under Cecil's leadership, Richard had become a regular at dog shows and the co-owner of a growing kennel. One of their prized dogs—Edgewood Cold Steel, a bull terrier known familiarly as the Kid (which was Richard's nickname for Charlie)—is the model for the hero of "The Bar Sinister."[24]

The Kid, who narrates the story in a lingo reminiscent of Gallegher's, is the son of a prize-winning English bull terrier and a streetfighting black-and-tan of dubious morals. (In heraldry, the bar sinister was thought to be a sign of bastard birth.) Adopted by a kindly Irish groom, the Kid is taken to live on a Long Island estate, where he enchants the wealthy daughter of the house. Miss Dorothy enters him in a grand dog show at the Madison Square Garden, which of course he wins. His greatest delight comes when he realizes that the dog he has defeated for best of class is his own father. Pampered by Miss Dorothy, he has only one remaining desire: to find his mother, who ran away years ago to escape the jeers of other dogs at the circumstances of his birth. One day, riding in a carriage, he gallantly jumps to the assistance of an old bitch being murderously attacked by three large dogs. He rescues her and then recognizes that he has at last found his mother. Seeing how attached he is to the old dog, Dorothy brings her back to the Long Island estate.

"The Bar Sinister" is an Ugly Duckling story with a weird Oedipal subtext. A son defeats his father (of English ancestry, like Clarke Davis) and rescues his mother. "All I know of fighting [writing?] I learned from mother . . . ," says the Kid. "No one ever was so good to me as mother." Because it is a "dog story," one may miss at first that "The Bar Sinister" is charged with more human feeling than anything else Davis wrote at the height of his career. It is the testament of a son's love for a mother who has become (in the Kid's words) "very old, and sick, and hungry, and nervous, as mothers are."

"The Bar Sinister" is the outstanding story in the collection that Scribner's published in July 1902; but because Davis wanted to publicize the name of "Ranson's Folly" to enhance its life on the stage, he gave that name to the book. It was one of the best sellers of the summer. Two months later, the Scribners published *Captain Macklin*, the novel that Davis had begun before the Spanish-American War. It was his "favorite" work, the one that he was counting on to fulfill his youthful promise.[25] He hoped that after it was published, he would never again have to hear himself described as "the author of 'Gallegher.' "[26] He dedicated it to his mother, who declared it "immortal."[27] But it turned out to be one of the shorter-lived of his literary progeny.

Davis made several daring advances in *Captain Macklin*. In place of the usual touched-up image of himself, his hero was a young man who was callow, boastful, and hot-headed—another portrait of the author, one might say, but a much less flattering one. And instead of his usual plot device of a *dea ex machina*, he amended this novel in its early stages to make it a bildungsroman. Age and experience, rather than the love of a good woman, would reform the hero. Had the Spanish-American War and Boer War not interrupted him, Davis might have written the book he wanted. The novel differs markedly in its beginning and its end—and the first half is better. One might think that Davis's observations of war would enrich *Captain Macklin*. Instead, the trite stories and farces that he produced during those years had a more obvious impact on his artistic achievement.

Captain Macklin is presented as a sequence of long journal entries, the first of them written when Macklin is twenty-three—the precocity of the memoirist being one sign of his vanity. Scion of a military family, Royal Macklin has never wanted anything but a military career; however, at the start of the book, he is expelled from West Point for a minor infraction. Unable to fight for his own country, he offers his services to another. Leaving his cousin Beatrice, for whom he entertains feelings that surpass the cousinly, he takes off for revolution-torn Honduras. There he links up with a gallant old soldier of fortune, the pointedly named General Laguerre, whose ragtag band of foreign legionnaires backs a rival to the corrupt president. Before long, Macklin discovers complexities in the situation. The rival is just as venal as the president; and both of them are merely puppets for conflicting Wall Street interests. He helps persuade Laguerre to strike out on his own, and the old man is installed as president. Laguerre makes a fine leader—the first honest president in memory, with a program that actually helps the people—but he is betrayed through the chicanery of American businessmen. Wounded, he flees. So does Macklin, who returns to Dobbs Ferry, New York, where he plans to marry Beatrice and enter business. Then he is invited to join a foreign legion campaign under Laguerre in Indochina. Breaking his engagement to Beatrice, he happily runs off to fight again.

The notices for *Captain Macklin* were mostly very good—the *Review of Reviews* reported "a general opinion that this is the most successful of Mr. Davis' sustained efforts in fiction"—but they did not salute the breakthrough that Davis thought he had achieved. Nor did *Macklin* sell as well as Davis's previous books.[28] There was far too much derring-do, especially in the second half, for the elite audience Davis hoped to entice. "I have always been afraid that I allowed my liking for military things to lead me into giving up too much space to that side of the expedition," he confessed.[29] He cut some of it, but he should have cut more. Having grown so accustomed to his alter-ego protagonists, his readers missed the variation in Royal Macklin. The Scribners didn't help matters with the initial advertisements for the book, which suggested that Macklin's adventures were based on Richard's own.[30] If the Scribner publicists missed these nuances, how could the general public be expected to understand?[31]

Too many readers dismissed *Macklin* as a retread of *Soldiers of Fortune* with a less attractive hero. "Nothing ever hurt me so much as the line used by many reviewers of 'Macklin' that 'Mr. Davis' hero is a cad, and Mr. Davis cannot see it,' " Davis wrote several years later to a friendly critic. "Macklin I always thought was the best thing I ever did, and it was the one over which I took the most time and care. Its failure was what, as Maggie Cline used to say, 'drove me into this business' of play writing. All that ever was said of it was that it was 'A book to read on railroad trains and in a hammock.' That was the verdict as delivered to me by Romeike from 300 reviewers, and it drove me to farces. . . . I tried to make a 'hero' who was vain, theatrical, boasting and self-conscious, but, still likable. But, I did not succeed in making him of interest, and it always has hurt me."[32]

As he reached out unsuccessfully for a new audience, Davis lost touch with his young female readers who were outraged by an "unhappy" ending in which the girl failed to get her man. Perhaps they also noticed that throughout the book, women were Macklin's antagonists. First the cadet is thrown out of West Point for meeting a girl after curfew. Then he is humiliated in Honduras by a rich American girl who treats his admiration with disdain. Finally, and most inauspiciously, he is almost trapped by his love for Beatrice into a humdrum commuter routine, and thinks: "I had sworn for her sake alone to submit to the life I hated."[33] Although the theme of women caging men inside "civilization" had appeared in the Davis canon from the start, it became more prominent in the early years of his marriage. In his story "Ranson's Folly," young Ranson, who "lived only to enjoy himself," contemplates giving up manly adventure for feminine domesticity—this for a girl whose father has become a highwayman so that he can afford to buy the luxuries that would "make a lady of her." A heroine who has emasculated one man and impoverished another suggests an author who is feeling a little resentful.[34]

He was. By this time, Richard recognized that his marriage to Cecil had settled into its permanent contours. It would never exceed a respectful, reserved friendship. Cecil was an independent woman. To get closer to her, Richard had adopted her interests of billiards and dog breeding, but those were merely shared hobbies. Emotionally, Cecil would give or take only so much. Richard apparently never wrote about it (to whom could he confide?), but, as his fiction suggested and later events would prove, he became unhappy in his marriage. It was a financial strain without domestic compensations: not least of the losses in a sexless marriage was the absence of children. Whether Cecil was similarly discontent is more mysterious. She was fond of Richard, but in a distant way. Intriguingly, her one finished portrait of him, holding a book, is rough and unaccomplished compared to her paintings of women, including some striking full-length portraits of women in masculine attire. Throughout her life, she enjoyed the company of intelligent, articulate men but reserved her deepest friendship for women; surviving Richard by many years, she would spend her last two decades with a female secretary-companion. Yet, given the choices available to a talented, ambitious, but largely conventional upper-class American woman at the turn of the century, she had good reason to be satisfied with her arrangement.

In the early winter of 1903, bitter that despite his labors on *Captain Macklin* he seemed fated to be seen as a lightweight, Richard renounced fiction to pursue riches in the theater. "I do not intend to write any more fiction—at least not for some time—some years," he wrote to his publisher,

Charles Scribner. "If any one wants them, and I find the subjects, I will write descriptive articles of travel, and war correspondence[,] but no more fiction for 'reading on trains' and in 'hammocks.' "[35] Even before this renunciation, he was doing as much travel writing for *Collier's* as he wished. Eager for his byline, Rob Collier in 1902 sent him to Venezuela and then to Europe for two coronations: Alfonso XIII in Madrid and Edward VII in London. (He never saw Edward's coronation; it was postponed when the king fell ill.)[36]

Most of his energies, however, went into writing plays. Jubilant over the success of *Soldiers of Fortune*, he tried to breathe theatrical life into his other pieces of fiction. He first adapted "The Lion and the Unicorn," which he had written after Cecil rebuffed his proposal of marriage. "It is not startling in any way but very seeable and attractive," was Cecil's measured verdict.[37] Henry Miller took the role of Phillip Carroll, who was the forerunner of a long line of Davis's poor but genteel suitors of rich young women. *The Taming of Helen*, as it was called, was the first full-length play written by Davis to be commercially produced. Although it was well received during its preliminary run in Toronto, Boston, and Philadelphia, the New York critics were fiercer. "It was the most aggravated case of breaking a butterfly that the town has seen this Winter," wrote a friendly observer in *Town Topics*, after the show opened at the Savoy on March 30, 1903.[38] Since he himself considered *The Taming of Helen* to be a mediocrity that he "was not proud of," Davis couldn't bellyache too much about the negative notices.[39] "Personally I dread no battle so much as I do a battle with the critics," he jocularly told a reporter after the opening of *Helen*.[40] At a luncheon in New York with Augustus Thomas, Dana Gibson, and Finley Peter Dunne, Thomas asked if Davis was making any money from *Helen*. With an air of mystery, Richard showed him a check for $541, for the one week that the play had made money. "That's last week's check," he said carelessly, as the others whistled and passed it around the table. "It made a hell of an impression on the very crowd I wanted to see it," Richard told Charles.*[41] As for impressing the critics, he looked ahead optimistically to his next production, a dramatization of *Ranson's Folly*.[42] Even more promising, he had begun his first theatrical piece not based on a previous work of fiction. It was a farce called *The Dictator*.

Although Davis took little pride in the workmanlike melodrama of *Ranson's Folly*, he pressed hard for a first-rate production.[43] A poor play could well turn a fine profit. Davis cordoned off his dramatic writing as a second-rate territory, judging it only by commercial standards. While he would fight bitterly over the tiniest details in his books, such as the illustrations and proofreading, he resigned himself to the inevitable compromises

---

*Despite initially positive audience response, the critical wounds were mortal: *Helen* succumbed in under a month.

of the theater. "I think it's hopeless in this business to get what you want," he reasoned, "and the only thing is to get what you can, and then quit it."[44] He had no objections when the star actor Raymond Hitchcock suggested a hokey love interest as the dramatic motor for "A Derelict," Davis's Spanish-American War story about a wire-service reporter and a Crane-like drunken genius.[45] By the same reasoning, he renounced any literary concerns when he assigned the theatrical rights to *Captain Macklin* to his friend, the proven playwright Franklin Fyles. "He will probably marry Macklin for the play, but I shall not object," Richard told his mother. "The book is all I care about. That is mine, written to suit myself, and the play is Fyles."[46]

Richard thought that lowering his values for plays would not affect his other work; but corrosion, once it starts, can be hard to check. Although always seeking popular acclaim for his fiction, he had written stories that he delighted in, stories that he was proud of. Now he was writing strictly for money. It's a well-established rule of commercial fiction that the authors who succeed are not those who tailor their work to the public taste, but those who, writing to please themselves, happily find that their own preferences are shared by the millions. When he became a playwright, Davis crossed over the line that separates those who please from those who pander.

Despite the playwright's private misgivings, *Ranson's Folly* was a popular success. Just before the play opened in Providence on January 11, 1904, Davis predicted that "this time we are going to come out without a very severe fall. It does not aim high enough to fall far."[47] His self-deprecating prophecy came to pass. The play opened in New York a week later to favorable notices and audiences. Not that Richard was satisfied. "The notices seem mildly 'good,' " he wrote his mother. "They will have to be 'better' for the Dictator or the American stage will lose a playwright and the novel reading public again will suffer." He surmised, however, that the production would "increase in public interest," and here, once again, he was correct.[48] "As you guess, I like a theatre," Richard remarked to Rebecca later that month, "and when the 'House Full' sign is out, and it is *your* show, the theatre proves most attractive."[49]

The experience with *The Dictator* was even more gratifying. As Davis said, it was a better play—in fact, it was the best he would ever write. Not constricted by the girders of an existing story, he built a purely theatrical device with surprising deftness, a farce of mistaken identities set in the mythical Latin American town of Porto Banos. With just one act finished, he was already thinking of a production for *The Dictator*. The actor he had in mind was William Collier, an idiosyncratic light comedian who had recently joined the Weber and Fields company at a salary of a thousand dollars a week.[50] Despite his doubts about giving the farce to a vaudeville company, Davis was willing to compromise if Collier would put on the play as soon as it was finished. But before anything was settled, Collier, miserable over a disastrous season, bolted the company and retained Charles Frohman as his manager. So it was Frohman who bought the play for Collier, giving Davis the star and producer of his choice. Frohman shared Davis's mania for authenticity of detail (a real motorboat engine was used in *The Dictator* to ensure that the noise would be accurate).[51] He also did not stint on casting. The talented company of *The Dictator* included John Barrymore, Ethel's younger brother, who made his reputation overnight as an addled wireless operator. It was ironic, considering Barrymore's lifelong bout with the bottle, that his big moment in *The Dictator* was a drunk scene.

The out-of-town tryouts in New Haven and Boston went so well that everyone was confident of a hit. At the premiere in New Haven, the laughter of the audience drowned out the dialogue at the end of the second act. "It might have been a pantomime," Davis quipped. When it was over, Frohman addressed Davis formally before the company. "Mr. Davis, I have produced a good many plays," he said, "and I have never produced one with so many laughs in it." He told him that no revisions were needed: "Your part is done, go home and get some sleep."[52] Richard was heading in that direction at 1:30 A.M. when he went to the aid of a horse that had fallen down; and who should come riding by in a motorcar but Ethel Barrymore. She was so ecstatic over the dual success of her old friend and younger brother that she insisted on taking Richard to supper. They celebrated until 4:30. Without bothering to sleep, he read the morning newspapers and went off to the racetrack. It was quite an opening night.

Of course, it couldn't rival the real opening night in New York, which happened two months later. The reviews were the reviews of a playwright's dreams. The tone was set by the New York *World*, which called it "the most humorous piece produced in the last twelve months."[53] When he read the notices, Davis punched himself to make sure he was awake, and looked around for someone to blow to a drink. But there was no one to be seen except Belgian diplomats and Japanese servants. On April 4, 1904, the night that *The Dictator* opened in New York, Davis was on the other side of the world—in Tokyo, with a flock of reporters squawking like caged geese, trying futilely to get to the front to cover the Russo-Japanese War.[54]

A war correspondent who reads of mobilizing troops is like a Dalmatian that hears the clang of a fire bell: the ears perk up, the tail starts to wag, and he's off and running. In the summer of 1903, at the same time that he was revising one play and completing another, Davis was anxiously following the reports of imminent hostilities between massive, senescent Russia and upstart, aggressive Japan. From a journalist's perspective, it was just like the Boer War. The conflict in East Asia was so far away that it made sense for Davis to go only if he was sure war would break out and would last until he arrived. By year's end he had largely decided to go. When he wasn't shopping for props and uniforms for his two productions, he was purchasing olive-green padded coats for a Manchurian winter.[55] He had received many offers to go to Japan, but none could possibly compete with Rob Collier's colossal stipend of a thousand dollars a week.[56] Collier pursued his big-name literary trophies like a great white hunter, and he wasn't about to let Davis get away. "I find that of all the people who write for us we get better returns from your work," he told Richard.[57] Motivated by Collier's mix of flattery and lucre, Davis agreed to start writing fiction once again (he also informed the Scribners that he was back in the market) and to report overseas for *Collier's*.[58] The Japanese war was his first big assignment for the *Weekly*. He signed on for three months.[59]

As late as the New Haven opening of *The Dictator* on February 8, Davis was scouting the newspapers for auguries of war, uncertain of his plans. Reassured by the martial red on the horizon, he and Cecil, accompanied once again by Cecil's trusty and footloose maid, Hubert, departed Boston by train on February 20. They were headed for San Francisco, where they would board a ship to Japan.[60] The journey from Boston to Tokyo, with a stopover in Hawaii, would take three weeks. "Somehow we cannot take this trip seriously," Richard wrote his mother from the train. "It is such a holiday trip all through not grim and human like the Boer war. Just quaint and queer. A trip of cherry blossoms and Geisha girls."[61] San Francisco impressed him—as it has generations of tourists before and since—as "one of the few cities that lives up to it's [*sic*] reputation in every way." Making the rounds from the Cliff House to Chinatown to the Golden Gate, he thought it "the most interesting city, with more character back of it than any city on this continent."[62]

On the crowded steamer to the Orient, Cecil had a stateroom to herself, while Richard shared one with a stranger.[63] The weather was cold and damp, the food was wretched, the quarters were cramped and musty. Virtually all the white passengers were war correspondents.[64] Talking to them during the dismal passage, Richard had forebodings of failure. "It seems to be the consensus of opinion among the 89,000 war correspondents on board, many hundreds of whom have been in Japan, that it is going to be most difficult to get news back," he wrote Charles. "I am really very fearful I will not be able to earn my salary as I should like to do."[65] Later he would wish that he had acted on his hunches and turned back home.

Among the warbound correspondents on the ship was John Fox, Jr., a friend since Cuba who had attended Richard and Cecil's wedding. Gaunt, sickly, and acerbic, Fox at first glance seemed to have little in common with the florid, burly Davis. Born a year and a half before Richard, he was raised in Kentucky and graduated from Harvard College. Like so many college-educated young men with ambitions in journalism, he apprenticed on the New York *Sun*. He learned quickly that he had little talent for news-gathering but a bent for descriptive, anecdotal writing. His great love was

the Appalachian hill country, and his greatest fame came from his sentimental novels, *The Little Shepherd of Kingdom Come* and *The Trail of the
Lonesome Pine*. But like Davis, Jack London, and Stephen Crane (who
would most likely have been in Tokyo had he not died in 1900), Fox happily
interrupted his work on fiction to follow the call of war. Beyond these
professional parallels, his greatest resemblance to Davis was the intensity
of his maternal attachment. "The most beautiful thing in his life was his
love for his mother," Fox's sister wrote. "She was always first with him. . . ."
Uncannily echoing Davis, Fox would often say, "Mother, no one understands you or me; we just understand each other." In the rough fraternity
of war correspondents, it's not surprising that these two men took a liking
to each other. "He is one of the best men when you get to know him, as
we have, of my acquaintance," Richard wrote home from Japan. "Out here
they always speak of him as the Little Shepherd because he spends his time
rescuing drunkards, beach combers and remittance men, and his money
too."[66]

The ship stopped to refuel in Honolulu, an outpost of the new American empire. In 1893, after Queen Liliuokalani was toppled, President Cleveland thwarted the efforts of American sugar planters to bring the Hawaiian
Islands under the American flag; but President McKinley signed an annexation treaty on July 7, 1898. Although Richard (and *Harper's Weekly*, where
he was managing editor) shared Cleveland's distaste for imperial adventures
back in 1893, now that the deed was done he was eager to see how his
country administered a faraway colony of brown-skinned natives.[67] He was
disappointed. "I have decided we are as little adaptable as the English," he
wrote his mother. "Imagine the '*New England Bakery*' set in a grove of date
palms, the sign obscuring the entire front of the garden. The houses built
by the American residents are all taken from the *Ladies Home Journal* school
of art." He and Cecil finally saw two lovely homes, with broad cool roofs
and wide porches, painted a deep green and nestled in a garden of tropical
plants. They exclaimed to their driver on the appropriateness and beauty
of these dwellings. "Yes," he replied, "Chinese man live in them houses."
Richard thought that the American military men and shopkeepers, and their
"pale, overdressed American wives," faced a big problem in Hawaii. "We
have given them a wonderful public school, fine apartments, good roads,
splendid cable car service, but the natives don't care for any of those things,"
he wrote perceptively, "and all of them to whom I talked spoke of the
monarchy and the Queen with the most deep regret."[68] The American faith
in technical progress and material comfort would not satisfy all the desires
of a dominated people: an obvious insight, perhaps, but one that was
considerably less obvious to most upper-class Americans at the turn of the
century.

After a rainy and dull ten days, the Davises' first glimpse of Japan was
an irregular line of purple mountains against a yellow sky. "In spite of the

Sunday papers, and the interminable talk on board, the guide books and maps which had made Japan nauseous to me," Davis wrote, "I saw the land of the Rising Sun with just as much of a shock and thrill as I first saw the coast of Africa." He was so eager "to see the kimonos and temples and geishas and cherry blossoms" that he was "almost hoping the Government won't let us go to the front and that for a week at least Cecil and I can sit in tea houses with our shoes off and draw $1000 a week from Collier while the nesans [serving-girls] bring us tea and the geishas rub their knees and make bows to us."[69] His wish was fulfilled with a vengeance.

Checking into the Imperial Hotel (in its pre–Frank Lloyd Wright incarnation), the Davises found it full of war correspondents, none of whom had seen a hint of war. Some of the men had been waiting for months to go to the front. The war—which excited enormous interest back in the United States—was not to be seen in Tokyo. There were no soldiers. Three days after arriving, Davis woke to find the streets filled with flag-waving Japanese. He rushed to ask his interpreter if Port Arthur had fallen. The man eyed him reprovingly. "Today is the spring festival," he said. The people were cheering the blossoms on a plum tree at the Temple of Kawasaki. The only war news available in Tokyo came, weeks late, on the rebound from London.[70] Richard's old friend Lloyd Griscom—his fellow gringo in Central America a decade before—had grown up to become the American minister to Japan; so Richard trusted that "if any [reporters] get up Lloyd will let me be one."[71] Still, it was a big "if." And the rainy, snowy, chilly city of Tokyo was a poor place to wait for an uncertain payoff. The gray houses, bare limbs of the trees, and dark clothes of the people created a colorless, cheerless scene.[72] "It is a city as big as London, 14 miles across, and is without beauty, filled with flying dust, and great stinking moats, and miles and miles of little shops of one story open to the street," Davis wrote. "Having seen one block, you have seen it all."[73]

The Japanese military staff had announced that three groups of correspondents were to accompany different armies. Thanks to Griscom's efforts, six of the first band of sixteen would be Americans. Chosen (before Davis's appearance) according to priority of arrival, length of experience, and importance of publication, the first group included Frederick Palmer, a *Collier's* correspondent who landed in Tokyo six weeks before Davis; Jimmy Hare, who was taking photographs for *Collier's*; and Jack London, who was working for Hearst.[74] Davis was assigned to the group that would travel with the second army out. To his dismay, he observed that not even the first squad showed any signs of forward motion.[75]

At the urging of the Japanese, Davis and the other correspondents obtained interpreters, servants, horses, outfits, and provisions, and then they waited at the hotel which they dubbed the Imperial Tomb. Because the order to go might come at any time, they didn't dare travel further than Yokohama harbor, which was eighteen miles away. When the first batch of correspondents at last departed on April 1, "their going cleared the atmosphere like a storm in summer," Davis wrote his mother. Still, he wasn't sure the first group would be allowed to see anything, and he didn't know when his second group would be permitted to follow. He worked off his frustration by perfecting his kit, supplementing the gear he had purchased in New York, Boston, and San Francisco. The war outfit of Richard Harding Davis, which was much admired and derided during his lifetime, may have reached its apotheosis in Japan. The inspiration of the superbly organized Japanese people, the opportunity provided by months of free time, and the very generous Japanese baggage allowance of sixty-six pounds all contributed to this achievement.[76]

There are practical reasons for a correspondent in the field to suit up as comfortably as possible. So Davis argued when he wrote for publication about his kit. This rational skein, however, couldn't mask his mania for equipment and uniforms, which was romantic, not practical. It dated from his earliest boyhood, as did his love of theater, costumes, and military decorations. Buying a kit was like dressing for a part. Davis had gone to war in Cuba with only two saddlebags, but that was due to the cruel restrictions on the transport ships. To cover the Boer War in South Africa, he acquired a beautiful tent with window panes, ventilators, clothes lines, inside pockets, and doors that looped up. It was colored "a lovely green" and was accented by red knobs. His equipage during that campaign included two tables, two chairs, a bathtub, a folding bed, two lanterns, and a Cape cart; and his staff of three black boys featured one who did nothing but polish his boots, gaiters, and harness to the luster level of a British officer.[77]

Good as that kit was, in Japan Davis outdid himself. He reported that "everybody here voted it the greatest ever seen" and that "all the Jap saddlers, tent makers and tinsmiths have been copying it."[78] When news of this remarkable kit reached the highest military echelons, General Fukushima asked the American correspondent to bring his complete outfit to the War Office. As Davis spread the items out on the floor, Fukushima "with unerring accuracy" selected the three most valuable articles: a folding cot, a folding armchair, and a cleverly combined water bottle and cooking kit. He asked if he might borrow them; and Richard complied, assuming the general wanted them for his personal use. Later, the Japanese general staff informed Davis that their army had introduced many replicas of his chairs, water bottles, and cooking kits—without paying a cent of royalties to the inventors.[79]

So that Cecil would not have to live alone in the hotel when Richard was at the front, the couple in early May rented a small house on a hill near the foreign legations. Cecil readily admitted that she was not "an eager sightseer."[80] However, while Richard awaited his marching orders, there was little to do but visit the celebrated tourist attractions of greater Tokyo.

Davis forlornly mailed his prosaic travelogues back to New York.[81] "Nothing I have sent home has been good," he wrote Charles. "If it has been published, it no doubt hurt my reputation."[82] He called himself, self-deprecatingly, a "cherry blossom correspondent."[83]

It took him a few weeks of impatient waiting to realize that, behind their screen of elaborate courtesy, the Japanese general staff viewed the foreign correspondents with mistrust and contempt. In their shrewd, scientific prosecution of the war, they made little allowance for Western opinion. The reporters regarded themselves as the tribunes of the English and American people, and expected to be treated respectfully. To the Japanese, they were at best gnats, at worst spies. The generals didn't deny the reporters' requests flat out, because a direct no would be a breach of Japanese etiquette. Instead, they put off their petitioners again and again with vague promises and apologetic shrugs. A man more experienced with Japanese mores would have realized sooner what was happening. For Davis, it was a painfully protracted education.

In mid-May the first group of correspondents returned from the front with discouraging tales. The Japanese general staff had required them to hire, at the cost of eleven gold dollars a day, a contractor to dispense food and supplies.[84] This contractor promptly disappeared when they reached Manchuria, forcing the Westerners to return to Tokyo prematurely. The reporters were nevertheless able to see a battle and to mine successfully for local color. The material was there, but the Japanese placed obstacles all along the way.[85] In a letter to President Roosevelt at the end of May, Davis complained that the Japanese had "imposed restrictions that put us a little higher than naughty children and a little lower than spies."[86]

Spring, with cherry blossoms that Cecil thought "much overrated," turned into a sweltering Tokyo summer; and still there was no word of when the second group of reporters would depart.[87] On June 21, Davis and John Fox cabled President Roosevelt to ask him to intercede with the Japanese Minister on behalf of all the American correspondents.[88] It was Richard's idea; by this time, he had been in Japan three months, his stipend from Collier's had just been halved (on a pay schedule arranged before his departure) to five hundred dollars a week, and he was willing to try almost anything. Through Secretary of State John Hay, Roosevelt wrote a note to Griscom in support of the hamstrung reporters, and he sent a sympathetic letter directly to Davis; but he wouldn't do anything more, for fear of exciting the Japanese. The Japanese minister of foreign affairs gave Griscom a hearing but refused to intervene, explaining that it was a question for the War Office. Richard was left where he had started, feeling "helpless and hopeless."[89]

Many of the other Americans gave up and left—including Jack London, who (Richard wrote) "is very bitter against the wonderful little people and says he carries away with him only a feeling of irritation."[90] Twice Davis had interceded on behalf of the quarrelsome London: once with Griscom, after the Japanese police confiscated London's camera; and then with Roosevelt, after London was court-martialed for knocking down a Japanese groom who he said was stealing supplies. Returning now to San Francisco, London bid good riddance to what he called a lousy war, hardly fit for white men to observe.[91] Davis, Fox, and a few others lingered, envying those who were homeward bound but longing to retrieve something from the fiasco.

Had the Japanese stated at the outset that they would not permit foreign correspondents to accompany their troops, Davis and his colleagues would have had no grievance. "No one in this world would have been better pleased had they when war was declared announced frankly that we would not be allowed to go," Davis wrote, "but it is there [sic] letting us come all the way over here and lying to us week after week when they knew we were to be held up here for months that makes my case against them."[92] They were the best soldiers in the world, he thought: "as cold-blooded in making war as Hill or Morgan are in a deal on Wall Street."[93] But they were not gentlemen. "Apparently it is easier to make a general than a gentleman," he sniped, "and we require more of a gentleman than merely to rub his knees and smile."[94]

Racism was so prevalent at the turn of the century that few Anglo-Saxon men remained untainted. But Davis wore his prejudices lightly— that is, until he got to Japan.* To his credit, he didn't bolt at the idea of taking commands from nonwhites. What angered him was the duplicity of the orders, not the color of the men issuing them. "I've no objection to a Filipino, a negro or a dago, but these people are uncanny; and I cannot get next to them at any point," he wrote his mother. "They don't like us; they know their superiority, and what we call the 'finer feelings' they look upon as weaknesses." He found the Japanese alloy of science and fanaticism extremely unsettling. "It's like a man with the intelligence to play the best chess," he explained vividly, "and with the lack of balance 'to cut his throat if he makes a false move.' "[95] He had always admired the Japanese. As early as his Lehigh days, he had extolled two Japanese exchange students as "very polite people and very grateful for anything that's done for them . . . [with] a certain self respect and decision which is very pleasent [sic]."[96] His experiences during the war changed his mind. Afterward, he denounced the Japanese as "a half-educated, half-bred, conceited, and arrogant people."[97]

While they might blame the queer Japanese for denying them "that

---

*For instance, amidst the furor aroused by President Roosevelt's luncheon invitation to the black educator Booker T. Washington, Davis wrote to congratulate Roosevelt, saying, "I would not insult you nor myself, by saying you were right to ask to your table a gentleman who has done as much for his people, and through them, for the good of his country, their country, and yours and mine, as has Booker Washington." (RHD to Theodore Roosevelt, Oct. 17, 1901; Theodore Roosevelt Papers, Library of Congress.)

freedom we have enjoyed in other wars,"[98] Davis and his colleagues would realize later that the Russo-Japanese War was not an aberration but a harbinger, and that the manners of the Japanese were an irritating, not a determining, factor. Those days of gamboling without credentials on the trail of the Greek army, of galloping alone across the veldt to Ladysmith— those days were gone with the last century, a casualty of progress in communications. Even before his immobilization in Japan, Davis (during his frustrating wait on the British side during the Boer War) had contemplated writing an article to be called, "The Passing of the War Correspondent." His argument was that the war correspondent "must either disappear altogether like the vivandiere or be allowed to do his work. . . . Either [the generals] should persuade the Government that their objections to him are weighty and suppress him altogether, or recognize him as a part of the outfit."[99] It took him a decade to write the article, by which time the Russo-Japanese War had furnished him with more evidence to clinch his case.

The problem was the quickness with which news now traveled from one end of the world to the other. As long as the correspondent relied upon the mails, he was permitted to see everything; because, by the time his articles appeared in print, the events were already history. "But the day his cable from Cuba to New York was in an hour relayed to Madrid the war correspondent received his death sentence," Davis wrote, "and six years later the Japanese buried him." In the brief space of nine years, covering six campaigns, Davis had seen the status of the war correspondent "utterly changed," from being an independent and respected free-lance to being "a prisoner and a suspected spy." He rightly predicted that in the next war, the Japanese method of dealing with the press would be widely copied.[100] Had he lived longer, he would have seen only further corroboration of his thesis. Writing in 1956, one of Richard's *Collier's* colleagues in Japan looked back over half a century and dated the origins of the decline of the war correspondent to the Russo-Japanese War: "It was the start of the secrecy which in the world wars to come barred reporters from the front lines, so that no public should ever know the truth."[101]

Made "damned miserable and nervous" by the disappointment and uncertainty, Davis issued one more ultimatum to the Japanese general staff.[102] On July 3, he announced that unless he received a pass to go to the front, he would quit Japan on July 17, exactly four months after he had arrived.[103] Probably it was coincidence (although he never knew for sure) that on July 18, he and his colleagues assigned to the Second Army sailed out of Yokohama, headed toward the fighting. (Cecil was grievously disappointed by the extension of her exile. Very weary of a life in which lessons in drawing and flower arranging were the primary diversions, she too left Tokyo, to take a brief tour of China.) Dining at a Kobe hotel that Kipling had celebrated, sailing across the Inland Sea and through the Shimonoseki Strait, swimming in opalescent waters with jagged islands on the horizon,

Davis and his friends washed off the gloom that had silted down on them over the idle months.[104] At Shimonoseki, Davis and John Fox shared a huge room in a Japanese-style hotel—the room in which the Shimonoseki treaty ending the Sino-Japanese War had been signed. It was a historic jumping-off point for their quest to see history being made.

The eighteen correspondents, along with their servants, interpreters, and horses, boarded a transport at Shimonoseki. Slowly, very slowly, the ship moved north and then halted for three days. Life on board the transport was crisscrossed with rules: the Japanese stopped Richard from diving for tossed coins after the captain discovered a regulation—a regulation obviously intended for soldiers—that forbade bathing. Despite such annoyances, the reporters couldn't help but be happy. They were only a ten-hour sail from Port Arthur. When the ship started moving again and the men could see the rocky coast of Manchuria, they cheered loudly. At the sound of a big gun moaning in the distance, they were so thrilled that they forgot the long, tedious months of waiting.

Some of their excitement dissipated once they landed at Talienwan and learned from their food contractor that they were not headed for Port Arthur. What their destination was he would not say. They set out on horseback the next morning. Only later did they discover that they were following General Oku's army, which was marching north to Liao-yang— the opposite direction from Port Arthur. For twelve hard days, they pushed through muddy roads, oppressed by the August heat and torrential rains. They slept in dirty, fly-ridden villages and ate foul food. When they reached the walled city of Haicheng, they were brought to a compound and given an identifying sleeve badge—"the Red Badge of Shame," they called it. They could wander anywhere in the city, but they couldn't venture outside without a pass, and then only under guard. "Some of our common soldiers, never having seen a foreigner before, are not able to distinguish between you and Russians," said one of their three guards, a University of Chicago alumnus. "We wish to provide against accidents." And he laughed. "You have had a very hard time," he said, "but I think the fight at Liao-yang will recompense you." He said it would be far more important than Port Arthur. Liao-yang was twenty-nine miles from Haicheng.

General Oku sent them gifts: a dozen bottles of champagne, four dozen bottles of beer, a package of flypaper, and a live sheep. Except for the sheep, which died before the canteen man could slaughter it, the presents were much appreciated. The reporters were escorted out of Haicheng to be introduced to the general, who was camped in a small Chinese village. Melton Prior, a distinguished magazine artist, Bennett Burleigh, who was a veteran of many campaigns, and Davis all wore ribbons over their left breast. Each of the eighteen journalists was first presented individually to Prince Nashimoto, who was with Oku. "Melton Prior," said the elderly illustrator, and the prince, who had been educated in Paris, thrust out his hand. Burleigh, bending low, whispered almost confidentially, "Burleigh." Richard came last. "Mr. Davis," he said.

Oku had a sad face, which looked kindly in profile, relentless straight on. He reminded Fox of Lincoln. The reporters asked if they would see much fighting. "I think so—from a high place," Oku said. "You cannot see in the valleys—the *kow-liang* [millet-fields] is too high to see over even on horseback. Yes, you will see the fight." They waited for twelve days in Haicheng, knowing that only ten miles away, cannons were booming and men were dying. And then they were woken at dawn and ushered out of the city by their three guards—at last to see a fight. After a two-hour march, they crawled to the top of a little hill and saw that eight miles away, the battle of Ashantien was being waged. From that distance, one could not determine if the cigarette puffs of smoke were incoming or outgoing, from Russian or Japanese shells. For feature writers dependent on human-interest tidbits, the trip was worthless. It was the first battle Davis had ever witnessed, he said, in which he wasn't compelled to smoke calmly to conceal his fear. To the dismay of their guards, some of the correspondents napped, while others, with their backs to the battle, read about the St. Louis Exposition in old newspapers. That night they sent a round-robin letter to Oku demanding to be allowed closer to his army.

While awaiting his reply, they were summoned at 3:00 A.M. to observe a predawn attack. They stumbled in rain and fog through dripping cornfields, chilled by a damp wind. The trail ended at a slippery hill, so steep that if the men sat, they slipped slowly downward. They waited two hours for trees and rocks to materialize out of the mist. But as the fog rolled back, they saw nothing but miles of millet fields and the tracks of the Siberian Railroad. There were four hundred thousand men within thirty miles of them, but they could see nothing. That night, a Japanese major informed them that the Russians were fleeing in retreat from Liao-yang, heading for Mukden. Japanese troops had occupied Liao-yang bloodlessly, he said. There would be no fighting until the Japanese reached Mukden in ten days. The next morning, word came from Oku: the correspondents had gotten as close to the fighting as they would ever be permitted to get. That settled it. Davis and Fox (along with two British correspondents) returned to Haicheng, where the general in charge happily gave them passes back to Japan.

It was a slow, muddy trip to the coast, and then a voyage across the Gulf of Pe-chi-li to Chefoo on the Shantung peninsula. Chefoo was the first town from which Davis could cable New York. He went at once to the telegraph office and asked if his name was listed to send a collect cable to *Collier's*. It was, said the Chinese man in charge. When Richard began to write, the man added with grave politeness, "I congratulate you." As a chill crept down his spine, Davis, not lifting his eyes, waited for the blow to fall. "Why?" he asked. The man bowed. "Because you are the first," he said.

"You are the only correspondent to arrive who has seen the battle of Liao-yang." Seized with nausea, Davis protested, although he knew instinctively that his protest was pointless. "There was no battle," he insisted. "The Japanese told me themselves they had entered Liao-yang without firing a shot." The cable operator spoke with gentle sympathy. "They have been fighting for six days," he said. Davis walked to a bench and sat down.

Three days after he left Manchuria, the greatest battle since Gettysburg and Sedan had commenced. It lasted ten days, with two hundred thousand men on each side. The reporters who persisted a few days longer were now witnessing it. Davis had waited six months, only to be cheated by a lie.[105]

10

A House of His Own

*H*AVING EARNED SO MUCH AND REPORTED SO LITTLE, Richard massaged his knotted conscience by bringing Robert Collier a handsome and expensive inlaid cigarette case from Japan. Not long afterward, burglars broke into Collier's sumptuous Gramercy Park apartment and stole all of his jewelry—except the cigarette case. At their club the next day, Finley Peter Dunne urged Collier not to report the crime to the police if he wished to keep it out of the newspapers. The group agreed that the one amusing thing about the heist was the way the burglars had spurned Davis's expensive gift. Davis, who was there, endured the teasing for a time and then excused himself. He walked to a telephone and called the *Sun* city editor.

"I didn't see anything in your paper this morning about Mr. Collier being robbed," he said.

"We haven't heard anything about it. Who are you?"

"Never mind who I am. Mr. Collier was robbed last night of all his jewelry except a single handsome cigarette case, given him by Richard Harding Davis, and of which he thinks so much that he sleeps with it under his pillow."

"Well, that's a great story!" the editor said. "I'll hustle a man up to see about it. Now tell me who you are."

"Never mind about that," Davis said. "The story is true, all right, and you had better find out about it. Be sure to tell the reporter who goes to get it to ask what the policeman on the beat was doing at the time of the robbery."

"Well, if you won't tell me who you are, thanks anyway," said the city editor, ringing off.

Returning to the table, Davis soon found an excuse to leave. They were joking about the crooks' discrimination when he departed. "They probably didn't want to break my heart altogether," said Collier, laughing. "Whatever you do," Dunne repeated for the twentieth time, "take my tip and don't tell the police, for then it will get into the newspapers."

Later in the day, Davis called up the *Sun* city editor again. "This is the man who told you this morning about the Collier robbery," he said. "Did you look it up?"

"Yes, we got it. That was a peach of a story. Who are you?"

"Never mind about me. Did you get a scoop on it?"

"Sure we did."

"Did you have your reporter ask what the policeman on the beat was doing at the time of the burglary?"

"Wait a minute and I'll see," the editor said. "Oh, O'Malley!" A moment later: "Our man, O'Malley, says he forgot to inquire about that."

"I'm sorry," Davis complained.

"Why?" The city editor now feared that he had missed out on an important angle.

"I would like to have known that," Davis said, "because I am the man who got the jewelry." And he hung up.

The *Sun* not only printed the news of the robbery, with inside details on how Collier saved Davis's precious Japanese curio; it also ran an editorial on the boldness of New York burglars, who, after they stole a man's belongings, bragged about it to the newspapers. It is safe to assume that when Collier heard the whole story, he was amused, and therefore, appreciative. He was a man who liked to be amused.[1]

The Collier circle was defined by two points: a taste for luxury and a fondness for practical jokes. The silver-haired eminence of the coterie was Mark Twain, who had fled celebrity hounds by moving to Stormfield, a Connecticut house fifty miles from New York. Once there, though, he complained of loneliness. "You ought to have a friendly animal in the house," Collier told him solicitously. "It would be company for you in the long winter evenings—something you could talk to, but that won't talk to you. Not a dog, a dog wouldn't be it. It must be the most intelligent animal in the world. Ah, I know—I'll get you a baby elephant. It'll be a Christmas present to you. I'll fix it all up; it won't be any trouble at all." Not wanting to offend his enthusiastic young friend, Twain did not object. Instead, he expressed his worries to Finley Peter Dunne and *Collier's* editor Norman Hapgood. "I can't have a damn baby elephant up there," he said. "The thing would grow up. The ceilings of the house are low. You fellows have got to head Collier off." To which they replied: "You know how he is when he gets going; there's nothing we can do about it; you'll just have to take the elephant, for a while anyhow." Collier gleefully attended to the details. First he dispatched a load of hay to Stormfield. Next he outfitted a swarthy printer in turban and pajamas, taught him to babble in a fake foreign lingo, and sent him to Stormfield a day or two before Christmas to impersonate a mahout. The baby elephant arrived on Twain's doorstep on Christmas morning. It was made of cotton.[2]

In late 1904, when Davis returned from Japan, Rob Collier and his magazine were fizzy with confidence and success. Under the gallant Collier, the *Weekly* waged progressive crusades for the income tax, child labor laws, direct election of senators, and women's suffrage; and against noxious patent medicines, corrupt congressional power brokers, the blackmailing society gossip sheet *Town Topics*, and chicanery in the Department of the Interior.[3] Because Collier was, at least in his youth, so idealistic, the writers who accepted the high sums he offered didn't think they were selling out. One young journalist who came to Collier's attention, the socialist Upton Sinclair, described the seduction process: "The running of his magazine 'on a personal basis' amounted to this: a young writer would catch the public fancy, and Robbie would send for him, as he sent for me; if he proved to be a possible person—that is, if he came to dinner in a dress-suit, and didn't discuss the socialization of 'Collier's Weekly'—Robbie would take him up and introduce him to his 'set,' and the young writer would have a perpetual market for his stories at a thousand dollars per story; he would be invited to country-house parties, he would motor and play golf and polo, and flirt with elegant young society ladies, and spend his afternoons loafing in the Hoffman House bar. I could name not one but a dozen writers and illustrators to whom I have seen that happen. In the beginning they wrote about America, in the end they wrote about the 'smart set' of Fifth Avenue and Long Island. In their personal life they became tipplers and café celebrities; in their intellectual life they became bitter cynics; into their writings you saw creeping year by year the subtle poison of sexual excess—until at last they became too far gone for 'Collier's' to tolerate any longer, and went over to the 'Cosmopolitan,' which takes them no matter how far gone they are."[4] Of course, Rob Collier did not seduce Richard Harding Davis in this way; by the time they met, Davis had chosen his subject matter and his social milieu, and his sexual mores were made of a granite too stern to be eroded by money and liquor. But Collier gave Davis the opportunity to indulge himself as a squire—just as he lured younger men with the dream of emulating Richard Harding Davis.

In the year following his return from Japan, Davis was preoccupied with the completion of his house in Mount Kisco. When he wasn't selecting wallpaper or debating the merits of gas and electricity, he was fixing the cracks in the dam for the lake or purchasing additional parcels of land. The stories and plays that he wrote at the time should be regarded less as literary works than as black-ink entries in a depressing financial ledger. Despite encouraging words from the Scribners, he ruled out a book on Japan, resolving "to let it all go, and forget it, and help others to forget it too."[5] Living in Marion while the Mount Kisco house slowly took form, he struggled with a farce that he hoped would duplicate the success of *The Dictator*. He set it in Greece, during the war with Turkey which he remembered so fondly. The protagonist was a war correspondent loosely based on Stephen Crane. He fretted that it was "old farce tricks and very like the Dictator only not a fifth as original, nor so funny."[6]

The death of his father on December 14, 1904, brutally interrupted Richard's money chasing and house building. Clarke, sixty-nine, had been ailing for about a year (to some extent, he had been ailing for decades). A man who took comfort in routine, he had undergone an unsettling career change two years before, when George W. Childs Drexel sold the *Public Ledger* to Adolph Ochs, the owner of the New York *Times*. Clarke had been the editor of the *Public Ledger* for almost eleven years. The shock knocked him down. How rattled he was can be seen in the letter he wrote to Rebecca, who was visiting in Marion: "My Dear, Dear Wife and Darling: I have seen Mr. Drexel. He has sold the Ledger to Oxe [*sic*] of the New York and the Phila. Times. This is what I thought and feared was the case when you told me of the telegram. That night, when I could not sleep, I got up and read it over with great study and care and was convinced that it meant ill for us. . . . Of course, for the present [Ochs] is unlikely to make any changes in the staff, but equally of course, he will begin at the top, naturally wanting a man of his own selection to carry out his different views. But it is inevitable that the reduction of salaries will begin at once. He is strictly a business man. . . . Like old and wise folk we are going to accept the situation with courage and, if God helps us, cheerfully."[7] When Drexel announced the sale to the staff, terrified employees came in groups to see Clarke, saying how happy they were that he was staying. "They think I may save them," he told Rebecca. "So I shall—as many as I can, and I shall save all worth the saving, but the worthless need it most God help them. It is the most pitiful situation you ever saw."[8]

Richard sent a telegram that Clarke placed where he could read it at any time, and followed it with a letter praising him effusively, a letter that Clarke sobbed over. Rebecca rushed back to Philadelphia to be by her husband's side, and quickly realized that despite his near hysteria, the change would be entirely for Clarke's good. Bitter that Ochs was "a Jew and not a gentleman," Clarke went to meet the new publisher with a mostly closed mind. Their first conference, which was attended by the other senior editors, surprised him. Ochs announced that he wanted to make the *Ledger* as good as it could be. "Does he want to make it commoner or lower in tone?" Rebecca asked her still distressed husband, when he came home that evening. "Oh heavens, no!" Clarke replied. "His ideas are high and broad and he has carried them out on the *Times* and will on the *Ledger*." "But he isn't a gentleman, you said?" Rebecca prodded, a little mischievously. Clarke hesitated. "His motives are honorable and he stands on the right side—if that is being a gentleman," Clarke conceded. "But his grammar is bad?" she persisted. "By no means," Clarke said. "He talks well and straight to the point." By the end of their conversation, Rebecca inferred that "the defect was that he was a business man, pure & simple, and *a stranger.*" She told Richard, "As far as I can see nothing could be more deferential than he has been with Dad or nicer." The high-strung Clarke soon recovered his composure. Accepting Rebecca's analysis, he decided that his opportunities would be greater in the Ochs era than under Drexel or the previous proprietor, George W. Childs.[9] The Ochs years proved to be the happiest of his editorial career.

Unfortunately, there were only two of these years. Ill throughout his Marion summer holiday in 1904, Clarke by November was (Richard reported) "greatly depressed in spirits." Going down to Philadelphia, Richard found him so excitable that visits had to be limited to a few minutes at a time.[10] He was suffering from heart disease, which was, of course, serious, but no one realized how serious: the fatal heart attack was unexpected. Richard and Charles, both away when he died, hurried back to Philadelphia.[11] As the condolence messages streamed in, from prominent men in journalism and politics, Richard looked back on his father's life with wistful sentiment.

Richard was already predisposed to reflection. Earlier that year he had turned forty, a momentous passage for a man preoccupied with youthfulness. Now that he was entering middle age himself, it was natural for him to compare the "purity" and "nobility" of his father's career (the words cropped up repeatedly in the published tributes) with his own more celebrated accomplishments. The author of thousands of unsigned editorials, Clarke had never sought personal fame. His ambition flowed underground into political channels, into battles for the causes that engaged him all his life. He loved to champion the helpless and the disenfranchised. In his youth, he had been a vehement abolitionist. In old age, one of his prouder achievements was a successful campaign against the lax Pennsylvania laws governing involuntary commitment to mental institutions. "He belonged to that class of publicists who prefer to sink their own personality and strive rather for general and not personal results," one of the more insightful eulogists noted.[12] To his son, who was so much not that way, these qualities shone brighter by contrast. "Dear Dad, you do not know how I love you and wish I could be like you and that I could follow you in your good deeds and noble spirit," Richard wrote a few years before Clarke's death.[13] Afterward, he told Rebecca that Clarke "was the finest and best man I ever knew, and more of a saint, and more of a Christian gentleman."[14] His father's death was the first misfortune to scar the smooth surface of Richard's life.[15]

Bolstered by her religious faith, Rebecca withstood the blow of Clarke's death with dignity—"very sensibly and calmly," thought Cecil.[16] In deference to Clarke's aversion to wearing mourning, his widow did not even dress in black; although, as Cecil remarked, "Dick of course does."[17] Richard helped sort and sell Clarke's pictures, furniture, and fishing tackle; and then Rebecca encouraged him to escape south, away from the cold weather which, even in better times, depressed him.[18] Cancelling plans to cover the presidential inauguration for *Collier's* (Roosevelt had been elected to his first full term the previous November), Richard booked passage with Cecil on a February 16 boat to Havana. In an extra berth in his stateroom, he took as his guest Frank Fyles, Jr., the theater-loving son of the writer of *The Girl I Left Behind Me*.

Havana was so packed with American tourists that it took them six tries to find a hotel. Like their fellow Americans, they toured the sites that testified to Spanish brutality: the torture chambers, underground vaults, and firing-squad walls. "Of course, Cecil would go first until she and the soldier butted in to an oak beam with their teeth," Richard reported to Rebecca. "It had been there 300 years and after that Cecil was content to keep behind. Later she delighted the ferry man by sailing his boat around the harbor and filled Fyles with admiration." They traveled to Santiago, a city that Davis had not entered since his trip with William Thurston in 1886. Cecil stayed in town while Richard and Frank rode horses over the San Juan hills, photographing trees covered with the names of Rough Riders.[19]

Sending Frank home, the Davises proceeded to Panama, hoping to see the American-financed canal under construction. An outbreak of yellow fever sent them scurrying for the first boat that would take them—a Spanish steamer bound for Venezuela.*[20] (The best way to dig a canal, Cecil proposed, would be to sink the isthmus with everyone on it.)[21] Because of the yellow-fever quarantine and the Venezuelan detour, Richard missed a Rough Rider reunion in San Antonio that he had been planning to attend. But he was longing for home, anyway—and, in particular, for his new home, the Mount Kisco farm.

Three years after he bought the land, his dream house was nearing completion. He and Cecil had designed and dictated every aspect of it: the farm was their great creative collaboration. Richard took charge of the landscaping, bringing in engineers to dam a stream and flood a cow pasture, thus creating a five-acre lake. The house was sited, after much dithering, on a height overlooking the lake; though Richard had wanted it nearer the water, that would have placed it close by the road. Even in this pastoral setting, he already heard "possible trolley cars clanging at our front gate."[22] Could he see Mount Kisco today, he would congratulate himself on his prescience. He and Cecil had mapped out the floor plan with felt on the

---

*The eradication of yellow fever would be a triumph comparable to the building of the canal. By September of that year, William C. Gorgas had eradicated the *Stegomyia fasciata* mosquito—and with it, yellow fever in Panama.

lawn at Marion, firing one architect who designed (in Cecil's words) "quite the most stupid & conventional villa style ever seen with large double doors everywhere and impossibly small rooms." Working from Cecil's detailed plans, a second architect came up with a two-story shingled frame house eighty-five feet long and thirty-five feet deep. There were nine master bedrooms and five master baths, six top-floor servants' bedrooms ("as beautiful as the Waldorf," Richard boasted), two dining rooms, a music room with a Steinway piano, and a billiard room with a Collender pool table. (To Richard's relief, Cecil, after paying myriad other bills, still had enough of her father's money left to buy a billiard table.) Richard and Cecil's bedroom and bath suites on the second floor were separated by Richard's writing room. On the property of 204 acres, they built a tennis court, stables, kennels, and a garage.[23]

From the house site, one had a twenty-five-mile view over the boulder-strewn hills of the Westchester countryside, with Long Island Sound and the Palisades in the distant background. Cows grazing on far-off meadows resembled, one visitor thought, "scenic cattle painted on their green-bronze pasture to give an aspect of husbandry to the scene." There wasn't a neighbor in sight.[24] (J. Borden Harriman and Charles Scribner were among the invisible neighbors.) Most of the property was woods, which Richard stocked with quail to hunt. He seeded his little lake with three thousand black bass, and he bought three small boats to help catch them.

The Davises spent the summer of 1905 in Marion. In late August, Richard moved down in advance, leaving Cecil behind to oversee the final packing. He told his mother that the day he arrived in Mount Kisco to take possession of the farm was "one of the grandest days of my life."[25] It was also one of the more chaotic. Over the next two weeks, he raced to unpack boxes faster than new ones arrived. The house cleaners he hired had camped out indefinitely, and he saw no way to remove them. "As they seem to be ladies of road house fame I dare not use severe methods for fear they will blackmail me," he joked to Charles. "And I never dare go where they are unchaperoned. Most of the time they sit gazing out of a window singing Hiawatha, and whenever I pass they say to each other, 'This is a much more elegant house than Mrs. Harriman's.' "[26]

A torrential rainstorm began over Labor Day weekend to greet Cecil as she arrived, but it couldn't dampen her elation over her new home. "Cecil loves it," Richard told his brother. "I never saw her so interested and pleased before."[27] Her first observation was: "It is the most distinguished looking house I know." By Cecil's second night, hot food was being served in the dining room, and the lady and gentleman of the house—she in beads and dinner dress, he in dinner jacket—were supping as they would at Marion. "No one would have thought," Richard remarked, "that an hour before we had our sleeves to our shoulders breaking open barrels and freight."[28]

Even before Richard moved in, the dam had sprung a leak. It would not be the last leak, and each time he paid to raise the level of his lake, the level of his bank account dropped significantly. But what is a country house without a prospect of water? And the prospect must be properly framed, which required him to construct a wide brick terrace, decorated with bay trees in terra-cotta pots. Within a month, he had bought additional land (to protect the seclusion of his property), built a private road (so the house could be approached, as in England, through a park and not from the public highway), and acquired a Cadillac car and chauffeur (so he could motor about the countryside like his rich neighbors).[29] Clearly, the huge costs he incurred once he began building the house would not stop now that he resided there. The chain was unending: the new car, for instance, would necessitate the construction of a garage, as it was unsafe to keep an auto and gasoline near flammable straw in the barn.[30] Murmuring in the background was the trickle of salaries paid to the laundress, cook, maid, coachman, chauffeur, and kennel man.

And yet, he never regretted buying Crossroads Farm. When his travels forced him to leave it, he pined for the farm as much as he longed for his family. He had always lived in someone else's house—with his parents, in a rented flat, at his in-laws'. Now, at the age of forty, he had his own house, and it was one that he had carefully designed to fit his self-image. After Richard's death, Charles reflected: "As far back as I can remember it was Dick's ambition to have a home of his own and this was realized in Crossroads farm. . . . It was a very big part of his life and I do not think he was ever quite happy away from it."[31]

During the summer of 1905, when he wasn't preparing the Mount Kisco house, Richard was trying to pay for it by completing his Greco-Turkish War farce. Although plotted less well than *The Dictator*, it had clever dialogue and colorful props, providing commercial possibilities. Faithfully re-created on the stage, the reading room of the Hotel Angleterre in Athens, the boxes piled up at the Piraeus wharf, the little news kiosk, and the romantically garbed soldiers all satisfied the public appetite for exotic spectacle in these last days of precinema theater. In the cast of stereotypes, the most interesting character is the vainglorious war correspondent Kirke Warren, who combines Davis's appearance with Crane's sexual irregularity. (Similarly, when he wrote of this war in his deservedly forgotten novel *Active Service*, Crane created a self-conscious, grandstanding hero modeled on both himself and Davis.)[32] *The Galloper*, which is what Davis called the new farce, was declined by William Collier and his manager, Charles Frohman, and then offered to Raymond Hitchcock.[33] A musical-comedy star with extramusical ambitions, Hitchcock had asked Davis for a farce back when *The Galloper* was promised to Collier.[34] Reading it now, he loved it and "begged for the play," Richard reported.[35] Lanky and lantern-jawed, Hitchcock had a nasal, drawling voice and a wealth of queer mannerisms. With Davis's help, he transformed a play that had been written for another man into a custom-made vehicle for his own talents. Although not a smash, *The Galloper* was a solid success, and Hitchcock deserved much of the credit.

A successful play earned Davis four hundred to eight hundred dollars a week. While this was a splendid rainfall, it followed a prolonged drought. During the second half of 1905, Davis worked on only *The Galloper* and "The Spy" (his first short story since the disappointment of *Captain Macklin*).[36] With nothing new to sell, he was living off the income from his old books, a stipend that would have been woefully inadequate were it not for the ingenuity of Harper and Brothers. Adapting P. F. Collier's idea of selling book sets on installment, the Harpers had offered low-priced sets of Mark Twain to new subscribers to their magazine, and in ten months had sold fifteen thousand. They proposed in May 1902 that Davis accept a similar arrangement. They would publish a clothbound uniform set of eight of his volumes, mostly travel writings, and sell it for twelve dollars, which would include a four-dollar subscription to *Harper's Magazine* or *Weekly*. They would give him a reduced royalty—only fifty cents for each eight-dollar set; but the sales volume should compensate handsomely. After some bickering, and a futile attempt to buy back the plates of his nine Harpers books (the publisher demanded the outrageous ransom of forty thousand dollars), Davis accepted an advance of five thousand dollars against royalties.[37] The money helped him over his first wave of house expenses.

At Davis's prompting, the Scribners soon prepared a uniform edition of their own Davis books. *Scribner's* had been luring subscribers with cheaper books for which the publisher paid no author's royalties. When Richard approached Charles Scribner, however, Scribner couldn't say no. It was the summer of 1903, when Davis was building the dam for his lake and beginning construction on the house, and every week the architect and workmen presented him with new bills. Desperate for ready money, he got the Scribners to make up a subscription set of six volumes, on which he would earn a forty-cent royalty. Against this they paid him an advance of four thousand dollars, plus another thousand-dollar advance for an elaborate Christmas edition of *The Bar Sinister*. Thanks to the Scribner set, he was able to keep his head above water through 1903—but just barely. In July, a month after sending him five thousand dollars, the Scribners surprised Davis with another large check; yet by November, he was once again imploring them to send whatever money might be owed him, as his funds were "all tied up to pay builders and plasterers."[38]

The set proved to be a big moneymaker for the Scribners. For Davis, it financed the farm. By the time he moved into Mount Kisco in the summer of 1905, he had earned royalties of twenty thousand dollars on sales of fifty thousand sets. Those figures were so impressive that Charles Scribner brandished them proudly to persuade another popular writer, Thomas

Nelson Page, to accept a low royalty rate on a subscription set: the Davis edition had demonstrated that this was a way to breathe new life into books that had ceased to move in the stores.[39] Yet despite all this income, Davis was saving nothing. When Frohman rejected *The Galloper* in the fall of 1905, Richard had to ask Scribner for a two-thousand-dollar advance on money that was not due him until next spring. Without the theatrical royalties he had counted on, he couldn't pay his bills.[40] Raymond Hitchcock unexpectedly stepped in and put on *The Galloper*, alleviating the cash crisis; but it was merely a remission in a chronic money shortage that would plague Davis until his death.

One of the perquisites of a star reporter is the freedom to travel like a wealthy man without spending a penny. In March 1906, the Davises fled the snows of winter by going to Cuba on the *Collier's* tab. On the voyage out, they struck up a friendship with the new American minister to Cuba, Gerald Morgan, a bachelor who occupied a beautiful old Spanish house on the seashore near Havana. Before the trip was over, Morgan invited Richard and Cecil to be his guests; they accepted for the first week of their visit.[41] Staying with American ministers was another perquisite of a star reporter.

The highlight of Richard's sojourn in Cuba was a nostalgic tour. Leaving Cecil behind in a Havana hotel, he went to Santiago with a friend from Marion to revisit the scene of the fighting in the Spanish-American War. It was a more thorough inspection than he had made a year earlier with Frank Fyles, Jr. For two days he rode over rough terrain, exploring woods and fields that bore little resemblance to the landscape imprinted in his memory. In part, that was because the landscape had changed. In the eight years gone by, unusually heavy rains had flooded the San Juan River. The "bloody bend" was gone. There were new fords and new landmarks. The approach to the blockhouse on the San Juan hills, where so many Americans had been shot down, was no longer a meadow of high grass. Davis belatedly realized that before the battle, the Spaniards had chopped down the trees and cleared out the brush, to prevent the enemy from approaching stealthily. Now the trees and bushes had grown back. It was as if a golf course had become an orchard. When he rode out to Las Guásimas, however, Davis discovered that the site of the Rough Riders' first battle had kept its old contours. He could pinpoint exactly where he had tied his horse, where he had seen his first Spaniard, where he had come across injured men.

But all of the terrain was altered profoundly by the absence of war. Some of it was subjective. A landscape looks different to a tourist on horseback than it does to a man on foot in stifling heat with the whine of Mauser bullets and the cries of the wounded pressing against his ears. Davis was amazed to retrace his steps from the blockhouse, where he had climbed to watch the American artillery in action, down to the safer terrain where he had retreated to join Colonel Wood. He would have guessed the distance to be three-quarters of a mile; in fact, it was about seventy-five yards. Other changes were more tangible. Davis was distressed to see that such sacred spots as the crest of Kettle Hill had been profaned by the banalities of peacetime life: kitchen gardens, wooden gates, mud-and-twig shacks. American tourists who wanted to see the places of which they had read in the newspapers would find it hard to imagine the wartime scene. They could expect little help from the caretaker of the small public park on San Juan Hill, who spoke only Spanish, or from the Cuban guides at the hotels, who spouted misinformation and pretended that the Cubans had been on the edge of victory when the Americans arrived to claim all the credit. Davis suggested that metal markers with descriptions be erected on the most significant sites.[42]

In only eight years, the outlines of wartime glory had been blurred and obscured. As on the battlefields of the San Juan hills, so with Davis himself. He was stockier now, more a burgher than a soldier. He had been softened and thickened by the unpicturesque impositions of everyday life. The scrubby growth of farces concealed the more promising literary work of his youth. There were no bronze tablets to commemorate "Gallegher," or the Van Bibber stories, or *Captain Macklin*. There was only a famous name, a stirring past, and an uncertain future.

If Richard needed another reminder of the transience of modern celebrity, he found it soon after he returned home. On June 25, 1906, in the rooftop theater of the Madison Square Garden, a stocky, middle-aged man with a bristle moustache and a thatch of bright red hair sat alone at his customary table watching the chorus girls kick, strut, and sing. It was the opening night of *Mamzelle Champagne*, an entertainment in which the title character emerged dramatically and fetchingly from a giant papier-mâché bottle of Pommery Sec. The show was crammed with many comic songs—including the suggestive "I Could Love a Thousand Girls"—and with many more comely girls. When a tall pale man in a long overcoat approached the red-haired man's table, pulled out a revolver, and fired three bullets at close range, many in the audience rubbernecked and tittered, thinking it was part of the show. The red-haired man, after all, was Stanford White, the architect of Madison Square Garden. He maintained a studio in the tower and appeared regularly at the garden girl shows; it was not implausible that, as a quasi-host, he had been recruited to enliven the evening's entertainment. This was not, of course, the case. The young man in the long overcoat was Harry K. Thaw, the deranged heir to a Pittsburgh fortune; and he had murdered White to avenge—or so he said—the tarnished honor of his wife, the beautiful soubrette Evelyn Nesbit Thaw. She had been ravished by White, he claimed, five years earlier, when she was only fifteen. White was a pervert and a satyr, Thaw declared. He deserved to die.

Since, even in our own day of uncinched corsets, we scrutinize and all too often vilify the morals and character of the victim of a sex-related crime, we should not be surprised at the public reaction in 1906 to the scandalous death of Stanford White. Overnight, a man who professionally was one of the greatest architects that America has produced, who from the arch in Washington Square to the Bronx campus of New York University had done more than anyone of his generation to mold the face of New York City; a man who was the life of countless parties and the mainstay and confidant of many friends; a man who cultivated the rich, in both senses, by winning their confidence and elevating their taste; overnight, this leader of New York society became a nonperson, a name no one dared mention, a ghost no one ventured to defend. His partner, Charles McKim, was one of the few prominent men to attend the funeral, but he would make no statement to the press. Cooper Hewitt, a close friend who shared space in the Madison Square Garden tower, also declined comment. Such kindred bon vivants as Jimmy Breese and Thomas B. Clarke lay low. Meanwhile, the newspapers, especially Hearst's *Journal* and *American* and Bennett's *Herald*, made headlines with lurid "confessions" of chorus girls who testified to the monstrous lechery of the dead man. In numerous interviews, antivice crusader Anthony Comstock related the horrific findings of his own "investigations."[43]

It was Davis, and Davis alone, who spoke out against these slanders. For about a decade, he had been a friend of White's, though hardly an intimate. Probably the last time they spent together was the previous election day, when Davis for two hours joined White in driving up and down Broadway. They passed much of the time in the campaign headquarters of the patrician district attorney William Travers Jerome, who was up for reelection.[44] Less than eight months later, Jerome was prosecuting Harry Thaw for the murder of his friend Stanford White.

The licentious White hardly seems like someone Davis would befriend or champion. But that was not the White he knew. His White was a model gentleman, scion of an old New England family which traced its arrival in this country back to 1632. Far from being a "voluptuary" who amused himself in "harems," the man Davis knew was a sportsman whose "greatest pleasure was to stand all day waist deep in the rapids of a Canadian river and fight it out with the salmon." White was an enthusiast. It was a quality that Davis shared and appreciated. "He loved life and got more out of it in more intelligent and in more different ways than any other man of his day in New York City," Davis wrote. "He admired a beautiful woman as he admired every other beautiful thing that God has given us." Just how his admiration for beautiful women manifested itself was a point that Davis avoided. There is a story, perhaps apocryphal, that William Dean Howells was standing beside Stanford White on a ferry deck when a stoker fell off the stern of a tug and was mashed by the screw into a bloody iridescent slick on the water. "Oh, poor devil!" White shouted. Then he smashed both palms on the ferry rail, and exclaimed: "My God! What color!"[45]

That was Stanford White; and there was ample room for Davis's White and Thaw's White within the same lusty body.

Sickened by the incessant vilification of White in the yellow press, and even more by the silence that greeted it, Davis wrote an eloquent eulogy that began: "One who is permitted to write a few true words about a man who never spoke an unkind one resents the fact that before he can try to tell what Stanford White was, he must first tell what Stanford White was not." He bemoaned the fact that lies about White could be manufactured and disseminated with impunity, because a dead man cannot be libeled. "These charges are so impossible that were they not hideous they would be absurd," he continued. "Had some of them been true Stanford White would have been the first to cut his own acquaintance; had others been true he would have cut his own throat." (Davis had used this bloodthirsty rhetorical figure a decade before to disarm his own critics.) He testifed to White's modesty and generosity, praising him as "a big-hearted, generous, gentle man." It was a sober, temperate piece, and reading it today, one has difficulty imagining the stir it caused.

Davis offered it to Rob Collier doubtfully. Collier had been discouraged when Daniel H. Burnham and Augustus Saint-Gaudens would not offer testimonials to White; mentors and colleagues, these eminent men had been far closer to White than Davis ever was. What stiffened Collier's resolve to publish was Davis's hint that he might place the piece elsewhere. When Collier insisted on having it, Davis urged him to consider the *Weekly*. "To hell with the *Weekly*!" Collier retorted bravely. He then for the first time read the article, and congratulated himself on having the good sense to publish it.[46] The piece provoked the anticipated uproar. As if they had been waiting for someone to make the first noise, some of White's friends— including Saint-Gaudens—joined Davis's chorus, applauding the article and belatedly defending their dead friend.[47] But the broader response was hostile. A New Jersey librarian dumped all of Davis's books off the shelf and threw them into the gutter. A prep-school headmaster warned his students to avoid the "foul emanations of a depraved romancer."[48] "Depraved" was a strange description of the superclean Davis. However, a man with a darker private life and a less chivalrous public image might have been tarred far worse—and, consequently, might have hesitated to expose himself to calumny.

The ensuing trial of Harry Thaw further blackened the name of White. Evelyn Nesbit testified vividly how the middle-aged seducer spiked her champagne while she was admiring the art in his studio. When she awakened, she found herself undressed in his bed. As she began to scream, White, who was naked beside her, put on a kimono and tried to hush her. "It is all over now," he said—making her sob even louder. In the courtroom, Nesbit described White's mirrored bedroom and graphically established that, at the time she entered it, she was a virgin.[49] Even today, this is powerful stuff. Back then, it boggled the mind. After one hung jury, Thaw was tried again and found not guilty because of insanity. He was committed to a lunatic asylum. However, the verdict did not dry up what Rebecca called the "outpouring of filth" in the yellow press.[50] Thaw's myriad appeals and consequent court appearances kept the story alive for another decade.[51] In all this croaking, snickering, hooting commotion, Davis's article sounded the sole high note.[52]

Just as it was unique in the discussions of White's death, so the article was anomalous in Davis's own work of the time. All the rest of it was done purely for money. For a thousand dollars apiece, he wrote six articles (cut-and-clip jobs, really) for *Collier's*; for an advance of two thousand dollars, the Scribners published them as a book under the self-explanatory title, *Real Soldiers of Fortune*.[53] In October 1906, he returned to Cuba for *Collier's* to cover the occupation of the island by American troops. Sounding a bit old and testy, he washed his hands of the Cubans. "From now on it would be better if there were less of the hand of velvet and more of the carpet slipper," he wrote. No longer believing the Cubans capable of self-government, he favored American annexation.[54]

Lured by money, not art, he also returned to writing fiction. As his mother, generalizing from her own experience, had grimly prophesied, he was now writing strictly as a business venture. His stories were vapid but quick reads. In this, he was a creature of his time. In the words of *Life*, 1911: "This is a get-things-done-quick age. It is a ready-to-put-on-and-wear-home age, a just-add-hot-water-and-serve age, a new-speed-record-every-day age, a take-it-or-leave-it-I'm-very-busy age."[55] On his first visit to New York, Charlie Chaplin was stunned by the city's "slick tempo": "The shoe black flips his polishing rag with alacrity, the bartender serves a beer with alacrity, sliding it up to you along the polished surface of the bar. The soda jerk, when serving an egg malted milk, performs like a hopped-up juggler."[56] These hectic urban rhythms permeated Richard's writing as strongly as they syncopated ragtime. The fiction of Rebecca's day—the novels of Hawthorne and Melville, for instance—meandered at a relaxed pace. By Richard's time, fiction, like everything else, was in a hurry. A story had to *move*. Often a short story appeared for the first time in a newspaper or newsweekly; it competed for the reader's eye with tales of passionate murders and photographs of battlefields. "The long introductions of a Scott or a Thackeray are done away with," Davis in his maturity told an interviewer. "Nowadays a man begins his story where they ended. His first sentence is, 'He was bankrupt. He did not know where to turn,' or 'She no longer loved him but she—.' He jumps right into the middle of his story at the first phrase, and just where the older writers left off."[57]

Typically, Davis disparaged the glittery, insubstantial literary world through which he had risen so buoyantly. He was nostalgic for the rarefied literary circles that once existed in Concord and Cambridge, the world that his mother had visited before the tug of family obligations drew her to Philadelphia and literary commerce. He had himself gone to Boston in 1891, just before taking over at *Harper's Weekly*, and he had been greeted warmly by the surviving old crowd (including Oliver Wendell Holmes, Sr., and Julia Ward Howe), both as his mother's son and as an emissary from the new world. America's literary locus had already shifted from Boston to New York, from "the Athens of America" to the financial capital. (William Dean Howells's move from the *Atlantic* to *Harper's* in New York at about this time is conventionally cited as epitomizing Boston's eclipse.)[58] Back then, Richard had joked that the only person he could find in Boston who had read one of his stories was Maurice Barrymore, and he was a New Yorker.[59]

Now in middle age, Richard had a different perspective on what had happened to American fiction. "Some authors take themselves too seriously," he remarked. "That was all very well in days of Hawthorne, Lowell, Holmes, Emerson and the rest. They were great writers, at least Hawthorne was, and they were regarded almost with reverence by the people of their day, especially by those in Massachusetts. Another point is that the material rewards for writing were less in those days. The law of compensation operates in these matters as in every situation in life. These men, Hawthorne and the others, gained respect, social position, reverence even, but small material rewards. To-day so many people write [because] the material rewards are very great, but no one pays much attention to writers. That is as it should be. . . . That's the law of compensation operating. When you get the material reward you don't get the other. The writer to-day sells his story. But he doesn't stop there. He sells its newspaper rights. He makes it into a play and sells that. He sells it over in England. He keeps on selling it. The returns pile up. . . . He puts his money in an auto or a farm. He travels abroad, gets whatever he likes best. That's his reward for his work. But if he tries to hang laurels on his plough he makes a mistake. He ought to do his ploughing and not bother about the laurels. . . . We have no great writers now, no writers like Hawthorne. The men now manage to tell a story with some human interest in it, that's about all."[60]

This assessment of the literary scene by a very successful writer might be compared to the laments of an industrialist over the ravaged environment, or the complaints of a tourist about the overtrafficked showplaces, or the gripes of a Newport grande dame over the lost civilities of her village. It is a nostalgia for the world that one has helped to destroy. It's a very fin-de-siècle sensibility, and a very modern one. And it is the essence of Davis's worldview.

In the last weeks of 1906, three commercial magazines, ravenous for serial fiction by celebrated authors, pursued Richard Harding Davis. He accepted four thousand dollars from *Collier's*, supplemented by a thousand-dollar Scribner advance.[61] Writing to his mother, he announced his return to fiction writing in this way: "Today I ordered work on the terrace begin, and grading. I think I will work on a three part novelette. Both Princess Aline and In the Fog were very much liked and it is a handy form in which to tell a story."[62] Obviously, the exigencies of financing a terrace are at least as relevant to the new work as are the literary precedents of "The Princess Aline" and "In the Fun." Beyond the terrace there was his purchase in September of a half-interest in twenty-seven contiguous acres to protect the privacy of his farm. That set him back another fifteen hundred dollars.[63]

As a frame for his triptych, Davis came up with the notion of a touring automobile. Although it wasn't an original idea (C. N. and A. M. Williamson had invented the formula with a 1903 novel about a motor tour of Europe), it was a clever marketing strategy.[64] Advertisements for automobiles played a role of increasing importance in the finances of magazines. The automobile was still a novelty and, until Henry Ford began mass-producing his Model T in 1913, still a plaything of the rich—as this 1904 *Life* parody indicates:

> *Half a block, half a block,*
>   *Half a block onward,*
> *All in their motobiles*
>   *Rode the Four Hundred.*
> *"Forward!" the owners shout,*
> *"Racing car!" "Runabout!"*
>   *Into Fifth Avenue*
>   *Rode the Four Hundred.*
>
> *"Forward!" the owners said.*
> *Was there a man dismay'd?*
> *Not, though the chauffeurs knew*
>   *Some one had blundered.*
> *Theirs not to make reply,*
> *Theirs not to reason why,*
> *Theirs but to kill or die.*
>   *Into Fifth Avenue*
>   *Rode the Four Hundred.*[65]

To the less privileged classes, the automobile was not only ostentatious— it was terrifying. When inexperienced drivers plowed into unprepared pedestrians, it was the pedestrians who suffered. On March 1, 1906, Woodrow Wilson, who was then president of Princeton University, said that the motorist was "a picture of the arrogance of wealth, with all its independence and carelessness," and declared that "nothing has spread socialistic feeling in this country more than the use of the automobile."[66]

To the car owner, by contrast, the chief peril of motoring was the likelihood of mechanical breakdown. As a popular joke of the time had it, a man inspecting a lunatic asylum entered the ward for crazed motorists and was puzzled to find it completely empty. "Where are the patients?" he asked the director. "Oh," that gentleman replied, "they're all under the cots, fixing the slats."[67] This was the humor of motorists, and the point of view of Davis's three-part story, "The Scarlet Car." The protagonists of "The Scarlet Car" are the owner of the vehicle, his St. Paul's classmate, the classmate's sister, and her fiancé. Their adventures in the first two parts are occasioned by the automobile's breakdown, and those in the third by a collision with a drunken pedestrian.[68] Otherwise, there is not much to say about these stories, except that they helped to pay for Davis's terrace. Uncharacteristically, he was late on the third installment because he simply couldn't think of a plot.[69]

Travel was a way to find inspiration and, secondarily, to reduce household expenses. Rob Collier would send Davis anywhere. The problem was deciding where. Collier suggested shipping Richard and Cecil in an automobile to a place that had never seen an automobile—Persia, Turkey, or Abyssinia were all possibilities. Like a bubble, the scheme grew larger, until it assumed the form of a Cape-to-Cairo journey up the east coast of Africa, driving along unfinished railroad tracks. And then the bubble burst, punctured by its own impracticality and by the unexpected death of Richard's uncle, Hugh Wilson Harding, who had tutored him so many years before at Lehigh University. When the idea of the trip was revived, it was simpler in concept, though every bit as daunting. The destination was still Africa, but now more specific: the so-called Congo Free State, which was administered by Belgium. And the purpose of the expedition was not merely to sightsee, but to investigate.[70]

Investigative reporting was not Richard's strength. Even if it had been, this trip as conceived was an impossible task. Only on the ship to England did he commence reading about the alleged atrocities committed against the natives under Prince Leopold's rule. He began to comprehend how difficult these charges would be to prove. In London, a missionary's wife told him that it was absurd to try to see anything in less than six months: one must travel three weeks inland from the Congo River to reach the real country. Richard was so alarmed that he went to Cook's to see if he could substitute another interesting destination for the Congo, but he was unsuccessful.[71] In a mood as cold and gray as the snowy morning, he boarded the Belgian ship on January 25. "Cannot remember departing on a trip with less pleasure at doing so," he confessed in his diary. "It is absurd to try and get at the truth of this matter in a few weeks, and the trip seems [a] waste of time." He shared a cabin with a young English clerk; Cecil had one to herself.[72] (She wanted to go to the Congo, and although Richard didn't know what she would do there, he knew that the cost of six weeks on the ship to and from Africa equaled two weeks of expenses in London. So Cecil, with her maid, came along.)[73]

They arrived at the mouth of the Congo River on February 12. In dazzling heat, they began the voyage up the river, reaching first Boma and then Matadi, which was as far as the steamer could go before the cataracts and rapids began.[74] Cecil stayed behind in Boma, a squalid and unhealthy coastal town, waiting for a slow steamer that would stop at the interesting ports of West Africa on the way back to England. Richard would leave for England later on a much faster ship. Now he went by train to Léopoldville (Kinshasa), where the Congo became navigable again. He was headed up the Kasai River, hoping to root out stories of massacre and torture. In that, he was unsuccessful, but the Kasai did offer a gorgeous panoply of wildlife. On the Kasai, Davis's misguided mission to investigate Belgian atrocities metamorphosed into a more feasible attempt to shoot a hippopotamus.

There were hippos everywhere, along with crocodiles, monkeys, scarlet cranes, and giant flamingoes. It was amazing. Having seen hippos only in the zoo, Davis was first thrilled, then covetous. He wanted to shoot one as badly as, twenty-six years earlier in the Adirondacks, he had longed to kill a buck; and he went about it with the same mix of tenacity and clumsiness. The main problem in bagging a hippo was timing: to shoot one as it ventured on or near land. If killed in the river, a hippo would sink like a very large stone, not surfacing for days. Parsimony had kept Richard from purchasing a high-powered rifle when he was in London. Consequently, he was armed with only a Winchester, not the weapon of choice against such a thick-skinned beast.[75]

His chance came one morning, as he and the other passenger, an Italian officer, breakfasted with the boat captain. Looming in front of them, large as a haystack, a hippo lumbered on a white sand island. The captain jumped with excitement and ordered the ship to shore, as the passengers raced for their weapons. Alerted too late, the hippo tried to get back to the river. At close range, Davis shot the beast twice in the head and, when they opened, in the jaws. After the last shot, the captain brought his ship broadside to the bank, where the hippo lay motionless. With great gusto, the black soldiers and woodboys laid out the gangplank and rushed to the bank, where they danced around the hippo, hacking with knives at its tail to make it bleed to death more quickly. At the captain's urging, Davis ran back to his cabin for more cartridges. "It seemed an absurd precaution," he wrote. "I was sure I had the head of that hippo as I was sure that my own was still on my neck. My only difficulty was whether to hang the head in the front hall or in the dining-room. It might be rather too large for the dining-room. That was all that troubled me."

Three minutes later, he was back on the river bank. Twenty black men stood around the motionless hippo, and three were sawing off its tail, as the women chanted a song celebrating the return of the triumphant hunter. The Italian passenger snapped one photo, and Richard was just heading back to the cabin for his camera when he heard a shout of amazement and alarm. The hippo had opened its eyes and raised its head. Wishing to put the animal out of its misery, Davis put his rifle close to its head and fired. He needn't have bothered. "The bullet affected him no more than a quinine pill," Davis wrote. "What seemed chiefly to concern him, what apparently had brought him back to life, was the hacking at his tail. That was an indignity he could not brook. His expression, and he had a perfectly human expression, was one of extreme annoyance and of some slight alarm, as though he were muttering: 'This is no place for *me*,' and, without more ado, he began to roll toward the river." Because of the crowd of people, Davis could not shoot. The natives beat at the animal with firewood and tried to rope it with a steel hawser. It was all futile. The hippopotamus reached the bank and rolled into the muddy water. There was a great splash, then it was seen no more. Davis's only memento was the photograph taken by the Italian officer. In telling the story, he concluded: "I am still undecided whether to hang it in the hall or the dining-room."[76]

Davis's trip up the Kasai ended at Dima, the headquarters of the Kasai concession. He had gone there to see a rubber plantation. Now he was informed that it was a four-day trip to the plantation, and the boat wouldn't leave for six days. He had also heard that there was an American mission nearby. In fact, the mission was a month's trip upriver. Dima was a clean, efficient town, but not at all picturesque; and the only steamer heading back to Léopoldville in the next ten days was departing the following morning. With a squealing of gears, Davis abruptly changed course. Ending his exploration of the Dark Continent, he headed back to the coast, where he joined Cecil and embarked on a leisurely trip up the shoreline of West Africa. A touch of fever hampered his sightseeing, but he saw enough to squeeze out another magazine piece.[77]

Davis's *Collier's* articles were gathered by the Scribners into *The Congo and Coasts of Africa*, a volume that may be his worst book. Lacking the rigor of investigative reporting and the color (except for the hippo shooting) of good travel writing, it is an ill-favored bastard. Of the generally negative reviews, the consensus was most wittily expressed by Ambrose Bierce, who wrote in *Cosmopolitan*: "Mr. Richard Harding Davis, who went to the Congo country to expose the wickedness of King Leopold, did not see any 'atrocities,' nor any one who had seen any, but he has made a blood-addling book about them, all the same. As an observer Mr. Davis is a peerless rhetorician, with all a great thinker's scorn of personally conducted attention."[78]

The failure of the Congo trip served to underline that what Davis now did, primarily, was write for the theater. Just before leaving for the Congo, he had reworked *The Galloper* into a musical. His leading man, Raymond Hitchcock, had welcomed a farce as an artistic stretch. Distressed by the modesty of *The Galloper*'s success, Hitchcock now wanted to return to his old tricks.[79] Since Hitchcock was most famous for his role in a musical comedy called *The Yankee Consul*, the producers hired the lyricist from that show and titled the new effort *The Yankee Tourist*. As one reviewer noted, in *The Galloper* Davis had invented "a new dramatic form—a musical play without music."[80] The quaintly costumed Greek soldiers were already on stage. How much effort was required to make them sing?

The *Yankee Tourist* opened on the road while the Davises were in the Congo, but they were back for the Broadway debut on August 12, 1907. The night was sweltering hot. "Personally, on such a night I would not have sat through any other play on earth!" Richard joked. He could afford to joke. *The Yankee Tourist* was the colossal hit that everyone had hoped for, the smash musical comedy of the season. Hitchcock had scored "one of the biggest successes ever seen on Broadway," proclaimed the New York *Telegraph*. So great was the demand for seats that, even two months after the opening, tickets were being sold six weeks in advance.[81] Author's royalties of three hundred to five hundred dollars a week helped Davis stay afloat at a time when a financial panic had tightened up the money supply.[82] So it was with a sense of rising alarm that he watched an ugly scandal envelop his star and threaten his show.[83]

Like Stanford White, Hitchcock was accused of taking indecent liberties with an underage girl. More than six months earlier, he had accosted twelve-year-old Elsie Voecks and her girlfriend as they passed the stage door. With the novelty of a drive in a motorcar, he enticed them to his country house in Great Neck, Long Island. That much he admitted. There, the girls alleged, he assaulted them. That he denied. The story surfaced when Elsie's brother tried to blackmail Hitchcock, and the star called in the police. Soon afterward, Hitchcock was arrested and charged with assaulting Elsie's fifteen-year-old friend. Released on three thousand dollars' bail, he appeared as usual that night at the Astor Theater. But his troubles were only beginning. Sources in District Attorney Jerome's office revealed to the press that a grand jury was considering charges involving four or five other girls. Learning from Finley Peter Dunne that Jerome would be dining with Rob Collier at Delmonico's, Richard, after eating with Charles at Sherry's, crossed the street and joined Jerome and Collier at their table. Hitchcock was "in bad," Jerome said, and he should get a savvy criminal lawyer. Visiting the theater that evening, Richard found Hitchcock "quite dazed." His wife, Flora Zabelle—who was also his costar in *The Yankee Tourist*—was weeping. The audience for the show had shrunk, and one of Hitchcock's songs that night did not get an encore. "I'm a dead dog, Richard, I'm a dead dog," he said. He felt that his fans had abandoned him.[84] A day later, a warrant was issued for Hitchcock on six indictments, but before it could be served, the actor disappeared. Mrs. Hitchcock said he had left their apartment to take a Turkish bath and had not come back.

His name was taken off the marquee of the Astor Theater. (He was replaced in the part by a young man from the chorus, Wallace Beery.) The newspapers speculated wildly about Hitchcock's whereabouts: suicide? kidnapping victim? on the lam in Canada? On October 31, District Attorney Jerome declared him a fugitive from justice.

Thinking that *The Yankee Tourist* was about to close, bringing an end to his weekly royalties, Richard asked Charles Scribner for as much money as the publisher could spare—"at a time when [because of the Panic] no one has any money."[85] He had no sooner posted the letter than, at about 11:00 A.M. on November 6, Charles called up to announce jubilantly that Hitchcock had returned. "It's a great instance of the tragic to the ridiculous," Richard observed. "Apparently he came back because he was 'lonely.' Said in the Tombs I can at least have company." Posting bail of seventy-five hundred dollars, Hitchcock rushed to the theater for the matinee performance and pranced on stage with the chorus. That night, Beery was demoted and Hitchcock was back in his old role. Making a speech to the audience, the fugitive star received a fine hand.[86] In the play, there was a scene in which the character played by Flora Zabelle is supposed to enter unobserved by Hitchcock. Instead, Zabelle walked up to her husband and threw her arms around his neck. He then stooped and kissed her, while the audience cheered, whistled, and stomped. The story was on the front page of all the next day's papers—a capital piece of publicity for *The Yankee Tourist*. Hitchcock rode out the scandal. Perhaps because of the unreliability of the witnesses, the charges against him didn't stick.

And Richard survived the tight-money squeeze of 1907. The financial panic, in the big picture, was a spasm provoked by the unexpected closing of a trust company in October. The stock market crashed, and as depositors withdrew their funds from banks and trust companies, many of these institutions went under. Although it was the biggest banking crisis since the Civil War, the underlying economy was essentially sound.[87] Seen from Davis's street-level vantage point, the panic of 1907 meant having to argue to cash a check for $100 when the clerk at the Waldorf-Astoria wanted to restrict him to $50.[88] By late November, Richard heard, the banks in Philadelphia were limiting account withdrawals to $50; and the Chicago banks were issuing $1 and $2 certificates.[89] The press of monthly expenses weighed heavy on Davis. His outlay for October was $1,365, for November $1,500— a huge sum when you consider that a first-rate dinner for four with two bottles of champagne cost $20, and four tickets to the theater went for $7.50. "I have decided to live in a tent," he wrote in his diary. "I never want to hear of a servant's wages, a ton of coal or a bag of oats again." He vowed, as one new economy, to invite fewer guests. That evening, Cecil told him that her brother, Bruce, and his wife had asked if they could visit for the weekend with another couple, and she had said yes. Charles would also be coming out with a friend.[90] Richard was about as successful at economizing as his fictional alter ego Van Bibber had been. On the Saturday that his guests arrived, he served no champagne; but by Sunday, it was flowing again.[91]

To keep solvent, he began a light novel, which he called *The White Mice*. "The White Mice is disgracefully light weight, but, one more light weight novelette cannot damn me," he told Charles.[92] When his mother revealed her grand hopes for his novel, he hastened to correct her. "Please do not tell me you expect something from me in the story line this time, that is 'high,' " he wrote. "It is only a silly, foolish story and not at all high. You scare me, and I blush with confusion."[93] Well might he blush, for *The White Mice* was his weakest novel, a dilute tincture from a formula that had lost its strength.[94] In the novel, four American youths band together to rescue an imprisoned Latin American statesman. Before it's over, one of them marries the man's conveniently available and beautiful daughter. "It is, what the reviewers always call my books, 'one suited to the hammock or railroad train,' " Davis told his publisher.[95] Even in a hammock, it reads poorly.

But *The White Mice* was from the first a sideshow to Davis's main ambition—his first try at a serious play. Although he had begun crafting plays strictly to make money, Davis—now that *all* of his writing was solely for money—had belatedly developed dramatic aspirations. Despite his pressing bills, he couldn't stand himself if he did nothing but hack work. He began researching *Vera, the Medium* in 1907, soon after returning from the Congo. Wanting to advance beyond foreign wars, and recognizing that his slight dramatic talent required the padding of local color, he lighted on the phenomenon of the occult, with its promising séances, trances, and apparitions. The world of mediums and hypnotists was hardly virgin territory. To cite just two examples: Davis's Tokyo comrade Jack London had exploited it for his 1900 short story, "Planchette," and Davis's *Soldiers of Fortune* collaborator, Augustus Thomas, had mined the same vein for his 1907 play, *The Witching Hour*.[96] But a trademark of the Davis style was the ability to march across posted land with the bravura of a pioneer. He threw himself into his research, visiting crystal-ball gazers, interviewing "spooks," and—best of all—attending a séance in which the participants sat in a circle and held wrists, as balls of fire played around them and strange voices and guitar chords floated through the air.[97] The *Tourist*'s grand success when it opened in August freed Davis for *Vera*. Besides releasing blocks of time, the hit show eased his financial anxiety. "This play I am at now, will not be a money maker," he confided to Charlie. "And, I am not trying to make it one. I want to write it after my own idea of how it should be written; and the good money coming in from the 'Tourist' enables me to do that. . . . I want to treat myself to a 'success of esteem.' "[98]

He read the first act of the play to Ethel Barrymore, hoping that she would insist upon playing Vera. She was noncommittal.[99] He read the completed play two months later to Charles Frohman, who rejected it.[100] At this point, realizing that the reception to *Vera* was even chillier than he had predicted, Davis hit upon the idea of reworking the material into a novella. He could market just about anything in print. The Scribners were delighted to pay him four thousand dollars for the book and magazine rights to a novelized version of *Vera*.[101]

Unlike the book, the play required a star; and, eventually, it found one—the beautiful Eleanor Robson. This was to be one of Robson's last appearances on the stage, because early in 1910 she would retire from the theater to assume the full-time role of wife to millionaire August Belmont, Jr. Sadly, *Vera* proved to be one of her less successful parts. Reflecting on it many years later, she wrote: "I was hopelessly miscast and I knew it, a dreadful feeling for an actor. The public did not like to see a star they had put on a pedestal portray a person with any stain on her character. The attitude current was that you might accept bad behavior in private life from people you loved, but you did not have to pay to see it in the theater."[102] The character of Vera was only mildly tainted—by our standards, she is mawkishly pure. An orphan who has become a very successful medium, she has been hired to stage a séance in which spooky voices will instruct a doddering millionaire to leave his money to scoundrels. The handsome district attorney, arguing that Vera should renounce her shady life, shows up on the night of the séance and announces that he will wait for her downstairs "to congratulate you—on your failure." And in the middle of the séance, Vera tears off her wig and confesses her fraud. (Derivative as well as ludicrous, *Vera* is a cartoon version of Henry James's *The Bostonians*.)

Like *Captain Macklin, Vera* ventured far enough from the Davis formula to alienate an unthinking audience, but not nearly enough to captivate an intelligent one. The book appeared in serial form in the spring of 1908. The play was produced that fall. Davis novelized his play hurriedly, and the book contains such uncharacteristically unreadable sentences as: "He was deeply concerned lest the distinguished cross-examiner should think that from him of his lurid past he could withhold anything."[103] He spent more time on the play, rewriting constantly through rehearsals and the out-of-town tryouts to adjust to audience reactions and to Robson's nonmelodramatic style. "Never was a play so rewritten," Robson later reminisced. "Practically every time the company met we had a new version, at least a new scene or two." The theatrical manager and Davis stopped speaking, using Robson as their intermediary. In the end, a play doctor was called in to perform last-minute emergency surgery. Davis gave his consent but, not caring to witness the operation, he sailed for London.

Vera never opened in New York. It was deemed incurable, and Robson finally abandoned the play to star as an innocent Cockney street waif in Frances Hodgson Burnett's *The Dawn of a Tomorrow*. It was her last stage role and, unlike *Vera*, it was a triumph.[104] "*Vera* was a failure; at least, with

Miss Robson in it," Richard sadly concluded. "She is too sweet, and too innocent. The audiences would not have her as a crook, nor, could she persuade anyone that she was capable of deceit. I saw that was the trouble the first two weeks, and even when they thought they were coming into New York with a great money maker, I told them they never would open with Miss Robson on Broadway. Unfortunately, I was right." Davis had sacrificed popular appeal in hopes of a critical success, but he wound up with neither.[105]

11

A Wild,

Fantastic, Headlong Dance

C ECIL AND RICHARD SAILED SEPARATELY TO LONDON.
   To Eleanor Robson, Richard explained Cecil's early departure in this manner: "Mrs. Davis very wisely believes that the way to get me to London, is to go there herself, and so, she is sailing Wednesday to hire houses, maids and flats, which probably means two rooms in Russell Square!!!"[1] But no amount of hysterical punctuation could conceal a deepening marital crisis. Richard and Cecil might have continued until the end in a wedlock of mutual respect, some shared interests, and no sexual contact. Cecil would have been satisfied, so long as she could pursue her painting career and show her dogs. Richard was so bound by duty and convention that, without a triggering factor, he might have carried on, uncomplaining. But in the spring of 1908, half a year before the move to London, he met the triggering factor. Her name was Bessie McCoy.

Actually, that was her stage name. She was born Elizabeth Genevieve McEvoy, the daughter of circus and vaudeville performers, and she began her acting career at the age of five. By her teens she was a veteran trouper, appearing in a vaudeville dance duo with her sister, Nellie. The act was so successful that producer Sam Shubert urged the sisters to separate. When they did, Bessie's career took off. In fast-paced sequence, there was a chorus-girl slot behind Fritzi Scheff, a soubrette's role at the Hippodrome, and then, in the 1908 musical *The Three Twins*, overnight stardom as "The Yama-Yama Girl." Wearing a Pierrot suit adorned with a white bow at the neck, three giant pom-poms, a chapeau with a pom-pom, and more pom-poms on her shoes, Bessie danced out on stage and sang, in a husky, boylike voice, a nonsense tune called "The Yama-Yama Man." (The Yama-Yama Man was a bogeyman who jumped out from dark corners.)

> *Mary had—a lit—tle lamb—*
> *She took it on—the 'L.'*

> *And when they got—up to—the Bronx*
> *That lamb was black—as He-e-e—*

At which her eyes widened and her mouth puckered in an aghast "O," only to dissolve into sheepish laughter, a rollicking chorus of "Oh-h-h-h, Ya-a-ma, Ya-a-ma man," and a sudden dance. The dance is what attracted the most attention. It was, one observer wrote, "a wild, fantastic, headlong dance—the dance of a crazy king's clown, half girl, half wild boy. . . . The black satin of her bloomers fills like sails, and they ripple and flatten against her body. Her hair flies in loose flax around her face. . . . Her face flickers with changing moods. Her feet might be bounding white balls, carrying her body with them in their tireless, leaping flight. She circles madly around the boards, touching lightly and rebounding from the jutting points of the painted mock scenery, impatiently, hurriedly, like an imprisoned moth, or an elf hunting for some lost thing and fearful of being caught."[2] She danced in broken movements, like a somnambulist, seemingly unaware of the audience that filled the Herald Square Theatre.

From the first, Richard was smitten. He went back again and again to see the "Yama-Yama Man" number. For a well-off man to pay conspicuous court to a lady of the stage was nothing unusual. During the phenomenal run of *Florodora* back in 1900 and 1901, a gaggle of millionaires would flock into the theater nightly, just a few moments before the big chorus-girl number. All six of the original *Florodora* chorus eventually married millionaires.[3] They must have been cagey as well as beautiful, for few of the gentleman connoisseurs of the musical comedy had matrimonial intentions. Stanford White was unusually unlucky, but not otherwise unusual, as a married man in the pursuit of fetching young talent. But Davis? Perhaps it was the influence of Rob Collier, who, although married to a granddaughter of Mrs. William Astor, rivaled White as a chaser of chorus girls. Perhaps it was the frustration of his sterile partnership with Cecil. Perhaps it was simply the last grasp for life of a middle-aged man who had been denied the joys of passion and fatherhood. By 1907, for whatever reasons, Davis was casting his eye beyond the hearth in search of feminine companionship. But unlike Collier and White, he was not looking for a dalliance. He was hoping for a wife.

He was too earnest, particularly in his chivalry toward women, to consider anything else. His moral ballast insured that if he fell, he would fall hard. By 1907, he had acknowledged the failure of his marriage. There is a cryptic note in his diary of May 27: "Had a talk with Cecil in which she proposed a method vivendi." He says nothing more of it; but over the next months, he and Cecil spent increasing amounts of time apart. Richard would stay in town and dine with Charlie or Rob, while Cecil returned to the farm. Although they both moved to Marion in August, Richard came back to New York in late September and Cecil stayed on. They were pulling at their double harness; breaking free, however, was a more serious matter.

Divorce was on the rise in the United States—more than seventy-two thousand in 1906, compared with some twenty-five thousand in 1886—but it was still quite rare.[4] And the stigma attached to it was real. Before wedding Edith Carow, whom he married some time after the death of his first wife, Alice, Theodore Roosevelt self-reproachfully declared that second marriages "augured weakness in a man's character" and he bemoaned his own "inconstancy and unfaithfulness."[5] If these were the feelings of a widower, imagine the thoughts of a man contemplating divorce. Richard's Lehigh pal Mark A. De Wolfe Howe, who had become a prominent man of letters in Boston, broke off his friendship with the younger writer John Marquand after Marquand divorced his wife. About that time, there were a couple of celebrated Boston divorces, and the men paid a stiff social penalty: one was banished from the board of trustees of the Boston Symphony Orchestra, the other from the Corporation of Harvard College. Asked by his daughter why a man's private life was of public concern, Howe said, in substance: "It's a matter of *trust*. If a man is not trustworthy in one relationship it's fair to question whether he might not prove untrustworthy in another."[6]

By deferring to society's hypocrisy and philandering discreetly, a married man could avoid ostracism. In the theater community, where Davis passed much of his time, chorus girls and "professional beauties" abounded; if he was fishing for a lover, he was in the right waters. When Eva Fallon, a soubrette in *The Yankee Tourist*, told him of a married man who was pursuing her, Richard replied that she was right to be indignant, but he guessed that the man was all right, too.[7] He himself was quite infatuated (apparently only from afar) with a beauty named Daisy Green.[8]

But the bewitchery of Bessie McCoy dissolved all his discretion. She was not a conventionally beautiful woman. Her nose was a little large, and her yellow hair was dyed. By all accounts, however, she was captivating. Her deep, throaty voice and her large blue eyes, her slender figure and her graceful movements worked as powerfully on an audience of one as on the crowds at the Herald Square. She had a childlike curiosity and self-effacing manners, the freshness of an ingenue. When Davis first saw her, she was only twenty. Although forty-four himself, he reacted like a boy her age. He was so lovesick that he felt near bursting; if he didn't declare his passion, he might explode. Two months after *The Three Twins* opened, he joked to his mother that he had brought a friend to a performance by "a young lady named Bessie McCoy, whom I intend to buy, and keep on the farm."[9] Having dropped this hint to his mother, he then announced his adoration to the readership of *Collier's*. In a piece about curmudgeonly critics, he digressed very oddly to speak of one critic who was exceptional in his generosity. "When a few months ago a New York critic rolled up his sleeves, and, casting caution and tradition to the winds, proclaimed the triumph of Bessie McCoy to his several hundreds of thousands of readers, I could have walked a good many miles to thank him," he wrote. "I had not then seen that young lady, I had not heard her sing. I was not then, as I am now, with the rest of the world, kneeling at her feet. . . ."[10]

Davis attended *The Three Twins* repeatedly before he secured an introduction to Bessie. The man who introduced them—probably at Churchill's restaurant on Broadway—was Frank O'Malley, star reporter on the *Sun*.[11] O'Malley was dining with Miss McCoy when Davis, at a table nearby, came up to say hello. An introduction followed. O'Malley asked them both to accompany him that night to the Larry Mulligan ball, one of the annual bashes sponsored by Tammany Hall. They agreed; and before the night was over, they both served as judges of the beauty pageant that was a highlight of the affair.[12] In the weeks that followed, Davis paid court at the Herald Square Theatre to a reticent princess. Unless otherwise detained, he would appear nightly at ten-thirty "to see the story of my life sing the Yama Yama Man."[13] To this burning ardor, Bessie responded coolly. He was old enough to be her father, and he was married. His motives were, to say the least, suspect. But over time, his persistence paid off.

When he left for his London sojourn in December 1908, Richard won Bessie's assurance that she would write him.[14] For Christmas, he commissioned Charlie to buy for her a pigskin-encased gold traveling clock at Tiffany's, with her initials stamped on it in gilt; and as a reward, he invited Charlie "to take Bessie McCoy out to supper, *at my expense*, on the condition, you *both drink my* health."[15]

His thoughts and dreams were with Bessie back in New York, while he maintained a shadow life in London. The first in his chain of London obligations was finding a suitable house. (Despite what he told Eleanor Robson, house hunting was not something Cecil did.) He discharged his duty handsomely, leasing for fifty dollars a week the house on Cheyne Walk in Chelsea that had once belonged to the painter William Turner. It was very far from the fashionable West End, which was the part of London Richard knew, but they took it because Cecil wanted to paint, and there was a huge studio connected to the residence, with a squash court in between. The three-story house was all oak and rafters, the walls paneled and painted green, and brass knobs everywhere. There were more rooms than they could use. "Our view is the river, and the gulls wheel and whirl and complain all day in front of the window," Richard wrote. "The river flows past the place where the houses would be if there were houses opposite. When I woke up this morning I fancied I was on a steamer just making port." Most of the house was cold and drafty, but Richard had a tiny workroom that, when stoked furiously with coal, became toasty enough to permit him to write.[16]

In that room, he dutifully cranked out the final pages of *The White Mice* and daydreamed about Bessie. The energy absent from his fiction was funneled into his internal moral debate. He resolved in January that he would divorce Cecil. He wrote to tell Charlie the news and waited with anxiety for the response. "When it came, it made me cry with relief, and with happiness, to know you are so true to me," he wrote back gratefully.[17] He also informed Cecil, who was less understanding. Bitter that he should prefer another, let alone a vaudeville star, she proudly declared that she would not stand in his way.[18] The way would be long and twisting; in the meantime, the Davises lived married but estranged, together but apart. "As the man says, 'We might have been so happy if we hadn't been so damned miserable,' but in spite of being miserable I am damned happy," Richard told Charles in January. "Never more so, at any time. How it is going to end, the good Lord only knows, but I am happy now, and grateful."[19]

Despite his lame efforts to economize, he was "Living awful close," squeaking by with royalty checks that arrived in the mail unpredictably.[20] In January he panicked and broadcast an appeal for any funds due him from his various publishers and theatrical managers; the resulting windfall kept him solvent until, upon submission of the last segment of *The White Mice* in mid-February, he received twenty-five hundred dollars from the *Saturday Evening Post*.[21] When not writing short stories, he was working out a musical version of *The Dictator* with his old friend, the comic actor Seymour Hicks. He was hopeful that war might break out in the Balkans— eager not for the pageantry of the battlefield but for the large paychecks from *Collier's*.[22]

Cecil had retained a young painting teacher, and she spent her days painting portraits. Social London being a small world, she invited John Sargent in one day for advice on changing the pose of one of her models. "Cecil had the nerve to ask him to sketch her the pose he wanted, and with a piece of charcoal in ten minutes he made the most exquisite drawing . . . which he left Cecil," Richard wrote his mother-in-law. "She was blowing fixitive [*sic*] on it before he had left the house."[23] Richard had promised Cecil he would stay in London for three months. When his duty was up in early March, she tried to persuade him to reenlist, returning with her to America at the end of April. There were strong arguments in her favor: with Sargent's encouragement, she was completing two portraits to submit to the spring exhibition at the Royal Academy; and the rent on the studio and house had been paid in advance through April 25.[24] This logic made Richard vacillate, but it did not change his mind. He left Cecil in the London house in mid-March and sailed for New York. "Cecil was perfectly splendid about letting me go," he wrote his mother-in-law. "She appreciated I was very homesick, and with my novel finished, and, the new version of the 'Dictator' completed, anxious to begin work."[25]

He had resumed writing stories as his chief source of income. The tales he composed during this period of marital estrangement and financial anxiety leave little doubt about his concerns. Romance and money are the themes. All too frequently, the protagonist is a poor young writer who loves a rich woman; and often, the deserving young man (of good, albeit impoverished, stock) acquires a miraculous money-making gift. An indigent Yalie writer marries the richest girl in America, who is promptly disinherited; but their fortunes rise dramatically when he finds that he cannot lose at the racetrack.[26] Another penniless fellow, this one a Harvard man, falls in love with another fabulously rich girl, and mysteriously acquires another supernatural talent: this time, mind reading.[27] A struggling writer feels he cannot marry the rich girl who loves him, until he stumbles into an espionage scheme and sells a purloined treaty.[28] A young reporter courts a beautiful girl he believes to be poor, but—oh, happy fate!—she is as rich as she is lovely.[29] (This plot brought in the element of mistaken identity, a staple of Davis's farces. In 1915, he wrote much the same story again, using as his hero not a reporter but a romance writer.)[30] A reporter in London rescues an imprisoned heiress and wins her love along with her liberty.[31] Another rich young woman pretends to be poor to test the love of an estranged sweetheart (he passes the test).[32] Are these short stories or wish fulfillments? Should they be analyzed by a literary critic or a psychologist? At the same time that he was contemplating a divorce from a rich wife to marry a woman without money, when he was examining each day's mail hoping for checks and usually finding only bills, Davis was dreaming up a processional of heiresses and marching them down the aisle on the arms of indigent writers.

The most painful hurdle on the road to divorce was the necessity of breaking the news to his elderly, ailing mother. By 1910, Rebecca was in physical decline. Her most vexing problem was failing eyesight; surgery alleviated the problem, but only temporarily. She was forced to reduce, though not abandon, the writing and reading that she had kept up in her old age. One remaining pleasure was wintering in Warm Springs, Virginia, usually accompanied by her daughter, Nora. Another great joy was staying with Richard in Mount Kisco, where mother and son would take rides in a horse-drawn carriage and talk quietly on the porch. When he could, Richard would visit her in the old Philadelphia row house that she and Nora still shared. "Dear boy, I know you went away last night but somehow you don't seem to be gone," she wrote him after one such visit. "You never *are* quite away from me. It's curious. No matter what happens I always feel as if 'Dick knows. Dick understands.' When God gave me my first child he gave him for keeps. All your love for Cecil never has dulled your love for us at home—has it? You are the best husband alive in the world today. But you are as near to us as you ever were. When one gets old like me life is really made up of only a few things we know of God and half a dozen people. If I only could tell you what you children are in my narrow life!"[33]

When they were separated, Richard wrote to his mother virtually every day. It was an era in which sons were typically more demonstrative to their mothers than they are now. Even so, the mutual devotion of Richard and Rebecca was considered remarkable. "Dick Davis's mother was the controlling influence of his life and no one could fully understand him without knowing about her," wrote the reporter Martin Egan. "The bond between them was an amazingly strong one and never in my life have I known a man who had greater devotion for his mother than Dick had."[34] It was more than the usual hyperbole when Richard assured Rebecca, near the end of her life: "No son ever loved a mother as this son loves you, just remember that, for in all the world there is nothing so true."[35]

Old age and its narrowing outlook merely intensified the way Rebecca had always felt. Much as she loved her other children, she placed her first-born first. They had a special understanding, to which they frequently and fondly referred. Richard would write effusive letters to Rebecca not only on her birthday but on his own. He perceived—quite sensibly, really—that his birthday had as much to do with her as it did with him. As a holiday, its deepest significance was to commemorate their closeness.

Apparently, Rebecca remained unaware of the widening cracks in Richard's marriage. He protected her from the news, dreading the day he would have to tell her. The day never came. In early 1910, she suffered a slight stroke. Because of her age, her children feared the worst, but in the coming months, Rebecca once again displayed her enormous resilience and vitality. By that summer, she was making a busy round of visits: to Manasquan, to Germantown, to Connecticut, and finally, to Crossroads Farm. It was there that she fell ill again. She asked Richard to take her home to Philadelphia, and though he promised to do so as soon as she improved enough to travel, this time she did not improve. On September 29, 1910, at the age of seventy-nine, Rebecca died of heart failure at Richard's home.[36]

His mother was Richard's greatest admirer and most attentive critic. She was the person he sought most to please and to whom he felt closest. She was a formidable personality, and she dominated not only Richard, but all her children. Indeed, since the younger children were weaker, she enthralled them all the more. "[Charlie] ought to have a wife & a patch of ground of his own," Rebecca once told Richard. "If he doesn't it won't be for lack of my pushing & prodding."[37] Yet only after her death did Charlie and Nora, both in their forties, break the bonds of childhood and marry. Much the same can be said of Richard, whose unsatisfying first marriage was to someone who, from girlhood on, had been known and endorsed by Rebecca. His mother's death threw Richard into a depression, in which the natural grief at her loss was muddied by the guilty knowledge that the last obstacle to his own conjugal happiness was now removed. He would not have to wound her with the shocking announcement that he was divorcing a sober, respectable wife to marry a vaudeville star. Her pain would not taint his joy.

He was not, however, the first Davis child to rush to the altar after Rebecca's death. That distinction went to Nora, now in her early forties and for the first time on her own. Having grown up in the shade cast by her eldest brother, Nora was delicate and retiring. In an accomplished family, she could boast of no exceptional talent. Conforming to that familiar Victorian pattern, she took to her bed in recurring collapses; sometimes, in such a state, she would stay with Richard and Cecil at Crossroads Farm. "All of her friends . . . say how lucky she is when she breaks down to have a beautiful country house open & in full running order for her to get well in," Rebecca wrote to Richard on one such occasion.[38]

You might think that her mother's professional success would have inspired and liberated Nora; but, just as easily, such a model can intimidate and paralyze. Especially when the mother has subordinated her own career to family and is vicariously relishing the success of her famous son. On a voyage to Europe with her mother in 1906, a woman came up to Nora in the salon, where a group was singing around a piano, and said, "Won't you play for us?"

"Thank you, I don't play," Nora said.

"Then you sing?"

"No, I don't sing."

"Perhaps you recite?"

"I can't recite."

"Oh, then you will tell a story."

"No, I can't tell stories."

"And yet," the woman announced to the listening room, "and yet she is Richard Harding Davis's sister!"

Perhaps the most revealing fact about this anecdote is that it was related to Richard by his mother, who added this commentary: "Then everyone talked & said how they had read every word you wrote & this one liked the Van Bibber stories & that Gallegher—& so on. Noll came down laughing at them. But I saw she was very much pleased. Every time when I go up somebody comes & talks to me of you boys."[39] Being constantly compared to one's illustrious brother would be hard enough; how much crueller would it be to live with a son-besotted mother who thrived on these encounters and assumed her youngest child felt the same?

Nora was the plain, dutiful daughter who tends to her parents and slips unobtrusively into spinsterhood. It was a surprise that she married. Her choice, though, was less remarkable. Just as Richard for his first wife had selected Cecil, so Nora wed someone who had been almost a member of the Davis family. F. Percival Farrar was a son of the Reverend Frederic

W. Farrar, a celebrated Dean of Westminster Abbey and the author of *The Life of Christ*. Dean Farrar had been a close friend of George W. Childs, the proprietor of the Philadelphia *Public Ledger*. As Childs was childless and Farrar had eight children, the Philadelphian offered to take one of the Farrar boys into the newspaper business. And so, in 1892, Percival was dispatched to Philadelphia, where he lived with Childs and worked first as a reporter and then as the private secretary to the paper's managing editor— L. Clarke Davis.

Later it was said that a romance budded between the young man and his employer's only daughter. At the least, they became friends. But not long afterward, Percival was called back to England by his father to study for the ministry. He took his orders and rose rapidly in the Church of England. Although he exchanged letters with Nora, he rarely saw her.[40] The geographical distance that divided them, and the chronological gap (Nora was a couple of years his senior), provoked comment later, when the marriage was rocked by scandal, and some suggested that it had never been more than an alliance of convenience.

Percival had the most important sponsor an Anglican clergyman could hope for: the king of England. His simple eloquent sermons were favored by Edward VII and Queen Alexandra. Bright and charming, he became a confidant of the king. He was made rector of Sandringham, the site of the king's favorite house, and was appointed domestic chaplain to the king. King Edward died in May 1910, but his son, George V, retained Farrar as his personal chaplain. When Richard gave his sister, Nora, in marriage to Percival in a ceremony at Saint Andrew's, Westminster, in July 1911, there were gifts from King George V and Queen Mary, and from Queen Alexandra. While the newlyweds enjoyed their honeymoon trip, Queen Alexandra personally supervised the renovation of the rectory at Sandringham.[41]

After such an auspicious start, Richard was baffled and alarmed by a desperate, cryptic telegram that he received from Nora in late November, less than five months after the wedding. She was in great trouble; could he or Charles come at once? He boarded the *Mauritania* two days later, fearing that she was seriously ill. A day or two into the voyage, he received a wireless message from Charles intimating the nature of the trouble: "that it was not illness," Richard said, "but far more serious." How serious it was he did not discover until he arrived in England.[42]

The day that Richard received Nora's telegram, the Farrars had de-camped from Sandringham. On the next day, it was announced that Percival had been dismissed as the chaplain to the king. Not in modern memory had the king's chaplain been so perfunctorily sacked.[43] The reason for his disgrace was (as one New York newspaper described it) "of such a character that it can only be whispered." Although the details were suppressed— "hushed up, as is the usual policy of the authorities in such cases," said the press report—it seems clear that detectives, acting upon rumors, observed him in a homosexual encounter. "He was caught flagrante delicto," related another press account, in "an unprintable offense." Homosexual acts were criminal in England, but the police declined to press charges, on the understanding that Farrar would leave the country within twenty-four hours.[44]

By the time Richard reached London, Percival was in hiding. Nora, distraught, was debating what to do. Richard urged her to return to the United States to live with him at Crossroads Farm; to his regret, she decided that her duty was to join her husband. "In time, I think, she will see that her duty lies in another direction," Richard told a New York *Times* reporter. "I have not seen her husband nor communicated with him in any way, and I never shall." Besides his worries for his sister's future, Richard feared that he himself would appear at fault in the lurid light of the scandal. "What affects me most is that people who do not know my brother and myself may think that we did not make sufficient inquiries about the history of the man my sister married," he told the *Times* man. "But I had met him fifteen years before, and knew him as a splendid type of Englishman, a first-rate athlete, fond of outdoor exercises and sports. The next time I saw Farrar was at the wedding a few months ago. He seemed to be the same fine man, only more developed and making great headway in the Church. Would any one under the circumstances think of making inquiries, bearing in mind that the man was a clergyman, the King's Chaplain, and what his family was?"[45]

Richard sounded defensive because some people, under the circumstances, thought that inquiries would have been very much in order. According to rumor, Percival's "transgressions" were widely known and condoned in the morally permissive court of Edward VII. Under the stricter reign of George V and the puritanical Queen Mary, Farrar thought it wise to take a wife. Indeed, the story went, Nora was quite aware of her husband's past and entered the partnership with open eyes. This proper domestic façade was demolished by an enemy who brought evidence of the clergyman's secret life to the king's private secretary. An investigation followed as a matter of course. Perhaps Edward would have protected his friend and chaplain. Certainly George did not.[46]

Nora stayed with Percival, moving to British Columbia and returning to England when the notoriety had passed. Richard went back to New York alone. Compared to these wretched intrigues, his own domestic affairs were merely conventionally unhappy. It was almost two years before his divorce came through. For Richard, they were years of waiting, of aimless traveling, of financial anxiety, of hack writing. He visited Panama and Cuba. Twice he went to Aiken, South Carolina, to stay at the winter home of Gouverneur and Elsie Morris. In Aiken, not too far from the home turf of the Wright brothers, Richard in 1911 was taken on a ride in a Wright biplane. The thought of it made him queasy; only the promise of a check from *Collier's* stiffened his shaky legs. Crawling between a crisscross of wires to a tiny seat, he grasped a wooden upright with his right hand. With his left he could hold on to nothing but his seat. His feet rested on a steel crossbar. And that was it. "Had I placed myself in such a seat on a hotel porch, I would have considered my position most unsafe," he wrote, "to occupy such a seat a thousand feet in mid-air while moving at fifty miles an hour struck me as ridiculous." The plane raced on bicycle wheels down a polo field. "You are in the air!" the pilot announced, and Davis, not believing him, braced himself to look down. It was true—they were two feet off the ground; and then the landscape dropped off below them as the plane quickly gained altitude. The experience was unlike gazing down from a skyscraper or from a train on a trestle—his points of comparison—because now there was only air between him and the ground. Indeed, a flight on a Wright biplane resembled a modern parachute drop far more than, say, a ride in a DC-10. It was, Davis wrote, "the sense of power, of detachment from everything humdrum, or even human; the thrill that makes all the other sensations stale and vapid."[47]

It was a rare uplifting moment in a stale, vapid period. The interminable divorce played itself out in the glare of gossipy publicity, as newspapermen projected the future by hinting at Richard's new attachment and rhapsodized the past by recalling the ocean-hopping Jaggers and the storybook wedding in the Marion chapel. The newspapers had more trouble reporting the events of the present because neither Richard nor Cecil would talk. In November 1910, less than two months after Rebecca's death, Cecil filed for divorce in New York State and began to wait out the mandatory separation period. Mysteriously, in May 1912, she dropped the suit, provoking a flurry of newspaper conjectures about a reconciliation. The real explanation was less romantic. To avoid the stringent New York divorce laws, which demanded proof of infidelity, Cecil moved back to Chicago and filed for divorce there on grounds of desertion. On June 18, 1912, the divorce decree was signed. There was no alimony awarded.[48] Abandoning New York, a city she had never much liked, Cecil stayed in Chicago with her parents and returned to Marion (now off-limits to Richard) each summer. Despite the wound to her pride, she could now concentrate on her primary passion—painting.

As it happened, the month that his divorce became final in Chicago, Richard was in that city covering the convention of the Republican Party for Scribner's.[49] Theodore Roosevelt's decision to challenge the renomination of President Taft, his hand-picked successor, had divided Republicans against each other and sowed dissension among friends and within families. For Davis, of course, there was no question: his loyalty lay with the man who had stormed Kettle Hill, the man whose legend he had helped weave. Matters were more complicated for the Republicans, who hesitated to renounce an incumbent president and to give Roosevelt an unprecedented third term in the White House. After the convention remained faithful to

Taft, Roosevelt bolted, starting his own Progressive Party. It was nicknamed the Bull Moose Party when Roosevelt, one of the most quotable figures in American history, responded to a reporter's routine question about his health and spirits by bellowing, "I'm feeling like a bull moose." Davis returned to Chicago in August to cover the convention of the Progressives for *Collier's*.[50] "We stand at Armageddon, and we battle for the Lord," Roosevelt told the delirious audience.

It was a bitter campaign. Nowhere were the divisions sharper than at *Collier's*, where they did not emerge until the conventions were over. A triumvirate of Rob Collier, Norman Hapgood, and Mark Sullivan ran *Collier's*, and all three backed Roosevelt over Taft. *Collier's* had earned Taft's lasting enmity by exposing the corruption in his Interior Department—a major scandal that severely damaged Taft's chances for reelection. In a three-man race, however, the problem was choosing between Roosevelt and the Democratic candidate, Princeton University president Woodrow Wilson. Both men preached enlightened, progressive ideas. Mark Sullivan had been an early backer of Wilson; but once Roosevelt entered the race, he supported the Bull Moose Party. Still, he focused his fusillades on Taft and refrained from attacking Wilson. Collier, who objected to what he called Wilson's "professorial" quality, would have liked a few more swipes at the Democrats, but he supported Sullivan's policy. Only Norman Hapgood, who wrote the editorials, favored Wilson. And unlike his colleagues, Hapgood didn't limit himself to criticizing Taft. He peppered Roosevelt. Hapgood also objected to the number of pro-Progressive feature articles (like Davis's) that *Collier's* was running.

The breaking point came in October, after a gunman wounded Roosevelt in Milwaukee. Refusing to go to a hospital, Roosevelt delivered his scheduled speech and only then sought medical attention. It was thought that the incident would win him the election. Writing his *Collier's* editorial, Hapgood expressed his regret that a madman's act might outweigh the reasoned arguments of the campaign. In condemning the act of violence, he also deplored the violent rhetoric of Roosevelt's speeches. Outraged by this editorial, which he read in proof, Collier wrote one of his own to run alongside it, and he inserted it after Hapgood left for the day. Hapgood resigned. In the back-and-forth public statements that ensued, Hapgood began by saying that he had quit because commercial interests were dominating the weekly. He then went further in diagnosing the ills of *Collier's*. Bankers had been able to penetrate the editorial sanctum, he charged, because of Rob Collier's "degenerating from his former high ideals through influences which I do not care to discuss . . . a surrender which I believe to be the result entirely of undesirable modes of life." Mocking one of Collier's statements, he sniped that "the public must wonder just what state he was in when he wrote it." It was a public airing of the dark secret that had been plaguing *Collier's*, the rot at the core that would eventually topple the whole enterprise.

For everything that Hapgood said was true. P. F. Collier had died in 1909. Rob took over the business, but he was no businessman, and soon he was asking for money from his banker friends the way he had from his father. Had he wanted the money for magazine expenses, his sins would be pardonable, but in fact he was treating the *Collier's* till as a piggy bank to fund his drinking and womanizing. In a long binge of self-destructive dissipation, he exhausted his health and his fortune. He rarely appeared at the office, yet he wouldn't delegate authority. The cashier would delay payment on manuscripts. By the time Rob died in 1918, he had bankrupted his magazine along with his mind and his body.*[51]

For Davis, Rob Collier's decline was on the one hand a personal tragedy, the self-destruction of a friend and colleague. More mundanely and importantly, it eliminated a chief source of his income. Money was more of a problem than ever. He would have been better off had Cecil taken the farm (which she didn't want) rather than leave him to make the payments on it. But he loved Crossroads Farm, and it was there that he brought his new bride on July 8. His wedding followed his divorce by less than three weeks.

To elude reporters, he kept the site for the ceremony a secret (although he did divulge the date a week in advance). On the appointed morning, having woken at five, he was taken by car from Mount Kisco to the house of Gouverneur Morris, his best man, nearby in Bedford. After drinking champagne, the wedding party—which now filled two automobiles—proceeded over the state line to Greenwich, Connecticut, where a judge who went to Yale with Morris would officiate. On the way, Richard bought a white ribbon and toothache medicine. The day already was scorching, the hottest of the year. Sedated by the heat, the drink, and perhaps the medicine, Richard to his amazement napped in the car. Escorted by matron of honor Ethel Barrymore Colt (who had married a scion of the Colt firearm fortune), Bessie came to Greenwich by train. She too was faint from the heat. "B. very wonderful and sweet and pretty," Richard noted in his diary. She wore

---

*He bequeathed the *Weekly* to three men who had been running it during his prolonged final breakdown; but the beneficiaries, once they learned how small was his estate, gave it to his widow. Relying in large part on the advice of her good friend Charlie Davis, Mrs. Collier sold the *Weekly* on the cheap to the Crowell Publishing Company. Finley Peter Dunne, one of the original beneficiaries, gnashed his teeth, but could change nothing. He was all the more bitter at the role played by Charlie, whom he thought a "chump." "But to be destroyed by Charlie Davis!" he wailed to a friend. "I am like the antique hero who died at the bite of a louse." Although *Collier's* survived until 1956, its glory days were over.

a white lace sunbonnet tied with a pink ribbon and a gown of white embroidered lace over silk, and she carried a colossal bouquet of lilies of the valley, roses, and sweet peas. He wore a blue blazer, white flannels, and white yachting shoes. Following what Richard deemed a "very solemn ceremony," the party, now in three cars, went back to Westchester for a luncheon at the home of the Morrises. A larger celebration, which they didn't attend, was held at Coney Island, where fifty lower East Side mothers and their two hundred children romped at the beach. At Bessie's request, Richard underwrote this tenement children's outing—an event, as one newspaper noted, that was in the spirit of his own story, "Van Bibber and the Swan-Boats," in which the dapper clubman treated three little lower East Side girls to a boat ride in Central Park.[52] Bessie's secretary-companion, Louise Frey, had brought Bessie's clothes to Crossroads Farm the day before the wedding. "Strange sensation of finding women's slippers skirts hairbrushes lying about," Richard had written in his diary.[53] Arriving now herself, Bessie was delighted with her bedroom. The honeymoon began.

It did not last long. Exchanging the name of Bessie McCoy for Mrs. Richard Harding Davis was not so easy. Bessie had met Richard on Broadway, that ecumenical boulevard where bluebloods and showgirls walked as equals. Off Broadway, however, matters were more complicated. The theater world that Richard frequented for fun and business was the only world that Bessie knew. Richard expected her to give it up and retire from the stage. In place of her career, she would preside over a large house in the country and entertain the friends of her social and literary husband. "I knew nothing but the theatre," she later confessed. "Believe me, I had very far to grow to be a fitting companion for Richard Harding Davis." When she worried about behaving correctly among bookish, well-bred people, Richard reassured her. "You will never make any mistakes because you are considerate," he said. "Consideration for others is the essence of good breeding."[54] In Arcadia, perhaps, but not in New York.

Richard was twice her age and set in his ways. He began his day by breakfasting alone, with a copy of the London *Graphic* propped against the toast tray. After breakfast, he and Bessie would meet, fully dressed, for a walk to the lake or the apple orchard. Then they would return to the house, with Richard retiring to work in his study, Bessie administering the household. They would meet again at one for an informal lunch, after which Richard would read the New York papers that reached Mount Kisco in the afternoon. "Bessie, interrupt me in the middle of a story if you must, but never talk when I'm reading the papers," he would tell her. "It's part of my business to read them, and I can't be disturbed." Once the papers were read, he returned to his work, breaking off sharply at five. At that time precisely, he would call for Bessie to join him, axe in his hand, for a tramp through the woods or a cross-country carriage ride. By the time they returned, it was time to start preparing for dinner.[55]

Even about little things he had strong views. His desk was fastidiously arranged, with scissors, erasers, and sharpened pencils all in place. He forbade Bessie to use it; she had a desk of her own. He was so neat that he would blot his letters only on the underside of the blotter, so the smears wouldn't show.[56] His likes and dislikes might take her a lifetime to learn. He hated patent leather, for example, and often insisted that she change her belt. Extolling "the realities of life," he encouraged Bessie to let her hair grow back to its natural brown. "When we walked in the woods," she later recalled, "he liked me to wear a gown that would harmonize with the colors of the woods."[57] Accommodating his sartorial predilections was simpler than penetrating his circle of intimates. She was jealous of his friends and family, whom she suspected of secretly disapproving of her. She was right about Nora, who did not conceal her misgivings. She misjudged Charlie, however. He signed on wholeheartedly to anything that his big brother endorsed. Perhaps the mere fact of their extraordinary closeness threatened Bessie unacceptably. She was very insecure.

Had she continued her dancing, she might have maintained her equilibrium. But Richard didn't want his wife on the stage. He removed Bessie from her natural surroundings, and, like some delicate tropical bird, she languished. She developed nervous complaints, she stopped eating, she fell into severe depressions. He loved her dearly. Unfortunately, once he possessed her, she became one more thing for him to worry about.

Among the late manuscripts of Richard Harding Davis there are worksheets which, blunt and stark, depict a man shoring up against a deluge of bills. At the end of each day, Richard would mark the number of pages he had completed and, estimating $10 a page, calculate his earnings. On some astounding days, he would total $100, or even, once, $150; on drier days, only $20. Usually, $50 or $60 was the figure. It was never enough. He typically spent two to three weeks to finish a story.[58]

He wrote another play, *Who's Who*, specifically for William Collier, who had scored such a success in *The Dictator*. This time, Collier said, he wanted to stretch himself with more than a farce. He wanted human situations and real emotions. So instead of stringing together gag lines, Davis tried (always within the boundary lines of farce) to create plausible characters and episodes. But when it came time to play this cowboy-and-bandit piece, Collier couldn't tolerate the moments when the audience wasn't rolling in the aisles. In tryouts in Toronto, Davis toiled bitterly to rewrite his play to suit his star's changed ideas. "I'll bet I've lost twenty pounds, and gained ten years," Richard grumbled to Charles. "It now is a fair farce, but no knock out. Had he declared at the start he wanted nothing but laughs, it would have been much easier. But he told us he wanted 'drama' and he wanted love scenes. When he found he was unsuited to either, he blamed the play, and walked through the part. . . . He has got to have laughs or he dies; smiles and 'interest' he despises; he must have guffaws, or he passes away."[59] Charles Frohman, who produced *Who's Who*, put Davis's full name on the Broadway marquee in electric lights a foot and a half high.[60] This did not prevent the farce from closing a few weeks after it opened in September 1913. More than six months of work had come to naught.[61] Not since *The Yankee Tourist* back in 1907 had Davis enjoyed a hit—and that was a retread of the earlier *Galloper*. He would never write a hit again.

The birth of motion pictures, late in Davis's career, was a gift from providence. Then as now, movie producers needed material, and nothing could be better than fiction by a famous author. Davis's *Soldiers of Fortune* was one of the first full-length features to be produced by the fledgling movie industry. The screenwriter and director was none other than Augustus Thomas, the highly successful playwright who had helped Davis adapt *Soldiers* for the stage and who had just finished filming his own hit play, *Arizona*. The leading man was Dustin Farnum, a matinee idol who had starred in Owen Wister's *The Virginian* on Broadway. This was Farnum's first film and (perhaps intimidated by the strange machinery and situations) he was a far more tractable star than Collier. The movie was filmed in Santiago, Cuba, using many of the real settings that had inspired the fiction. For Richard, who came along to advise the crew and to write an article for *Scribner's*, the responsibilities were limited and the situation was novel. It was a lark.

The mechanics of filmmaking fascinated him. What's interesting, reading about it now, is to see how little has changed. The peculiar lingo which we associate with Hollywood actually predates Hollywood (the movie business was still centered in New York). The Cuban settings were known as "locations," the actors were woken for their morning "call," the "director-general" required the actors to "register" various emotions on film. For Richard, whose specialty was costumes, an especially interesting item was the looseleaf-bound book in which, next to each numbered scene, there appeared the names of the characters appearing in the scene and the costume each would wear. Since the movie was being filmed out of sequence—a weird occurrence for these stage actors—it was the most efficient way to make sure that a character who was wearing boots when he left the house would not be wearing lace-ups once he emerged on the street.

Going back to the Hotel Venus, the villa La Cruz, and the Juragua Iron Company was evocative in itself for Richard. He was even more thrilled when "the characters I had imagined so long ago began to walk around the real mines as I had made them walk in fiction, and ride engines, and work ore trains, and make love."[62] Shooting movies on location is commonplace now; but precinema, a stage play would have been the only conceivable "real-life" translation from the page, and that was far from "real." On location in Cuba, Richard felt like a dreamer, transported to the places that had inspired him, seeing men and women who owed their existence to his imagination now living and breathing like Pygmalion's Galatea. It was eerie to watch the actor playing MacWilliams—whom Davis had based on the engineer Kirkpatrick—walk over to Kirkpatrick's grave, dressed in the mining boots, blue shirt, and sombrero that Kirkpatrick always wore. It was more amusing and characteristic when the director found that Farnum, playing Clay, had none of the clothes suitable for a dashing Davis hero. Everyone knew immediately where to find such clothes. Over the next few days, Farnum—who was fortunately the right size—stripped Davis of his coat, sombrero, riding boots, leather gaiters, gauntlets, khaki coats, pongee coats, gray flannel shirts, white flannel trousers, tan shoes, tennis shoes, riding whip, raincoat, and revolver. No one dressed more like a Davis hero than Davis.[63]

Thomas said that he believed *Soldiers of Fortune* would be the greatest film yet made in America.[64] However, when the All Star Picture Corporation, an independent distributor, premiered it in Manhattan in January 1914, the scenery stole the show. Critics found the scenario confusing and wordy. It was not a hit.[65]

Returning to Mount Kisco from make-believe fighting in Cuba, Davis once again was distracted by the off-stage noises of a real war. Military strongman Victoriano Huerta had seized power in Mexico, outraging President Wilson and his secretary of state, William Jennings Bryan. Wilson refused to recognize Huerta's presidency. But how far would he go, as he put it, "to teach the Latin-American republics to elect good men"?[66] Davis joked that with the two thousand men loaned to the movie company in Cuba, he had been tempted to march into Mexico City. "Why, with 2,000 men and a machine gun, you'd clean up the whole country," he told a reporter.[67] Talking more seriously, Richard complained to Charles of Wilson's "contemptible" policy of all bluster, no follow-up. "I don't mean that I want war," he insisted, "but I hate being made to look abjectly afraid and by such a pair as Wilson and Bryan."[68]

Wilson was waiting for an "incident." A dispute involving American sailors in the port of Tampico gave him what he wanted, and on April 14, he ordered the U.S. fleet to Tampico. The American newspapers vibrated in anticipation of war. By the hour, Richard was being telephoned with lucrative proposals. The New York *Tribune*, in combination with a newspaper syndicate headed by John N. Wheeler, signed him up for the extravagant sum of a thousand dollars a week for the first four weeks, and five hundred dollars for each week thereafter. He insisted on one important stipulation, which he thought made the whole contract moot: he would go only if war broke out. He was confident that Huerta would back down, but he was wrong.[69] Unflinching, Mexico and the United States faced off. On April 21, although there was still no declaration of war, American marines and sailors captured the port of Veracruz. On the same day, no longer able to resist the enthusiastic importunings of his employers, Davis boarded a train to

New Orleans, heading toward the action. "In one way it is a relief," he wrote, "for months waiting for this has upset my plans and kept me daily, almost hourly, in doubt. I never knew whether I would spend the day at work on the farm, or on a train to El Paso, or a boat to Vera Cruz. So, now like having a tooth out, *that* worry is behind me."[70] Only the timing bothered him. On January 14, without giving Richard any warning, Charles had married Pauline Ada Turgeon, known as Dai, the goddaughter of Mrs. Rob Collier. The wedding took place in England (Richard was notified by cable), where the couple honeymooned. In April they would be returning to New York for the first time as man and wife. It made Richard "sick at the stomach" that he found out too late to cancel his plans and welcome them.[71]

How much greater was his disappointment to discover, upon arriving in Veracruz on the same ship with Brigadier-General Frederick Funston, that war had not been declared and nothing was happening. The countries had submitted the dispute to mediation. "It was a terrible blow to all, especially to me," Richard wrote home to Bessie. "I hoped for a quick advance on Mexico City, and then back to you. Now, God knows how long they will be!"[72] He was once again being paid huge sums to walk around an uninteresting city. "Not that I want to catch bullets in my teeth, but I *did* expect quick action and something to write about," he told Charles. "*Nothing* hurts a man more than writing routine stuff, when the readers deserve to have thrills." The situation was so murky that General Funston and the press censor asked *him* what news he had had from home.[73] He missed Bessie, and he worried about her fragile nervous state. He was not happy in Mexico.

To his colleagues of the press, he was a semimythical creature. He was the first journalist accredited to travel with the army—a fact duly published by the Associated Press. On the voyage from Galveston to Veracruz, he was the only correspondent given his own cabin, and at meals he was placed to the left of General Funston (a colonel sat on the general's right).[74] In Veracruz, he stayed at the Hotel Diligencia in a large room with a balcony overlooking the plaza.[75] Despite the heat, he would, every evening promptly at six, put on a dinner jacket—"the only black coat and pleated shirtfront within five hundred miles," sniped one unimpressed colleague[76]—and dine with invited companions (usually General Funston) or, more often, by himself, at his reserved table under the crowded *portales*, or arcades, of the Diligencia. "In town he was Van Bibber, as he was Captain Macklin at the front," observed journalist Frederick Palmer. If alone, he would write letters to Bessie, to discourage interlopers from approaching. As insurance, he carried a large roll of cable blanks: if a "bore" threatened to sit down at his table, he would pretend to be composing urgent messages. "I *hate* people I don't like at my dinner and so I dine alone," he wrote Bessie. "And no one dares come near me."[77]

If he wished, however, he could be an amusing, self-deprecating com-

panion. In Veracruz, he befriended Chicago cartoonist John McCutcheon—the younger man thought their main bond was his long
acquaintance with Cecil Clark. McCutcheon was surprised to find Davis
"wholly congenial, friendly and unspoiled," and not, as advertised, "conceited, a little brother of the gods."[78] Certainly, wherever he went, he was
pointed out, his distinctive appearance making him a marked man. "He
dressed and looked the 'war correspondent,' such a one as he would describe in one of his stories," wrote McCutcheon. "He fulfilled the popular
ideal of what a member of that fascinating profession should look like. . . .
He carried his bath-tub, his immaculate linen, his evening clothes, his war
equipment—in which he had the pride of a connoisseur—wherever he
went. . . ."[79]

He had played the role of Richard Harding Davis so long that he
performed it instinctively. One afternoon, Palmer and Davis walked ten
miles under a blazing sun to visit a camp of marines. They had removed
their collars and swung their coats over their arms. Every inch of their
clothing was soaked through. As they neared the camp, Davis put his collar
back on, over Palmer's protests. "Everybody in camp will be dripping and
in negligée, too," Palmer said. "Why make yourself uncomfortable? You
are putting on too much style for the occasion." "Yes," Davis agreed. "But
you haven't my reputation of a good dresser to live up to." "Why not put
a flower in your buttonhole?" Palmer baited him. "It is not in regulation
to put a flower in the buttonhole of a military blouse," Davis replied calmly.
"I am a stickler for regulations."[80] It was the same self-deprecating humor
with which he had defused criticism of his flamboyant dress since childhood.
When the wife of the American *chargé d'affaires* poked fun at the blue
polka-dot Rough Rider puggaree that he wore on his hat, saying it was "the
loudest thing in town and can be spotted at any distance," Davis simply
chuckled and quipped: "But isn't recognition what is wanted in Mexico?"[81]

If he were simply showboating, his colleagues would have despised
Davis. However, the middle-aged celebrity worked as hard as any cub.
When the Wheeler Syndicate scheduled, through the Brazilian and English
ambassadors in Mexico City, an interview with Huerta in the capital,
Wheeler cabled to see if Davis would make the long, risky trip. His brief
reply came within two hours: "Leaving for Mexico City tomorrow afternoon
at three o'clock."[82] Less laconically, he wrote Charles: "The papers say they
have arranged for me to interview Huerta, but I doubt it. Anyway, there is
no news here. And the trip will be very interesting, and beautiful."[83]

It would also be very arduous for a gray-haired correspondent who
was no longer young. The journey to Mexico City was the first of a sequence
of physical shocks that Davis endured, as he pushed his weakening body
ever harder. Accompanied by Medill McCormick, a Chicago man writing
for the *Times* of London, and veteran war correspondent Frederick Palmer,
Davis left Veracruz by train on May 7. The reporters got as far as Paso del

Macho, where they were arrested and marched single file under the guard of four barefoot boys brandishing rifles and bayonets. "I have written many stories about Latin America and in them some one always gets shot against a stone wall," Davis wrote in his debonair newspaper account. "As we marched through the village I recalled this and it seemed to me I never had visited a place with so few houses and so many stone walls." He eyed his runty guards with contempt. "Isn't it about time we did something?" he called over his shoulder. Neither McCormick nor Palmer thought he was joking. "We don't want to be drawn into any Soldier of Fortune stuff, Dick," McCormick warned.

They were detained in a cell while a general decided their fate. He sent Palmer, who was carrying only an American passport, back to Veracruz. However, he was impressed by the letters from the British and Brazilian ambassadors in Mexico City that both Davis and McCormick were carrying. He let them proceed on a packed, freezing train that passed through the mountains. In Mexico City, they were immediately arrested and ordered to take the first train back to Veracruz, which was leaving in twenty-four hours. Having gone two days without decent food or berth, Davis protested irately until he was permitted to go to the Café Sylvain, a restaurant "the fame of which," he wrote, "had reached even Paris." If he failed to get his interview, he would at least get a good meal.

The drama of the correspondents' capture had been played up big in war-hungry newspapers starved for incidents. This was pure Hearstian sensation—"the journalism that acts"; but if Davis was bothered by it, he didn't say. Back in Veracruz, as soon as he filed his first-person account, he showed up in the bar of the *portales*, still in his dusty khakis, and, without another word of introduction to the crowd of newsmen, all of them painfully aware that he had made it to Mexico City, he asked nonchalantly, "Ever been to Sylvain?" "I hear the revolution ruined it," said one man willing to take the bait. "Down at the heel—awful," Richard responded, and he launched into the tale of how he had lost Palmer, missed Huerta, landed in the jug, and then found *the* place for champagne.[84]

Not until mid-June did his employers accept Davis's assessment that nothing newsworthy was likely to happen, and permit him to sail home. He returned to a wife shaken by nervous complaints and an intimidating mountain of bills. During the last stretch of Richard's Veracruz sojourn, Bessie fled the farm to escape the servants and the isolation and, on her doctors' advice, went to Atlantic City. Charlie tried to look in on her in Mount Kisco, but she rebuffed him, jealous of his closeness to her husband. "Poor soul, she is so much more her own enemy than any person I ever knew, and, suffers so much more than any of us guess," Richard wrote apologetically to Charlie. "We all know that jealousy is to those who observe it, the most hateful of diseases, but, none of us appreciate how cruel it is to the person who suffers from it. Not only the farm, but trying to pay off my debts has been a big strain on her, too. . . ."[85] She spent two weeks at a "milk farm" in Summit, New Jersey, drinking milk and bathing in it. The milk cure seemed to work: she gained ten pounds, her headaches disappeared, and she talked of going back into vaudeville; but two weeks later, the headaches had returned, with painful swelling around the eyes, and no doctor could supply a diagnosis.[86]

Since the pressure of managing a large house and staff was contributing to Bessie's mental distress, and the house was also the biggest drain on the family finances, Richard reluctantly faced up to the prospect of selling. "Money coming in, but debts also, and think must sell farm," he confided to his diary on June 25.[87] His financial position was so precarious that any unexpected expense could topple him. The latest scare had come the previous October, during the filming of *Soldiers of Fortune*. While Richard was in Cuba, his chauffeur had struck and injured a girl, and in the absence of auto insurance, Richard was personally liable. This was the second time his car had been in an accident. Back in 1909, his father-in-law, John Clark, had negotiated the settlement.[88] Now he was on his own, in the worst circumstances: the chauffeur, drunk, had run away after the accident. In February, Davis paid five hundred dollars in medical expenses, while waiting for the aggrieved family to estimate the lost wages of the convalescing victim. When they at last demanded a thousand dollars, he was relieved: he had feared a bill for five thousand dollars, which would have forced him to sell part of the farm.[89]

Such narrow escapes were better suited to the movie reels than to the domestic arrangements of a man of fifty. In July, Richard rode around the neighborhood, hunting for a smaller place, but saw nothing that would in any way console him for the loss of Crossroads.[90] He put off the decision. He was hoping that something unforeseen would occur, something that would make the house sale unnecessary.

12

Shrapnel,

Chivalry, Sauce Mousseline

*H*AVING JUST RETURNED FROM A DUD WAR, Richard squinted cynically at the ominous reports out of Europe in the summer of 1914. "Of course, the WAR is at it again, and, the same excitements of April," he wrote to Charles on July 29. "All the papers that had me in Mexico are wanting me again, and others. But, I said I would not go until someone hit someone, and not at all until the big powers got engaged."[1] On the very day he wrote those words, Austria declared war on Serbia and bombarded Belgrade. "I do hope only Servia and Austria will be in this," Richard wrote on July 31. "As I want to stay where I am."[2] The next day, Germany announced herself at war with Russia, and France mobilized her forces. The precarious peace of Europe, built on uneven timbers and riddled by secret diplomacy, was collapsing with horrifying force. On August 4, Great Britain declared war on Germany, and all of Europe was sucked into the conflagration.

Even as he was hoping for peace, Davis was arranging passage to England for himself and Bessie should war come. The small band of professional war correspondents, the men who smoked and sweated and complained together in Tokyo and Veracruz, now scurried to reach the theater of war. They sensed that this was it, the real thing; but they wondered if they would be permitted to see it. The glory days of the war correspondent were over. Writing an obituary of his short-lived vocation back in 1911, Davis noted that the first famous war correspondent—William Howard Russell, who covered the Crimean War for the *Times* of London in 1854—outlived his profession. While journalists would still be sent to wars, everything had changed. The quick transmission of news by cable provoked the nations at war into censoring and delaying each dispatch so "that it will furnish information neither to the enemy nor to any one else."[3] That was the painful lesson of the Russo-Japanese War.

The telegraph wires enmeshed correspondents in another way as well.

On the battlefield, Russell and his peers were beyond an editor's grasp. Now, Davis wrote, "the correspondent moved with a cable from the home office attached to his spinal column, jerking him this way and that." A war correspondent in the heroic era had been a man alone, racing dangerously to the battlefield without an official escort, shepherding his dispatch over hostile territory to mail it home. Davis's beau ideal was J. A. MacGahan, an American who traversed the frozen steppes and scorching deserts of Russia and Central Asia to join the Russian army on its campaign into Turkestan. In the modern age such men, even if they were still made, were no longer needed. The transmission of the news was the responsibility of a syndicate. What was required of the reporter was an eye for detail and the ability to write. Ever romantic, Davis bemoaned the diminution of his profession. Yet the talents currently desired were those he abundantly possessed, which was why he was the most famous and highly paid war correspondent in the world.

The snags and obstacles that confronted the war correspondent of 1914 were not very picturesque. He vied for bookings on the luxury ocean liners that would take him to the battlefront. He scrambled for a stash of gold dollars: the European crisis had closed down the stock exchanges and frozen the money supply, making letters of credit worthless. (Three banks in which Davis for years had maintained accounts refused him a hundred dollars in gold, or even—for whatever good it might have done him—a letter of credit.)[4] In the fiercest competition of all, the newsmen jockeyed for official credentials from the bureaucracy-heavy great powers. Each feared that unless he won one of the few available places, he would be prevented from witnessing the action later. The French were not yet permitting any reporters, even French ones, to visit their front lines. The British were a bit more accommodating, but not much: only one American reporter, to be selected by the U.S. government, would be accredited to the British army. Davis wanted to be the one. He had his publishers—the Wheeler Syndicate and the Scribners—petition the Wilson administration. However, after his escapade in Mexico, Davis was not very popular with the Wilson administration. The coveted slot went to Frederick Palmer. It would seem that the famous luck of Richard Harding Davis was giving out; but in fact, Palmer's plum proved to be a padlock, chaining him to the rear far behind the British lines, preventing him from seeing anything.[5]

The Wheeler Syndicate was paying Davis six hundred dollars a week plus expenses, and *Scribner's* contracted for four articles at a thousand dollars each.[6] To be sure of getting off, Richard double-booked passage on the *Lorraine* and the *St. Paul* for Bessie and himself. The Wheeler Syndicate agreed to foot Bessie's traveling expenses, and she wanted to accompany Richard as far as she could. To her general nervousness and her dislike of pastoral solitude, there was an added cause for skittishness: she was five months pregnant. With her doctor's approval, she yearned for a last fling before her confinement. So it was with a pregnant wife and twenty-five hundred dollars in gold double eagles but no official credentials that Richard sailed from New York on August 4. Despite their alternative bookings, the Davises went on a third ship, the *Lusitania*, the pride of the British Cunard line. They chose the *Lusitania* because it was destined for England, where Richard could settle Bessie and check on the well-being of his sister, Nora. Also, the accommodations on the *Lusitania* were unsurpassed: he and Bessie occupied a royal suite, which in peacetime cost a thousand dollars.[7]

Davis didn't learn for certain that he had been denied credentials until he reached London. This self-described "stickler for regulations" agonized not a moment about the ethics of eluding Allied censorship. He thought it outrageous that democratically elected governments would presume to wage war in secret. Once he found London lodgings for Bessie, he arranged to travel to Brussels with Gerald Morgan, an American veteran of Veracruz and Tokyo who was representing the London *Daily Telegraph*. In the first days of the war, German troops had surprised the world by sweeping from the north into neutral Belgium, heading first for Brussels and then for France. Davis would go unofficially in an attempt to witness the German advance.

Reporters were streaming into Brussels as the tourists fled. Like other American journalists, Davis was welcomed into the home of the American minister, Brand Whitlock, a former Radical mayor of Toledo, Ohio, who was tall, lanky, and, in his tortoise-shell glasses, sensitive-looking. Brussels was a city of contradictions. At the Palace Hotel, where Davis occupied a huge room and bath, the lights blazed at night and the sidewalk cafés were full. However, signs of the impending war were everywhere: in the Boy Scouts directing traffic to replace the men at arms, in the Red Cross nurses and English aviators impatiently waiting to be sent to the front, in the private automobiles filled with ammunition and chalked "For His Majesty."

The war was a short drive away. In the past, Davis had followed war into the mountains of Greece, the jungles of Cuba, the veldt of South Africa, and the milletfields of Manchuria; but never had he seen it fought so close to civilization.[8] Each morning, he would leave his hotel and, with Morgan, ride in a hired automobile toward the front, studying the morning papers like racing forms to decide where to go. They carried French, Belgian, and Russian flags; as soon as they spotted an army, they raised the appropriate banner and pursued at sixty miles an hour. They would pass women harvesting the grain, and whitewashed houses with red-tiled roofs, and pear trees bent over with fruit. When they lost the trail or blew a tire, they would stop for an omelette washed down with red wine. At night, they would return to the city, to enameled bathtubs, shaded electric lights, and iced champagne, and watch the nightlife promenade past.

On such a night, two days after he arrived, Davis saw the first crowd of refugees enter Brussels, wearing wooden shoes and balancing bundles.

From their midst the word rippled out: "The Germans! The Germans are at Louvain!" That was inconceivable. Davis had cabled to his home office that afternoon that there were no Germans near Louvain, which was less than twenty miles to the northeast. "Refugees always talk like that," said the correspondents.

In his hotel room the next morning, August 19, Davis awoke to the sound of honking horns and speeding automobiles, all heading northwest, toward Ghent, Bruges, and the coast. By nine the traffic had tripled. By ten the horns and sirens "issued one long, continuous scream," the roar of a gale, the sound of panic. From the front of the hotel, Davis could see the taxis, limousines, and sports cars full of the women and children of the rich. When he walked out, he found the side streets jammed with peasant carts and well-to-do carriages. Davis's eye, ever attuned to niceties of dress, noticed that the servants on the box of a carriage were dressed in the disordered livery in which they served dinner, and the grooms and footmen, although coatless, still wore striped waistcoats and silver buttons.

Watching from their little iron tables on the sidewalks, the people of Brussels were unperturbed. The Germans are no nearer than Liège, they repeated to each other. But Whitlock, the American minister, knew better. On his advice, most Americans in Brussels moved their belongings to a hotel opposite the legation. Not taking any chances, Davis reserved for his own use a green leather sofa in the legation itself. The city seemed unchanged, except that the Belgian officers and the English correspondents (whom the Germans would have arrested) could no longer be seen in the cafés. Even the next morning, August 20, the shops opened and the streets were crowded. The people did not yet know that, overnight, the king of Belgium had sent word to surrender, and that the gendarmes were turning in their rifles and their uniforms. At ten, "as if a wand had waved," the boulevards emptied and the houses closed behind their shutters. And then, an hour later, the advance guard of the German army came down the Boulevard Waterloo: a captain and two privates on bicycles, rifles slung across their shoulders, looking as carefree as tourists. Behind them, so close together that one couldn't cross the street, followed the mounted Uhlans, the infantry, and the guns. Returning to his hotel, Davis dashed off a six-hundred-word dispatch and entrusted it to a woman bound for Ostend.[9] He then returned to the center of town to watch the Germans.

He gazed at the procession for two hours until, cross-eyed from the monotony of it, he retreated to his hotel. An hour passed, and he could still hear the army rumbling below. Two hours passed, and boredom gave way to wonder. For the rest of the day, he watched, and all night, in his bed, he listened. The next day he sent off a dispatch that became a legend of war reporting.[10]

"The entrance of the German army into Brussels has lost the human quality," he began. At the time of his writing, this gray-green torrent had been flowing through the Belgian capital for twenty-six hours. It was like a tidal wave, an avalanche, or—the inevitable Davis simile when describing a disaster—like the swollen waters of the Conemaugh Valley that swept through Johnstown. At first, this lack of human quality had glazed his reporter's eye, which was trained to pick out the bits of human interest; but then, the total absence of human aspect gripped him with an uncanny fascination. He was watching an army, but he could have been studying the fog as it rolled over the sea. "The gray of the uniforms worn by both officers and men helped this air of mystery," he wrote. "Only the sharpest eye could detect among the thousands that passed the slightest difference. All moved under a cloak of invisibility. Only after the most numerous and severe tests at all distances, with all materials and combinations of colors that give forth no color could this gray have been discovered. . . . It is the gray of the hour just before daybreak, the gray of unpolished steel, of mist among green trees. I saw it first in the Grand Place in front of the Hotel de Ville. It was impossible to tell if in that noble square there was a regiment or a brigade. You saw only a fog that melted into the stones, blended with the ancient house fronts, that shifted and drifted, but left you nothing at which you could point."

It was a distinguishing characteristic, a thumbprint of Davis's reporting style, to dwell on people's clothing. In his maturity, he had become a little self-conscious about this point. "If I appear to overemphasize this disguising uniform," he wrote defensively, "it is because of all the details of the German outfit it appealed to me as one of the most remarkable." The selection of this disappearing color was but an example (albeit a favorite example) of the ways in which the Germans had mustered the best equipped and best organized army that Davis had ever encountered. When the secretary of the American legation joined him on the sidelines and consulted him as a martial expert, he confessed that, while he thought he knew the last word in war equipment, much of what he was seeing he had never seen before.[11] Even to the most ignorant eye, however, the German army presented a picture of perfect discipline. After three weeks on active service, the soldiers displayed not a chinstrap nor a horseshoe missing. As they marched, cooks prepared meals on rolling stoves and distributed the steaming-hot food. Post-office carts fell out of the column to deliver letters and collect postcards. On motortrucks, cobblers mended boots and farriers beat out horseshoes. The infantrymen sang "Fatherland, My Fatherland," and between each line of the song, they took three steps. At times there were two thousand men singing in perfect harmony; their iron-clad boots clanged in unison against the granite street.

He lacked the time for careful composition in his hotel room in Brussels. But when he revised the story for *Scribner's*, Davis tried to suggest in his prose the repetitive, crushing impact of the German march through the city: "All through the night, like the tumult of a river when it races between the cliffs of a canyon, in my sleep I could hear the steady roar of the passing army. . . . This was a machine, endless, tireless, with the delicate organization of a watch and the brute power of a steam-roller. And for three days and three nights through Brussels it roared and rumbled, a cataract of molten lead. The infantry marched singing, with their iron-shod boots beating out the time. In each regiment there were two thousand men and at the same instant, in perfect unison, two thousand iron brogans struck the granite street. It was like the blows from giant pile-drivers. The Uhlans followed, the hoofs of their magnificent horses ringing like thousands of steel hammers breaking stones in a road; and after them the giant siege-guns rumbling, growling, the mitrailleuse with drag-chains clanking, the field-pieces with creaking axles, complaining brakes, the grinding of the steel-rimmed wheels against the stones echoing and re-echoing from the house-front. When at night for an instant the machine halted, the silence awoke you, as at sea you wake when the screw stops. For three days and three nights the column of gray, with fifty thousand bayonets and fifty thousand lances, with gray transport wagons, gray ammunition-carts, gray ambulances, gray cannon, like a river of steel cut Brussels in two."[12]

With its impressionistic splashes of evocative details and its onomato-poetic play of language, Davis's description of the German entry into Brussels was an instant classic, and it has been anthologized and excerpted ever since. A dozen years afterward, his onetime rival Frederick Palmer declared it "unsurpassed among bits of classic war description."[13] Another colleague proclaimed it "the most vivid piece of writing of the war."[14] What the anthology readers can't appreciate is Davis's adroitness in getting the original newspaper dispatch out of Brussels. The Germans forbade reporters to depart until the army had passed through. To elude this three-day blackout, Davis found an English boy—shades of Jaggers—who agreed to take the manuscript (plus a letter to Bessie) to Ostend. E. A. Dalton was the boy's name. At dusk on Friday, he left the capital on the road to Ghent, a road jammed with lines of German infantry. Despite many detours and a difficult mile in which he crept in the undergrowth by the roadside for fear of discovery, he was arrested three times. At midnight, he returned to Brussels in defeat, and Davis sent him off for a second try with the American deputy consul. This time, Dalton succeeded. He reached Ostend and boarded a government refugee boat to Folkestone. From there, he quickly arrived at the *Tribune*'s London office on Sunday with Davis's copy.[15]

The Germans entered Brussels on the day that Davis, through Whit-lock's intercession, was to receive press credentials from the Belgian govern-ment. Unfortunately, the government had fled to Antwerp without leaving behind papers for the celebrated American correspondent. Gerald Morgan was in the same fix. Both reporters had passes from General Thaddeus von

Jarotzky, the new German military governor of Brussels, permitting them to go through German military lines in Brussels and its environs. But how far did the "environs" extend? Hearing rumors that the French and English were already in Belgium and that the English had reached Halle and fought Germans there, the Americans decided to put it to the test by driving the eleven miles to Halle.[16]

On Saturday, August 22, they rehearsed by driving out of town and scouting the road. The next day, in a taxi, they rode to Halle, intending to leave the taxi there and set out on foot to try to join the Allied armies. But when they reached Halle, a German officer rode up to the taxi brandishing an automatic and placed them under arrest. He ordered four wounded soldiers to guard them, and all of them climbed into the cab. Were the Americans actually under arrest? It was hard to be certain. They drove until the street became too narrow to contain both the cab and the regiment; and then the wounded soldiers left the car and disappeared. Davis paid the cabman and, with Morgan, followed the regiment as openly as possible. They hoped that their candor would demonstrate their innocence. The column extended for fifty miles. Clearly, there had been no battle at Halle. To judge from the army's behavior, no battle was expected.

At noon the army halted at Brierges. They were unquestionably outside the environs of Brussels. "If we go any farther, the next officer who reads our papers will order us back to Brussels under arrest, and we will lose our *laissez-passer*," Morgan argued. "Along this road there is no chance of seeing anything. I prefer to keep my pass and use it in 'environs' where there is fighting." Davis wanted to turn back, too. He decided, however, that he should keep going until he could report that he had been ordered back by "Colonel This" or "General That." It would add a smattering of color to a drab tale. He would later rue this vanity.

Soon after Morgan left, Davis, eating a sandwich beneath a tree by the side of the road, was taken prisoner by four German soldiers carrying automatics. One jabbed him in the stomach with a revolver and brought him to a colonel who had just finished lunch in a café. The colonel gave the soldier a drink for making the arrest, and Davis a drink for being arrested. He wrote on Davis's passport permission to proceed to Enghien, which was two miles away. No more than two hundred yards further, Davis was arrested again but allowed to continue to Enghien. He went there, planning to stay overnight and continue in the morning. It seemed he could continue indefinitely, perhaps following the German army to the gates of Paris. His reception at Enghien should have warned him to turn back. The Germans scowled at him. The Belgians winked at him. The owner of the town's only hotel called him "suspect" and wouldn't give him a room. Davis went to the burgomaster, who wrote him a pass authorizing him to spend one night at Enghien. "You really do not need this," he said, "as an American you are free to stay here as long as you wish." He winked. "But I am an

American," Davis insisted. "But certainly," the burgomaster said gravely, and winked again.

You could hardly blame them for thinking he was a spy. He certainly looked the part, as he perched on a mossy stone bridge until nightfall, watching wave after gray wave of the German army. The next morning he sat on his bed, wondering whether to continue. He still wanted someone in authority to order him to turn back. So at six, thinking he was on the road to Soignies, he went off, a speck on the fast-flowing German stream. He greeted a group of German officers seated by the road, and they returned his hello. A hundred yards down the road, he was stopped by one of them, who had galloped ahead to ask for his papers. With relief, he handed them over. Finally he would be ordered back to Brussels. He calculated that if he found a taxi at Halle, he could be at the Palace Hotel in time for lunch. "I think you had better see our general," the captain said. "He is ahead of us." Thinking the captain meant a few hundred yards ahead, Davis was secretly pleased that it would be a general ordering him back.

He was placed in the ranks and for the next five hours forced to advance at a steady trot. He now realized that he had surprised the army in a surprise maneuver. These men had been marching at this speed for two days. Many of them seemed semicomatose. During their frequent halts, they would drop to the stony ground as if hit by clubs, some instantly falling asleep. At this rate, the column could cover thirty miles a day. They passed a wrecked British airplane, surrounded by German staff officers. Davis's papers were given to them, but Davis was not permitted to speak. He continued marching with the column. A few minutes later, the officers in their automobiles passed on their way to the front. With them went Davis's papers. Whether or not that was a misfortune, it was hard to say. Since he was miles beyond the environs of Brussels, the papers incriminated more than they exonerated. He had obviously disobeyed orders.

At noon, a very blond, very distinguished-looking officer wearing a monocle came speeding back from the front. In perfect and polite English, he asked Davis to come with him to the general staff. For the first time, Davis realized his danger. They were paying much too much attention to him. Before entering the car, he decided upon his strategy: feign total ignorance. "It was really too stupid of me," he gushed apologetically. "I cannot forgive myself. I should not have come so far without asking Jarotzky for proper papers. I am extremely sorry I have given you this trouble. I would like to see the general and assure him I will return at once to Brussels." He did not allude to the fact that he was being taken to the general at sixty miles an hour. The blond officer smiled uneasily and examined the sky through his monocle.

At headquarters, the staff were lunching, some in their luxurious automobiles, others on the roadside. In their dress uniforms, gloves, and flowing cloaks, they were a superior race to the dusty gray men marching by, and they knew it. Whenever they spoke, they saluted, heels clicking, waists bending. They reminded Davis of priests breathing incense. As he stood in the middle of the road, he was approached by a dark young man, handsome and smooth-shaven, in a tight uniform of light blue and silver, with high patent-leather boots. Lithe and slender-waisted, he bowed, shrugged, and gesticulated as he spoke in perfect English. He had been charged with disposing of Davis's case. "You are an English officer out of uniform," he began. "You have been taken inside our lines." He pointed his index finger at Davis's stomach and wiggled his thumb. "And you know what *that* means!" Davis abandoned the role of the fool at once. "I followed your army because it's my business to follow armies," he said, "and because yours is the best-looking army I ever saw." The young officer bowed and grinned mockingly. "We thank you," he said. "But you have seen too much." "I haven't seen anything that everybody in Brussels hasn't seen for three days," Davis retorted. The German shook his head and pointed to the group of officers. "You have seen enough in this road to justify us in shooting you now." With that exit line, he rejoined the group.

Only now Davis realized that at Enghien he had taken the wrong road. The Belgians had painted out the names on the signposts to confuse the Germans, but it was the American reporter who was fooled. Instead of going southeast to Soignies, Davis had headed southwest toward Ath. In so doing, he had stumbled across the German army making a quick turning movement to surprise the English. The Germans thought he was a British spy who had followed them from Brussels and now wanted to slip back to warn his fellows. They assumed that by seeing the Count de Schwerin, commander of the Seventh Division, on the road to Ath, he knew that the army corps of which the Seventh was a part had separated from the main army and was speeding south to attack the English flank at Mons.

For the rest of the day, the Germans argued over his fate. The handsome young officer wanted him shot. His prosecutorial points: Davis's pass was merely stamped, not signed, by a German commander in Brussels; his American passport had been issued not in Washington but in London; and in his passport photograph, he was wearing a British officer's uniform. The uniform in the picture was most damning. Davis explained that the photograph was eight years old. In it, he displayed a uniform that he had first seen on the west coast of Africa, worn by the West African Field Force. It was unlike any known uniform and as cool as a golf jacket, so he had had it copied. Since then, however, it had been adopted by the English Brigade of Guards and the Territorials. His adversary smiled with delight. "Do you expect us to believe that?" he asked. "Listen," Davis replied. "If you could invent an explanation for that uniform as quickly as I told you that one, standing in a road with eight officers trying to shoot you, you would be the greatest general in Germany." The others laughed.

"Very well, then, we will concede that the entire British army has changed its uniform to suit your photograph," said his prosecutor. "But if you are *not* an officer, why, in the photograph, are you wearing war ribbons?" It was a question that Davis answered with enthusiasm. "They prove that I *am* a correspondent," he argued, "for only a correspondent could have been in wars in which his own country was not engaged." "Or a military attaché," said his adversary, trumping him instantly, as the others smiled and nodded. Accusingly, the officer then pointed to the clothes in which Davis was now dressed. They were English, he charged. Indeed, they were, but they were unmarked, so the Germans could not be sure. As for the felt Alpine hat—Richard couldn't remember whether he had bought it in London or New York. He took if off and fanned himself but didn't dare to inspect it. Then a German plane passed overhead. As the others looked up, he quickly glanced inside the hat and saw, to his relief, "Knox, New York" stamped in gold on the leather. He returned it to his head and removed it a few minutes later, saying, "If I were an Englishman would I cross the ocean to New York to buy a hat?"

How like a Richard Harding Davis story, for the suspect to be implicated and exculpated by his clothes! The gimmick was as old as "Gallegher." Recognizing a good yarn when they heard one, Knox Hats later produced an advertising flyer with a dashing picture of Davis being quizzed by two black-moustached, spike-helmeted brutes and the slogan "That hat saved him . . . a hat 'made in America' with a prestige so great in foreign lands that in the critical period of a great war it serves as a pass-port to safety."[17] In real life, sadly, Davis's freedom did not emerge magically from the hat.

Whispering frequently among themselves, the Germans appeared to be divided. The youthful prosecutor wanted him shot. Others argued that he was stupid but harmless. They decided to refer the case to the general of the army corps, who was still a long drive off. Placing Davis in an automobile, they went to Ath, and then five miles south to the village of Ligne, all the time straying further and further from the "environs" of Brussels. In Ligne, confined to a stone-floored room with whitewashed walls, under the distrustful eye of an itchy-fingered guard, Davis bound his foot, badly cut on the instep during his forced march, and bathed, shaved, and donned dry clothes to look better for his meeting with the general. A German reservist who had studied at an American university spoke to him sympathetically. "What nonsense!" the German said earnestly. "Any one could tell by your accent that you are an American! The staff are making a mistake. They will regret it." Saying that he hoped to avoid regrets and mistakes, Davis gave the man a letter addressed to Brand Whitlock, written in the most familiar style. It was aimed not at the American minister but at Davis's German captors, who he was sure would read it. The friendly German kept saying that he thought Davis would be set free, but as he spoke, tears rolled down his cheeks. It was very disconcerting.

At nightfall, the reservist brought a candle and left, taking the guard with him. Alone for the first time, Davis sorted through his knapsack, looking for any incriminating items. His notebook was uncontroversial. His only other paper had been on his mind all day: a letter of introduction from Theodore Roosevelt to President Poincaré of France. Roosevelt was much admired by the kaiser; but Poincaré? Unsure if the letter would be his vindication or his death warrant, Davis chose to keep it in reserve until the last moment.

Escape was impossible. Even if he could bribe his way past the sentries, the German staff held his passport and his *laissez-passer*. Without documents, he couldn't go a hundred yards. The plan he devised, and expressed to the friendly German reservist, was this: give him a pass to Brussels, stating that he was a suspected spy. If he was found off the direct road to Brussels—and if he was not in Brussels reporting to the military governor by midnight, August 26, two days hence—he could be shot on sight. Since passes were checked constantly, he would be as much a prisoner on the road as he was in this room. It was fifty miles to Brussels. As a civilian could not hire a bicycle, automobile, or cart, he would have to walk as fast as he could. The reservist endorsed this scheme vociferously, and suggested that Davis might be able to hitchhike on a truck or ambulance returning to Brussels. He left, and Davis never saw him again.

Night fell, and nothing happened. As it grew later, Davis persuaded himself that nothing would happen until morning. He stretched himself out on a bundle of straw that the Germans had tossed on the floor. At midnight he was roused suddenly by the beam of an electric flashlight. It was strapped to the chest of a guard who spoke only German and angrily ordered Davis to come with him. As he ventured out beneath the black sky, Davis thought there could be only one reason to take him out in the middle of the night.

In silence, they entered an automobile and drove down a country road, until they reached a grand château in a huge park. Its electric lights weren't working; it was lit only by candles. Inside, some soldiers slept in the hall on bundles of wheat, while others charged up and down the marble staircase. Davis was seated in the hall on a huge silk-and-gilt armchair, between two gray soldiers. Whenever the doors of the drawing room opened, he could see a long table, illuminated by silver candlesticks, strewn with many maps and open bottles of champagne. Around the table, standing and seated, were brilliantly uniformed staff officers, much older and higher ranking than any Davis had seen. They were eating, drinking, gesticulating, leaning over the maps; and some, despite the tumult, were sleeping, totally exhausted. It was out of a painting from the Franco-Prussian War, thought Davis, whose mind even in extremity was always alert to the picturesque.

He had come at an inopportune moment. The Germans had been surprised, and seemed close to panic. *"Die Englischen kommen!"* someone shouted. Officers carrying electric flashlights rushed in and out to make their reports. Richard was almost relieved when the young German officer who was his nemesis emerged from the drawing room. *"Mr. Davis,"* he began—he always emphasized "Mr. Davis" to show that he knew it wasn't a real name—*"Mr. Davis,* you are free." As he seemed cheerful, Richard waited. "You are free under certain conditions." The conditions seemed to raise his spirits. They were the ones Davis had devised, no doubt proposed by the friendly reservist as an original idea. Without his intercession . . . it was better not to think about it.

With a charming smile, the sadistic officer added: "And you will start in three hours!" "At three in the morning!" Davis cried. "You might as well take me out and shoot me now!" "You will start in three hours," the officer repeated with a grin. "A man wandering around at that hour wouldn't live five minutes," Davis protested. "It can't be done. *You* couldn't do it." "You will start in three hours, *Mr. Davis.*" The prisoner was put back in the automobile and driven to his improvised cell in Ligne. He paced the room until a little after three, and then tiptoed down the stairs, expecting to be challenged by sentries. They had gone. As he reached the garden of the totally dark house, a voice spoke to him in French. It was the owner of the house. "The animals have gone, all of them," he said. "I will give you a bed now, and when it is light you shall have breakfast." Davis said that he had been ordered to leave at three. "But it is murder!" the Belgian cried. With those encouraging words in his ears, Davis stepped out.

In his left hand, he held a matchbox and the pass, folded to display the red seal of the general staff. In his right hand were a couple of ready matches. Halted by a sentry, he would strike a match quickly and raise it to the seal. Speaking no German, he could do no more; but each time the match flashed, he feared the sentry would shoot. After repeating this maneuver three times, he lost his nerve and took cover behind a haystack until dawn. In daylight, the march to Ath was less threatening, though hardly pleasant. The sentries waved him through as soon as they saw the seal. The officers, who could read, cursed him and ordered him on. Twice they searched his knapsack; after the second time, he removed Roosevelt's letter, tore it up into tiny pieces, and swallowed it. Any Belgian peasants that he approached for food or assistance fled in fear, believing him to be German. Lacking food and sleep, limping on his bloody foot, he realized by noon that he would not be able to make it.

So he waited for the next German car headed toward Brussels. Flagging it down, he held up his pass. The red seal performed its magic. Without bothering to read the pass, an old, kindly-looking general who spoke no English and little French invited him to climb in next to him. They were going to Halle. Walking, he had hoped to reach Halle the next day. Now he would be there within two hours. "It was a situation I would not have used in fiction," he later wrote.[18] To his diary, he confided: "It was God's gift."[19] At Halle, the steps of the Hotel de Ville were crowded with generals in flowing cloaks and spiked helmets. Richard feared them. His general, too, seemed annoyed. "I am going on to Brussels," the general said. "Desire you to accompany me?" In dazed gratitude, Davis rode into Brussels, sighting the Palais de Justice with the emotions one reserves for the Statue of Liberty. Not until he reached the inner boulevards did he feel entirely safe. Bidding goodbye to his general, he went at once, unwashed and unshaven, powdered gray with dust from head to toe, to see Whitlock. Later Whitlock escorted him to the offices of General the Baron Arthur von Lutwitz, who had just assumed command of the city. Whitlock assured the general that Davis was not an English spy, but—as the secretary of the American legation quipped—"on the contrary, probably the greatest writer that ever lived, not excepting Shakespeare or Milton." The general, having read some of Davis's short stories, promptly cleared the American's honor.[20] But Davis seemed to have aged several years in the space of three days.[21]

There was no reason to stay in Brussels. German censors embargoed all dispatches until their news value was lost. Smuggling manuscripts out with travelers to Holland sometimes worked (as it had with Dalton), but usually not. On top of this, the American legation had heard a rumor that all neutral correspondents in Belgium were to be arrested and deported to Germany.[22] It would be best to leave immediately. The way out was on empty troop trains returning to Aachen (Aix-la-Chapelle), just over the German border; and from Aachen, to Holland and freedom. Luckily for the reporters, the route passed through the old Belgian town of Louvain— a fact which made the trip irresistible. In Brussels that morning, the military governor told Whitlock and Davis that rooftop snipers in Louvain had fired the day before on German troops, killing and wounding fifty. Louvain was to be destroyed in retribution. Davis drove off for the station in a *fiacre*. "It was drawn by the sorriest pair of nags I ever saw, and yet he sat there as calm and distinguished as if he were driving up Fifth Avenue," observed Whitlock, who wrote fiction in his spare time. "And I thought of Van Bibber, and of how the Avenue looks in the late afternoon when the throngs are going up Murray Hill. Ah, me! Did that gay insouciance still exist anywhere in the world?"[23]

The trip from Brussels to the German border normally took three hours. The train that left at midday on August 27 didn't arrive in Aachen until twenty-six hours later. Along with Davis, it carried Gerald Morgan, Will Irwin of *Collier's*, Arno Dosch-Fleurot of *World's Work* (later of the New York *World*), and Mary Boyle O'Reilly. Forbidden to leave the train, unable to obtain food and water, barred from the carriages with cushions (which were reserved for wounded German soldiers), the American correspondents slept on wooden benches and on the floor. The journey was uncomfortable, but "the chief irritation," Irwin thought, "was the mood and behavior of Richard Harding Davis," which he found "shockingly, incredibly rude." Sulky and surly when depressed, Davis walled himself off from his companions. "True, he had been through a shattering experience the day before, and his nerves must have been still shaky," wrote Irwin, bridling at the memory almost thirty years later. "But that hardly excuses the general discourtesy toward us."[24]

Ten miles from Brussels they saw the first burning houses.[25] They reached Louvain at seven in the evening. It was a town that Davis had admired ten days before. Its narrow, twisting streets were lined with smart shops and cafés. Its white-walled, green-shuttered, red-roofed houses were set in flower gardens. Its ancient university had been a Jesuit center. Its Church of Saint Pierre dated from the fifteenth century, and its five-hundred-year-old Gothic town hall, recently restored, was more famous than that of Bruges or Brussels. As the train pulled into the platform of Louvain, the reporters were ordered not to leave the train. But even before they reached Louvain, the story could be plainly seen in the flames that lit the evening sky.

The heart of the city was a smoldering ruin, from which sparks rose and fell in leisurely columns. Excited soldiers rushed through the station, drunk from destruction as well as from liquor. Some carried candles, and the officers bore searchlights; there was no electricity, because the power station had been destroyed. "English?" one soldier shouted at the correspondents. "Americans from the United States," said Dosch-Fleurot in German. "We are not enemies." "All who do not speak German well are enemies," the soldier replied, loosening his revolver. The reporters looked about in concern for a superior officer, afraid to say one more word in bad German. But as soon as the belligerent lout freed his revolver, another soldier noticed and pushed him aside, saying, "He's drunk."

They turned their gaze to the more ominous tableau outside the window. The Louvain station was situated alongside the town square, where a long line of about 150 civilians was being assembled in a circle. Here and there one was ordered to step forward. Watching this firelit pantomime, the reporters couldn't determine the criteria for selection, but the purpose was all too clear. At that moment their view was blocked by two soldiers leading a cow to the station entrance. Then one soldier-butcher thrust his bayonet into the cow's neck; as the animal collapsed, the reporters could see again. In the square, a dozen civilians were bunched to one side, and the others were being led past them. Dosch-Fleurot spotted one soldier on the platform who was watching the scene, alone among the hundreds passing through the station. He asked what was happening. "Oh, those are some of the people who came back to town to snipe again," the soldier said. "We caught them here in the ruins and are going to shoot some of them." His tone was nonchalant and detached. Outside, the civilians had completed the circuit, and the doomed dozen were led off to the right, followed by a firing squad. A few minutes later, there were shots. "Hear that," said the soldier. "What did I tell you?" Meanwhile, in a phantasmago-ric, candlelit scene by the train, two soldiers were skinning and carving up the cow. A pool of blood spread on the platform.[26]

Their train pulled out of Louvain an hour later. As the glow faded from the windows, Davis stretched out full length between the seats of the compartment and told the others to put their feet on him. After a long, sleepless night, they arrived in Aachen and received military passes to Maastricht in the Netherlands, where they stayed overnight while waiting for a train to the coast. Exploring the town while the others slept, Dosch-Fleurot was arrested and escorted back to the hotel by a policeman. The Dutch, who were fiercely guarding their neutrality, sent the policeman back to the hotel the next day to chaperone the reporters out of the country. Davis promptly commandeered him as a sort of valet—to reserve seats in the train, and, when they changed trains at Boxtel, to find the best restaurant for lunch. (Davis explained later that he was so fatigued, he mistook the policeman for a railroad porter, and wondered idly over the next two days why the Dutch porters in each town looked exactly alike.) As lunch was being prepared, Dosch-Fleurot took a tour of Boxtel with Davis. Dosch-Fleurot—who was, in Davis's phrase, "a Socialist of the Harvard school"—was fascinated by the older man. He found Davis to be "a strange mixture, a superb snob with a romantic soul." Passing a stagnant canal, Dosch-Fleurot remarked that the Dutch seemed to wash everything, but they washed it all with dirty water. Davis gazed scornfully at the youngster. "Don't look at the dirt," he said. "Admire the picturesque. That's what I do, and that is why I am getting a thousand dollars a week and you are getting—whatever it is you are getting."[27]

Davis demonstrated another reason for his success late in the day, when the reporters reached Flushing (now Vlissingen). The ship to Folkestone was crammed with passengers. Davis walked up to the purser's desk, where a dozen people were clamoring for cabins. He returned with two keys, giving one of them to Dosch-Fleurot and Irwin, keeping a single cabin for himself. "What luck," said Dosch-Fleurot, thanking him.

"Not at all," Davis replied. "I wired for them."

"But still, in this crowd," the other man persisted.

Davis leaned over, smiling. "I signed my wire," he said, "Sir Richard Davis."[28]

On the passage over, Davis wrote a heated story vilifying the Germans for burning Louvain, and he fantasized about his reunion with Bessie, who had been waiting for him in London all this time. He had cabled her at each stop of the three-day journey out of Brussels, wiring last from Folkestone to request a supper of cold meat and champagne. Arriving at her hotel, he saw the light in her room and bounded in. To his dismay, he found no cold meat, no champagne, and no Bessie. Instead there was the hotelkeeper, tearfully holding the Folkestone telegram. Very few of his cables had gotten through; and, unfortunately, the last one that had reached Bessie informed her that he could not return in time, because the Germans were not allowing trains out of Brussels. That had all changed—but she could not know. She was already at sea, on her way home.[29]

The reunion was the one thing he had been looking forward to. His contract with the Wheeler Syndicate until October 1 stretched before him as a sentence that he must serve out, trying to cover a war that he was not permitted to see. Then he could go home, to his wife and farm. In the meantime, he would do his best to rouse Americans out of torpid neutrality by describing the horrors that he had seen the Germans perpetrate. He would report this war as he had the ones in Cuba and South Africa: as a struggle between the right and the wrong. He had a distinctive double vision, detecting details and fragments that others overlooked and then placing them, like bits of stained glass, in a large simple framework. He had long disliked the Germans, at least as far back as 1896, when he wrote of "the envy and uncharitableness of the Austrian and German mind."[30] He would not pretend to the slightest "objectivity" in reporting this war. The day after arriving in London, he wrote a virulently anti-German dispatch. This sentence conveys its tone: "When a mad dog runs amuck in a village it is the duty of every farmer to get his gun and destroy it, not to lock himself indoors and preserve toward the dog and those who face him a neutral mind."[31] Winston Churchill, who for his first World War was serving in the Office of the Admiralty, wired Davis his congratulations and thanks. From New York, though, Richard received a less enthusiastic telegram from the head of the Wheeler Syndicate. Wheeler tried to avoid offending Davis, but under the circumstances, that was a futile hope. "Though anti-German and deeply appreciating your viewpoint, papers for obvious reasons request you be neutral if possible, letting your wonderful pen pictures [of] what you have seen as at Louvain point moral," Wheeler beseeched him.

Sickened by what he had seen and exhausted by what he had endured, Davis was not in a receptive mood for criticism. He fired back this hot-tempered response: "Tell Tribune and other papers of your syndicate dictation unexpected. My articles will continue [to] be anti-German. They can go to name of place censored. Sorry if [I] have embarrassed you. If you desire, release you from contract tonight." The syndicate backed down hurriedly, assuring Davis that the *Tribune* opposed Germany in its editorials, but that the papers were "having awful time with German population." All the same, the syndicate was "not slightest embarrassed" and had "no desire release you."[32] To Bessie, Richard wrote bitterly: "As I am not interested in the German vote, or in advertising of German breweries (such a hard word to *say*), I thought, considering the *exclusive* stories I had sent them, instead of kicking, they ought to be sending me a few bouquets. . . .

Considering that without credentials I was with French, Belgian and German armies and saw entry of Germans into Brussels and sacking of Louvain and got arrested as a spy, they were a bit ungrateful. I am now wondering *what* I would have seen *had I had* credentials."[33]

There was nothing to see in London, of course. It was simply a rest. "Never in all my years, have I felt so rushed," Richard wrote Charles. "I did not sleep at all for one week, and I have not caught up yet. . . . It is the hardest game I ever played; it moves so fast and is so vast."[34] Although he had written many stories, full of color and human interest and suffering, none of them described any actual *fighting*. For a war correspondent, that was a serious omission. He departed for Paris on September 8, hoping—despite his lack of credentials—to witness action on the front before going home.

Paris in wartime was beautiful but lifeless. The theaters and most of the famous shops were shuttered, the streets were empty. Fleeing the approaching Germans, the government had moved to Bordeaux. The men had been mobilized into the army, the wealthier families had packed up their households and retreated. "Paris is like one of those Newport palaces out of season," Davis wrote. "The owners have temporarily closed it; the windows are barred, the furniture and paintings draped in linen, a caretaker and a night watchman are in possession."[35] Davis checked into the imperial suite of the Hotel de l'Empire, where he had once stayed with Cecil for 49 francs, or $9.80, a day. The rate now was 8 francs. (On the other hand, a chicken dinner cost 12 francs, and rolls—thought to be an inefficient use of flour—were unavailable.)[36] Gerald Morgan was in Paris, along with Ellis Ashmead-Bartlett, a sharp-eyed, sharp-witted Englishman, and Granville Fortescue, another old friend, who had fought with the Rough Riders and served as an American military attaché with the Japanese army at Port Arthur. None of them could obtain credentials, none had anything to do. The French officials made only one concession: they provided each reporter with a little round permit issued by the general staff, which authorized the bearer to go twice a day to headquarters for the official bulletin.

Gerald Morgan ventured to see whether the little round pass could carry him any further. Hiring a motorcar, he drove out of Paris toward the front. At checkpoints he would wave his piece of paper with the seal of the general staff, and the sentries would motion him on. He actually came close to the town of Soissons, about fifty miles northeast, and saw some fighting. When he reported his good fortune to his colleagues that night in Paris, they resolved to duplicate his feat.

On the next morning, piling into a chauffeured limousine paid for by Davis, the correspondents hurtled toward the gates of the city. They brandished the pass. The gates opened! They rode out into the countryside, soon passing fields that just a few days before had been battlefields. The huge poplars that lined the road bore mute testimony to the ferocity of the fighting. Their fallen branches littered the road for four miles. Many of the giant trunks seemed to have been split by lightning, or torn in half "as with your hands you could tear apart a loaf of bread." Through some, solid shells had cut clean holes. "Others looked as though drunken woodsmen with axes from roots to topmost branches had slashed them in crazed fury," Davis wrote. Alongside the smashed branches stood abandoned wicker baskets of German ammunition, bloody bandages and clothing, heaps of boots, and the bodies of dead German soldiers. The Germans had retreated in a hurry. They were retreating still.[37]

None of the inhabitants had returned to the villages, abandoned by the Germans only the day before. The streets were piled with grain, on which the soldiers had slept. In a château, a table in the garden had been set for twelve, with fine china and many half-emptied wines and liqueurs. Some alarm had summoned the officers. Unwatched, the candles burned down to the silver candlesticks. The coffee went untasted. Surrounded by flowers in the cheerful sunlight, the deserted table and the stately château reminded Davis of a bewitched castle in a fairy tale.[38]

Soldiers materialized a few miles onward—first the picturesquely garbed Algerians and Moroccans, who were executing a turning movement, and then the advance line of the French army. It was the second day of the battle for Soissons, a town that the Germans had held for two weeks. From a height, Davis watched the artillery battle, of a thundering intensity that he had never experienced. The tumult was so overwhelming that it acted as an anesthetic. Even though shells were falling two hundred yards away, and villages burned in the distance, those Frenchmen not manning the guns hunted for souvenirs, shouting gleefully to their comrades whenever they found a spiked helmet. Oblivious to the horror, they were like children picking daisies.[39] The firing ceased in the late afternoon. By the end of the day, the Allies had recaptured Soissons.

And by the end of the day, Davis was back in Paris, where the Taverne Royale and Maxim's were open as usual, serving dinner to famished correspondents. One of the odder anomalies of this war was the way it catered to reporter-commuters. There was no need for elaborate kits and portable stoves for correspondents on the Western front. The posh dining rooms at night were easily accessible, just an hour's drive from the artillery fire. Not only correspondents but officers on a day's leave could substitute the odors of "truffles, white wine, and 'artichaut sauce mousseline' " for "the smell of camp-fires, dead horses and unwashed bodies." Listening to gruesome stories as he sat back on the red velvet cushions of Maxim's or La Rue's, Davis found it incredible that these young men in uniform, surrounded by gilded mirrors and gold-and-white walls, would be back in the trenches in a few hours. What a strange twist it was on an old Davis fictional device:

the raconteur who entertains his dinner companions with tales of recent adventure. Who could have imagined adventures so recent; or, indeed, such adventures?

Most of the officers to whom Davis spoke at Maxim's were English, and they epitomized the upper-class British values that he had emulated all his life. There was a right way to fight a war and a right way to order wine, and a gentleman knew both. The posh dining rooms of Paris were bustling with exemplars. There was the subaltern who had bought so many gifts for his fellow officers that he was down to his last five francs. Soon afterward, Davis met him and inquired after his finances. "I've had the most extraordinary luck," the youth replied. "After I left you I met my brother. He was just in from the front, and I got all his money." "Won't your brother need it?" Davis asked. "Not at all," the boy said cheerfully. "He's shot in the legs, and they've put him to bed. Rotten luck for him, you might say, but how lucky for me!" And then there was the English major, hit in three places by a bursting shell, who was asked by the doctors, "This cot next to yours is the only one vacant. Would you object if we put a German in it?" "By no means," said the major. "I haven't seen one yet." These English aristocrats shared Davis's code: self-deprecating wit and reserved grace in the face of adversity.[40]

Later, when he published his war reports as a book, Davis was parodied with wicked effectiveness for his glorification of these upper-class paragons, and for his epicurean style of war correspondence. In an on-target review cleverly titled "Richard the Lion-Harding," Philip Littell lampooned Davis's code: "A perfect day, for Mr. Davis, would consist of a morning's danger, taken as a matter of course; in the afternoon a little chivalry, equally a matter-of-course to a well-bred man; then a motor dash from hardship to some great city, a bath, a perfect dinner nobly planned. Shrapnel, chivalry, *sauce mousseline*, and so to work the next morning. . . . Richard Coeur-de-Lion would not have disliked such a day, once he was used to shrapnel." Nothing deflates glamour faster than ridicule. The Davis image of virtue unalloyed by irony was wearing badly in the twentieth century. As Littell asked his readers: "Have you never, although you may be rather chivalrous yourself, in a modest way, risen from the perusal of Mr. Davis on chivalry with a determination never again, no matter how infirm the woman standing in front of you might be, or how heavy-laden, to rise from your seat in the car for her sake?" Among the younger readers of these lines, few would not have chortled in agreement.[41]

Of the reporters' excursions from Paris, the one to Reims on September 18 was the most productive. Davis chose the destination. The others wanted to return to Soissons to pursue the fighting, but Davis insisted on visiting the bombarded cathedral. "You are seeing something of greater news interest than any battle," he assured them.[42]

Once again, the combination of a grand motorcar and an official-looking pass greased their way out of the city. To avoid the British army, which was sandwiched between Reims and Soissons, they traveled first to Meaux, a town ravaged by shells and littered with torn bits of uniforms and empty cartridge boxes, and then on a road that followed the green banks of the Marne. So many bridges had been destroyed that the fifty-six-mile trip took most of the day. Their first view of Reims, the venerable center of champagne production, came in the late afternoon—clouds of black smoke masking the towers of the cathedral. Cannons boomed from the east and southeast. Hundreds of refugees on the road slowed the reporters' progress. Their faces taut with strain and fear, the refugees called to each other in nervous excitement. Their fever infected Davis. He questioned them in jerky sentences of English and phrasebook French, and then called on Morgan to translate the voluble replies. To the chauffeur, he kept shouting, *"Vite! Vite! À Reims, à Reims!"*

The Germans had occupied Reims on September 4 and held it until September 12, when they retreated to the neighboring hills. Now they were bombarding the city; and the French, to the north and east of the town, were firing back. As their car crossed the canal bridge into Reims, the reporters saw squads of blue-bloused red-pantalooned soldiers hurrying through the city, bicyclists racing with dispatches, horse soldiers galloping across the cobbled streets, and artillery pieces being dragged to the front. Although few citizens were to be seen, their homes remained. Many houses were still standing, the walls pierced by the neat hole of a shell, which, on exploding, had reduced the interior to a shapeless mass of brick and wood. This, however, was not the story. The war was less than two months old, and smashed houses were already old news. The story—and the reporters' destination—was the cathedral.

The cathedral of Reims ranked among the grand monuments of Europe. A French Gothic masterpiece, it was begun in the thirteenth century and completed in the fifteenth. For centuries, the kings of France had been crowned at Reims: there, in 1429, Joan of Arc had witnessed the coronation of Charles VII. A favorite destination of tourists, the cathedral was famous for its remarkable stained-glass windows, which sparkled with reds and blues of a purity and richness that cannot be duplicated, since the medieval process is lost. The glass is irreplaceable. As the correspondents entered the cathedral, it crunched beneath their feet.

German shells had been raining on the cathedral since the day before, and they were falling still. Although the French priests had converted the building into a nursing station for wounded German soldiers, the Red Cross flag flying from the spire did not deflect the artillery fire. On the contrary, it seemed to attract it. A shell bursting inside the cathedral had killed two injured Germans. The bodies lay under heaps of dirty straw, the pointed toes of the boots peeking out grotesquely. Other Germans, bloody and haggard, but alive, lay on straw near them. A young, white-haired priest led the reporters through the cathedral, on a tour that bitterly echoed the routine of Baedeker-riffling tourists. Shells had torn out some windows entirely—sash, glass, and stone frame—leaving only jagged holes. Leaden window sashes lay tangled on the stone floor like coils of barbed wire. A great brass candelabra, its supporting steel chain shot away, had tumbled to the floor. Fragments of stone from carvings and flying buttresses lay in the dust. Everywhere there was broken glass, glittering amidst the straw, the mud, the caked blood. Instead of the filtered blue-and-red rays that once softly illuminated the interior, great streams of bright daylight shone directly on the rubble, outlining it with unwonted and unwanted clarity.

The correspondents walked about, stooping to collect shards of the precious glass. (Fortescue filled his musette bag, presenting it many years later to John Barrymore to be made into a fire screen.) As they gleaned, the whistle of an incoming shell brought them to attention. There was a deafening explosion, followed by a torrent of falling glass. The huddled Germans shuddered, and a dying officer groaned involuntarily. Then there was another shell, more breaking glass, and the sound of shattered masonry from outside. Davis stood next to Ashmead-Bartlett, gazing in silence upon the unearthly scene. "Do you know," he said suddenly, "this is the first cathedral that has ever interested me."[43]

They spent the night in the Hotel du Nord, the one hotel open in the deserted city. No reservations were required. They each received a room overlooking the garden, where they proceeded, after dinner, to write what they had seen. Filed the next day in Paris, then approved in due course by the censors, these dispatches would be the first authoritative report of the destruction in Reims.[44]

On September 21, again at Davis's suggestion, the quartet returned to Reims. They spent three hours surveying the damage to the cathedral, leaving only after shrapnel fell perilously near them. To his diary, Davis conceded that Morgan was "probably right in saying it was because [the Germans] saw us on roof of the cathedral," viewing the French and German artillery lines stretched out across the plain below.[45] Fortescue agreed that the correspondents had provoked this deliberate shelling of the cathedral tower. Seen through binoculars from a great distance, the reporters would resemble Allied officers directing French artillery against the Germans. Ashmead-Bartlett even wore a British tunic. They made plausible targets.[46] What he confided to his diary, however, Davis did not share with his reading public. To them, what he wanted to convey was the inexcusable and wanton destruction of a treasured, hallowed place by the ruthless German commanders. In his second dispatch from Reims, he emphasized that there was no military justification for the bombardment of the cathedral.[47]

Having spent the night again in the Hotel du Nord, Davis went to visit the American consul, from whom he obtained, in addition to a summary of the events of the past few days, three bottles of excellent champagne and three of a rare old Burgundy. Before departing Reims, Davis noted amidst the devastation the odd picturesque details that enlivened his reportage. A sliver of wall, all that remained of one house, bore the sign, "This house is for sale; elegantly furnished." Another house had been totally destroyed except for the drawing-room mantel, on which sat a terra-cotta harlequin, legs spread, arms folded, head thrown back in laughter. "Of all the fantastic tricks played by the war," he wrote of that clay figure laughing in the ruins, "it was the most curious."

Hearing that they might see a French attack on a German position north of town if they took the road to Fismes, the quartet decided, over Morgan's objections, to risk it. They were soon in the midst of a marching French army. Their car was frequently stopped by sentries, but a wave of the document with the seal of the general staff always sufficed. They stopped for a hitchhiker in civilian clothes, who stood in the center of the road. "I have a farm about five miles on which overlooks the Aisne and the entire battlefield," he said, when they told him of their mission. "If you come with me, I will take you there, and you will have a magnificent view if there is an attack." Thanking him for his generosity, they welcomed him into the front seat of their car. They drove on for about five miles, into thicker concentrations of troops, until they ran into the general and his staff. They went no further. A staff member demanded to see their pass. He took them to the general who, affably but firmly, told them to return to Reims at once. Expecting worse, they obeyed with alacrity. Their hitchhiker, however, was detained. Later, they learned that he was a suspected German agent. They never determined his fate.

They retraced the route to Reims without incident and proceeded on the direct road to Paris. But their luck had run out. Three or four miles on, they ran into an entire French army corps on its way to the front. They crept along, always ceding the right of way, until a suspicious officer demanded to see their passes. Their round cardboard discs failed to impress him. "These do not entitle you to be with the army at the front," he said, "they merely authorize you to go to the quartier general for news in Paris itself." He placed them under arrest.

Interrogated by the chief of staff and other officers, they produced their press credentials and loudly affirmed the purity of their motives. They made little headway. Their passports could be forged. As for their motives . . . who was to say? The situation was deteriorating when an officer came up and said, "Are you not Ashmead-Bartlett, and were you not attached to

the French army in Morocco in 1907? I remember you very well there."
From that point on, the tone of the inquisition improved, but the outcome
was nonetheless unfavorable. Only the general could decide what to do
with them, said the chief of staff. In the meantime, they would have to be
detained. They were led down a lane to a farmyard full of dirty straw,
surrounded by even filthier animal sheds.

It had been frightening to be arrested by the Germans, but to be
detained by the French, whom he supported, was humiliating and maddening. Davis was apoplectic. He swore he would never enter the pigsty,
and he swore much else besides. Fortunately, his French was so bad that
his captors could not understand most of what he said. Acting as spokesman,
Morgan won permission for the prisoners to remain by the roadside and
send for their lunch, which was in the car. After lunch, however, the chief
of staff returned with word from the general. There was a standing order
from General Joseph Joffre that any unauthorized persons found at the
front must be kept as prisoners for eight days lest news of troop movements
leak out. They were to be detained in the farmyard for eight days.

At this, Davis almost choked with rage. Partly in French, partly in
English, he kept on repeating, "I am Richard Harding Davis. I am an
American. No one has the right to lock me in a farmyard. I am a free-born
American citizen. I refuse to be treated in this manner. I demand my
immediate release, or that I be allowed to communicate at once with Mr.
Herrick, my Ambassador in Paris. I have come all the way from America
to help France. I have done my best, and now you wish to lock me in a
dirty pigsty. I will never enter it." Fortescue was even more abusive. Neither
was much understood, but their vehemence made an impression. The chief
of staff went off again to confer with the general. Returning hours later, he
announced that they would be returned that night under police escort to
the military authorities in Paris.

Their cortege of military cars lost its way several times on the road to
Paris and made several stops for liquid refreshment at the expense of the
correspondents. It was after midnight when they arrived, and the military
governor of the city could not be located. Over their loud protests, they
were sent to the old stone military prison of Cherche-Midi to await the
governor's return in the morning. Davis had worked himself into a fine rage.
"I am Richard Harding Davis," he kept repeating, the typical American in
a foreign country who thinks that if he says something often enough in his
own language, the foreigners will eventually understand. "They have no
right to keep me here. I demand to be allowed to communicate with my
Ambassador."

Once the guards realized that their curious prisoners posed no danger,
they became very friendly. They persuaded the military staff officers, who
had sentenced the reporters to this prison, to take one journalist (Fortescue
was selected) on a search for the American ambassador, Myron T. Herrick.

Davis pitched a tent at Ladysmith, where he saw the relief of the besieged British outpost, a highlight of the Boer War. Cecil waited behind in Cape Town.
(Kehrig Collection)

This 1904 caricature in Life *lampooned Davis's extreme chivalry and upper-class affectations.*

Traveling to Japan in 1904 to cover the war with Russia, Davis spent most of his time in tea houses, waiting for permission to go to the front.
(Special Collections, Lehigh University Libraries)

Davis shared the frustration in Tokyo with John Fox, Jr. (center), and Jack London (right).
(Poett Collection)

The construction and maintenance of Crossroads Farm in Mount Kisco, seen here just after the house was finished in 1905, consumed much of Davis's income for the last decade of his life. (Poett Collection)

Richard gives his younger sister, Nora, an assist on a bicycle. (Kehrig Collection)

With a pair of sheepdogs, Richard and Cecil tramp through the woods at their Mount Kisco home. (Poett Collection)

His parents' forty-one-year marriage was for Richard a model of conjugal happiness—one he could not equal.
(Kehrig Collection)

A native servant assisted Davis on his unsuccessful Congo trip in 1907. (Kehrig Collection)

This photograph is the only relic of the hippopotamus that Davis shot in the Congo. (Kehrig Collection)

The loyal brothers, Richard and Charles, late in life. (Kehrig Collection)

Richard's second wife, Bessie McCoy, won stardom as "The Yama-Yama Girl." (Kehrig Collection)

BESSIE McCOY
as
"THE YAMA GIRL."

Bessie angled artfully in the lake at Crossroads Farm. (Kehrig Collection)

On location in Cuba for the filming of
Soldiers of Fortune *in 1913, Davis coached
the actors who played his fictional
characters. (Kehrig Collection)*

*In regulation dress
despite the heat,
Davis inspected the
outskirts of Vera-
cruz during the
1914 incident that
almost led to war
between Mexico
and the United
States. (Kehrig
Collection)*

*Davis (front row, second from right)
trained at General Leonard Wood's war-
preparedness camp in Plattsburg in 1915.
Carrying a forty-pound pack on a nine-day
hike in the August sun, he admitted, "I'm a
little bit afraid I've overdone."
(Kehrig Collection)*

*Davis standing at the entrance to a trench
in Arras, France, in November 1915.
(Kehrig Collection)*

Bessie McCoy Davis with daughter Hope.
(Kehrig Collection)

Richard became a father at an age when
most men are grandfathers.
(Kehrig Collection)

The seasoned war correspondent near the end of his life.
(Kehrig Collection)

They permitted the reporters to send out to the Ritz for a champagne supper, and when it arrived, they gratefully accepted the invitation to join the feast. The stone-walled, stone-floored, stone-roofed chamber, lit only by two oil lanterns, made a picturesque setting for a festive late supper. By the time they had eaten the meal and drained the champagne bottles, the guards and captive reporters were on the best of terms. Even Davis's spirits had revived.

Aware that the famous, middle-aged American war correspondent was at heart a little boy, with an education that was, to be charitable, spotty, Ashmead-Bartlett had an inspiration. "Davis, you have the chance of your life," he said. "Do you know this is the very prison in which Marie Antoinette was interned, and it was from here that she was taken to the guillotine?" Davis brightened. "No, is that really true?" "Yes, absolutely," Ashmead-Bartlett replied. "Now, with your imagination and your powers of description, think of the story you could write if you spent the night in her cell." Davis was overcome by excitement at this notion. "He became like a joyous schoolboy who has been promised an extra half-holiday," Ashmead-Bartlett later reminisced, "and instead of regarding a night in the cells with horror and dismay, it became the one obsession of his mind."

An hour and a half elapsed before Fortescue returned with the staff officers. The mission had failed. But as Fortescue gobbled his belated dinner, the staff officers consulted with the jailers and at last they spoke up. They had concluded that the cells of Cherche-Midi were too grim. They would take the correspondents to a converted girls' dormitory that was being used to detain captured officers. In the morning, they would be brought to their ambassador. All the reporters greeted this news with elation. All, that is, but Davis.

He had his heart set on sleeping in the historic cell in which Marie Antoinette had passed her final night. Rising to his feet, he shouted, "*No. Je refuse absolutely de partir ici. Je désire dormir avec Marie Antoinette. Je refuse de partir.*" He continued to repeat, "*Je désire dormir avec Marie Antoinette,*" as the guards, the staff officers, and Fortescue stared in amazement. Had he lost his mind? Ashmead-Bartlett and Morgan (who was in on the gag) strained to keep from exploding in laughter. They waited until Davis had whipped himself into a fierce lather, and then they confessed the practical joke. Everyone found it very amusing. Everyone, that is, but Davis. He was furious with Ashmead-Bartlett for days.

But they spent an agreeable night in the dormitory, and in the morning, Ambassador Herrick vouched for them all. The only sticking point was General Joffre's requirement that any unauthorized person found at the front must be incarcerated for eight days. Through negotiation, it was agreed that they could serve their detention at large in Paris, so long as they gave their word that they would not leave the city limits within that time. As sentences go, it was rather lenient. Each day they gathered at Maxim's,

La Rue's, Voisin's, or the Café de la Paix. Davis wrote up his past experiences for *Scribner's* and penned bland, inspirational pap for the Wheeler Syndicate. On September 29, the last night of their parole, Davis hosted a farewell dinner at the Hotel de l'Empire. The next day he left for England, and from there a week later he sailed home. He was emotionally bankrupt and terribly tired: "So tired," he wrote in his diary in London, "that cried in the streets for nothing."[48]

13
The Final Blessing

*I*N THE CATHEDRALS OF BELGIUM, FRANCE, AND ENGLAND, Richard had lit candles for "the Blessing." On January 4, 1915, in New York, the blessing materialized—a daughter, as he had hoped.[1] Hope is what the happy parents named her, after the pure-minded tomboy heroine of Richard's most popular novel, *Soldiers of Fortune*.[2] Richard and Bessie had agreed readily on the name, but had the Blessing been a boy, they would have been unprepared. "One evening I stood at a window looking out at the river," Bessie later recalled. "I thought, that shall be The Blessing's name. It is a fine, strong name, like the river. We will call him Hudson. But Richard would not have it. On his writing-table, where he knew I would see them, I found the written words, 'Hudson, Blank, No.' "[3]

You couldn't see the Hudson River from the Davis farm in Mount Kisco, but that is not where Richard and Bessie were spending the winter. They closed up the farm and rented an apartment way uptown in Manhattan, at 730 Riverside Drive, relieving the expectant mother of the threat of isolating snowdrifts. Although not terribly convenient, the apartment was closer to midtown than the farm, and a lot cheaper and easier to run. Davis was still racing to keep ahead of his creditors. Just before departing for Europe, he had signed a year's exclusive contract for his fiction with the *Metropolitan*, a flashy monthly that billed itself as "the liveliest magazine in America." *Metropolitan* agreed to pay Davis the lively sum of two thousand dollars a story, and, on top of that, presented him with a three-thousand-dollar bonus upon signing.[4] All too quickly, however, the bonus money trickled away, and Richard was having trouble thinking of ideas for stories.[5] Distracted by the disturbances of the city, he found it difficult to write. Encumbered by the expenses of "the staff and 'establishment' of a baby," he was ever more conscious of the need to work.[6] And, in the background, in thunderous amplification of his anxieties, the war news from Europe hammered away at his nerves.

Against all that was the miracle of his daughter. It did seem a godsent blessing that at this stage of his life, when the years had weathered him gray and craggy, there should spring up, as bright and unexpected as an alpine flower, an adorable baby—*his* adorable baby. "You have a lot of fun ahead of you," wrote Charles Dana Gibson, one of the many friends who had reached this bend of the river years before.[7] It was another sign of Richard's reluctance to grow old that, at an age when men become grandfathers, he was celebrating paternity for the first time. Looking at the photographs, you might at first take this middle-aged, well-dressed fellow to be the grandfather of the chubby little baby he is holding—that is, until you notice the tenderly uncertain way he grasps her, and the fond, bemused smile that flickers on his lips. "No event in my brother's life had ever brought him such infinite happiness . . . ," Charles wrote.[8] The birth of Hope confirmed (if confirmation were needed) that he had been wise to dissolve the barren union with Cecil. "He was touchingly sweet with children," wrote his friend Gouverneur Morris. "I think he was a little afraid of them. . . . But when they showed him that they trusted him, and, unsolicited, climbed upon him and laid their cheeks against his, then the loveliest expression came over his face, and you knew that the great heart . . . throbbed with an exquisite bliss, akin to anguish."[9]

Despite the gap in years, Richard had less problem than most fathers in communicating with his little girl. In so many ways, he was still a child himself: "none of us seem to grow any wiser, or older," he wrote when he was forty-four.[10] One of his favorite organizations in these years was the Boy Scouts, which Lord Baden-Powell had established in 1908. John Wheeler, paying a visit to Crossroads Farm in the summer of 1914, found Boy Scouts camping everywhere. The Scouts were there on a two-week visit, and Davis, abandoning his Sunday guests, ate with the boys, and preached to them the ethos of the outdoors, a faith in which he deeply believed.[11]

His favorite afternoon activity was to walk through the woods collecting boughs of evergreens and laurel to decorate the house. When Bessie accompanied him, she learned not to gossip or speak frivolously. "Dear, this is the woods," he would chide her. "Nothing of that in God's woods."[12] Like the Scouts, Richard loved to dig for "buried treasure," which might turn out to be a broken arrowhead or piece of chipmunk skull.[13] In the winter, he would hike in the snow to track the marks left by the birds, foxes, woodchucks, and squirrels. Infuriated by poachers, he applied in August 1915 to become a "special game protector."[14]

He celebrated the Scouts in a short story—perhaps it would be more accurate to call it a short piece of propaganda—about a Boy Scout named Jimmie who tracks down a German spy in Westchester County. Of course, the man *can't* be a spy, the adults tell the Scout, and, with no hard feelings on either side, Jimmie's prisoner is released. A few minutes later the Secret Service agents drive up: the spy has given them the slip once again.[15] The short story is so farfetched that you might think only a preadolescent boy could believe it; but—and probably this exception proves the rule—Davis believed it. Like his fictional Scout, he was obsessed with German spies infiltrating the United States. He placed a classified ad in the New York *Herald* in which he claimed to be a retired German-American army officer named Henry Wagner who was offering for sale confidential plans and patents. At the Wheeler Syndicate headquarters he enlisted the office boy as an amateur detective to inquire at the *Herald* if there was any mail for Mr. Wagner. On the way back, Davis instructed, the boy should walk around the block and see if anyone was tailing him. "If I receive a reply and can arrange for a meeting, I will get General Wood, who is a friend of mine, to give me some phoney plans of fortifications," Davis explained to Wheeler while the boy was out. "I will try to sell them. If I do, it will be a great story of German spies in America for you."* The boy returned: no mail, and no one on his trail. "Maybe my bait wasn't right for hooking them," Davis fretted. "I'm sure they are here just the same."[16]

In the same spirit (although he would have been offended by the analogy) Davis was an enthusiastic supporter of General Wood's training camps for war preparedness. As early as August 1909, he participated in war games staged near Middleboro, Massachusetts, close by Marion. Although war then was a distant thunderhead, Wood hoped that these exercises would expose the feeble state of the American armed forces. However, the Massachusetts maneuvers suffered from a handicap that would continue to cripple Wood's efforts: people had trouble taking them seriously. These were grown men dividing up into the Red and Blue teams to stage "battles" in which umpires determined when a soldier was "dead." Davis, too, had trouble writing about the war games. "If you take them seriously it bores people," he explained, "and, I refuse to make fun of them, which any cheap Jack can do, and, for the last week, has done."[17]

Jokers were still ridiculing Wood and his maneuvers six years later in the summer of 1915, when Davis once again accepted a *Collier's* assignment to pitch camp as a participant-observer.[18] Congregating at the U.S. Army post at Plattsburg in upstate New York, these recruits were older than their predecessors. Most were community leaders, nicknamed the T.B.M.'s— tired businessmen. About twelve hundred of them paid thirty dollars for the monthlong program, which was too short a time to convert novices into officers but long enough to demonstrate how badly the T.B.M.'s needed training. Like a revival camp, Plattsburg aimed to spread the word of the gospel—in this case, the gospel of preparedness, according to Wood.

It was the same call to arms that, ever since his return to America, Davis had been sounding in letters to the editor, in public appeals for

---

*Leonard Wood was commissioned as a brigadier-general on July 9, 1898, a week before the Spanish army surrendered in Cuba.

French and Belgian war relief, in journalism, and in fiction.[19] He stated openly at the outset that his article on Plattsburg was "frank propaganda." He insisted that he was aiming "to prepare against war," not to promote war; but, like Wood, he was being disingenuous. The preparedness movement was driven by East Coast establishment figures who, imbued all their lives with English and French culture, seethed at President Wilson's reluctance to intervene on behalf of the Allies.[20] Wood's old comrade-in-arms, Theodore Roosevelt, gave a speech at Plattsburg to an audience of Fishes, Chanlers, and many other familiar faces. Indeed, the T.B.M.'s might as easily have been dubbed "middle-aged Rough Riders." There was something distinctly déjà vu about these millionaires digging trenches and dining on bacon and potatoes in democratic fraternalism. The cavalry squad in which Davis enrolled included two Maryland fox-hunting squires, a master of hounds, a gentleman jockey from Boston, and the nation's two leading steeplechase riders. Older and fatter than the fighting men in Cuba, the Plattsburg recruits may have suffered even more. No tropical fever raged in upstate New York; that aside, the month in Plattsburg exhausted Davis more than his tour in Cuba. His stamina was slipping. "This is a very real thing, and *strenuous*," he wrote to Charles.[21] To those scoffers who dismissed the whole affair as a picnic, he replied in *Collier's*: "If it was a picnic it was the first one I ever attended at which any of the picnickers lost fifteen pounds."

Carrying a forty-pound pack on a nine-day hike in the August sun, he admitted to a photographer friend, "I'm a little bit afraid I've overdone." He was suffering from chest pains, and a younger man observed that his face grew livid and stern. But there was never any question of his backing down.[22]

Nor was there any doubt that he would return to the battlefields of Europe. When he left the previous fall, he said that a correspondent couldn't work under such conditions. "No more front for me," he grumbled to an acquaintance. "I have been arrested and locked up, and God knows what else. War correspondents can do nothing."[23] But how could he reconcile the fact that "war correspondents can do nothing" with his fierce need to do something? The sinking of the *Lusitania* by a German torpedo on May 7, 1915, enraged him. Among the 1,195 who perished (124 of them American) was Richard's longtime business acquaintance, the theater producer Charles Frohman. Traveling with Frohman was a good friend of Richard's, the short-story and romance writer Justus Miles Forman, whose anti-German play *The Hyphen* was a success in New York. Another friend, the socialite Alfred Gwynne "A. G." Vanderbilt, also died. Over the next two days, as sketchy reports solidified into a reliable list of survivors, Richard conceded reluctantly that these men were lost. When he met his brother Charlie for lunch at Delmonico's on May 10, he found the place aghast over the sudden death of Frohman, who had towered like a titan over Broadway.

"He said goodbye to me the day before he sailed," murmured the washroom boy. Charlie, who had seen Frohman off at the dock, was the last person to talk to him on American soil. He couldn't speak of it without tears.[24]

It was all well and good to write propaganda for the Allies in New York and march with other middle-aged enthusiasts in Plattsburg, but it was not enough. There had been a time when the opportunity to cover a great war would have lured Davis irresistibly, as a way to garner experience and to advance his career. There had been a time, more recently, when he grudgingly accepted war assignments as the surest way to earn money. But he returned to the European front in the fall of 1915 for a different reason—a sense of obligation. He empathized with the French and the British as if they were his own people. He had more close friends in London, after all, than in any American city but New York. When he covered the Spanish-American War, he had done so with partisanship, but without any tinges of hysteria or desperation. Even in those moments when American victory was uncertain, the United States had never been threatened to the slightest degree. France and England, by contrast, were battling Germany to the death. He felt that he belonged by their side, doing what he did best: telling the story.

The Wheeler Syndicate was delighted to send him back, at the same salary of six hundred dollars a week (calculated from the time of his departure in mid-October 1915, until his return to New York), plus one thousand dollars in expenses.[25] From the Scribners, he took an advance of five hundred dollars but made no promise to supply magazine articles from the field—a duty which had nagged at him during his previous hectic tour.[26] Another irritant on that trip was the New York *Tribune*, which had been the preeminent subscriber to his services through the Wheeler Syndicate. In Europe he found their men to be "worse than useless" and "lazy, stupid and jealous." "Not only they dont [*sic*] help," he complained to Charlie, "but the[y] harm me all they can."[27] A few hours after Richard sailed for France, Wheeler arranged for his articles to be published in New York by the *Times*. Davis was delighted.[28]

Hard as it had been to bid farewell to Bessie in the past, it was doubly difficult now to part from his wife and daughter. He left them not at Crossroads Farm, since Bessie hated living alone in the big place, but in a cottage nearby that was owned by Arthur Scribner and rented at one time by Charlie. After his departure, Richard wrote to Bessie: "I want you to keep saying to yourself all the time, 'This is the most serious effort he ever made, because the chances of seeing anything are so *small*, and because never had he such a chance to help. But, all the time, every minute he thinks of me. . . .' "[29] The chances of seeing something were indeed small. The military positions, which were fluid during Davis's first visit at the start of the war, had hardened into an appalling stalemate. The French were resisting months of massive German assaults at Verdun. In July, the British

had launched a bloody and ultimately inconclusive attack on German positions on the Somme. The trench warfare was dull and brutal. Even worse,
from the reporter's standpoint, it was cut off by an iron screen of military
regulations and censorship.

On the slow boat to Bordeaux, Richard broke the cap on a front tooth
and endured stomach pains that he attributed to "ptomaine poisoning"
brought on by (what else?) German sauerkraut.[30] The trip was beginning
badly. The day that he arrived in Bordeaux, the French government announced a new cabinet, purging the gentlemen to whom Davis was carrying
letters of introduction.[31] Still, he was able on the strength of his pro-Allies
reputation to obtain in Paris what no previous reporter had been granted:
a wartime interview with President Raymond Poincaré. Upon leaving, Davis
presented a letter written by Colonel Roosevelt and noted that, as he had
swallowed the last such letter when captured by the Germans, he had this
time asked Roosevelt to write on thinner paper. Stroking the letter between
thumb and forefinger, Poincaré smiled and said, "This one is quite digest-
ible."[32]

The Poincaré interview was a "darn good story," Davis thought, "one
of the best things I have pulled off."[33] He would have enjoyed this triumph
more if the censor had not delayed the story's transmission.[34] And it was
hard to feel exultant when he was so homesick and so *cold*. He had always
hated winter. But now, after dinner, he welcomed crawling into bed and
shivering beneath the bedclothes. "I have not only to warm the bed with
my body, but all of Paris," he wrote to Bessie. "Anyway that's what it feels
like."[35] Chilly, too, was the welcome from Wythe Williams, the *Times*
man in Paris. Understandably, Williams responded suspiciously to a star
correspondent muscling in on his beat. "You know them all, don't you?"
he said sarcastically, when the duchess of Marlborough greeted Davis on
the platform of the Gare du Nord. Davis was decked out in his paramilitary
khaki uniform and war ribbons at the time.[36]

But whatever the appearances, Davis's fame and exalted connections
helped him do his job. To see the war up close, he won a place alongside
other journalists on a three-day guided tour of the labyrinth of trenches
near Arras in the Artois. Better yet, he was promised a later visit, alone, to
the French forces in the Reims sector. On the way to Arras, he saw how
the war had changed during his year's absence.[37] It had become part of the
routine, an element of the landscape. The peasants no longer raised their
heads at the sound of the ambulances, the gray-painted troop buses, the
truck-borne heavy guns. They tended their fields and mended the roads. A
French airplane eluding German shrapnel failed to interest them. It wasn't
their concern. "Since this war began shrapnel, when it bursts, has invariably
been compared to balls of cotton," wrote Davis, whose concern it was,
"and as that is exactly what it looks like, it is again so described." Like the
war itself, writing about the war had become conventional.

But Davis worked hard to make it new. Sometimes he slipped into his old clichés: the clay-caked uniforms of the soldiers reminded him of "those of football players on a rainy day at the end of the first half." Usually, though, he succeeded in conveying the desolation of those winter days, a misery that mocked comparison with football and undermined his cheerful countenance. "A cold rain was falling and had turned the streets of Ablain and all the roads to it into swamps," he wrote. "In these were islands of bricks and lakes of water of the solidity and color of melted chocolate. Whatever you touched clung to you. It was a land of mud, clay, liquid earth. A cold wind whipped the rain against your face and chilled you to the bone. All you saw depressed and chilled your spirit." If war was a wave of cheering men and galloping horses, then this did not suggest war. The trenches might have been a mining camp during spring rains; and for all the attention that the men paid, the shells bursting nearby might have been the sounds of miners blasting rock.

In France only two weeks, he had already interviewed the president and gathered good local color. Yet on returning to Paris he found not congratulations but a "long annoying cable."[38] The New York *Times*, under the leadership of managing editor Carr Van Anda, was proving to be far more troublesome than the *Tribune* had ever been. A formal, thin-lipped man with a high forehead and rimless eyeglasses, Van Anda was a polymath who liked to direct his troops personally.[39] Bored by the unnovel news in France, he was pressing Wheeler to send Davis to Salonika in northern Greece, where the Allies were launching a new campaign in the Balkans.[40] Davis's patience was threadbare. "It is most disheartening getting cables to go here and go there," Richard wrote to Bessie, "when you have been working 28 hours a day to get stories in France."[41] Correspondents who had been to Salonika told Davis that they were bottled up there, unable to reach the front. Davis had previously passed on this information to Wheeler, with the closing threat: "syndicate seems impatient hard to please if not satisfied my judgment best I make other connections." Wheeler had mollified his thin-skinned star reporter but continued to relay the unrelenting demands of his obstreperous chief client. Now he conveyed the *Times*'s view that a trip to Salonika would be worthwhile even if Davis couldn't travel outside the city. He went so far as to suggest specific story ideas.[42]

Realizing that Wheeler would not be forwarding these "suggestions" if he didn't tacitly endorse them, Davis decided to leave for Greece five days later. The interval allowed him to obtain his visas and make his scheduled trip to Reims.[43] Traveling the same roads where a year ago he had feared arrest at every crossing, he now carried a blue slip of paper that, to his amazement, conveyed him to the front trench. The next morning, the general in Reims asked what he had seen, and then exclaimed, "Nothing! You have seen nothing. When you return from Servia, come to Champagne again and I myself will show you something of interest." Richard lamented to Bessie that "had they not devilled the spirit out of me with cables, I believe I could have written such a lot of stories of France that no one else has had the opportunity to write."[44]

He had, out of pique, cabled Van Anda of the *Times* before departing for Reims: "As you ignorant of conditions here suggest discontinue cables of advise [*sic*] have already told Wheeler am going Greece when work here finished. . . ." Unlike Wheeler, Van Anda had no inclination—or financial motive—to pamper his prima donna, and he fired back this icy response: "Not aware that I have sent you cables of advice of any nature. Had I done so your message would be quite justified for our contract is with Wheeler and it is to him not to you that we look for its execution. Wheeler sent you cables stating *Times* 'wishes' but it was of his own construction and was merely assented to here because he thought it might aid him in carrying out his contract. It would have been more accurate had he professed to express not our wishes addressed to you but our demands upon him for compliance with his agreement. Should he be unable to comply we shall take prompt and appropriate measures. In the meantime I must insist that you send no insulting messages to this office or indeed messages of any kind except such as will enable Wheeler to execute his contract with us."[45]

This "very rude cable" greeted Davis in Paris, as did a nervous telegram sent a day later by Wheeler, expressing "intense indignation" at Van Anda's "wholly unjustified response," and assuring Davis that Wheeler was "perfectly satisfied" with him. These rousing words did little to assuage Richard's anger or restore his self-confidence. Because of the vagaries of the censor, he was already rattled by not knowing *if* his dispatches were being received. Now he also fretted over *how* they were being received. "Nothing worries me so much as the feeling that the Man Who Pays is not satisfied I am giving him his money's worth," he wrote (to a different employer) about this time.[46] That uncertainty galled him constantly throughout this second tour of service for the Wheeler Syndicate.

The twelve-day trip to Salonika, which he undertook so half-heartedly, became more attractive once his train escaped the snowy environs of France and entered the warm landscape of southern Italy.[47] But everything, starting with the weather, changed in Salonika. The boat that brought him there passed through "a giant funnel of snow, through which the wind roared." The icy gusts frosted the woodwork, the velvet cushions, and even the blankets on the ship.[48] When he bathed, the steam rose off him.[49] "Cold simply corpse like," he wrote in his diary.[50] It was said to be the coldest winter in Salonika since the seventeenth century.[51] Crowded under normal circumstances, Salonika was full to bursting with foreigners. Appearing late at night, Davis found no rooms available in the deluxe Olympos Palace Hotel. The porter kept asking if he wanted to see "New York gentlemans."

Although Davis assured him he did not, the insistent porter opened a door and announced, "A man to see you, misters." Blinking in the bright light, Davis saw who was inside and roared, with his up-to-date slang, "You sons o' guns! You sons o' guns!" The "New York gentlemans" were no gentlemen at all. They were war correspondents—John McCutcheon, Jimmy Hare, and William G. Shepherd. They were camping out in a large front room, forty feet long by twenty feet wide, that had formerly been the Austrian Club. They invited Davis to join them. He accepted gratefully, and they improvised an extra bed out of a sofa and chair.[52] Early the next morning, the correspondents woke to the sound of violent splashing, accompanied by deep grunts and shuddering gasps. Turning toward the source of the disturbance, they saw, from the vantage point of their snug beds, that it was Davis. He had produced his portable rubber bathtub and was sitting in it, sloshing his body with jugs of ice-cold water. He would maintain this ritual throughout his stay in Salonika. In the frigid room, a cold bath seemed imprudent; but it was a part of Richard's discipline, an element of a personal code that he would uphold until his death.[53]

Although he "would not admit it to Wheeler, or the Times," Davis was glad to be in Salonika.[54] It was the "most remarkable" and "most picturesque" spot he ever saw.[55] Along with his journalistic colleagues, he was taken to the Balkan front at the point where Greece, Serbia, and Bulgaria converge. Sharing an automobile with Jimmy Hare, he visited an English battery dug in beneath a covering of branches and snow. In command were two boy officers: one not yet eighteen, and his superior, who was nineteen. With a handful of men and a gun that jammed, they had been left to defend this abandoned outpost against Bulgarian forces who were four thousand yards away. "You don't seem to have any supports," Davis said solicitously. The younger boy, aware that his men were listening, waved his hand toward the dark hills and said nonchalantly, "Oh, they're about—somewhere." He added proudly, "You might call this an independent command."

The French chauffeur was blaring his horn for departure. Feeling "as must the robbers who deserted the babes in the wood," Davis offered the boys the best cigars sold in Greece. Although they weren't very good cigars, the boys must take them, he explained, for they were called the King of England. "I would take them if they were called the 'German Emperor,' " one of the child officers replied. Richard was chilled by guilt as he and Hare waved farewell from their car. "I felt I had meanly deserted them—that for his life the mother of each could hold me to account," he wrote. "But as we drove away from the cellar of mud, the gun that stuck, and the 'independent command,' I could see in the twilight the flashes of the guns and two lonely specks of light. They were the 'King of England' cigars burning bravely."[56] They were burning as brightly as the cigarette of the executed Rodríguez, the cigarette that, two decades earlier, Davis had described smoldering in the Cuban dirt; but they were burning with a more ambiguous light. In Davis's eyes, Rodríguez had been a noble young man who made an inspiring sacrifice to help win his people's freedom. For these child-officers in Serbia, lost in a menacing landscape for reasons beyond their comprehension, he could feel only pity. Pity, and the guilt of the man who observes without commitment—the guilt of the reporter.

On the Balkan front, Davis recognized that this was a war that was dangerous without being picturesque. That was true not only for the combatants but also for the correspondents. The reporters' chauffeur drove at sixty miles an hour on a road congested with troops and scarred by washouts and shells. "In these days of his downfall the greatest danger to the life of the war correspondent is that he must move about in automobiles driven by military chauffeurs," Davis wrote, with mordant, self-deprecating humor.[57] He was driven to Hill 516, the highest point of the French front, inside enemy Bulgarian territory. Looking out in the fog toward Bulgaria, he could see only snowy mountains. There were no blockhouses, no villages, no columns of men for the batteries to fire upon. But somewhere in that haze lay the invisible Bulgars, who, seeing the flashes from Hill 516, fired shells that landed within forty feet of where Davis stood. As the explosions came closer, the official guides hurried the correspondents out of the trenches and drove them to Serbia and safety. Long after dark they reached an army post where a large hospital tent had been prepared for them. Each newsman had a cot with fresh linen. The tent was heated by a stove. Thinking of the men in the mud of Hill 516, Davis once again "felt like a burglar who, while the owner is away, sleeps in his bed."[58]

If it was any consolation to his conscience, he spent the next night without blankets on the floor of an unheated cattle car that was lit only by candles, traveling seven agonizing hours to cover the fifty-five miles back to Salonika. Like his arrest in Mexico, his forced march in Belgium, and his nine-day hike in Plattsburg, the freezing journey was another insult to his battered body. "I don't believe Davis ever really got thawed out," McCutcheon later wrote. Salonika remained in the icy grip of a fierce winter. With bribes, Richard obtained a room of his own in the Olympos Palace— quite an accomplishment, for the hotel halls were crowded with cots for foreign officers. He bought a small oil stove that warmed his room as hot as an oven. Yet even wearing several sweaters, and placing the stove between his knees as he wrote, Davis shivered. The ice-water baths did not help.[59]

Most nights, the reporters dined together in the Olympos Palace restaurant. Richard would call for *Mastika!*, a Greek drink distilled from mastic gum. A peremptory *Du beurre!* was his second order. He brought his own bread to these meals, a coarse brown variety that he preferred to the fancier white bread served in the hotel; and he slathered it with butter. With drink and buttered bread in hand, he would entertain the others for hours with stories of his experiences throughout the world—tales that McCutcheon recalled as "intensely vivid, with the remarkable 'holding' quality of description which characterizes his writings." While Richard tactfully downplayed his own role in these narratives, it was plain to McCutcheon that he took great pride in "the width and breadth of his personal relation to the great events of the past twenty years." Senior in experience, he was instinctively deferred to, the alpha wolf in a pack of correspondents.[60]

Their daytime den was the large salon once shared by Davis. Still occupied by Hare, McCutcheon, and Shepherd (with occasional supplements), the oversized room had become a local headquarters for visiting Americans in Salonika, and was visited by the American consul and many British officers. It was a living room, a workroom, a club room, and, occasionally, a dining room. Davis was chatting there with his colleagues one morning when the porter made the standard announcement—"A man to see you, misters"—and in wandered an unremarkable-looking American youth in a British army uniform, who would inspire Richard's most memorable story of the war. "I simply had to come and talk American for a while," the young man said, extending his hand. Like McCutcheon, whom he greeted first, he had attended Purdue University in Indiana. By pretending to be Canadian, he had joined the British army and was now a sergeant in the British medical corps. He had seen action on the French and Belgian fronts. About six miles outside Salonika, he and his comrades were camped out in tents in the mud. "We haven't got any work to do now, and so we're only waiting for something to turn up," he said.

"Waiting is the toughest part of a soldier's life, isn't it?" Davis said affably.

"Well, fighting is bad enough," the boy replied. He said he had witnessed so much horror in the trenches that he wondered if he could ever become a quiet, decent American citizen again. This leave was his first in six weeks. Homesick for the United States, he hoped to quit as soon as he could. He asked if he might, on his next leave, borrow American clothes to visit the U.S. consul to ask assistance. He would hate to go in a British uniform. Although Davis was many sizes too big, McCutcheon offered shoes and a cap, Shepherd had an extra suit, and Hare could supply spare socks. Saying he would return on his next leave, the youth bid them good night and set off on his six-mile hike to camp.

The correspondents were having breakfast early the next morning when the porter announced, "A man to see you, misters," and in walked the young sergeant. Telling them to continue eating, he shaved off his jaunty little moustache, complaining cheerfully about the dullness of his razor. The correspondents did not know that in shaving the moustache, the soldier was violating a military rule that could bring him at least ten days' detention. "Now for the clothes," he said, pulling the promised articles out of the various trunks and then tearing off the muddy uniform that he had worn every day for a year. "You don't know how sick a man can get of a suit of clothes," he complained. He said it was worse than shell fire.

Departing for the errands that constituted their work in Salonika, the correspondents told the soldier to make himself at home. When they returned in the early afternoon, he was sitting in an armchair, dressed in their clothes, reading a newspaper, and smoking. Their first inkling that something was wrong came when he asked if they would mind holding on to his uniform for three or four days, then sending it by courier to his camp. "Isn't everything all right?" asked Shepherd. "Didn't the consul give you an American passport?"

"No, he can't issue passports. He said I would have to go to the American embassy at Athens for one. There's a boat sailing for Athens this afternoon, and I'm going on it."

"Going this afternoon?" asked McCutcheon.

"Yes, I am. I can't stand this any longer." He pointed out the window to the *Helleni*, a Greek steamer docked across the street. It sailed in three hours for Athens, which was neutral territory. Once he boarded that boat, he would be free to go to the United States.

The awkward silence that fell over the room was broken by Davis. "Me for lunch," he declared, and the other reporters went with him, leaving the soldier behind in the room. At lunch, it was Davis who first used the word "deserter." "It's none of our business, I suppose," he added. "He's his own boss." They talked of other things.

But after lunch, back in the room, McCutcheon cleared his throat and asked the boy if he wasn't afraid of being shot as a deserter as he walked to the ship. The young soldier replied that he had taken too many risks to worry—and if he stayed in the army, he was certain to be shot, anyway.

The correspondents took another tack. Knowing that the young man hoped to write of the war, Shepherd said, "Son, this war is some war. It's the biggest war in history, and folks will be talking about nothing else for the next ninety years; folks that never were nearer it than Bay City, Michigan. But you won't talk about it. And you've been all through it."

"I won't?" the youth demanded. "And why won't I?"

"Because of what you're doing now," Shepherd said. "Because you're queering yourself. Now you've got everything." Shepherd and his colleagues would give their eyeteeth to have seen all that the soldier had seen. "And you're throwing all that away."

The youth turned to McCutcheon in furious appeal. "I'm no quitter," he protested. "But, if I'm ready to quit, who's got a better right? What do you fellows know about it? You *write* about it, about the 'brave lads in the trenches'; but what do you know about the trenches? What you've seen from automobiles. That's all. That's where *you* get off! I've *lived* in the trenches for fifteen months, froze in 'em, starved in 'em, risked my life in

'em, and I've saved other lives, too, by hauling men out of the trenches."
He ran to the closet and dragged out his uniform, still so caked with mud
and snow that it splashed when it hit the floor like a wet bathing suit. "How
would you like to wear one of those?" he cried. "Stinking with lice and
sweat and blood; the blood of other men, the men you've helped off the
field, and your own blood."

He tore off his coat and vest and pulled up his shirt, baring his stomach
to display a scar as long as a football seam, cross-hatched with stitches.
"Look at that scar!" he almost yelled. "Look at that scar and tell me if that
doesn't entitle me to freedom and to go back to my father and mother at
home! What the hell do you fellows know about how I feel?" He had spent
three months in the hospital. "You don't even know what I'm talking
about," he said. "Why, you can't. Here you are, with your five beds and
your decent meals, and you can come and go as you please. What the hell
right have you to advise me?"

"Do you mean to say after you've got a magnificent scar like that one,
that you're going to desert and get your name on the blackbook?" Davis
persisted. "Why, you won't dare to show that scar to anybody. How can
you ever be proud of it, if you sneak away now?" The argument continued,
rising in heat, until McCutcheon motioned to the others to go outside. In
the hall, he urged them to leave him alone with the boy. "The boat sails in
an hour," he said. "Please don't come back until she's gone."

They went to a movie house next door to the hotel, although they
couldn't concentrate on the picture. A more suspenseful drama was un-
folding in their room. When they emerged to the wan glow of streetlamps
in the twilight, they saw an empty berth where the *Helleni* had docked.
They hurried back to the hotel to see the ending to the story.

Impatiently, Davis pushed open the door to the room. The young
soldier stood there in his old khakis. Shepherd's suit lay on the floor. "How
was the moving-picture show?" McCutcheon asked.

"Rotten, as usual," Davis replied. They discussed the appalling level
of the cinema in Salonika while the soldier finished dressing. As he donned
his overcoat, the young man spoke up. "It's bad enough to get into these
things again, after I said goodby to them, but my trouble is only beginning,"
he said. He had returned that day without a leave of absence, he told them.
And on top of that, he had shaved off his moustache, which was a military
offense.

"Tell them you got drunk and shaved it off because a girl wanted you
to," one reporter said. The youth said nothing, walking to the door.

"If there's anything we can do for you, let us know, won't you?" said
McCutcheon, clearing his throat.

"Well, there is one thing you can do," the boy said.

"What is it?" the reporters eagerly replied.

"You can all go to hell," he said. And he closed the door behind him.

They stood in their room, awkwardly eyeing the comfortable beds. "Some wrench!" Davis exclaimed. "It took some wrench of the will for that fellow to change his mind." The Turkish carpets looked hideously effeminate. "This is my story!" Davis suddenly shouted. "This is my story. I yelled first. Best war story I ever knew."

For certain, it was the best war story he ever wrote. He waited until he was back home in New York to work on it. He streamlined the incident, eliminating the soldier's first visit and the shaving of the moustache. He muted the baring of the scar; in his story, the soldier merely draws his finger across his shirt to indicate the wound. But he did not sweeten the story with sentiment. When McCutcheon and Shepherd later wrote their versions, they both saw this as a cautionary tale of a young man who, in a weak moment, loses his moral bearings. They saw it, in short, as a Richard Harding Davis story. That is the plot of " 'There Were Ninety and Nine' " and "The Miracle of Las Palmas" and "The Card-Sharp" and "The Long Arm."[61] In the end, the young man is always brought to his senses and redeemed. And in the nonfiction accounts set forth by McCutcheon and Shepherd, the young man—encountered some months later—is grateful to the reporters for setting him straight. There is a happy ending.

To his great credit, Davis refused to tack on a happy ending—although he did contemplate it.[62] He made such a resolution impossible by focusing not on the young man but on the older reporters. The correspondents "win," but the soldier has presented arguments they cannot refute. They are in no position to advise him. They have not seen his war. They praise courage that they cannot comprehend. They traffic in platitudes.

With a directness that he had not displayed since his youthful story, "The Other Woman," Davis in his final tale examined the moral hypocrisy of his own kind. The lean, straightforward prose style is nothing new for him. But in this story, because the subject matter is the sordid, unheroic reality of war, it is clear how much his style anticipates the modern style—and, in particular, the style of Ernest Hemingway.[63] "We heard the door slam, and his hobnailed boots pounding down the stairs," the story ends. "No one spoke. Instead, in unhappy silence, we stood staring at the floor. Where the uniform had lain was a pool of mud and melted snow and the darker stains of stale blood." Even the original title of this short story—"The Man Who Had Everything"—exhibits a tough irony atypical of Davis.[64]

Was it the brutality of this war that changed him? Was it the maturity of his added years, or of fatherhood? To some degree, all of that is true. In a more revealing sense, though, Davis had not changed. His gift was always an uncanny instinct for the desires of his audience. Throughout his life, his readers had demanded happy endings and spiritual redemption. While Davis was writing of moral regeneration and Central American derring-do, other writers, with the vision and fortitude to look, had observed darker truths. They rejected the forced optimism of the late Victorian age, and substituted irony, bitterness, discontent, pessimism: the humors that we recognize as modern. These authors—Crane, Adams, Garland, Norris, and Bierce, among other—tend to be the ones we read today.

The conditions of the modern age already existed before the advent of the Great War, but it took the shock of that war for most people to see the world in a different way.[65] It was only now, as his readership was shifting, that Davis, like a passenger on the same ship, could change direction, too. Sadly, he was approaching the end of his voyage. He finished "The Man Who Had Everything," his last short story, two weeks before his death.

When he left Salonika on December 18, traveling to Athens on a jam-packed little Greek steamer, Davis looked back on his visit to the Balkan front and reckoned it a failure. He believed that had he stayed in France, he would have produced good news stories. Instead, he had wasted most of his time traveling.[66] "Personally, I got a lot out of it," he reflected, "but I am not sent over here to improve my knowledge of Europe, but to furnish news and stories and that has not happened."[67] Once he reached Paris, he reviewed his published articles and compared them to the competition. This exercise depressed him. "My stuff seems so weak after reading [John] Reed," he wrote in his diary. "Awfully, awfully tired."[68] He was distressed to receive a list of story suggestions from the Wheeler Syndicate. "Know have not sent them anything, but, did not know they knew that," he worried privately. He cabled Wheeler, demanding to be told frankly if the newspapers were dissatisfied with his service; and, not trusting the reply, sent telegrams asking Charlie and Bessie to investigate and report back to him. "Everybody pleased but you," Bessie cabled reassuringly. He was not reassured.[69]

He did some more work in France, taking advantage of his reputation as a passionate Francophile to travel to the trenches along the five-hundred-mile front. He saw everything except Flanders, but on such a superficial level that, from a professional standpoint, he saw little: after more than a year of war, the basics of trench fighting were commonplace.[70] In Paris, he interviewed charity workers—the same angle that he had explored in Johnstown, the first big story of his career. His purpose now was pure propaganda, to encourage American contributions to French war relief efforts. He was effective. Visiting a committee of French and American art students who were selling postcard watercolors, he donated some cash; but when he announced that he planned to write about them, they erupted in glee. A Davis story would fetch thousands in American donations.[71]

Writing about charities, he was unapologetically interested in the well-born. The poor appealed to him only if they were bohemian or otherwise picturesque. This genteel attitude was not only morally dubious, it was old-fashioned; it invited parody (of the *sauce mousseline* variety) and attack. He was at his worst when defending a charity for blind officers. "It is not unfair to the *poilu* to say that the officer who is blinded suffers more than the private," he wrote. "As a rule, he is more highly strung, more widely educated; he has seen more; his experience of the world is broader; he has more to lose. Before the war he may have been a lawyer, doctor, man of many affairs. For him it is harder than, for example, the peasant to accept a future of unending blackness spent in plaiting straw or weaving rag carpets."[72]

That is Davis at his most blinkered and class-bound. At his next stop in London, by contrast, his views on the status of women were much more agreeably modern. Arriving there after a year's absence, he was surprised most of all by the many women who were employed. In Paris, women had long worked; but in London, the only female workers had been showgirls, barmaids, typists, or governesses. Now they did everything—operating elevators, driving vans. There were even women police officers! Their advances outpaced the sharpest jests of the comics and the wildest dreams of the suffragists. And, as Davis quickly realized, there was no turning back. "If, after this, women in England want the vote, and the men won't give it to them, the men will have a hard time explaining why," he wrote.[73]

In both Paris and London, he was pathetically eager to return home. On New Year's Eve, he dined by himself at the Café de la Paix; when the clock struck midnight, he was alone in his hotel room. Outside the streets were absolutely silent.[74] Four days later, he awoke suddenly at four in the morning, imagining that he heard Hope crying for her mother. He was so spooked that he turned on all the lights, and then checked the time by three watches. It was (in New York) one hour shy of his daughter's first birthday. Unable to fall back asleep, he lay in bed, homesick and forlorn.[75] He had been tired and moody through much of this trip. Some people thought that he seemed happy only when he was showing off photographs of Hope.[76] He visited an orphanage near Salonika and carried a few little children in his arms, thinking of Hope and feeling much better.[77] He joked that the Parisian nannies in the Bois skittered in alarm as he approached their baby carriages: from the hungry look in his eyes, they took him for a childnapper.[78] He had missed Hope's first Christmas and her first birthday. He swore that it would never happen again, not knowing that he would never have the chance to make it up.[79]

The stomach problems that had plagued him two months earlier on his voyage to Europe recurred at the end of his trip. He blamed the pain, once again, on ptomaine poisoning; and he did not seek a doctor.[80] His last week abroad he spent in London, giving much of his time to his sister, Nora, who was living with Percival in Kent. The relations between brother and sister had been strained over the last few years. Apart from Nora's marital difficulties, there was Richard's own divorce. Nora was a dear friend of Cecil.

But Richard was in an elegiac mood when he saw his sister in January

1916. They hadn't spent so much time together—certainly not alone—since they were children. As they reminisced about their parents and the old house in Philadelphia, Nora felt nearer to him than she had ever felt before. In this haze of nostalgia, he talked to her also of Cecil. When they dined at the Savoy, he harkened back to the good times he had known there with his first wife. On the day he sailed for New York, Nora came to his hotel, and he asked her which rooms Cecil had occupied on her visit to the same hotel the previous winter; as his cab to the station turned out of the street, he leaned back to look at the former rooms of his former wife. If Nora's account to Cecil (in a condolence letter after Richard's death) can be trusted, he "spoke of his life, simply as a matter of course, since the divorce as maimed through his own fault and as his idea of life was to now 'gather up the fragments that remain.' " He said Cecil had given him "the best I know or have," and that he "must have been the hardest man in the world to live with." He had seen life as a drama. Cecil had viewed it otherwise, and only now did he realize the difference. Uncomplaining, he accepted his responsibilities for his actions, and his obligations to Bessie. But he told Nora—if she is to be believed—that Cecil had been the spirit of his life.[81]

Richard excelled at telling listeners what they wished to hear; and for Nora, who was ruffled by the divorce, these words would have smoothed bent feathers. Even so, her account stretches credulity. Could Richard, at the same time that he was writing lovesick letters to "the best of women, with the best of daughters," be sighing to his sister that the spirit of his life had departed with Cecil?[82] Probably Nora exaggerated Richard's remorse, but she didn't invent his bittersweet nostalgia. In leaving Cecil for Bessie, he had gained a child and created a new family. The price was sacrificing his old family. Though his parents were already dead, they had known and approved of Cecil. To divorce her was to step out of their world. (That world included Cecil's parents, to whom Richard had been close in a way he could never be with Bessie's mother, who was a faded, uneducated hoofer.) The estrangement from Nora, while distressing, was tangential; far worse, Bessie jealously had banned Charlie from Crossroads Farm. For all his life, Richard had known only one intimate male friend—his brother. It was cruel and foolish for his wife to try to make him choose between her and Charlie. Of course, Richard continued to write to Charlie, and to see him in town. By ostracizing him, though, Bessie made it clear that Richard's new family would replace, not supplement, his old one.

Much as he loved Bessie and Hope, they represented an unstoppable drain, emotionally and financially. Cecil, who had given little emotionally, demanded little in return. As an educated, "modern" woman, she had insisted on being included in Richard's professional life. She had accompanied him to battlefields and to dinner parties, always holding her own (although she definitely preferred the battlefields). She had also pursued her own career. Unlike Bessie's vaudeville dancing, Cecil's painting was thoroughly respectable socially, and Richard didn't attempt to stop her. (He wouldn't have succeeded had he tried.) Socially established, financially secure, professionally independent, Cecil had slipped smoothly into the spinning spheres that made up Richard's work and social life. Her distance, her coolness, her autonomy—the very qualities that alienated him during the marriage—undoubtedly seemed more attractive now that he was tied to a woman who was hysterically jealous and totally dependent. But while he may have missed some of Cecil's qualities, Richard did not mourn the marriage. It hadn't been a real marriage. If he needed any reminder of that, he had only to reach for the nearest photograph of his lovely little daughter.

The day of reunion with Hope and Bessie had beckoned to him during his freezing days on the front and his lonely nights in hotel rooms. When at last it came, on February 5, it was inevitably a blend of light and shadows. His daughter, beautiful though she was, didn't recognize him. His wife, glad as she was to see him, was harboring a list of resentments. And, of course, a pile of bills awaited him at the door. The constant keening of the creditors was one of Bessie's main vexations. She had paid the most pressing bills shortly before her husband's return, using twenty-five hundred dollars supplied by Wheeler at Richard's cabled request. With the remaining twenty-eight hundred dollars that Wheeler now gave him, Richard could go some way toward discharging the rest of his debts. Most of them, though, he had to put off. Every unproductive moment weighed on his conscience. "No work attempted," he wrote in his diary on February 10. "Each idle day costs $150 at 12 pages a day."

Richard's family was another of Bessie's peeves. Since she would not allow Charles and his wife, Dai, to visit them in Mount Kisco, Richard went to his brother's new house in Ho-Ho-Kus, New Jersey, spending the night there. When he returned home the next day, Bessie was sick with headache.[83] A week later, he recorded in the diary: "B. still unhappy about my family."[84] She never relented. Unable to see his brother in Mount Kisco, Richard was forced to travel to New York City for lunchtime reunions.

That winter, the weather was not kind to travelers. On February 14, the mercury dropped to four degrees below zero. A month later, the temperatures were still frigid: at six degrees, New York City suffered the coldest March 18 then on record. The Davises were living in the Scribner cottage, having closed up Crossroads for the winter. The subzero February weather froze the water pipes. Richard was just as cold in the writing room of the cottage as he had been at the Olympos Palace Hotel in Salonika. No matter how much clothing he put on, he was unable to work up a sweat.[85]

He still loved Crossroads Farm, but he could feel it slipping away from him. If he wanted to make ends meet, he would have to move to a smaller establishment. As he wrote in his diary: "Easiest way is to cut down to a different sphere of living reducing in every way."[86] Besides the expense, living at the farm was terribly impractical. Situated on a private road, it was inaccessible in snow or mud for months at a time.[87] Bessie hated being there alone. In March, as they made preparations to move back in, American troops rushed to the Mexican border in an incident that threatened war. Richard was weighing the merits of covering the war as a correspondent against serving as an army officer when Bessie announced that she refused to return to the farm unless he assured her that he would not go to Mexico in any capacity. He told her that if she couldn't feel safe there, they should sell and find a place closer to civilization. (And he promised that he would not leave home unless a full-scale war broke out.)[88]

Undoubtedly, part of Bessie's recalcitrance about living at Crossroads stemmed from jealousy. She was jealous of his family, because their relationship with Richard antedated her own. She was jealous of his writing, because when he closed his study door, that "wooden rival" reminded her that she did not hold exclusive rights to his attention.[89] How could she not be jealous of the house he had planned and built with his first wife? It's surprising she agreed to live there in the first place. Although they did move back into Crossroads in March, Richard resigned himself to selling the farm. The first advertisement for it (with no price) appeared in the April 1 edition of *Town and Country*.[90]

In addition to all of these problems (or was it in consequence of them?), Richard felt dreadful. On March 25, after a bite of a lobster croquette at a New York lunch, he was consumed by the "acutest indigestion and ptomaine poisoning." He suffered terrible chest pains later that day and sought refuge in the Brook Club, where he sipped hot water. He was beginning to wonder about these strange recurrent bouts of "ptomaine poisoning." Despite the discomfort, he went that night as planned to Madison Square Garden to see Jess Willard fight Frank Moran in the heavyweight championship bout. Everyone in the fashionable, journalistic, and theatrical communities seemed to be there, and before the boxing began, Davis mingled happily at Delmonico's Café. "I believe I know more people than anyone else in New York," he wrote in his diary, "or anyway more strangers know me." But there was no doubt that his jealous wife, shaky finances, and rotten health were undermining his social profile. He was no longer a cynosure in the New York social constellation. Just a month before, he had marched out of Delmonico's when the headwaiter told him that his usual corner table was reserved for someone else.[91]

The day after the Willard fight, Richard was gripped by "awful pains" during lunch at the Algonquin Hotel. "Ice cold cocktails drove me crazy," he recorded in his diary. He warmed the champagne and got by. But when he had another attack that night at Crossroads "for nothing," he cancelled his plans to go to New York the next day to see Charles and Dai, who were just back from a vacation at Rob Collier's house in the Bahamas. Bessie would not allow them to come see Richard at the farm.[92]

Despite his illness, he was able to keep working. In the two months following his return from Europe, he completed the articles he owed *Scribner's* and revisions on what would be his final book of journalism, *With the French in France and Salonika*. He also wrote "The Deserter," beginning it on March 1 and finishing it on March 27. The tale earned him two thousand dollars from the *Metropolitan*. (*Pictorial Review* had offered him twenty-five hundred dollars a story; he used the bid to squeeze more advertising out of the *Metropolitan*.)[93] He went to town the day after finishing "The Deserter" to meet Charles and Dai for lunch. Once again, he could not tolerate iced drinks. The next night, despite the opiates he swallowed, he was seized for half an hour by awful pain. He identified it as "acute indigestion" in his diary, but he placed the phrase in quotation marks. The doctor told him not to eat, drink, or smoke.[94]

Over the next week, the attacks became more frequent and more severe. Although the doctor never informed him, the cause was not indigestion or ptomaine poisoning, but angina pectoris—a restriction of the coronary arteries, for which there was no cure. After one nighttime seizure he wrote in his diary that he now knew "how men feel who will 'lick the boots' of the man that gives 'em morphine." On April 5, the doctor ordered him to remain in bed and warned that if the pain worsened, he would require opiate injections. He made the best of being an invalid. With Hope crawling over his chest, he rummaged through letters that he had written to his mother twenty years earlier and that she had carefully preserved. Rereading them now, what struck him was how impulsively he had traveled when he was young, and how he had never worried about money.[95]

An unusual storm on April 8 smothered the landscape in snow. It seemed as though the winter would never end. Bessie, who had dismissed Hope's nanny, was on the brink of exhaustion from lack of sleep and from worry over money. If he wrote a new story, that would bring in two thousand dollars, but he could not think of a plot. Lying in bed, chafing under the doctor's ban on alcohol, working on a theatrical version of O. Henry's *Cabbages and Kings*, Richard speculated about his illness. "I think the attack was brought on by the cold, which I *cannot* stand, and worry at Bessie's not understanding why I was away, and at not getting a[n idea for a short] story," he wrote in his diary. "I am tired all over, and have had a sort of a warning that I am getting on."[96]

After several days of bed-bound discomfort, he felt well enough on Tuesday, April 11, to be up and working. He began an article which, point by point, refuted those misguided souls who confused preparedness with militarism. It was the first, he said enthusiastically, in a series of pieces on American preparedness. After dinner, he chatted with Bessie in the billiards room. When she went upstairs to put Hope to bed, he returned to his library to dictate a telegram on a matter that had been on his mind. The New York *Times* reported the day before that a Pennsylvania labor leader, in a speech at a New York high school, had said, "Down with the Stars and Stripes!" That morning Davis was pleased to read in the paper that the mayor of New York had demanded an investigation. He telephoned a congratulatory cable to the mayor. He later had a conversation with a newspaperman friend who noticed that the conversation ended abruptly but suspected nothing. He was sending a telegram to a journalist staying at the Harvard Club, to say that he was unable to write anything at present and would explain later, when he was stricken by a massive heart attack.[97]

Upstairs, Bessie, who had learned not to interrupt her husband in his study, assumed that Richard had settled in to read after finishing on the telephone. At midnight, she called to him. Getting no reply, she went down to his study, and found him wedged in the telephone booth, slumped on the floor beneath a dangling receiver. In falling, he had scraped heavily against the plaster wall; clouds of dust whitened his body. Hysterical, she called the doctor, who came from Mount Kisco to confirm the cruelly obvious. Richard had died, most likely instantly. He was one week shy of his fifty-second birthday.[98]

A ringing telephone roused Charles and Dai at 1:00 A.M. Wednesday in Ho-Ho-Kus. Dai took the call. When she heard the news, she told Charles only that Richard had been stricken, and they hired a car to drive them to Mount Kisco. Not until they were on the road did she reveal that Richard was already dead. Arriving at Mount Kisco at 7:00 A.M., they found Bessie emotionally crumpled by the shock. She welcomed Charles gratefully. Too late, the jealous wife was brimming with repentance for having barred the devoted brother from Crossroads.[99]

A small memorial service was held at the farm the next day. Of the old crowd of high-living friends who had strutted across New York at the turn of the century, only Charles Dana Gibson (with his wife, Irene, and their daughter, Babs, Richard's godchild) attended the service. Nan Clark, the wife of Cecil's brother, represented the Marion days. Not counting staff, there were fewer than a dozen people in the house. Richard had never approved of large, formal funerals. Years earlier, after attending one such "awfully painful" affair, he wrote his mother: "I certainly do not want to have any of my family at a church service over me. It is a cruel assault on the feelings and all wrong. . . ." As it turned out, that wish was in part honored, for Bessie was too distraught to attend the funeral service and unable on Friday to travel with Charles and Dai to Philadelphia, where the body was cremated. On Saturday, with only Charles and Dai present, Richard's ashes were interred in Leverington Cemetery, in a grave next to that of his parents.[100] The site overlooks the Wissahickon Creek, where Rebecca and Clarke had gone boating during their courtship.

Besides the emotional blow, Bessie had to cope with financial distress.

She had about $35 at her disposal. Most of Richard's assets were tied up in the house, which could not be liquidated immediately. His bank account contained $797.09, an amount far smaller than his outstanding debts. Moreover, by the terms of his will, that bank balance—along with the rest of his assets, including the proceeds from an eventual house sale and all of his future royalty earnings—went into a trust. Bessie would receive the income of the trust until Hope's twenty-first birthday; from then on, the yield would be divided evenly between mother and daughter. Should Bessie remarry, the income and principal would go to Hope alone. While it may have been prudent to safeguard against Bessie's financial naïveté, this arrangement left her as dry as a beached whale. Davis had lived on current income. Without it, and with all royalties on old work siphoned directly into the trust, Bessie hadn't the wherewithal to pay her daily expenses. The trust didn't amount to anything until Crossroads was sold for $74,434, a process which took more than a year. And once the debts and administrative costs were paid, Richard's entire estate (which had been estimated at $250,000 when he died) amounted to just $50,375.11. He had earned $26,000 in 1915. Temperamentally incapable of saving, he left little behind for his widow.[101]

Richard's death was, as Charles put it, "a complete calamity to her," and Bessie had trouble getting back on her feet.[102] She moved out of Crossroads immediately. Charles found her a cottage in nearby Port Chester, and rented the farm until it could be sold.[103] Without Richard, Bessie's life wobbled like a spun-out top. Beyond the matter of what to do for money, there was the question of how to fill her time. Now that her career as Mrs. Richard Harding Davis was abruptly snipped, could she pick up the thread she had dropped when she married? She quickly determined to try. In the summer of 1916, a few months after Richard's death, she wrote to the theater impresario Florenz Ziegfeld, Jr., for advice on breaking into the movies. He responded with an idea that could benefit them both. With Bessie's old mentor, Charles Dillingham, Ziegfeld ran the Century Theatre on Central Park West. If Bessie wanted a movie contract, Ziegfeld counseled, she should refresh the public's memory by returning, at least briefly, to the stage. Naturally, he had just the vehicle: a musical review, to be called *Miss 1917*.[104]

When *Miss 1917* opened in November of that year, Bessie McCoy Davis was a featured player and she won headlined rave reviews. However, *Miss 1917* was not the prelude to a movie career. It led instead to more stage and vaudeville work until, in the early 1920s, after an injury, Bessie retired from the theater, and moved with Hope to France, settling near Biarritz in the town of St. Jean de Luz. Although she never became a movie star, the motion-picture industry helped finance her retirement: the sales of Richard's stories to movie producers swelled the trust fund. When Bessie died in France in 1931, at the age of forty-four, the Davis estate had almost tripled, with movie and dramatic rights to Richard's fiction netting his heirs sixty-five thousand dollars since February 1918.[105]

It was a comfortable inheritance for Hope. In 1933, when she was eighteen, she married a French neighbor in St. Jean de Luz. He was the son of an affluent industrialist. Unfortunately, his family fortune was lost in World War II, and the young couple emigrated to New York and then to Lincolnville, Maine. There Hope produced a son, but not the books that her mother hoped would carry on the Davis legacy. Inculcated with the family tradition, she tried—in genres as disparate as screenplays and letters to the editor—to revive the fame of her parents. Unsuccessful, she died by her own hand in 1976.

Charles Belmont Davis outlived his brother by a decade, dying in 1926. He had no children. Nora Davis Farrar survived the Second World War in England. She died, childless, in 1958. After the deaths of her parents, Cecil Clark Davis adopted Marion as her primary residence, although she continued to maintain studios in London, Chicago, and Rio de Janeiro. Upon Bessie's death, she offered to adopt Hope, but was rebuffed. Never remarrying, she lived for two decades until her death in 1955 with Frederica Poett, a secretary-companion from an old California family. In the last years of her life, Cecil was plagued by a mysterious degenerative disease that she was thought to have contracted in the tropics. She assuaged the pain with alcohol. Until her death, she continued to be known as Mrs. Richard Harding Davis.

Like his fortune, Richard's reputation was consumed almost as quickly as it was made. His journalism, by its nature, was ephemeral. His fiction, for the most part, was an extension of his personality; its popularity died when he was no longer there to promote it. Had his legend been tarnished by sexual scandal or neurotic eccentricity, it would have shone brighter in the modern world. Instead, it quickly gathered dust, like an Eastlake chair in grandmother's parlor. His hearty, boyish optimism clashed irreconcilably with the furnishings of the modern mind.

"He was one of those magnetic types, often otherwise second-rate, who establish patterns of living for others of their kind," wrote the critic Van Wyck Brooks in 1952, "and the notion of the novelist as war-correspondent which prevailed so long in American writing began in the early nineties undoubtedly with him. It was . . . he who convinced Frank Norris that the journalist came in closer touch with the raw material of life than other people. . . . There was something of Davis too in Jack London and Stephen Crane, . . . and his legend was part of the atmosphere in which John Reed grew up, like Vincent Sheean, like Ernest Hemingway. . . . One of the most influential of writers, not as a writer but as a man, Davis was like the reporter who made himself king, for he was the hero of college boys who gathered from him that the journalist's life was the most picturesque and exciting of all careers."[106]

Davis's steadfast allegiance to an outdated code made him, for the next generation, one of the many fond illusions of youth to be shed with maturity. Norris, who traveled to South Africa in 1895 under Davis's influence, three years later wrote in his autobiographical novel *Blix* that he had in his youth "suffered an almost fatal attack of Harding Davis."[107] Sinclair Lewis dropped out of Yale to sail steerage to Panama, in hopes of living like a Richard Harding Davis hero;[108] and Theodore Dreiser as a young man joined the New York *World* inspired in part by the literary success of journalist Davis.[109] By the time they were mature, however, both Lewis and Dreiser most likely would have agreed with their literary champion H. L. Mencken (himself once one of the cub reporters who worshiped Davis as the "hero of our dreams") that Davis was a "cheese-monger" purveying "servant-girl romanticism" of "almost inconceivable complacency and conformity." Mencken joked that in the great Baltimore fire of 1904, he "lost a suit of clothes, the works of Richard Harding Davis, and a gross of condoms."[110] On the road to oblivion, the first station is ridicule.

The Scribners published a collected Crossroads Edition of Davis's fiction in 1916. It sold well enough that volumes are still easily found in almost any second-hand book shop, covered with decades of dust. The passage of time is not likely to restore Davis's reputation as a writer of fiction. As a reviewer noted back in 1908, Davis did not fulfill the promise of his youth. He never progressed beyond a boyish, ingratiating superficiality. "The material is not of a durable kind, but it is well-tailored; it puts up a good Fifth Avenue front, and is perfectly at home on Broadway," this prescient critic wrote. "In short, it is literature according to the *boulevardier* of the island of Manhattan, and may be hailed good-naturedly as such."[111]

The novels are all forgettable. Of the stories, only a handful—chiefly, "Gallegher," "The Other Woman," "An Unfinished Story," "In the Fog," "The Bar Sinister," and "The Deserter"—deserve a second look. The journalism, which is more difficult to locate, has worn better. Anyone curious about New York in the 1890s, Cuba and the Spanish-American War, the pageantry of Europe at the turn of the century, the first years of the Great War—interested, in short, in any of the events that Davis covered—would do well to dig up his accounts.

Yet his writing was not his major achievement. "His books were sold in great numbers, but it might be said in terms of the trade that his personality had a larger circulation than his literature," observed his friend Finley Peter Dunne. "He probably knew more waiters, generals, actors and princes than any man who ever lived, and the people he knew best are not the people who read books. They write them or are a part of them."[112] Davis's outsized personality, neither ironic nor introspective, is grounded in a time just before our own. Looking back on that life and those years, we might be adults recalling our own adolescence. We recognize the features that, blurred and altered, persist. Still, it seems a long time ago.

Notes

THE BULK OF THE LETTERS WRITTEN by Richard Harding Davis and the members of his family are in the Richard Harding Davis collection, Clifton Waller Barrett Library, Manuscripts Division, Special Collections Department, University of Virginia Library (Barrett Collection). The second most important holdings, including diaries and scrapbooks, are in the possession of Davis's grandson, Kristen Kehrig of Orleans, California (Kehrig Papers). Letters by and to Cecil Clark Davis and her mother, Louise Clark, heretofore unseen by researchers, are owned by Frederica D. Poett of Santa Barbara, California (Poett Papers). E. Anthony Newton of Palm Beach, Florida, has a smaller group of letters, most of which pertain to the Boer War (Newton Papers). Davis's long relationship with the firm of Charles Scribner's Sons is documented in the Archives of Charles Scribner's Sons, Princeton University Library (Scribner Archive). A group of letters in Special Collections, Lehigh University Libraries, relates primarily to Davis's association with Harper and Brothers. The clippings collection in the Billy Rose Theatre Collection, New York Public Library for the Performing Arts (Theatre Collection, New York Public Library), has been another essential source.

In identifying letters, I refer to Davis as RHD and to members of his immediate family by first names: his parents, L. Clarke and Rebecca Harding Davis; his brother, Charles Belmont Davis, and sister, Nora Davis Farrar; and his first wife, Cecil Clark Davis, and second wife, Bessie McCoy Davis.

The standard edition of Davis's fiction is the twelve-volume Crossroads Edition published in 1916 by Charles Scribner's Sons. I have used it as the source for notes, with the obvious exception of those stories not included in it. A year after Davis's death, his brother, Charles Belmont Davis, published a heavily edited selection of his letters, *Adventures and Letters of Richard Harding Davis*. I have indicated when the letters I cite are reprinted there; since I have quoted from the originals, there will be discrepancies that (except in the most blatant cases) I do not mention. The best bibliography of Davis's work is Henry Cole Quinby, *Richard Harding Davis: A Bibliography*, published in 1924; Quinby identifies unsigned newspaper stories written by Davis using scrapbooks no longer in existence. A very useful compilation of secondary sources on Davis was compiled by Clayton L. Eichelberger and Ann M. McDonald in *American Literary Realism* 4 (Fall 1971), 313–90. There are two previously published biographies of Davis: Fairfax Downey's *Richard Harding Davis: His Day* (New York: Charles Scribner's Sons, 1933) and Gerald Langford's *The Richard Harding Davis Years* (New York: Holt, Rinehart and Winston, 1961). More useful, however, is an unpublished work: the extremely thorough 1953 University of Kentucky Ph.D. dissertation by Scott C. Osborn, "Richard Harding Davis: The Development of a Journalist."

When quoting from letters, I have retained the original spelling and punctuation, calling attention to errors only when I feared there might be confusion. All conversations and dialogue have been transcribed from the indicated sources.

Introduction

1. "About People We Know," *Town and Country* 71 (Mar. 20, 1916): 22.

2. Booth Tarkington, intr. to Richard Harding Davis, *Van Bibber and Others* (New York: Charles Scribner's Sons, 1916), ix.

3. RHD to Mark De Wolfe Howe, n.d. [c. Jan. 9, 1886]; Houghton Library, Harvard University.

4. Edward W. Bok, "The Author of 'Gallegher,' " *Ladies' Home Journal* 11 (Aug. 1894): 5.

5. John D. McCutcheon, intr. to Richard Harding Davis, *The Lost Road* (New York: Charles Scribner's Sons, 1916), xiii.

6. Ellis Ashmead-Bartlett, *Some of My Experiences in the Great War* (London: George Newnes, Ltd., 1918), 33. Much the same point was made by John Fox, Jr.: "He was easily the first reporter of his time—perhaps of all time. Out of any incident or situation he could pick the most details that would interest the most people and put them in a way that was pleasing to the most people; and always, it seemed, he had the extraordinary good judgment or the extraordinary good luck to be just where the most interesting thing was taking place." John Fox, Jr., intr. to Richard Harding Davis, *The White Mice* (New York: Charles Scribner's Sons, 1916), vii–viii.

7. Cited by Harry Thurston Peck, "Richard Harding Davis," *Bookman* 5 (Aug. 1897): 468; and later by Arthur Bartlett Maurice, "Representative American Story Tellers, I—Richard Harding Davis," *Bookman* 23 (Apr. 1906): 145.

8. This point is well made by Larzer Ziff, *The American 1890s: Life and Times of a Lost Generation* (New York: The Viking Press, 1966), 173–82. For more on the virility anxiety of the American upper class at the turn of the century, see T. J. Jackson Lears, *No Place of Grace: Antimodernism and the Transformation of American Culture, 1880–1920* (New York: Pantheon, 1981) and Tom Lutz, *American Nervousness, 1903: An Anecdotal History* (Ithaca, N.Y.: Cornell University Press, 1991).

9. For more on this point, see Walter E. Houghton, *The Victorian Frame of Mind, 1830–1870* (New Haven: Yale University Press, 1957), 305, 310.

10. "The Stroller," Philadelphia *Call*, Feb. 7, 1898: 4.

11. Winston Churchill, *The Celebrity* (New York: The Macmillan Company, 1898), 190.

Chapter 1

1. Helen W. Sheaffer, "Rebecca Harding Davis: Pioneer Realist" (Ph.D. diss., University of Pennsylvania, 1947), 9–16, 19–24, 31–32. Rebecca Harding Davis, *Bits of Gossip* (Cambridge, Mass.: The Riverside Press, Houghton, Mifflin Company, 1904), 65–69, 102–4, 205.

2. [Rebecca Harding Davis], *Margret Howth: A Story of To-day* (Boston: Ticknor and Fields, 1862), 17.

3. Rebecca Harding Davis, *Life in the Iron Mills* (Old Westbury, N.Y.: The Feminist Press [1861], 1972).

4. Rebecca to RHD, n.d. [c. Aug. 1888]; Kehrig Papers. Reprinted in Charles B. Davis, ed., *Adventures and Letters of Richard Harding Davis* (New York: Charles Scribner's Sons, 1917), 40.

5. Rebecca to James T. Fields, n.d. [c. Nov. 30, 1861]; Barrett Collection.

6. Mark Antony De Wolfe Howe, *Memories of a Hostess* (Boston: The Atlantic Monthly Press, 1922), 11; Van Wyck Brooks, *The Flowering of New England, 1815–1865* (New York: E.P. Dutton & Co., 1937), 479.

7. Rebecca to James T. Fields, Nov. 26, 1861; Rebecca to James T. Fields, Apr. 14 [1862]; Barrett Collection. Gibson Lamb Cranmer, ed., *History of Wheeling City and Ohio County, West Virginia and Representative Citizens* (Chicago: Biographical Publishing Company, 1902), 188–91.

8. Rebecca to James T. Fields, Apr. 14 [1862]; Barrett Collection.

9. Rebecca to James T. Fields, May 1 [1862]; Rebecca to Annie Fields, May 15 [1862]; Rebecca to James T. Fields, May 27 [1862]; Barrett Collection.

10. Rebecca to Annie Fields, Dec. 6, 1862; Barrett Collection.

11. Helen Howe, *The Gentle Americans* (New York: Harper & Row, 1965), 74; Davis, *Bits of Gossip*, 54; Brooks, *Flowering*, 479.

12. Rebecca to Annie Fields, Jan. 10, 1863; Rebecca to Annie Fields, Oct. 25, 1862; Rebecca to Annie Fields, Dec. 6, 1862; Rebecca to James T. Fields, n.d. [c. Nov. 30, 1861]; Barrett Collection.

13. Davis, *Bits of Gossip*, 32–36.

14. Davis, *Bits of Gossip*, 56–57, 62–64. Rebecca to Annie Fields, June 27 [1864]; Barrett Collection.

15. Rebecca to Annie Fields, Aug. 21 [1862]; Rebecca to Annie Fields, Aug. 22 [1862]; Rebecca to Annie Fields, Tuesday [June 24, 1862]; Barrett Collection.

16. Clarke to Annie Fields, Nov. 4, 1864; Barrett Collection.

17. Philadelphia *Public Ledger*, Dec. 15, 1904; Philadelphia *Press*, Dec. 15, 1904; Philadelphia *Telegraph*, Dec. 15, 1904; clippings in Kehrig Papers. Rebecca to Annie Fields, n.d. [late Jan. or early Feb., 1863]; Barrett Collection.

18. Rebecca to Annie Fields, Jan. 10 [1863]; Barrett Collection.

19. Rebecca to Annie Fields, Feb. 18 [1863]; Mar. 18 [1863]; Barrett Collection.

20. Rebecca to Annie Fields, Monday evening [Jan. 1863]; Barrett Collection.

21. For "The Second Life," a serial written in two weeks, *Peterson's* gave her $300. The *Atlantic* paid her $200 for "David Gaunt," a story almost as long, which she reworked for months. Rebecca to James T. Fields, June 4 [1862]; Rebecca to James T. Fields, Oct. 20 [1862]; Barrett Collection.

22. Sheaffer, "Rebecca Harding Davis," 108–10.

23. Rebecca to Annie Fields, Apr. 21 [1863]; Rebecca to Annie Fields, n.d. [late Apr. or early May 1863]; Rebecca to Annie Fields, May 1 [1863]; Barrett Collection.

24. Clarke to Annie Fields, n.d. [Spring 1865]; Barrett Collection.

25. Rebecca to Annie Fields, Aug. 22 [1862]; Barrett Collection.

26. Rebecca to Annie Fields, May 11 [1863]; Rebecca to Annie Fields, July 27 [1863]; Rebecca to Annie Fields, May 6 [1863]; Rebecca to Annie Fields, n.d. [May 1863]; Barrett Collection.

27. [Rebecca Harding Davis], "The Wife's Story," *Atlantic* 81 (July 1864): 1–19. Rebecca wrote the story after her convalescence and sent it to the *Atlantic* in February 1864. Rebecca to James T. Fields, Feb. 25 [1864]; Barrett Collection.

28. Rebecca to Annie Fields, n.d. [late Aug. 1863]; Barrett Collection.

29. Rebecca to Annie Fields, n.d. [early Sept. 1863]; Barrett Collection.

30. Rebecca to Annie Fields, n.d. [Dec. 1863]; Rebecca to Annie Fields, n.d. [Christmas 1863]; Rebecca to Annie Fields, n.d. [Jan. 11 1864]; Rebecca to Annie Fields, n.d. [Feb. 14 1864]; Barrett Collection.

31. Sheaffer, "Rebecca Harding Davis," 95–96.

32. Rebecca to Annie Fields, May 17 [1864]; Rebecca to Annie Fields, June 27 [1864]; Barrett Collection.

33. Rebecca to Annie Fields, two letters, n.d. [Summer 1864]; Barrett Collection.

34. Rebecca to Annie Fields, Sept. 23 [1864]; Barrett Collection.

35. Rebecca to Clara Wilson Baird, Nov. 30 [1866]. Quoted in Sheaffer, "Rebecca Harding Davis," 102–3.

36. Davis, ed., *Adventures and Letters*, 1. The house is still standing.

37. Davis, ed., *Adventures and Letters*, 5–8. Sheaffer, "Rebecca Harding Davis," 163–67. Rebecca to Annie Fields, Aug. 10 [1865]; Rebecca to Annie Fields, Sept. 16 [1871?]; Barrett Collection.

38. Rebecca to James T. Fields, Mar. 15, 1861; Barrett Collection.

39. Philadelphia *Public Ledger*, Dec. 15, 1904; clipping in Scrapbook, Kehrig Papers. Sheaffer, "Rebecca Harding Davis," 107, 358–63. Rebecca to James T. Fields, Nov. 26 [1866]; Barrett Collection.

40. [Rebecca Harding Davis], "The Promise of the Dawn," *Atlantic* 11 (Jan. 1863): 20. Rebecca to James T. Fields, Oct. 20 [1862]; Rebecca to Annie Fields, Dec. 6 1862; Barrett Collection.

41. She wrote of Wheeling that "in a town like this it is easy to come into direct contact with every class." Rebecca to Annie Fields, Dec. 6, 1862; Barrett Collection.

42. Rebecca to Annie Fields, n.d. [Feb. 1864]; Barrett Collection.

43. Rebecca Harding Davis Diary, Feb. 2, 3, 1870; Barrett Collection.

44. Rebecca to Annie Fields, Apr. 21 [1866]; Barrett Collection.

45. Rebecca to Annie Fields, n.d. [Feb. 1866]; Barrett Collection.

46. Rebecca Harding Davis Diary, n.d.; Barrett Collection.

47. Rebecca to Annie Fields, Nov. 6 [1864]; Barrett Collection.

48. Rebecca Harding Davis Diary, n.d.; Barrett Collection.

49. Rebecca to Annie Fields, June 10 [1865]; Rebecca to Annie Fields, May 18 [1865]; Barrett Collection.

50. Rebecca Harding Davis Diary, Jan. 5, 1867; Barrett Collection.

51. Clarke wielded national influence in the theater. He was among the first to hail the comic genius of Joseph Jefferson. His panegyric of *Pinafore* in 1878, reprinted by the producers, fanned the public fervor that kept the show in the Broad Street Theatre all winter. "Penn.," "Men and Things," Philadelphia *Evening Bulletin*, Dec. 16, 1904: 6; Nathaniel Burt, *The Perennial Philadelphians: The Anatomy of an American Aristocracy* (Boston: Little, Brown and Company, 1963), 444–47.

52. Davis, ed., *Adventures and Letters*, 4, 10.

53. Rebecca Harding Davis Diary, May 4, 1871, and n.d.; Barrett Collection.

54. Rebecca Harding Davis Diary, n.d.; Barrett Collection.

55. RHD to Charles, n.d.; Barrett Collection.

56. Rebecca Harding Davis Diary, Feb. 9, 1871; Barrett Collection.

57. Scott C. Osborn, "Richard Harding Davis: The Development of a Journalist" (Ph.D. diss., University of Kentucky, 1953), 53n.; Davis, ed., *Adventures and Letters*, 2.

58. Rebecca Harding Davis Diary, June 7, 1879; Barrett Collection.

59. Davis, ed. *Adventures and Letters*, 14–15; Registrar's Office, Lehigh University, *Book Z, Record of the Standing of Students in Lehigh University, Nov. 1880 to 1891*, 49.

60. Catherine Drinker Bowen, *A History of Lehigh University* (Bethlehem, Pa.: Times Publishing Company, 1924), 8–9. For a broader view of the boom in engineering education, see David F. Noble, *America by Design* (New York: Alfred A. Knopf, 1977), 24.

61. In the torchlight procession that each June followed the mathematics exam and featured the trial and burning in effigy of King Calculus, his classmate Mark Howe later remembered the cries of "Here comes Davis!" and the "volley of objects harder than words" that rained down. RHD to Charles, n.d. [c. 1882]; Barrett Collection. Mark A. De Wolfe Howe, *A Venture in Remembrance* (Boston: Little, Brown, 1941), 69–71; Bowen, *Lehigh*, 44; Richard Harding Davis, "Richard Carr's Baby" in Davis, *Stories for Boys* (New York: Charles Scribner's Sons, 1891), 118.

62. RHD to Clarke, n.d. [1880]. Reprinted in Davis, ed., *Adventures and Letters*, 3.

63. RHD to Clarke, n.d. [c. Feb. 1882]; Barrett Collection. Reprinted in Davis, ed., *Adventures and Letters*, 21–26. RHD to Family, n.d. [c. Oct. 1882]; Kehrig Papers. Lehigh *Burr* 3 (Sept. 1883): 2. Lehigh *Burr* 3 (Oct. 1883): 20. H. S. Fisher, "History of '87," *The Epitome of '85* (Lehigh University), 36. Richard Harding Davis, "The History of the Sophomores," *The Epitome of '86* (Lehigh University), 33. [Richard Harding Davis], "The Cane Rush" Bethlehem *Daily Times*, Sept. 30, 1882: 1.

64. Caspar Whitney, "Walter Camp," *Harper's Weekly* 36 (Mar. 5, 1892): 226–27; Howard Mumford Jones, *The Age of Energy: Varieties of American Experience, 1865–1915* (New York: The Viking Press, 1971), 343–44.

65. "The roughness with which they seize the bearer of the ball is impossible to imagine without having witnessed it," a French traveler wrote in the 1890s. Paul Bourget, *Outre-Mer: Impressions of America* (New York: Charles Scribner's Sons, 1895), 330.

66. Richard Harding Davis, "The Early Days of Foot-ball at Lehigh," *Lehigh Quarterly* 1 (Apr. 1891): 82–83.

67. Davis, "Foot-ball," *Lehigh Quarterly*, 84–86.

68. Elwood Worcester, *Life's Adventure: The Story of a Varied Career* (New York: Charles Scribner's Sons, 1932), 123–24; E. Digby Baltzell, *Philadelphia Gentlemen: The Making of a National Upper Class* (Glencoe, Ill.: The Free Press, 1958), 104–5, 120.

69. RHD to Family, n.d. [Oct. 1882]; Barrett Collection.

70. RHD to Rebecca, Feb. 4 [1883 or 1884]; Barrett Collection. Davis, ed., *Adventures and Letters*, 28; C. Belmont Davis, "The Early Drama at Lehigh," *Lehigh Quarterly* 1 (June 1891): 125–26.

71. Lehigh *Burr* 4 (June 1885): 109. RHD to Family, n.d. [June 1885]; Barrett Collection.

72. Davis, ed. *Adventures and Letters*, 7.

73. There is a copy in the Barrett Collection. It has been reprinted, with an introduction by Joseph McElrath, Jr., in *American Literary Realism* 14 (Autumn 1981): 195–215. The volume is undated. Both McElrath and Osborn ("Richard Harding Davis," 279) thought the trip occurred in the summer of 1880. But a letter in the Kehrig Papers, written by Richard to Charles from Lake Placid on July 29, contains an illustration in which Richard wrote "1881." Since he was already playing

tennis and asking for an English cane at the time, the later date seems much more likely.

74. RHD to Family, n.d. [Winter 1881–82]; Kehrig Papers. [Richard Harding Davis], "Unappreciated Zeal," Lehigh *Burr* 2 (Oct. 1882): 18–20.

75. The following stories by Davis were published without a byline: "A Disciple of Theodore Hooks," Lehigh *Burr* 2 (Feb. 1883): 64–66; "Conway Maur as Thespian," Lehigh *Burr* 2 (Mar. 1883): 79–81; "An Ass in Lion's Clothing," Lehigh *Burr* 2 (May 1883): 103–5; and "A Commencement Boomerang," Lehigh *Burr* 2 (June 1883): 115–18.

76. RHD to Family, n.d. (2 letters); Barrett Collection. Davis, ed., *Adventures and Letters*, 18. Henry Cole Quinby, *Richard Harding Davis: A Bibliography* (New York: E.P. Dutton, 1924), 17. A copy of *Adventures of My Freshman*, with an inscription by Davis that explained the failure of his parents to finance a second edition, was listed in a catalogue: "Benefit Sale for the Belgian Sufferers. Under the Auspices of the Authors Club." The Anderson Galleries, May 20, 1915; Barrett Collection.

77. "An Editor's Vagaries," New York *Times*, Jan. 8, 1885: 2; "The Liberty Bell Goes South," New York *Times*, Jan. 24, 1885: 4.

78. RHD to Family, n.d. [Jan. 17, 1885]; RHD to Family, [Jan.] 23 [1885]; Barrett Collection.

79. "The 'Epitome,' " Bethlehem *Daily Times*, May 26, 1885: 1. RHD to Rebecca, n.d. [May 1885]; Barrett Collection. Lehigh *Burr* 4 (June 1885): 109. "A Lawyer Caned," Bethlehem *Daily Times*, June 17, 1885: 1.

80. RHD to Family, n.d. [Sept. 1882]; Kehrig Papers.

81. *Book Y, The Faculty's Official Record of Standing of Students, 1876 to 1885,* 133–34, 157–58, 171–72; *Book Z, Lehigh University,* 49.

82. Richard Harding Davis, "The Grand Cross of the Crescent" (1912), in Davis, *The Red Cross Girl* (New York: Charles Scribner's Sons, 1916), 50–94.

83. *Book Z, Lehigh University,* 49; Worcester, *Life's Adventure,* 119.

Chapter 2

1. "How 'Dick' Davis Got His First Job," Brooklyn *Eagle*, Apr. 23, 1916, 3: 7.

2. Talcott Williams, *The Newspaperman* (New York: Charles Scribner's Sons, 1922), 190.

3. RHD to Family, n.d. [late Fall 1885]; Kehrig Papers. RHD to Family, n.d. [late Fall 1885]; Barrett Collection.

4. RHD to Rebecca, n.d.; RHD to Clarke, n.d.; RHD to Family, n.d. [Fall 1885]; RHD to Clarke, n.d. [c. Dec. 1885]; RHD to Rebecca, n.d. [Winter 1885–86]; Kehrig Papers. RHD to Family, n.d. [Spring 1886]; RHD to Rebecca, n.d. [Winter 1885–86]; Barrett Collection.

5. Rebecca to Annie Fields, July [1865]; Rebecca to Annie Fields, July 25 [1867]; Barrett Collection.

6. Charles Blancke, "Cricket in America," *Harper's Weekly* 35 (Sept. 26, 1891): 725–6, 732; Burt, *Perennial Philadelphians,* 303–8; Baltzell, *Philadelphia Gentlemen,* 199–200.

7. RHD to Family, n.d. [c. Mar. 1886]; Kehrig Papers. RHD to Family, n.d. [Spring 1886]; Barrett Collection.

8. RHD to Family, n.d. [Dec. 1885]; Barrett Collection. Still, at this point at Johns Hopkins (as in his early days at Lehigh) he felt distressingly out of place: "a third rate grind where grinding is the rule, a football player where football playing is considered an evidence of a weak intellect and a bad dancer though a good talker where good dancers are as numerous as the flowers in May (tra la) and where good talking is considered an evidence of bohemianism." RHD to Mark De Wolfe Howe, n.d. [c. Jan. 9, 1886); Houghton Library, Harvard University.

9. RHD to Family, n.d. [Mar. 1, 1886]; Barrett Collection. RHD to Family, n.d. [1886]; Kehrig Papers.

10. RHD to Family, n.d. [Spring 1886]; Barrett Collection.

11. Rebecca Harding Davis Diary, n.d. and Oct. 13, 1879; Barrett Collection.

12. RHD to Family, n.d. [c. Fall 1885]; Kehrig Papers.

13. RHD to Family, n.d. [c. Feb. 1886]; Barrett Collection. R. H. Davis, "His Little List," *Life* 7 (Mar. 4, 1886): 133.

14. RHD to Family, n.d. [c. Jan. 1886]; Barrett Collection. Richard H. Davis, *Current* (Chicago), Jan. 9, 1886: 26–7.

15. Rebecca to RHD, n.d.; Kehrig Papers. Reprinted in Davis, ed., *Adventures and Letters,* 34.

16. RHD to Family, n.d. [Mar. 2 1886]; RHD to Family, n.d. [c. Feb. 1886]; Barrett Collection. Davis, "Richard Carr's Baby," 117–29.

17. Rebecca to RHD, n.d. [c. Jan. 1887]. Reprinted in Davis, ed., *Adventures and Letters,* 33–35.

18. Rebecca to James T. Fields, Aug. 17 [1861]; Rebecca to James T. Fields, n.d. [early Jan. 1862]; Rebecca to James T. Fields, Jan. 16 [1862]; Rebecca to James T. Fields, Mar. 18 [1862]; Rebecca to James T. Fields, n.d. [late Sept. 1862]; Rebecca to James T. Fields, Nov. 26 [1866]; Barrett Collection.

19. Philadelphia *Inquirer,* Dec. 16, 1904; New York *Times,* Dec. 15, 1904; clippings in Kehrig Papers.

20. RHD to Clarke, Oct. 18, 1878; Kehrig Papers.

21. RHD to William Young, April 11, 1887; Special Collections, Lehigh University Libraries.

22. RHD to Family, n.d. [Fall 1885]; Kehrig Papers.

23. Davis, ed., *Adventures and Letters,* 35.

24. Bethlehem *Daily Times,* June 12, 1885: 4. Richard Harding Davis, "Breaking

into the Movies" *Scribner's* 55 (Mar. 1914): 275, 282. William Harley Porter, "Mr. Davis and the Real Olancho," *Bookman* 15 (Aug. 1902): 558–61. R.H.D. [Richard Harding Davis], "Sights of Santiago de Cuba," Philadelphia *Press*, Aug. 14, 1888: 8. Robert Edeson, "Soldiers of Fortune Founded on Facts," Philadelphia *Press*, Feb. 22, 1903, Color Sec.: 2.

25. Joseph Jackson, "When Richard Harding Davis Made His Press Debut," Philadelphia *Public Ledger*, May 7, 1916, Magazine Sec.: 4.

26. [Richard Harding Davis], "A Tobacconist Disappears," Philadelphia *Record*, Sept. 10, 1886: 1.

27. "Authorship as a Business," New York *Sun*, Aug. 18, 1911: 7.

28. "How 'Dick' Davis," Brooklyn *Eagle*, 7. James O. G. Duffy, "Harding Davis as Friends Knew Him," Philadelphia *Press*, Apr. 13, 1916: 1, 12.

29. "Stars of Long Ago," Philadelphia *Press*, Dec. 26, 1886: 7; "In the Park and Zoo, The Beautiful Easter Sunday," Philadelphia *Press*, Apr. 11, 1887: 7; "Helping the Helpless," Philadelphia *Press*, Nov. 25, 1887: 3; "Five Trees Planted," Philadelphia *Press*, Apr. 23, 1887: 5; "Sliding in Toboggans," Philadelphia *Press*, Dec. 19, 1886: 3; "Almost in Mutiny," Philadelphia *Press*, Nov. 19, 1887: 7

30. Jackson, "When Richard Harding Davis," Philadelphia *Public Ledger*, 4.

31. Elizabeth Dunbar, *Talcott Williams: Gentleman of the Fourth Estate* (privately published, 1936), 195.

32. Norman Hapgood, "The Reporter and Literature," *Bookman* 5 (Apr. 1897): 120.

33. "The Life of the Giller," Philadelphia *Press*, May 1, 1887: 10; "Is Dunham Insane?" Philadelphia *Press*, Feb. 6, 1888: 2.

34. "Creston Clarke Talks," Philadelphia *Press*, Feb. 6, 1888: 4; "A Chat with Dixey," Philadelphia *Press*, Jan. 3, 1887: 2; "Changers of Money," Philadelphia *Press*, July 31, 1887: 17.

35. Gouverneur Morris, intr. to Davis, *Red Cross Girl*, xx.

36. "Placid Walt Whitman," Philadelphia *Press*, Aug. 11, 1887: 3.

37. Walt Whitman to Talcott Williams, Aug. 11, 1887. Autograph letter listed in catalogue, "Benefit Sale for the Belgian Sufferers."

38. "Walt Whitman's November," Philadelphia *Press*, July 29, 1888: 8.

39. Horace Traubel, *With Walt Whitman in Camden*, 2 (New York: D. Appleton and Company, 1908), 34.

40. RHD to Rebecca, May 16, 1897, Barrett Collection. Reprinted in Davis, ed., *Adventures and Letters*, 211. Rebecca Harding Davis, "Some Hobgoblins in Literature," *Book Buyer* 14 (Apr. 1897), 230–31; cited in Osborn, "Richard Harding Davis," 136.

41. "What Is the Best Short Story in English?" New York *Times*, Jan. 25, 1914, 5: 2, 6.

42. "Dead with His Dog," Philadelphia *Press*, July 20, 1887: 3. Stevenson's letter was reprinted in Allen Sangree, "Richard Harding Davis," *Ainslee's* 7 (Feb. 1901): 9; and, later, in Davis, ed., *Adventures and Letters*, 41.

43. "Dunham Convicted," Philadelphia *Press*, Feb. 5, 1888: 2.

44. "Confiding 'Crooks,' " Philadelphia *Press*, Dec. 18, 1887: 10.

45. Rebecca Harding Davis, "A Reporter's Work," *Independent* 42 (Jan. 16, 1890): 1.

46. Davis wrote "The Dives' Harvest," Philadelphia *Press*, Mar. 28, 1887: 3; and, possibly, "Night in the Dives," Philadelphia *Press*, Mar. 27, 1887: 1–2. For more on the campaign against dives and policy shops, see also, in the Philadelphia *Press*: "The Dives Will Go," Mar. 20, 1887: 6; "Policy Running Riot," Mar. 25, 1887: 1; "The War on the Dives," Mar. 31, 1887: 3; "Policy and the Dives," Apr. 3, 1887: 1; "The Dives Have Gone," Apr. 15, 1887: 1–2.

47. For details of the costume, including a photograph, see "Notes on R.H. Davis," *Bookman* 43 (June 1916): 355. For Davis's self-assessment, see "Confiding Crooks," 10. The account of Davis's undercover work also comes from this story in the *Press*.

48. "How 'Dick' Davis," Brooklyn *Eagle*, 7; "Notes," *Bookman* 43 (June 1916): 355; and Davis, ed., *Adventures and Letters*, 38.

49. In a scrapbook that has since disappeared, Henry Cole Quinby found a *Press* article headlined "Confiding, but Guilty. Charles Toohey Once Told a 'Press' Man Too Much." Although Quinby dated it Dec. 1887, I could not locate the story. See Quinby, *Bibliography*, 138.

50. Bourget, *Outre-Mer*, 195.

51. The details of the deal are in RHD to Charles, n.d. Reprinted in Quinby, *Bibliography*, 12–13. Original not located. See also Jackson, "When Richard Harding Davis," Philadelphia *Public Ledger*, 4.

52. The "Lime Light Man" columns, in the order they are mentioned, appeared in the following issues of the *Stage*: Oct. 13, 1888; Oct. 20, 1888; Dec. 1, 1888.

53. For the fourth issue, dated October 20, 1888, MacMichael assumed the title of publisher along with editor. Warburton left at the start of 1889, and Davis severed ties to the paper a few months later. The *Stage* played on for the remainder of the year, but in 1890 MacMichael folded it into the *Jester*, a humor magazine he had begun a few weeks before. Probably MacMichael was as responsible as Richard for their parting. However, as he had demonstrated in the mutiny of the Lehigh *Burr*, Richard was not the sort of first mate to let the captain breathe easily.

54. Duffy, "Harding Davis," Philadelphia *Press*, 12.

55. David McCullough, *The Johnstown Flood* (New York: Simon & Schuster, 1968), 177–81.

56. "Hundreds Dead," Philadelphia *Press*, June 1, 1889: 1.

57. H. S. Brown, "Pushing to the Front," Philadelphia *Press*, June 5, 1889: 1–2.

58. F.J.C. [F. Jennings Crute], "In the Ruined City," Philadelphia *Press*, June 4, 1889: 1.

59. RHD [Richard Harding Davis], "A Vision of Virginia Desolation," Philadelphia *Press*, June 5, 1889: 2.

60. "How the Correspondents Live," New York *Times*, June 9, 1889: 2; " 'Press' Men in Clover," Philadelphia *Press*, June 9, 1889: 2.

61. "Purifying the City," New York *Times*, June 8, 1889: 1.

62. "How the Correspondents Live," New York *Times*, 2.

63. R. H. Davis, "Philadelphia's Tribute," Philadelphia *Press*, June 8, 1889: 1.

64. Richard Harding Davis, "Philadelphians at Work," Philadelphia *Press*, June 9, 1889: 1; "Homes for the Orphans," Philadelphia *Press*, June 7, 1889: 4.

65. A. E. Watrous [although the real author was F. Jennings Crute], "A Lieutenant's Disgrace," Philadelphia *Press*, June 6, 1889: 1; "Lieutenant Jackson's Case," Philadelphia *Press*, June 7, 1889: 1; F. J. Crute, "Lieutenant Jackson's Disgrace," Philadelphia *Press*, June 8, 1889: 2.

66. RHD to Rebecca, n.d. [early 1890]; Barrett Collection.

67. Rebecca Harding Davis, "A Reporter's Work," 1.

68. RHD to Rebecca, n.d. [c. Jan. 15, 1890]; Barrett Collection.

69. A. B.[Arthur Brisbane], "Richard Harding Davis," *Book Buyer* 8 (June 1891): 198; Antoinette M. Reazin, "Richard Harding Davis: Brief Biography," Philadelphia *Inquirer*, Sept. 10, 1898: 7.

70. McCullough, *Johnstown Flood*, 51–58, 76–77, 247–50.

Chapter 3

1. Fairfax Downey, *Richard Harding Davis: His Day* (New York: Charles Scribner's Sons, 1933), 48.

2. "Philadelphia Society has probably the longest record of snobbish exclusiveness in America; more compact and effectively implemented than New York, it is more lavish and more overtly materialistic than Boston." Dixon Wecter, *The Saga of American Society* (New York: Charles Scribner's Sons, 1937), 143.

3. Lloyd Morris, *Incredible New York* (New York: Random House, 1951), 151–54, 190–93.

4. Thomas Beer, *Stephen Crane* (New York: Alfred A. Knopf, 1923), 67.

5. Edith Wharton, *The Custom of the Country* (New York: Charles Scribner's Sons, [1913] 1941), 74.

6. Frederic Cople Jaher, "Style and Status: High Society in Late Nineteenth-Cen-

tury New York," in Jaher, ed., *The Rich, the Well Born and the Powerful* (Urbana, Ill.: University of Illinois Press, 1973), 269.

7. A Philadelphia journalist noted that "no one having indisputably held social prestige in this town has ever lost it for want of money. Wealth may socially 'make' a family in Philadelphia, but the lack of it never 'unmakes' them." "Life on $15,000 a Year," Philadelphia *Press*, March 11, 1888: 13.

8. "Because one's social position [in post–Civil War New York] was not fixed, 'activities which are known as social functions' came to dominate society. To be a member of society, one had to act as society decreed and attend events that defined society. One's social status came not from one's rank but from acceptance by others into a private round of balls, dinners, and parties that distinguished the rich from everyone else." Lewis Erenberg, *Steppin' Out: New York Nightlife and the Transformation of American Culture, 1890–1930* (Westport, Conn.: Greenwood Press, 1981), 12. The young Richard Harding Davis showed an intuitive grasp of the subject when he wrote: "Society is an indefinite number or class or condition of existence, in which the subscribing members mutually bind themselves to conform to certain rules and restrictions, and to observe certain amenities which they find make the life they lead move more smoothly and pleasantly for themselves and everybody else." "The Lime Light Man," *Stage*, Nov. 17, 1888: 5.

9. Foster Coates, "Journalism of To-day," Philadelphia *Press*, Nov. 27, 1887: 13. Forty years later, three New York managing editors were earning salaries of $40,000 to $50,000; in Philadelphia, Boston, and Chicago, their counterparts were making between $7,500 and $15,000. A beginning reporter would get $20 to $25 a week in New York, between $12 and $20 in the smaller cities. Talcott Williams, *The Newspaperman* (New York: Charles Scribner's Sons, 1922), 160–61.

10. Gunther Barth, *City People: The Rise of Modern City Culture in Nineteenth Century America* (New York: Oxford University Press, 1980), 90–96.

11. Edward P. Mitchell, *Memoirs of an Editor* (New York: Charles Scribner's Sons, 1924), 229.

12. Piers Brendon, *The Life and Death of the Press Barons* (New York: Atheneum, 1983), 29.

13. Brendon, *Press Barons*, 97.

14. E. A. Ross in the *Atlantic* (Mar. 1910) estimated that advertising had constituted less than half the earnings of daily newspapers in 1880. By 1910, it made up at least two-thirds, and in some larger papers, nine-tenths of total revenues. Cited by Upton Sinclair, *The Brass Check* (Pasadena, Calif.: Privately published, 1919), 293. Sinclair has much to say on the relationship between department stores and newspapers. See especially the amusing anecdotes on p. 227 and p. 283. Charles Dudley Warner discusses the importance of advertising to newspapers in "The American Newspaper" (1881) in *Fashions in Literature* (New York: Dodd, Mead and Company, 1902), 39.

15. Allen Churchill, *Park Row* (New York: Rinehart and Company, 1958), 43.

16. W. A. Swanberg, *Pulitzer* (New York: Charles Scribner's Sons, 1967), 163 cited in Brendon, *Press Barons*, 97.

17. Philadelphia *Public Ledger*, Dec. 15, 1904; clipping in L. Clarke Davis Obituary Scrapbook, Kehrig Papers.

18. Davis, ed. *Adventures and Letters*, 42–43. David A. Curtis, "Richard Harding Davis," *Author* 2 (Jan. 15, 1891): 17–18. Charles Davis says that, having been rejected by many editors, Richard was sitting on a park bench and planning to return to Philadelphia when Brisbane happened to pass by. Curtis, who got his story from Brisbane, reports that before he reached the *World* with his letter from Childs, Davis ran into Brisbane, who persuaded him to join the *Evening Sun*. Probably, Brisbane chose not to divulge Richard's failures. A detailed but totally inaccurate account was given after Davis's death in "Richard Harding Davis Drops Dead in His Home," New York *Evening Post*, Apr. 12, 1916: 6.

19. Oliver Carlson, *Brisbane: A Candid Biography* (New York: Stackpole Sons, 1937), 87.

20. Charles J. Rosebault, *When Dana Was the Sun* (New York: Robert M. McBride and Company, 1931), 166.

21. Candace Stone, *Dana and the Sun* (New York: Dodd, Mead and Company, 1938), 53.

22. Rosebault, *Dana*, 292.

23. Mitchell, *Memoirs*, 126.

24. Rosebault, *Dana*, 160.

25. Carlson, *Brisbane*, 87–92.

26. Mitchell, *Memoirs*, 373.

27. "Caught the Baby on a Fly," New York *Evening Sun*, Sept. 6, 1890: 1. For a baby who fell into a copy of the *Evening Sun* that a reader was perusing on the front stoop, see "Honora Fell Five Stories," New York *Evening Sun*, July 2, 1890: 1.

28. Rosebault, *Dana*, 167–68.

29. Norman Hapgood, *The Changing Years* (New York: Farrar and Rinehart, 1930), 121–22.

30. Rosebault, *Dana*, 254–55. Isaac F. Marcosson, *David Graham Phillips and His Times* (New York: Dodd, Mead and Company, 1932), 96.

31. Stephen Bonsal, *Heyday in a Vanished World* (New York: W.W. Norton and Company, 1937), 429.

32. Rosebault, *Dana*, 246.

33. Rosebault, *Dana*, 262–65. Marcosson, *Phillips*, 98.

34. [Brisbane], "Richard Harding Davis," *Book Buyer*, 198.

35. Davis, ed., *Adventures and Letters*, 43.

36. Bok, " 'Gallegher,' " *Ladies' Home Journal*, 5.

37. Bourget, *Outre-Mer*, 194.

38. "In one day he became famous," wrote Edward W. Bok. " 'Gallegher,' " *Ladies' Home Journal*, 5.

39. "Our Green Reporter," New York *Evening Sun*, Nov. 2, 1889: 1. "Tried to Bunco a Reporter," New York *News*, Nov. 2, 1889: 4. "Mr. 'Sheeny Mike's' Victim," New York *Times*, Nov. 3, 1889: 5. RHD to Family, n.d. [c. Nov. 3, 1889]; Kehrig Papers.

40. Davis, ed., *Adventures and Letters*, 45.

41. RHD to Family, n.d. [c. Nov. 3, 1889]; Kehrig Papers.

42. John H. Girdner, *Newyorkitis* (New York: The Grafton Press, 1901), 120.

43. "Editor's Easy Chair," *Harper's New Monthly* 13 (July 1856): 272; cited in Barth, *City People*, 31.

44. Bourget, *Outre-Mer*, 25.

45. Girdner, *Newyorkitis*, 128–29.

46. "Three High Kickers," New York *Evening Sun*, May 27, 1890: 2. "Carmencita and Otero," New York *Evening Sun*, Oct. 1, 1890: 4. "And Here Comes the Otero," New York *Evening Sun*, Oct. 2, 1890: 4. Edward Marshall, "Niblo's Garden," *Harper's Weekly* 36 (June 25, 1892): 614. Fairfax Downey, "Carmencita: Patron Saint of Vaudeville," unpublished manuscript, Scribner Archive. Thomas Beer, *The Mauve Decade* (New York: Alfred A. Knopf, 1926), 31–32. Davis mentions enjoying Carmencita's dancing in RHD to Rebecca, n.d. [c. May 16, 1890]; Barrett Collection. Reprinted in Davis, ed., *Adventures and Letters*, 52.

47. Mark Sullivan, *Our Times: Pre-War America* (New York: Charles Scribner's Sons, 1930), 350–51.

48. "Not Worth the Money," New York *Evening Sun*, Sept. 23, 1890: 3. This story, which echoes the judgment expressed in Davis's later article, "Harrigan's Tough Girl," is written in his style. Although it cannot be proven to be his work, this line deprecating the model's striped chemisette is virtually his signature: "It looks as much like the human flesh as does an orange and black striped jersey on a Princeton half-back."

49. "Succi Is Now Fasting," New York *Evening Sun*, Nov. 6, 1890: 2; "Succi a Sickening Sight," New York *Evening Sun*, Dec. 19, 1890: 1. The sequence of New York attractions appears in "Harrigan's Tough Girl," New York *Evening Sun*, Jan. 5, 1891: 4. Although not cited by previous researchers, this article was definitely Davis's work, written in his distinctive style and quoting one of his favorite phrases: "the new step on the floor and the new face at the door." He wrote another article praising the "tough girl," Ada Lewis, two months later. See Richard Harding Davis, "Edward Harrigan and the East Side," *Harper's Weekly* 35 (March 21, 1891): 210.

50. Journalists were overrepresented among the overdressed: David Graham Phillips, Lincoln Steffens, even Charles Dana were all renowned for their fastidious attire. The young Theodore Roosevelt was also a clotheshorse. For Phillips, see Marcosson, *Phillips*, 22–26, 63–64, 99. For Steffens, Justin Kaplan, *Lincoln Steffens: A Biography* (New York: Simon & Schuster, 1974), 23, 41, 50, 59. For Dana, Rosebault, *Dana*, 7. For Roosevelt, Edmund Morris, *The Rise of Theodore Roosevelt* (New York: Coward, McCann & Geoghegan, 1979), 88, 110, 260, 426, 506; and Mark Sullivan, *Our Times: America Finding Herself* (New York: Charles Scribner's Sons, 1927), 226–32.

51. RHD to Rebecca, n.d. [c. May 1890]; Barrett Collection. Richard was soon on very familiar terms with his young boss. Late one night another reporter, Stephen Bonsal, who had crashed in Brisbane's splendiferous Victorian apartment while his host went off to gamble, was awakened by a deferential pulling of his big toe. "I'm sorry to wake you up, Briz—but it is a case of must," said the intruder, in a most ingratiating tone of voice. "I'm going down to Lakewood by the first train. It's just the sweetest story you ever heard of and I think it will be a 'scoop.' I shall try to be back at eleven but hold the forms as long as you can and set aside at least two columns—and let me have a little more leeway if you can." Richard was shocked when he realized that he had mistakenly spilled the beans to a man from the rival *Herald*; but, calmed by Bonsal's reassurances, he soon befriended this friend of Brisbane's. Bonsal, *Vanished World*, 430.

52. Davis, ed., *Adventures and Letters*, 45–46.

53. RHD to Rebecca, n.d. [c. May 16, 1890]; Barrett Collection. Reprinted in Davis, ed., *Adventures and Letters*, 51–52.

54. Grover Cleveland to RHD, Feb. 5, 1891; Rare Book and Manuscript Library, Columbia University. William W. Ellsworth, *A Golden Age of Authors* (Boston: Houghton Mifflin Company, 1919), 18–19.

55. RHD to Rebecca, Tuesday, n.d. [c. early Jan. 1890]; Barrett Collection.

56. RHD to Rebecca, n.d.; Barrett Collection. In 1900, Helen Benedict wed Thomas Hastings, the architect.

57. "The Goddess in Mid-Air," New York *Evening Sun*, May 13, 1890: 3.

58. Morris, intr. to Davis, *Red Cross Girl*, viii.

59. RHD to Rebecca, n.d. [c. May 16, 1890]; Barrett Collection. Reprinted, with the last names of the girls excised, in Davis, ed., *Adventures and Letters*, 52–54. The last line is an allusion to the song "Little Annie Rooney," which appeared in 1890. The verse goes: "She's my sweetheart, I'm her beau,/She's my Annie, I'm her Joe,/Soon we'll marry, nev-er to part/Little Annie Rooney is my sweetheart!" Mark Sullivan, *Our Times: The Turn of the Century, 1900–1904* (New York: Charles Scribner's Sons, 1926), 255. The song was a favorite of Davis's. At about this time, he sang "Little Annie Rooney" in a gathering at Grover Cleveland's house. Bonsal, *Vanished World*, 432.

60. Marcosson, *Phillips*, 91–92. Carlson, *Brisbane*, 93.

61. "The Master and the Man," New York *Evening Sun*, Mar. 1, 1890: 5.

62. "Van Bibber's Box Party," New York *Evening Sun*, May 3, 1890: 3. Reprinted in Davis, *Stories for Boys*, 177–83, with the title "The Van Bibber Baseball Club."

63. Arthur Pendennis takes a working-class girl to Vauxhall Gardens and is delighted to see her intense enjoyment. "What would I not give for a little of this pleasure?" says the blasé young man to himself, eyeing the beautiful girl. The sexual overtones in Thackeray, of course, are expunged in the Davis translation. William Thackeray, *The History of Pendennis* (London: Macmillan and Co., 1925; facs. of 1848 edition), 526–28.

64. "Van Bibber on a Swan Boat," New York *Evening Sun*, June 7, 1890: 5. Reprinted as "Van Bibber and the Swan-Boats" in Richard Harding Davis, *Van Bibber and Others* (New York: Charles Scribner's Sons, 1916), 110–16.

65. These are the stories, in the order described. "The Hungry Man Was Fed," New York *Evening Sun*, June 21, 1890: 3; reprinted in Davis, *Van Bibber*, 42–49. "Van Bibber at the Races," New York *Evening Sun*, July 7, 1890; reprinted in *Van Bibber*, 50–58. "Van Bibber Economizes," New York *Evening Sun*, July 11, 1890: 4; reprinted as "An Experiment in Economy," *Van Bibber*, 59–66. "Van Bibber as Best Man," New York *Evening Sun*, July 26, 1890: 3; reprinted in *Van Bibber*, 130–39. "Van Bibber's Burglar," New York *Evening Sun*, Dec. 13, 1890: 4; reprinted in *Van Bibber*, 117–29.

66. With Van Bibber too suave to play the fool, Davis created the fumbling Travers, along the lines of the original Van Bibber. Travers first appeared in "Mr. Travers Was Not in It" New York *Evening Sun*, Aug. 30, 1890: 3, a tale in which he behaves foolishly during amateur theatricals. In subsequent stories, Van Bibber and Travers have adventures together, and the differences between them gradually blur. So much so that while Travers was the hero of "Love Me, Love My Dog" when it appeared in the New York *Evening Sun*, Jan. 1, 1891: 4, his name—and nothing else—was changed to Van Bibber when the story was republished in *Van Bibber and Others*.

67. Curtis, "Richard Harding Davis," *Author*, 18.

68. Cited in "Chronicle and Comment," *Bookman* 16 (Sept. 1902): 9; and again, by Arthur Bartlett Maurice, "Representative American Story Tellers," *Bookman* 23 (Apr. 1906): 137.

69. Clara S. J. Moore ("Mrs. H. O. Ward"), *Sensible Etiquette of the Best Society*, 10th rev. ed. (Philadelphia: Porter & Coates, 1878), 144; cited in Arthur M. Schlesinger, Sr., *Learning How to Behave: A Historical Study of American Etiquette Books* (New York: The Macmillan Company, 1947), 29.

70. Harry Thurston Peck, "Richard Harding Davis," *Bookman* 5 (Aug. 1897): 465. As a literary assessment of Davis, the essay, which appears on pages 462–68, remains unsurpassed.

71. Peck, "Richard Harding Davis," *Bookman*, 467.

72. RHD to Rebecca, n.d.; Barrett Collection.

73. Tudor Jenks, "Holiday Books for Young People," *Book Buyer* 8 (Dec. 1891): 544.

74. Beer, *Crane*, 78.

75. RHD to Family, n.d. [early May 1890]; Barrett Collection.

76. "A Vile Den to Be Closed," New York *Evening Sun*, Apr. 17, 1890: 2. The Haymarket wasn't permanently closed until 1913. See Erenberg, *Steppin' Out*, 22. A previously unidentified story about the closing of a Twenty-ninth Street tavern is written in the distinctive Davis style. It begins: "Tracey's dive, the most picturesquely 'tough' place in the Tenderloin district, has been closed, and one of the sights to which the New Yorker was sure to lead his Philadelphia cousin when he wanted to shock and surprise him has been taken away. There are very few of such places left and they are dying fast." "Last Days of 'Tracey's,'" New York *Evening Sun*, Sept. 1, 1890: 2.

77. RHD to Rebecca, n.d. [Apr. 3, 1890]; Barrett Collection. Reprinted in Davis, ed., *Adventures and Letters*, 47–48.

78. The account of the tour is based on two reports which, although they describe evenings more than three years apart, are quite similar. "The Inspector's Museum," New York *Evening Sun*, May 16, 1890: 6; and Bourget, *Outre-Mer*, 195–205. A similar tour is described in RHD to Rebecca, n.d. [c. May 17, 1890]; Barrett Collection. In that one, Richard took a crowd of eleven through police headquarters. In April 1890, he escorted four female Shippens (the three girls and their mother) through the Tombs Prison. See "Young Ladies in the Tombs," New York *Evening Sun*, Apr. 3, 1890: 3; and RHD to Rebecca, n.d. [Apr. 3, 1890]; Barrett Collection; reprinted in Davis, ed., *Adventures and Letters*, 48.

79. "New York's Front Stoop," New York *Evening Sun*, June 10, 1890: 2. Davis's "tough" stories of this period include "The Jump at Corey's Slip," New York *Evening Sun*, July 5, 1890: 3; "The 'Trailer' for Room 8," New York *Evening Sun*, July 15, 1890: 3; "How Hefty Left the Island," New York *Evening Sun*, Aug. 22, 1890: 4; "My Disreputable Friend, Mr. Raegen," *Scribner's* 8 (Dec. 1890): 685–89; and "How Hefty Burke Got Even," New York *Evening Sun*, Jan. 3, 1891: 5. They were republished, some with new titles, in his first three collections of short stories. Responding to his mother's criticisms of "How Hefty Left the Island," Richard wrote: "I could not understand why you did not like 'Hefty' because if I understood you it was his being such a tough that you objected to. But you must remember that while the Van Bibber tales appeal to those who are limited to a few hundreds the East River and the Island are very actual to many thousands and the clump of bushes where the boys hide their clothes and the Half Hose social and the Jolly Fellows Pleasure Clubs are all real places just as much as Martin's or Delmonico's and make the paper popular. The story was only meant to amuse anyway and I think I must have misunderstood you." RHD to Rebecca, n.d. [Aug. 26, 1890]; Barrett Collection.

80. [Charles T. Copeland], "The Short Story," *Atlantic* 69 (Feb. 1892), 268. Cited disapprovingly in "The Rambler," *Book Buyer* 12 (June 1895): 284.

81. Marcosson, *Phillips*, 219.

82. Richard Harding Davis, "The Reporter Who Made Himself King" (1891), reprinted in Davis, *The Exiles and Other Stories* (New York: Charles Scribner's Sons, 1916), 251.

83. Edwin L. Shuman, *Steps into Journalism* (Evanston, Ill.: Correspondence School of Journalism, 1894), 123; cited in Michael Schudson, *Discovering the News: A Social History of American Newspapers* (New York: Basic Books, 1978), 79.

84. "Where Is Mr. Bradley?" New York *Evening Sun*, Sept. 29, 1890: 3. RHD to Charles Davis, n.d. [c. Oct. 1, 1890]; Barrett Collection. Reprinted in Davis, *Adventures and Letters*, 48–49.

85. For cynicism among reporters, see Hapgood, "The Reporter and Literature," *Bookman*, 119–21.

86. Davis, "Van Bibber's Burglar," New York *Evening Sun*, Dec. 13, 1890: 4. Reprinted in Davis, *Van Bibber*, 119–20.

87. According to Chester Lord of the *Sun*, Davis's "enthusiasm and naïveté, his rigidity of code and self-dramatization . . . clashed with the cynicism and surface sophistication of many newspapermen and caused them to dislike him." Churchill, *Park Row*, 174.

88. Sangree, "Davis," *Ainslee's*, 4–5, relates this anecdote. Inaccuracies in Sangree's account have been corrected from the story itself: "Smothered in His Sleep," New York *Evening Sun*, Nov. 8, 1890: 1. Quinby, *Bibliography*, 289–90, reprints the story, with the first two paragraphs omitted.

89. This account of Kemmler's execution is based on the following stories in the New York *Evening Sun*: "Kemmler Must Die," Mar. 21, 1890: 1; "His Last Week," Apr. 26, 1890: 1; "Kemmler Is Ready," Apr. 28, 1890: 1; "Extra. He Has a Respite," Apr. 29, 1890: 1; "Respited!" April 29, 1890, Sporting and Financial Extra: 1; "Kemmler's Apathy," Apr. 30, 1890: 1; "How We Won the Day," Apr. 30, 1890: 1; "Kemmler's Lawyer Talks," Apr. 30, 1890: 2; "No Hope for Kemmler," May 23, 1890: 1; "All Up With Kemmler," June 24, 1890: 2; "Kemmler Breaking Down," July 26, 1890: 1; "The Machine All Ready," Aug. 1, 1890: 1; "Is Kemmler Insane?" Aug. 2, 1890: 1; "To See Kemmler's End," Aug. 4, 1890: 1; "In Death's Shadow," Aug. 5, 1890: 1; "Writhed," Aug. 6, 1890: 1; "How the Town Got the News," Aug. 6, 1890: 3; "First Shock Didn't Kill," Aug. 7, 1890: 1. There are two letters in the Barrett Collection from Davis to his family describing the preparations for the execution. Because they are undated, previous writers have assumed that Davis was in Auburn in August. But his references to the cool weather indicate that he was there in April. Describing the press shenanigans, he told his family, "Brisbane has promised to let me write the story of all this when it is all over and it ought to make funny reading." Because of the similarities between his letters and the *Evening Sun* article "How We Won the Day," which appeared on April 30, it seems likely that Davis was the author.

90. "Queer Crimes of a Year," New York *Evening Sun*, Dec. 31, 1890: 5.

91. This account of Annie Goodwin's death and Dr. Henry G. McGonegal's trial is based on the following articles, all in the *Evening Sun*: "Hid the Victim's Body,"

July 22, 1890: 1; "Her Body Resurrected," July 23, 1890: 1; "Resurrected!" July 23, 1890, Sporting and Financial Extra: 1–2; "Who Killed Annie Goodwin?" July 23, 1890: 2; "Who Killed Annie Goodwin?" July 24, 1890: 2; "Annie Goodwin's Romance," July 24, 1890: 1; "Sadie Tells Her Story," July 25, 1890: 1; "What Will Be Done With McGonegal?" July 25, 1890: 2; "Where Is Detective Price?" July 26, 1890: 1; "Hot Shot for McGonegal," July 28, 1890: 1; " 'Lynch Him!' Was the Cry," July 29, 1890: 1; "The Sweet Reasonableness of It," July 30, 1890: 2; "Following Up the Case," Aug. 4, 1890: 2; "M'Gonegal Indicted," Aug. 6, 1890: 2; "McGonegal's Trial Begins," Sept. 23, 1890: 1; "Old Dr. M'Gonegal's Fate," Oct. 4, 1890: 1; and "M'Gonegal Gets 14 Years," Oct. 15, 1890: 1.

92. Duffy, "Harding Davis," Philadelphia *Press*, 12. Some *Evening Sun* reporters believed that the model for Gallegher was a boy named "Daddy" Reaper, who worked on that paper and was devoted to Davis. "Chronicle and Comment," *Bookman* 43 (June 1916): 359. Perhaps during his numerous revisions, Davis incorporated some traits of "Daddy" Reaper into Gallegher.

93. "Chronicle and Comment," *Bookman* 43: 356.

94. Richard Harding Davis, "The Lime Light Man," *Stage*, Feb. 16, 1889: 4.

95. "Mr. Richard Harding Davis," Boston *Sunday Herald*, Apr. 12, 1896: 26.

96. For the spelling error, see Bonsal, *Vanished World*, 430. For the story, see Richard Harding Davis, "Gallegher," in Davis, *Gallegher and Other Stories* (New York: Charles Scribner's Sons, 1916), 3–53.

97. See, for example, H. L. Mencken, *Newspaper Days, 1899–1906* (New York: Alfred A. Knopf, 1941), 12.

98. Rebecca to RHD, n.d. [Summer 1888]; Kehrig Papers. Reprinted in Davis, ed., *Adventures and Letters*, 40.

99. Beer, *Mauve Decade*, 216.

100. Ellsworth, *Golden Age*, 144.

101. Bok, " 'Gallegher,' " *Ladies' Home Journal*, 5. According to another, probably less reliable account, six editors of lesser magazines had refused "Gallegher" before *Scribner's* accepted it. Francis Arthur Jones, "How They 'Broke into Print,' " *Strand* 49 (July 1915): 760.

102. Frank Luther Mott, *A History of American Magazines, 1885–1905* (Cambridge, Mass.: The Belknap Press of Harvard University Press, 1957), 717.

103. W. D. Howells, "The Man of Letters as a Man of Business," in *Literature and Life* (New York: Harper & Brothers, 1902), 7–9. Donald Sheehan, *This Was Publishing: A Chronicle of the Book Trade in the Gilded Age* (Bloomington: Indiana University Press, 1952), 41–44.

104. E. L. Burlingame to RHD, March 17, 1890. The payment is recorded in Mss. Record Book 11, Apr. 4, 1890, p. 53; Scribner Archive.

105. Rebecca to RHD, n.d. [c. Mar. 18, 1890]; Kehrig Papers.

106. "Mr. Richard Harding Davis," Boston *Sunday Herald*, 26. In this interview, Davis is quoted: "I do not think I ever wrote a whole story at a sitting, except one. Do you remember 'A Walk up the Avenue'? I wrote that on the back piazza of a hotel in Syracuse, whither I had gone to see a man hung. That fact got me out of a scrape, too, for a friend accused me of having used an incident in his own life, and was deeply hurt. Fortunately, I could prove, by the hotel paper on which it was written, that I wrote the story before the incident happened." Despite the discrepancy between hanging and electrocution, and Syracuse and Auburn, the fact that Davis wrote the story in April 1890, when he was covering the Kemmler case, suggests that he or his interlocutor confused a few details six years after the event.

107. RHD to Rebecca, n.d. [late April or early May 1890]; Barrett Collection. Richard Harding Davis, "A Walk up the Avenue," *Harper's Magazine* 81 (Aug. 1890): 388–90. Davis's romance with Alden did not last long. In October, Alden summoned him for another interview, this time at his home in Metuchen, New Jersey. This is Richard's report to his mother: "You should know what Mr. Alden wanted at once and you will rejoice with me. No wonder he would not talk it over hurriedly in his office but waited until he had me to himself in his New Jersey home. He wants me to write a story for Harper's for December after next!!!! And for this I travelled to Metuchen and listened to metaphysics and philosophy and the sighs of Mrs. Alden who is now absolutely well again and the sweet nothings of her daughter and viewed the pigs and the cows and got my patent leathers covered with the mud of his estate. I thought at least he wanted a novel, and when I found I had been decoyed into their lonely home in the pine woods to be told he would like a Christmas story year after next I boiled within and swore I had to get back to the city that night. And when I at last escaped from the seer and got into the smoking car cityward bound I kicked the stuffing out of the chair in front and laughed with glee although the laugh was on myself." RHD to Rebecca, n.d. [c. Oct. 1890]; Barrett Collection.

108. RHD to Rebecca, n.d. [mid-May 1890]; Barrett Collection.

109. RHD to Rebecca, n.d. [late April or early May 1890]; Barrett Collection.

110. The drawing, which was published in the issue of May 22, 1890, is reproduced in Downey, *Davis: His Day*, 81.

111. Charles Dana Gibson, "The First Glimpse of Davis," intr. to Davis, *Exiles*, vii. The date of the meeting is corroborated in Richard Harding Davis, "The Origin of a Type of the American Girl," *Quarterly Illustrator* 3 (Jan.–Mar. 1895): 3.

112. See Lois Banner, *American Beauty* (New York: Alfred A. Knopf, 1983), 162.

113. Fairfax Downey, *Portrait of an Era as Drawn by C.D. Gibson* (New York: Charles Scribner's Sons, 1936), 100–101.

114. Bok, " 'Gallegher,' " *Ladies' Home Journal*, 5.

115. [W. D. Howells], "Editor's Study," *Harper's* 83 (Sept. 1891): 640.

116. "Journalism and American Literature," *Critic* 18 (Feb. 7, 1891): 71.

117. Bourget, *Outre-Mer*, 194.

118. Frank Luther Mott, *Golden Multitudes: The Story of Best Sellers in the United States* (New York: The Macmillan Company, 1947), 184–88. RHD to Rebecca, n.d. [c. May 16, 1890]; Barrett Collection. Reprinted in Davis, ed., *Adventures and Letters*, 52.

119. For more on Merrill, see Grant C. Knight, *The Critical Period in American Literature* (Chapel Hill: University of North Carolina Press, 1951), 20–21; Sir William Rothenstein, *Men and Memories*, 1 (London: Faber & Faber, 1931), 94; and Alfred Kazin, "American Fin-de-Siecle," *Saturday Review of Literature* 21 (Feb. 3, 1940): 4.

120. RHD to Rebecca, n.d. [c. Apr. 15, 1890]; Barrett Collection.

121. E. L. Burlingame to RHD, May 16, 1890; Scribner Archive. RHD to Rebecca, n.d. [mid-May 1890]; Barrett Collection. Richard Harding Davis, "A Summer Night on the Battery," *Harper's Weekly* 34 (Aug. 2, 1890): 594.

122. RHD to Rebecca, n.d. [c. Aug. 26, 1890]; Barrett Collection.

123. E. L. Burlingame to RHD, Aug. 8, 1890; Scribner Archive. RHD to Rebecca, n.d. [c. Aug. 20, 1890]; Barrett Collection.

124. Richard Harding Davis, "My Disreputable Friend, Mr. Raegan," reprinted in Davis, *Van Bibber*, 153–81. Rebecca to RHD, Wednesday, n.d.; Kehrig Papers. RHD to Rebecca, n.d. [c. Aug. 20, 1890] and RHD to Rebecca, n.d. [c. Sept. 1, 1890]; Barrett Collection.

125. RHD to Rebecca, n.d. [early Sept. 1890]; Barrett Collection.

126. RHD to Family, n.d. [Oct., 1890]; Barrett Collection.

127. E. L. Burlingame to RHD, Nov. 7, 1890; Scribner Archive.

128. Richard Harding Davis, "Broadway," *Scribner's* 9 (May 1891): 585–604. It bears a notable similarity to "The Broadway Parade," New York *Evening Sun*, Mar. 7, 1890: 3, an article which Davis probably wrote.

129. See Lately Thomas, *Delmonico's: A Century of Splendor* (Boston: Houghton Mifflin Company, 1967), esp. 76–77, 86–88, 134, 148–49, 155–64, 191.

130. RHD to Family, n.d. [early May 1890]; Barrett Collection.

131. RHD to Family, n.d. [early May 1890]; Barrett Collection.

132. RHD to Family, n.d. [c. Sept. 10, 1890]; Barrett Collection. Reprinted in Davis, ed., *Adventures and Letters*, 49–50.

133. Peter Lyon, *Success Story: The Life and Times of S. S. McClure* (New York: Charles Scribner's Sons, 1963), 99.

134. Lyon, *Success Story*, 97.

135. RHD to Rebecca, Sept. 15, 1890; Barrett Collection.

136. RHD to Family, n.d. [c. Sept. 16, 1890]; Barrett Collection. Reprinted, with excisions, in Davis, ed., *Adventures and Letters*, 50. Instead of Davis, McClure hired another reporter, Walter Dohm. In his promotion, all McClure could say was that

Dohm was "champion amateur middle distance runner of the United States." Lyon, *Success Story*, 104.

137. RHD to Rebecca, n.d. [late Fall 1890]; Barrett Collection.

Chapter 4

1. For more on Curtis, see Edward Cary, "George William Curtis," *Harper's Weekly* 36 (Sept. 10, 1892): 870–71; and the editorial on p. 866 of the same number. See also Stow Persons, *The Decline of American Gentility* (New York: Columbia University Press, 1973), 168–70; and Eugene Exman, *The House of Harper* (New York: Harper & Row, 1967), 80–81. For background on *Harper's Weekly*, see Mott, *A History of American Magazines*, 469–84. "Only an occasional visitor" is from Curtis to L. Clarke Davis, Jan. 26, 1891; Barrett Collection.

2. Charles Davis states that Richard left the paper in "late December." Davis, ed., *Adventures and Letters*, 56. The last identified story that Richard wrote for the *Evening Sun* is "A Recruit at Christmas," which ran on Dec. 24, 1890.

3. "Journalism and American Literature," *Critic* 18 (Feb. 7, 1891): 71.

4. RHD to Ripley Hitchcock, Jan. 11, 1891; Rare Book and Manuscript Library, Columbia University.

5. Sheehan, *This Was Publishing*, 66–67.

6. RHD to Charles Scribner, June 16 [1891]; Scribner Archive.

7. RHD to S. S. McClure, n.d. [c. early Jan. 1891]; Barrett Collection. This is apparently Davis's own copy of the note he sent to McClure, saying he must abandon the idea of a syndicated letter because he has chosen to accept the *Weekly* job.

8. The offices are described in J. Henry Harper, *The House of Harper* (New York: Harper & Brothers, 1912), 26, 104–6; and J. Henry Harper, *I Remember* (New York: Harper & Brothers, 1934), 17–39.

9. Gertrude Atherton, *Patience Sparhawk and Her Times* (1895), quoted in Van Wyck Brooks, *The Confident Years: 1885–1915* (New York: E.P. Dutton & Co., 1952), 103n.

10. Schlesinger, *Learning How to Behave*, 37–38; and Banner, *American Beauty*, 235–37.

11. Booth Tarkington, intr. to Davis, *Van Bibber*, x–xi.

12. Richard Hofstadter makes these points and others in the essay "Cuba, the Philippines, and Manifest Destiny," in *The Paranoid Style in American Politics* (New York: Alfred A. Knopf, 1965), 145–87.

13. "Richard Harding Davis," *Book News* 10 (July 1892): 469.

14. Bonsal, *Vanished World*, 436.

15. RHD to Rebecca, n.d. [c. Feb. 3, 1891]; Barrett Collection.

16. RHD to Rebecca, n.d. [c. Feb. 3, 1891]; Barrett Collection.

17. Caspar Whitney began his weekly "Amateur Sport" column in *Harper's Weekly* 35 (Feb. 14, 1891): 127. M. A. De Wolfe Howe, Jun., "The Bishop of Massachusetts," *Harper's Weekly* 35 (Oct. 24, 1891): 830. "The Lounger," *Critic* 18 (Mar. 21, 1891): 157. David Graham Phillips, "The Sioux Chiefs Before the Secretary," *Harper's Weekly* 35 (Feb. 21, 1891): 142. David Graham Phillips, "The Rescue of the Jeanville Miners," *Harper's Weekly* 35 (Mar. 7, 1891): 177–78. Richard Harding Davis, "Lieutenant Grant's Chance," *Harper's Weekly* 35 (May 16, 1891): 363. Richard Harding Davis, "The Story of Two Collegians," *Harper's Weekly* 35 (July 4, 1891): 495. For more on the "fast set" at Harvard, see Alick Quest, "The Fast Set at Harvard University," in *The Sporting Set* (New York: Arno Press, 1975). Quest, whose article is reprinted from the *North American Review* of 1888, estimates that only one of 20—or about 100 in all—belonged to Harvard's "fast set." But they were as conspicuous and obnoxious as Davis intimates. "Young Men of New York," *Harper's Weekly* 35, supp. (Aug. 22, 1891): 649–52, 662–63.

18. RHD to Family, n.d. [late Apr. 1883]; Kehrig Papers.

19. Both Curtis, *Author*, 18, and Brisbane, *Book Buyer*, 197, say that Davis while on the *Evening Sun* wrote the best football stories in New York. Davis mentioned his football notes for *Week's Sport* in RHD to Family, n.d. [c. Sept. 10, 1890]; Barrett Collection.

20. Visiting the Yale locker room in 1893, Richard saw that most of the boys were held together with rubber bandages and sticking-plasters; etched with tincture of iodine, their bodies resembled the stamped and cancelled envelopes in the dead-letter office. Richard Harding Davis, "A Day with the Yale Team," *Harper's Weekly* 37 (Nov. 18, 1893): 1110.

21. Richard Harding Davis, "Out of the Game," *Harper's Weekly* 35 (Oct. 31, 1891): 843. As a Lehigh sophomore, Richard had ridiculed the Harvard faculty for its attempt to modify the rules of football to reduce the risk of injury. Conway Maur [Richard Harding Davis], "What Might Have Been," Lehigh *Burr* 3 (Dec. 1883): 40.

22. "The Game Is Only a Week Off Now," New York *Evening Sun*, Nov. 20, 1890: 4. In a short story of that time, Davis has his clubman Travers gulp so many swigs from a pocket flask that he sleeps through the game. On the way out, Van Bibber and company find their friend snoring in a hired hansom and get set for a good laugh. Rubbing his eyes incredulously, Travers asks who won, then shouts with glee at Yale's triumph. "And somehow his friends do not feel as if their laugh was as hearty as they had expected," Davis wrote. To revel in the parties and sleep through the game might be the best way to enjoy football on Thanksgiving Day. Richard Harding Davis, "Mr. Travers at the Game," New York *Evening Sun*, Nov. 29, 1890: 5.

23. Richard Harding Davis, "The Thanksgiving-Day Game," *Harper's Weekly* 37 (Dec. 9, 1893): 1170–71.

24. Charles to Rebecca, n.d. [July 6, 1891]; Kehrig Papers.

25. Charles to Rebecca, n.d. [July 6, 1891]; Rebecca to RHD, July 19 [1891];

Charles to Rebecca, n.d. [early July 1891]; Kehrig Papers. RHD to Clarke, n.d. [early Aug. 1891]; Barrett Collection. Davis, ed., *Adventures and Letters*, 59.

26. For instance, two weeks before the publication of Richard's first collection of short stories, the editor of *Scribner's* informed him regretfully that he had rejected a story by Charles, and that he wished he could have another story by Richard. E. L. Burlingame to RHD, Mar. 31, 1891; Scribner Archive.

27. RHD to Charles, Nov. 29 [1893]; Barrett Collection.

28. [W. D. Howells], "Editor's Study," *Harper's* 83 (Sept. 1891): 640.

29. Richard Harding Davis, "The Other Woman," in Davis, *Exiles*, 94–117.

30. RHD to Mark A. De Wolfe Howe, Apr. 27 [1891]; Houghton Library, Harvard University.

31. Peck, "Davis," *Bookman*, 466. Richard wrote his family: "Letters continue to come in about the 'Other Woman.' I am getting quite fond of her." RHD to Family, Mar. 17 [1891]; Barrett Collection.

32. RHD to Nora, n.d. [c. Jan. 1891]; Barrett Collection. That judgment was echoed two decades later by a critic who deemed it "surely his high-water mark of intense, significant writing." W. R. Rogers, "The Potency of Youth and R.H. Davis," *Book News Monthly* 29 (Apr. 1911): 514. For a while Richard even thought of writing a sequel, which would force him to "decide whether the other woman's husband died and he married her or whether the other woman was 'impossible' and died herself or whether he found he cared for the bishop's daughter." RHD to Mr. Bancroft, Mar. 11 [1891]; Special Collections, Lehigh University Libraries. He never wrote it, and perhaps he was wise to let the question hang in the air, for the mystery added to the story's appeal. "It may settle one anxious point to say here that that 'Other Woman' was not married," Arthur Brisbane wrote erroneously, while noting that female readers by the thousands sided with either the girl at the door or the "other woman" to the north. Brisbane, *Book Buyer*, 198.

33. See Knight, *Critical Period*, and Ziff, *The American 1890s.*

34. Charles Scribner to RHD, May 20 [1891]; Scribner Archive.

35. Charles Scribner to RHD, Apr. 21, 1892; Scribner Archive. The book was published virtually simultaneously in paper at half the price (fifty cents instead of a dollar), a practice that has wisely been revived a century later for fiction aimed at a similar youthful readership. An unsigned scrap of paper in the Scribner Archive, which seems to be a draft memorandum on Davis's account with Scribners, reports as of Sept. 15, 1891, cloth sales of 1,484 and paper sales of 7,300, yielding author's royalties of $590.

36. Charles recounts this in Davis, ed., *Adventures and Letters*, 59. He recalls it was the first royalty check, which was mailed on Sept. 15, 1891; but that was for $590, not the "nine hundred and odd dollars" he states. Since the second check, mailed on April 20, 1892, and covering royalties for both *Gallegher* and *Stories for Boys*, was indeed for $919.23, this is probably the one he remembers. The figures appear on an undated memorandum in the Scribner Archive. (Although the sum

on the memorandum for the second period is actually $926, the small discrepancy was caused by charges against Davis's account, probably for the purchase of Scribner books.) See also a telegram from Richard to Rebecca, Apr. 21, 1892; Barrett Collection, which reads: "Scribners latest payment on both books is nine hundred and twenty dollars if the band is playing Dick."

37. In a postscript, she added: "Anyhow $1000 for 12,500 words is not a *great* price." Rebecca to RHD, n.d.; Kehrig Papers. Reprinted in Davis, ed., *Adventures and Letters*, 55.

38. RHD to Family, n.d. [June 1891]; Barrett Collection. Reprinted in Davis, ed., *Adventures and Letters*, 63. Richard Harding Davis, "The Reporter Who Made Himself King," in Davis, *Exiles*, 249–325. The Van Bibber tale was "Her First Appearance," and it was only about half the length of "The Reporter."

39. Lyon, *Success Story*, 90–91, 99.

40. RHD to Charles Scribner, n.d. [c. Aug. 17, 1891]; Scribner Archive.

41. RHD to Charles Scribner, n.d. [c. Aug. 1, 1891]; Scribner Archive.

42. RHD to Charles Scribner, Aug. 27 [1891]; Scribner Archive. RHD to Family, n.d. [c. Apr. 11, 1892]; Barrett Collection.

43. Richard Harding Davis, "An Unfinished Story," in Davis, *Van Bibber*, 259–89.

44. "The Lounger," *Critic* 19 (Nov. 7, 1891): 253.

45. Richard Harding Davis, "An American in Africa," *Harper's* 85 (Mar. 1893): 632–35. See also Lately Thomas, *A Pride of Lions: The Astor Orphans* (New York: William Morrow & Co., 1971). On p. 155, Thomas states that Davis visited Chanler in London in the summer of 1891; but in his own account, Davis says it was the summer of 1892, and mentions that Chanler discussed the coming American presidential election. Davis was in London both in September 1891, and in May and June 1892. As Chanler left London to begin his journey on June 11, 1892, the meeting could have occurred at either time. Most likely, however, Thomas erred. Incidentally, Thomas deprecates Davis as "merely the copy of an original, gotten up for popular consumption—and the original was William Astor Chanler."

46. RHD to Family, n.d. [Nov. 24, 1891]; Barrett Collection. Reprinted in Davis, ed., *Adventures and Letters*, 66.

47. E.W.F., "Mr. Davis's Western Series & London Series," undated memorandum; Special Collections, Lehigh University Libraries. For the camera, see RHD to J. Henry Harper, Jan. 12 [1892]; Harper Brothers Collection, Rare Book and Manuscript Library, Columbia University.

48. RHD to Rebecca, Tuesday, n.d. [Jan. 19, 1892]; Barrett Collection. Rebecca to RHD, Feb. 5 [1892]; Kehrig Papers.

49. "A Trip Through Spain," New York *Evening Sun*, Jan. 27, 1890: 4. The inspiration was a notorious remark by Matthew Arnold that America was "uninteresting"; and Arnold's defensive explanation afterward that he meant only that from

a railroad car window, you saw none of the cottages or hedgerows that enlivened the English countryside.

50. "If I could travel over the West for three years, I might write of it with authority," he confessed to his readers, "but when my time is limited to three months, I can only give impressions from a car-window point of view, and cannot dare to draw conclusions." Richard Harding Davis, *The West from a Car-Window* (New York: Harper & Brothers, 1892), 3–4.

51. "The Garza Revolution," *Harper's Weekly* 36 (Jan. 16, 1892): 51. "300,000 Reward," *Harper's Weekly* 36 (Jan. 23, 1892): 93. See also Davis, *West*, 41.

52. RHD to Family, Jan. 23, 1892; Barrett Collection.

53. RHD to Rebecca, Tuesday, n.d. [Jan. 19, 1892]; Barrett Collection.

54. RHD to Family, n.d. [Jan. 22, 1892]; Barrett Collection. Reprinted in Davis, ed., *Adventures and Letters*, 68–70.

55. RHD to Family, Jan. 23, 1892; Barrett Collection.

56. Davis, *West*, 17–18.

57. RHD Notebook, "Anecdotes. Roosevelt." [Written probably in 1915 or 1916.] Davis noted that Roosevelt "spoke of my story of Gallegher at the dinner I think quoting the line of the police chief who said Why I've even got to arrest the President of the young man's Republican Club, the man that put this coat on me. To the civil service commissioner that difficulty of the political policeman was the part of the story he remembered."

58. RHD to Charles, Jan. 27 [1892]; Barrett Collection.

59. RHD to Rebecca, Feb. 2 [1892]; Barrett Collection. Reprinted in Davis, ed., *Adventures and Letters*, 71–72.

60. RHD to Rebecca, Feb. 9 [1892]; Kehrig Papers. Davis, *West*, 14–15, 122, 144–48.

61. Davis, *West*, 93, 112. RHD to Family, Feb. 26 [1892]; Barrett Collection. Reprinted in Davis, ed., *Adventures and Letters*, 77.

62. Davis, *West*, 154, 158. RHD to Family, Feb. 26 [1892]; Barrett Collection. Reprinted in Davis, ed., *Adventures and Letters*, 77–78.

63. Davis, *West*, 165–67.

64. Davis, *West*, 8–11.

65. Davis, *West*, 135–36, 158, 225–26. RHD to Family, Feb. 9 [1892]; Kehrig Papers.

66. RHD to Rebecca, Feb. 13 [1892]; Barrett Collection. RHD to Family, Mar. 7 [1892]; Barrett Collection. Reprinted in Davis, ed., *Adventures and Letters*, 79–80.

67. RHD to Family, n.d. [c. Mar. 21, 1892]; Barrett Collection.

68. Davis, *West*, 60.

69. Davis, *West*, 72–73. RHD to Family, Mar. 7 [1892]; Barrett Collection. Reprinted in Davis, ed., *Adventures and Letters*, 82.

70. Davis, *West*, 59–61, 65, 74.

71. Davis, *West*, 82.

72. RHD to Mr. Harper, n.d. [late Mar. 1892]; Barrett Collection. Davis said that two Harvard men would be going, including Nathaniel Curtis, the son of a former president of the Somerset Club.

73. RHD to Family, May 10 [1892]; Barrett Collection. Italics original. Davis mentions that he spent only a week in New York in RHD to Rebecca, n.d. [June 1892]; Barrett Collection.

74. RHD to Family, May 23 [1892]; Barrett Collection. Reprinted in Davis, ed., *Adventures and Letters*, 84. H. J. Whigham, who was an Oxford student at the time, recalled Davis's social success in "Notes and Comment," *Town and Country* 71 (May 1, 1916): 24. See also Osborn, "Richard Harding Davis," 334–37.

75. Richard Harding Davis, *Our English Cousins* (New York: Harper & Brothers, 1894), 106–7.

76. Davis, *Our English Cousins*, 114, 127.

77. RHD to Family, June 3 [1892]; Barrett Collection. Reprinted in Davis, ed., *Adventures and Letters*, 88.

78. In my account of the Souls, I have relied on two gossipy histories: Anita Leslie, *The Marlborough House Set* (Garden City, N.Y.: Doubleday & Company, 1973), which was published the previous year in London by Hutchison and Company as *Edwardians in Love*; and Angela Lambert, *Unquiet Souls* (New York: Harper & Row, 1984).

79. R. W. B. Lewis, *Edith Wharton: A Biography* (New York: Harper & Row, 1975), 243.

80. Leslie, *Marlborough House*, 246.

81. RHD to Family, n.d. [late Jan. 1893]; Barrett Collection.

82. Davis, *Our English Cousins*, 57.

83. Thomas Beer, "Richard Harding Davis," *Liberty* 1 (Oct. 11, 1924):16.

84. Davis, *Our English Cousins*, 57. In May 1893, Davis wrote, "By the death of the heir at the age of 30, Harry Cust has become the next to inherit Belton, Ashridge and the House of Carlton House Terrace as well as the title. To be editor of the Pall Mall, an M.P. and Earl of Brownlow in prospective is about as much of a good thing as I know. I am glad. I like Cust." RHD to Rebecca, May 16 [1893]; Barrett Collection.

85. RHD to Rebecca, n.d. [posted June 8, 1892]; Barrett Collection.

86. RHD to Rebecca, n.d. [June 17, 1892]; Barrett Collection.

87. Davis, *Our English Cousins*, 88, 90.

88. Davis, *Our English Cousins*, 94–105.

89. Wanting to reprint Cust's likeness along with his own in *Harper's*—because "everyone over here knows me more or less and it is the same with you in England"—Richard rigged his request so that no answer would be a tacit approval. (As a result, the two men are unmistakably depicted in an illustration of a victory rally.) RHD to Henry Cust, n.d. [c. Oct. 20, 1892]; Ray Collection, Rare Book and Manuscript Library, Columbia University. For the illustration, see Davis, *Our English Cousins*, 97.

90. The aggrieved woman, Nina Welby-Gregory, wrote to Balfour and Lord Haldane, both leaders of the government, saying she was pregnant and Cust must marry her. "[Arthur] Pollen tells me that our Candidate only married the girl because Lewis and Lewis threatened a breach of promise suit and not because Balfour told him he was a cad," Richard wrote to Charles in June 1894. This was not the generally accepted belief at the time, nor has it become so. RHD to Charles, June 6 [1894]; Barrett Collection.

91. "Mr. Richard Harding Davis," Boston *Sunday Herald*, 26.

92. "Mr. Richard Harding Davis," Boston *Sunday Herald*, 26.

93. M. A. Lane, "The Chicago Fair," *Harper's Weekly* 36 (July 2, 1892): 643; John Gilmer Speed, "Feeding the Multitudes," *Harper's Weekly* 37 (Aug. 26, 1893): 284.

94. Richard Harding Davis, "The Dedication Exercises," *Harper's Weekly* 36 (Oct. 29, 1892): 1038. Although the Columbian Exposition may not have worshiped Edison, it did make good use of his electric lights for nighttime illumination.

95. Richard Harding Davis, "The Last Days of the Fair," *Harper's Weekly* 37 (Oct. 21, 1893): 1002.

96. Louis H. Sullivan, *The Autobiography of an Idea* (New York: Dover Publications, [1924], 1956), 324–25. See also Ziff, *The American 1890s*, 21–22.

97. RHD to Cust, n.d. [c. Oct. 20, 1892]; Ray Collection. See also RHD to Family, n.d. [Oct. 12, 1892]; Barrett Collection. Reprinted in Davis, ed., *Adventures and Letters*, 94, where it is misdated as Oct. 2.

98. "It is very much to be deplored," sighed an editorial in *Harper's Weekly*, "that during the best part of the time since its opening the business crisis sweeping over the country should have so filled the minds of many of our people with harassing cares as to exclude all thoughts of enjoyment." "The Columbian Exposition," *Harper's Weekly* 37 (Sept. 16, 1893): 878.

99. For a recent account of the Exposition, see Robert W. Rydell, *All the World's a Fair: Visions of Empire at American International Expositions, 1876–1916* (Chicago: University of Chicago Press, 1984), 38–71. As his subtitle suggests, Rydell sees the Midway rather differently from Davis—as a display of American racism.

Chapter 5

1. RHD to Charles Scribner, June 16 [1891]; Scribner Archive.

2. RHD to Family, n.d. [Oct. 12, 1892]; Barrett Collection. Reprinted in Davis, ed., *Adventures and Letters*, 94.

3. Harper, *House of Harper*, 639. Davis was instead hoping for a tribute from William Dean Howells. RHD to Howells, n.d.; Houghton Library, Harvard University.

4. From a clipping dated Nov. 14, 1891, in a no longer extant file at the Columbia School of Journalism, Scott C. Osborn identified the story as J. C. B. Andrews, "The Dead That Did Not Die," *Harper's Weekly* 35 (Nov. 7, 1891): 865–66. See Osborn, "Richard Harding Davis," 197n. Soon afterward, Davis asked a young writer for references "to avoid accepting translations and stories that have already appeared in print." RHD to Albert Bigelow Paine, n.d. [Nov. 1891]; Huntington Library.

5. Richard Harding Davis, "The Editor's Story," in Davis, *Van Bibber*, 308–9.

6. Stephen Bonsal confirmed his part in this incident in an interview with Scott C. Osborn. See Osborn, "Richard Harding Davis," 197. The episode is also recounted in Harper, *House of Harper*, 608–9; and in Stanhope Searles, "Literary Conquest and the Idea in the Air," *Bookman* 20 (Sept. 1904): 62.

7. RHD to J. Henry Harper, Jan. 11, 1893; E.W.F., "Mr. Davis's Western & London Series," n.d.; Special Collections, Lehigh University Libraries. Instead of expenses of $550 for the West and $200 for London, he now wanted $1,000 for the Mediterranean and $400 for Paris.

8. Harper & Brothers to RHD, Jan. 12, 1893; Barrett Collection. See also John Gilmer Speed, "Theodore Child," *Harper's Weekly* 36 (Nov. 19, 1892): 1121.

9. RHD to Harper & Brothers, n.d. [received Jan. 12, 1893]; Special Collections, Lehigh University Libraries.

10. "As to the Cold Weather," *Harper's Weekly* 37 (Jan. 28, 1893): 75.

11. RHD to Rebecca, n.d. [late Jan. 1893]; Kehrig Papers.

12. RHD to Rebecca, Feb. 12 [1893]; Barrett Collection. This is excised from the version printed in Davis, ed., *Adventures and Letters*, 96–100.

13. Richard Harding Davis, *The Rulers of the Mediterranean* (New York: Harper & Brothers, 1894), 2. RHD to J. Henry Harper, Feb. 26 [1893]; Special Collections, Lehigh University Libraries. RHD to Family, n.d. [late Jan. 1893]; Barrett Collection. RHD to Rebecca, Feb. 12 [1893]; Barrett Collection. Reprinted with some errors in Davis, ed., *Adventures and Letters*, 98–99.

14. RHD to Rebecca, n.d. [Feb. 15, 1893]; Barrett Collection.

15. RHD to Rebecca, n.d. [Feb. 15, 1893]; Barrett Collection. They lunched at "such an inn as Don Quixote used to stop at, with the dining-room over the stable and a lot of drunken muleteers in the courts." RHD to Rebecca, Feb. 23 [1893]; Barrett Collection. Reprinted in Davis, ed., *Adventures and Letters*, 104.

16. Davis, *Rulers*, 7.

17. Davis, *Rulers*, 40.

18. RHD to Rebecca, Feb. 15 [1893]; Barrett Collection. Reprinted in Davis, ed., *Adventures and Letters*, 106. Davis, *Rulers*, 46.

19. RHD to Rebecca, Feb. 15 [1893]; Barrett Collection. Reprinted in Davis, ed., *Adventures and Letters*, 107. His guide's costume is described in Davis, *Rulers*, 43. Because of his Western accoutrements, Davis wrote, "Mahamed was not even picturesque. . . . This hurt my sense of the fitness of things very much."

20. Davis, *Rulers*, 56–71. RHD to Rebecca, Feb. 23 [1893]; Barrett Collection. Reprinted in Davis, ed., *Adventures and Letters*, 105.

21. RHD to Rebecca, Feb. 25 [1893]; Barrett Collection. RHD to Rebecca, n.d. [Mar. 4, 1893]; Barrett Collection. Reprinted in Davis, ed., *Adventures and Letters*, 110. RHD to J. Henry Harper, Feb. 26 [1893]; Special Collections, Lehigh University Libraries.

22. RHD to Rebecca, Feb. 25 [1893]; Barrett Collection.

23. RHD to Rebecca, Mar. 11, 1893; Barrett Collection. Reprinted in Davis, ed., *Adventures and Letters*, 112.

24. RHD to Rebecca, Mar. 11, 1893, and Mar. 28 [1893]; Barrett Collection.

25. RHD to Rebecca, Mar. 19, 1893; Barrett Collection. Reprinted in Davis, ed., *Adventures and Letters*, 113. Davis, *Rulers*, 107, 134.

26. RHD to Rebecca, Mar. 11, 1893; Barrett Collection. Reprinted, with incorrect punctuation, in Davis, ed., *Adventures and Letters*, 112–13.

27. Davis, *Rulers*, 163–64, 170. RHD to Rebecca, Mar. 19, 1893; Barrett Collection. Reprinted in Davis, ed., *Adventures and Letters*, 115. RHD to Charles, Mar. 21 [1893]; Barrett Collection.

28. RHD to Rebecca, Mar. 19, 1893; Barrett Collection. Reprinted in Davis, ed., *Adventures and Letters*, 114.

29. Davis, *Rulers*, 193–94.

30. Lloyd Griscom, *Diplomatically Speaking* (Boston: Little, Brown and Company, 1940), 37.

31. RHD to Rebecca, Apr. 3 [1893; misdated "Mar. 3" by RHD on the letter]; Kehrig Papers.

32. RHD to Rebecca, Apr. 7 [1893]; Barrett Collection. Davis, *Rulers*, pp. 207–8. RHD to Rebecca, Apr. 14 [1893]; Barrett Collection. Reprinted in Davis, ed., *Adventures and Letters*, 120, with a deletion that reads, ". . . and I hated putting myself under obligation to Thompson or to his cad of a secretary and I was tired of being civil to them."

33. RHD to J. Henry Harper, Mar. 24 [1893]; Special Collections, Lehigh University Libraries.

34. RHD to Charles, n.d. [c. Apr. 25, 1893]; Barrett Collection.

35. RHD to Rebecca, Apr. 23 [1893]; Barrett Collection. Before leaving Cairo, he

wrote the Harpers asking for a $1,000 advance on his *Weekly* articles and $200 for a Christmas short story he had sent in to the *Monthly*. RHD to J. Henry Harper, Mar. 24, 1893; Special Collections, Lehigh University Libraries. Paris (how little do things change) turned out to be "an awfully expensive place." RHD to Rebecca, May 29 [1893]; Barrett Collection.

36. RHD to Charles, n.d. [c. Apr. 25, 1893]; RHD to Rebecca, n.d. [c. May 6, 1893]; Barrett Collection.

37. "Do not put me in any more illustrations of Mediterranean," he angrily wired J. Henry Harper. RHD to Harper & Brothers, Apr. 24, 1893, cable; Special Collections, Lehigh University Libraries. "I confess to having been somewhat hurt at the silence which has met all the letters I have sent the office," Davis then wrote his publisher. "The only answer to the three personal letters I sent you has been a printed slip from a paper criticising an article written by my brother. I should have supposed that you would have at least let me know of the important change you have made in the illustrations. Hereafter I shall confine my communications to those of strictly a business nature and I regret that it should have to be so." RHD to J. Henry Harper, Apr. 24, 1893; Special Collections, Lehigh University Libraries.

38. RHD to Charles Scribner, Sept. 22 [1891]; Scribner Archive.

39. David Kiehl, *American Art Posters of the 1890s* (New York: The Metropolitan Museum of Art, 1987), 13.

40. RHD to [J. Henry] Harper, May 18 [1893]; Special Collections, Lehigh University Libraries. He also argued that Charles Dana Gibson's illustrations had sold Constance Cary Harrison's satirical novel of New York society, *The Anglomaniacs*, which was a best seller in 1890.

41. Charles Scribner had in fact informed Davis in advance of his plans for illustrations; when confronted with a copy of Scribner's earlier letter, which he had somehow overlooked, Davis scrawled, "I am covered with confusion and offer many and hearty apologies." RHD to Charles Scribner, undated note, marked "Oct. 15, 1891" by the Scribners; written on a copy of a Sept. 8 letter from Charles Scribner to Davis; Scribner Archive. In the same archive, RHD to Charles Scribner, Sept. 22 [1891]; RHD to Charles Scribner, n.d. [Oct. 11, 1891]; Charles Scribner to RHD, Oct. 12 [1891]; and RHD to Charles Scribner, n.d. [Oct. 13, 1891], all deal with this matter.

42. RHD to Charles, n.d. [c. Apr. 25, 1893]; Barrett Collection.

43. "I really think when he knows how much I count on what he thinks that he might have written me about the new story and about the articles," Richard wrote his mother. "I know I am over sensitive about people's not writing but when they know that, I cannot see why they do not gratify my weaknesses." RHD to Rebecca, Apr. 23 [1893]; Barrett Collection.

44. Grover Cleveland to L. Clarke Davis, Jan. 3, 1893; typed copy, Kehrig Papers.

45. Allan Nevins, *Grover Cleveland: A Study in Courage* (New York: Dodd, Mead and Company, 1932), pp. 515–16.

46. RHD to Rebecca, Apr. 23 [1893]; Barrett Collection. Grover Cleveland to L. Clarke Davis, May 4–5, 1893; Grover Cleveland to L. Clarke Davis, Sept. 7, 1893; Grover Cleveland to L. Clarke Davis, Oct. 14, 1893; typed copies, Kehrig Papers.

47. RHD to Rebecca, June 13 [1893]; Barrett Collection. Reprinted in Davis, ed., *Adventures and Letters*, 130–31.

48. Davis, *Our English Cousins*, 195; Lord Dufferin and his son are not identified by name. RHD to Rebecca, May 16 [1893]; RHD to Rebecca, June 1 [1893]; Barrett Collection.

49. "I find it harder here than in London to get material but I am making many notes and seeing all there is to see," Davis wrote his publisher. "Our new Ambassador helps me very much as does the English Ambassador." RHD to J. Henry Harper, May 19, 1893; Special Collections, Lehigh University Libraries.

50. RHD to Rebecca, May 5 [1893]; Kehrig Papers. Omitted from the letter reprinted in Davis, ed., *Adventures and Letters*, 125–26.

51. "With us the foreigner may get into society if he settles down and does us the honor of preferring our country to his own," remarked Paul Bourget. "As for him who is simply passing through not to return, it takes us some time to overcome a certain distrust; we do not, without a thorough acquaintance, pass over from formal courtesy to intimacy." Bourget, *Outre-Mer*, 48.

52. Richard Harding Davis, *About Paris* (New York: Harper & Brothers, 1895), 208–10. For Richard's own design taste, see RHD to Charles, Dec. 28 [1893]; Barrett Collection. RHD to Charles, Oct. 21 [1894]; Nov. 5, 1894; Kehrig Papers. "Mr. Richard Harding Davis," Boston *Sunday Herald*, 26. Although Frazier is not named, Davis, ed., *Adventures and Letters*, 125, identifies the portrait-painter Kenneth Frazier as a friend of Richard's in Paris, and Osborn, "Richard Harding Davis," 380, reveals that Davis knew Frazier from Lehigh.

53. Sir William Rothenstein, *Men and Memories*, 1 (London: Faber & Faber, 1931), 123–24, 126. See also Davis, ed., *Adventures and Letters*, 129.

54. RHD to Rebecca, May 29 [1893]; Barrett Collection.

55. Davis, *About Paris*, 182–97.

56. RHD to Rebecca, May 11 [1893]; Barrett Collection. Reprinted in Davis, ed., *Adventures and Letters*, 127.

57. RHD to Rebecca, May 29 [1893]; Barrett Collection. Of course, Davis was hardly the first Anglo-Saxon to dislike Paris. The capital of sensuality drew a similar response from Thomas Hughes, the author of *Tom Brown's Schooldays*, who wrote: "I get mad to smash some of the mirrors on the boulevards and to punch the heads of some of the little coxcombs who sit sipping and smoking all along the Cafe fronts." From E. C. Mack and W. H. G. Armytage, *Thomas Hughes: The Life of the Author of Tom Brown's Schooldays* (London: Benn, 1952), 176, cited in Walter E. Houghton, *The Victorian Frame of Mind, 1830–1870* (New Haven: Yale University Press, 1957), 215.

58. RHD to Rebecca, June 1 [1893]; Barrett Collection.

59. RHD to J. Henry Harper, June 22 [1893]; Special Collections, Lehigh University Libraries.

60. He wrote to Charles Scribner asking for any *Gallegher* royalties due him, noting, "Money goes so fast over here and mine is as quick to go as other people's." RHD to Charles Scribner, June 16 [1893]; Scribner Archive.

61. RHD to Rebecca, n.d. [c. early Aug. 1893]; Barrett Collection.

62. RHD to J. Henry Harper, Oct. 2, 1893; J. Henry Harper to RHD [draft of a response to RHD's Oct. 2 letter]; RHD to J. Henry Harper, Oct. 5, 1893; Special Collections, Lehigh University Libraries.

63. RHD to Clarke, n.d. [c. Sept. 30, 1893]; Special Collections, Lehigh University Libraries.

64. RHD to Charles, Jan. 5 [1894]; Barrett Collection.

65. RHD to Rebecca, n.d. [Summer 1893]; Barrett Collection.

66. Charles Hoffmann, *The Depression of the Nineties: An Economic History* (Westport, Conn.: Greenwood Publishing Corp., 1970), 58, 109. H. Roger Grant, *Self-Help in the 1890s Depression* (Ames, Iowa: Iowa State University Press, 1983), 7–8.

67. "The Rebellion at Homestead," *Harper's Weekly* 36 (July 16, 1892): 674–75; and "The Law of Treason," *Harper's Weekly* 36 (Oct. 22, 1892), 1010–11.

68. RHD to Rebecca, n.d. [c. Aug. 1893]; Barrett Collection.

69. For this summary, I have relied primarily on George Frederick Drinka, *The Birth of Neurosis: Myth, Malady, and the Victorians* (New York: Simon & Schuster, 1984); Tom Lutz, *American Nervousness, 1903: An Anecdotal History* (Ithaca, N.Y.: Cornell University Press, 1991), 3–7, 31–37; and F. G. Gosling, *Before Freud: Neurasthenia and the American Medical Community, 1870–1910* (Urbana and Chicago: University of Illinois Press, 1987), 9–29.

70. Charles Dudley Warner, "The American Newspaper" (1881), in *Fashions in Literature* (New York: Dodd, Mead and Company, 1902), 57. The journalist Ida Tarbell observed that the attempt on the life of industrialist Henry Frick in 1892 caused a "general nervousness." Lutz, *American Nervousness*, 213.

71. For Tarkington and Phelps, see Henry F. May, *The End of American Innocence: A Study of the First Years of Our Own Time, 1912–1917* (New York: Alfred A. Knopf, 1959), 77–78, 97. For Steffens, see Kaplan, *Lincoln Steffens*, 95, 280.

72. For more on neurasthenia among the upper classes of late-nineteenth-century America, see T. J. Jackson Lears, *No Place of Grace*, 56–57, 215, 221–22.

73. RHD to Rebecca, n.d. [c. Dec. 26, 1892]; Barrett Collection.

74. RHD to Rebecca, n.d. [Summer 1893]; Barrett Collection. This is the letter in which Davis wrote of the clouded financial futures of the Benedict and Fairchild families.

75. RHD to Rebecca, n.d. [c. early Nov. 1893]; Barrett Collection.

76. RHD to Rebecca, n.d. [late Nov. 1893]; Barrett Collection. Richard Harding Davis, "The Story of the Horse Show," *Harper's Weekly* 37 (Nov. 25, 1893): 1120, 1122. It was William Dean Howells who observed that the horses appeared more patrician than the swells in the ringside boxes. W. D. Howells, "The Horse Show," in *Literature and Life* (New York: Harper & Brothers, 1902), 206–15.

77. RHD to Charles, [Dec.] 28 [1893]; Barrett Collection.

78. RHD to Rebecca, n.d. [Jan. 2, 1894]; Barrett Collection.

79. RHD to Charles, Jan. 5 [1894]; Barrett Collection. RHD to Charles, Jan. 7 [1894]; Kehrig Papers.

80. RHD to Charles, Jan. 16 [1894]; Barrett Collection.

81. RHD to Rebecca, Jan. 24 [1894]; Barrett Collection.

82. RHD to Charles, Mar. 7 [1894]; Barrett Collection.

83. RHD to Charles, Feb. 7 [1894]; Barrett Collection.

84. RHD to Charles, Mar. 1 [1894]; Barrett Collection. RHD to Charles, Mar. 5 [1894]; Barrett Collection; reprinted in Davis, ed., *Adventures and Letters*, 134.

85. "Did you see that Princess Alix of Hesse was engaged," Richard later wrote to Charles. "She is the Princess Aline and her dresses are described in the Story and her names and titles and her jewels and orders. So I will not be allowed in Russia. I am broken hearted for I loved her picture dearly." RHD to Charles, Apr. 26 [1894]; Barrett Collection.

86. RHD to Charles, Mar. 16 [1894]; Barrett Collection.

87. *The Princess Aline* was the fifth-best-selling novel in America in 1895. Alice Payne Hackett, *Fifty Years of Best Sellers, 1895–1945* (New York: R.R. Bowker Co., 1945), 11. Davis borrowed the name of his heroine, which he eventually learned to spell, from the Countess Aline Petrovna Kuzmishchova, a grande dame who had married an American naval officer and moved with him from St. Petersburg to Marion. For more on the Countess Aline, see Alice Austin Ryder, *Lands of Sippican* (Marion, Mass.: Sippican Historical Society, [1934], 1975), 262. The classic statement on the importance of the American female reader is by William Dean Howells: "The man of letters must make up his mind that in the United States the fate of a book is in the hands of the women. It is the women with us who have the most leisure, and they read the most books. They are far better educated, for the most part, than our men, and their tastes, if not their minds, are more cultivated. . . . As I say, the author of light literature, and often the author of solid literature, must resign himself to obscurity unless the ladies choose to recognize him." W. D. Howells, "The Man of Letters as a Man of Business," in *Literature and Life*, 21.

88. Richard Harding Davis, "The Princess Aline," reprinted in Davis, *Gallegher*, 127–28.

89. RHD to Charles, Apr. 26 [1894]; Barrett Collection. RHD to Charles, Nov. 5, 1894; Kehrig Papers.

90. Richard Harding Davis, "The Romance in the Life of Hefty Burke," in Davis, *The Scarlet Car* (New York: Charles Scribner's Sons, 1916), 315–45.

91. Richard Harding Davis, "Miss Delamar's Understudy," in Davis, *Exiles*, 238, 246 [214–48 for the entire story]. It first appeared in *Scribner's* in August 1895. Davis declared that he had finished writing it in RHD to Charles, Dec. 9 [1894]; Barrett Collection.

92. Richard Harding Davis, "Our Suburban Friends," *Harper's* 89 (June 1894): 155–57.

93. Richard Harding Davis, "His Bad Angel," in Davis, *The Exiles and Other Stories* (New York: Harper & Brothers, 1894), 121–53. This story was not included in the 1916 edition of the collected works.

94. Morris, intr. to Davis, *Red Cross Girl*, xx.

95. John N. Wheeler, "Richard Harding Davis, *Pearson's* 33 (June 1915): 682.

96. Fox, intr. to Davis, *White Mice*, viii.

97. For example, he had his mother read his Paris articles (RHD to Rebecca, n.d.; Barrett Collection) and "The Editor's Story" (RHD to Rebecca, n.d. [Spring 1894]; Barrett Collection) before publication.

98. Morris, intr. to Davis, *Red Cross Girl*, xviii–xix.

99. RHD to Rebecca, n.d. [posted Feb. 3, 1893]; Barrett Collection. Reprinted, with errors, in Davis, ed., *Adventures and Letters*, 96.

100. RHD to Clarke, n.d.; Kehrig Papers.

101. Rebecca to RHD, Aug. 12 [1891]; Kehrig Papers.

102. Clarke to RHD, Feb. 15, 1892; Kehrig Papers. Reprinted, with deletions, in Davis, ed., *Adventures and Letters*, 76–77.

103. RHD to Charles, Apr. 17 [1894]; Barrett Collection. Davis described his plans for the story (which he never wrote) in RHD to Charles, Dec. 28 [1893]; Barrett Collection.

104. RHD to Charles, Apr. 19 [1894]; Barrett Collection.

105. RHD to Charles, Apr. 26 [1894]; Barrett Collection.

106. RHD to Charles, Apr. 19 [1894]; Barrett Collection.

107. RHD to Charles, May 9 [1894]; Barrett Collection.

108. RHD to Charles, Apr. 26 [1894]; Barrett Collection.

109. RHD to Charles, May 28 [1894]; Barrett Collection.

110. Elmer Ellis, *Mr. Dooley's America: A Life of Finley Peter Dunne* (New York: Alfred A. Knopf, 1941), 168.

111. RHD to Charles, Apr. 9 [1894]; Kehrig Papers.

112. RHD to Charles, Apr. 26 [1894]; Barrett Collection.

113. Davis tells slightly variant versions of this tale in RHD to Rebecca, Wednesday [Apr. 24, 1895], Barrett Collection; and RHD to Charles, Apr. 27 [1895], Kehrig Papers. Reprinted in Davis, ed., *Adventures and Letters*, 166–67.

114. RHD to Charles, May 9 [1894]; Barrett Collection.

115. RHD to Charles, May 1, 1894; Barrett Collection.

116. "Mr. Richard Harding Davis," Boston *Sunday Herald*, 26.

117. Davis, "The Exiles," in Davis, *Exiles*, 1.

118. Davis, "The Exiles," in Davis, *Exiles*, 21.

119. RHD to Charles, Apr. 3 [1894]; Kehrig Papers.

120. RHD to Charles, May 28 [1894]; Barrett Collection.

121. RHD to Rebecca, July 2 [1894]; Barrett Collection.

122. RHD to Rebecca, May 29, 1890. Barrett Collection. Reprinted in Davis, ed., *Adventures and Letters*, 54. In 1890, probably after a second Marion holiday the last week of July and the first week of August, Richard wrote his mother: "Today I have been seeing my old friends and except Brisbane I find them a bit unprofitable after the intellectualities of Marion. . . . I am sure this has been the best vacation I have had and I am so glad I had Marion instead of England which is saying a great deal." RHD to Rebecca, n.d. [Summer 1890]; Barrett Collection. The following year, a previously unidentified *Harper's Weekly* article in praise of Marion can be stylistically identified as Davis's work. See "Cape Cod Neighbors," *Harper's Weekly* 35 (Aug. 8, 1891): 598. In 1901, Davis said that he had been summering in Marion since 1890. Sangree, "Davis," *Ainslee's*, 10. For more general and historical information on Marion, see Ryder, *Lands of Sippican*, and Rosamond Gilder, ed., *Letters of Richard Watson Gilder* (Boston: Houghton Mifflin Company, 1916).

123. RHD to Rebecca, n.d. [c. May 1890]; Barrett Collection.

124. "Out of Town for the Summer," *Harper's Weekly* 37 (Aug. 5, 1893): 734.

125. RHD to Rebecca, n.d. [1891]; Barrett Collection.

126. RHD to Miss Peabody, Mar. 7, 1903; Houghton Library, Harvard University.

127. For more on the ascendance of the summer "cottage" over the resort hotel among the fashionable rich in the early 1890s, see "The Rise of the Summer Cottage," *Harper's Weekly* 36 (Aug. 20, 1892): 795. The article notes that although the Mount Desert vogue was greater than ever, several of the Bar Harbor hotels had remained shuttered that summer, because the "best people" all lived in cottages. The writer adds: "What is true to an exceptional degree at Bar Harbor is noticeable at other summer places."

128. *The Mikado: A Centenary Celebration.* Exhibition at the Pierpont Morgan Library, May 31–July 31, 1985; catalogue by Reginald Allen.

129. RHD to E. L. Burlingame, Oct. 5 [1894]; Scribner Archive.

130. RHD to Rebecca, n.d. [c. Sept. 26, 1894]; Barrett Collection.

131. "Why He Is Not a War Correspondent," New York *Tribune*, Sept. 27, 1894: 5.

132. RHD to Charles, n.d. [c. Sept. 27, 1894]; Barrett Collection.

133. RHD to E. L. Burlingame, Oct. 5 [1894]; Scribner Archive. RHD to Charles, Oct. 6, 1894; Barrett Collection.

134. RHD to Charles, Dec. 9 [1894]; Barrett Collection.

135. RHD to Charles, Nov. 5, 1894; Kehrig Papers.

136. He received $300 from *Harper's* for "The Writing on the Wall": RHD to Charles, Jan 7 [1894]; Kehrig Papers. *Scribner's* paid $400 for "Miss Delamar's Understudy": RHD to Charles, Dec. 22, 1894; Barrett Collection.

137. Having written about three chapters, Davis estimated that "if I had written as much and put it into short stories I would be from $900 to $1200 ahead of the game." RHD to Charles, Nov. 5, 1894; Kehrig Papers.

138. RHD to Charles, Nov. 12 [1896]; Barrett Collection.

139. RHD to Charles, Dec. 22, 1894; Barrett Collection. RHD to Rebecca, n.d. [c. Dec. 23, 1894]; Barrett Collection.

140. RHD to Charles, Oct. 21 [1894]; Kehrig Papers.

141. RHD to Charles, Dec. 9 [1894]; Barrett Collection.

142. Richard Harding Davis, *Three Gringos in Venezuela and Central America* (New York: Harper & Brothers, 1896), 27–28. Griscom, *Diplomatically Speaking*, 72–73.

143. Griscom, *Diplomatically Speaking*, 41.

144. Griscom, *Diplomatically Speaking*, 72–74.

145. Arthur Brisbane, "Three Gringoes at Home," New York *World*, May 4, 1895: 3.

146. Davis, *Gringos*, 38–39, 74. RHD to Family, n.d. [Jan. 17, 1895]; Barrett Collection. Reprinted in Davis, ed., *Adventures and Letters*, 140–41.

147. RHD to Rebecca, n.d. [Jan. 20, 1895]; Barrett Collection.

148. Davis, *Our English Cousins*, 186.

149. Mark Sullivan, *Our Times: Pre-War America*, 518.

150. RHD to Family, n.d. [Jan. 21, 1895]; Barrett Collection. Reprinted, with deletions, in Davis, *Adventures and Letters*, 143–44. Further details on Howland that were deleted from the book *Three Gringos* can be found in Richard Harding Davis, "Three Gringos in Central America," *Harper's Magazine* 91 (Sept. 1895): 494. See also Griscom, *Diplomatically Speaking*, 77.

151. Griscom, *Diplomatically Speaking*, 78–80.

152. RHD to Family, n.d. [Jan. 21, 1895]; Barrett Collection. Reprinted, with deletions, in Davis, ed., *Adventures and Letters*, 143–44.

153. RHD to Family, Feb. 13 [1895]; Barrett Collection. Deleted from the letter reprinted in Davis, ed., *Adventures and Letters*, 152–55.

154. Griscom, *Diplomatically Speaking*, 82.

155. Davis, *Gringos*, 139, 146–48.

156. RHD to Family, Feb. 13 [1895]; Barrett Collection. Reprinted in Davis, ed., *Adventures and Letters*, 154. Griscom, *Diplomatically Speaking*, 83.

157. See the not quite congruent accounts in RHD to Family, Feb. 13 [1895]; Barrett Collection. Reprinted in Davis, ed., *Adventures and Letters*, 154. Also, Davis, *Gringos*, 173; Griscom, *Diplomatically Speaking*, 83–84; and an anonymous letter to the editor, "Author and Hotel Keeper," New York *Sun*, Feb. 11, 1911: 8.

158. Griscom, *Diplomatically Speaking*, 84.

159. Davis, *Gringos*, 205–6.

160. "Giblin Will Not Hang," New York *Evening Sun*, Nov. 21, 1889: 1. For an amusing history of Giblin's law firm, see Richard H. Rovere, *Howe & Hummel: Their True and Scandalous History* (New York: Farrar, Straus and Giroux, [1947], 1985).

161. Davis, *About Paris*, 98–107.

162. Davis, *Gringos*, 212–15.

163. Griscom, *Diplomatically Speaking*, 85–87. See RHD to Rebecca, Feb. 28 [1895]; Barrett Collection. Reprinted in Davis, ed., *Adventures and Letters*, 161–63. Also discussed in Davis, *Gringos*, 212–16.

164. RHD to Rebecca, n.d. [Feb. 21, 1895]; Barrett Collection. Reprinted in Davis, ed., *Adventures and Letters*, 157.

165. See Griscom, *Diplomatically Speaking*, 89; and Thomas, *Delmonico's*, 260.

166. *Bookman* 3 (June 1896): 369.

167. RHD to Charles, n.d. [Dec. 31, 1895]; Barrett Collection. Reprinted in Davis, ed., *Adventures and Letters*, 170–72.

168. Davis, *Gringos*, 281.

169. RHD to Charles, n.d. [Dec. 31, 1895]; Barrett Collection. Reprinted in Davis, ed., *Adventures and Letters*, 170.

170. Visiting the site in 1914, Augustus Thomas said that Davis "had guessed at nothing. Everywhere he had overlaid the facts with adventure and with beauty, but he had been on sure footing all the time." Augustus Thomas, intr. to Richard Harding Davis, *Soldiers* (New York: Charles Scribner's Sons, 1916), xiv. Similarly, the mansions and restaurants of the capital of Olancho are all landmarks of Santiago de Cuba. See James F. J. Archibald, "Localities and Scenes of Richard Harding Davis's Stories," *Book Buyer* 25 (Sept. 1902): 115–21.

171. At his death, *Soldiers of Fortune* was still "the book by which Mr. Davis is best known. It has been said of this romance of American commercial success in Latin-America that it has made more bad engineers out of first-rate clerks than all the correspondence schools. Like Anthony Hope's 'Prisoner of Zenda,' it founded a school of adventurous fiction, which bears every indication of flourishing indefinitely." "Richard Harding Davis Drops Dead in His Home," New York *Evening Post,* Apr. 12, 1916: 6.

172. Knight, *Critical Period,* 120–21. James Lane Allen's historical romance, *The Choir Invisible,* outsold it.

173. RHD to Charles, Nov. 5, 1894; Kehrig Papers.

174. See, for example, Knight, *Critical Period,* 122; and W. Arthur Boggs, "Prologue to an Unpleasant Image," *Phylon* 24 (Summer 1963): 197–200. Lambasting *Soldiers* from a literary standpoint, H. L. Mencken set it up as a straw man for Joseph Conrad's thematically related *Nostromo,* in "Conrad, Bennett, James Et Al," *Smart Set* 36 (Jan. 1912): 153–58.

175. Davis, *Gringos,* 162–65.

176. Davis contrasted the idealism of the engineer with the compromised pragmatism of the politican and businessman in 1899 in "The Man with One Talent." In that story, an idealistic young engineer tries to win a senator's support for American intervention on behalf of the Cuban rebels. After agreeing to take a tour of Cuba, the senator changes his mind. Big industrialists fearing that a war would disrupt the economy have persuaded him not to rock the boat. The engineer vilifies "the money-changers in the temple of this great republic." Richard Harding Davis, "The Man with One Talent," in Davis, *Van Bibber,* 222–58. And in *Soldiers of Fortune,* the businessman Langham tries to avoid fighting, a "policy of non-interference" that the young men find distasteful. Davis, *Soldiers of Fortune,* 210. Making the same point, from the perspective of a later historian, is a well-known essay: John P. Mallan, "The Warrior Critique of the Business Civilization," *American Quarterly* 8 (Fall 1956), 216–30.

177. Davis, *Gringos,* 197.

178. A handwritten draft of the first chapter and the start of the second chapter of *Soldiers of Fortune* is in the Poett Papers. Davis's first title for the book was "The Self-Made Man," which he then crossed out in favor of "The Revolutionists." He also early on considered the title "Young Lochinvar." RHD to Charles, n.d. [c. Dec. 1894]; Barrett Collection.

179. Davis, *Soldiers of Fortune,* 69, 30.

180. Davis, *Soldiers of Fortune,* 61–62.

Chapter 6
1. RHD to Charles, Sept. 14 [1895]; Barrett Collection.

2. Interview with Frederica Poett, Santa Barbara, Calif., Mar. 28, 1985.

3. RHD to Rebecca, [Sept.] 10 [1895]; Barrett Collection.

4. RHD to Charles, Sept. 29 [1895]; Barrett Collection.

5. Quoted in Beer, *The Mauve Decade*, 58.

6. Banner, *American Beauty*, 277.

7. Bourget, *Outre-Mer*, 93.

8. Davis, *Soldiers of Fortune*, 85.

9. Interview with Frederica Poett, Santa Barbara, Calif., Mar. 28, 1985.

10. Richard Harding Davis, "The Buried Treasure of Cobre" (1913), in Davis, *The Lost Road* (New York: Charles Scribner's Sons, 1916), 205; Davis, *The White Mice* (New York: Charles Scribner's Sons, [1909], 1916), 115; and Davis, "Ranson's Folly" (1902), in Davis, *Ranson's Folly* (New York: Charles Scribner's Sons, 1916), 17.

11. Richard Harding Davis, "The Vagrant" (1899), in *Ranson's Folly*, 212.

12. Davis, *White Mice*, 130–31.

13. Richard Harding Davis, "Vera, the Medium" (1908), in Davis, *Scarlet Car*, 282.

14. Davis, *Soldiers of Fortune*, 348.

15. RHD to Charles, n.d. [Dec. 31, 1895]; Barrett Collection. Reprinted in Davis, ed., *Adventures and Letters*, 170. In that letter, Richard says he is receiving an advance of $5,000. In fact, he got a total of $7,500, with $2,000 paid on delivery of the completed manuscript and the remaining $5,500 paid in two installments, in February and March. E. L. Burlingame to RHD, Dec. 17, 1895; RHD to Charles Scribner, Dec. 6 [1895]; Scribner Archive.

16. RHD to Charles, Oct. 21 [1894]; Kehrig Papers. RHD to J. Henry Harper, Mar. 2 [1895]; Special Collections, Lehigh University Libraries.

17. RHD to J. Henry Harper, Aug. 14 [1895]; Special Collections, Lehigh University Libraries.

18. RHD to J. Henry Harper, June 28 [1895]; Special Collections, Lehigh University Libraries.

19. [Edward W. Townsend], "Major Max Is Angry," New York *Sun*, Nov. 3, 1893: 4. "This Is Dreadful," New York *World*, Nov. 12, 1893: 2.

20. "Notes," *The Chap-Book* 1 (Aug. 15, 1894): 172.

21. "Mr. R.H. Davis and His Comrades," *Critic* 29 (Sept. 26, 1896): 185. Davis's open letter was also published in the New York *Tribune*, Sept. 27, 1896, 2: 4. The source of the malicious paragraph appears to be a burlesque that ran in the New York *Evening World* and was later quoted by a Pittsburgh paper as if it were an actual interview. That extract was then copied by other papers, and the story made the rounds. "A Literary Ghost," New York *Evening World*, Oct. 10, 1896: 6.

22. "Mr. Richard Harding Davis," Boston *Sunday Herald*, Apr. 12, 1896: 26.

23. "Mr. R. H. Davis and His Comrades," *Critic* 29 (Sept. 26, 1896): 186.

24. W. A. Swanberg, *Citizen Hearst* (New York: Charles Scribner's Sons, 1961), 55–59, 62.

25. Swanberg, *Hearst*, 61; Churchill, *Park Row*, 77.

26. Charles H. Brown, *The Correspondents' War* (New York: Charles Scribner's Sons, 1967), 14–15.

27. Davis, ed., *Adventures and Letters*, 170.

28. Richard Harding Davis, "How the Great Football Game Was Played," New York *Journal*, Nov. 24, 1895: 1–2.

29. RHD to Charles, n.d. [Dec. 31, 1895]; Barrett Collection. Reprinted in Davis, ed., *Adventures and Letters*, 172.

30. RHD to Charles, n.d. [Dec. 31, 1895]; Barrett Collection. Reprinted in Davis, ed., *Adventures and Letters*, 170.

31. Swanberg, *Hearst*, 81–82; Churchill, *Park Row*, 71–75, 81–82.

32. RHD to Clarke, n.d. [Jan. 1896]; Barrett Collection. His dream, though, was to save enough money to cover a war "independently of any periodical." RHD to Charles, Apr. 14 [1895]; Barrett Collection.

33. RHD to Charles, Apr. 14 [1895]; Barrett Collection.

34. RHD to Charles, Jan. 21 [1896]. Barrett Collection. To his mother, Richard wrote: "I am so glad you told me about the name so decidedly. It does sound silly but as I knew it was used in the story I was sort of used to it." RHD to Rebecca, n.d. [late Jan. 1896]; Barrett Collection. Although "The Reporter Who Made Himself King" had appeared five years earlier in the juvenile-oriented *Stories for Boys*, it was needed to pad out this collection.

35. Richard Harding Davis, "The Princess Aline," reprinted in Davis, *Gallegher*, 154.

36. RHD to Rebecca, n.d. [Feb. 21, 1895]; Barrett Collection. Reprinted in Davis, ed., *Adventures and Letters*, 159.

37. RHD to Charles, n.d. [c. Jan. 21, 1896]; Barrett Collection.

38. RHD to Charles, n.d. [early May 1896]; Barrett Collection.

39. RHD to Charles, May 17 [1896]; Barrett Collection. Reprinted, with slight alterations, in Davis, ed., *Adventures and Letters*, 177–80.

40. RHD to Charles, May 17 [1896]; Barrett Collection.

41. RHD to Charles, n.d. [May 26, 1896]; Barrett Collection. Reprinted in Davis, ed., *Adventures and Letters*, 181–82.

42. Richard Harding Davis, *A Year from a Reporter's Note-book* (New York: Harper & Brothers, 1898), 43.

43. Davis, *A Year*, 55–60.

44. Richard Harding Davis, "The Crowning of the Czar," New York *Journal*, May 27, 1896: 1–2.

45. Richard Harding Davis, "Moscow in a Blaze of Glory," New York *Journal*, May 23, 1896: 1–2.

46. RHD to Charles, n.d. [May 26, 1896]; Barrett Collection. Reprinted in Davis, ed., *Adventures and Letters*, 181.

47. RHD to Family, May 8 [1896]; Kehrig Papers. Reprinted in Davis, ed., *Adventures and Letters*, 184. For a description of the Khodynka disaster, see Robert K. Massie, *Nicholas and Alexandra* (New York: Atheneum, 1967), 54–56.

48. RHD to Charles, Sept. 28 [1896]; Barrett Collection.

49. Richard Harmond, "Progress and Flight: An Interpretation of the American Cycle Craze of the 1890s," *Journal of Social History* 5 (Winter 1971–72): 250.

50. F. P. Prial, "Cycling in the United States," *Harper's Weekly* 34, supp. (Aug. 23, 1890): 672.

51. James B. Townsend, "The Social Side of Bicycling," *Scribner's* 17 (June, 1895): 705–6.

52. "Authors Who Ride," *Critic* 24 (Oct. 12, 1895): 226.

53. RHD to Rebecca, n.d. [June 1895]; Kehrig Papers.

54. RHD to Charles, Sept. 19 [1895]; Barrett Collection.

55. RHD to Charles, Aug. 11 [1896]; Barrett Collection.

56. Harmond, "Progress and Flight," 240.

57. RHD to Charles, n.d. [early Nov. 1896]; and RHD to Charles, Nov. 12 [1896]; Barrett Collection.

58. Swanberg, *Hearst*, 84–90.

59. Joseph E. Wisan, *The Cuban Crisis as Reflected in the New York Press (1895–1898)* (New York: Columbia University Press, 1934), 65–66.

60. Brown, *Correspondents' War*, 27–28, 44.

61. Hearst announced the acquisition of the *Vamoose* on Nov. 24, 1896. The *Journal* was the first newspaper to charter a press boat. See Brown, *Correspondents' War*, 55, 446–47.

62. RHD to Rebecca, Dec. 19 [1896]; Barrett Collection. Reprinted with deletions in Davis, ed., *Adventures and Letters*, 186–88. Davis's reassurances to his mother were disingenuous. When the time came to write about Cuba, he admitted, "It is as dangerous to seek for Gomez as Stanley found it to seek for Livingston, and as few men return from the insurgent camps as from the arctic region." He noted that he felt free to praise those who succeeded because he had failed in his own effort to reach Gómez. Richard Harding Davis, *Cuba in War Time* (New York: R.H. Russell, 1897), 116.

63. RHD to Family, n.d. [Dec. 26, 1896]; Barrett Collection.

64. Augustus Thomas, "Recollections of Frederic Remington," *Century* 86 (July 1913): 357.

65. RHD to Rebecca, telegram, Dec. 30, 1896; Barrett Collection.

66. RHD to Rebecca, Jan. 1, 1897; Barrett Collection. Reprinted in Davis, ed., *Adventures and Letters*, 190.

67. RHD to Family, Jan. 2, 1897; Barrett Collection. Reprinted in Davis, ed., *Adventures and Letters*, 191–93.

68. RHD to Rebecca, Jan. 4 [1897]; Barrett Collection. For more on Gómez's sword, see Brown, *Correspondents' War*, 65–69, 76.

69. RHD to Rebecca, Dec. 19 [1896]; Barrett Collection. Reprinted in Davis, ed., *Adventures and Letters*, 186.

70. For details of the *Commodore* disaster, see Brown, *Correspondents' War*, 69–74; and R. W. Stallman, *Stephen Crane: A Biography* (New York: George Braziller, 1968), 244–54.

71. RHD to Rebecca, Jan. 9 [1897]; Barrett Collection.

72. James Creelman, *On the Great Highway* (Boston: Lothrop Publishing Company, 1901), 158, 162, 168.

73. RHD to Rebecca, Jan. 10, 1897; Barrett Collection.

74. RHD to Rebecca, Jan. 10, 1897; Barrett Collection.

75. Creelman, *Great Highway*, 177–78.

76. "Mr. Hearst's Tiff with the London 'Times,' " *Literary Digest* 35 (Dec. 14, 1907): 903.

77. RHD to Rebecca, n.d. [Jan. 15, 1897]; Reprinted, with errors, in Davis, ed., *Adventures and Letters*, 193.

78. Richard Harding Davis, "A Day with the Yale Team," *Harper's Weekly* 37 (Nov. 18, 1893): 1110.

79. Peggy and Harold Samuels, *Frederic Remington: A Biography* (Garden City, N.Y.: Doubleday & Company, 1982), 245.

80. RHD to Rebecca, n.d. [Jan. 15, 1897]; Barrett Collection. Deleted from the letter reprinted in Davis, ed., *Adventures and Letters*, 193–94.

81. RHD to Rebecca, Jan. 16 [1897]; Barrett Collection. Deleted from the letter reprinted in Davis, ed., *Adventures and Letters*, 194–99.

82. RHD to Rebecca, Jan. 16 [1897]; Barrett Collection. Reprinted in Davis, ed., *Adventures and Letters*, 195.

83. Davis, *Cuba in War Time*, 25. RHD to Rebecca, Jan. 16 [1897]; Barrett Collection. Reprinted in Davis, ed., *Adventures and Letters*, 197.

84. RHD to Rebecca, Jan. 19 [1897]; Barrett Collection.

85. Davis, *Cuba in War Time*, 40. Written after Davis fell out with Hearst, this chapter was excerpted as "Unpublished Cuban Letters by Richard Harding Davis," New York *Sunday World*, Apr. 11, 1897: 39.

86. Davis, *Cuba in War Time*, 50.

87. "Richard Harding Davis Amid the Horrors of the Cuban War," New York *Journal*, Jan. 31, 1897: 33–34; Wisan, *Cuban Crisis*, 236.

88. "Davis and Remington Tell of Spanish Cruelty," New York *Journal*, Feb. 2, 1897: 1–2. Working from Davis's dispatch, Remington made his sketches in New York.

89. With minor changes, the *Journal* story is reprinted as "The Death of Rodriguez" in Davis, *Cuba in War Time*, 99–113.

90. RHD to Charles, n.d. [c. Jan. 26, 1897]; Barrett Collection.

91. RHD to Rebecca, Jan. 24 [1897]; Barrett Collection. See also Brown, *Correspondent's War*, 85–87, for details on the adventures of Scovel and Rea. After getting through to see the insurgent general Gómez and relaying a story that appeared in the January 19 *World*, Scovel was arrested in Tunas in early February.

92. "Richard Harding Davis and Frederic Remington in Cuba for the Journal," New York *Journal*, Jan. 17, 1897: 33.

93. RHD to Rebecca, Jan. 24 [1897]; Barrett Collection.

94. RHD to Charles, n.d. [c. Jan. 26, 1897]; Barrett Collection.

95. Davis, *Cuba in War Time*, 113–33.

96. RHD to Rebecca, Jan. 20 [1897]; RHD to Rebecca, Jan. 24 [1897]; Barrett Collection.

97. "Tale of a Fair Exile," New York *World*, Feb. 15, 1897: 1.

98. Brown, *Correspondents' War*, 93.

99. "Tale of a Fair Exile," New York *World*, Feb. 15, 1897: 1.

100. "Good Men Gone Sadly Wrong," New York *Evening World*, Feb. 15, 1897: 6.

101. Wisan, *Cuban Crisis*, 191.

102. Richard Harding Davis, "Does Our Flag Shield Women?" New York *Journal*, Feb. 12, 1897: 1–2. The *Journal* article contained a number of other errors, including the statement that the women had been searched three times, rather than twice. Davis was also mistaken in arguing that international law forbade the Spanish from exercising authority over a foreign vessel docked in their harbor. When he reprinted the article in a book, Davis specified that "a female detective" had conducted the searches. He wrote: "For the benefit of people with unruly imaginations, of whom there seem to be a larger proportion in this country than I had supposed, I will state again that the search of these women was conducted by women and not by

men, as I was reported to have said, and as I did not say in my original report of the incident." Davis, *Cuba in War Time*, 121–22. Corroborating Miss Arango's account, another woman who was searched told her story to the *Times*. "Cuban Women Ill Treated," New York *Times*, Mar. 2, 1897. For Hearst's lack of remorse, see Willis J. Abbot, *Watching the World Go By* (Boston: Little, Brown and Company, 1934), 214.

103. A few months later, when the Harpers were publishing in book form his newspaper dispatches from Greece, he requested a note that he had been there as a correspondent of the London *Times*, and explained, "I want American readers to know that I was not employed by the *Journal*." RHD to J. Henry Harper, June 30 [1897]; Special Collections, Lehigh University Libraries.

104. Although he began his trip sympathetic to President Cleveland's nonintervention policy, Davis soon reported that he was being "slowly converted" to the opposite viewpoint. He wrote: "I guess that man Dad used to take fishing at Marion [i.e., Cleveland] is wrong about this and pretty soon he will have to do something." RHD to Rebecca, n.d. [Jan. 15, 1897]; Barrett Collection (deleted from the version published in Davis, ed., *Adventures and Letters*, 193–94). A day later, Davis reiterated that only American intervention could stop the devastation. RHD to Rebecca, Jan. 16 [1897]; Barrett Collection. Reprinted in Davis, ed., *Adventures and Letters*, 196–98. Yet, within a few days, he had once again decided that he agreed with the President, "although I doubt if he arrived at his decision by the same means I did." RHD to Rebecca, Jan. 20 [1897]; Barrett Collection.

105. Davis, "Does Our Flag Shield Women?" 2.

106. "What Mr. Davis says of the fate of the *pacificos* is enough to stir the most sluggish blood and to make one feel like shouldering a musket and joining the insurgents; but other questions beside those of sentiment are to be considered before a civilized nation can go to war," wrote one cool-headed reviewer of *Cuba in War Time*. "Mr. Davis's partisanship does credit to his heart, but great countries, he must remember, are not ruled from the heart." [Review] "Cuba in War Time," *Critic* 30 (Apr. 24, 1897): 286.

107. RHD to J. Henry Harper, Feb. 16 [1897]; Special Collections, Lehigh University Libraries. E. L. Burlingame to RHD, Mar. 4, 1897; Scribner Archive.

108. RHD to Charles, Mar. 5 [1897]; Barrett Collection.

109. Richard Harding Davis, *A Year*, 145–46, 160–61, 164.

110. RHD to Charles, Mar. 7 [1897]; Barrett Collection. Davis's impression of Mrs. McKinley at the inauguration was widely shared. See Margaret Leech, *In the Days of McKinley* (New York: Harper & Brothers, 1959), 117.

111. RHD to Family, n.d. [c. Mar. 25, 1897]; Barrett Collection.

112. RHD to Rebecca, Apr. 15 [1897]; Barrett Collection.

113. Clipping from the *Daily Mail*, Mar. 26, 1897; Barrett Collection.

114. RHD to Charles, Sept. 28 [1896]; Barrett Collection.

115. RHD to Rebecca, n.d. [late Mar. 1897]; Barrett Collection. Without stating his source, Thomas Beer wrote that Davis and Crane first met at the Lantern Club in New York in 1895. Beer, *Stephen Crane*, 124. If this encounter took place, Davis (who was then far better known) did not remember it less than two years later. Beer interviewed Davis for his book on Crane, and most likely Davis provided this erroneous recollection two decades after the fact. The Cuban trip prevented Davis from meeting Crane earlier, at the dinner that Elbert Hubbard's Philistine Society gave in Crane's honor on December 19, 1896, in Buffalo, New York. RHD to Harry Taber, n.d. [Dec. 1895]; Stephen Crane Collection, Rare Book and Manuscript Library, Columbia University. For details of the Philistine Society dinner, see Stallman, *Stephen Crane*, 159–65.

116. Stallman, *Stephen Crane*, 24.

117. Stallman, *Stephen Crane*, 29.

118. The struggle between idealism and realism in the literature of the turn of the century is the subject of Grant C. Knight, *Critical Period*.

119. Stallman, *Stephen Crane*, 197–98.

120. RHD to Family, Apr. 1 [1897]; Barrett Collection. Reprinted in Davis, ed., *Adventures and Letters*, 200.

121. RHD to Family, Apr. 1 [1897]; Barrett Collection. Deleted from Davis, ed., *Adventures and Letters*, 200.

122. Her story is told at length in Lillian Gilkes, *Cora Crane: A Biography of Mrs. Stephen Crane* (Bloomington: Indiana University Press, 1960).

123. Frederick Palmer, *With My Own Eyes* (Indianapolis: The Bobbs-Merrill Company, 1933), 24–25.

124. RHD to Family, Apr. 1 [1897]; Barrett Collection. Reprinted in Davis, ed., *Adventures and Letters*, 200. RHD to Rebecca, Apr. 30 [1897]; Barrett Collection.

125. RHD to Louise Clark, n.d. [Apr. 1897]; Poett Papers. See also Davis, ed., *Adventures and Letters*, 201.

126. RHD to Family, Apr. 28, 1897, original not located. Reprinted in Davis, ed., *Adventures and Letters*, 204.

127. RHD to Charles, n.d. [Apr. 21, 1897]; Barrett Collection.

128. RHD to Charles, [April] 22 [1897]; Barrett Collection. See also Davis, ed., *Adventures and Letters*, 201.

129. RHD to Charles, n.d. [Apr. 29, 1897]; Kehrig Papers.

130. RHD to Family, Apr. 28, 1897; original not located. Reprinted in Davis, ed., *Adventures and Letters*, 202.

131. Davis, *A Year*, 226.

132. RHD to Charles, n.d. [Apr. 28, 1897]; Kehrig Papers.

133. RHD to Charles, n.d. [May 7, 1897]; Kehrig Papers. Reprinted in Davis, ed., *Adventures and Letters*, 206.

134. RHD to Rebecca, Apr. 30 [1897]; Barrett Collection.

135. Stallman, *Stephen Crane*, 275, 277.

136. RHD to Charles, n.d. [Apr. 28, 1897]; Kehrig Papers.

137. RHD to Family, May 14 [1897]; Barrett Collection. Deleted from the misdated letter reprinted in Davis, ed., *Adventures and Letters*, 207.

138. RHD to Charles, May 4 [1897]; Kehrig Papers. See also [Richard Harding Davis], "The Fighting at Velestino," London *Times*, May 20, 1897: 13.

139. It was well known in its day. See F. Lauriston Bullard, *Famous War Correspondents* (Boston: Little, Brown and Company, 1914), 29.

140. [Davis], "The Fighting at Velestino."

141. RHD to Family, May 14 [1897]; Barrett Collection. Reprinted, and misdated May 16, in Davis, ed., *Adventures and Letters*, 208–9.

142. Misreading Davis's ambiguous letter home of May 14 (misdated May 16 in *Adventures and Letters*), Scott C. Osborn mistakenly states that Crane arrived on the afternoon on May 4, the first day of fighting. Scott C. Osborn, "Stephen Crane and Cora Taylor: Some Corrections," *American Literature* 26 (Nov. 1954): 416. For independent corroboration that Crane didn't arrive until the second day, see Crane's own account in Stallman, *Stephen Crane*, 280.

143. RHD to Family, May 14 [1897]; Barrett Collection. Deleted from the misdated letter reprinted in Davis, ed., *Adventures and Letters*, 209. After Crane's death, Davis softened his opinion of Cora. In a 1913 letter, he wrote, "Any decent man will tell you she was a loyal wife to Crane as long as he lived." Published in Thomas Beer, "Mrs. Stephen Crane," *American Mercury* 31 (Mar. 1934): 291, cited in Gilkes, *Cora Crane*, 49.

144. Stallman, *Stephen Crane*, 279.

145. RHD to Family, May 14 [1897]; Barrett Collection. Deleted from the misdated letter reprinted in Davis, ed., *Adventures and Letters*, 211. Bass nonetheless found something to say about Crane in an article, "How Novelist Crane Acts on the Battlefield," which appeared in the *Journal* of May 23, 1897.

146. RHD to Family, May 14 [1897]; Barrett Collection. Reprinted and misdated in Davis, ed., *Adventures and Letters*, 210–11.

147. RHD to Charles, n.d.; Barrett Collection.

148. RHD to Family, May 30 [1897]; Barrett Collection.

149. RHD to Louise Clark, [May 16, 1897; misdated May 15 by Davis]; Poett Papers. RHD to Family, n.d. [May 20, 1897]; Barrett Collection.

150. RHD to Rebecca, June 21 [1897]; Barrett Collection. Reprinted in Davis, ed., *Adventures and Letters*, 214. Davis, *A Year*, 263–37.

151. RHD to Rebecca, June 25 [1897]; Barrett Collection. Reprinted in Davis, ed., *Adventures and Letters*, 216.

152. For the date of publication, see Quinby, *Bibliography*, 44.

153. Davis, ed., *Adventures and Letters*, 60; Quinby, *Bibliography*, 102. RHD to Rebecca, n.d. [c. Nov. 7, 1892]; Barrett Collection. RHD to Charles Scribner, n.d. [c. Nov. 4, 1892]; Scribner Archive.

154. It was produced by the Theatre of Arts and Letters. Quinby, *Bibliography*, 102–3. RHD to Rebecca, Apr. 7 [1893]; Barrett Collection.

155. RHD to Charles, Feb. 7 [1894]; RHD to Charles, Feb. 16 [1894]; Barrett Collection.

156. RHD to Charles, Apr. 19 [1894]; Barrett Collection.

157. RHD to Charles, n.d. [Jan. 1, 1895]; Barrett Collection. In Quinby, *Bibliography*, 103, Hilliard, when interviewed two decades later, places the first performance of "The Littlest Girl," as he called it, in Cleveland in the fall of 1895. In fact, it was the first New York performance that took place at that later date.

158. RHD to Louise Clark, Oct. 28, 1895; Poett Papers. Quinby, *Bibliography*, 104, erroneously states that the play was written for Nat Goodwin.

159. RHD to Charles, n.d. [early Nov. 1896]; Barrett Collection.

160. RHD to Louise Clark, Dec. 7 [1896]; Poett Papers.

161. RHD to Rebecca, n.d. [early Dec. 1896]; Barrett Collection.

162. RHD to Rebecca, Oct. 6 [1897]; RHD to Family, n.d. [Oct. 10, 1897]; Barrett Collection.

163. RHD to Rebecca, n.d. [Oct. 14, 1897]; Barrett Collection.

164. RHD to Family, n.d. [Dec. 1, 1897]; Barrett Collection.

165. Richard Harding Davis, "The King's Jackal," in Davis, *Gallegher*, 175–306. First printed in *Scribner's* 23 (Apr.–July 1898). He was already working on the story by the end of 1896. RHD to Rebecca, n.d. [Jan. 15, 1897]; Barrett Collection. Deleted from the letter reprinted in Davis, ed., *Adventures and Letters*, 194.

166. Maurice, "Representative American Story Tellers, I: Richard Harding Davis," *Bookman*, 140.

167. RHD to Charles, n.d. [Jan. 1, 1895]; Barrett Collection.

168. RHD to Rebecca, n.d. [c. Dec. 29, 1897]; Barrett Collection. Reprinted in Davis, ed., *Adventures and Letters*, 218–23.

169. Cecil Clark Davis to Louise Clark, May 12 [1901]; Poett Papers. "In the Fog" was first published in *Collier's* 28 (Nov. 23, 1901): 6–8, 10; (Nov. 30, 1901): 10–11, 14; (Dec. 7, 1901): 23, 25, 27; and as a book by R.H. Russell in New York in 1901. Scribners republished it in the *Ranson's Folly* story collection in 1902. For the standard edition, see Davis, *Ranson's Folly*, 224–320.

170. RHD to Rebecca, [Jan.] 26 [1898]; Kehrig Papers.

171. RHD to Rebecca, n.d. [early Feb. 1898]; Barrett Collection.

172. RHD to Rebecca, n.d. [c. Feb. 7, 1898]; Barrett Collection.

173. RHD to Rebecca, Jan. 11 [1898]; Barrett Collection.

174. RHD to Rebecca, n.d. [c. Mar. 20, 1898]; Barrett Collection.

175. RHD to Rebecca, Feb. 24 [1898]; Barrett Collection.

Chapter 7

1. Walter LaFeber, *The New Empire* (Ithaca, N.Y.: Cornell University Press, 1963), 385–87. A March 17 speech by Vermont Senator Redfield Proctor on the destruction he had witnessed in Cuba (observations very similar to those that Davis had made a year earlier) was credited by contemporaries as the most important event in the push toward war. See Gerald F. Linderman, *The Mirror of War: American Society and the Spanish-American War* (Ann Arbor: University of Michigan Press, 1974), 37–59. Richard Harding Davis, "The Man with One Talent," reprinted in Davis, *Van Bibber*, 222–58.

2. RHD to E. L. Burlingame, Apr. 16 [1898]; Apr. 30, 1898; Scribner Archive. RHD to John D. Long, May 14, 1898; reprinted in *Papers of John Davis Long, 1897–1904* (Norwood, Mass.: The Massachusetts Historical Society, v. 78, 1939), 122. RHD to Family, Apr. 26 [1898]; Barrett Collection. Reprinted in Davis, ed., *Adventures and Letters*, 232. For the record of the *Herald*, see Wisan, *Cuban Crisis*, 121–22, 300, 341, 345, 350, 368–69, 376–77, 386.

3. The photograph appeared in *Critic* 32 (Apr. 23, 1898): 283. The commentary is in *Critic* 32 (May 7, 1898): 318–19.

4. G. J. A. O'Toole, *The Spanish War* (New York: W.W. Norton & Company, 1984), 197.

5. Richard Harding Davis, *The Cuban and Porto Rican Campaigns* (New York: Charles Scribner's Sons, 1898), 12.

6. RHD to Rebecca, n.d. [Apr. 24, 1898]; Barrett Collection. Reprinted in Davis, ed., *Adventures and Letters*, 227.

7. RHD to Family, Apr. 26 [1898]; Barrett Collection. Reprinted in Davis, ed., *Adventures and Letters*, 229–30.

8. RHD to Family, Apr. 26 [1898; the letter was dated and begun on this day, but completed on the day following]; Barrett Collection. Reprinted in Davis, ed., *Adventures and Letters*, 232–33.

9. "Matanzas Batteries Bombarded and Silenced by American Ships," New York *Herald*, Apr. 28, 1898: 5, 11. See also Richard Harding Davis, "Fighting Seen from the Flagship," New York *Herald*, Apr. 28, 1898: 5, 11.

10. RHD to Family, Apr. 30 [1898]; Barrett Collection. Reprinted in Davis, ed., *Adventures and Letters*, 236.

11. Davis, *Campaigns*, 30–34.

12. "Matanzas Batteries Bombarded." RHD to Family, Apr. 30 [1898]; Barrett Collection. Reprinted in Davis, ed., *Adventures and Letters*, 234. Ralph D. Paine, *Roads of Adventure* (Boston: Houghton Mifflin Company, 1922), 200. "Herald Brings News," New York *Herald*, Apr. 28, 1898: 5.

13. Paine, *Roads of Adventure*, 202; Stallman, *Stephen Crane*, 351–52.

14. RHD to Family, Apr. 30 [1898]; Barrett Collection. Deleted from Davis, ed., *Adventures and Letters*, 235.

15. Samuels, *Remington*, 266.

16. RHD to Family, Apr. 30 [1898]; Barrett Collection. Deleted from the letter reprinted in Davis, ed., *Adventures and Letters*, 238.

17. "The Herald Was Right," New York *Herald*, May 5, 1898: 12. In a letter complaining about the failure to advertise his books, Davis later wrote: "Then your editor had me turned off the flagship on the ground that I represented an English paper when he knew I represented as well an American magazine and twenty-five American newspapers. This only a few weeks after he had been offered and refused my services." RHD to J. Henry Harper, n.d. [c. Nov. 17, 1898]; Special Collections, Lehigh University Libraries.

18. *Long Papers*, 122–23.

19. Davis himself disparaged the Spaniards as "a comic opera people" subject to "fits of hysterics . . . with all of a child's unreasonable rage." Richard Harding Davis, "Spain's Children in Comic Opera," New York *Herald*, May 4, 1898: 8.

20. R. A. Alger, *The Spanish-American War* (New York: Harper & Brothers, 1901), 29.

21. Gen. William R. Shafter, "The Capture of Santiago de Cuba," *Century* 57 (Feb. 1899): 612; Graham A. Cosmas, *An Army for Empire* (Columbia, Mo.: University of Missouri Press, 1971), 193–94.

22. Cosmas, *Army for Empire*, 55–62.

23. Virgil Carrington Jones, *Roosevelt's Rough Riders* (Garden City, N.Y.: Doubleday & Company, 1971), 49–51.

24. Davis, *Campaigns*, 46–53, 60. RHD to Nora, May 3, 1898, original not located. Reprinted in Davis, ed., *Adventures and Letters*, 238.

25. RHD to Nora, May 3, 1898, original not located. Reprinted in Davis, ed., *Adventures and Letters*, 238.

26. RHD to Charles, May 2 [1898]; Barrett Collection.

27. RHD to Nora, May 3, 1898, original not located. Reprinted in Davis, ed., *Adventures and Letters*, 238. RHD to Family, May 7, 1898; Barrett Collection.

28. RHD to Rebecca, May 14, 1898; Barrett Collection.

29. RHD to Charles, n.d. [c. May 15, 1898]; Kehrig Papers.

30. RHD to Charles, n.d. [c. May 15, 1898]; Kehrig Papers.

31. RHD to Charles, n.d. [c. May 17, 1898]; Barrett Collection. Reprinted, and misdated, in Davis, ed., *Adventures and Letters*, 241.

32. RHD to Charles, n.d. [c. May 17, 1898]; Barrett Collection. Reprinted, and misdated, with the concluding remark deleted, in Davis, ed., *Adventures and Letters*, 240–41.

33. RHD to Family, n.d. [c. May 21, 1898]; Barrett Collection. Beer, *Crane*, 183.

34. RHD to Family, n.d. [c. May 21, 1898]; Barrett Collection.

35. Walter Millis, *The Martial Spirit* (Boston: Houghton Mifflin Company, 1931), 214–15; Cosmas, *Army for Empire*, 158–59.

36. Richard Harding Davis, "Serious Defects of Our Volunteer Regiments," New York *Herald*, June 5, 1898, 5: 3. See also RHD to Charles, May 29 [1898]; Barrett Collection. Reprinted in Davis, ed., *Adventures and Letters*, 242.

37. RHD to Charles, May 29 [1898]; Barrett Collection. Reprinted in Davis, ed., *Adventures and Letters*, 241–44.

38. RHD to Family, n.d. [c. May 21, 1898]; Barrett Collection.

39. Poultney Bigelow, "Shall Politics and Incompetence Command Our Army?" New York *Herald*, June 5, 1898, 5: 1. Poultney Bigelow, "In Camp at Tampa," *Harper's Weekly* 42 (June 4, 1898): 550.

40. RHD to Clarke, n.d. [c. May 10, 1898]; Barrett Collection.

41. Richard Harding Davis, "Davis Replies to Bigelow," New York *Herald*, June 6, 1898: 5. At about this time, Davis wrote to his editor at *Scribner's* that the truth "cannot be told now, but when the war is over there will be some terribly sad things to write of incompetence and lack of preparation that is only equalled by that of the French in '72" [*sic* for '70—he always got this date wrong]. RHD to E. L. Burlingame, n.d. [c. May 29, 1898]; Scribner Archive.

42. Samuels, *Remington*, 169, 177.

43. Poultney Bigelow, *Seventy Summers* (New York: Longman, Green & Co., 1925), 286–88.

44. RHD to Family, n.d. [June 10, 1898]; Barrett Collection.

45. RHD to Family, June 9, 1898; Barrett Collection. Deleted from the letter reprinted in Davis, ed., *Adventures and Letters*, 246.

46. Poultney Bigelow, "Bigelow Charges Gross Incompetency," New York *Herald*, June 9, 1988: 9.

47. Brown, *Correspondents' War*, 230.

48. Poultney Bigelow, "Are Our Military Bureaus Offices for Political Jobbery?" New York *Herald*, June 12, 1898, 5: 2.

49. John D. Miley, *With Shafter in Cuba* (New York: Charles Scribner's Sons, 1916), 6.

50. The censorship is described in Brown, *Correspondents' War*, 225–28.

51. This and the following reminiscences by Davis of Roosevelt come from a notebook in the Kehrig Papers that was written by Davis, probably in 1915 or 1916, and is labeled, "Anecdotes. Roosevelt." Roosevelt corroborates his admiration for "Gallegher" in the introduction to Richard Harding Davis, *Captain Macklin* (New York: Charles Scribner's Sons, 1916), vii–viii. He writes that he was "immediately drawn" to "the power and originality" of the story.

52. Theodore Roosevelt, "A Colonial Survival," *Cosmopolitan* 14 (Dec. 1892): 229–36.

53. Theodore Roosevelt to James Brander Matthews, Dec. 6, 1892; reprinted in Elting E. Morison, ed., *The Letters of Theodore Roosevelt*, 1 (Cambridge, Mass.: Harvard University Press, 1951), 298.

54. Theodore Roosevelt to James Brander Matthews, Jan. 30, 1894, reprinted in Morison, ed., *Letters of Theodore Roosevelt*, 1, 358.

55. Morris, *Rise of Roosevelt*, 518–21.

56. Norman Hapgood, *The Changing Years* (New York: Farrar and Rinehart, 1930), 226.

57. Brown, *Correspondents' War*, 205.

58. Jones, *Rough Riders*, 5, 26–27, 35; Edward Marshall, *The Story of the Rough Riders* (New York: G.W. Dillingham Co., 1899), 28–29.

59. RHD to Charles, n.d. [June 5, 1898]; Barrett Collection. Reprinted in "Adventures and Letters," *Metropolitan* 46 (July 1917): 53.

60. RHD to Family, n.d. [June 10, 1898]; Barrett Collection.

61. RHD to Charles, n.d. [June 5, 1898]; Barrett Collection. Reprinted in "Adventures and Letters," *Metropolitan* 46 (July 1917): 53. Jones, *Rough Riders*, 3, 23; Marshall, *Story*, 35.

62. RHD to Charles, n.d. [June 5, 1898]; Barrett Collection. Reprinted in "Adventures and Letters," *Metropolitan* 46 (July 1917): 53. The two men he entertained were intimate family friends, who made the mistake of wearing their uniforms to dinner. See Jones, *Rough Riders*, 59.

63. Morris, *Rise of Roosevelt*, 623.

64. Davis, *Campaigns*, 83.

65. Brown, *Correspondents' War*, 265–66.

66. Cosmas, *Army for Empire*, 195.

67. Brown, *Correspondents' War*, 267–68.

68. RHD to Family, n.d. [June 10, 1898]; Barrett Collection.

69. RHD to Rebecca, n.d. [June 8, 1898]; Barrett Collection.

70. Miley, *With Shafter*, 45.

71. RHD to Family, June 9, 1898; Barrett Collection. Reprinted in Davis, ed., *Adventures and Letters*, 245.

72. Shafter, "Capture of Santiago," *Century*, 614.

73. RHD to Family, June 9, 1898; Barrett Collection. Reprinted in Davis, ed., *Adventures and Letters*, 244–46.

74. Davis, *Campaigns*, 86.

75. Albert E. Smith, *Two Men and a Crank* (Garden City, N.Y.: Doubleday & Company, 1952), 56–57.

76. Davis, *Campaigns*, 86. The size of the force comes from Miley, *With Shafter*, 43–44.

77. RHD to Charles, June 12, 1898; Barrett Collection.

78. Jones, *Rough Riders*, 82.

79. Davis, *Campaigns*, 86–94. RHD to Family, June 21 [1898]; Barrett Collection.

80. Davis, *Campaigns*, 103–8; Richard Harding Davis, "Shafter and Sampson Go Ashore to Confer with General Garcia," New York *Herald*, June 22, 1898: 5. RHD to E. L. Burlingame, June 21 [1898]; Scribner Archive. The other correspondents on the scene were Stephen Bonsal, Frederic Remington, and Caspar Whitney. For an excellent discussion of changing American attitudes toward the Cuban rebels, see Linderman, *Mirror of War*, 127–47.

81. Davis, *Campaigns*, 115. For the real-life models of the places in *Soldiers of Fortune*, see Archibald, "Localities and Scenes," *Book Buyer*, 116–17. Disagreeing, William Harley Porter identifies the inspiration for the iron pier as the nearby port of Siboney, in "Mr. Davis and the Real Olancho," *Bookman* 15 (Aug. 1902): 558–61.

82. Shafter, "Capture of Santiago," *Century,* 615.

83. Brig. Gen. E. J. McClernand, "The Santiago Campaign," in Society of the Army of Santiago de Cuba, *The Santiago Campaign* (Richmond, Va.: Williams Printing Company, 1927), 10–11. Shafter, "Capture of Santiago," *Century,* 620. The quoted dialogue is taken from McClernand's reminiscences.

84. The shipboard incident "doubtless materially affected the future reputation of the General," McClernand later concluded. McClernand, "Santiago Campaign," 10; Shafter, "Capture of Santiago," *Century,* 620. Some journalists agreed. Burr McIntosh blamed Shafter's widespread unpopularity with correspondents on the edict that barred them from landing with the troops. Burr McIntosh, *The Little I Saw of Cuba* (London and New York: F. Tennyson Neely, 1899), 55. In an article published four months after the invasion, Frederic Remington wrote: "When the first landing was made, General Shafter kept all the correspondents and the foreign military attaches in his closed fist, and we all hated him mightily. We shall probably

forgive him, but it will take some time." Frederic Remington, "With the Fifth Corps," *Harper's* 97 (Nov. 1898): 963.

85. RHD to Charles, June 26 [1898]; Barrett Collection. Reprinted in Davis, ed., *Adventures and Letters*, 247–48.

86. Davis, *Campaigns*, 136; Marshall, *Story*, 76–84; Theodore Roosevelt, *The Rough Riders* (New York: Charles Scribner's Sons, [1899] 1921), 78–79.

87. Davis, *Campaigns*, 136.

88. Marshall, *Story*, 92.

89. Davis, *Campaigns*, 138–42; Marshall, *Story*, 91–100.

90. Davis. *Campaigns*, 143–44.

91. Davis, *Campaigns*, 144–45.

92. Roosevelt, *Rough Riders*, 90–91. Although Roosevelt's account of the Las Guásimas fight is chronologically confused, Davis's reporter's notebook from the Spanish-American War, in the Kehrig Papers, establishes that the incident took place at this point.

93. Davis, *Campaigns*, 150–51.

94. Dr. James Robb Church, Princeton '88, was the son of the librarian of the U.S. Senate. He had played tackle on the football team for two years. After graduation, he lived in the woods of Washington State, returning East to earn a medical degree from Columbia University in 1893. "Dr. Church, Rough Riders," New York *Herald*, June 30, 1898: 6.

95. Davis, *Campaigns*, 149–50.

96. Davis, *Campaigns*, 155–60; Richard Harding Davis, "How Hamilton Fish and Allyn Capron Died, Fighting Bravely," New York *Herald*, June 26, 1898, 1: 3.

97. Davis's Spanish-American War notebook; Kehrig Papers.

98. Marshall, *Story*, 116. On July 1, another reporter—James Creelman of the *Journal*—led a charge on the fort at El Caney. He wrote: "This was hardly the business of a correspondent; but whatever of patriotism or excitement was stirring others in that place of carnage had got into my blood too." Creelman, *Great Highway*, 203–7.

99. Marshall, *Story*, 120.

100. Davis, *Campaigns*, 162–63; Marshall, *Story*, 143; Stallman, *Stephen Crane*, 383.

101. Marshall, *Story*, 143; Brown, *Correspondents' War*, 321.

102. Davis, *Campaigns*, 164–69.

103. RHD to Charles, June 26 [1898]; Barrett Collection. Reprinted in Davis, ed., *Adventures and Letters*, 251.

104. RHD to Family, n.d. [c. June 25, 1898]; Kehrig Papers. Reprinted, with

Crane's name omitted and some punctuation added, in Davis, ed., *Adventures and Letters*, 255.

105. Marshall, *Story*, 137–38.

106. The Americans sent 998 men into battle. The number of Spaniards is unclear. Estimates ranged from 1,200 to 4,000. Davis used the highest figure of 4,000. Roosevelt and most of the Rough Riders accepted the figure of 2,000 provided by the Spanish General Toral, although Wood thought it much too low, and offered 2,850 as a closer figure. Davis, *Campaigns*, 171; Jones, *Rough Riders*, 145.

107. Charles Sanford Diehl, *The Staff Correspondent* (San Antonio, Tex.: The Clegg Company, 1931), 139–40.

108. RHD to Family, n.d. [c. June 25, 1898]. Reprinted and misdated in Davis, ed., *Adventures and Letters*, 255. Unlike the Associated Press, the *Herald* reported Roosevelt's praise for Davis. See "Gallant Work by Our Troops," New York *Herald*, June 26, 1898, 1: 4.

109. Roosevelt, intr. to Davis, *Captain Macklin*, vii.

110. [Finley Peter Dunne], *Mr. Dooley's Philosophy* (New York: Harper & Brothers, 1900), 15.

111. Davis, "How Hamilton Fish and Allyn Capron Died." Caspar Whitney accompanied the regulars. Although Davis doesn't mention him, one other reporter— Kennett F. Harris of the Chicago *Record*—was with the Rough Riders at Las Guásimas, but apparently so far in the rear that he missed the ambush and much of the fighting. Brown, *Correspondents' War*, 313–14, 317. Charles Sanford Diehl of the Associated Press states that Davis, Marshall, and Dunning were the only three correspondents to see the Guásimas battle. Diehl, *Staff Correspondent*, 276.

112. Jones, *Rough Riders*, 135, 138.

113. Davis, *Campaigns*, 132–34.

114. Davis, "How Hamilton Fish and Allyn Capron Died."

115. Richard Harding Davis, "Rough Riders Gave Spaniards a Sample of American Pluck," New York *Herald*, June 28, 1898: 3.

116. RHD to Family, n.d. [c. June 25, 1898]; Kehrig Papers. Reprinted and misdated in Davis, ed., *Adventures and Letters*, 254.

117. RHD to Charles, June 26 [1898]; Barrett Collection. Reprinted in Davis, ed., *Adventures and Letters*, 249.

118. RHD to Theodore Roosevelt, Apr. 21, 1899; Theodore Roosevelt to RHD, Apr. 22, 1899; Theodore Roosevelt Papers, Library of Congress.

119. David F. Trask, *The War with Spain in 1898* (New York: Macmillan, 1981), 222.

120. Eight of the dead and thirty-four of the wounded were Rough Riders. Davis, *Campaigns*, 171. The Associated Press, whose man Dunning was on the scene, reported that "as perfect an ambuscade as was ever formed in the brain of an

Apache Indian was prepared, and Lieutenant Colonel Roosevelt and his men walked squarely into it." "Many Spanish Buried by Our Troops," New York *Herald,* June 27, 1898: 4. Marshall, another Roosevelt fan, used comparable scholastic reasoning when he concluded that, since Cuban scouts had reported sharpshooters in the woods and an entrenchment just beyond the meeting of the two trails at Las Guásimas, the battle "was not technically an ambush, although it is true that the American troops met the Spaniards before they had expected to." Marshall, *Story,* 90.

121. Davis, *Campaigns,* 173–77; RHD to Clarke, June 29 [1898]; Barrett Collection. Reprinted in Davis, ed., *Adventures and Letters,* 253. According to another reporter, a two-ounce package of tobacco was auctioned for $47.50. Marshall, *Story,* 161.

122. RHD to Clarke, June 29 [1898]; Barrett Collection. Deleted from the letter reprinted in Davis, ed., *Adventures and Letters,* 254.

123. Richard Harding Davis, "The Battle of San Juan," *Scribner's* 24 (Oct. 1898): 397. This was deleted when the article was reprinted in *The Cuban and Porto Rican Campaigns.*

124. Davis, *Campaigns,* 120–32.

125. Davis reported this inspection as occurring on June 29, but all other accounts date it June 30. Davis, *Campaigns,* 183; Miley, *With Shafter,* 101; Trask, *War with Spain,* 234; French Ensor Chadwick, *The Relations of the United States and Spain: The Spanish-American War,* 2 (New York: Charles Scribner's Sons, 1911), 69.

126. Jones, *Rough Riders,* 155.

127. Davis, *Campaigns,* 185.

128. Shafter, "Capture of Santiago," *Century,* 625.

129. Chadwick, *Relations,* 74, 77, 85. Five days before the battle, Davis had heard Major-General Adna Chaffee explain that if the troops were sent down the two trails that snaked through the woods, they would emerge into the clearing, one after another, like ducks in a shooting gallery. Chaffee urged that small trails be cut throughout the front of the woods, so the whole army could appear at once. His advice was ignored. Instead, everyone was led through just *one* of the two trails. Davis, *Campaigns,* 181–82.

130. McIntosh, *Little I Saw,* 116. Frank Collins, a Boston *Journal* correspondent who later died of fever, persuaded a mule driver to transport Davis in his wagon. Richard Harding Davis, "Our War Correspondents in Cuba and Puerto Rico," *Harper's* 98 (May 1899): 945.

131. Davis, *Campaigns,* 190–94; Richard Harding Davis, "Troops Marched at Night to Form the Battle Line," New York *Herald,* July 3, 1898, 1: 5. RHD to Charles, n.d. [Sept. 1898]; Barrett Collection.

132. Davis, *Campaigns,* 196, 199.

133. Davis, *Campaigns,* 204–11.

134. Davis, *Campaigns*, 212–13.

135. Davis, *Campaigns*, 212–14.

136. Roosevelt, *Rough Riders*, 119–30; Davis, *Campaigns*, 214–17. Roosevelt's own recollection of what he said is pithier: "Then let my men through, sir."

137. Davis, *Campaigns*, 217.

138. Richard Harding Davis, "Dashing Bravery of Rough Riders," New York *Herald*, July 14, 1898: 4.

139. RHD to Rebecca, July 9 [1898]. Barrett Collection. Reprinted in "Adventures and Letters," *Metropolitan* 46 (July 1917): 53–54. Davis, *Campaigns*, 227; McIntosh, *Little I Saw*, 130.

140. Davis, *Campaigns*, 218–20, 223.

141. Chadwick, *Relations*, 93; Roosevelt, *Rough Riders*, 134–39.

142. RHD to Rebecca, July 9 [1898]; Barrett Collection. Reprinted in "The Adventures and Letters of Richard Harding Davis," *Metropolitan* 46 (July 1917): 53–54. See also Richard Harding Davis, *Notes of a War Correspondent* (New York: Charles Scribner's Sons, 1910), 122; Davis, *Campaigns*, 235–36.

143. Years later, Davis muddied the distinction further by writing: "San Juan Hill is not a solitary hill, but the most prominent of a ridge of hills, with Kettle Hill a quarter of a mile away on the edge of the jungle and separated from the ridge by a tiny lake. In the local nomenclature Kettle Hill, which is the name given to it by the Rough Riders, has always been known as San Juan Hill, with an added name to distinguish it from the other San Juan Hill of greater reknown." Davis, *Notes*, 116.

144. Davis, *Campaigns*, 217.

145. Davis, "Dashing Bravery."

146. Chadwick, *Relations*, 97; Alger, *Spanish-American War*, 165–66.

147. Davis, *Notes*, 125; Beer, *Crane*, 191–92. Hare claimed that he, not Davis, shamed Crane into lying down. Cecil Carnes, *Jimmy Hare: News Photographer* (New York: The Macmillan Company, 1940), 73. Several of his colleagues thought Crane wanted to be shot. He talked academically of the points of entry for a bullet on his body. The night before Guásimas, he shocked Henry Carey and Acton Davies by saying it would be interesting to be shot. He had noticed that with chest wounds, men ran ahead for a while before falling; with abdominal injuries, they crumpled. Davies, a fat theatrical critic, was sunburned pink and red, freckled, and blistered. Rubbing linseed oil on his shoulders, Crane remarked, "You'd look bully if a shell hit you, ol' man. Like a squashed peony." Beer, *Crane*, 190.

148. Carnes, *Jimmy Hare*, 57, 73–74; Davis, *Notes*, 128.

149. Chadwick, *Relations*, 100.

150. Davis, *Campaigns*, 247.

151. Brown, *Correspondents' War*, 369–70.

152. Chadwick, *Relations*, 106. "It has often happened that an army has asked the navy to assist it in an assault upon a fortified port," Davis wrote. "But this is probably the only instance when a fleet has called upon an army to capture another fleet." Davis, *Campaigns*, 120.

153. Chadwick, *Relations*, 100.

154. Alger, *Spanish-American War*, 172–75; Chadwick, *Relations*, 108–10.

155. RHD to Rebecca, July 9 [1898]; Barrett Collection. Reprinted in "Adventures and Letters," *Metropolitan* 46 (July 1917): 54.

156. Davis, *Campaigns*, 249–50.

157. Richard Harding Davis, "Our Brave Men Defy Hardships," New York *Herald*, July 7, 1898: 11.

158. Davis, *Campaigns*, 251.

159. Alger, *Spanish-American War*, 180.

160. Shafter, "Capture of Santiago," *Century*, 626.

161. "A Richard in the Field," New York *Sun*, July 14, 1898: 6.

162. Editorial, *Harper's Weekly*, July 16, 1898, cited in Brown, *Correspondents' War*, 395.

163. Davis, *Campaigns*, 277–78; Richard Harding Davis, "Made No Charge on the Trenches," New York *Herald*, July 12, 1898: 4; Richard Harding Davis, "Dashing Bravery." RHD to Rebecca, July 9 [1898]; Barrett Collection. Reprinted in "Adventures and Letters," *Metropolitan* 46 (July 1917): 54.

164. Chadwick, *Relations*, 234, 253; Miley, *With Shafter*, 146.

165. Davis, *Campaigns*, 256–57; Richard Harding Davis, "Soldiers Eager for 'More Hustle,'" New York *Herald*, July 14, 1898: 4. Richard Harding Davis, "Santiago Likely to Capitulate," New York *Herald*, July 8, 1898: 6. I have printed the Rough Rider's quote as it appeared in Davis's *Herald* dispatch of July 14. In *Campaigns*, he bowdlerized it into: "Now that we got those Mexicans corraled, why don't we brand them?"

166. RHD to Rebecca, July 9 [1898]; Barrett Collection. Reprinted in "Adventures and Letters," *Metropolitan* 46 (July 1917): 54.

167. Miley, *With Shafter*, 144–47.

168. RHD to Rebecca, July 11, 1898; Barrett Collection. Reprinted in "Adventures and Letters," *Metropolitan* 46 (July 1917): 54.

169. RHD to Family, n.d. [June 10, 1898]; Barrett Collection.

170. Davis, *Campaigns*, 265–70.

171. "Adventure Filled Life of Richard Harding Davis," New York *Evening Post*, Apr. 15, 1916, 1: 5.

172. Richard Harding Davis, "Rode in Triumph Through the Lines," New York *Herald*, July 9, 1898: 5.

173. Crane, "War Memories"; cited in Brown, *Correspondents' War*, 397.

174. Brown, *Correspondents' War*, 401–4.

175. RHD to Charles, July 26 [1898]; Barrett Collection.

176. Davis, *Campaigns*, 291.

177. RHD to Charles, July 26 [1898]; Barrett Collection.

178. RHD to Charles, July 26 [1898]; Barrett Collection.

179. Davis, *Campaigns*, 296–305.

180. Chadwick, *Relations*, 285–86, 299–300.

181. Richard Harding Davis, "Miles Fooled Spaniards," New York *Herald*, Aug. 2, 1898: 5. He reiterated the invidious comparison in Richard Harding Davis, "Ponce Surrenders to Miles and Greets Him With Cheers and Music," New York *Herald*, July 5, 1898: 3. He later remarked that the Puerto Rico campaign began brilliantly but ended prematurely, due to Spain's surrender. Davis, *Campaigns*, 331–32.

182. For the fullest account, see Richard Harding Davis, "The Taking of Coamo," in Davis, *Notes*, 101–12. An earlier, sketchier account, with some conflicting details, appears in Davis, *Campaigns*, 337–48. Since Davis wrote in "The Taking of Coamo" that he was at last giving a complete report, I have relied on the later version when they diverge.

183. In the Puerto Rico campaign, which he covered for the New York *Journal*, Stephen Crane took a town of his own. Writing about that escapade, Davis quipped, "It was not safe for an American wearing anything that resembled a uniform to approach a Porto Rican stronghold unless he was prepared to have it fall prostrate at his feet." Richard Harding Davis, "How Stephen Crane Took Juana Dias," reprinted in R. W. Stallman and E. R. Hagemann, eds., *The War Dispatches of Stephen Crane* (New York: New York University Press, 1964), 196–99.

184. "The War with Spain," *Critic* 34 (Apr. 1899): 361.

185. Pitts Duffield, "Witnesses of the War," *Book Buyer* 17 (Jan. 1899): 615.

186. E. L. Burlingame to RHD, Aug. 30, 1898; Scribner Archive.

187. For a concurring opinion, see Knight, *Critical Period*, 139.

188. Richard Harding Davis, "Our War Correspondents in Cuba," 941.

189. Richard Harding Davis, "On the Fever Ship," *Scribner's* 25 (Jan. 1899): 21–28; reprinted in Davis, *Exiles*, 118–43.

190. Richard Harding Davis, "A Derelict," *Scribner's* 30 (Aug. 1901): 131–52; reprinted in Davis, *Ranson's Folly*, 101–52.

191. "A Disgruntled Reporter," New York *Daily Tribune*, Aug. 19, 1901: 8.

192. Beer, *Crane*, 246.

193. For a convincing analysis of the parallels between Davis's character of Channing and his perception of Crane, see Scott C. Osborn, "The 'Rivalry-Chivalry' of Richard Harding Davis and Stephen Crane," *American Literature* 28 (Mar. 1956), 50–61.

Chapter 8

1. Sangree, "Richard Harding Davis," *Ainslee's*, 9.

2. *Notable Men of Chicago and Their City* (Chicago: Chicago Daily Journal, 1910), 81.

3. Interview by the author with Miss Frederica Poett, Mar. 28, 1985.

4. RHD to Louise Clark, Nov. 6 [1898]; RHD to Louise Clark, Nov. 12 [1898]; Poett Papers.

5. Poett Papers. Capitalized and punctuated as in the original. The verse is a take-off on a popular song, Charles Graham's "The Picture That Is Turned to the Wall."

6. RHD to Louise Clark, Nov. 12 [1898]; Poett Papers.

7. RHD to Rebecca, n.d. [c. Dec. 11, 1898]; RHD to Family, n.d. [mid-Dec. 1898]; Barrett Collection.

8. RHD to Louise Clark, n.d. [c. Dec. 15, 1898]; RHD to Louise Clark, [Jan.] 10 [1899]; Poett Papers.

9. RHD to Charles, n.d. [c. Feb. 2, 1899]; RHD to Charles, Feb. 10 [1899]; Barrett Collection. RHD to Louise Clark, n.d. [c. Jan. 18, 1899]; Poett Papers. RHD to J. Henry Harper, cable, Jan. 30, 1899; Special Collections, Lehigh University Libraries.

10. On Jan. 20, 1899, Scribners was typesetting "The Lion and the Unicorn." See Charles Scribner to RHD, Jan. 20, 1899; Scribner Archive.

11. Richard Harding Davis, "The Lion and the Unicorn," in Davis, *Exiles*, 144–203. The story first appeared in *Scribner's* 26 (Aug. 1899): 129–52.

12. RHD to Charles, n.d. [mid-Mar. 1899]; Kehrig Papers.

13. Davis, ed., *Adventures and Letters*, 255–56; C. Lewis Hind, *Authors and I* (New York: John Lane Company, 1921), 80–85.

14. RHD to Charles, Mar. 15, 1899; original not located. Reprinted in Davis, ed., *Adventures and Letters*, 256–57; and more completely in "Adventures and Letters," *Metropolitan* 46 (Aug. 1917): 27.

15. RHD to Charles, Mar. 15, 1899; original not located. Reprinted in Davis, ed., *Adventures and Letters*, 257.

16. RHD to Charles, Mar. 15, 1899; original not located. Reprinted in "Adventures and Letters," *Metropolitan* 46 (Aug. 1917): 27. Daniel Frohman had once attracted free publicity by sending a bogus district messenger boy to London with souvenirs

of the hundredth performance of *The Highest Bidder*. Davis wrote about this in "The Lime Light Man," the *Stage*, Oct. 27, 1888: 5.

17. Davis, ed., *Adventures and Letters*, 256.

18. "The St. Louis Has a Rough Trip," New York *Daily Tribune*, April 9, 1899, 1: 4.

19. "Davis Drops Dead," New York *Evening Post*, 6.

20. RHD to Louise Clark, Mar. 21 [1899]; Poett Papers.

21. "St. Louis," New York *Daily Tribune*, 4; RHD to Charles Scribner, telegram Apr. 12, 1899; Scribner Archive.

22. Boston *Sunday Journal*, May 14, 1899, Photographic Section: 1,4,5. Information on the size and acreage of the Clark house, which has since been demolished, was provided by Miss Frederica Poett in an interview with the author on Mar. 28, 1985.

23. "Curious Kink in 'Dickie' Davis' Character," Cleveland *Leader*, May 7, 1916. Theatre Collection, New York Public Library.

24. Beer, *Mauve Decade*, 54.

25. RHD to Rebecca, n.d. [May, 1899]; Barrett Collection. Reprinted, with an unjustifiably specific date, in Davis, ed., *Adventures and Letters*, 260.

26. RHD to Louise Clark, n.d. [c. May 7, 1899]; Poett Papers.

27. RHD to Rebecca, n.d. [May, 1899]; Barrett Collection.

28. RHD to Louise Clark, July 28 [1899]; Poett Papers.

29. Davis, *Soldiers of Fortune*, 356.

30. Erenberg, *Steppin' Out*, especially 33–43; and Thomas, *Delmonico's*, especially 266–82. See also "An American Palace," *Harper's Weekly* 37 (Mar. 25, 1893): 283; Howard Mumford Jones, *The Age of Energy: Varieties of American Experience, 1865–1915* (New York: The Viking Press, 1971), 130; and Lloyd Morris, *Incredible New York* (New York: Random House, 1951), 239.

31. RHD to Family, July 18 [1900]; Barrett Collection.

32. Interview with Frederica Poett, Mar. 28, 1985.

33. Harper & Brothers to RHD, cable, July 29, 1899. RHD to Harper & Brothers, cable, Aug. 10, 1899; Harper Brothers Collection, Rare Book and Manuscript Library, Columbia University.

34. RHD to J. Henry Harper, Aug. 25 [1899]; Special Collections, Lehigh University Libraries.

35. RHD to J. Henry Harper, Nov. 7 [1900]; Special Collections, Lehigh University Libraries.

36. RHD to Rebecca, Feb. 9, 1900; Newton Papers.

37. RHD to Charles, Dec. 27, 1899; Barrett Collection. RHD to Charles Scribner,

n.d. [c. Nov. 20, 1899]; RHD to Charles Scribner, Dec. 11 [1899]; RHD to Charles Scribner, n.d. [c. Dec. 18, 1899]; RHD to Charles Scribner, Dec. 20 [1899]; RHD to Charles Scribner, Dec. 27 [1899]; RHD to Charles Scribner, cable, Jan. 10, 1900; Scribner Archive.

38. RHD to Rebecca, [Jan.] 10 [1900]; Newton Papers.

39. RHD to Rebecca, Friday [Jan. 12, 1900]; RHD to Rebecca, Saturday [Jan. 13, 1900]; Newton Papers.

40. RHD to Louise Clark, Wednesday [Jan. 17, 1900]; Poett Papers.

41. RHD to Nora, n.d. [c. Jan. 22, 1900]; Newton Papers. RHD to Louise Clark, n.d. [c. Jan. 28, 1900]; original not located. Reprinted in "Adventures and Letters," *Metropolitan* 46 (Aug. 1917): 28.

42. Cecil to Louise Clark, [Jan.] 19 [1900]; Poett Papers. RHD to Nora, n.d. [Jan. 19, 1900]; Newton Papers.

43. Hind, *Authors and I*, 80–82.

44. RHD to Charles Scribner, Dec. 20 [1899]; E. L. Burlingame to RHD, July 10, 1900; Scribner Archive.

45. RHD to Nora, n.d. [c. Jan. 22, 1900]; Newton Papers.

46. Cecil to Rebecca, Tues. [Jan. 23, 1900]; Newton Papers.

47. RHD to Nora, Jan. 31 [1900]; Newton Papers.

48. Richard Harding Davis, "Jameson's Fatal Error," New York *Sun*, Sept. 6, 1896, 1: 1. Reprinted as *Dr. Jameson's Raiders vs. the Johannesburg Reformers* (New York: R.H. Russell, 1897), 7. See also *The Autobiography of John Hays Hammond* (New York: Farrar and Rinehart, 1935), 412–13.

49. RHD to Charles, Sept. 28 [1896]; RHD to Clarke, Sept. 8 [1896]; Barrett Collection.

50. Charles Belmont Davis, intr. to Quinby, *Bibliography*, xv–xvi. Although Charles Davis reported the sum as $400 and did not name the "very rich man" and "leader in a famous cause" that his brother had interviewed, there can be no doubt that he was alluding to Hammond in this account written two decades later. However, there is no contemporary corroboration of this anecdote.

51. RHD to Rebecca, n.d. [early Spring 1897]; Barrett Collection.

52. RHD to Rebecca, Aug. 10 [1896]; Barrett Collection.

53. RHD to Charles, Aug. 11 [1896]; Barrett Collection.

54. "Mr. Harding Davis on Trans-Atlantic Friendship," London *Daily Mail*, Jan. 20, 1900; clipping in Kehrig Papers.

55. "Marion Loves Him," Boston *Herald*, Aug. 12, 1900: 36; "Returning Americans and Visitors Tell of Their Plans and Experiences," New York *World*, Aug. 5, 1900: 5.

56. RHD to Nora, Jan. 31 [1899]; Newton Papers.

57. RHD to Louise Clark, n.d. [c. Jan. 28, 1900]; original not located. Reprinted in "Adventures and Letters," *Metropolitan* 46 (Aug. 1917): 28.

58. RHD to Rebecca, Feb. 14 [1900]; Newton Papers. Cecil to Louise Clark, Jan. 31 [1900]; Poett Papers.

59. RHD to Rebecca, Feb. 18 [1900]; Newton Papers.

60. RHD to Rebecca, Feb. 14 [1900]; Newton Papers.

61. RHD to Rebecca, Feb. 18 [1900]; Newton Papers.

62. Cecil to Rebecca, Feb. 20 [1900]; Newton Papers.

63. Cecil to Louise Clark, Feb. 21 [1900]; Poett Papers.

64. Cecil to Rebecca, Feb. 20 [1900]; Newton Papers.

65. Cecil to Louise Clark, Mar. 1 [1900]; Poett Papers.

66. RHD to Rebecca, Feb. 23 [1900]; Newton Papers.

67. Richard Harding Davis, *With Both Armies in South Africa* (New York: Charles Scribner's Sons, 1900), 2–5.

68. Davis, *With Both Armies*, 6–7.

69. RHD to Rebecca, n.d. [c. Feb. 28, 1900]; Newton Papers.

70. RHD to Rebecca, Mar. 4 [1900]; Newton Papers. Reprinted in Davis, ed., *Adventures and Letters*, 273.

71. RHD to Rebecca, n.d. [c. Feb. 28, 1900]; Newton Papers. Reprinted in Davis, ed., *Adventures and Letters*, 270.

72. Davis, *With Both Armies*, 12.

73. RHD to Rebecca, Mar. 4 [1900]; Newton Papers. Reprinted in Davis, ed., *Adventures and Letters*, 273.

74. RHD to Rebecca, n.d. [c. Feb. 28, 1900]; Newton Papers. Reprinted in Davis, ed., *Adventures and Letters*, 270–71.

75. RHD to Theodore Roosevelt, Mar. 1 [1900; misdated 1910]; Theodore Roosevelt Papers, Library of Congress.

76. RHD to Rebecca, Mar. 5 [1900]; Newton Papers. Reprinted in Davis, ed., *Adventures and Letters*, 275.

77. Davis, *With Both Armies*, 61–72. RHD to Rebecca, Mar. 3 [1900]; Newton Papers. Reprinted in Davis, ed., *Adventures and Letters*, 271–72.

78. RHD to Rebecca, Mar. 3 [1900]; Newton Papers. Reprinted in Davis, ed., *Adventures and Letters*, 271–72.

79. Davis, *With Both Armies*, 73–74.

80. RHD to Rebecca, Mar. 3–4 [1900]; Newton Papers. Reprinted in Davis, ed., *Adventures and Letters*, 272–74.

81. RHD to Rebecca, Mar. 5 [1900]; Newton Papers. Reprinted with deletions in Davis, ed., *Adventures and Letters*, 274.

82. Davis, *With Both Armies*, 39–40. RHD to Rebecca, Mar. 15 [1900]; Newton Papers. Reprinted with deletions in Davis, ed., *Adventures and Letters*, 277.

83. RHD to Rebecca, Mar. 15 [1900]; Newton Papers. Reprinted in Davis, ed., *Adventures and Letters*, 277. Davis, *With Both Armies*, 86–87. In a news story on his return to the United States, Davis was quoted as saying that he "went over to the Boers after [he] had endured English censorship as long as [he] could," but he denies that convincingly in *With Both Armies*. See "R.H. Davis on Boer War," New York *Daily Tribune*, Aug. 5, 1900, 1: 10.

84. RHD to Rebecca, Mar. 30 [1900]; Special Collections, Lehigh University Libraries.

85. RHD to Family, Mar. 25 [1900]; Newton Papers. Reprinted in Davis, ed., *Adventures and Letters*, 279.

86. Cecil to John Clark, Mar. 28 [1900]; Poett Papers.

87. RHD to Family, Wednesday, n.d. [Jan. 20, 1892]; Barrett Collection. Ricardo L. Trumbull, "Should the United States Help Chili?" *Harper's Weekly* 35 (Aug. 22, 1891): 638–39; "The Revolution in Chili," *Harper's Weekly* 35 (Aug. 29, 1891): 654; "The Victory of the Congressionalists," *Harper's Weekly* 35 (Sept. 5, 1891): 684; Richard Harding Davis, "Minister Patrick Egan," *Harper's Weekly* 35 (Sept. 12, 1891): 696; "Our Minister in Chili," *Harper's Weekly* 35 (Sept. 19, 1891): 702; "The Valparaiso Incident," *Harper's Weekly* 35 (Nov. 7, 1891): 862; Richard Harding Davis, "The Crew of the Baltimore," *Harper's Weekly* 35 (Nov. 14, 1891): 891–92; "Chili and the United States," *Harper's Weekly* 35 (Dec. 26, 1891): 1034; "Chili and War," *Harper's Weekly* 36 (Jan. 9, 1892): 26; "The United States and Chili," *Harper's Weekly* 36 (Jan. 30, 1892): 98; "Why Was Chili Hostile?" *Harper's Weekly* 36 (Feb. 6, 1892): 122; "Chili Again," *Harper's Weekly* 36 (May 28, 1892): 506; "An Indemnity for Chili," *Harper's Weekly* 36 (July 30, 1892): 722.

88. Davis, *With Both Armies*, 125.

89. RHD to Family, Apr. 4 [1900]; Newton Papers. RHD to Rebecca, Apr. 5 [1900]. Newton Papers. Reprinted in Davis, ed., *Adventures and Letters*, 281–82. Davis, *With Both Armies*, 86–91.

90. Davis, *With Both Armies*, 92–93. RHD to Rebecca, Apr. 18, 1900; Barrett Collection.

91. RHD to Rebecca, Apr. 23 [1900]; Newton Papers.

92. Cecil to Louise Clark, Apr. 22 [1900]; Poett Papers. Davis, *With Both Armies*, 119.

93. Cecil to Nora, Apr. 25 [1900]; Newton Papers.

94. RHD to Family, May 4 [1900]; Newton Papers.

95. RHD to Family, May 8 [1900]; Newton Papers. RHD to Family, May 18 [1900]; Newton Papers. Reprinted in Davis, ed., *Adventures and Letters*, 282. Davis, *With Both Armies,* 174–75.

96. RHD to Family, May 18 [1900]; Newton Papers. Reprinted in Davis, ed., *Adventures and Letters*, 282–88. See also Davis, *With Both Armies*, 185–211.

97. Davis, *With Both Armies*, 224.

98. Davis, *With Both Armies*, 215–19.

99. Davis, *With Both Armies*, 157–62.

100. RHD to Rebecca, Jan. 11 [1898]; Barrett Collection.

101. Richard Harding Davis, "What 'Peace on Earth, Good Will to Men' Really Means," New York *Herald*, July 8, 1900, 5: 2. When the article was republished in *With Both Armies*, the section on Lord Rosslyn was deleted. For Rosslyn's rebuttal of Davis's charges, see "Earl of Rosslyn Contradicts and Criticises Mr. R. Harding Davis," New York *Herald*, Sept. 7, 1900: 9. Davis answered Rosslyn—in particular, his charge that Davis wore Greek medals to which he wasn't entitled—in "A Question of Decorations," New York *Daily Tribune*, Sept. 9, 1900, 1: 9.

102. Richard Harding Davis, "Pretoria in War-Time," *Scribner's* 28 (Aug. 1900): 176. This hyperbole was deleted from the book.

103. Davis, *With Both Armies*, 140–44, 147–48.

104. Davis, *With Both Armies*, 148–56.

105. RHD to Rebecca, June 8 [1900]; Newton Papers. Reprinted in Davis, ed., *Adventures and Letters*, 288–89. See also Davis, *With Both Armies*, 220; and Richard Harding Davis, "Kruger's Last Day in Pretoria," New York *Herald*, Aug. 5, 1900, 5: 2.

106. Davis, *With Both Armies*, 231.

107. Davis, *With Both Armies*, 88, 125–26, 138, 178, 194–96, 237.

108. RHD to Rebecca, June 8 [1900]; Newton Papers. Reprinted in Davis, ed., *Adventures and Letters*, 289.

109. Davis, *With Both Armies*, 195–96, 233.

110. Davis, "Kruger's Last Day in Pretoria."

111. Davis, *With Both Armies*, 233–35.

112. RHD to Rebecca, Mar. 5 [1900]; Newton Papers. Reprinted in Davis, ed., *Adventures and Letters*, 276.

113. RHD to Rebecca, June 21 [1900]; Newton Papers.

114. RHD to Rebecca, June 8 [1900]; Newton Papers. Deleted from the letter reprinted in Davis, ed., *Adventures and Letters*, 289.

115. RHD to Rebecca, June 8 [1900]; Newton Papers. Deleted from the letter reprinted in Davis, ed., *Adventures and Letters*, 289. Richard Harding Davis, *The*

Congo and the Coasts of Africa (New York: Charles Scribner's Sons, 1907), 180–83. Cecil to Louise Clark, July 1 [1900]; Poett Papers.

116. RHD to Rebecca, June 12 [1900]; Newton Papers.

117. "Returning Americans and Visitors Tell of Their Plans and Experiences," New York *World*, Aug. 5, 1900: 5.

118. Davis, *Congo*, 208–11.

119. RHD to Rebecca, June 21 [1900]; Newton Papers. See also Davis, *Congo*, 218.

120. RHD to Rebecca, June 29 [1900]; Newton Papers. Deleted from the letter reprinted in Davis, ed., *Adventures and Letters*, 291. See also Davis, *Congo*, 219.

121. RHD to Nora, June 25 [1900]; RHD to Rebecca, June 29 [1900]; Newton Papers.

122. "R.H. Davis on Boer War," New York *Daily Tribune*.

123. "Dick thinks he has done some very good work but I suppose there is no interest left for the Boers now that the Chinese war is on," Cecil remarked in July. Cecil to Louise Clark, July 1 [1900]; Poett Papers.

124. To cite merely a few instances: the drawn yellow skin of the men at Ladysmith is mentioned on pp. 69, 73, and 83; the fact that General Buller needs weeks to travel twelve miles over rough terrain is stated on pp. 29 and 45; and the comparison of the Englishman's motives to a thief coveting another man's gold watch and chain is made on pp. 125–26 and 194. Even more jarring, the early part of the book retains the usage of "our" forces, referring to the British army, that appeared in the original articles in the *Daily Mail*. See p. 50.

125. This clipping, from Nov. 10, 1900, and many similar ones were found in the Poett Papers.

126. *Outlook* 66 (Nov. 17, 1900): 714.

127. RHD to Rebecca, Mar. 15 [1900]; Newton Papers. Reprinted in "Adventures and Letters," *Metropolitan* 46 (Aug. 1917): 29.

Chapter 9
1. RHD to Louise Clark, Nov. 27 [1900]; RHD to Louise Clark, n.d. [Dec. 6, 1900]; Poett Papers.

2. Sothern had cast a Davis play and was set to start rehearsals the previous December; Mansfield had promised to open another Davis play in Chicago in May; and Hackett had said he would bring a third to New York next September. RHD to J. Henry Harper, Nov. 7 [1900]; Special Collections, Lehigh University Libraries.

3. RHD to J. Henry Harper, Nov. 7 [1900]; Special Collections, Lehigh University Libraries. See also Quinby, *Bibliography*, 104. RHD to Louise Clark, [Nov.] 7 [1900]; RHD to Louise Clark, Nov. 27 [1900]; Cecil to Louise Clark, Tues. [Dec. 11, 1900]; Poett Papers.

4. RHD to Louise Clark, Jan. 20 [1901]; Poett Papers.

5. Mark Sullivan, *Our Times: The Turn of the Century, 1900–1904* (New York: Charles Scribner's Sons, 1926), 531, 580–81.

6. Augustus Thomas, intr. to Davis, *Soldiers of Fortune*, x. See also Augustus Thomas, *The Print of My Remembrance* (New York: Charles Scribner's Sons, 1922), 431.

7. "The Passing Throng," New York *Daily Tribune*, Feb. 13, 1902: 7. "Soldiers of Fortune," Baltimore *Herald*, Nov. 11, 1902; clipping in Kehrig Papers. For Richard's attention to the uniforms, see RHD to Rebecca, n.d. [c. Jan. 20, 1902]; Barrett Collection.

8. RHD to Rebecca, Apr. 29 [1902]; Barrett Collection. RHD to Louise Clark, Apr. 30 [1902]; Poett Papers.

9. RHD to Rebecca, Feb. 14 [1902]; RHD to Rebecca, Feb. 22 [1900]; Barrett Collection.

10. Sheehan, *This Was Publishing*, 97–98.

11. Harry Thurston Peck, "Then and Now," *Bookman* 30 (Feb. 1910): 595.

12. Henry F. May, *The End of American Innocence: A Study of the First Years of Our Own Time, 1912–1917* (New York: Alfred A. Knopf, 1959), 68–70.

13. Ziff, *American 1890s*, 120.

14. Mark Sullivan, *Our Times: The War Begins, 1909–1914* (New York: Charles Scribner's Sons, 1932), 92–100.

15. Hapgood, *Changing Years*, 174–75.

16. Carnes, *Jimmy Hare*, 257; Mark Sullivan, *The Education of an American* (New York: Doubleday, Doran & Co., 1938), 205.

17. Fairfax Downey, *Portrait of an Era as Drawn by C.D. Gibson* (New York: Charles Scribner's Sons, 1936), 275–78

18. RHD to Rebecca, two letters, n.d. [Summer 1902]; one letter, n.d. [late 1903]; Barrett Collection.

19. Cecil to Louise Clark, Tuesday [Jan. 15, 1901]; Poett Papers. Carnes, *Jimmy Hare*, 110.

20. Richard Harding Davis, "The Trouble in Venezuela," *Collier's* 26 (Feb. 16, 1901): 5, 23.

21. RHD to Louise Clark, Aug. 8 [1901]; Poett Papers.

22. The asphalt controversy did not go away. Visiting Caracas four years later, Davis discounted rumors that the United States was about to invade Venezuela on behalf of the aggrieved asphalt trust. "Let us ask ourselves the question: Do we or do we not desire to go to war, in order that the asphalt trust may thrive and flourish?" he wrote. "For that is all there is to it." Richard Harding Davis, "The Asphalt Scandal," *Collier's* 35 (May 13, 1905): 20–21. In a short story "The Spy,"

about a controversy over nitrates that is in thin disguise the asphalt dispute, an eminent American lawyer believes (as did Davis) that "between preserving the nitrate beds for the trust, and preserving for his country and various sweethearts one brown-throated, clean-limbed bluejacket, I was for the bluejacket." Richard Harding Davis, "The Spy" (1905), in Davis, *The Bar Sinister* (New York: Charles Scribner's Sons, 1916), 88–120.

23. Davis mailed the story to *Scribner's* on January 1, 1902. RHD to E. L. Burlingame, Jan. 1, 1902; Scribner Archive. It was first published in *Scribner's* 31 (Mar. 1902): 307–26, and is reprinted in Davis, *Bar Sinister*, 1–55.

24. See Davis, *Bar Sinister*, 2; "Mr. Davis's Bull Terrier Dead," New York *Daily Tribune*, June 16, 1903: 3. Sired by the purebred Lord Minto of a black-and-tan dam of doubtful pedigree, Edgewood Cold Steel was the only white puppy in a litter of black-and-tans. At his first dog show, in Toronto in 1900, he took a first. He won forty prizes during his lifetime. Jimmy Jocks, the English bull terrier in "The Bar Sinister," was based on Woodcote Jumbo, better known as Jaggers.

25. RHD to Charles Scribner, July 16 [1902]; Scribner Archive.

26. RHD to Rebecca, n.d. [early Feb. 1898]; Barrett Collection.

27. Rebecca to RHD, n.d. [early Fall 1902]; Kehrig Papers.

28. *Review of Reviews*, Dec., 1902; clipping in Kehrig Papers. See Arthur Bartlett Maurice, "Four Novels of the Moment," *Bookman* 16 (Oct. 1902): 175–79; and Norman Gask, *Critic* 42 (Jan. 1903): 68.

29. RHD to E. L. Burlingame, June 17 [1902]; Scribner Archive.

30. "I notice in the paragraphs sent out that it is announced the adventures are partly my own," Davis complained to Charles Scribner. "This I fear is a mistake in judgement, as well as in fact. The paragraph I read at your office said that I had made use of what I had seen of military life, and of the country described, but that is very different from saying that what happened to my hero, has happened to me." RHD to Charles Scribner, Oct. 25 [1901]; Scribner Archive.

31. See Maurice, "Four Novels of the Moment"; and Gask, *Critic*.

32. RHD to Arthur Bartlett Maurice, Apr. 9, 1906; typescript in Kehrig Papers. Reprinted in Davis, ed., *Adventures and Letters*, 317–18.

33. Richard Harding Davis, *Captain Macklin: His Memoirs* (New York: Charles Scribner's Sons, [1902] 1916), 309, 325.

34. Richard Harding Davis, "Ranson's Folly" (1902), in Davis, *Ranson's Folly*, 1–100.

35. RHD to Charles Scribner, n.d. [c. Feb. 8, 1903]; Scribner Archive. In this letter, Davis tells Scribner that he has "refused others"—presumably Collier—on the same grounds.

36. Richard Harding Davis, "The Coronation of Alfonso XIII," *Collier's* 29 (June 21, 1902): 4–5; Richard Harding Davis, "Echoes of the Spanish Coronation,"

Collier's 29 (June 28, 1902): 15; Richard Harding Davis, "England's Tragedy," *Collier's* 29 (July 5, 1902): 15.

37. Cecil to Louise Clark, n.d. [c. Jan. 6, 1903]; Poett Papers.

38. "At the Play," *Town Topics* 49 (Apr. 2, 1903): 13.

39. RHD to Rebecca, n.d. [late Mar. 1903]; Barrett Collection.

40. "Davis Says He Dreads Critics," New York *Daily Tribune*, Apr. 5, 1903, 1: 6.

41. RHD to Charles, Mar. 3 [1903]; Barrett Collection.

42. RHD to Rebecca, n.d. [late Mar. 1903]; Barrett Collection.

43. RHD to Charles, n.d. [Oct. 29, 1903]; Barrett Collection.

44. RHD to Charles, Friday [Oct. 30, 1903]; Barrett Collection.

45. RHD to Charles, Saturday [Oct. 24, 1903]; Barrett Collection. This project never went beyond the talking stage.

46. RHD to Rebecca, n.d. [c. Oct. 1, 1902]; Barrett Collection. Fyles completed only the first act of the play. Quinby, *Bibliography*, 55.

47. RHD to Rebecca, Sunday [Jan. 10, 1904]; Barrett Collection.

48. RHD to Rebecca, n.d. [Jan. 19, 1904]; Barrett Collection.

49. RHD to Rebecca, n.d. [late Jan. 1904]; Barrett Collection.

50. This and other facts about Collier come from the clippings in the Robinson Locke Collection, Theatre Collection, New York Public Library.

51. Arthur Edwin Krows, *Play Production in America* (New York: Henry Holt and Company, 1916), 227.

52. RHD to Louise Clark. Feb. 5, 1904; original not located. Reprinted in "Adventures and Letters," *Metropolitan* 46 (Sept. 1917): 22–23.

53. " 'The Dictator' Is Immensely Funny," New York *World*, Apr. 5, 1904. Clipping, Theatre Collection, New York Public Library.

54. RHD to Charles, May 10 [1904]; Barrett Collection.

55. RHD to Louise Clark, Jan. 6 [1904]; Poett Papers.

56. RHD to Louise Clark, Feb. 5, 1904; original not located. Reprinted in "Adventures and Letters," *Metropolitan* 46 (Sept. 1917): 22–23. RHD to Charles, Mar. 5 [1904]; Barrett Collection.

57. RHD to Rebecca, n.d. [early Dec., 1903]; Barrett Collection.

58. RHD to Family, n.d. [late 1903]; Barrett Collection.

59. RHD to Charles Scribner, June 29 [1904]; Scribner Archive.

60. Cecil to Louise Clark, Feb. 8 [1904]; Poett Papers.

61. RHD to Rebecca, Monday night [Feb. 22, 1904]; Barrett Collection. Reprinted in Davis, ed., *Adventures and Letters*, 298.

62. RHD to Rebecca, [Feb.] 26 [1904]; Barrett Collection. Reprinted in Davis, ed., *Adventures and Letters*, 298–99.

63. RHD to Rebecca, [Feb.] 26 [1904]; Barrett Collection. Deleted from the letter reprinted in Davis, ed., *Adventures and Letters*, 299.

64. RHD to Rebecca, Mar. 1, 1904; original not located. Reprinted in "Adventures and Letters," *Metropolitan* 46 (Sept. 1917): 23.

65. RHD to Charles, Mar. 4 [1904]; Barrett Collection.

66. The biographical details come from Elizabeth Fox Moore, "John Fox, Jr.: Personal and Family Letters and Papers" (Lexington, Ky.: University of Kentucky Library Associates, 1955), especially 1–6, 17, 30, 76. RHD to Rebecca, July 6 [1904]; Barrett Collection.

67. Nevins, *Grover Cleveland*, 549–62. "The Hawaiian Business," *Harper's Weekly* 37 (Feb. 25, 1893): 170; "The Annexation Policy," *Harper's Weekly* 37 (Mar. 18, 1893): 246.

68. RHD to Rebecca, Mar. 5 [1904]; Barrett Collection.

69. RHD to Rebecca, Mar. 17 [1904]; Barrett Collection. Reprinted and misdated with deletions in Davis, ed., *Adventures and Letters*, 299–300.

70. Cecil to John M. Clark, Mar. 21, 1904; Poett Papers. Richard Harding Davis, "Bottled Up in Tokio Where No One Hears of War," *Collier's* 33 (Apr. 23, 1904): 10.

71. RHD to Charles, Mar. 5 [1904]; Barrett Collection.

72. Cecil to John M. Clark, Mar. 21, 1904; Poett Papers.

73. RHD to Charles, Mar. 29 [1904]; Barrett Collection.

74. Palmer, *With My Own Eyes*, 234, 237; Richard O'Connor, *Jack London: A Biography* (Boston: Little, Brown and Company, 1964), 207.

75. RHD to Rebecca, Mar. 22 [1904]; Barrett Collection. Reprinted with deletions in Davis, ed., *Adventures and Letters*, 300–301.

76. Richard Harding Davis, "A War Correspondent's Kit," in Davis, *Notes*, 244. Davis had told his mother that he would have a baggage allowance of 400 pounds, but that seems to have been an overly optimistic prediction. RHD to Rebecca, Apr. 2 [1904]; Barrett Collection. Deleted from Davis, ed., *Adventures and Letters*, 302. He carried 400 pounds when reporting from the English side in the Boer War. See Davis, *Notes*, 243.

77. RHD to Rebecca, Mar. 5 [1900]; RHD to Rebecca, n.d. [c. Feb. 28, 1900]; Newton Papers.

78. RHD to Rebecca, Apr. 2 [1904]; Barrett Collection. Reprinted in Davis, ed., *Adventures and Letters*, 302.

79. RHD to Rebecca, May 9 [1904]; Barrett Collection. Davis, *Notes*, 258–59.

80. RHD to Charles, Apr. 28 [1904]; Barrett Collection. Cecil to Louise Clark, Apr. 28, 1904; Poett Papers.

81. Richard Harding Davis, "Marking Time in Tokio: The Temple of Daishi," *Collier's* 33 (Apr. 30, 1904): 13; Richard Harding Davis, "Marking Time in Tokio: The War Dogs Dine Out," *Collier's* 33 (May 7, 1904): 9; Richard Harding Davis, "Marking Time in Tokio: A War Drama," *Collier's* 33 (May 14, 1904): 11–12; Richard Harding Davis, "Marking Time in Tokio: The Tea House of the Hundred and One Steps," *Collier's* 33 (May 28, 1904): 10–11; Richard Harding Davis, "Marking Time in Tokio: The Wrestlers of Japan," *Collier's* 33 (June 4, 1904): 6–7; Richard Harding Davis, "The Ladies of the Golden Screens," *Collier's* 33 (Aug. 13, 1904): 6.

82. RHD to Charles, Apr. 28 [1904]; Barrett Collection.

83. John Fox, Jr., *Following the Sun-Flag* (New York: Charles Scribner's Sons, 1905), 50; and Fox, intr. to Davis, *White Mice*, vi.

84. RHD to Charles, May 7 [1904]; Barrett Collection.

85. RHD to Charles, June 14, 1904; Barrett Collection.

86. RHD to Theodore Roosevelt, May 26 [1904]; Theodore Roosevelt Papers, Library of Congress.

87. Cecil to Louise Clark, Apr. 28, 1904; Poett Papers.

88. The cable read: "Could you through Japanese Minister help us have been detained here thirteen weeks in idleness acting at request all American correspondents accredited second and third armies respectfully ask we be sent front or sent home Harding Davis John Fox." Richard Harding Davis, "Japan Diary," June 21; Kehrig Papers.

89. Hay's letter to Griscom read: "The President is interested in Harding Davis and John Fox and other correspondents who are anxious to go to the armies to which they have been accredited. He, of course, asks nothing against public policy but authorizes you to use such good offices as may be convenient in the interests of these gentlemen. Tell Davis. John Hay." Richard Harding Davis, "Japan Diary," June 24; Kehrig Papers. Roosevelt informed Davis that he was "strongly tempted" to advise the Japanese minister that it was in Japan's own interest to treat Western correspondents well. Theodore Roosevelt to RHD, June 29, 1904; Theodore Roosevelt Papers, Library of Congress; reprinted in Morison, ed., *Letters of Theodore Roosevelt*, 4, 849–50. For Roosevelt's intercession, see RHD to Charles, June 22 [1904]; RHD to Rebecca, June 25 [1904]; Barrett Collection. For Davis's salary cut, see RHD to Rebecca, [June] 13 [1904]; Barrett Collection. Deleted from the letter reprinted in Davis, ed., *Adventures and Letters*, 305.

90. RHD to Rebecca, [June] 13 [1904]; Barrett Collection. Reprinted in Davis, ed., *Adventures and Letters*, 305.

91. RHD to Theodore Roosevelt, May 26 [1904]; Theodore Roosevelt Papers,

Library of Congress. O'Connor, *Jack London*, 207–8, 218–21. Griscom, *Diplomatically Speaking*, 245–46.

92. RHD to Rebecca, July 6 [1904]; Barrett Collection.

93. RHD to Rebecca, May 2, 1904; original not located. Reprinted in "Adventures and Letters," *Metropolitan* 46 (Sept. 1917): 25.

94. RHD to Rebecca, July 6 [1904]; Barrett Collection.

95. RHD to Rebecca, June 29, 1904; original not located. Reprinted in "Adventures and Letters," *Metropolitan* 46 (Sept. 1917), 64.

96. RHD to Clarke, n.d. [Sept. 1883]; Kehrig Papers.

97. Davis, *Notes*, 234.

98. RHD to Rebecca, Aug. 14 [1904]; Barrett Collection. Reprinted in Davis, ed., *Adventures and Letters*, 309.

99. RHD to Rebecca, Mar. 15 [1900]; Newton Papers.

100. Richard Harding Davis, "The War Correspondent," *Collier's* 48 (Oct. 7, 1911): 21–22, 30.

101. Robert Dunn, *World Alive* (New York: Crown Publishers, 1956), 115.

102. Richard Harding Davis, "Japan Diary," July 9; Kehrig Papers.

103. Richard Harding Davis, "Japan Diary," July 3; Kehrig Papers.

104. The following account is based on Richard Harding Davis, "Battles I Did Not See," in *Notes*, 213–35; and Fox, *Sun-Flag*, 74–189. I have retained the Chinese place-names that were used in 1904.

105. Davis did not inform *Collier's* of his fiasco in time to avert the following editor's note, which ran with Davis's final Manchurian dispatch (devoted largely to his disappointment at not seeing the fall of Port Arthur and to a description of local villages), datelined August 17: "Mr. Davis joined General Nodzu's army and was present at the battle of Liao-Yang. As this battle was fought less than two weeks after the present letter was written, it is probable that we shall receive in about two or three weeks Mr. Davis's account of what he saw of the greatest battle of modern times." *Collier's* 34 (Oct. 8, 1904): 14. It wasn't a total loss for *Collier's*: Frederick Palmer, the correspondent with the Japanese First Army, witnessed the battle of Liao-Yang. See Frederick Palmer, "The Greatest Battle Since Gettysburg," *Collier's* 34 (Nov. 5, 1904): 11–14, 26–30; and Palmer, *With My Own Eyes*, 250–51.

Chapter 10
1. John N. Wheeler, "Richard Harding Davis, Writer and War Correspondent," *Pearson's* 33 (June 1915): 683–84. All the quotes are taken from Wheeler's account.

2. Sullivan, *Education*, 232–33.

3. Sullivan, *Education*, 212–19; Hapgood, *Changing Years*, 178–79; Mott, *A History of American Magazines*, 459–62.

4. Sinclair, *Brass Check*, 30. Even Sinclair credited *Collier's* with a "generous spirit."

5. Arthur H. Scribner to RHD, Oct. 19, 1904; Scribner Archive. RHD to Rebecca, Oct. 21 [1904]; Barrett Collection.

6. RHD to Charles, n.d. [c. Dec. 4, 1904]; Barrett Collection.

7. Clarke to Rebecca, July 21, 1902; Kehrig Papers.

8. Clarke to Rebecca, July 22, 1902; Kehrig Papers.

9. Rebecca to RHD, Wednesday [July 23, 1902]; Kehrig Papers. All of the quoted dialogue, including the pauses in the conversation, is taken from this letter.

10. RHD to Charles, n.d. [mid-Nov. 1904]; Barrett Collection.

11. A collection of obituaries in the Kehrig Papers contains, most notably, those from the Philadelphia *Public Ledger* and Philadelphia *Press*, both of Dec. 15, 1904.

12. Philadelphia *Inquirer*, Dec. 16, 1904; clipping in Kehrig Papers.

13. RHD to Clarke, n.d. [Sept. 1900]; Barrett Collection.

14. RHD to Rebecca, n.d.; Kehrig Papers.

15. This point is made explicitly by Charles Davis in Davis, ed., *Adventures and Letters*, 312.

16. Cecil to John M. Clark, Friday [Dec. 23, 1904]; Poett Papers.

17. Cecil to Louise Clark, Thursday [Jan. 12, 1905]; Poett Papers.

18. RHD to Charles, n.d. [late Dec. 1904]; Barrett Collection.

19. RHD to Rebecca, Feb. 21, 1905; RHD to Rebecca, Feb. 23, 1905; RHD to Rebecca, Mar. 2 [1905]; Barrett Collection.

20. David McCullough, *The Path Between the Seas* (New York: Simon & Schuster, 1977), 447–49; Sullivan, *Our Times: Turn of the Century*, 461–64.

21. RHD to Rebecca, Mar. 10 [1905]; RHD to Charles, Mar. 10 [1905]; Barrett Collection.

22. RHD to Rebecca, n.d. [early Feb. 1903]; Barrett Collection.

23. Cecil to Louise Clark, Wednesday [Feb. 18, 1903]; Poett Papers. RHD to Rebecca, Feb. 4 [1903]; RHD to Rebecca, Tuesday [Aug. 22, 1905]; RHD to Rebecca, Sept. 2 [1905]; Barrett Collection. Advertisement in *Town & Country* 71 (Apr. 1, 1916): 5. "A Campaigner Under Many Skies," *Outing* 46 (May 1905): 183.

24. Davis, ed., *Adventures and Letters*, 313–15. The description Charles Davis cites is from Justus Miles Forman's novel *The Blind Spot*.

25. RHD to Rebecca, Thursday [Aug. 24, 1905]; Barrett Collection.

26. RHD to Charles, Wednesday [Aug. 30, 1905]; Barrett Collection.

27. RHD to Charles, n.d. [Sept. 3, 1905]; Barrett Collection.

28. RHD to Rebecca, n.d. [Sept. 4, 1905]; Barrett Collection.

29. RHD to Rebecca, Sept. 13 [1905]; RHD to Rebecca, [Sept.] 19 [1905]; RHD to Charles, [Sept.] 26 [1905]; RHD to Rebecca, Sept. 27 [1905]; Barrett Collection. RHD to Charles Scribner, Sept. 27 [1905]; Scribner Archive.

30. RHD to Rebecca, Fri. [May 31, 1907]; Barrett Collection.

31. Charles to Arthur H. Scribner, July 26, 1916; Scribner Archive. See also Morris, ed., "Adventures and Letters," *Metropolitan* 46 (Oct. 1917): 24.

32. Richard Harding Davis, *The Galloper* (New York: Charles Scribner's Sons, 1909). Stephen Crane, *Active Service* (New York: Frederick A. Stokes Company, 1899).

33. RHD to Charles, May 30 [1905]; RHD to Charles, June 1 [1905]; RHD to Rebecca, Saturday [Nov. 11, 1905]; Barrett Collection. As one writer noted when the play opened: "The title is confusing and non-understandable to those who have not been in touch with European war correspondents. A 'galloper' is a correspondent who does 'stunts' on horseback in the way of getting his news to the telegraph station." New York *Herald*, Jan. 23, 1906. Clipping in the Robinson Locke Collection, Theatre Collection, New York Public Library.

34. RHD to Rebecca, June 2 [1905]; Barrett Collection.

35. RHD to Rebecca, Tuesday [Nov. 14, 1905]; Barrett Collection.

36. RHD to Charles Scribner, Nov. 6 [1905]; Scribner Archive.

37. Harper & Brothers to RHD, May 6, 1902; Harper & Brothers to RHD, July 8, 1902; Harper & Brothers to RHD, July 29, 1902; RHD to Harper & Brothers, July 31, 1902; George Harvey to RHD, Nov. 10, 1902; J. Henry Harper to RHD, Nov. 24, 1902; RHD to J. Henry Harper, Dec. 5, 1902; Harper & Brothers to RHD, Dec. 8, 1902; memo of agreement between RHD and Harper & Brothers, Dec. 10, 1902; Barrett Collection. In January 1906, having sold the original 10,000 sets, Harpers published a second edition. "F.A.D." to RHD, May 8, 1906. Harper Brothers Collection, Rare Book and Manuscript Library, Columbia University. By 1909, Harpers had sold 13,000 sets, but sales had fallen off sharply over the last two years. RHD to Harper & Brothers, May 8 [1909]; Harper & Brothers to RHD, May 14, 1909. Harper Brothers Collection, Rare Book and Manuscript Library, Columbia University.

38. RHD to Charles Scribner, June 14 [1903]; Charles Scribner to RHD, June 17, 1903; RHD to Charles Scribner, June 19 [1903]; Charles Scribner to RHD, June 23, 1903; RHD to Arthur Scribner, July 29 [1903]; RHD to Charles Scribner, cable, Nov. 4, 1903; RHD to Charles Scribner, Nov. 4, 1903; Scribner Archive.

39. Charles Scribner to RHD, Jan. 14, 1905; Scribner Archive. Sheehan, *This Was Publishing*, 191–92.

40. RHD to Charles Scribner, Nov. 6 [1905]; Scribner Archive.

41. RHD to Rebecca, Feb. 2 [1906]; RHD to Rebecca, Mar. 6 [1906]; Barrett Collection.

42. Richard Harding Davis, "The Passing of San Juan Hill," *Scribner's* 38 (Aug.

1905): 142–53. Reprinted in Davis, *Notes* 113–34. RHD to Charles, n.d. [c. Mar. 29, 1906]; RHD to Charles, n.d. [c. Mar. 31, 1906]; RHD to Rebecca, Mar. 31 [1906]; Barrett Collection.

43. Frederick L. Collins, *Glamorous Sinners* (New York: Ray Long & Richard R. Smith, 1932), 42–44, 79; Gerald Langford, *The Murder of Stanford White* (Indianapolis: The Bobbs-Merrill Company, 1962), 44.

44. RHD to Rebecca, n.d. [Nov. 8, 1905]; Barrett Collection.

45. Beer, *Crane*, 100.

46. RHD to Charles, July 19 [1906]; Barrett Collection.

47. Collins, *Sinners*, 42.

48. Richard O'Connor, *Courtroom Warrior: The Combative Career of William Travers Jerome* (Boston: Little, Brown and Company, 1963), 199–201.

49. Collins, *Sinners*, 170–73.

50. Rebecca to RHD, Feb. 13 [1907]; Barrett Collection.

51. Sullivan, *Our Times: Pre-War America*, 447–51.

52. I paraphrase the actress Maude Adams, who told Rebecca: "There has been but one fine high note struck in the whole thing. And that was Dick's paper." Rebecca to RHD, Feb. 4 [1907]; Barrett Collection.

53. RHD to Rebecca, n.d.; Barrett Collection. RHD to Arthur Scribner, June 24 [1906]; Scribner Archive. Richard Harding Davis, *Real Soldiers of Fortune* (New York: Charles Scribner's Sons, 1906).

54. Richard Harding Davis, "The Army of Pacification," *Collier's*, 38 (Nov. 3, 1906): 18–19. For more on this episode, see Russell H. Fitzgibbon, *Cuba and the United States, 1900–1935* (Menasha, Wis.: George Banta Publishing Co., 1935), 112–24.

55. *Life,* July 6, 1911, quoted in Mark Sullivan, *Our Times: The War Begins* (New York: Charles Scribner's Sons, 1932), 288.

56. Charles Chaplin, *My Autobiography* (New York: Simon & Schuster, 1964), 120–21.

57. "Authorship as a Business," New York *Sun*, Aug. 18, 1911: 7.

58. See, for example, Kenneth Lynn, *William Dean Howells: An American Life* (New York: Harcourt Brace Jovanovich, 1971), 141; and Ziff, *American 1890s*, 24.

59. RHD to Rebecca, Jan. 21, 1891; Barrett Collection. Reprinted, but incorrectly dated, in Davis, ed., *Adventures and Letters*, 61.

60. "Authorship as a Business," New York *Sun*.

61. RHD to Louise Clark, Nov. 24 [1906]; Poett Papers. RHD to Charles, Jan. 18 [1907]; Barrett Collection. Charles Scribner to RHD, Dec. 18, 1906 [copy]; Scribner Archive.

62. RHD to Rebecca, n.d. [Nov. 1906]; Barrett Collection.

63. RHD to Louise Clark, July 1 [1906]; Poett Papers. RHD to Rebecca, Sept. 20 [1906]; RHD to Charles, Jan. 18 [1907]; Barrett Collection.

64. Grant C. Knight, *The Strenuous Age in American Literature* (Chapel Hill: University of North Carolina Press, 1954), 98, 139.

65. Sullivan, *Our Times: Turn of the Century*, 497–98.

66. Sullivan, *Our Times: Pre-War America*, 431.

67. Sullivan, *Our Times: Pre-War America*, 432.

68. Richard Harding Davis, "The Scarlet Car" (1907), reprinted in Davis, *Scarlet Car*, 1–106.

69. RHD to Charles Scribner, Apr. 21 [1907]; Scribner Archive.

70. RHD to Louise Clark, Dec. 4 [1906]; RHD to Louise Clark, n.d. [Dec. 5, 1906]; RHD to Louise Clark, Dec. 11 [1906]; RHD to Louise Clark, n.d. [Dec. 20, 1906]; RHD to Louise Clark, Dec. 25 [1906]; Cecil to Louise Clark, Dec. 26 [1906]; Poett Papers. RHD to Rebecca, Dec. 6 [1906]; RHD to Rebecca, n.d. [Dec. 20, 1906]; Barrett Collection.

71. RHD Diary, 1907, Jan. 17, Jan. 18; Kehrig Papers.

72. RHD Diary, 1907, Jan. 25; Kehrig Papers.

73. RHD to Charles, n.d. [c. Jan. 24, 1907]; Barrett Collection.

74. RHD Diary, 1907, Feb. 15, Feb. 16; Kehrig Papers. Davis, *Congo*, 60.

75. RHD to Charles, Mar. 2 [1907]; Barrett Collection.

76. Davis, *Congo*, 118–41. RHD Diary, 1907, Feb. 28; Kehrig Papers. Reprinted in Davis, ed., *Adventures and Letters*, 329–30. Davis apparently did bring back a trophy; and when guests at the farm admired it, he would say, "That is the one I shot in Central Africa with a fifty-dollar bill." Frederick Palmer, "Richard Harding Davis," *Scribner's* 80 (Nov. 1926): 475.

77. RHD Diary, 1907, Mar. 1; Kehrig Papers. Davis, *Congo*, 138.

78. Ambrose Bierce, "Small Contributions," *Cosmopolitan* 45 (July 1908): 220.

79. RHD to Rebecca, n.d. [Dec. 20, 1906]; Barrett Collection. RHD to Louise Clark, n.d. [Dec. 20, 1906]; Poett Papers.

80. Boston *Transcript*, Dec. 26, 1905. In the New York *American* of Jan. 27, 1906, Alan Dale wrote that *The Galloper* was "a comic opera, played 'straight,' and without a suspicion of music." Both clippings are in the Robinson Locke Collection, Theatre Collection, New York Public Library.

81. New York *Telegraph*, Oct. 19, 1907. Clipping in Robinson Locke Collection, Theatre Collection, New York Public Library.

82. RHD to Charles Scribner, n.d. [c. Nov. 5, 1907]; Scribner Archive.

83. The account of Hitchcock's troubles is based on newspaper clippings in the Robinson Locke Collection, Theatre Collection, New York Public Library.

84. RHD Diary, 1907, Oct. 29; Kehrig Papers.

85. RHD to Charles Scribner, n.d. [c. Nov. 5, 1907]; Scribner Archive.

86. RHD Diary, 1907, Nov. 6; Kehrig Papers.

87. Chester Whitney Wright, *Economic History of the United States* (New York: McGraw-Hill Book Co., 1949), 707–8.

88. RHD Diary, 1907, Nov. 4; Kehrig Papers.

89. RHD Diary, 1907, Nov. 19; Kehrig Papers.

90. RHD Diary, 1907, Dec. 5; Kehrig Papers. The prices for dinner at Rector's and the theater, given for 1906, appear in Thomas, *Delmonico's*, 298.

91. RHD Diary, 1907, Dec. 7–8; Kehrig Papers.

92. RHD to Charles, n.d. [Oct. 1908?]; Barrett Collection.

93. RHD to Rebecca, Apr. 14 [1908]; Barrett Collection.

94. Richard Harding Davis, *The White Mice* (1909), reprinted in Davis, *The White Mice*. The youths call themselves the White Mice after the mouse kept in an engine room to detect leaking sulfuric gas. Their mission, too, is to save life.

95. RHD to Charles Scribner, Feb. 28 [1909]; Scribner Archive.

96. Knight, *Strenuous Age*, 11, 161. For many other instances of turn-of-the-century fiction about the supernatural, see Lutz, *American Nervousness*, 129, 169, 177–78, 202, 233.

97. RHD to Rebecca, Wednesday [June 5, 1907]; Barrett Collection.

98. RHD to Charles, Sept. 20 [1907]; Barrett Collection.

99. RHD Diary, 1907, Aug. 18; Kehrig Papers.

100. RHD Diary, 1907, Nov. 18, 20, 21, 22, 25, Dec. 3, 4; Kehrig Papers.

101. RHD Diary, 1907, Dec. 9; Kehrig Papers.

102. Eleanor Robson Belmont, *The Fabric of Memory* (New York: Farrar, Straus and Cudahy, 1957), 61–62.

103. Richard Harding Davis, *Vera, the Medium* (1908), reprinted in Davis, *The Scarlet Car*, 238.

104. Belmont, *Fabric*, 62, 77. Clippings in the Robinson Locke Collection, Theatre Collection, New York Public Library.

105. RHD to Louise Clark, Jan. 21 [1909]; Poett Papers. Davis rewrote *Vera, the Medium* as a melodrama. Titled *The Seventh Daughter*, it was premiered unsuccessfully by comedienne Chrystal Herne in 1910.

Chapter 11

1. RHD to Eleanor Robson, Nov. 19 [1908]; Belmont Collection, Rare Book and Manuscript Library, Columbia University.

2. Nell Brinkley, New York *Evening Journal*, July 6, 1908; clipping in Bessie McCoy Theatre Scrapbook, Kehrig Papers.

3. Allen Churchill, *The Great White Way* (New York: E.P. Dutton & Co., 1962), 3–10.

4. Knight, *Strenuous Age*, 196.

5. Morris, *Rise of Roosevelt*, 339.

6. Helen Howe, *The Gentle Americans* (New York: Harper & Row, 1965), 322.

7. RHD Diary, 1907, Oct. 2; Kehrig Papers.

8. RHD Diary, 1907, June 5, 7, 8, 10, Aug. 11; Kehrig Papers.

9. RHD to Rebecca, Aug. 13 [1908]; Kehrig Papers.

10. Richard Harding Davis, "On a Certain Ingratitude in Critics," *Collier's* 42 (Oct. 24, 1908): 11. Further exhibiting his obsession, he wrote of Bessie McCoy a couple of months later in a letter to his mother-in-law. RHD to Louise Clark, Jan. 21 [1909]; Poett Papers.

11. Shortly before marrying Bessie, Davis wrote to O'Malley: "I have a secret to tell you, which no one has a better right to know than yourself (I wonder if you know why) but, I can't tell you yet." RHD to Frank Ward O'Malley, June 1 [1912]; Kehrig Papers.

12. "Mrs. Richard Harding Davis Dies," New York *Sun*, Aug. 18, 1931; clipping in Theatre Collection, New York Public Library. As this authoritative-sounding account appeared in O'Malley's paper, he was most likely the source. Bessie later said that the meeting took place in Union Square, as she was leaving a music store in the company of an escort (O'Malley, although she didn't name him) and Davis was passing by. O'Malley called out, and Davis stopped. He and Bessie were introduced, and they chatted for a few moments on the curb, before Bessie proceeded uptown to the theater. That afternoon, Richard called on her at the theater, and—in the presence of her mother, she insisted in her reminiscence—he talked about his farm in Mount Kisco. She thought he was a farmer until someone told her otherwise. He returned that evening to the theater with Charlie, and met Bessie and her mother as they left the stage door. Bessie McCoy Davis, "The Grave Defying Romance of Richard Harding Davis and His Dancer Wife," Los Angeles *Examiner*, Oct. 14, 1917; clipping in Theatre Collection, New York Public Library. Most likely Bessie, not wishing to seem in the least bit improper when she later told the tale, cautiously moved the scene from raucous Churchill's and assigned the initial overture to O'Malley.

13. RHD to Charles, Labor Day [Sept. 7, 1908]; Kehrig Papers.

14. RHD to Charles, Feb. 5 [1909]; Kehrig Papers.

15. RHD to Charles, Dec. 6, 1908; Kehrig Papers.

16. RHD to Louise Clark, Jan. 21 [1909]; Poett Papers. RHD to Charles, Dec. 25 [1908]; Kehrig Papers. See also RHD to Rebecca, Dec. 25 [1908] and RHD to Rebecca, Dec. 29 [1908]; originals not located. Reprinted in Davis, ed., *Adventures and Letters*, 336–38.

17. RHD to Charles, Jan. 29 [1909]; Kehrig Papers. Richard's earlier letter and Charles's response seem not to have survived.

18. George Martin, *The Damrosch Dynasty* (Boston: Houghton Mifflin Company, 1983), 198. Walter Damrosch to Cecil, Mar. 10, 1909; Poett Papers.

19. RHD to Charles, Jan. 19, 1909; Kehrig Papers.

20. RHD to Charles, Feb. 5 [1909]; Kehrig Papers.

21. RHD to Charles, Jan. 10 [1909]; Barrett Collection. RHD to Charles, Mar. 2 [1909]; Kehrig Papers. RHD to Charles Scribner, Jan. 16, 1909; Scribner Archive.

22. RHD to Charles, Jan. 19, 1909; Kehrig Papers.

23. RHD to Louise Clark, Feb. 23 [1909]; Poett Papers. See also RHD to Rebecca, Feb. 23, 1909; original not located. Reprinted in Davis, ed., *Adventures and Letters*, 340–41. The Sargent sketch is now in the collection of the University of California at Santa Barbara.

24. RHD to Charles, Mar. 2 [1909]; Kehrig Papers.

25. RHD to Louise Clark, Mar. 18 [1909]; Poett Papers.

26. "The Man Who Could Not Lose" (1910), reprinted in Richard Harding Davis, *The Man Who Could Not Lose* (New York: Charles Scribner's Sons, 1916), 1–61.

27. "The Mind Reader" (1912), reprinted in Davis, *Red Cross Girl*, 188–226.

28. "The God of Coincidence" (1913), reprinted in Davis, *Lost Road*, 157–88.

29. "The Red Cross Girl" (1912), reprinted in Davis, *Red Cross Girl*, 1–49.

30. "The Log of the 'Jolly Polly' " (1915), reprinted in Davis, *Man Who Could Not Lose*, 312–65. Other tales from this period that rely on farcical mistaken identities include "The Amateur" (1909) and "The Make Believe Man" (1910), reprinted, respectively, in Davis, *Bar Sinister*, 189–225 and 226–75.

31. "The Lost House" (1911), reprinted in Davis, *Man Who Could Not Lose*, 223–311.

32. "The Lost Road" (1912), reprinted in Richard Harding Davis, *The Lost Road*, 1–29.

33. Rebecca to RHD, Friday [Dec. 1908?]; Barrett Collection.

34. Downey, *Davis: His Day*, 301n.

35. RHD to Rebecca, Apr. 13 [1908]; Barrett Collection.

36. Sheaffer, "Rebecca Harding Davis," 342–43.

37. Rebecca to RHD, n.d.; Barrett Collection.

38. Rebecca to RHD, Thursday [Mar. 1908]; Barrett Collection.

39. Rebecca to RHD, May 1 [1906]; Barrett Collection.

40. "Royal Chaplain Has Disappeared," New York *Times*, Nov. 23, 1911: 1; "Farrar's Career Here," New York *Daily Tribune*, Nov. 23, 1911: 3.

41. "Royal Chaplain Has Disappeared," New York *Times*, 1; "Miss Davis Weds Chaplain to the King," New York *Times*, July 7, 1911: 9; "Farrar Scandal Only Whispered in London," New York *World*, Nov. 24, 1911: 18.

42. "R.H. Davis to Bring Mrs. Farrar Home," New York *Times*, Nov. 30, 1911: 13.

43. "Royal Chaplain Loses Post," New York *Times*, Nov. 22, 1911: 1; "Royal Chaplain Has Disappeared," New York *Times*, 1.

44. "Farrar Scandal Only Whispered in London," New York *World*, 18; "Farrar Had to Quit England," New York *Sun*, Nov. 24, 1911: 2.

45. "Mrs. Farrar with Husband," New York *Times*, Dec. 5, 1911: 6; "R.H. Davis to Bring Mrs. Farrar Home," 13.

46. "Loved a Girl Whom He Could Not Marry," New York *World*, Nov. 24, 1911: 18. The writer attributes Farrar's "grave errors" in recent years to the "derogatory effect upon the rector's character" of a long-term illicit relationship with "a young woman of obscure position."

47. Richard Harding Davis, "The New World," *Collier's* 47 (Sept. 16, 1911): 19–20.

48. "Mrs. Davis Drops Separation Suit," New York *Herald*, May 11, 1912; "R. Harding Davis's Wife Begins New Suit for Divorce," New York *World*, May 30, 1912; "Divorce from Author Ends Childhood Romance," Cincinnati *Commerical Tribune*, June 18, 1912; clippings in the Robinson Locke Collection, Theatre Collection, New York Public Library. For the account of a comparable divorce at about the same time, see Sinclair, *Brass Check*, 111, 333.

49. Richard Harding Davis, "The Two Conventions at Chicago," *Scribner's* 52 (Sept. 1912): 259–73.

50. Richard Harding Davis, "The Men at Armageddon," *Collier's* 49 (Aug. 24, 1912): 10–11.

51. Sullivan, *Education*, 296–314; Will Irwin, *The Making of a Reporter* (New York: G.P. Putnam's Sons, 1942), 171–72; Sinclair, *Brass Check*, 31; Ellis, *Mr. Dooley's America*, 252–55; Hickman Powell, "Collier's," *Scribner's* 105 (May 1939): 20.

52. RHD Diary, 1912, July 8; clippings in Davis Wedding Scrapbook; Kehrig Papers. Although newspapers reported 500 mothers and children treated to a beach outing, a letter to Davis from the general agent of the New York Association for Improving the Condition of the Poor fixed the numbers at 50 mothers and 200 children. John A. Kingsbury to RHD, July 9, 1912; Davis Wedding Scrapbook. Back in 1908, Bessie had organized a benefit performance of *The Three Twins* for the same cause.

53. RHD Diary, 1912, July 7; Kehrig Papers.

54. Bessie McCoy Davis, "Grave Defying Romance," Los Angeles *Examiner*.

55. Zoe Beckley, " 'Yama-Yama' Girl, Lured Away by Love, Back to Stage, as 'There's No Other Place' "; clipping in Bessie McCoy Theatre Scrapbook, Kehrig Papers.

56. Beckley, " 'Yama-Yama' Girl."

57. Bessie McCoy Davis, "Grave Defying Romance," Los Angeles *Examiner*.

58. Richard Harding Davis, Worksheets, 1912–15; Barrett Collection.

59. RHD to Charles, Sept. 5 [1913]; Barrett Collection.

60. RHD to Charles, Aug. 6 [1913]; Barrett Collection.

61. RHD to Charles, Oct. 18, 1913; Barrett Collection.

62. RHD to Charles, Oct. 18, 1913; Barrett Collection.

63. Richard Harding Davis, "Breaking into the Movies," *Scribner's* 55 (Mar. 1914): 275–93.

64. RHD to Charles, Oct. 24, 1913; Barrett Collection.

65. DeWitt Bodeen, "The Farnum Brothers," *Films in Review* 34 (Nov. 1983): 515. Clippings in the Chamberlain and Lyman Brown Scrapbooks, Dustin Farnum, Reel 27; Theatre Collection, New York Public Library.

66. Dexter Perkins, *A History of the Monroe Doctrine* (Boston: Little, Brown and Company, 1963), 258.

67. Count Mourik de Beaufort, "R.H. Davis 'Almost' Takes Mexico," New York *American*, Nov. 6, 1913: 5.

68. RHD to Charles, Nov. 20 [1913]: Barrett Collection.

69. RHD to Charles, Apr. 17 [1914]; RHD to Charles, Apr. 21 [1914]; Kehrig Papers.

70. RHD to Charles, Friday [Apr. 24, 1914]; Barrett Collection.

71. RHD to Charles, Jan. 14 [1914]; Barrett Collection. RHD to Charles, Apr. 21 [1914]; Kehrig Papers.

72. RHD to Bessie McCoy Davis, n.d. [c. Apr. 27, 1914]; typescript in Kehrig Papers.

73. RHD to Charles, Apr. 30 [1914]; Barrett Collection.

74. RHD to Charles, Friday [Apr. 24, 1914]; Barrett Collection.

75. RHD to Charles, Apr. 30 [1914]; Barrett Collection.

76. Dunn, *World Alive*, 199.

77. Palmer, "Richard Harding Davis," 474. RHD to Bessie, May 20, 1914; original not located. Reprinted in Davis, ed., *Adventures and Letters*, 363. RHD to Bessie,

May 17, 1914; original not located. Reprinted in "Adventures and Letters," *Metropolitan* 46 (Oct. 1917): 26.

78. John T. McCutcheon, *Drawn from Memory* (Indianapolis: The Bobbs-Merrill Company, 1950), 297.

79. John T. McCutcheon, intr. to Davis, *Lost Road*, x–xi.

80. Palmer, "Richard Harding Davis," 474–75.

81. Downey, *Davis: His Day*, 240.

82. Wheeler, "Richard Harding Davis," 679.

83. RHD to Charles, May 6 [1914]; Barrett Collection.

84. Richard Harding Davis, "R.H. Davis Tells Story of Arrest by Huerta's Police," New York *Tribune*, May 12, 1914: 1, 5; Richard Harding Davis, "When a War Is Not a War," *Scribner's* 56 (July 1914): 41–52; Palmer, *With My Own Eyes*, 292–94; Palmer, "Richard Harding Davis," 473–74; Dunn, *World Alive*, 203. Reminiscing forty years afterward, Dunn identified the restaurant as Prendes, but Davis's contemporary account establishes that it was Sylvain.

85. RHD to Charles, May 30 [1914]; Kehrig Papers.

86. RHD to Charles, Feb. 26 [1914]; RHD to Charles, Mar. 15 [1914]; Kehrig Papers.

87. RHD Diary, 1914, June 25; Kehrig Papers.

88. RHD to John M. Clark, Nov. 18 [1909]; Poett Papers.

89. RHD to Charles, Oct. 24, 1913; RHD to Charles, Oct. 26, 1913; RHD to Charles, Nov. 20 [1913]; RHD to Charles, Nov. 27 [1913]; Barrett Collection. RHD to Charles, Feb. 5 [1914]; RHD to Charles, Feb. 18 [1914]; Kehrig Papers.

90. RHD to Charles, July 10 [1914]; Barrett Collection.

Chapter 12
1. RHD to Charles, July 29 [1914]; Kehrig Papers.

2. RHD to Charles, July 31 [1914]; Kehrig Papers.

3. Richard Harding Davis, "The War Correspondent," *Collier's* 48 (Oct. 7, 1911): 21–22, 30.

4. Richard Harding Davis, *With the Allies* (New York: Charles Scribner's Sons, 1914), 158.

5. RHD to Scribner's, Aug. 15–16, 1914, cable; Scribner Archive. Palmer, *With My Own Eyes*, 301, 306–18. RHD Diary, 1914, Aug. 15; Kehrig Papers.

6. RHD Diary, 1914, Aug. 4, 10; Kehrig Papers.

7. RHD to Charles, Aug. 4 [1914]; Kehrig Papers. RHD to Charles, Aug. 8, 1914; original not located. Reprinted in Davis, ed., *Adventures and Letters*, 367–68.

8. The following account is based on Davis, *With the Allies*, 12–30.

9. RHD Diary, 1914, Aug. 20; Kehrig Papers. Richard Harding Davis, "Germans Got Cold Cheer in Brussels," New York *Tribune*, Aug. 25: 2. Delayed in transmission, this article was published a day later than Davis's famous dispatch on the German entry into Brussels.

10. With variations, this account appears as Davis, "Saw German Army Roll On Like Fog," New York *Tribune*, Aug. 24, 1914: 1,3; "The Germans in Brussels," *Scribner's* 56 (Nov. 1914): 569–70; and *With the Allies*, 22–30. Unless otherwise noted, my quotations are taken from the newspaper version.

11. Hugh Gibson, *A Journal from Our Legation in Belgium* (Garden City, N.Y.: Doubleday, Page & Company, 1917), 102.

12. Davis, "Germans in Brussels," *Scribner's*, 570. Davis had used similar metaphors fourteen years earlier in his description of the British military machine—"something entirely lacking in the human element"—advancing on the Boers in the battle of the Sand River. Davis, *With Both Armies*, 203.

13. Palmer, "Richard Harding Davis," 477.

14. Arno Dosch-Fleurot, *Through War to Revolution* (London: John Lane, The Bodley Head, 1931), 19.

15. "How Courier Dodged Germans to Get Dispatch to Cable Office," New York *Tribune*, Aug. 24, 1914: 3. RHD Diary, 1914, Aug. 21; Kehrig Papers.

16. The following account is based on Davis, *With the Allies*, 31–79.

17. Scrapbook, RHD Trip to the Western Front, 1914; Kehrig Papers.

18. Davis, *With the Allies*, 76.

19. RHD Diary, 1914, Aug. 25; Kehrig Papers.

20. Brand Whitlock, *Belgium: A Personal Narrative*, 1 (New York: D. Appleton and Company, 1919), 148–50; Gibson, *Journal*, 152.

21. Irwin, *Reporter*, 227.

22. Irwin, *Reporter*, 227.

23. Whitlock, *Belgium*, 1, 153.

24. Irwin, *Reporter*, 234.

25. The following account is based on Davis, *With the Allies*, 80–95, and supplemented by the other sources cited.

26. Dosch-Fleurot, *Through War*, 28–30.

27. Dosch-Fleurot, *Through War*, 31–32. Richard Harding Davis, "Eight American Writers Arrested," New York *Tribune*, Sept. 4, 1914: 1.

28. Dosch-Fleurot, *Through War*, 33.

29. RHD to Bessie, Aug. 31 [1914]; typescript in Kehrig Papers. Reprinted in Davis, ed., *Adventures and Letters*, 371–72. For the Louvain article, see Richard

Harding Davis, "Horror of Louvain Told by Eyewitness; Circled Burning City," New York *Tribune*, Aug. 31, 1914: 1, 4.

30. Davis, *A Year*, 73.

31. Richard Harding Davis, "Tells Experience as War Prisoner," New York *Tribune*, Sept. 2, 1914: 1.

32. These cables are all contained in the Davis 1914 War Scrapbook; Kehrig Papers.

33. RHD to Bessie, Sept. 3 [1914]; typescript in Kehrig Papers. Reprinted in Davis, ed., *Adventures and Letters*, 374.

34. RHD to Charles, Sept. 4 [1914]; Kehrig Papers.

35. Davis, *With the Allies*, 96.

36. RHD to Charles, Sept. 15, 1914; Kehrig Papers. Reprinted in Davis, ed., *Adventures and Letters*, 377. Richard Harding Davis, "Paris Standing Strain of War Complacently," New York *Tribune*, Sept. 5, 1914: 1–2.

37. Davis, *With the Allies*, 106–8.

38. Davis, *With the Allies*, 111–12.

39. Davis, *With the Allies*, 192–93.

40. Davis, *With the Allies*, 193–97. A bad speller even in his own language, Davis spelled the French word for artichoke as "artechant," and no proofreader caught it.

41. Philip Littell, "Richard the Lion-Harding" (1915), in *Books and Things* (New York: Harcourt, Brace and Howe, 1919), 231–32, 235–36.

42. RHD Diary, 1914, Sept. 18; Kehrig Papers. For confirmation, see Ashmead-Bartlett, *Experiences*, 35. Writing much later, Granville Fortescue says, unconvincingly, that going to Reims was his idea. Granville Fortescue, *Front Line and Deadline* (New York: G.P. Putnam's Sons, 1937), 121. The Fortescue account of the reporters in Reims, which (among other gross errors) conflates the events of two different trips, is in general unreliable. The following account is based on Davis, *With the Allies*, 118–48, and Ashmead-Bartlett, *Experiences*, 34–58, with a few seemingly trustworthy details from Fortescue, *Front Line*, 120–47.

43. Ashmead-Bartlett, *Experiences*, 41.

44. Emmet Crozier, *American Reporters on the Western Front* (New York: Oxford University Press, 1959), 87; Ashmead-Bartlett, *Experiences*, 46. See also Richard Harding Davis, "Vivid Description of the Shelling of Rheims Cathedral," New York *Tribune*, Sept. 22, 1914: 1, 3.

45. RHD Diary, 1914, Sept. 21; Kehrig Papers.

46. Fortescue, *Front Line*, 130.

47. Richard Harding Davis, "Rheims a Wreck Around Cathedral," New York *Tribune*, Sept. 29, 1914: 1, 2.

48. RHD Diary, 1914, Oct. 2; Kehrig Papers.

Chapter 13
1. Fortescue, *Front Line*, 151.

2. Bessie McCoy Davis, "How My Baby Killed the Terrible Yama Yama Man," Chicago *Herald*, Oct. 21, 1917; clipping, Theatre Collection, New York Public Library.

3. Bessie McCoy Davis, "Grave Defying Romance," Los Angeles *Examiner*.

4. Carl Hovey to RHD, July 29, 1914; Barrett Collection.

5. RHD Diary, 1914, Dec. 27; Kehrig Papers.

6. RHD to Charles Scribner, Mar. 4 [1915]; Scribner Archive.

7. C. D. Gibson to RHD, n.d. [c. Jan. 8, 1915]; Scrapbook, Kehrig Papers.

8. Davis, ed., *Adventures and Letters*, 380.

9. Morris, intr. to Davis, *Red Cross Girl*, x. Perhaps Morris was detecting Davis's sadness that he lacked little ones of his own, for when Richard visited the two Morris daughters, he was childless.

10. RHD to Charles, Dec. 13 [1908]; Barrett Collection.

11. Wheeler, "Richard Harding Davis," 681.

12. Bessie McCoy Davis, "Grave Defying Romance," Los Angeles *Examiner*.

13. Morris, intr. to Davis, *Red Cross Girl*, xviii.

14. Correspondence between RHD and W. S. Carpenter, Confidential Secretary, N.Y. State Conservation Commission, Aug.–Oct. 1915; Barrett Collection. Davis's candidacy foundered in red tape and press agentry.

15. Richard Harding Davis, "The Boy Who Cried Wolf" (May 1916), in Davis, *Red Cross Girl*, 251–76.

16. Wheeler, "Richard Harding Davis," 683.

17. Richard Harding Davis, "The Capture of Boston," *Collier's* 43 (Sept. 4, 1909): 10–11. RHD to Rebecca, Aug. 20 [1909]; Barrett Collection. See also RHD to Rebecca, [Aug.] 19 [1909]; Barrett Collection. Reprinted in Davis, ed., *Adventures and Letters*, 343–44. Davis wrote a forgettable short story, "Peace Manoeuvres," of a guttering romance that is reignited by the Massachusetts war games. It was published in *Scribner's* in May 1910 and reprinted in Davis, *Bar Sinister*, 276–306.

18. Richard Harding Davis, "The Plattsburg Idea," *Collier's* 56 (Oct. 9, 1915): 7–9, 31, 33. For more on Plattsburg, see Mark Sullivan, *Our Times: Over Here, 1914–1918* (New York: Charles Scribner's Sons, 1933), 209–18; and Millis, *Road to War*, 93–95, 199, 209–11.

19. Davis's anti-German or anti-Wilson letters to the editor appeared in the New York *Times* of Nov. 8, 1914, 3: 2; Nov. 12, 1914: 4; Jan. 8, 1915: 10; Feb. 22, 1915: 6; May 11, 1915: 6; June 9, 1915: 3; and July 19, 1915: 8. For one of his

appeals written for the French Secours National, see Davis, ed., *Adventures and Letters*, 378–80. Besides the previously cited "The Boy Who Cried Wolf," his anti-German fiction in this period included "Somewhere in France" (June 1915), in Davis, *Lost Road*, 271–307. The protagonist is a truly evil woman—both promiscuous and German. Besides the Plattsburg piece in *Collier's*, he wrote two magazine articles urging American preparedness: "Not Too Proud—But Unprepared," *Metropolitan* 42 (July 1915): 9–11, 66; and "Our Eagle Without Wings," *Metropolitan* 43 (Nov. 1915): 78–79.

20. Millis, *Road to War*, 209–10; and May, *End of American Innocence*, 363–65.

21. RHD to Charles, n.d. [Aug. 1915]; Barrett Collection. Reprinted in Davis, ed., *Adventures and Letters*, 381.

22. Downey, *Davis: His Day*, 279–80.

23. "R.H. Davis Abandons War to Its Fate," a clipping from an unidentified October 3, 1914, newspaper, in the RHD 1914 World War scrapbook; Kehrig Papers. Another unmarked clipping in the book quotes him as saying that "there is no work for a war correspondent over here."

24. RHD Diary, 1915, May 7–10; Kehrig Papers.

25. RHD Diary, 1914, Oct. 19; Kehrig Papers.

26. Charles Scribner to RHD, Oct. 12, 1915; Robert Bridges to RHD, Mar. 2, 1916; Scribner Archive. Before leaving, however, he persuaded Scribners to commit to publish a third edition of his writings, this time encompassing only his fiction. It would contain his Van Bibber stories, *The Princess Aline*, and other well-known works published by the Harpers. Although these subscription sets had fallen out of favor in a glutted marketplace, Scribners advanced him $4,000 against a reduced royalty rate of 20 cents a set. Arthur H. Scribner to RHD, Aug. 6, 1915, with addendum of Aug. 8, 1915; Scribner Archive.

27. RHD to Charles, Sept. 4 [1914]; Kehrig Papers.

28. RHD 1915 Diary, Oct. 18; John N. Wheeler to RHD, Oct. 20, 1915, in the RHD 1915–16 World War scrapbook; Kehrig Papers.

29. RHD to Bessie, Oct. 18, 1915; original not located. Reprinted in Davis, ed., *Adventures and Letters*, 387.

30. RHD to Charles, Oct. 25, 1915; Barrett Collection. RHD Diary, 1915, Oct. 24; Kehrig Papers.

31. RHD to Bessie, Oct. 30, 1915, typescript; Kehrig Papers.

32. RHD Diary, 1915, Nov. 5; Kehrig Papers. Richard Harding Davis, *With the French in France and Salonika* (New York: Charles Scribner's Sons, 1916), 34.

33. RHD Diary, 1915, Nov. 5; Kehrig Papers.

34. RHD to Bessie, Nov. 8, 1915; typescript, Kehrig Papers.

35. RHD to Bessie, Nov. 6, 1915; typescript, Kehrig Papers.

36. RHD Diary, 1915, Nov. 10; Kehrig Papers.

37. Davis's description of what he saw in the Artois, including the passages quoted here, can be found in Davis, *With the French*, 35–54.

38. RHD Diary, 1915, Nov. 13; Kehrig Papers.

39. Gay Talese, *The Kingdom and the Power* (New York: The World Publishing Company, 1969), 35, 165.

40. Davis left New York on Oct. 18. On Oct. 24, five days before the ship landed at Bordeaux, Wheeler cabled him in Paris: "Arrangements made by Paris representative New York Time[s] for Balkan trip optional with you of course." Davis World War 1915 scrapbook; Kehrig Papers. Davis received this communication when he arrived in Paris on Oct. 30. RHD Diary, 1915, Oct. 30; Kehrig Papers.

41. RHD to Bessie, Nov. 8, 1915, typescript; Kehrig Papers.

42. Davis ignored the first hint that he should go to Greece. On Nov. 6, Wheeler cabled: "Big chance Greece advise leaving Marseilles Wednesday." Davis wired back the next day that to leave now would "waste efforts obtain me special facilities" but he was "later willing go Greece on [Wheeler's] responsibility." In his own judgment it would be an "absolute waste [of] time." Wheeler replied on Nov. 9 that "Syndicate satisfied you use your judgement Greece suggestion simply cabled at request one or two newspapers." The next day he sent Davis the "long annoying" cable urging him to go to Greece, saying it was at the *Times*'s request. All of these cables are in the RHD 1915 World War scrapbook; Kehrig Papers.

43. RHD Diary, 1915, Nov. 13; Kehrig Papers.

44. RHD to Bessie, Nov. 17, 1915, typescript; Kehrig Papers.

45. RHD to Carr Van Anda, cable, Nov. 15, 1915; Carr Van Anda to RHD, cable, Nov. 16, 1915; RHD 1915 World War scrapbook; Kehrig Papers. Unlike the other telegrams in this series, the Van Anda salvo was fully punctuated (with "stops" and "quotes") and not abbreviated to save cable costs.

46. RHD to Robert Bridges, Mar. 8 [1916]; Scribner Archive. The context was a disagreement over how much Davis was owed for a *Scribner's* article.

47. RHD to Charles, Nov. 25 [1915]; Barrett Collection.

48. Davis, *With the French*, 112.

49. RHD to Charles, Nov. 30 [1915]; Kehrig Papers. Reprinted in Davis, ed., *Adventures and Letters*, 395.

50. RHD Diary, 1915, Nov. 28; Kehrig Papers.

51. Davis, *With the French*, 119–20.

52. RHD Diary, 1915, Nov. 30; Kehrig Papers. RHD to Bessie, Nov. 30, 1915, typescript; Kehrig Papers. Reprinted in "The Love Letters of Richard Harding Davis to Bessie McCoy Davis," *Metropolitian* 46 (Nov. 1917): 15. William Gunn Shepherd, "The Scar That Tripled," *Metropolitan* 46 (July 1917): 7–8. McCutcheon, *Drawn from Memory*, 293–94.

53. McCutcheon, intr. to Davis, *Lost Road*, xvii–vxiii; Carnes, *Jimmy Hare*, 245.

54. RHD to Charles, Nov. 30 [1915]; Kehrig Papers. Deleted from the letter reprinted in Davis, ed., *Adventures and Letters*, 394–95.

55. RHD to Bessie, Nov. 30, 1915, typescript; Kehrig Papers. Reprinted in "Love Letters," *Metropolitan* 46 (Nov. 1917): 15. RHD to Charles, Nov. 30 [1915]; Barrett Collection. Reprinted in Davis, ed., *Adventures and Letters*, 394.

56. Davis, *With the French*, 161–64.

57. Davis, *With the French*, 165.

58. Davis, *With the French*, 169–71.

59. McCutcheon, *Drawn from Memory*, 294–95; McCutcheon, intr. to Davis, *Lost Road*, xvii–xviii. RHD to Charles, Dec. 6, 1915; Barrett Collection. RHD to Bessie, Dec. 6, 1915, typescript; Kehrig Papers. Reprinted in Davis, ed., *Adventures and Letters*, 395–97.

60. Davis, *With the French*, 146–47; McCutcheon, intr. to Davis, *Lost Road*, xx–xxii.

61. " 'There Were Ninety and Nine' " (1891), in Davis, *Scarlet Car*, 373–401; "The Miracle of Las Palmas" (1913), and "The Long Arm" (1912), in Davis, *Lost Road*, 30–60 and 137–56; and "The Card-Sharp" (1914), in Davis, *Red Cross Girl*, 277–96.

62. "Had meant to finish it with happy ending but decided leave it in doubt," he wrote in his diary after completing the story. RHD Diary, 1916, Mar. 27; Kehrig Papers.

63. For Davis's influence on the writing style and subject matter of the young Hemingway, see Peter Griffin, *Along with Youth: Hemingway, the Early Years* (New York: Oxford University Press, 1985), 29, 39, 127. The connection goes further, as is noted by Jay Martin, *Harvests of Change: American Literature, 1865–1914* (Englewood Cliffs, N.J.: Prentice-Hall, 1967), 55: "Hemingway not only followed Davis by traveling to and writing about countries Davis had romanticized, but he also assumed as his own the romantic, athletically masculine persona which Davis had projected."

64. The narrative above is based on Shepherd, "The Scar That Tripled," *Metropolitan*, 7–8, 56–57, 60; and John T. McCutcheon, intr. to Richard Harding Davis, *The Deserter* (New York: Charles Scribner's Sons, 1917), vi–xvi. The account in Carnes, *Jimmy Hare*, 249–50, related long after the event, is an unreliable rehash of the earlier versions, with some of the leading lines transferred to Jimmy Hare. The quoted dialogue in my account is taken from Shepherd, except for the heated argument between the soldier and the correspondents. Relying on Shepherd's assurance that Davis had reported that conversation "with a masterly faithfulness to detail, spirit, and even actual words," I have taken that dialogue directly from the short story. "The Man Who Had Everything" was published originally in the *Metropolitan* of Sept. 1916, and reprinted in Davis, *Lost Road*, 308–30. It was later published in book form as *The Deserter*, the title by which it is better known.

McCutcheon confirms that the model for Davis's Hamlin was a Purdue man, son of the superintendent of a Standard Oil plant in Indiana, in John T. McCutcheon to Charles Scribner's Sons, Sept. 15 [1917]; Scribner Archive.

65. This argument is eloquently made by May, *End of American Innocence.* See, for example, p. 393.

66. RHD to Charles, Dec. 18, 1915; Barrett Collection.

67. RHD to Charles, Dec. 31, 1915; Kehrig Papers. Reprinted in Davis, ed., *Adventures and Letters,* 403.

68. RHD Diary, 1915, Dec. 28; Kehrig Papers.

69. RHD Diary, 1915, Dec. 29; telegrams in RHD World War 1915 Scrapbook; Kehrig Papers.

70. RHD to Charles, Jan. 6 [1916]; Kehrig Papers. Davis, *With the French,* 211.

71. RHD to Bessie, Nov. 1 [1915], typescript; Kehrig Papers. Reprinted in Davis, ed., *Adventures and Letters,* 388–89. Davis, *With the French,* 241. A leader of the postcard painters later wrote Davis that his article had generated orders for the illustrated cards from all over the United States. Ronald Simmons to RHD, Mar. 24, 1916; Barrett Collection.

72. Davis, *With the French,* 231–32.

73. Davis, *With the French,* 257–62.

74. RHD Diary, 1915, Dec. 31; Kehrig Papers.

75. RHD to Bessie, [Jan. 4, 1916; misdated as Jan. 3], typescript; Kehrig Papers. Reprinted in "Love Letters," *Metropolitan* 46 (Nov. 1917): 61.

76. Carnes, *Jimmy Hare,* 249.

77. RHD to Bessie, Dec. 14 [1916], typescript; Kehrig Papers.

78. RHD to Bessie, Jan. 5, 1916, typescript; Kehrig Papers. Reprinted in Davis, ed., *Adventures and Letters,* 405–6.

79. RHD to Bessie, Dec. 6 [1915], typescript; Kehrig Papers. Reprinted in Davis, ed., *Adventures and Letters,* 397.

80. RHD Diary, 1916, Jan. 11; Kehrig Papers.

81. Nora to Cecil, Apr. 15 [1916]; Poett Papers. Corroboration of Nora's account is made more difficult by the fact that the Davis 1916 diary, which is mostly intact, is missing the pages for the entire week that Davis spent in London. These entries were probably torn out by the jealous Bessie after Richard's death. The page for February 4 and 5, when he returned to his home, is also removed.

82. RHD to Bessie, Dec. 24, 1915, typescript; Kehrig Papers. Reprinted in Davis, ed., *Adventures and Letters,* 402.

83. RHD Diary, 1916, Feb. 12; Kehrig Papers.

84. RHD Diary, 1916, Feb. 18; Kehrig Papers.

85. RHD Diary, 1916, Feb. 13, 14; Mar. 3; Kehrig Papers.

86. RHD Diary, 1916, Feb. 12; Kehrig Papers.

87. RHD Diary, 1916, Mar. 30; Kehrig Papers.

88. RHD Diary, 1916, Mar. 13, 17; Kehrig Papers.

89. Bessie McCoy Davis, "Appreciation of the Late Richard Harding Davis," New York *Tribune*, Nov. 23, 1919; clipping, Theatre Collection, New York Public Library.

90. *Town and Country* 71 (Apr. 1, 1916): 5. The ad appeared two more times, on Apr. 10 and 20.

91. RHD Diary, 1916, Feb. 22, Mar. 25; Kehrig Papers.

92. RHD Diary, 1916, Mar. 26; Nora to Charles, May 6 [1916]; Kehrig Papers.

93. RHD Diary, 1916, Feb. 16; Kehrig Papers. Paul Reynolds to RHD, Mar. 16, 1916; Barrett Collection.

94. RHD Diary, 1916, Mar. 29; Kehrig Papers.

95. RHD Diary, 1916, Apr. 5; Kehrig Papers.

96. RHD Diary, 1916, Apr. 8, 10; Kehrig Papers.

97. "The Last Message of Richard Harding Davis," *Collier's* 57 (Aug. 5, 1916): 19; Downey, *Davis: His Day,* 293–94; Leonard Wood, intr. to Davis, *Man Who Could Not Lose,* v; "Dick Davis Dies While at 'Phone,' " New York *Tribune,* Apr. 13, 1916: 14; "Last Thoughts for Flag," New York *Herald,* Apr. 13, 1916: 7; "R.H. Davis, Novelist, Dies at Telephone, New York *Times,* Apr. 13, 1916: 13; RHD to Van S. Merle-Smith, Harvard Club, New York [marked by Charles Davis, "Telegram which R.H.D. was telephoning at the time of his death"]; Kehrig Papers. As a footnote to a footnote to history, we should mention that, apparently, the *Times* reporter had misquoted James H. Maurer, the president of the Pennsylvania Federation of Labor. In his speech, Maurer described the disruption by state constables of the funeral of a Spanish-American War veteran during a bitter miners' strike. Seeing the military honors at the miner's burial, the constables had shouted (Maurer said) "Down with the Stars and Stripes!" In the news accounts, this slogan was placed, unmediated, in Maurer's mouth. See Sinclair, *Brass Check,* 343–45; and Downey, *Davis: His Day,* 293.

98. "Richard Harding Davis Drops Dead in His Home," New York *Evening Post,* Apr. 12, 1916: 6; "Does Richard Harding Davis Guide the Daily Career of Little Hope?" New York *Herald,* Mar. 19, 1922, 7: 9.

99. Nan Clark to Cecil, Thursday [Apr. 13, 1916]; Poett Papers.

100. RHD to Rebecca, n.d. [Oct. 1897?]; Barrett Collection. Nan Clark to Cecil, Thursday [Apr. 13, 1916]; Poett Papers. "Ashes of Davis Rest Near Parents' Grave," Chicago *Tribune,* Apr. 16, 1916; clipping in Poett Papers. "Simple Rites at Funeral of R.H. Davis," New York *Telegraph,* Apr. 14, 1916; Clipping, Robinson Locke Collection, Theatre Collection, New York Public Library.

101. Bessie to Arthur H. Scribner, Mar. 1, 1917; Scribner Archive. "Harding Davis Left $250,000," Philadelphia *Press*, Apr. 19, 1916; "Buys 360 Acre Farm of Richard H. Davis," New York *Telegraph*, Sept. 19, 1917; "Richard Harding Davis Estate Nets His Heirs $50,375," New York *American*, Mar. 2, 1918; clippings, Robinson Locke Collection, Theatre Collection, New York Public Library. RHD Diary, 1916, Feb. 24; Kehrig Papers.

102. Charles to Louise Clark, Oct. 28, 1916; Poett Papers.

103. Nora to Charles, May 9 [1916]; Kehrig Papers.

104. Florenz Ziegfeld, Jr., to Bessie, Aug. 23, 1916; Bessie McCoy Davis Theatre Scrapbook, Kehrig Papers.

105. "Bessie M'Coy Dies; Widow of Davis," New York *Post*, Aug. 18, 1931; clipping, Theatre Collection, New York Public Library.

106. Van Wyck Brooks, *The Confident Years, 1885–1915* (New York: E.P. Dutton & Co., 1952), 103–4.

107. James D. Hart, ed. *A Novelist in the Making: Frank Norris* (Cambridge, Mass.: The Belknap Press of Harvard University Press, 1970), 11–12, 114; and Franklin Walker, *Frank Norris: A Biography* (New York: Russell & Russell, 1963), 72–73, 104–5.

108. Mark Schorer, *Sinclair Lewis: An American Life* (New York: McGraw-Hill Book Co., 1961), 131.

109. Theodore Dreiser, *A Book About Myself* (New York: Boni and Liveright, 1922), 490.

110. Mencken, *Newspaper Days*, 239–40; H. L. Mencken, *Prejudices: Second Series* (New York: Alfred A. Knopf, 1920), 43; H. L. Mencken, *Prejudices: Fourth Series* (New York: Alfred A. Knopf, 1924), 286; H. L. Mencken to Upton Sinclair, Sept. 9 [1926], in Guy J. Forgue, ed., *The Letters of H.L. Mencken* (New York: Alfred A. Knopf, 1961), 295.

111. "Current Fiction," *Nation* 86 (June 25, 1908): 579. *Vera, the Medium* was the work under review.

112. Finley Peter Dunne, intr. to Davis, *Scarlet Car*, vii.

Acknowledgments

I AM ESPECIALLY GRATEFUL TO those who provided me use of letters and photographs in their possession: Kristen Kehrig, the grandson of Richard Harding Davis; Frederica D. Poett, the secretary-companion of Mrs. Cecil Clark Davis; and E. Anthony Newton, the son of Pauline Ada Turgeon Newton, former wife of Charles Davis. Among the many librarians who assisted me, I must single out Martha Monte of the Rathbun Free Library in East Haddam, Connecticut, and Philip A. Metzger, Curator, Special Collections, Lehigh University Libraries.

Wendy Lesser scrutinized the manuscript with great intelligence and care. I am indebted also to my editor, Barbara Grossman, and her assistant, Joy Smith, for encouragement and astute advice; my agent, Peter Matson; Jean Strouse, Mark Stevens, and Annalyn Swan, for their suggestions; and Stephen Davis, Harvey Ginsberg, Anthony Scaduto, and Edmund Tripp, for directing me to sources I otherwise might not have found.

The National Endowment for the Humanities supported this book with a fellowship.

My thanks most of all to David Hollander.

Index

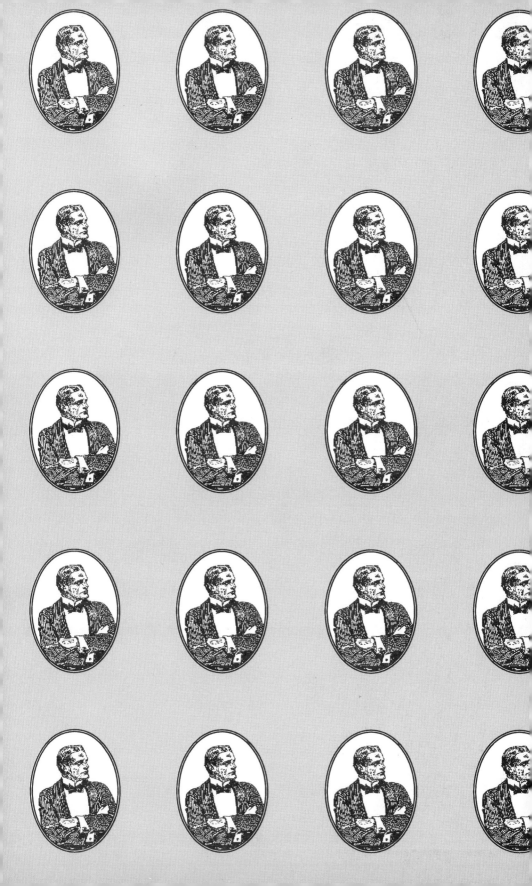